Oil Is Not a Curse

MW00334195

This book makes two central claims: First, that mineral-rich [states] ~~~
by their wealth per se but rather by the ownership structure they chose to manage their mineral wealth; and second, that weak institutions are not inevitable in mineral-rich states. Each claim represents a significant departure from the conventional 'resource curse' literature, which has treated ownership structure as a constant across time and space and presumed that mineral-rich countries are incapable of either building or sustaining strong institutions – particularly fiscal regimes. The experience of the five petroleum-rich Soviet successor states (Azerbaijan, Kazakhstan, the Russian Federation, Turkmenistan, and Uzbekistan) provides a clear challenge to both of these assumptions. Their respective developmental trajectories since independence demonstrate not only that ownership structure can vary even across countries that share the same institutional legacy, but also that this variation helps explain the divergence in their subsequent fiscal regimes.

Pauline Jones Luong is Associate Professor in the Department of Political Science at Brown University. Previously she was Assistant Professor at Yale University. At Harvard University, where she received her doctorate, she was an Academy Scholar from 1998 to 1999 and from 2001 to 2002. Her primary research interests are institutional origin and change, identity and conflict, and the political economy of development. Her empirical work to date has focused on the former Soviet Union. She has published articles in several leading academic and policy journals, including the *American Political Science Review*, *Comparative Political Studies*, *Current History*, *Foreign Affairs*, *Politics and Society*, and *Resources Policy*. Her books include *Institutional Change and Political Continuity in Post-Soviet Central Asia* and *The Transformation of Central Asia*. Funding from various sources has supported her research, including the National Science Foundation, the John T. and Catherine D. MacArthur Foundation, the National Council on East European and Eurasian Research, and the Smith Richardson Foundation.

Erika Weinthal is Associate Professor of Environmental Policy at the Nicholas School of the Environment at Duke University. From 1998 to 2005, she taught in the Department of Political Science at Tel Aviv University. Her research focuses on environmental and natural resources policy in the former Soviet Union and the Middle East. She has published widely in journals such as *Perspectives on Politics*, *Comparative Political Studies*, *American Political Science Review*, *Foreign Affairs*, *Ground Water*, *Global Environmental Politics*, and *Journal of Environment and Development*. She is the author of *State Making and Environmental Cooperation: Linking Domestic Politics and International Politics in Central Asia*. She has received funding from a variety of institutions to support her research, including the National Research Council for Europe and Eurasia, the United States Institute of Peace, the John T. and Catherine D. MacArthur Foundation, the Fifth Framework Programme of the European Union, and the United States Department of Agriculture. She is a member of the UNEP Expert Advisory Group on Environment, Conflict, and Peacebuilding.

Cambridge Studies in Comparative Politics

General Editor
Margaret Levi *University of Washington, Seattle*

Assistant General Editors
Kathleen Thelen *Massachusetts Institute of Technology*
Erik Wibbels *Duke University*

Associate Editors
Robert H. Bates *Harvard University*
Stephen Hanson *University of Washington, Seattle*
Torben Iversen *Harvard University*
Stathis Kalyvas *Yale University*
Peter Lange *Duke University*
Helen Milner *Princeton University*
Frances Rosenbluth *Yale University*
Susan Stokes *Yale University*

Other Books in the Series
David Austen-Smith, Jeffry A. Frieden, Miriam A. Golden, Karl Ove Moene, and Adam Przeworski, eds., *Selected Works of Michael Wallerstein: The Political Economy of Inequality, Unions, and Social Democracy*
Andy Baker, *The Market and the Masses in Latin America: Policy Reform and Consumption in Liberalizing Economies*
Lisa Baldez, *Why Women Protest: Women's Movements in Chile*
Stefano Bartolini, *The Political Mobilization of the European Left, 1860–1980: The Class Cleavage*
Robert Bates, *When Things Fell Apart: State Failure in Late-Century Africa*
Mark Beissinger, *Nationalist Mobilization and the Collapse of the Soviet State*
Nancy Bermeo, ed., *Unemployment in the New Europe*
Carles Boix, *Democracy and Redistribution*
Carles Boix, *Political Parties, Growth, and Equality: Conservative and Social Democratic Economic Strategies in the World Economy*
Catherine Boone, *Merchant Capital and the Roots of State Power in Senegal, 1930–1985*
Catherine Boone, *Political Topographies of the African State: Territorial Authority and Institutional Change*
Michael Bratton and Nicolas van de Walle, *Democratic Experiments in Africa: Regime Transitions in Comparative Perspective*
Michael Bratton, Robert Mattes, and E. Gyimah-Boadi, *Public Opinion, Democracy, and Market Reform in Africa*

Continued after the Index

Oil Is Not a Curse

Ownership Structure and Institutions in Soviet Successor States

PAULINE JONES LUONG

Associate Professor
Brown University
and

ERIKA WEINTHAL

Associate Professor
Nicholas School of the Environment
Duke University

CAMBRIDGE
UNIVERSITY PRESS

CAMBRIDGE UNIVERSITY PRESS
Cambridge, New York, Melbourne, Madrid, Cape Town, Singapore,
São Paulo, Delhi, Dubai, Tokyo, Mexico City

Cambridge University Press
32 Avenue of the Americas, New York, NY 10013-2473, USA

www.cambridge.org
Information on this title: www.cambridge.org/9780521148085

© Pauline Jones Luong and Erika Weinthal 2010

First published 2010

Printed in the United States of America

A catalog record for this publication is available from the British Library.

Library of Congress Cataloging in Publication data
Jones Luong, Pauline.
  Oil is not a curse : ownership structure and institutions in Soviet successor states / Pauline
  Jones Luong and Erika Weinthal.
    p.   cm.
  Includes bibliographical references and index.
  ISBN 978-0-521-76577-0 – ISBN 978-0-521-14808-5 (pbk.)
    1. Petroleum industry and trade–Soviet Union.   2. Commonwealth of Independent
  States.   I. Weinthal, Erika.   II. Title.
  HD9575.S65.J66 2010
  333–dc22   2010020088

ISBN 978-0-521-76577-0 Hardback
ISBN 978-0-521-14808-5 Paperback

For Minh, my unlimited source of energy, and for our two natural treasures, Arista and Alexander (Pauline Jones Luong)

For Emma and Adam (Erika Weinthal)

Contents

List of Tables		*page* xi
List of Figures		xii
List of Maps		xiii
1	Rethinking the Resource Curse: Ownership Structure and Institutions in Mineral-Rich States	1
2	Why Fiscal Regimes: Taxation and Expenditure in Mineral-Rich States	31
3	State Ownership with Control versus Private Domestic Ownership	45
4	Two Versions of Rentierism: State Ownership with Control in Turkmenistan and Uzbekistan	77
5	Petroleum Rents without Rentierism: Domestic Private Ownership in the Russian Federation	121
6	State Ownership without Control versus Private Foreign Ownership	181
7	Eluding the Obsolescing Bargain: State Ownership without Control in Azerbaijan	219
8	Revisiting the Obsolescing Bargain: Foreign Private Ownership in Kazakhstan	259
9	Taking Domestic Politics Seriously: Explaining the Structure of Ownership over Mineral Resources	299
10	The Myth of the Resource Curse	322
Appendix A	List of Authors' Interviews	337
Appendix B	Variation in Ownership Structure in Developing Countries	345

Appendix C Responses to Select Life in Transition Survey
           (LiTS) Questions by Age Group   351
Appendix D Ranking Basis for Determining which Countries
           are Included in Our Database   357

Works Cited   361
Index   399

Tables

1.1	Claimant Status under Different Ownership Structures	*page* 11
1.2	Oil and Gas Production and Proven Reserves in the CIS in 2006	23
4.1	Potential Energy Rents (selected Caspian Basin countries) 2000 (in percent of GDP)	79
4.2	Effective Tax Rates on Key Economic Sectors in Turkmenistan, 1998	89
4.3	Implicit Taxes on Foreign Trade in Uzbekistan, 1997–1999 (in percent of GDP)	95
4.4	Oil and Gas Ministers of Turkmenistan, 1994–2005	107
4.5	Support for State Ownership in Uzbekistan	111
4.6	Perceived Effects of Privatization in Uzbekistan	112
5.1	Stages of Reform in the Russian Oil Sector, 1992–1998	127
5.2	Percentage of Government Stake in Russian Oil Companies	130
5.3	Government Finances, 2001–2005 (percent of GDP)	146
6.1	Predicted Fiscal Outcomes under P_2 and S_2, 1900–2005, by Time Period	184
6.2	Hybrid Fiscal Regimes under S_2 from 1990–2005	213
6.3	Hybrid Fiscal Regimes under P_2 from 1990–2005	214
8.1	Overview of Most Prominent Early Deals with FOCs	266
8.2	Budget Revenue from Oil and the NFRK (current US$ millions)	279
9.1	Domestic Determinants of Ownership Structure	304
9.2	Control Variables	313
9.3	Descriptive Statistics	317
9.4	OLS Estimates	318
10.1	Average Democracy Scores: Voice and Accountability, 1996–2005, and Freedom House, 1991–2005	327

Figures

1.1	Variation in Ownership Structure, 1900–2005	*page* 8
1.2	Performance of Petroleum-Rich versus Petroleum-Poor States in the FSU	19
1.3	Performance of Petroleum-Rich versus Petroleum-Poor States in the FSU (excluding Turkmenistan and Uzbekistan)	19
4.1	Indirect versus Direct Taxation in Turkmenistan (as a Percentage of Total Revenue)	92
4.2	Indirect versus Direct Taxation in Uzbekistan (as a Percentage of Total Revenue)	93
5.1	PIT as a Percentage of GDP, 1995–2005	141
5.2	Number of SMEs Using Simplified Tax System	142
7.1	Azerbaijan Oil Production (Actual and Projected), 2000–2024	225
7.2	Indirect versus Direct Taxation in Percent of Total Non-Oil Tax Revenues	231
8.1	PIT as a Percentage of GDP	270
8.2	Breakdown of CIT as a Percentage of GDP	271
8.3	PIT Relative to VAT (Percentage of GDP)	272
10.1	Distribution of Oil-Rich Democracies and Autocracies	325
10.2	Petroleum Wealth and Level of Democracy in the Soviet Union and Russian Federation, 1960–2005	325
10.3	Non–Hydrocarbon Sector Revenue as a Function of Hydrocarbon Sector Revenue, 1992–2005	332
10.4	Spending Levels, 1960–2005	333

Maps

1.1	Commonwealth of Independent States (CIS)	*page* 5
5.1	Russian Oil Fields	125
5.2	Russian Gas Fields	126
7.1	Azerbaijan Oil Fields	223
8.1	Kazakhstan Oil and Gas Fields	262

Rethinking the Resource Curse

Ownership Structure and Institutions in Mineral-Rich States

> Petro-states share a similar path-dependent history and structuration of choice ... the exploitation of petroleum produced a similarity in property rights, tax structures, vested interests, economic models, and thus frameworks for decision-making across different governments and regime types.
>
> – Terry Lynn Karl (1997, 227)

> For the quality of our understanding of current problems depends largely on the broadness of our frame of reference.
>
> – Alexander Gershenkron (1962, 6)

The negative consequences of mineral abundance in developing countries – poor economic performance, unbalanced growth, impoverished populations, weak states, and authoritarian regimes – are widely accepted among highly respected academics, international nongovernmental organizations (INGOs), international financial institutions (IFIs), and even representatives of the popular media. This is particularly true of petroleum.[1] Indeed, some have gone so far as to declare that the resource curse is "a reasonably solid fact" (Sachs and Warner 2001, 837), while others have proclaimed that there is a "Law of Petropolitics" whereby "[t]he price of oil and the pace of freedom always move in opposite directions in oil-rich states" (Friedman 2006, 31). Nigeria's experience with petroleum provides a vivid illustration of this so-called "curse" of wealth. Although its government has accrued $350 billion in oil revenues since independence in 1960, between 1970 and 2000 its economy shrank dramatically, its poverty rate "increased from close to 36 percent to just under 70 percent" (Sala-i-Martin and Subramanian 2003, 3) and its political regime "has become increasingly centralized and oppressive" (Jensen and Wantchekon 2004, 819).

---

[1] Petroleum and oil are often used interchangeably to connote hydrocarbons more generally that can be separated into various forms of energy, including natural gas. Throughout this book, we conform to this common practice.

But few seem to agree as to exactly why mineral wealth allegedly produces such negative outcomes. The most prominent explanations for economic stagnation focus on the direct effect that export windfalls have on the real exchange rate. In short, by shifting production inputs to the booming mineral sector and nontradable sector, they reduce the competitiveness of the nonbooming export sectors and hence precipitate their collapse (i.e., "Dutch Disease") (see Auty 2001b). Others stress the indirect effects that export windfalls have on retarded economic growth through promoting corruption and indebtedness while discouraging productive long-term investment (see Gylfason 2001, Leite and Weidmann 1999). On the political side, the prevalence of authoritarian regimes in mineral-rich states, for example, is largely attributed to the effect that centralized access to export revenue, particularly during a boom, has on regime type by increasing the government's fiscal independence and consequently decreasing both the ability and willingness of the general population to hold its leaders accountable (see Ross 2001a, Wantchekon 1999).

The diversity of explanations posited in the vast literature on the resource curse, however, masks the fact that underlying all of them are institutions.[2] More precisely, these seemingly disparate explanations share the recognition, either implicit or explicit, that weak (or nonexistent) institutions are the key intervening variable between mineral abundance and the negative economic and political outcomes associated with this wealth.[3] In short, mineral-rich countries are "cursed" because they do not possess the "right" set of institutions. This is because either such institutions did not exist prior to an export boom, and state elites have no incentive to build them once they start to reap the benefits of their wealth (see Acemoglu et al. 2002, Karl 1997, Shafer 1994), or if such institutions did exist before an export boom, state elites would have a strong incentive to dismantle or undermine them (see Chaudhry 1989, Karl 1997, Ross 2001c). Even those scholars who distinguish among types of natural resource wealth and their effects argue that weak institutions are endogenous to mineral wealth. Isham et al. (2003), for example, conclude that because weak institutions are inevitable in countries rich in "point source" resources (i.e., fuels, minerals, and plantation-based crops), they cannot escape terms of trade shocks and thus are doomed to suffer from poor economic growth (see also Bulte et al. 2003). In sum, weak institutions are both a direct consequence of mineral wealth and the primary reason that this wealth inevitably becomes a curse.

That the weakness (or absence) of institutions is widely viewed as the underlying cause of the resource curse in the developing world is most readily apparent in how this literature deals with the exceptions – that is, those few developing countries that have managed to escape the resource curse, such

---

[2] Sachs and Warner (1995) is a notable exception.
[3] For a concurring view of the resource curse literature, see Brunnschweiler and Bulte 2008, 249.

as Botswana, Chile, and Malaysia.[4] Consider the case of Botswana. In contrast to both its mineral-rich and mineral-poor neighbors, Botswana has experienced rapid and sustained growth, moving from the twenty-fifth poorest country in 1966 to an upper-middle income country within 30 years (Sarraf and Jiwanji 2001). As is well recognized, the most immediate cause of this economic success story is Botswana's sound macroeconomic policies. It has mitigated the effects of Dutch Disease by managing its exchange rate policy through the accumulation of foreign reserves and has avoided both wasteful spending and indebtedness by running budget surpluses that were set aside for stability spending during periods of busts. At the same time, it has invested wisely in infrastructure, education, and health. But the success of these policies is widely attributed to strong political and economic institutions (see Harvey and Lewis 1980), including an insulated and autonomous technocracy committed to long-term developmental goals (see Eifert et al. 2003, Gelb and Associates 1988, Stevens 2003), a legislature that exercises control over the budgetary process (Sarraf and Jiwanji 2001, 12), and "institutions of private property" (Acemoglu et al. 2003, 84).

Recent critics of the established resource curse thesis also cite strong political and economic institutions as the main reason why some mineral-rich countries experience positive developmental outcomes. They argue, for example, that resource dependence can stimulate economic growth when governments have both the will and capacity to make the right investment choices – for example, in education and the development of new technologies (Wright and Czelusta 2004) – or promoting economic diversification (Lederman and Maloney 2003). Their point of departure from the conventional literature on the resource curse, then, is not their emphasis on the role of institutions (as they often suggest), but their treatment of institutions as exogenous, rather than endogenous, to mineral wealth (see Mehlum et al. 2006, Robinson et al. 2006). Nonetheless, both proponents of the resource curse and its critics treat institutions in mineral-rich states as stagnant – in other words, good developmental outcomes will only result in mineral-rich states that already possess and manage to sustain good institutions. Consider again the case of Botswana. In this view, its exceptionalism is a product of its colonial past, which bequeathed many of the aforementioned strong political and economic institutions that have allowed it to succeed where others have failed.

Proponents of the resource curse thesis and its critics also agree that the crucial institutions mineral-rich countries typically lack are essentially of two types: (1) those that constrain the ruling elite or chief executive from relying exclusively on the mineral sector and engaging in wasteful spending; and (2) those that enable the government to make sound investment decisions and recover from economic crises. Foremost among these are strong fiscal regimes,

---

[4] Studies that seek to explain the success of Norway also focus on the strength of its institutions in contrast to mineral-rich states in the developing world (see Sala-i-Martin and Subramanian 2003).

which encompass institutions that regulate the state's ability to both tax and spend. The widespread assumption is that all mineral-rich states will become rentier or distributive states whereby revenue is generated exclusively from natural resource export rents and then distributed widely, albeit unequally, across the population (see Vandewalle 1998). Thus they are incapable of building or sustaining fiscal regimes that contribute to good macroeconomic policies, rational public spending decisions, and the government's ability to respond effectively to a commodity shock (see Isham et al. 2003). Such strong fiscal regimes would include, for example, legal limits on government spending and foreign borrowing (see Manzano and Rigobon 2001), stabilization funds into which excess revenue is placed during booms to make up for budgetary shortfalls during busts (see Katz et al. 2004, Mikesell 1997), or savings funds aimed at determining an "optimal share" of mineral rents consumed by each generation (see Matsen and Torvik 2002), and a broad-based tax regime that provides an alternative source of government revenue so as to reduce budgetary reliance on mineral exports and facilitate economic recovery during a bust (see Chaudhry 1989, Karl 1997).

Yet despite this consensus, our understanding of the relationship between mineral wealth and institutions remains limited. Are weak institutions endogenous to mineral wealth? In particular, are weak fiscal regimes, and thus the negative outcomes they are presumed to generate, inevitable in mineral-rich states? If they are not endogenous, what then accounts for the prevalence of weak fiscal regimes in mineral-rich states? And finally, if they are exogenous, under what conditions are mineral-rich states that inherit weak fiscal regimes likely to develop strong ones?

This book seeks to advance the literature on the resource curse by utilizing the experience of the Soviet successor states to address each of these seminal questions. When the Soviet Union collapsed in 1991, it generated not only fifteen newly independent states but also a new set of petroleum-rich developing countries – Azerbaijan, Kazakhstan, the Russian Federation, Turkmenistan, and Uzbekistan. Alongside their petroleum-poor counterparts, these five former Soviet republics inherited universally weak institutions – most notably, fiscal regimes. Their experience suggests not only that weak institutions are not endogenous to mineral wealth but also that even those mineral-rich states that do not inherit strong institutions can nonetheless build them. Most importantly, the divergent development of fiscal regimes in each of these states from the early 1990s through 2005 also provides ample support for our contention that institutions in mineral-rich states are not a product of their wealth per se, but rather ownership structure – that is, who owns and controls the mineral sector. As we elaborate below, largely due to its focus on a single time period during which mineral wealth was predominantly state-owned (i.e., the late 1960s to early 1990s), the resource curse literature has ignored this possibility. Yet, a broader view of the empirical evidence suggests otherwise. In the Soviet successor states and throughout the developing world, there is actually significant variation in ownership structure over petroleum wealth throughout the twentieth century.

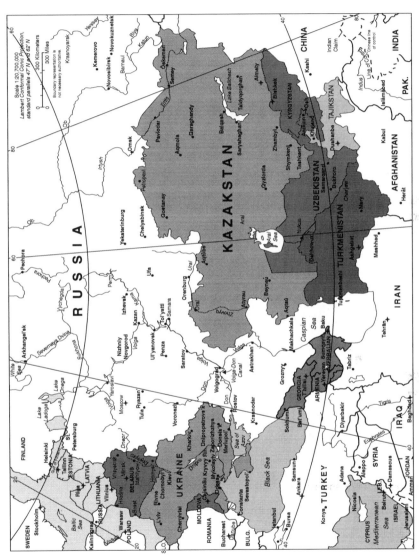

MAP I.I. Commonwealth of Independent States (CIS).

A BROADER VIEW: THE "CURSE" OF OWNERSHIP, NOT WEALTH

Our central claim is that mineral-rich states are "cursed" not by their wealth but rather by the structure of ownership they choose to manage their mineral wealth. This represents a significant departure from the conventional resource curse literature, which has largely ignored the potential impact of ownership structure over mineral reserves because it assumes that this does not vary across resource-rich states in the developing world and often conflates state ownership with control. Two separate, yet reinforcing, logics underlie this consensus.

The first concerns the overwhelming constraints that the very nature of the mineral sector imposes on leaders of capital-poor countries. Because extraction and development are capital-intensive, leaders must secure foreign direct investment or loans from international banks, which requires state ownership because only the state can satisfactorily guarantee the investment climate and loan repayment (see Karl 1997). At the same time, the need for significant amounts of capital creates greater barriers to entry, such that ownership will necessarily be concentrated (see Auty 2001b). Add to this mix the tendency for mineral reserves themselves to be clustered within a single region of the country and for this sector to dominate the country's economy, and the recipe for state ownership and centralized control is complete (see Shafer 1994).

Perhaps somewhat ironically, the second rationale stems from the prevalent, albeit often implicit, assumption that leaders in developing countries operate under very few, if any, domestic constraints. Given the enormous rents associated with the export of mineral wealth, predatory state leaders will undoubtedly want to capture these rents for themselves (see Beblawi and Luciani 1987, Mahdavy 1970, Vandewalle 1998). The strong presumption, moreover, is that the desire for state ownership and control is easily translated into the ability to do so – either because these leaders do not have to confront any sociopolitical forces that are strong enough to oppose them (see Klapp 1987, Robinson et al. 2006) or because there is no "distinction between public service and private interest in these countries" (Beblawi 1987, 55). Indeed, that mineral rents necessarily accrue directly to the central government is the central premise of an entire body of literature on the "rentier state" within and outside of the Middle East (see Karl 1997, Mahdavy 1970, Yates 1996).[5]

The overwhelming presumption of state ownership is both fostered and reinforced by the fact that most of the resource curse literature focuses on the same historical period – that is, roughly from the late 1960s to the early 1990s. The attractiveness of this period is understandable considering the conventional views of the relationship between resource endowments, economic growth, and state building at the height of post-colonialism. Scholars sought to explain the

---

[5] By definition, a rentier state is one in which "the government is the principal recipient of the external rent in the economy" (Beblawi 1987, 52).

apparent paradox that, contrary to the expectations of developmental economists in the 1950s and 1960s, the economies of resource-rich countries in the
less developed countries (LDCs) were growing more slowly than resource-poor
ones and that, despite a sustained oil boom in the 1970s, mineral-rich countries
in the developing world were experiencing economic decline and political tur-
moil in the 1980s and 1990s (see Auty 1993, Gelb and Associates 1988, Karl
1997). Yet it provides a skewed picture of the empirical reality because this is
also the time period during which the vast majority of mineral-rich countries
did, in fact, exercise state ownership over their mineral reserves.

Thus, with few exceptions, ownership structure has heretofore been viewed
as a constant rather than a variable. And yet the empirical reality is that ownership structures vary greatly both within and across mineral-rich states over
time. If one takes a broader and more nuanced view, it becomes clear – at
least regarding petroleum-rich states – not only that state ownership is not
inevitable, but also that it is accompanied by varying degrees of state control.
Figure 1.1 provides such a view. It is based on our own analysis of ownership
structure in petroleum-rich states throughout the developing world over the
course of the twentieth century, in which we disaggregate ownership and control into four possible resource development strategies.

1. *State ownership with control (S₁).* The state must own the rights to
   develop the majority of petroleum deposits and hold the majority of
   shares (> 50 percent) in the petroleum sector. Foreign involvement in
   the petroleum sector is limited either to participating in contracts that
   restrict their managerial and operational control, such as carried interest or joint ventures (JVs), or to operating as service subcontractors.
2. *State ownership without control (S₂).* The state must own the rights
   to develop the majority of petroleum deposits and hold the majority
   of shares (> 50 percent) in the petroleum sector. Foreign investors are
   allowed to participate through more permissive contracts, such as production-sharing agreements (PSAs), which grant them significant managerial and operational control.
3. *Private domestic ownership (P₁).* Private domestic companies can own
   the rights to develop the majority of petroleum deposits and hold the
   majority of shares (> 50 percent) in the petroleum sector.
4. *Private foreign ownership (P₂).* Private foreign companies can own the
   rights to develop the majority of petroleum deposits and hold the majority of shares (> 50 percent) in the petroleum sector, usually via concessionary contracts.

As these four ideal types should make clear, our decision rule for classifying a petroleum sector as under state ownership versus private ownership is
whether legislation (broadly construed)[6] mandates that the state own rights to

---

[6] In other words, this can include any promulgation by an official organ of the state, such as a
presidential decree.

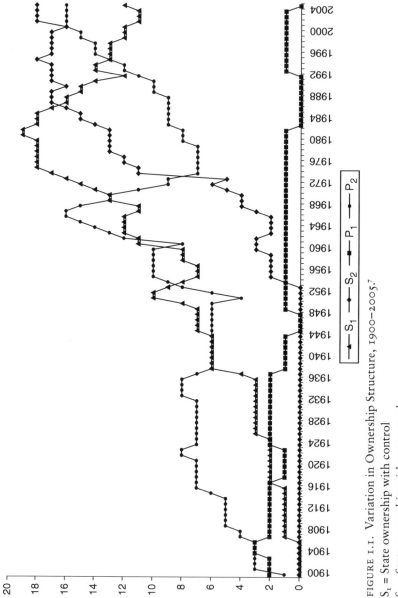

FIGURE 1.1. Variation in Ownership Structure, 1900–2005.[7]

S_1 = State ownership with control
S_2 = State ownership without control
P_1 = Private domestic ownership
P_2 = Private foreign ownership

develop the majority of petroleum deposits and hold the majority of shares in the petroleum sector, and classifying a state as "with control" versus "without control" depends on whether legislation limits the form of foreign oil companies' participation (that is, the types of contracts they can sign). Relying on legislation has two important implications for how we classify a change in ownership structure that deserve special emphasis here. First, because there is often a time lag between the adoption of ownership structure and its full implementation, we are more concerned with a legislative change that signals intent than actual practice. Second, the adoption of a new ownership structure occurs only when there is a legislative change in the rules governing ownership and control. When the private oil companies that initially owned the majority of shares sell off some (or even all) of their shares to other private oil companies, for example, this is a continuation rather than an abrogation of private ownership. Similarly, altering the terms of an existing contract with foreign investors is not sufficient to constitute a change in the degree of state control.

The neglect of ownership structure as a potential variable has deterred scholars from making explicit connections between the structure of ownership and the negative political and economic outcomes that they attribute to mineral wealth. Yet, as this book demonstrates, which form of ownership structure a country adopts is arguably the first and the most important choice that mineral-rich states make because it shapes incentives for subsequent institution building. In particular, it affects the type of fiscal regime that emerges and hence the prospects for building state capacity and achieving long-term economic growth.

OWNERSHIP STRUCTURE AND FISCAL REGIMES

Why should we expect ownership structure to influence the types of institutions that emerge in mineral-rich states? In particular, why should who owns and controls the mineral sector affect the emergence of fiscal regimes that vary in terms of their ability to constrain and enable the state? Our theory rests on three building blocks.

Ownership Structure Is a Set of Social Relations

First, we conceptualize ownership as a set of social relations among multiple claimants to the benefits derived from the exploitation of the asset in

---

[7] Based on the authors' codings for each of the 50 petroleum-rich countries in the developing world: Algeria, Angola, Argentina, Azerbaijan, Bahrain, Bolivia, Brazil, Brunei, Cameroon, Chad, Chile, China, Colombia, Republic of Congo, East Timor, Ecuador, Egypt, Equatorial Guinea, Gabon, Guatemala, Imperial Russia, India, Indonesia, Iran, Iraq, Kazakhstan, Kuwait, Libya, Malaysia, Mexico, Nigeria, North Yemen, Oman, Peru, Qatar, Romania, the Russian Federation, Saudi Arabia, South Yemen, the Soviet Union, Sudan, Syria, Trinidad and Tobago, Tunisia, Turkmenistan, the United Arab Emirates, Uzbekistan, Venezuela, Vietnam, and Yemen. To code each country's ownership structure, we rely on their respective constitutions, laws and regulations governing the mineral sector, and (where available) petroleum sector contracts with foreign oil companies.

question. As others have long recognized, whether it is public, private, foreign, or domestic, ownership is, above all, a form of exclusion (see Demsetz 1967, Umbeck 1981). Yet precisely because it confers upon an individual, group, or entity the sole right to exploit – and thereby to have direct access to the proceeds from – an asset to which society assigns worth, it is rarely an absolute one (see Furubotn and Pejovich 1972, 1139). Rather there will always be multiple claimants to the benefits derived from the exploitation of the asset in question. Those who enjoy ownership rights, moreover, cannot easily dismiss these claims because whether their rights persist is conditional upon some level of societal acceptance (see Ostrom and Schlager 1996, 130). As both the primary guarantor of property rights and responsible for protecting the public interest, the modern state has become the key to ensuring both that owners "respect" the claims of nonowners and that nonowners perform their "duty" to observe the owners' property rights (see Bromley 2006, 56). Although it has done so in a variety of ways throughout history, in the twentieth century the state has primarily performed this role either by taxing and regulating the private sector (see Alt 1983)[8] or by asserting public ownership (see Chaudhry 1993).[9] Thus, like Daniel Bromley (1989, 202), we view property rights as a triadic set of "social relations among members of a collectivity with respect to an array of items of social worth [that] link not merely a person to an object, but rather a person to an object against other persons." And yet, building on his insight, we argue that the triad of relations that property rights create necessarily includes the state and thus must also have a political content.

This is particularly true when it comes to mineral resources, such as petroleum, that are not only widely perceived as having an extremely high economic value but also portrayed as constituting the nation's wealth and hence property (see Wenar 2007). No matter who has the sole right to exploit and derive direct benefit from these resources, those who are excluded from ownership will thus seek to gain access to these benefits indirectly – albeit through different means. Chief among these claimants is the state, which has increasingly assumed the role of the protector of the public interest vis-à-vis the exploitation of mineral resources even when it does not own these resources outright. While not wholly a twentieth-century notion, the view that a country's mineral wealth ultimately belongs to the people who inhabit it was elevated to the international level during the postcolonial era when it was codified by the United Nations, for example, in the 1962 UN Resolution on Permanent Sovereignty over Natural Resources and then enshrined in the constitutions of newly independent mineral-rich countries in the developing world in the 1960s and 1970s (see Mommer 2002). The continued dominance of this sentiment is evident in Article 108 of the 2005 Iraqi constitution, which states that "[o]il and gas are the ownership of all the people of Iraq in all the regions and governorates."

---

[8] As James Alt (1983, 184) adeptly summarizes: "a tax is both a claim to ownership and an extraction of value."

[9] The state also plays an important role in enforcing communal ownership (see Ostrom 1990).

TABLE 1.1. *Claimant Status under Different Ownership Structures*

Ownership Structure	Direct Claimants	Indirect Claimants
S_1	Governing Elites + Enterprise Bureaucrats	Domestic Population
P_1	Domestic Private Owners	Governing Elites + Domestic Population
S_2	Foreign Investors + Governing Elites	Governing Elites + Domestic Population
P_2	Foreign Investors	Governing Elites + Domestic Population

Ownership structure in the context of mineral wealth, therefore, can be best understood as a set of relations between direct and indirect claimants to the proceeds (or rents) from the exploitation of this natural resource (see Table 1.1). Under state ownership with control (S_1), the relevant relationship is between governing elites and enterprise bureaucrats (usually managers of the national oil company – hereafter NOC), who serve as the direct claimants to the proceeds from mineral wealth, and the domestic population, which serves as the indirect claimant. In contrast, private domestic ownership (P_1) creates a triadic relationship among those who have a direct claim to the proceeds from mineral wealth (that is, the domestic private owners) and those who have only an indirect claim (that is, state elites and the domestic population). The triadic relationship under S_2 and P_2 includes the same set of actors – that is, foreign investors are the main direct claimants to the proceeds from mineral wealth, and both governing elites and the domestic population serve as the indirect claimants. Yet because the state often retains control over a portion of its mineral reserves under S_2 (which it produces via an NOC), governing elites also serve as a direct claimant to the rents it generates from these reserves (as under S_1). As we will explore in the second half of the book, this dual claimant status has important implications for the relationship between governing elites and the general population.

Institutions Are a Product of Both Supply and Demand

Second, we treat robust institutions as the product of both supply and demand. Since formal fiscal institutions are primarily generated at the state level, governments must have an incentive to supply them and nongovernmental actors must have an incentive to demand them. Each form of ownership structure is likely to produce a distinct fiscal regime, then, because each form generates divergent incentives for institution building among the relevant actors. More specifically, ownership structure generates the transaction costs (hereafter TCs) and societal expectations that influence whether the main claimants (direct and indirect) to the proceeds from mineral wealth have an incentive to support a fiscal regime that can effectively constrain and enable the state and the power relations that influence how such institutions emerge, and thereby serve to reinforce these incentives. For reasons we elaborate upon in Chapter 2, fiscal regimes can range from weak to strong in terms of their ability to constrain and enable the state. A weak fiscal regime consists of: (1) a tax system that is unstable, based largely, if not exclusively, on the mineral sector, and relies primarily on indirect and implicit taxation across sectors; and (2) a system of expenditures that undermines budgetary stability and transparency. The features of a strong fiscal regime are precisely the opposite: (1) a tax system that is stable, broad-based, and relies primarily on direct and explicit taxation; and (2) a system of expenditures that emphasizes budgetary stability and transparency.

S_1 fosters weak fiscal regimes because it creates low TCs and high societal expectations – that is, the popular perception that the state should have an enlarged state role in generating and allocating mineral rents. As a result, neither governing elites and enterprise bureaucrats (that is, the direct claimants) nor the general population (that is, the indirect claimants) have an incentive to supply or demand institutions that set effective limits on the state's ability to extract and spend the proceeds from mineral wealth. Under this form of ownership structure, governing elites and enterprise bureaucrats legitimate their privileged access to mineral rents through deliberately concealing taxation of the population while making the wide distribution of these rents as visible as possible. The fiscal regime that emerges, therefore, is most likely to include a tax system that not only focuses on the mineral sector, but also relies primarily on indirect and implicit forms of taxation within as well as outside the mineral sector, and a system of expenditures that emphasizes universal subsidies and massive public works or "national prestige" projects, which serve to undermine budgetary stability and transparency. States that adopt S_1, therefore, are most likely to conform to the popular notion that "[a]ll mineral [rich] states … are rentier or distributive states" (Karl 1997, 49).

Conversely, P_1 fosters strong fiscal regimes because it generates high TCs and low societal expectations – that is, the popular perception that the state should play a minimal state role in collecting and redistributing mineral rents. This combination provides domestic private owners (that is, the direct claimants) as well as governing elites and the general population (that is, the indirect claimants) with an incentive to supply and demand institutions that set effective limits on the state's ability to extract and spend the proceeds from mineral wealth. In contrast to S_1, the primary vehicle through which the former legitimate their property rights and the latter reap their perceived share of the proceeds from the exploitation of the country's mineral wealth is a viable (that is, stable, direct, and explicit) tax regime that is broad-based. A stable tax system in the mineral sector helps ensure that both domestic private owners and governing elites have access to predictable revenue streams so as to maximize company profits and the share of these profits that accrues to the state budget, respectively, while direct and explicit taxation serves to reassure the general population that governing elites are indeed extracting its fair share. Beyond the mineral sector, the mutual acknowledgement that only a portion of mineral rents captured by private actors will find its way into the state's coffers also facilitates support among governing elites and the population alike for a viable tax regime across sectors to generate additional revenue. The focus on taxation rather than expenditure to legitimate this form of ownership structure, moreover, relieves pressure on governing elites to engage in populist-style social spending, and thereby creates the opportunity for saving its share of mineral rents during booms to cover budgetary shortfalls during busts and/or investing them more wisely. States that adopt P_1, then, are least likely to fit the prototype of the rentier or distributive state.

Furthermore, weak versus strong fiscal regimes are likely to emerge and persist under S_1 and P_1, respectively, because the incentives that each form of ownership structure fosters vis-à-vis institution building are reinforced by the process through which these institutions are created. Although both forms of ownership structure produce interdependent power relations between the main actors and thus facilitate bargaining that produces distributional outcomes, the degree of transparency and accountability in this bargaining process varies considerably. Low TCs and high societal expectations under S_1 foster the mutual desire to hide information from the public and thus encourage implicit bargaining, which not only increases opportunities for corruption but also reinforces personalism as the basis for allocating resources. In contrast, high TCs and low societal expectations under P_1 foster the mutual desire to reveal information to the public and thus encourage explicit bargaining, which contributes not only to greater fiscal transparency but also accountability.

Ownership Structure Does Not Exist in a Historical Vacuum

The final building block of our theory is the recognition that the way in which ownership structure affects fiscal regimes depends upon the international context. In other words, ownership structure does not exist in a historical vacuum. Particularly where foreign investors are actively involved in the exploitation of mineral wealth – either as managers on behalf of the state under S_2 or as owners under P_2 – the effects of ownership structure on TCs, societal expectations, and power relations are mediated through the international system in which these foreign investors operate. As a result, S_2 and P_2 are distinct from S_1 and P_1 in two equally important ways. First, their effect on fiscal regimes is dynamic. As different actors gain and lose prominence in the mineral sector at the international level, they can transform the impact of ownership structure itself on the triadic relationship between the primary direct claimants to the proceeds from mineral wealth (here, foreign investors) and the primary indirect claimants (here, governing elites and the domestic population). Second, S_2 and P_2 can only produce fiscal regimes that are partially constraining and enabling – or what we call "hybrid" – because their primary influence is within the mineral sector – that is, on the size, stability, composition, and degree of transparency of the foreign investors' fiscal burden. For the specific case of petroleum, we identify three distinct time periods during which fundamental shifts in the dominant actors and norms at the international level have altered the type of hybrid regime we should expect to find under S_2 and P_2.

During the first time period (1900–1960), which is characterized by the financial and ideological dominance of a small number of large foreign oil companies (a.k.a. "the Majors"), fiscal regimes under S_2 and P_2 should look very similar because the effects of these two forms of ownership structure on TCs, societal expectations, and power relations are virtually identical. In sum: TCs are negligible due to the widespread use of a global template for contractual relations between foreign oil companies and host governments (a.k.a. the "model contract"); societal expectations are low vis-à-vis both the state and foreign investors owing to the immense secrecy with which foreigners enter into petroleum production agreements with host governments; and power relations decisively favor the foreign investors who are thus able to dictate the terms of their contracts. As a result, there is a strong likelihood for the ensuing fiscal regime to embody the foreign investors' preferences for a minimalist and stable fiscal burden. Indeed, the model contract that dominated this period granted the host government a fixed royalty on the amount of oil produced but not a share of the profits and did not require foreign investors to engage in social spending beyond providing higher salaries and occasionally housing and medical clinics for their own workers. Nor were governments tempted to engage in universal social spending or build national prestige projects in order to create the impression that the proceeds from mineral wealth were being widely distributed.

Beginning with the second time period (1960–1990), which came about with the rise of small foreign oil companies (a.k.a. the "independents") who eroded the Majors' control over the global oil supply and facilitated the foundation of the Organization of Petroleum Exporting Countries (OPEC), the expected fiscal regimes under S_2 and P_2 start to diverge. On the one hand, because TCs remained negligible due to the persistence of the model contract, and yet power relations shifted decisively in favor of the state, under both S_2 and P_2 we are likely to find that the foreign investors' tax burden is expanded to include profit sharing and is highly unstable. Thus, consistent with Raymond Vernon's (1971) theory of the "obsolescing bargain," governing elites should be able not only to extract a greater share of the proceeds upfront but also to increase the foreign investors' fiscal burden arbitrarily, thereby unilaterally changing the initial terms of their contracts. On the other hand, we are likely to see very different levels of state spending under S_2 and P_2 during this period due to differences in societal expectations.

Although the heightened publicity surrounding the petroleum industry in the developing world universally raised public awareness in host countries about the dominant role of foreign investors in petroleum production, it did not generate identical societal expectations. Under S_2, societal expectations are high vis-à-vis both the state and foreign investors, which fosters incentives for broader and more visible forms of social spending. Governing elites are thus more likely to engage in populist-style social spending and to build national prestige projects, while foreign investors are more likely to expand their social spending to include symbolic forms of philanthropy in the regions in which they operate. Under P_2, however, societal expectations are similarly high vis-à-vis the foreign investors, but because the state has relinquished both ownership and control over the petroleum sector, they remain low vis-à-vis the state. Thus, while we expect to see the same level of foreign investor spending as under S_2, we should see a much lower level on the part of the state. Low societal expectations also create *some* potential for broad-based taxation by reducing governing elites' disincentives for pursuing this policy option. Thus we might also see differences concerning the tax regime outside the mineral sector, although the ease with which the state can extract increasing amounts from foreign investors makes this unlikely under either S_2 or P_2.

The fiscal regimes likely to be generated under S_2 and P_2 continue to diverge in the third time period (1990–2005), which marks the proliferation of both new international norms concerning the obligations of foreign oil companies to host countries and INGOs and IFIs seeking to impose these norms. Although TCs remain negligible, direct pressure from INGOs and IFIs to incorporate corporate social responsibility (hereafter, CSR) transformed the model contract itself. Thus the foreign investors' fiscal burden specified in this contract was likely to go above and beyond that of the two preceding periods by including some form of broad social spending. Likewise, societal expectations differ from previous periods not in form but in content. While they remain high vis-à-vis foreign investors under both S_2 and P_2, due to direct pressure from INGOs and IFIs for foreign oil companies to assume greater responsibility for their host country's social and economic development, the requirements for satisfying societal expectations also expand. In other words, foreign investors must not only engage in *social* spending in the regions where they operate but also provide financial support that exceeds the spending obligations specified in their contracts. Foreign investors are thus more likely to develop a broader interest in shaping the fiscal regime – that is, to influence its composition and degree of transparency as well as its size and stability, and to do so within as well as outside the mineral sector. For example, because it affects the quantity and quality of their own fiscal contribution, they are more likely to be concerned with how the state allocates the proceeds it accrues from mineral sector taxation. This, in turn, makes foreign investors more likely to support international efforts to increase society's access to information about both how much revenue the state extracts from the mineral sector and how this revenue is spent. For those fully committed to CSR, moreover, there is an additional incentive to actively support similar international efforts to place restrictions on how governments can spend their money such that these foreign investors' own efforts to foster broad social and economic development are complemented rather than potentially undermined.

In sum, we would expect any fiscal regime that emerged from 1990–2005 to expand the state's reliance on the mineral sector by including expenditures. The extent of this fiscal reliance and the potential for foreign investors' spending to have a positive short- and long-term impact, however, are contingent on power relations, which this particular international context has also transformed. Whereas in the first two time periods the balance of power clearly favors one side over the other, during the third time period the dominant actor cannot be identified ex ante. Rather, both because international organizations no longer give uncompromising support to host governments over foreign investors and foreign investors have developed more effective strategies to counter the inevitability of the obsolescing bargain, there is a greater deal of uncertainty concerning which actor will exercise greater influence over the fiscal regime. The best-case scenario, it turns out, is when foreign investors who are fully committed to CSR can unilaterally enforce the terms of their contracts. Within the mineral sector, this fosters a tax regime that is more likely to promote both stability and transparency than in either of the two previous time periods. It is also more likely to result in spending that is directed toward improving society's welfare by alleviating poverty and promoting development. Outside the mineral sector, the inability of governing elites to arbitrarily extract increasing amounts from foreign investors, alongside pressures from INGOs and IFIs, means that there are also greater prospects for tax and expenditure reform than in either of the two previous time periods.

And yet, even under their respective "best-case" scenarios, S_2 and P_2 generate second-best outcomes. The reason is twofold. First, foreign investors' ability to foster strong fiscal regimes outside the mineral sector remains limited because it is highly dependent on whether governing elites have an incentive to constrain and enable themselves. Strong fiscal regimes are most likely to emerge under P_1 precisely because the combination of high TCs, low societal expectations, and explicit bargaining fosters a mutual incentive for doing so among governing elites, domestic private owners, and the population. Weak fiscal regimes, in contrast, emerge under S_1 because the combination of low TCs, high societal expectations, and implicit bargaining creates and reinforces a mutual disincentive to set effective limits on the state's ability to tax and spend. Thus, while the likelihood is greater under P_2 than under S_2 owing to the role of low societal expectations in ameliorating the political obstacles for governing elites to pursue broad-based taxation and limits on spending, it is not nearly as high as under P_1 or as low as under S_1. Second, there is an inherent danger that by strengthening the role of foreign investors in fostering more desirable social and economic outcomes from mineral sector development, the promotion of CSR via well-intentioned INGOs and IFIs is actually enervating the state. This stands in stark contrast to the development model of the 1960s through the 1980s, which not only recognized the primary role of the state in promoting economic growth but also emphasized the need for capacity building within states to achieve these goals (see Evans 1992).

PETROLEUM WEALTH AND FISCAL REGIMES IN THE SOVIET SUCCESSOR STATES

The collapse of the Soviet empire in 1991 and the emergence of five newly independent petroleum-rich states – Azerbaijan, Kazakhstan, the Russian Federation, Turkmenistan and Uzbekistan – present both an empirical puzzle and a theoretical opportunity for students of the resource curse. Making their debut just as the view that mineral wealth is more often a "curse" than a "blessing" was gaining prominence in the mid-1990s (see Auty 1993, Gelb 1988, Sachs and Warner 1995), the Soviet successor states endowed with abundant energy resources were easily slated to become the resource curse's newest victims. It was widely presumed, for example, that these five states would adopt the same kinds of counterproductive fiscal policies that universally doomed the OPEC members to "double-digit inflation, cost overruns on vast public projects, insolvent banking sectors, and a collapse of the agricultural and manufacturing sectors ... [as well as] high levels of state debt" by the end of the 1980s (Sabonis-Helf 2004, 159–60 citing Karl 2000, 35; see also Amuzegar 2001). Some notable experts even went as far as to issue "[a w]arning to the Caspian" that such a fate awaited them, particularly in the wake of an expected oil export boom (Amuzegar 1998), and to predict that "[h]istory [would] repeat itself ... [in] 'new' entrants to global energy markets like Azerbaijan and Kazakhstan" (Karl 1999, 46). Moreover, just as the OPEC countries are widely believed to have experienced a *much* slower growth rate due to their heavy reliance on mineral exports (see Auty 1993, Auty and Gelb 2001, Sachs and Warner 1995), so too were the petroleum-rich Soviet successor states expected to proceed *much* slower along the transition path from a planned to a market economy – and with much less success than their petroleum-poor counterparts (see Auty 1997b, Esanov et al. 2001, Sabonis-Helf 2004).

And yet, as it turns out, petroleum wealth is a poor predictor of both the pace and extent of social, political, and economic reform in the former Soviet Union (FSU). First, after over a decade of independent statehood, it is clear that Turkmenistan and Uzbekistan are much more poised to follow the development trajectory of the OPEC nations than Azerbaijan, Kazakhstan, or the Russian Federation. They are notorious not only for their bloated public sectors but also for their high levels of indebtedness and overzealous spending aimed at maintaining or expanding the cradle-to-grave welfare system they inherited from the Soviet Union and, particularly in Turkmenistan, building grandiose national prestige projects. Conversely, Kazakhstan and Russia are noteworthy for their continued efforts at shrinking the size of the public sector and controlling government spending despite a sustained oil boom in the first half of the 2000s (see CASE 2008). And yet, alongside petroleum-poor Kyrgyzstan and Tajikistan, Turkmenistan and Uzbekistan rank at the bottom of the list when it comes to both the Human Development Index (HDI)[10] and

[10] The HDI is calculated annually by the UNDP and can be found at http://hdr.undp.org

the share of the population living in poverty – that is, well below both the other petroleum-rich FSU countries and the Commonwealth of Independent States (hereafter CIS)[11] average.

Second, the difference in progress toward market-based reforms between the energy-rich and energy-poor Soviet successor states is actually quite small.[12] (See Figure 1.2.) And, more importantly, when you remove the two habitual laggards from the dataset, this difference disappears. Indeed, Turkmenistan and Uzbekistan drag down the aggregate results to such an extent that when they are eliminated, petroleum-rich countries in the CIS actually outperform the petroleum-poor countries when it comes to the extent of transition by the mid-2000s. (See Figure 1.3.) This is also the case concerning other relevant socioeconomic indicators, including HDI and Transparency International's Corruption Perceptions Index (CPI).[13]

Finally, some of the petroleum-rich countries in the CIS – most notably Kazakhstan and Russia – appear to be more advanced than many of their petroleum-poor counterparts. As of 2006, for example, both of these countries had made greater progress toward improving the business environment and reforming the financial sector than all other CIS countries except for Armenia and Ukraine, respectively.[14]

Our contention that mineral-rich states are "cursed" not by their wealth but rather by the structure of ownership they choose to manage this wealth suggests an alternative explanation for this finding. Turkmenistan and Uzbekistan are outliers among the Soviet successor states not only when it comes to their consistently sluggish approach to social, political and economic reform, but also their choice of ownership structure. They are unique among the petroleum-rich countries in that, following independence, they retained the ownership structure they inherited from the Soviet Union – state ownership with control (S_1). The other three petroleum-rich states each adopted one of the other three alternative forms of ownership structure we have identified: Azerbaijan chose state ownership without control (S_2); Russia pursued private domestic ownership (P_1); and Kazakhstan opted for private foreign ownership (P_2). Each of these five countries retained their initial ownership structure for at least a decade,[15] enabling us to draw inferences about the relationship between their choice of ownership structure and the fiscal regimes that emerged during the transition from Soviet rule.

[11] The CIS includes all the Soviet successor states except for the Baltic countries – Estonia, Latvia, and Lithuania.

[12] As measured by the European Bank for Reconstruction and Development's (EBRD) Transition Indicators, available at http://www.ebrd.com/country/sector/econo/stats/index.htm

[13] The CPI score and rank for petroleum-rich FSU countries in 2005, for example, improves by 10 percentage points when Turkmenistan and Uzbekistan are removed. For details concerning CPI scores and ranks, see http://www.transparency.org/policy_research/surveys_indices/cpi

[14] Based on EBRD Transition Indicators, op. cited.

[15] Uzbekistan changed to S_2 in 2001; Russia changed to S_1 in 2005; and Kazakhstan changed to S_2 in 2005. We offer a broad explanation for changes in ownership structure in Chapter 9.

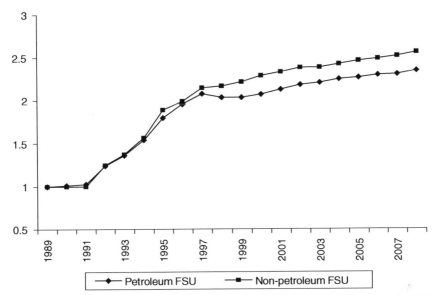

FIGURE 1.2. Performance of Petroleum-Rich versus Petroleum-Poor States in the FSU. *Source*: Authors' calculations from http://www.ebrd.com/country/sector/econo/stats/index.htm.

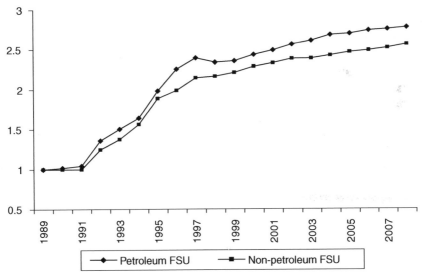

FIGURE 1.3. Performance of Petroleum-Rich versus Petroleum-Poor States in the FSU (excluding Turkmenistan and Uzbekistan). *Source*: Authors' calculations from http://www.ebrd.com/country/sector/econo/stats/index.htm.

This variation presents a "natural laboratory" for testing our hypotheses concerning the relationship between ownership structure and fiscal regimes, moreover, because the Soviet successor states share so much else in common. First and foremost, alongside their petroleum-poor counterparts, all five inherited universally weak institutions – most notably, fiscal regimes. In the context of the socialist command economy, "taxation was nearly non-existent ... [and] tax administration was anemic at best" (Authors' interview with Shatalov). Although the Soviet Union collected income taxes from its citizenry, these were nominal and collected directly from their place of employment (that is, state-owned enterprises), thereby attracting little attention and requiring little administration (see Holzman 1950, Newcity 1986). The most important taxes were the enterprise profit tax and the retail turnover tax from state stores – both of which were likewise collected directly from state-owned enterprises via their state-controlled bank accounts. At independence, then, none of the former Soviet republics possessed either a modern taxation system for the public sector or the capacity to tax the private sector. Instead, they inherited a tax administration ill-equipped to enforce compliance, a tax system based on negotiated rates between state officials and enterprise managers, and a population with little or no experience in paying taxes (for details, see Martinez-Vazquez and McNab 2000). Their inheritance on the expenditure side was equally debilitating. In order to sustain both a loss-generating industrial sector and an extensive welfare system that provided full citizen rights to benefits regardless of income or social status, the Soviet Union relied on a plethora of quasi-fiscal activities that served to undermine budgetary stability and accountability. Most importantly, these included implicit energy subsidies for both industrial and household consumers and soft budget constraints for public enterprises. Because one of the primary mechanisms for delivering the Soviet Union's extensive welfare system were state-owned enterprises, moreover, regional petroleum enterprises also incurred the cost of providing their employees and the surrounding community with a plethora of social and economic benefits, including subsidized housing, free healthcare, and all-expense-paid vacations.

Their common fiscal legacy is crucial because it enables us to assume a virtually identical starting point when it comes to fiscal reform, thereby facilitating our causal inferences concerning the link between ownership structure and the subsequent evolution of taxation and expenditure policies in each of the petroleum-rich Soviet successor states. Rather all five "had to design a tax system in dire circumstances of the USSR collapse, emergence of a new state and budget crisis, basically from scratch" (Shatalov 2006, 780) while contending with a preexisting cradle-to-grave welfare system financed in large part by petroleum rents (see Jones Luong 2000a) and delivered via regional petroleum enterprises. This has particular implications for societal expectations. On the one hand, there should be a strong popular aversion to the idea of taxation, particularly direct and explicit forms, making the barrier for instituting a broad-based tax regime universally high. On the other, societal

expectations concerning the allocation of petroleum rents should be universally elevated – even more so than in other petroleum-rich states that lacked
such an inheritance – regardless of ownership structure. The changes in societal expectations we predict in response to the change in ownership structure
in the Soviet successor states following independence, then, should be viewed
in relative rather than absolute terms.

Second, Azerbaijan, Kazakhstan, the Russian Federation, Turkmenistan,
and Uzbekistan emerged as new petroleum-rich states at exactly the same
time. This allows us to hold constant the international context and thus to test
systematically our specific predictions regarding the types of fiscal regimes
that should emerge under each form of ownership structure during this particular time period (that is, 1990–2005). *Ceteris paribus*, because these five
petroleum-rich states emerged simultaneously, they should all experience the
same international pressures. And yet we argue that because they chose different ownership structures, both the form and degree of these pressures will
vary and thus so too will the effects on their incentives to build constraining
and enabling fiscal institutions. Consider also the fact that, with the exception
of Uzbekistan,[16] all five states experienced a short-lived boom in the early-to-
mid-1990s, and then a bust in the late 1990s, followed by a sustained boom
through 2005.[17] While the conventional literature on the resource curse posits
that exogenous shocks caused by changes at the international level should
have the same deleterious effect across mineral-rich states – that is, to reinforce weak fiscal regimes – we posit that this effect will be mediated by ownership structure. More specifically, due primarily to the divergence in societal
expectations under S_1 versus P_1 discussed above, whereas the boom from 1999
to 2005 should exacerbate both the budgetary reliance on petroleum rents and
wasteful spending in Turkmenistan, it should facilitate broad-based tax reform
and the creation of an effective stabilization fund in the Russian Federation.

Focusing on this most recent time period also enables us to utilize a variety
of primary source materials in ascertaining whether the causal mechanisms
we specify are indeed at work. Given the emphasis of our argument on how
ownership structure shapes actors' institutional incentives via its effect on
TCs, societal expectations, and power relations, it is incumbent upon us to
demonstrate that the actors in question actually had and were motivated by
such incentives. This is inherently difficult, of course, but becomes impossible
without access to the words and thoughts of the actors themselves. And such
arguments can be made much more convincing when information and data
sources can be triangulated.

---

[16] Uzbekistan's decision to develop its petroleum primarily for domestic consumption (discussed
in Chapter 4) meant that it was effectively shielded from these exogenous shocks.

[17] Petroleum booms can be caused by various factors, including the transfer of assets, the influx
of foreign investment, and a marked increase in the international price of oil or the amount
of petroleum available for export. Whereas the initial boom these countries experienced was
the result of the first and/or second of these factors, the boom in the 2000s was primarily the
result of the third. For details, see von Hirschhausen and Engerer 1999.

This is particularly the case when it comes to demonstrating that different societal expectations influenced the type of fiscal regime that emerged in each of these countries. Here, we need to demonstrate not so much that the general population actually held the particular beliefs we hypothesize under each form of ownership structure, but more so that the actors in question perceived society to hold these beliefs, and that this perception drove their support for certain kinds of taxation and expenditure policies. Thus we marshal evidence from three different types of sources to assess whether this mechanism is at work for each of our five cases: (1) available mass survey and polling data; (2) our own in-depth interviews with, and surveys of, government officials, foreign investors, representatives of INGOs and IFIs, and various societal actors, supplemented by official interviews and speeches published in the local and international press; and (3) annual presidential addresses to the public. Mass surveys and public opinion polls are perhaps the best, or at least the most common, way to reveal what the population thinks. But they are not a perfect instrument, as both their availability and reliability tends to be very limited in countries with highly authoritarian regimes like Turkmenistan and Uzbekistan. Here we take advantage of the opportunity provided by the EBRD's 2005 Life in Transition Survey (LiTS).[18] Its many advantages include a cross-national perspective covering at least part of the time period under study for all the FSU countries except Turkmenistan. Interviews are clearly the most direct way to ascertain elite attitudes and perceptions, but must be done systematically and should not be relied upon exclusively. Thus we supplement our own interviews with those available in the local and international press. Due to greater difficulty in conducting reliable interviews with a cross section of government officials in some countries versus others, in order to ensure consistency across the five cases, we also rely on the president's annual speech to the legislature as an indicator of elites' perceptions of societal expectations.

Finally, Azerbaijan, Kazakhstan, the Russian Federation, Turkmenistan, and Uzbekistan are all rich in the same mineral – petroleum – though whether they are primarily endowed in oil versus gas varies. (See Table 1.2 for details.) Together with Iran, these five Soviet successor states make up the Caspian Basin, which is estimated to hold significantly larger oil and gas reserves than those in the North Sea (Gelb 2002).[19] Due to the distinctive features of petroleum, this both facilitates comparison across these countries and increases the broader significance of our findings. First, the economic, and hence political, magnitude of petroleum makes it a more volatile export not only than other primary commodities but also other kinds of minerals (see Isham et al.

---

[18] The full dataset and questionnaire are available at http://www.ebrd.com/country/sector/econo/surveys/lits.htm .

[19] DOE-EIA (2007) estimates that the Caspian holds proven oil reserves of 17–49 billion barrels, which is similar in size to Qatar on the low end and Libya on the high end, and proven natural gas reserves of 232 trillion cubic feet, which is comparable to those in Nigeria (see http://www.eia.doe.gov/cabs/Caspian/Full.html).

TABLE 1.2. *Oil and Gas Production and Proven Reserves in the CIS in 2006*

	Oil Production, Mt	Proven Oil Reserves, billion tons	Gas Production, bcm	Proven Gas Reserves, trillion cubic meters
	(Share of World Total, percent)	Share of World Total, percent)	(Share of World Total, percent)	(Share of World Total, percent)
Azerbaijan	32.5 (0.8)	1.0 (0.6)	6.3 (0.2)	1.35 (0.7)
Kazakhstan	66.1 (1.7)	5.5 (3.3)	23.9 (0.8)	3.0 (1.7)
Russia	480.5 (12.3)	10.9 (6.6)	612.1 (21.3)	47.65 (26.3)
Turkmenistan	8.1 (0.2)	0.1 (<0.05)	62.2 (2.2)	2.86 (1.6)
Uzbekistan	5.4 (0.1)	0.1 (<0.05)	55.4 (1.9)	1.87 (1.0)

Source: British Petroleum 2007.

2003, Verleger 1993).[20] Oil prices doubled from 1978 to 1981, for example, in response to the Iranian Revolution and the start of the Iran-Iraq war. Crude oil prices oscillated between $10.00 and $25.00 a barrel in the 1990s, and these fluctuations have been even more extreme in the 2000s, ranging from $25.00 in 2000 to $145.00 in 2008.[21] Particularly since the 1990s, natural gas prices have followed a similar trend, as they have been increasingly affected by many of the same factors that contribute to the volatility of oil prices (see Mastrangelo 2007 for details). Second, precisely because it can serve and has served as a valuable and attractive political weapon, the sheer size of rents that petroleum generates also tends to be much larger than other commodity or mineral exports. For instance, Gazprom's decision to cut off deliveries of natural gas to Ukraine in a dispute over gas prices during the winter of 2005–2006 immediately heightened European concerns that Russia could use the region's energy dependence on the gas monopoly to wield similar influence on pricing and supplies (see Spanjer 2007). This, in turn, has a magnifying effect on societal expectations. As we describe in Chapters 3 and 6, the popular perception of what the state actually yields from export rents, and hence the benefits society should reap, has increased over time with the greater publicity surrounding oil and gas exploration. In the context of the FSU, moreover, the preexisting cradle-to-grave welfare system means that societal expectations for the widespread allocation of rents were already quite high. Lastly, given

[20] Crude oil is also the world's most actively traded commodity, accounting for about 10 percent of total world trade (Verleger 1993).
[21] For details, see http://www.eia.doe.gov/emeu/international/crude2.html

the large number of petroleum producers in the developing world, testing our hypotheses concerning the link between ownership structure over mineral wealth and fiscal regimes on petroleum-rich countries means that there are a greater number of cases to which our results should apply.

Moreover, the variation in ownership structure across the Soviet successor states offers yet another theoretical opportunity because it violates a core assumption of the resource curse literature – specifically that ownership structure does not vary and thus can be treated as a constant across time and space. As such, it too begs explanation. Here their shared experience under Soviet rule is also key because this enables us to exclude the most plausible alternative explanations. Most importantly, because all natural resources were owned and controlled by the Soviet state, the leaders of all five newly independent states inherited the same political and institutional structure for the management of their petroleum reserves, as well as the negative consequences of this management structure – gross mismanagement of resources, dilapidated infrastructure, and primitive technology – which culminated in an acute production crisis in the 1980s (Gustafson 1989). This suggests that ownership structure prior to independence (that is, path dependency or institutional inertia) was not a decisive factor. Similarly, because all four countries chose different ownership structures within the same context of falling oil prices and trends toward privatization in the developing world, these commonly cited international pressures for policy convergence also clearly did not play a role. And yet, for all their similarities at independence, these countries' petroleum reserves exhibited many differences – particularly concerning their level of development, size, and degree of concentration, "quality" and difficulty of extraction, and access to foreign markets. None of these variables, however, help explain either why Azerbaijan, Kazakhstan, the Russian Federation, Turkmenistan, and Uzbekistan made different choices regarding ownership structure.

First and foremost, one might argue that Russia adopted domestic privatization because it had the most well-developed petroleum sector and thus the domestic expertise to continue to manage its development whereas the other four did not. Although it is true that the Soviet government prioritized oil production in the Russian Soviet Federated Socialist Republic (RSFSR) – particularly when it switched from coal to oil as its major energy source in the 1950s and 1960s (Lydolph and Shabad 1960)[22] – because these fields were both cheaper to exploit and more accessible to lucrative export markets in Western Europe (for details, see Goldman 1980), Russia is not the only former Soviet republic in which the petroleum industry has a long history. In fact, Azerbaijan has had a much longer history. The world's first oil well was drilled in 1848 near its capital (Baku) at Bibi-Heybat, and by the late 1800s,

---

[22] At this time, the Soviet government also switched its emphasis from the Caucasus and Caspian region to the Volga-Urals region and to newer fields in Western Siberia (Wakeman-Linn 2004, 8).

Azerbaijan had become one of the world's leading suppliers of oil, successfully challenging Standard Oil's international grip on oil production at the end of the nineteenth century (Nassibli 1998, Yergin 1991).[23] The Bolshevik Revolution and Azerbaijan's subsequent annexation into the Soviet Union in 1922 interrupted oil production around Baku, but output surged once more during World War II when Azerbaijan generated almost 75 percent of the Soviet Union's total production (Wakeman-Linn 2004, 8). Oil was discovered much later in Kazakhstan and Uzbekistan – at the end of the nineteenth century in Western Kazakhstan (Tasmagambetov 1999) and the Fergana Valley (Sagers 1994), respectively – albeit still prior to the Bolshevik Revolution in 1917.

While it is also the case that Azerbaijan and Kazakhstan contributed a mere pittance to total Soviet oil production prior to independence,[24] this did not necessarily translate into a dearth of local expertise or *neftyaniki* (oilmen). Many of the chief experts in the Soviet oil industry came from Azerbaijan. In fact, Vagit Alekperov – the president of Lukoil, Russia's largest private oil company and largest producer of oil since its creation in 1993[25] – was born in Baku and educated at the Azizbekov Institute of Oil and Chemistry in Azerbaijan. Those who either remained in or returned home to their native Azerbaijan after independence make up the core management in the national oil company SOCAR. Kazakhstan also inherited its share of oil sector expertise – enough, at least, to warrant the popular claim that "the Kazakhs [always] were the 'oil people'" or *neftyaniki* in Central Asia whereas the Uzbeks were the "water people" or *vodniki* (Weinthal 2002, 212). In any case, the availability of experts in the oil industry does not seem to have affected the choice of ownership structure, either in Russia or more broadly. As described in Chapter 5, the beneficiaries of Russia's privatization process were not solely *neftyaniki* but also bankers with little or no knowledge of the industry.

Second, there is considerable variation in both the size and the degree of concentration of proven reserves across these four countries. Based on Western conservative estimates of oil reserves prior to the Soviet Union's collapse (that is, rather than Soviet estimates), about 85 percent were within Russia, 9 percent in Kazakhstan, 2.3 percent in Azerbaijan, 2 percent in Turkmenistan and 1 percent in Uzbekistan (Sagers 1994). Thus Kazakhstan, Azerbaijan, Turkmenistan, and Uzbekistan combined comprised only 13.5–14 percent of the Soviet Union's "claimed explored reserves" (ibid). This is, of course, due largely to the greater degree of exploration that took place in the RSFSR during the Soviet period. Estimates of "probable reserve additions" that emerged after it became independent in the early 1990s put Kazakhstan's at 12 billion barrels – the same level as the United Kingdom and Qatar – and around

[23] Baku's output accounted for half of the world's oil production in 1900 (Sagers 1994, 268).

[24] Azerbaijan produced less than 3% and Kazakhstan produced just under 6% (World Bank 1993b, 8). Uzbekistan was a net importer of oil but the USSR's third largest producer of natural gas (Pomfret 2004).

[25] Another (now defunct) private oil company – Yukos – overtook Lukoil briefly from 2002–2004 as the country's largest producer of oil.

the twentieth place in the world (Sagers 1994). At this time, Azerbaijan and Uzbekistan were also suspected to have substantial "reserve additions" worthy of exploitation (ibid). That these estimates were taken seriously is evidenced by the influx of foreign oil companies into Kazakhstan and Azerbaijan in numbers that rivaled and then surpassed the number entering Russia (Jones Luong and Weinthal 2001).[26] Thus size alone does not seem to account for either greater foreign interest or attempts at state control.

The variation in concentration of reserves also does not seem to affect the choice of ownership structure. On a scale from least to most concentrated, Azerbaijan is at the far end of the spectrum, since its reserves are all located in the Baku region and primarily offshore. During the Soviet period, most of Azerbaijan's oil production was largely concentrated onshore along the Absheron peninsula and offshore in a shallow-water oil complex known as *Neft Dashlari*, or *Oily Rocks*, that was constructed in 1947 (see Hoffman 2000a). This site – extending more than 40 kilometers into the Caspian – produced over half of Azerbaijan's total crude oil at independence (ibid, 6). According to the conventional wisdom, then, this would suggest not only state ownership, but also the greatest degree of state control. However, Azerbaijan opted for S_2 – state ownership with the lowest degree of state control. The others are all near the middle of this spectrum, and yet they each adopted very different forms of ownership structure. Russia's onshore reserves are spread across more than a dozen regions, although the bulk of them are concentrated in West Siberia (see Chapter 5). Similarly, Kazakhstan's onshore reserves are largely in the western part of the country, but spread across five of its fourteen regions, one of which is located in the south-central part of the country. Both countries also have significant offshore reserves in the Caspian Sea. Uzbekistan's reserves are located in two distinct parts of the country – the Fergana Valley region and the Aral Sea basin.

Third, the petroleum reserves in these four countries also vary in terms of their "quality" and difficulty of extraction – two factors that are often highly correlated. The petroleum reserves in Kazakhstan's largest onshore field (Tengiz), for example, both have a high sulfur content and are very deep (Samoilov 1993). These factors are also commonly associated with the need for high levels of foreign investment to provide the necessary capital and technology. But here again, the structural features of the oil sector alone do not tell the whole story. At first glance, Azerbaijan and Kazakhstan are probably tied for having reserves that are the lowest in quality and most difficult to extract. And indeed, both opted for a high level of foreign involvement. Yet they opted for a different form of ownership – state versus private, respectively. A closer look at the variation in the difficulty of extracting petroleum reserves across the FSU further suggests that Russia is most in need of investment in advanced technology. Not only has the "easy oil" already been extracted from fields in

---

[26] Uzbekistan and Turkmenistan also received a fair share of interested foreign investors, but quickly turned them away. See Chapter 4 for details.

western Siberia and the Volga-Urals region, but the largest projected source of future reserves – offshore in the Far East (that is, Sakhalin Island) – is considered a challenge for even the large multinational oil companies. Nonetheless, Russia chose to privatize its oil sector to domestic actors and, as detailed in Chapter 5, has actively sought to limit foreign investment in Sakhalin.

Finally, with the exception of Russia, at independence, none of these countries had existing pipelines that provided ready-made access to foreign markets.[27] On the one hand, this might lend support to the widely accepted view that Russia was able to privatize because it did not need the same degree of investment in infrastructure that would require foreign capital. It does not help explain, however, why the other three former Soviet republics chose very different structures of ownership. On the other hand, a preexisting network of pipelines linking producing fields to international markets should facilitate maintaining state ownership with control.

In sum, the departure of the five petroleum-rich Soviet successor states from the conventional story of the resource curse – both in terms of ownership structure and fiscal regimes – presents us with a twofold opportunity for theoretical advancement. While the core of this book is dedicated to advancing and testing a set of hypotheses concerning the relationship between mineral wealth and fiscal regimes, in Chapter 9, we offer an alternative explanation for the variation in ownership structure over petroleum wealth that we document over the course of the twentieth century and test it using an original cross-sectional dataset. The statistical results serve to bolster our claim that none of the existing explanations, including prior ownership structure, international pressures, or the structural features of oil wealth itself, can account for the variation in ownership structure – both across the FSU and beyond. They should also allay any concerns about endogeneity by demonstrating that each form of ownership structure is chosen for reasons that are independent of the fiscal regime it generates.

RETHINKING THE RESOURCE CURSE

To recap, we argue that ownership structure is the key intervening variable between mineral wealth and institutional outcomes. The main implication of the research put forth in this book, then, is that the negative outcomes commonly associated with mineral wealth – particularly weak fiscal regimes, which are linked directly to poor economic growth, enfeebled states, and authoritarian regimes – should instead be attributed to who owns and controls the mineral sector. On the one hand, this is a significant departure from the widespread assumption that all mineral-rich states will inevitably become rentier or distributive states because they are incapable of building or sustaining fiscal regimes. On the other hand, it is consistent with the broader

---

[27] Only Russia and Azerbaijan inherited an integrated (domestic) pipeline system connecting the major oil-producing regions with refineries.

treatment of natural resources that acknowledges the variable impact of ownership. In particular, for more than half a century, the literature on common property resources (CPRs) has deliberated the effects of different types of property regimes on environmental management outcomes (such as conservation, depletion, and overexploitation) for natural resources as varied as forests, rivers, and fisheries (see Ostrom 1990). Yet the combination of viewing petroleum as an atypical resource and the role of the state as sanctimonious may account for why proponents of the resource curse thesis have overlooked ownership structure as a variable.[28] Thus we not only offer a more complete explanation for the economic and political pathologies associated with the so-called resource curse, but also bring the study of petroleum back into the mainstream natural resource literature.

Both of these insights suggest that the main shortcoming of the conventional resource curse literature is its focus on a single time period (that is, from roughly 1970 to 1990).[29] Conversely, taking a much broader view indicates that the entire notion of a "resource curse" is bounded temporally. First, the predominance of state ownership during this period may have blinded researchers' ability to consider ownership as a variable. According to our calculations, just under 80 percent of all petroleum-rich countries in the developing world had adopted either state ownership with (S_1) or without control (S_2) by the early 1970s. Second, the particular international context that framed this time period in which host governments' "interests" were fiercely protected over those of foreign investors reinforced both the choice of state ownership and the negative outcomes we argue that it promotes. Thus broadening our historical perspective lends credence to the contention that the record underperformance of resource-rich countries from the late 1960s until the early 1990s is a product of different modes of development in the post – WWII era, especially since prior to this they actually grew faster than their resource-poor counterparts (see Auty 2001b).

Thus, by documenting the variation in ownership structure over the course of the twentieth century, we do not merely provide an initial justification for exploring the links between ownership structure and fiscal regimes in mineral-rich states. We also make a compelling case for broadening our historical perspective concerning the experience of petroleum-rich countries. As we show in Chapter 6, it is not just that ownership structure varies across countries over time, but also that the very meaning of ownership structure changes in response to the international context. During the 1970s and 1980s, fiscal regimes under S_1 and S_2 looked remarkably similar because governing elites' preferences for weak fiscal regimes predominated. Due to the prevalence of the obsolescing bargain, whereby bargaining power shifted decisively from foreign investors to host governments once contracts were signed, whether the state exercised managerial control on paper mattered little in practice when

---

[28] For a recent example of the normative bias toward the state, see Humphreys et al. 2007.

[29] There are few exceptions, such as Haber and Menaldo (2008) and Dunning (2008).

it came to taxation and expenditure. Since the 1990s, however, the ability of some foreign investors to avert the obsolescing bargain combined with pressures for adopting CSR has fostered fiscal outcomes under S_2 that are qualitatively different and can be substantively better from the perspective of the population. In contrast to this prior period, not only do foreign investors' contracts automatically include a social spending component, where these investors can enforce their contracts and are fully committed to CSR, there is a much greater potential for mineral wealth not only to improve citizens' lives in the short term but also to contribute to long-term social and economic development.

PLAN OF THE BOOK

Because we focus on fiscal regimes in order to advance our understanding of the relationship between mineral wealth and institutions, the next chapter is dedicated to justifying this focus. On the one hand, the predominant emphasis on taxation and expenditure institutions in mineral-rich states is directly related to the almost immediate impact they can have on the quality of citizens' daily lives. On the other, the consensus that weak fiscal regimes are the primary cause of the so-called resource curse is consistent with the broader literature in political economy that links how states generate and allocate revenue directly to their long-term prospects for developing administrative capacity, sustaining economic growth, and promoting democracy. Chapter 2 seeks to illuminate and refine these causal connections both by disaggregating taxation and expenditure policies in mineral-rich states and explicating why some ways of taxing and spending are more likely to constrain and enable the state than others. Thus this chapter also serves to clarify our rationale for classifying fiscal regimes as "weak," "strong," or "hybrid" – each of which not only is an important outcome in its own right but also has unique implications for other long-term social, economic, and political outcomes.

The rest of the book is divided into two parts. In the first part, we turn our attention to the most common form of ownership structure – state ownership with control (S_1), and the least common – private domestic ownership (P_1). In Chapter 3, we develop our theory for how each of these two forms of ownership structure fosters weak and strong fiscal regimes, respectively, via three causal mechanisms: TCs, societal expectations, and power relations. The next two chapters utilize empirical evidence from our case studies to test our hypotheses concerning both fiscal outcomes and the mechanisms through which they are generated. Chapter 4 explores the causal link between S_1 and weak fiscal regimes in Turkmenistan and Uzbekistan. Chapter 5 explores the causal link between P_1 and strong fiscal regimes in the Russian Federation.

In the second part, we turn to the remaining forms of ownership structure in which foreign investors are directly involved in the exploitation of petroleum – state ownership without control (S_2) and private foreign ownership (P_2). Chapter 6 situates these forms of ownership within the international context and elucidates how changes at the international level mediate the direct effects of S_2 and P_2 on the same three causal mechanisms we identify in Chapter 3: TCs, societal expectations, and power relations. In Chapters 7 and 8, we test the effects of S_2 and P_2 on fiscal outcomes in Azerbaijan and Kazakhstan, respectively, during our third time period (1990–2005), in which new norms regarding the way that businesses conduct their operations abroad emerged, accompanied by new actors (INGOs and IFIs) actively seeking to diffuse these norms.

In Chapter 9, we shift the focus of the book to the prior question of where ownership structure itself comes from. We offer an alternative explanation for the variation in ownership structure over petroleum wealth over the course of the twentieth century that emphasizes the role of agency and domestic conditions. We then utilize an original cross-sectional dataset that includes all petroleum-rich countries in the developing world from the late 1800s through 2005 to test our explanation against competing hypotheses. As such, this chapter serves two crucial purposes: first, to demonstrate that ownership structure is not endogenous to fiscal regimes; and second, to add further credibility to our central claim that ownership structure cannot be taken for granted across time and space, but rather must be treated as a variable in our analysis of the development prospects for mineral-rich states.

Finally, we conclude in Chapter 10 by returning to our larger claim that we need to broaden our historical perspective concerning the resource curse. The chapters that follow make a compelling case that the conventional literature has erred in treating ownership structure as a constant rather than a variable, and thus has impeded our understanding of the relationship between mineral wealth and institutions. Yet it turns out that this is only one of several faulty presumptions that have contributed to the myth of the resource curse. These faulty presumptions, moreover, all share a common root – that is, the conventional literature's focus on a truncated timeline: roughly the late 1960s to the early 1990s. A reappraisal of the most significant of these suggests both that the entire notion that oil is a curse is bounded temporally and that the predominance of state ownership during the 1970s and 1980s holds the key to understanding why this particular period has shown such strong statistical support for the resource curse hypothesis.

2

Why Fiscal Regimes

Taxation and Expenditure in Mineral-Rich States

> The history of state revenue production is the history of the evolution of the state.
>
>   – Margaret Levi (1988, 1)

> All mineral states ... are rentier or distributive states.
>
>   – Terry Lynn Karl (1997, 49)

The conventional literature on the resource curse defines the problem of mineral-rich states as essentially a fiscal one. In short, because they can derive income exclusively from external rents, such states have no need to develop a viable tax system to tap into domestic sources of revenue. Fiscal independence from the domestic population, in turn, affords governing elites the freedom to distribute the state's income as they please. Mineral-rich states, therefore, are often classified as both rentier states and distributive states.

This focus on fiscal regimes, particularly the extractive side, is understandable considering the overwhelming emphasis on taxation in the general political economy literature. Beginning with Max Weber, it is widely recognized that the ability to generate revenue is a minimal requirement for modern statehood. Simply put: without revenue, state leaders would be unable to perform the basic tasks of staffing the bureaucracy, maintaining social order, and securing their borders (see Levi 1988, Tilly 1975), let alone to fulfill the broader goal of promoting societal welfare (see Skocpol and Amenta 1986). Not surprisingly, then, some have defined the state solely "in terms of [its] taxation powers" (Lieberman 2002, 92 referring to North 1981, 21).[1]

The source of this revenue, moreover, is considered to be of paramount importance because it affects not only state capacity but also the potential for long-term economic development and democratization (see Bates and Lien

---

[1] According to North, the state is "an organization with a comparative advantage in violence, extending over a geographic area whose boundaries are determined by its power to tax constituents".

1985, Levi 1988, North and Weingast 1989). Generally speaking, domestic sources of revenue generation are believed to have an advantage over external sources in this regard. First of all, when the state is forced to rely primarily on the domestic economy for its income, it is much more likely to adopt policies that foster economic growth across sectors. Secondly, because "the taxed devise ways of being represented" (Anderson 1992 cited in Waterbury 1997, 149), taxing the domestic population is more likely to foster demands for democracy from below. Likewise, the resource curse literature has also consistently cited the reliance on external sources of income as responsible for the prevalence of weak state capacity, unbalanced economic growth, and authoritarian regimes in mineral-rich states (see Beblawi and Luciani 1987, Karl, 1997, Mahdavy 1970, Ross 2001a).

Consistent with both sets of literature, then, our focus on fiscal regimes is motivated by the presumption that how states generate and allocate revenue has long-term developmental implications when it comes to administrative capacity, economic growth, and democratization. Yet our analysis is also based on two important points of departure.

First, departing from the resource curse literature, we seek to investigate rather than take for granted the types of taxation and expenditure institutions that emerge in mineral-rich states. In short, the contention that all mineral-rich states are necessarily rentier or distributive states offers an overly simplistic and one-dimensional view of taxation and expenditure in these states. Regarding the former, domestic taxation is treated as a zero-sum proposition – that is, deriving income from external rents precludes the government from taxing its citizenry. As it turns out, rentier states do, in fact, tax their citizens, and yet, because they tend to do so indirectly and implicitly, this is often overlooked or considered inconsequential (Waterbury 1997). We argue instead that the key is not whether the state derives income from domestic sources but how – specifically, whether it relies primarily on direct and explicit or indirect and implicit forms of taxation. Similarly, when it comes to expenditures, proponents of the distributive state thesis consistently emphasize the government's ability to spend at will and its tendency to do so wastefully, but do not specify the patterns of spending beyond large outlays for public works or ("national prestige") projects. And yet, here again, we highlight that the key problem is not that these states engage in broad social spending, but the fact that they do so overwhelmingly through providing implicit subsidies and universally available free (or heavily discounted) goods and services rather than explicitly targeting the poorest segments of society.

Second, departing from the general political economy literature, our emphasis on taxation and expenditure institutions in mineral-rich states is also motivated by the recognition that fiscal regimes are an important outcome in their own right. A system of taxation and expenditures based on transparency, for example, creates the possibility that governments can be held accountable for how they extract and allocate revenue, and thereby increases the cost of corruption and politically motivated spending decisions. It does not, however, necessarily promote democratic governance or sustained economic growth. When it comes to the expenditure side in particular, transparency alone does not guarantee that governments' spending priorities will embrace the short- or long-term developmental goals of international financial institutions (IFIs) and international nongovernmental organizations (INGOs) – that is, poverty alleviation and human capital formation. And yet promoting transparency has nonetheless become the mantra of IFIs and INGOs actively involved in the mineral sector since the 1990s (see Humphreys et al. 2007).

In sum, we contend that evaluating fiscal regimes in mineral-rich states requires a multidimensional perspective. Just as in other countries – developing and developed alike – they are the set of institutions that embody decisions about (1) the primary sources of government revenue, including the stability, scope, and composition of taxation; and (2) how this revenue is allocated, including how much is spent, on what it is spent, and how it is spent. These institutions, moreover, vary according to the degree to which they constrain and enable the state. In this chapter, we clarify why some ways of taxing and spending are more constraining and enabling than others and thus why they are not only inherently more desirable but also more likely to promote short-term benefits as well as long-term developmental outcomes. In doing so, we justify our definition of a strong fiscal regime as one that encompasses both: (1) a tax system that is stable, broad-based, and relies primarily on direct and explicit taxation, and (2) a system of expenditures that emphasizes budgetary stability and transparency.

TAXATION

When it comes to evaluating their political role, tax systems have three essential features: stability, scope, and composition.[2] Stability concerns both whether there is an official tax code and how frequently this code changes. Scope refers to the breadth or expansiveness of the tax base – specifically whether the state budget relies on a single sector or multiple sectors of the economy (see Andersson 1992). For mineral-rich states, it refers to the extent to which the state focuses its revenue collection primarily on the mineral sector. In practice, this reflects whether the official tax code integrates the mineral sector with other economic sectors or whether a separate tax code is devised solely for the mineral sector. Composition involves the types of taxes that comprise the tax system – that is, if they are direct or indirect, explicit or implicit. Direct taxes, including personal income and corporate profits tax as well as capital gains and property taxes, are "collected from those citizens who actually pay the tax burden themselves," whereas indirect taxes are essentially consumption taxes,

---

[2] In contrast, economists often evaluate them based on fairness, efficiency, administrative simplicity, adaptability, and transparency (see Di John 2006, McLure 1999, Peters 1991).

such as sales, excise, and the value added tax (VAT), that "are collected by intermediaries such as producers and firms" (Lieberman 2002, 105).[3] Implicit taxation differs from explicit taxation in that it does not directly affect the government budget and usually takes the form of subsidies, including directed credits, discounted production inputs, production quotas, and price and wage controls (see Rosenberg et al. 1999).

The links between the first two of these characteristics and whether the state is effectively constrained and enabled are fairly straightforward. When tax systems are stable, they provide an effective constraint not only on what the state can extract but also on how much it has to spend without turning to additional sources, such as foreign loans. Stable tax systems are also more enabling over both the short and long term because they ensure some degree of predictability for both state and private actors. With predictable revenue streams, both sets of actors can make more informed budgetary choices and sustained investments. A minimum requirement for successful human capital development, for example, is a sustained budgetary commitment (see Schultz 1961). And, as we will elaborate upon below, human capital development is intricately linked to economic growth. Similarly, private entrepreneurs need some assurance that their tax burden will not fluctuate and be assigned arbitrarily in order to willingly and openly grow their companies by increasing employment. It is well known, for example, that the informal economy is largest in those countries where this assurance does not exist (see Schneider 2002). The expansion of small and medium enterprises (SMEs), moreover, provides an alternative source not only of stable tax revenue and economic growth in the long term, but also of employment and poverty reduction in the short term (see Agbeibor Jr. 2006).[4]

Similarly, tax systems that rely on multiple sectors of the economy are more constraining and enabling than those that are limited to the mineral sector because they produce a more stable and predictable source of revenue. As is well established, export commodities, particularly "point source" natural resource exports such as minerals (see Isham et al. 2003), are prone to boom-and-bust cycles due to market volatility, subjecting the state budget to a great deal of instability (Karl 2004, Katz et al. 2004, Mikesell 1997). By providing the state with an alternative source of revenue, then, broad-based tax systems directly contribute to both the development of state capacity and long-term economic growth in two equally important ways. First, they stabilize the budget, without which it is impossible to build and sustain a well-functioning administrative apparatus (see Eshag 1983, Katz et al. 2004). Second, they provide governments with the means to recover from an economic crisis caused by

---

[3] This builds on the classic distinction of indirect from direct taxes as "assessed on *objects* rather than on individuals" (Musgrave 1969, 173).

[4] SMEs are one of the most important sources of both employment generation and poverty reduction in developing countries, where they "account for 50 to 60 percent of total employment" (ILO 2005, 225).

a sharp fall in commodity prices without incurring foreign debt. The tendency for governments to borrow from abroad or engage in deficit spending rather than cut current expenditures in response to a bust is one of the main reasons why, for example, those countries that rely primarily on mineral sector taxation tend to be heavily indebted in comparison to their resource-poor counterparts (see Katz et al. 2004, McMahon 1997, Sarraf and Jiwanji 2001).

When mineral sector taxation is integrated into the general tax code, however, even a taxation system that relies primarily on the mineral sector can provide some degree of constraint on the state. To understand why, consider the fact that when mineral sector taxation is relegated to a separate tax code, it is much less visible to the domestic population as well as international monitoring agencies. This serves both to conceal the true value of the rents that accrue from the mineral sector and to facilitate the diversion of these rents, for example, into secret bank accounts (see Global Witness 2004). Conversely, the inclusion of mineral sector taxation in the official tax code not only has the potential to reveal the true value of these rents but also subject them to greater public oversight. The short-term benefit is a reduced opportunity for governing elites to divert revenue from mineral sector taxation intended for the state's coffers because it increases governmental accountability. In the long term, creating institutionalized impediments to corruption helps both ensure that the government has more money to spend on matters of the state and prevent incumbents from utilizing mineral rents to build or sustain an authoritarian regime (Wantchekon 1999). As we discuss under expenditures, mineral sector taxation that is transparent is also enabling because it increases the likelihood that the state will make better allocational decisions.

The effect of different tax structures (that is, composition) on state behavior is more complex and somewhat more contentious. Direct taxation is more likely to constrain the state in both the short and long term by virtue of its visibility, which places both its extraction and spending patterns under greater scrutiny and thereby makes it easier for taxpayers to hold the state accountable. Conversely, indirect taxes are inherently less constraining because they are virtually invisible to taxpayers (Peters 1991, 37).[5] In fact, there is a broad consensus that indirect taxes are so prominent in the developing world precisely because their reduced visibility evokes little popular protest and thus minimizes the political costs of collection (see Fauvelle-Aymar 1999, Lieberman 2002).[6] The inability to hold government accountable, moreover, translates into spending patterns as well. The doctrine of fiscal illusion, for example, "contends that since indirect taxes hide the total amount paid, citizens are misled into paying more than they would otherwise pay" (Webber

---

[5] Some tax experts advocate the VAT, for example, because it "can raise revenue with the least noise" (Bagachi 1991, 246). In reality, of course, some indirect taxes are less invisible than others.

[6] In contrast, direct taxes are the largest single source of revenue in most industrialized countries (Peters 1991, 29).

and Wildavsky 1986, 578). Among other things, unrestrained government spending can result in a bloated state bureaucracy.

Direct taxation is also more likely to enable the state in both the short and long term because it is more difficult to administer, whereas indirect taxes are less enabling because they are much easier to collect. Indirect taxes based on consumption require little paperwork, reporting, and monitoring essentially because they are collected incrementally and at the point of purchase (see Peters 1991, 35). In contrast, assessing and collecting direct taxes, particularly personal income taxes (PIT), requires the state both to cultivate a group of local tax experts (McLure 1992) and to create and sustain an administrative apparatus, which in the modern era has required frequent upgrades in informational technology through which it can continually and accurately gather information about the employment status and earnings of private individuals (see DiJohn 2006, Slemod 1990). In addition to building administrative capacity, this requirement provides the state with crucial information, including who is employed and in what sectors of the economy, through which it can redistribute wealth and make better investment decisions (see Chaudhry 1989, Giddens 1987) – two of the most widely accepted justifications for state intervention in the economy (Eshag 1983, 11–16). In short, it is analogous to providing the state with an ongoing economic census whereby it has a clearer sense of both the current health and future potential of the economy. Although its long-term benefits have received much more scholarly attention, direct taxation can also serve to enable the state in the short term. Access to reliable economic information concerning the economic status of its citizens, for example, has an immediate effect on both the likelihood that the government will engage in social spending that targets the poor, and moreover, that this policy will be effective. Direct taxation (particularly PIT) can also provide revenue relatively quickly, which may be why it has been introduced so commonly during wartime (see Peters 1991, 228).

Some direct taxes, however, are arguably easier to assess and collect than others. There is a broad consensus that corporate income taxes (CIT) or enterprise profit taxes (EPT)[7] require considerably less administrative capacity than the PIT – particularly when the taxpayers in question are either state-owned enterprises (SOEs) or multinational corporations (MNCs). The reasons are twofold: first, these firms tend to be large and highly concentrated; second, due primarily to their size and high degree of concentration, they are subject to more stringent and enforceable reporting requirements.[8] Both SOEs and MNCs are thus considered to be "captive sources of tax revenue" in developing countries (Waterbury 1997, 153) because they cannot escape detection (see Musgrave 1969). Indeed, profit taxes imposed on SOEs can often be deducted automatically from state-controlled bank accounts, as they were

---

[7] In many countries, the EPT is the equivalent of the CIT for state-owned enterprises.

[8] In other words, corporations tend to keep better records than the average citizen (Peters 1991, 31).

in the Soviet Union. As a result, they "are required to comply with statutory accounting requirements from which the majority of small farmers and traders are exempt" (Burgess and Stern 1993, 777). Moreover, tax collection from MNCs is often facilitated by tax reporting requirements in their home countries that allow them to write off some portion of their overseas taxation (Tanzer 1969, 62).

The view that it requires less state capacity to collect CIT is consistent with the conventional wisdom that sectors largely determine the difficulty of taxation (see Fauvelle-Aymar 1999). By virtue of its concentration, the mineral sector is said to provide an easy source of CIT (see Shafer 1994). Thus the level of direct taxation is often inflated in mineral-rich countries.[9] According to this view, then, while relying on CIT in the mineral sector can be enabling in the short term because it provides a more immediate source of revenue, especially in the form of bonuses and royalties,[10] it is nonetheless disabling in the long term because of the effects on budgetary instability and unpredictability described above. What this perspective overlooks, however, is that the source of CIT can have varying effects. If MNCs are the main source, for example, the degree to which it can serve to enable the state depends on the stability of contracts between host governments and foreign investors. When the terms of these contracts are relatively fixed and compliance rates are high, CIT in the mineral sector can actually serve to enhance budgetary stability and predictability.

Income taxes are particularly enabling. First, they are both a more efficient and productive way of collecting taxes than taxes on consumption, such as tariffs and excises (Fauvelle-Aymar 1999, 392). At a minimum, they are based on economic productivity such that a government undermines its own tax base when it adopts policies that damage this productivity. An excessive CIT rate, for example, may undermine long-term economic growth by denying firms the capital to invest in the future of their companies (Peters 1991, 31) or encouraging them to move their operations abroad (see Andersson 1992). The adoption of a flat tax for both PIT and CIT, therefore, may serve not only "as a way of tying the government's hands in limiting the size of government" but also as a means to "renounce an activist stance of favoring particular activities or sectors" (Keen et al. 2006, 35), and hence provide the government with further incentive to stimulate economic growth across sectors. In addition, increasing reliance on the VAT rather than income tax has been criticized as regressive because it fails to capture revenue generated in the informal economy and thus acts as one more obstacle to promoting economic growth and building state capacity (Emran and Stigltiz 2005).

---

[9] This is precisely why Waterbury (1997) finds higher than expected levels of direct taxation in the Middle East and North Africa. Lieberman (2002) reports a similar finding regarding Venezuela.

[10] Countries may receive bonuses as soon as a contract is signed with an MNC and then royalties and potentially additional bonuses as soon as production commences.

Second, income taxes offer a more efficient way for the government to redistribute wealth among its citizens (than, for example, subsidies, which are discussed below). In fact, one of the primary reasons that income tax is considered a direct tax is that it "may be adjusted to the individual characteristics of the taxpayer, whereas indirect taxes are levied on transactions irrespective of the circumstance of buyer and seller" (Cremer et al. 2001, 781). Thus, income taxes are redistributional not only because they extract income from some members of the community to serve the entire community, but also because they can be made progressive, whereas indirect taxes can only be proportional (ibid, 782).[11] Taxes on consumption, by definition if not design, disproportionately affect the poorest segments of society because they tend to "devote more of their income to consumption than the rich" (Waterbury 1997, 150).[12]

Implicit taxation has many of the same short-term advantages and long-term disadvantages of indirect taxation. Like taxes on consumption, implicit taxes are essentially invisible – and perhaps even more so because they are often excluded from the official budget – and thus, unlikely to provoke political opposition. Precisely because implicit taxes are "hidden," their widespread use reduces governmental accountability. The population cannot hold its leaders accountable "for what does not officially exist and is therefore difficult to quantify" (Jones Luong 2003b, 14). Implicit taxation is also relatively easier to administer than explicit forms of taxation and thus does not contribute to building state capacity. In fact, some forms of implicit taxation, such as harassment by local tax authorities and the arbitrary use of fines for tax violations, thrive on weak administrative capacity.

EXPENDITURES

Government spending essentially consists of three different parts: (1) how much revenue is spent (rather than saved); (2) what it is spent on; and (3) how it is spent. When it comes to evaluating how much revenue is spent, for example, the literature on the welfare state in both the developed and developing world focuses primarily on determining levels of public expenditure – that is, what percentage of GDP and the total government budget is allocated toward social spending (see Garrett 1998, Kaufman and Segura-Ubiergo 2001). At the same time, this literature disaggregates levels of social spending according to what it is being spent on – specifically, expenditures on social protection (for example, pensions) versus human capital development (for example, health and education). Finally, as the efficacy with which spending alleviates poverty and builds human capital has become more central to the agenda of IFIs, research has turned increasingly to the question of how revenue is distributed – that

---

[11] This includes flat taxes, "the distributional effects of [which] are not unambiguously regressive, and in some cases they may have increased progressivity" (Keen et al. 2006, 1).

[12] The VAT can be designed to avoid this, however (see Bird and Gendron 2007, Ebrill et al. 2001).

is, whether social spending is implicit versus explicit or universal versus targeted – and by whom it is distributed – that is, state versus private actors (see Andrews and Ringold 1999, IMF 2007a). Each of these three components contributes to whether the state is effectively constrained and enabled due to its respective impact on budgetary stability and transparency.

When it comes to making expenditures more stable and transparent, there are a variety of institutional options that pertain to developed and developing countries alike, irrespective of mineral wealth. To prevent prolonged deficit spending and the accumulation of foreign debt, for example, states often set legal limits on government spending and borrowing, such as constitutional amendments requiring balanced budgets and parliamentary approval of sizable budgetary outlays (see Tanzi and Schuknecht 2000, Webber and Wildavsky 1986). They can also institute procedures, such as regular independent audits, for monitoring the budgetary process to ensure not only that spending limits are enforced but also that spending commitments are actually met (see Von Hagen and Harden 1996).

A method for enhancing budgetary stability and transparency particularly relevant for the developing world concerns the reduction or elimination of quasi-fiscal activities (hereafter QFAs). QFAs are activities that are not explicitly executed through budgetary mechanisms and can include implicit subsidies to consumers, preferential credits, tax arrears, and subsidized inputs for selected industries, as well as extrabudgetary funds. In mineral-rich states, these routinely come in the form of energy subsidies to households and enterprises (see IEA 1999). QFAs are problematic for two main reasons. First, they "divert public resources in an inefficient and non-transparent manner, undermining accountability and economic growth" (Andrews and Shatalov 2004). For example, governments often utilize QFAs in order to continue to finance "structurally or socially important enterprises, regardless of their performance" (ibid) or to "serve special interest groups" without parliamentary scrutiny (Freinkman et al. 2003, 3). Second, QFAs contribute heavily to the state's expanded role in the economy, and yet, by circumventing formal expenditure limits, they actually serve to deflate estimates of the size and scope of government (see Petri et al. 2002). IFIs have thus strongly encouraged the integration of QFAs into the state budget in the form of explicit subsidies and direct expenditures not only to constrain government elites from engaging in discretionary spending, but also to enable them to respond more effectively to an economic crisis (CASE 2008, 135, IMF 2007a, 36).

Another policy tool that is increasingly being applied to the developing world is targeted spending. Although IFIs initially welcomed government efforts to provide universal access to public goods and social services, by the 1990s a consensus emerged that universal social spending was not achieving the dual goals of alleviating poverty and building human capital (for details, see Bird and Zolt 2005, 1636–7, World Bank 1990). Thus, alongside encouraging developing countries to direct social spending toward providing a social safety net and building human capital, IFIs were increasingly advising developing countries to introduce "a program of well-targeted transfers" aimed at the neediest or most vulnerable segments of society in lieu of the universal provision of benefits (World Bank 1990, 4). This has also been the case in mineral-rich countries. For example, the primary aim of the World Bank's Chad-Cameroon Oil and Pipeline Project, which is designed to serve as the model for all oil-exporting countries, is to "promote poverty reduction through targeted use of oil revenues" (Gary and Karl 2003, 60).

Targeted spending is more likely than universal spending to constrain the state for several reasons. First of all, by definition, targeted spending places limits on government expenditures because it restricts the segment of the population that is entitled to certain public goods and social services. In short, it "deliver[s goods and services] selectively to those regarded as being in need," usually based on income (Mitchell et al. 1994, 315), whereas the latter "makes [these goods and services] available to rich and poor alike (i.e., regardless of income)" (Besley 1990, 119). Perhaps because the entitled population also tends to be less politically influential, targeted welfare payments are generally less generous than universal payments are, which reduces the government's spending commitments (see Saudner 1994). Yet designating a segment of the population as "eligible" also makes it harder for governments to renege on their commitments (see Tanzi and Schuknecht 2000, 71).[13] Targeted spending that relies on means testing or evidence-based programs furthermore makes it harder for leaders to direct spending toward their cronies or personal pet projects (see IBRD 2007, v). In contrast, universal spending often locks in high levels of spending, making it harder for governments to introduce cuts during times of economic crises, and instead may spur "wars of attrition," especially since those benefiting most will not want to see cuts in their benefits (see Alesina and Drazen 1991). Secondly, precisely because it designates the "winners" and "losers" of social spending, targeted spending is more transparent than universal spending, which not only enhances the cost effectiveness of social service provision, but also allows governments to focus on strategic policy decisions (Tanzi and Schuknecht 2000, 114, 139; see also IBRD 2007).

Targeted spending is also more likely than universal spending to enable the state because it is both more difficult to implement and more likely to be effective. In short, this is because it requires detailed information about the economic and social well-being of the population. Similar to the way in which direct taxation forces the state to build an administrative apparatus to collect information about the population's employment status – that is, in effect, to conduct an economic census – targeted spending requires the state to carry out a social census (in the form of a household survey).[14] A targeted

[13] This is most evident when targeting is based upon "categorical" criteria rather than "means-testing."

[14] It often requires greater capacity to acquire information about those outside of the cities – that is, the rural poor and more politically disenfranchised (see van der Berg 1998).

social safety net, for example, requires the state to develop the administrative capacity to determine eligibility and then to actually deliver the benefits to the designated population (see Andrews and Ringold 1999). Access to this information, in turn, enables the state to make better decisions regarding redistribution in both the short and long term (see Tanzi and Schuknecht 2000, IBRD 2007). Targeted programs are thus more likely to increase the quality of public goods and services, as well as to have a greater impact on alleviating poverty, because they are intended to reflect better the particular characteristics of different social groups (see Van de Walle 1998). In contrast, because it does not take into account income, universal spending can end up benefiting the middle class more than it does the poorest and most vulnerable segments of the population (Tanzi and Schuknecht 2000, 114),[15] particularly when it takes the common form of subsidies, such as price controls on basic goods including bread, dairy products, and meat.[16]

The quintessential institution designed for increasing the stability and transparency of expenditures specifically in mineral-rich states is the Natural Resource Fund (hereafter NRF), which has become an increasingly popular policy recommendation since the 1980s (for details, see Weinthal and Jones Luong 2006b). NRFs consist of stabilization or savings funds and often combine both. As a rule, stabilization funds aim to reduce the impact of commodity price volatility on the economy by smoothing out the budget. Simply stated, they reduce overspending when prices are high and borrowing when prices fall, because when commodity prices are high, excess revenue is placed in the fund, but when prices are low, revenue is transferred out to make up for budgetary shortfalls. Savings funds, in contrast, are intended to ensure that future generations enjoy a share of the nation's wealth, even after the mineral resources are depleted.

In theory, NRFs are constraining and enabling both over the short and long term because they improve budget predictability by simultaneously delinking expenditures from fluctuations in the world market price of mineral exports, thereby stabilizing spending patterns, and increasing transparency of the revenue stream. In the short term, they constrain the state by predetermining what percentage of rents the state can spend and providing a clear set of rules that the population (present and future) can utilize to hold the state accountable. Stabilization funds, in particular, also provide the state with an alternative to accumulating foreign debt during economic downturns to maintain current expenditure levels, which, in turn, affects prospects for long-term economic growth. This was a common problem across mineral exporters in the 1980s and 1990s because they were compelled to commit a significant percentage of their shrinking GDP to debt servicing (see Lewis 1984, Philip 1994). Over the

---

[15] This is also why narrow targeting may be more beneficial than broad targeting when it comes to providing assistance to those in extreme poverty (Van de Walle 1998).

[16] While often hailed as a direct benefit for the poor, such subsidies are often meaningless to the poorest segments of the population because they cannot afford these goods (Ahmed 1992).

long term, NRFs not only force state elites to prolong the utility of what is a finite resource to meet its financial needs and obligations, but also to ensure that some of the benefit derived from mineral wealth is preserved beyond the current generation. Thus NRFs are enabling in that they encourage the state to make better spending decisions – concerning capital investments as well as social service provision – because they cannot simply use resource windfalls to increase public expenditures at will.

Not all NRFs, however, are equally effective at limiting state spending and encouraging state leaders to spend widely (see Bacon and Tordo 2006). First and foremost, NRFs with formal oversight mechanisms, such as a "working" legislature or a truly independent advisory board, tend to be the most effective (Tsalik 2003). The second basic requirement for effective NRFs is transparency, which developing countries are usually advised to increase by establishing clear guidelines for how the money accumulated in the fund can be spent and increasing public involvement[17] in all spending decisions concerning the fund (see Heilbrunn 2002). This can serve both to deter governments from misappropriating revenue and to ensure that revenue is allocated toward public spending aimed at relieving poverty and building human capital. However, there is no guarantee that governments will actually decide to allocate funds in this way. For example, when particularistic interests are disproportionately represented, a greater public role in determining how much of the fund should be spent and exactly on what it should be spent can actually reduce the government's ability to make economically rational spending decisions. A third way of increasing transparency that has received much less attention but may actually be more effective is to integrate the NRF into the state budget, such that mineral rents must be reported and accounted for along with all other sources of government income and outlays (see Heilbrunn 2002, IMF 2007a).

Another means of enhancing budgetary stability and transparency in mineral-rich states concerns contractual relations between foreign investors and host governments. Although rarely viewed in this light, where foreign investors are directly involved in developing the mineral sector either as managers or as owners, the nature of their fiscal burden can play a decisive role in constraining and enabling the state. Stable contracts, for example, contribute to both budgetary stability and transparency because they impede governing elites' ability either to rely on foreign investors to routinely increase government spending and to finance large investment projects that exceed the state's own financial capacity, or to redirect these funds so as to benefit themselves and their political allies. Likewise, when foreign investors' fiscal burden is composed not only of taxation but also of social spending requirements,

---

[17] This can range from making financial information about the fund publicly available to institutionalizing direct participation in the decision-making process (see Bacon and Tordo 2006).

there is a greater likelihood that those communities most affected by mineral extraction will actually benefit. Moreover, when foreign investors can set their own priorities, and these priorities are consistent with those of IFIs and INGOs, there is a higher probability that their spending will be devoted to reducing poverty and promoting broad socioeconomic development in the host country. These efforts are far more likely to actually improve society's welfare in the host country when foreign investors partner with local activists to help determine their spending priorities. Decisions regarding the provision of schools and health clinics, for example, are often more efficacious when they are made with the open involvement of the people they are intended to help (IMF 2007a, 29–30).

Finally, the nature of foreign investors' fiscal burden can have a direct impact on budgetary transparency. First, the terms of foreign investors' contracts can be made publicly available so as to increase popular awareness and access to information regarding the size and nature of mineral sector rents to the state. One institutional mechanism for doing this is to require both foreign investors and governments to publish the royalties, income taxes, and bonuses that they pay and receive, respectively, and then to submit them to a neutral auditor for verification.[18] Another is to integrate foreign investors' expenditures into the state budget (IMF 2007a, 11). Even when foreign investors' spending requirements are specified in their contracts, if their expenditures remain outside of the budgetary process, they can distort overall spending priorities. Integrating them into the formal budgetary process, then, would be both constraining and enabling – that is, it would serve not only to increase government accountability vis-à-vis the population but also to encourage the government to make more economically rational spending decisions.

BEYOND RENTIERISM

In sum, not all fiscal regimes are created alike. Mineral-rich states in particular can adopt a variety of taxation and expenditure institutions that can serve – to varying degrees – to constrain the government from relying exclusively on the mineral sector and engaging in wasteful spending of mineral rents, and enable the government to invest the proceeds from mineral sector development wisely and to recover from economic crises precipitated by external commodity shocks. While the conventional resource curse literature rightly emphasizes the problem of weak fiscal regimes in such states, it artificially limits it to one of dependence on an external source of revenue that is spent wastefully – that is, to the problem of rentierism. This, we contend, is due to the overwhelming tendency in this literature to treat taxation as dichotomous and zero-sum

---

[18] Since 2002, this has been facilitated through the "Extractive Industries Transparency Initiative" (EITI). See Chapter 6 for details.

and to emphasize total government expenditures rather than to disaggregate both taxation and spending. In order to provide a more complete picture of fiscal regimes in mineral-rich countries and to illuminate their short- as well as long-term impact, we distinguish and evaluate tax systems according to their stability, scope, and composition, and expenditure systems according to not only how much revenue is spent but also on what and how it is spent.

3

State Ownership with Control versus Private Domestic Ownership

> Supposing we had oil and gas, do you think I could get the people to do this? No ... . If I had oil and gas I'd have a different people, with different motivations and expectations. It's because we don't have oil and gas and they know that we don't have, and they know that this [Singapore's economic] progress comes from their efforts.
>
> – Lee Kwan Yew, founder and first Prime Minister of Singapore, on why he was able to motivate his citizenry to work hard and expect less from the government (Mydans and Arnold 2007).

> The [resource curse] problem is exacerbated by the fact that natural resources tend to be controlled by state-run monopolies, which pretty much insures a low level of innovation and competitiveness, and encourages people to look to the state, instead of themselves, for solutions.
>
> – James Surowiecki (2001) on why countries like Saudi Arabia are hooked on oil.

The variation in ownership structure over mineral reserves across time and space in the twentieth century documented in Chapter 1 is not just an empirical fact. It also has theoretical import because it influences the institutional outcomes that follow – specifically, whether weak, strong, or hybrid fiscal regimes emerge in mineral-rich states. In sum, we argue that ownership structure fosters distinct fiscal regimes because it generates the transaction costs (hereafter, TCs) and societal expectations that influence what kinds of rules governing taxation and spending the main claimants to the proceeds from mineral wealth prefer, and the power relations that influence how such institutions emerge, and hence whether they persist. The purpose of this chapter, therefore, is twofold: first, to clarify how we conceptualize TCs, societal expectations, and power relations, and second, to provide a theory for how each of these causal mechanisms links different forms of ownership structure to various types of fiscal regimes.

As detailed in Chapter 1, our classification yields four different ideal types of ownership structure – state ownership with control (S_1), state ownership without control (S$_2$), private domestic ownership (P$_1$), and private foreign ownership (P$_2$). In this chapter, we focus exclusively on what have historically been its most common and least common forms, respectively: S$_1$ and P$_1$.[1] By 1970, for example, S$_1$ had well surpassed P$_2$ as the dominant form of ownership structure over petroleum wealth in the developing world – a position it retained for over 30 years.[2] In contrast, over the course of the entire twentieth century, only a handful of developing countries have adopted P$_1$.[3]

State ownership with control (S$_1$) is arguably the most coveted form of ownership from the perspective of governing elites because it provides the government with the greatest amount of decision-making authority over the mineral sector and most direct access to its proceeds. In other words, the government not only exercises the sole authority to make decisions about exploration, production, and export of the country's mineral reserves, but also enjoys the status of the direct claimant to the revenue generated from these activities. It usually performs this role via the relevant ministry and a large national vested company – that is, the ministry of petroleum and the national oil company (hereafter NOC) in the case of petroleum.[4] Indeed, the very first NOCs – Argentina's Yacimientos Proliferos Fiscales (YPF), formed in 1922, and Mexico's Petróleos Mexicanos (Pemex), formed in 1938 – were created precisely for this purpose.[5] Pemex, for example, was founded within a few months after nationalization to assume the management and production of the foreign oil companies' expropriated properties (Philip 1982, 221). Thus, while NOCs had become a common feature across petroleum-rich states regardless of ownership structure by the end of the twentieth century, numbering over 100 and "account[ing] for 73 percent of [world oil] production" (McPherson 2003, 185–6), they continued to perform a uniquely prominent role under S$_1$. In particular, because decisions regarding mineral sector development under S$_1$ are not solely based upon economic considerations, NOCs have often served to fulfill the state's political objectives (Pirog 2007). Finally, consistent with our depiction of ownership structure in Chapter 1 as a set of triangular social relations, under S$_1$ the petroleum ministry and NOC are joined by the population, which, as the indirect claimant to the proceeds from mineral wealth, is the other key actor needed to complete this triad.

---

[1] The two remaining forms of ownership structure (S$_2$ and P$_2$) are discussed in Chapter 6.

[2] In the early 1960s, S$_1$ and P$_2$ were nearly tied with each representing about half the total number of cases. By 1970, however, more than half of the petroleum-rich states had adopted S$_1$ whereas less than one-fifth had ownership structures that could be classified as P$_2$. See Appendix B for details.

[3] In addition to Russia (1993–2004), these are: Brazil (1891–1939), Venezuela (1904–1907), Romania (1924–1945), and Guatemala (1949–1983). See Appendix B for details.

[4] The relevant government entity may vary by country. There may also be more than a single ministry involved. And, in some cases, the NOC itself has the status of a government ministry and reports directly to the president.

[5] An important exception is Venezuela's Compañía Venezolana de Petróleo, formed in 1923, which President Gomex created to sell off the remaining national reserves to foreign investors (Lieuwen 1954, 34–6).

While the majority of petroleum-rich countries that have pursued S_1 have immediately developed the natural resource sector for export, the merger of ownership and control rights under S_1 also enables mineral-rich states in the developing world to pursue two other options: (1) to delay the development of the mineral sector and (2) to develop this sector primarily for internal consumption. In short, both of these strategies are facilitated by the minimal role that S_1 affords foreign investors, which means that under this ownership structure the state not only denies itself the upfront cash benefit of bonuses and royalties, but also takes on the burden of providing capital investment to the mineral sector, which may slow the pace of exploration and production as well as the development of export capacity. And yet they have been dismissed by the conventional literature owing to its tendency to equate resource wealth with export dependence (for details, see Chapter 9). This is an important oversight – both because these strategies have the potential to lead to a more productive economic trajectory and because the fact that they have seldom done so in the developing world highlights the importance of treating ownership structure as a variable. The domestic consumption of mineral resources as a basis for industrialization, in particular, has been credited with promoting economic growth in mineral-rich states in the (now) developed world such as Australia, Canada, and the United States (see Davis 1995, Irwin 2000, Watkins 1963, Wright and Czelusta 2004). But this experience has rarely been replicated elsewhere. A large part of the reason for this, we argue, is that those petroleum-rich countries in the developing world that have pursued this strategy – such as China, Mexico, and Uzbekistan – also adopted S_1 over their respective mineral sectors. As will become clear below, the potential benefits of this development strategy are undermined by the broad negative impact that S_1 tends to have on fiscal regimes.

Conversely, P_1 is among the least desirable forms of ownership structure from the perspective of governing elites. While it shifts the financial burden of capital investment away from the state, it places decision-making authority concerning the development of the country's mineral wealth in the hands of non-state actors who also enjoy the sole status of direct claimant to the proceeds generated from this wealth. Decisions about whether to produce petroleum primarily for export or internal consumption, for example, is thus left to these private actors rather than to governing elites, as under S_1, and based primarily on economic considerations, such as the size of the domestic market, rather than political factors. It is no coincidence that in all of the aforementioned cases where mineral wealth is associated with sustained economic growth, the private sector has been at the helm. In the United States, for example, the private oil industry's decision to produce for the domestic market in California, which at the end of the nineteenth century was a "remote, peripheral economy" was responsible for spawning massive growth in its manufacturing sector between 1900 and 1930 (Wright 2001, Wright and Czelusta 2003, 14). Under P_1, then, ownership and control are not vested in the government via the ministry of petroleum and the NOC, which may either not exist at all or serve merely as a holding company for minority shares retained by the state.[6] It is vested in the domestic private owners (hereafter, DPOs) and their shareholders. This is not to say that governing elites play little or no role in managing the mineral sector, but rather that because they serve as an indirect claimant alongside the population, their primary function is to tax and regulate. Thus here the triangular relationship is most likely to consist of DPOs, bureaucracies charged with matters of state finance, the environment, and trade (rather than petroleum per se), and the population.

At the same time, S_1 and P_1 are similar in that foreign investors play only a minimal role in the development of mineral sector. In fact, a defining feature of S_1 is that foreign investors are routinely shunned while under P_1 they are likely to serve only as minority shareholders and, in some cases, to be employed in a few high-level management positions.[7] In contrast to S_2 and P_2, therefore, the effects of these two forms of ownership structure on fiscal regimes are not mediated by the international context. Most importantly, this means that international financial institutions (IFIs) and international NGOs (INGOs) are unlikely to have a direct influence on the kinds of taxation and spending policies that countries under S_1 and P_1 adopt. It does not mean, however, that the international context has no influence on the behavior and choices of the relevant actors but rather that it is fairly minimal and largely indirect. The diffusion of norms embodied in the notion of "corporate social responsibility" (CSR) in the 1990s, for example, has affected not only the way that major foreign oil companies conduct business abroad, as discussed in Chapter 6, but also how domestic private oil companies conduct business in their home countries.[8] In practice, this means that in the twenty-first century domestic private oil companies are more likely to be held accountable to local populations for the potential damage their activities may cause to the natural environment than during prior exploration periods. U.S. oil companies drilling in the Gulf of Mexico, for example, have both initiated and supported broad conservation projects in the region.[9]

Not surprisingly, S_1 and P_1 tend to produce reverse institutional outcomes. S_1 fosters weak fiscal regimes – that is, fiscal regimes that are neither constraining nor enabling – because it creates low TCs and societal expectations for an

---

[6] If the state retains a small portion of reserves, the NOC or its functional equivalent might also manage these.

[7] Even in the most professional and international NOC, StatoilHydro, the majority of representatives on the Board of Directors and corporate executives are Norwegian citizens (see http://www.statoilhydro.com/en/aboutstatoilhydro/corporategovernance/pages/default.aspx).

[8] Conversely, in the first part of the twentieth century, domestic private oil companies were solely concerned with more traditional "Public Relations" (see Larson et al. 1971).

[9] Marathon, for example, has supported an initiative to protect a bird stopover habitat in the Gulf of Mexico (Marathon 2006), and Transocean joined The Gulf of Mexico Foundation that promotes local concerns regarding conservation in the Gulf of Mexico (http://www.csr-wire.com/News/9114.html).

enlarged state role in generating and allocating revenue such that neither the direct claimants (governing elites) nor the indirect claimants (the population) have an incentive to supply or demand institutions that set effective limits on the state's ability to extract and spend the proceeds from mineral wealth. In contrast, P_I fosters strong fiscal regimes – that is, fiscal regimes that are both constraining and enabling – because it creates high TCs and societal expectations for limited redistribution such that both the direct claimants (DPOs) and indirect claimants (governing elites and the population) have an incentive to supply and demand institutions that set effective limits on the state's ability to extract and spend the proceeds from mineral wealth.

Moreover, weak and strong fiscal regimes are likely to emerge and persist under S_I and P_I, respectively, because the incentives that each form of ownership structure fosters vis-à-vis institution building are reinforced by the process through which these institutions are created. Although both forms of ownership structure produce interdependent power relations between the main actors, and thus facilitate bargaining that produces distributional outcomes, the degree of transparency and accountability in this process varies considerably. Low TCs and high societal expectations under S_I foster the mutual desire to hide information from the public, and thus, encourage implicit bargaining, which not only increases opportunities for corruption but also reinforces personalism as the basis for allocating resources. Conversely, high TCs and low societal expectations under P_I foster the mutual desire to reveal information to the public, and thus encourage explicit bargaining, which contributes not only to greater fiscal transparency but also accountability.

The contention that S_I and P_I foster weak and strong fiscal regimes, respectively, contrasts sharply with the conventional view that mineral wealth is always a curse. According to this view, weak fiscal regimes are inevitable in mineral-rich states because the leaders of these countries, who become myopic and risk-averse as a result of this wealth, inevitably neglect institution building (see Karl 1997, Mitra 1994). The cyclical nature of booms and busts in international commodity prices then serves to exacerbate the perverse psychological effects of mineral wealth, causing these leaders to become fiscally overextended during booms and unable to curtail spending during busts. We argue that these outcomes should not be attributed to mineral wealth per se, but rather to who owns and controls the mineral sector. In sum, in mineral-rich states that adopt S_I, *weak* fiscal regimes are both more likely to emerge and to be reinforced by boom and bust cycles, whereas in mineral-rich states that adopt P_I, *strong* fiscal regimes are both more likely to emerge and to be reinforced by boom and bust cycles. As we elaborate upon in the concluding section to this chapter, shifting the analytical focus away from mineral wealth to ownership structure provides not only a more complete explanation for why specific types of taxation and spending policies emerge but also new insight into why the state has so often failed to serve as an effective engine of economic growth in mineral-rich countries.

TRANSACTION COSTS

Since the concept of transaction costs emerged from Ronald Coase's (1937) original inquiry into the firm, it has been applied to the study of institutions in essentially two ways: (1) TCs can generate the incentives for actors to build institutions; and (2) TCs can influence the actual design of these institutions. At the core of both applications of TCs is a prominent role for information because the notion of such costs is tied to the need for principals to constrain agents or prevent them from making decisions that contradict the principals' interests (see Eggertson 1990, North 1990, Williamson 1985).[10] In other words, TCs are a function of information asymmetries about other actors' interests, and hence behavior.[11] When these information asymmetries are high, they elevate the costs of exchange and thereby foster a desire on the part of economic and political actors to create institutions to help minimize these costs (see North 1981). More specifically, these actors have an incentive to establish institutions because they can supply information – for example, by monitoring actors' behavior – that will reduce their uncertainty and stabilize expectations (see Keohane 1988). At the same time, the information costs that economic and political actors face upon agreeing to create such an institution will influence their choice over alternative forms (see Levi 1988, North 1990).[12] The very origin of the theory of TCs, for example, is in finding an explanation for the proliferation of the firm in place of pure market transactions (Williamson 1981).

Although these two approaches are often conflated and the latter has been more prevalent in Political Science, we draw a clear distinction between them and adopt the former for two reasons. First and foremost, there are several possible institutional forms, particularly when it comes to fiscal regimes, that can serve to reduce TCs. Quasi-voluntary compliance is one very efficient way of reducing the TCs of collecting tax revenue (Levi 1988), for example, but there are several others such as introducing a flat tax rate. Thus, there is no reason to assume that efforts to lower TCs will result in a specific institutional outcome. In fact, the prevalent criticism of what amounts to a contractarian approach to the emergence of institutions is that, when there are multiple equilibria, it cannot explain why one particular outcome or institutional solution gets "selected" over the other possibilities (see Bates 1988, Knight 1992). We will return to this critique when we discuss the role of power relations in shaping how institutions emerge. What we want to emphasize here is that TCs

---

[10] Coase himself posited that in a world in which actors had perfect information, ad hoc agreements would prevail. North (1990, 27) states: "[T]he costliness of information is the key to the costs of transaction." Some, however, distinguish TCs from information costs (see Barzel 1977).

[11] "Moral hazard," for example, occurs because employers cannot observe postcontractual behavior (see Eggertson 1990, 44–5).

[12] This perspective reflects the work of Cheung (1969) on how TCs influence the choice of different contracts.

primarily affect the main actors' incentives to build strong versus weak fiscal regimes but not necessarily what these institutions look like or the exact form they take.

Second, we want to avoid the tendency to privilege the sovereign's decision-making calculus in accounting for the emergence of strong political and economic institutions, particularly fiscal institutions (see Campbell 1993, Levi 1988, North 1981). Although we share the recognition that within the modern state the prerogative to tax ultimately rests with the ruler (Brennan and Buchanan 1980), and therefore that the state is, by definition, one of the primary actors, we do not emphasize the state's role to the exclusion of other actors.[13] Rather we are equally concerned with what motivates a demand for strong institutions from non-state actors, without which it is improbable that the sovereign would ever willingly erect such institutions (see North and Weingast 1989, Root 1989). The lack of attention to the demand side in the study of fiscal institutions is most notable in the vast literature on the resource curse, which explains the prevalence of weak tax systems in mineral-rich states solely in terms of the overriding disincentive that large mineral rents flowing into state coffers creates for the state to tax its population (see Karl 1997). Yet, as we discuss below, ownership structure affects both the incentives of state actors to supply and non-state actors to demand fiscal institutions in mineral-rich countries in part because of the different level of TCs that each fosters.

As in both of the standard political economy approaches to TCs, however, information asymmetries are central to our conceptualization of TCs and the way in which ownership structure influences these costs. Simply put, ownership structure generates different levels of TCs by shaping the interests of the main claimants regarding how the asset in question (here, the mineral sector) should be managed. When their interests are aligned, the main claimants have little or no motivation to constrain each other's behavior because information asymmetries, and hence TCs, are low. Conversely, when their interests are not aligned, the main claimants have a compelling reason to constrain each other's behavior because information asymmetries, and hence TCs, are high.

Under state ownership with control (S_1), TCs are low because the main actors – governing elites (usually via cabinet ministers) and NOC managers – have a mutual interest in maximizing their discretion over the management of the mineral sector, regardless of whether they opt to develop the sector for export or for internal consumption. Although both of these actors are direct claimants to the proceeds from natural resource exploitation, neither is a residual claimant; that is, neither has an exclusive claim to the profits generated from the NOC (see Alchian and Demsetz 1972). Rather governing elites are the agents charged with serving the interests of the nominal principal – the population as a whole – to which these profits ultimately belong. They maximize their respective shares of revenue derived from the mineral sector,

---

[13] North (1981), for example, suggests that it is rulers who produce institutional change because, unlike societal actors, they do not face a free-rider problem.

then, not by maximizing the NOC's profits, but rather by maximizing their ability to utilize their privileged position vis-à-vis mineral rents to serve their own personal and political ends. Thus neither ministers nor NOC managers have an incentive to constrain effectively the behavior of the other in the form of strong fiscal regimes. Rather they prefer to maintain a tacit agreement to exchange "easy taxation" on the part of the government for "easy stealing" by the NOC managers. This type of intra-elite agreement was perhaps most overt in Zaire (present-day Democratic Republic of Congo) under the notorious dictator Mobutu Sese Seko who ruled the country for more than three decades. In 1976, he brazenly instructed his bureaucrats: "If you want to steal, steal a little cleverly, in a nice way. Only if you steal so much as to become rich overnight, will you be caught" (quoted in Shafer 1983, 328).

Governing elites maximize their share of the proceeds from mineral wealth, then, by maximizing their ability to exploit the NOC for noncommercial purposes, which in turn requires minimizing external and internal oversight of the company's operations. Cabinet ministers are prone to utilize the mineral sector as a key source of implicit taxation by requiring the NOC to supply free or heavily discounted fuel to other state-owned enterprises (SOEs) and the general public and by routinely treating the NOC's bank account as a source of extra budgetary funds to dole out patronage to their supporters (see Eller et al. 2007). In the Persian Gulf during the 1970s and 1980s, for example, fuel subsidies to industrial and household consumers alone "ran as high as 10 to 20 percent of GDP in some years" (Amuzegar 1998, 101)[14] and have remained this high in some of these countries, including Saudi Arabia, into the early 2000s (see Bjorvatn and Selvik 2007, 3). Where the petroleum sector is either underdeveloped or developed primarily for internal consumption, fuel subsidies are all the more important because, at least in the short term, they are likely to be the primary financial contribution of this sector to the state budget. For example, China had the second-highest levels of fuel subsidies worldwide in the early 1990s (Larsen and Shah 1992, 4).

Likewise, NOC managers are inclined to deliberately "mismanage" investment funds and arbitrarily transfer the company's assets to enrich themselves and their cronies. In Venezuela, Mexico, and Nigeria, for example, they were notorious for using their authority to hide capital and squander the company's earnings on large public works projects that never came to fruition (a.k.a. "white elephants" or "national prestige" projects) (Ascher 1990). Their ability to do so is, of course, dependent on a low degree of external as well as internal monitoring capacity. Yet it is also facilitated by implicit taxation because this entails making payments to the government in kind – that is, inherently less transparent financial transactions. NOC managers, for example, can deliver

[14] The Persian Gulf states include Bahrain, Iran, Iraq, Kuwait, Oman, Saudi Arabia, and United Arab Emirates (UAE), all of which had S_1 during this period except for Bahrain, Oman, and UAE, which had S_2 (Appendix B). Yet, as explained in Chapter 6, we would expect the effects of S_1 and S_2 to be very similar during this time period.

fuel to consumers outside of the state mandate for cash payments or even smuggle petroleum products abroad, where they can obtain the world market price to finance their own political agenda and siphon off part of the proceeds for themselves (see Marcel 2006, 154).

The daily interactions between the government and the NOC under S_1, moreover, are typically structured so that they not only reinforce these mutual incentives for discretion but also perpetuate low TCs and hence mutual incentives for weak fiscal regimes. The fact that government officials tend to chair the NOC's board of directors, appoint its other members, and are periodically rotated with the NOC's top management (Marcel 2006, van der Linde 2000),[15] for example, means that no matter at what side of the table you sit initially, you can expect to gain eventually from the other side's ability to exercise discretion over both the generation and use of the proceeds from mineral wealth. It also means that the boundaries between the officials who are charged with monitoring the NOC and those who are charged with managing it quickly become blurred. For example, John Entelis (1999, 17) described the relationship of Sonatrach (Algeria's NOC) to the state as "direct, intimate, and long-standing" owing to the fact that "high government officials and their counterparts in the national company exchange positions regularly." Mutual incentives for discretion are also reinforced by the internal structure of the NOC itself. Due to the ill-defined managerial structure and lack of objective criteria for determining managerial performance, governing elites can easily conflate the NOC's administrative tasks and their own political goals (see Boycko et al. 1996, Shleifer and Vishney 1994).[16] Sonatrach, for example, was charged with no less than "achieving socialism" (Madelin 1975, 128).

The causal link between S_1, mutual incentives for discretion, and weak fiscal regimes is perhaps most apparent when one considers what would happen if the interests of governing elites diverged under this ownership structure. Suppose, for example, that what NOC managers cared most about was the company's profitability even though they did not expect to benefit financially. Suppose these managers were motivated instead by the prestige and professional pride associated with competing internationally to win production contracts abroad, which would require the NOC to maintain better control over its own finances. They would not only be less inclined to steal from the company but also more likely to object to the government's siphoning off the company's investment capital for noncommercial uses and to support the creation of institutions that would effectively prevent such exploitation. At the very least, they would be more inclined to seek formal oversight mechanisms to shield the NOC's income from the government's arbitrary expropriation.

---

[15] In most cases, the petroleum minister serves as chair and the ministry is heavily represented on the board of directors, which is the *formal* decision-making body of the NOC (Marcel 2006, 82–5). This is also a reflection of the chronic blurring of boundaries between governing elites and NOC managers under S_1.

[16] This is compounded by the fact that managers do not face any hard budget constraints.

In other words, this divergence in interests would raise TCs and thereby create an incentive for strong fiscal regimes on the part of one of the two direct claimants to the proceeds from mineral wealth (that is, the NOC managers). This is the story of Venezuela in the 1980s and 1990s, during which the NOC Petróleos de Venezuela Sociedad Anónima (PdVSA) not only became a model of efficiency under the direction of technocrats who overtly prioritized the company's financial health over government spending, but also actively sought to impose institutional limits on the president's access to its investment funds.[17]

Such cases, however, are quite rare. When the interests of NOC managers and governing elites do diverge in this way, the most likely scenario is for the government to respond by reining in the company – even where it has previously supported the NOC's drive to attain greater efficiency and profitability. In the case of PdVSA, the company initially encountered little resistance from the executive branch when it launched an internationalization strategy to secure investment funds in the mid-1980s (Mommer 2002, 210). This ended rather abruptly, however, with the 1998 election of President Hugo Chavez, who began to reassert government control over PdVSA almost immediately, starting with the replacement of its CEO and culminating in the outright firing of over half the company's professional management and workforce by 2003 (Mares and Altimirano 2007, 6).[18] Part of the reason for this lies in the structure of interaction between the government and the NOC described above – in particular, that the NOC's management is routinely chosen by the government, and political goals are conflated with economic priorities. Yet it is also intimately related to the societal expectations that S_1 generates, and thus to the overwhelming "spending pressures" governing elites face, particularly during booms – a topic we discuss in detail in the subsequent section.

Thus, in the vast majority of cases, S_1 fosters a common interest in maximizing discretion and hence low TCs between governing elites and NOC managers. This promotes the establishment of a weak fiscal regime in two mutually reinforcing ways. First, it creates a disincentive for either of the direct claimants to the proceeds from the mineral wealth to support the establishment of a Natural Resource Fund (NRF) that would constrain their ability to allocate these proceeds. Even if an NRF is created under S_1, it will deliberately lack the transparency measures necessary to make it effective. Consequently, NRFs end up becoming slush funds for governing elites to serve their personal and political ends (see Tsalik 2003, 44–5). Second, low TCs under S_1 foster an energy sector that is dominated by quasi-fiscal activities (QFAs), usually via the NOC, including implicit taxation, fuel subsidies to households and enterprises, and extrabudgetary funds. To compound the problem, an ineffective

---

[17] Indeed, part of what prompted the professionalization of PdVSA was the forced seizure of its investment funds in 1982 by then President Luis Herrera Campins in response to an economic crisis (see Mommer 2002, 208–9).

[18] Some of this was in retaliation for the strikes launched in 2002–2003.

NRF can also serve as a source of extrabudgetary funds. Since Chavez reasserted state ownership and control over the petroleum sector in Venezuela, for example, the government has routinely transferred resources from the Venezuelan Investment Fund to subsidize public enterprises, particularly in the electricity sector (Davis et al. 2003, 293).

These perverse incentives, moreover, ultimately destroy the country's primary source of income – the NOC itself. It is no coincidence that in countries where S_1 prevails, the NOC is woefully undercapitalized and heavily indebted, thereby deprived of the capital needed for reinvestment (see Ascher 1990, Bentham and Smith 1986, Shafer 1983).[19] Heavy reliance on fuel subsidies, for example, not only amounts to less revenue for the state, but also means that "there is less money available for capital investments" for the NOC (Marcel 2006, 153). Mexico's NOC provides a vivid illustration. Even as world oil prices were soaring at the beginning of the twenty-first century, Pemex was only able to remain afloat economically through massive borrowing, accumulating $42.5 billion in debt (Smith 2004).

Conversely, under private domestic ownership (P_1), TCs are high because the main actors – DPOs and governing elites – have divergent interests regarding the management of the mineral sector. Like governing elites and NOC managers under S_1, DPOs are the direct claimant to the proceeds from mineral exploitation. Yet, because they are the sole principal, they are also the residual claimant and thus benefit directly from the profitability of their respective companies. Their primary interest concerning both the generation and use of the proceeds from mineral wealth, then, is to maximize profit, which entails minimizing their tax burden. Governing elites, however, want to maximize the share of these proceeds that accrues to the state budget, which they can only extract via taxation due to their status as an indirect claimant. The way in which DPOs typically interact with government officials, moreover, serves to reinforce these divergent interests and the high TCs they promote. In contrast to S_1, government officials generally do not have the authority to influence internal decisions such as who is chosen to manage the company or serve on its board of directors. While former government officials may indeed occupy important positions in private companies, this is most likely to be the result of their own desire to leave the public sector to pursue more lucrative opportunities in the private sector. The combination of the petroleum ministry's reduced status and lower salaries in the aftermath of privatization, for example, acts as a potentially strong impetus for ministry employees to defect to private oil companies.

At the same time, because maximizing profit also requires maximizing internal control over their company, DPOs have a strong incentive to monitor closely the agents they hire to manage their company, punishing and rewarding them based on the company's performance. Both because they can benefit

---

[19] In 2005, there was only one NOC (Petrochina) among the world's fifteen largest oil and gas companies when it comes to market capitalization (PFC Energy 2006).

directly from reinvestment and cannot depend on government financing, DPOs are also more likely to introduce international accounting standards in order to secure commercial loans to finance reinvestment (see Marcel 2006, 143). These positive incentives are reinforced when DPOs are held accountable to shareholders, who expect a return on their investment. In contrast to the internal structure of NOCs, then, private oil companies are more likely to be characterized by a well-defined managerial structure and objective criteria for determining managerial performance. Neither DPOs nor their managers, therefore, are likely to conflate administrative tasks with political goals. Likewise, because tax revenue is directly affected by the company's profitability, governing elites have less incentive either to divert the private companies' assets away from reinvestment or to undermine the DPOs' efforts to maximize efficiency and increase market capitalization.

Thus, in most cases, DPOs and governing elites have a mutual incentive to build strong fiscal institutions because in the absence of limits on each other's discretionary power, both would actually lose income through a costly ongoing "negotiation" process that would result in unpredictable revenue streams. Without a formalized tax regime, for example, governing elites and DPOs would be locked in a vicious cycle in which exorbitant tax rates encourage tax evasion, and tax evasion encourages even higher tax rates and threats of expropriation, leading DPOs to devise more elaborate and time-consuming schemes to hide their profits – as was the case in Russia by the end of the 1990s. As a result, the government expends considerable effort collecting a fraction of the tax revenue it expects, and the DPOs divert precious resources to unproductive activities while facing fluctuating tax rates. By negotiating a stable tax rate, then, both sides can capture the gains from more predictable revenue streams. This has two virtuous effects. First, as detailed in Chapter 2, budgetary stability enables the government to meet its current commitments and to plan for future investments in the economy. Second, it facilitates the DPOs' desire to reinvest in their companies so as to maximize future profitability – a sharp contrast to the image of a dilapidated NOC that is fostered under S_1.

Just as an NOC can behave like a private oil company under certain conditions, however, so can a private oil company behave like an NOC. This is most likely to occur, for example, where the mineral sector is privatized as a monopoly. On the one hand, granting a private company monopoly status means that it does not need to compete for market share to maintain its profitability. On the other hand, it lowers the costs of negotiation for both sides and thus the incentives for establishing formal institutions. As we discuss at length in Chapter 5, the privatization of the gas sector as a monopoly in Russia fostered a tacit agreement between the private company (Gazprom) and the government to exchange unfettered access to gas rents for subsidizing domestic gas and electricity consumption. It may also occur where the practice of government officials "defecting" to private oil companies become reciprocal – in other words, former company managers, in effect, exchange places with government officials who are charged with regulating the mineral sector, mimicking the problem of the "revolving door" that is so pervasive under S_1. This will not only contribute to the blurring of boundaries but also to DPOs' incentives to seek greater profits via government protection rather than via smarter business practices. As the example of the U.S.-based Enron Oil and Gas Company demonstrates, when the Board of Directors is not truly independent from the CEO, boundaries might also become blurred within the company itself. The private company can thus become as dilapidated as an NOC under S_1. In this case, however, the problem will be less political ambition than personal greed and, assuming this company operates under hard budget constraints and is in a competitive environment, the end result may be the company's demise, as occurred with Enron in 2001. Conversely, the Brazilian NOC's (Petrobras) financial strength and success in discovering new fields in the early twenty-first century can be attributed directly to the government's decision to abolish Petrobras's legal monopoly status in the late 1990s (Bridgman et al. 2008).

In addition to the desire for stability, high TCs create an incentive for governing elites and DPOs to support the development of a broad-based tax regime, such that mineral sector taxation is one part of an overarching system of revenue extraction, as a way of further constraining one another's behavior and reinforcing their agreement. From the perspective of governing elites, minimizing the government's budgetary dependence on the mineral sector limits the degree of political influence that DPOs can exert, including the ability to renegotiate their tax burden, while increasing the government's own policy options. In times of economic crises, for example, it would be able to turn to its tax base in other sectors rather than put pressure on DPOs to make up revenue shortfalls or borrow from foreign banks. DPOs are likely to support such efforts as a way not only to decrease their own tax burden over time[20] but also to reduce the government's temptation to renege on its commitment to a stable tax rate. In addition, DPOs are apt to favor a broad-based tax regime for several other interrelated reasons. One of the key reasons is that they are both more likely (than foreign investors) to have assets and make investments in other sectors of the economy and to rely on domestic supply networks to market their products (see UNCTAD 1999).[21] Domestic conditions such as the stability of tax regimes and health of the economy, therefore, affect not only their own company's capitalization but also their ability to generate profits beyond the mineral sector.

The desire for budgetary stability and independence also generates incentives to place institutional limits on spending. Governing elites are more likely to create an effective NRF under P_1 because it liberates the state budget from

---

[20] There is considerable evidence to suggest that the largest and wealthiest sectors prefer to shift the tax burden to other sectors of the economy in order to reduce their own (Burgess and Stern 1993, 801).

[21] Not all DPOs, of course, diversify their assets to the same degree (see Post 2008).

sharp fluctuations in commodity prices by smoothing out expenditures. From the DPOs' perspective, an effective NRF means that the state will be less likely to engage in deficit spending and thus ameliorates the need to raise mineral sector taxation to balance the budget. Their aforementioned links to the local economy provide an additional incentive for DPOs not only to support the creation of an effective NRF but also one that clearly designates that spending from this fund be targeted at developing the labor force (that is, on human capital formation) and providing a social safety net for workers (see Mares 2001). Thus even if some of the revenue accumulated in the NRF under P_1 is allocated to social spending, the chance that it will be spent productively is much greater than under S_1.

SOCIETAL EXPECTATIONS

Societal pressures on state spending, both direct and indirect, have increased universally over the course of the twentieth century (see Tanzi and Schuknecht 2000). In the context of the "spread" of the idea and reality of the welfare state, there has been a near-global convergence of expectations for the state to do much more than perform its "traditional" functions of maintaining social order and securing borders, including implementing social protection programs and, perhaps most importantly, orchestrating economic development (see Lindert 2005a, 2005b, Malloy and Borzutzky 1982, Skocpol and Amenta 1986). In the late-nineteenth century, government expenditures on social welfare focused on providing relief to the poor and public education (see Connell 1980). By the mid-twentieth century, they expanded to encompass benefits for the entire population and consisted, for example, of unemployment compensation, pensions, public health, and housing subsidies (Lindert 2005a). For advanced industrialized countries, this trend has been less consequential, because popular pressures to increase public spending did not emerge until after their governments had achieved "efficient resource allocation through budgeting and effective resource accumulation through income taxation" (Webber and Wildavsky 1986, 356). But it has had an enormous impact on developing countries, which were often confronted with these inflated expectations before they had built the capacity to extract sustained financing from their population and certainly well before the introduction of the income tax. In these countries, governments have felt pressured to spend more on social programs than the OECD countries spent at similar levels of purchasing power and with the same percentage of elderly in the population (Lindert 2005a, 218). For the developing world, then, being part of an international system in which the state's need to play an expanded role in promoting social and economic development was assumed meant that a crucial link between the state's extractive capacities and public spending commitments was severed.[22]

---

[22] As Oran Young notes: "A 'new' state ... has little choice but to join the basic institutional arrangements of the states system" (1986, 120).

Direct and indirect societal pressures in the mid-to-late twentieth century have been magnified in mineral-rich states. Given the immensity of (real and perceived) rents from oil and gas exports, this is particularly the case in petroleum-rich states. In these states, political leaders came to anticipate, if not internalize, such pressures, perceiving their newly acquired wealth as a mandate for state-led development, as well as an opportunity to "allocate oil windfalls ... in such a way as to optimize popular satisfaction" (Amuzegar 2001, 14). Societal expectations concerning the state's role, however, are not merely a function of mineral wealth, as is commonly presumed (see Beblawi and Luciani 1987, Gary and Karl 2003). Nor does mineral wealth in and of itself necessarily create "rentier societies" – that is, entire populations who are stripped of any entrepreneurial initiative by virtue of their country's discovery of mineral wealth, as the literature often portrays (see Mahdavy 1970, Okruhlik 1999, Shambayati 1994). Rather the form they take depends on who owns and controls this wealth – that is, on the structure of ownership – because it circumscribes societal claims to benefit from this wealth. In other words, although the population always has a legitimate right to expect some benefit from the country's natural resource endowments, and the state always has a duty to acknowledge these expectations (see Wenar 2007), ownership structure affects both the nature and scope of societal expectations vis-à-vis mineral wealth as well as the ways in which the state attempts to fulfill these expectations. This is consistent with our conceptualization of ownership structure as a form of property relations in which all owners (public or private, domestic or foreign) must legitimate their property rights to those who effectively relinquish these rights or entrust them to others. It is also consistent with our claim that the state, as the primary institution responsible for conferring such rights, plays a central role in this legitimation process. Here our point of departure from the literature on property relations is not recognizing that owners have both claims and obligations (see Bromley 1989, 203), but rather that societal actors, albeit indirect claimants, have expectations based on their relationship to these owners that all political leaders – even under authoritarian regimes – must recognize and take seriously.

When the state owns and controls mineral wealth on behalf of its population (S_1), societal expectations are high – that is, for widespread distribution of benefits and hardest to ignore or deny – because the state owes its status as direct claimant to its role as society's agent. In other words, by conferring property rights upon itself, the state has committed itself, at least nominally, to managing this wealth in society's (that is, the principal's) "best interest." While the baseline for what constitutes the state's social obligation toward its citizenry will, of course, vary by country, the state's need to legitimate its own property rights creates three mutually reinforcing ways in which societal expectations affect the type of fiscal regime that is likely to emerge under S_1 across states.

The first way concerns how the state allocates the proceeds from mineral wealth, including how much is spent versus saved, and on what it is spent.

Because the entire population feels entitled to enjoy the bulk of these proceeds, and state leaders need to demonstrate that they are acting in society's best interest by owning and controlling the country's natural resources, neither is likely to support limits on state spending.[23] As the nominal principal, the public at large expects to receive the lion's share of benefits from the exploitation of its mineral wealth in the form of improved living standards. Although this expectation can be met in a variety of ways – including building more hospitals and roads, providing access to free education, and guaranteeing job security (see Boycko et al. 1996, Shleifer 1998), in order to reassure society that it is dutifully performing its role as "agent," the state has a strong incentive to provide goods and services that make it appear that everyone is benefiting – even if some are actually benefiting more – either because they are made available to all citizens or because they have a high degree of visibility. This not only fosters widespread distribution in the form of universal subsidies, such as for fuel, basic foodstuffs, and housing, but also encourages grandiose public work projects (a.k.a. "white elephants") that are so prominent in mineral-rich states, such as "the largest airport in Saudi Arabia, the Great Man-made River Project in Libya, the Trans-Railway in Gabon, and a new capital city, Abuja, in Nigeria" (Gary and Karl 2004, 36). Because the NOC is the primary source of financing for these subsidies and politically motivated projects,[24] efforts to reform the NOC such that it operates on a commercial basis are unlikely to surface – and, if they do, are likely to be quickly squelched. For similar reasons, the emergence of an NRF that would effectively reduce the portion of mineral rents that could be spent in such a way is also highly unlikely. Simply put, the stronger society's claim to mineral rents, the harder it is to place institutional limits on public spending.

These spending patterns are reinforced, moreover, during boom-and-bust cycles. Pressures to increase spending during booms stem directly from the notion that government spending should be commensurate with state income via petroleum exports. In other words, the fact that the proceeds accruing to the state increase during booms means that there is a strong sense that benefits accruing to the population must also increase – or more correctly, that the population must perceive this to be the case, thereby making the expansion of universal subsidies and large public works projects all the more appealing. Beyond widespread fuel and food subsidies, the government of Nigeria, for example, ramped up spending on large investment projects in industry during the boom in the 1970s – the most notorious being the Ajaokuta steel mill built in the 1970s (Ascher 1999, 179) that never "produced a commercial ton of steel" (Sala-i-Martin and Subramanian 2003, 13). Similarly, pressures to maintain current spending levels during busts propel the state to borrow

---

[23] Simply put, it is harder to cap public spending when society has a strong claim to the rents (see Shafer 1983).

[24] Pemex, for example, was often considered just as much a "social service agency as an oil company," having run hospitals and schools (Golden 1991, D1).

against future production and revenue rather than reducing expenditures, and hence to oblige the NOC to increase production (at a significant loss per barrel) rather than improving its efficiency.[25] They also provide an even greater impetus for governing elites to pilfer the NOC, forcing it to become increasingly indebted in order to continue its operations. PdVSA in Venezuela again provides a vivid illustration. Immediately after the oil price began to fall in the early 1980s, rather than cutting expenditures, the government unilaterally appropriated the NOC's reserve fund to supplement the national budget, leaving it to turn to international capital markets for future investment funding (Karl 1997, 176). On the positive side, this contributed to the company's managers' desire for institutional guarantees against future government expropriation. Yet in this regard, PdVSA's experience is exceptional. In most cases, it is understood that the government will allow its direct control over the NOC's finances to wane during a boom but use the bust as an opportunity to temporarily reassert its authority (see Marcel 2006).

The second way concerns how the state pays for such goods and services. Under S_1, the fact that the state owns and controls what is considered to be the country's most valuable asset places limits on its ability to extract additional resources to pay for such goods and services. From society's perspective, not only should mineral rents be sufficient to finance the state – whether derived via exports abroad, taxation, or international loans – but also the state, rather than the population, should be the primary source of revenue. As a result, while taxation is a sensitive issue for any government interested in its own survival,[26] it is especially precarious where the mineral sector is under S_1 because both taxation outside the mineral sector (that is, broad-based) and forms of taxation that are more visible to the taxpayer (that is, direct and explicit) become politically risky. State leaders, therefore, prefer to utilize less visible forms of taxation (that is, indirect and implicit) across sectors – such as multiple exchange rates and public procurement of agricultural goods at administered prices, which function as implicit taxes on exporters and farmers, respectively – and to borrow both internally and from abroad in order to either expand the role of government or make up for budgetary shortfalls. Saudi Arabia serves to illustrate the extent to which the state is deterred from taxing its population directly under S_1. When the government tried to introduce an income tax in 1988, owing to public outcry, they were forced "to rescind the income tax *within three days of its announcement*" (Chaudhry 1997, 274). Rather, in order to maintain high levels of government spending, the Saudi Arabian government has borrowed both on the domestic market, such that its domestic debt in 2000 exceeded more than 100 percent of its

---

[25] Even during the economic crisis in the early 1990s, the Libyan government continued to spend approximately one-third of its oil revenues on large public works projects (Vandewalle 1998, 161).

[26] George H. W. Bush made this painfully clear with his successful U.S. presidential campaign pledge: "Read my lips. No new taxes."

GDP, and from abroad, leveraging the borrowing power of its NOC (Gause 2000, 83).[27] In sum, both the state and the population under S_1 eschew direct and explicit forms of taxation beyond the mineral sector that would provide the former with a more reliable income stream and enhance the latter's ability to hold its leaders accountable.

Societal expectations regarding both state spending and taxation will, however, be diminished where the mineral sector in question is either at an earlier stage of development or being developed primarily for internal consumption. Because it is not receiving large windfalls from export rents, the perception and reality of the country's wealth are also diminished. This serves to elongate the time horizons of both governing elites and the population vis-à-vis reaping benefits. Although expenditures will still take the form of universal subsidies, in such cases there is less immediate pressure on the state either to embark upon a massive expansion of the status quo provision of public goods and social services or to promote white elephants. These elongated time horizons might also enable mineral-rich states to develop more rational spending programs, such as those targeted at the neediest segments of the population, which can lead to better social outcomes, including poverty reduction. By insulating the economy from fluctuations in the international price of the commodity in question, the government also insulates itself from societal pressures to expand spending during a boom. At the same time, the state has more latitude – and potentially more capacity, given that the traditional sectors continue to dominate the economy – to collect taxes from other sectors.[28] Thus taxation will initially appear to be more broad-based than in most mineral-rich states under S_1. It might also encounter less opposition where taxes are perceived as necessary – at least in the short term – to supplement state efforts in providing social services.

Thirdly, state ownership and control over the mineral sector fosters the widespread belief that the state should be the chief source of economic activity. Broadly speaking, this shared view promotes the conflation of public spending with private interests beyond the mineral sector. More specifically, it has two related effects on the emergence of fiscal regimes. The first is that it promotes state-sponsored industrialization via publicly owned enterprises and import substitution (ISI), whereby the bulk of state investment in industry is devoted to replacing imports rather than promoting exports (see Quinn 2002). This industrialization strategy, in turn, reinforces the state's reliance on implicit subsidies and taxation, because these fiscal tools facilitate the transfer of assets from the mineral sector or traditional sector (usually agriculture) to manufacturing in order to build and sustain this sector. It is often the role of the NOC, for example, not only to provide subsidized fuel to industrial consumers but also to finance the deficit in the non-hydrocarbon sector (see

[27] It obtained $4.6 billion in international loans in 1998 (Gause 2000, 83).

[28] As we demonstrate in Chapter 9, a viable alternative source of revenue is one of the key variables that explains why some countries choose to adopt S_1.

Marcel 2006). Overreliance on the NOC for fostering inward-oriented development policies further reinforces the decrepitude of the NOC, as it does not base its investment decisions on comparative advantage but rather on political objectives (see Quinn 2002).[29]

Manufacturing thus becomes a "subsidized sector" (Auty 2003, 257) not because protecting this sector is an instinctive policy response to Dutch Disease, but rather because under S_1, governments in developing countries feel pressured to forge industrialization from above rather than in conjunction with private industry.[30] It is common in oil-rich countries, like Saudi Arabia, that adopted S_1 for such policies to protect the manufacturing sector to emerge well before the onset of Dutch Disease (Auty 2001). The cumulative result is that S_1 in the mineral sector directly promotes the growth of the public sector at the expense of the private sector throughout the economy, thereby circumscribing the government's tax base to SOEs and their employees. And yet, for reasons we describe in Chapter 2, this particular form of direct taxation does not contribute to either building state capacity or promoting economic growth.

The conviction that the state should dominate the economy is so prominent under S_1 that governing elites who opt to develop the petroleum sector for internal consumption nonetheless have a strong temptation to adopt ISI. Indeed, as in Mexico following the nationalization of its oil industry, state-led industrialization has often become a central part of the explicit rationale for pursuing this strategy, although there are often political motivations underlying it. As Esperanza Durán (1985, 147) underscored in her study of Pemex, "[b]etween 1938 and 1976, the prime objective [of the oil industry] was to satisfy internal demand and to support [ISI] through very low, subsidized prices. Oil was regarded as a tool for inward-looking development, a means to supply industry and consumers with cheap fuel." This tendency is in fact one of the main reasons why the economic successes of such a growth strategy for mineral-rich states in the developed world, like the United States, Canada, and Australia, are rarely replicated in the developing world. In these countries, the internal consumption of petroleum served to foster innovation rather than rent seeking, and thus contributed to technological and industrial development via the growth of an autonomous private sector (see Maloney 2002, Wright 2001).

The second effect is that the concentration of mineral rents in the state's hands combined with its enlarged economic role fosters pervasive rent seeking

---

[29] The inefficiencies of the NOC are best captured by how much revenue they receive per barrel. SaudiAramco, for example, only receives $.40/boe (barrel of oil equivalent) compared to Shell's $21.67/boe (Eller et al. 2007).

[30] As is well known, ISI was not unique to Latin America, where it has been blamed for a host of economic and social problems. In fact, nearly every country that industrialized after Britain went through a stage of ISI (Baer 1972, 95–6.) The key is that in those cases that were successful, this was temporary and aimed at fostering competition. The "East Asian tigers" are a vivid illustration (see Hughes 1988).

(see Beblawi 1987, Karl 1997). Societal actors thus focus their energies on currying favor with the state to gain privileged access to its financial largess. As a
result, even privately owned enterprises become financially dependent on the
public sector for their survival. Indeed a common strategy in adopting ISI is to
incorporate domestic capitalists who then become both its chief beneficiaries
and proponents (see Alarcon and McKinley 1992). Here too, the NOC plays a
central role, often serving as the primary vehicle for distributing such patronage, whether in the form of relatively well-paying government jobs or lucrative
service and construction contracts (see Auty 1990, Stevens 2007). Moreover,
since privileged access to the state's financial largess is often granted through
implicit forms of taxation, such as directed credits and targeted subsidies,
it amounts not only to providing some citizens – particularly civil servants,
contractors, and the business elite – with an additional share of rents accruing
from the country's mineral wealth (see Beblawi 1987) but also to deluding the
majority of other citizens into paying the costs of that access. Thus the universal provision of visible benefits does not preclude – and may even facilitate –
some segments of society benefiting more than others.

The practice of providing particularistic benefits is exacerbated by booms
and busts. Booms not only encourage rent seeking among societal actors, but
also embolden states to increase the provision of such benefits. As a result,
the expansion of state spending when oil prices are high is not limited to the
population at large. Rather, enlarged universal subsidies are often accompanied by the creation of new government jobs and the extension of directed
credits to new enterprises. During the 1970s oil boom, for example, Nigeria
and Ecuador – both of which adopted S_1 just prior to the boom – witnessed a
dramatic increase in the share of government employment (Gavin 1993, 241,
Gelb 1988, 185). This, in turn, makes it that much more difficult for governments like Saudi Arabia – where by 1994, 95 percent of the national workforce
was employed in the public sector and "public sector wages absorbed one-fifth
of GDP" (Auty 2001, 83) – to adjust during busts by cutting expenditures. Not
only has government spending reinforced societal expectations for widespread
benefit, it has also generated a broad array of "special interests" that have
a stake in maintaining their particularistic benefits and the organizational
capacity to lobby for their interests. Because the NOC is so often an important source of such benefits, it also magnifies the aforementioned obstacles to
support for internal restructuring (Marcel 2006).

In sum, strong fiscal institutions are unlikely to emerge under S_1 because
governing elites have no incentive to supply them and the population at large
has no incentive to demand them. Rather, high societal expectations reinforce
the governing elites and NOCs' managers' mutual disincentive, stemming
from low TCs, to support the emergence of either institutions that would effectively restrict the state's spending capacity vis-à-vis mineral rents, including a
commercially based NOC and a NRF, or a stable, broad-based tax regime
based on a combination of direct and indirect taxes that would enable the
state to stabilize its revenue stream and promote long-term economic growth.

As in the case of Libya, the purpose of the institutions that emerge is "not to extract [or even to preserve] wealth but [rather] to spend it" (Vandewalle 1998, 7). Citizens thus become detached from the revenue-generating process and yet wholly dependent upon the allocation process. In other words, citizens become clients of rather than contributors to the state. This, in turn, fosters a distinctive form of "fiscal illusion" whereby the perception that someone (or in this case, something) else is shouldering the tax burden reinforces societal support for unbridled state spending.

Whereas societal expectations are high under S_1, they are best described as low under private domestic ownership (P_1), both because the direct claimant is not charged with managing mineral wealth in society's best interest, and because the state is only an indirect claimant, albeit the most important one. Thus in effect, societal expectations are filtered through a third party, DPOs. These owners legitimize their property rights primarily by paying taxes through which society reaps its perceived share of the proceeds from the exploitation of the country's mineral wealth, while the state fulfills its duty to society by ensuring that this tax revenue is collected. Society's position vis-à-vis the two main claimants (DPOs and the state) shapes its expectations in three fundamental ways, all of which foster support for strong fiscal regimes.

First, the population does not feel entitled to receive the bulk of these proceeds via *distribution* but rather a portion of them via *redistribution*. The conferral of private property rights in the mineral sector, regardless of how they emerge, serves as a powerful signal that the benefits of mineral wealth will neither be distributed widely nor allocated equally across the population. Society is thus forced to recognize that the individuals who acquire ownership rights in the mineral sector will receive a greater share of the benefits from the country's mineral wealth than the population at large. It also indicates that the state's ability to ameliorate this inequality depends largely on its capacity to extract revenue from the private actors who own and operate this sector.[31] Therefore, by virtue of their ownership and control status, DPOs will benefit disproportionately from the exploitation of mineral wealth, minus what they are obligated to pay in taxes. At the same time, because the extent to which they benefit from mineral sector exploitation depends on how much DPOs contribute to the state budget, the population at large has a strong incentive to support the emergence of a viable taxation system. In particular, both the state and society have an incentive to supply and demand, respectively, explicit forms of taxation in the mineral sector – that is, taxation that is more visible, such as corporate profits tax and mineral extraction tax – in order to assure the public that its interest vis-à-vis the DPOs is being protected. Conversely, the greater emphasis placed on the extractive role of the state means that governing elites have little incentive to build large public works projects as a way of demonstrating that the population is benefiting from the country's mineral

[31] The state can also address this disparity by effectively regulating the mineral sector – for example, making sure that DPOs do not violate environmental regulations.

wealth. The expectation of inequality also relieves pressure on the state to engage in populist-style social spending rather than to save and invest its share of mineral rents, thereby making both the establishment of a working NRF and broad social sector reform aimed at reducing entitlements and targeting benefits more likely.

This is not to say that implicit forms of taxation, such as consumer subsidies, will not exist under P_1. Yet if they do, they are likely to be minimal in comparison to what we would find under S_1, for two reasons. First, privatization to domestic owners complicates one of the simplest, and hence most common, ways in which petroleum-rich states can explicitly share their wealth with the population, regardless of ownership structure – that is, direct consumer subsidies for fuel and electricity. Simply put, in order to provide these subsidies under P_1, governing elites either have to rely on DPOs or the state's own relatively small share of oil and gas production – assuming this exists. Both, however, are highly problematic.[32] Unlike NOCs operating under S_1, private domestic companies are likely to insist on a reduction of their explicit tax burden as compensation for forfeiting a portion of their oil and gas production to domestic consumers at subsidized prices. This, in turn, reduces the state's overall take from the petroleum sector. Moreover, there is no guarantee either that the state has retained sufficient industry shares or can produce enough oil or gas from the portion of reserves it might have retained via an NOC to satisfy domestic demand. Second, implicit forms of taxation cut against the governing elites' need to make taxation of private owners in the petroleum sector highly visible. Regardless of how the government provides consumer subsidies, the perception is that these come directly from the state and thus do little to boost public confidence that the government is adequately performing its duty to tax and regulate the DPOs. Moreover, once fuel prices are subsidized, the public tends to have little sense of the relative cost of fuel. Thus privatization to domestic owners makes implicit taxation not only logistically much more difficult than under S_1, where the state itself can provide direct energy subsidies to consumers via an implicit tax on the NOC, but also less appealing politically.

The second way in which P_1 affects societal expectations concerns the relative contribution of the mineral sector to the state budget. In contrast to S_1, under P_1 the population does not expect the proceeds from mineral production and export to make up its entirety. In short, because society's ability to reap the benefits of mineral wealth is essentially a function of the state's ability to extract revenue from DPOs, there is a general recognition that its share of these proceeds will always amount to less than 100 percent. Put even more starkly, whereas state ownership and control conflates the state's budget with the mineral sector's income, privatization drives a wedge between them,

---

[32] Governments can also subsidize fuel prices under P_1 by issuing very low taxes on fuel, as is the case in the United States. But this too has its limitations. For example, lifting the tax during an oil price boom does little to lower the cost of fuel to consumers.

paving the way for other parts of the domestic economy to make up the difference. As a result, it is less politically risky for the state to tax the population alongside the mineral sector. This complements governing elites' own desire to develop a source of revenue beyond the mineral sector in order to stabilize their budget. A fiscal regime that is both broad-based and relies on explicit forms of direct and indirect taxation, therefore, is more likely to emerge. Low societal expectations in this regard also make it less politically risky for governing elites to institute an effective NRF. In fact, coupled with a broad-based and explicit tax regime, doing so actually has political benefits. Where citizens are important financial contributors to the state rather than merely its clients, they have both a greater desire and ability to hold the state accountable for its fiscal policies. They are thus more likely to support measures to promote fiscal transparency, such as the creation of an effective NRF, which enhances this ability.

Third, private domestic ownership over the mineral sector fosters the perception that the state is neither the sole nor the chief source of economic activity. This has three positive effects on the development of private enterprise in other sectors of the economy, which can contribute to long-term economic growth. The first is that, even if it initially adopts ISI, the state is more likely to not only engage but also promote the private sector in its industrialization strategy such that there is no inherent trade-off in the growth of the public and private sectors. The government thus has the potential to expand its tax base as well as the incentive to develop a taxation capacity beyond SOEs and their employees. The second effect is that it reduces incentives and opportunities for societal actors to engage in rent seeking. Simply put, the dispersion of mineral wealth increases the costs and diminishes the benefits of focusing one's energies on currying favor with the state rather than building a competitive business. This shift in focus, moreover, provides entrepreneurs with a direct stake in the emergence of a viable tax regime so as to reduce their tax burden and stabilize their revenue stream. Finally, the government will be more inclined to enlist the private sector in welfare reform, moving the provision of goods and services away from the state toward the market.

In sum, in contrast to S_1, private domestic ownership (P_1) fosters societal expectations that bolster governing elites' incentives, stemming from high TCs, to build a strong fiscal regime – that is, institutions that both constrain state spending and enable the state to stabilize its revenue stream. Precisely because societal expectations emphasize the extractive rather than the distributive role of the state, booms and busts also serve to reinforce these incentives.

During booms, governments will feel pressured not so much to expand social spending, but rather to increase the tax burden of DPOs in the mineral sector. An important and widely used vehicle for doing so is the excess profits (or windfall) tax, which refers to a tax levied against industries, usually commodity-based, that experience extraordinarily high profits. In the United States, for example, as both oil prices and their profits skyrocketed in the mid-2000s, fomenting consumer outrage, executives of the largest private oil companies were forced to testify before Congress and threatened with a new tax on windfall profits (Herszenhorn 2008). The debates that transpired were, in fact, reminiscent of the 1970s oil boom when Congress similarly responded to political pressure by attempting to introduce a windfall tax on oil companies' profits (Shanahan 1974). Because there is less pressure on the government to ramp up social spending, governing elites are also more likely utilize the opportunity of a boom to establish an NRF in which, for example, they can set aside the revenue from a windfall tax. Finally, the reduced role of the state in the economy under P_i means that booms can provide a greater opportunity for the expansion of private enterprise. This too is characteristic of the U.S. experience (for details, see Wright 2001, Wright and Czelusta 2003).

During busts, governments under P_i will have a greater incentive to enact policies that facilitate the mineral sector's ability to adjust. Relieving the DPOs tax burden, for example, is both a viable and a legitimate way for governments to respond to busts, because the state budget is neither wholly dependent on the mineral sector nor expected to be. Governments are also more inclined to utilize this opportunity to "lock in" the DPOs tax burden, perhaps by pegging the tax rate to the price of a barrel of oil, in order to foster budgetary stability for both parties. At the same time, governing elites have less incentive to pilfer NRFs, if they exist, in order to make up for budgetary shortfalls than they do under S_i.

What about the DPOs? How do these societal expectations affect their institutional preferences – specifically, the likelihood that they will also support strong fiscal institutions? The short answer is that, as the direct claimants to what is undoubtedly one of the country's most valuable assets, DPOs have a keen interest in securing society's tacit approval for retaining their private ownership and control rights. To some extent, they are in a similar position as the state vis-à-vis society under S_i – with the crucial difference that they are not charged with "protecting the public interest." Gaining such approval is particularly acute where private property rights are newly acquired and insecure. Paying taxes can be a relatively "cheap" way for DPOs to do this – provided that their tax burden is not extortionist. Contrary to the recent literature (see Acemoglu and Robinson 2005, Boix 2003) that builds on the assumption that the chief fear motivating capitalists is redistribution (originally conceived by Charles Beard in 1913), we argue that DPOs can actually embrace taxation as a way of making amends to or placating society. This does not mean that they are willing to see their taxes routinely raised in order to cover an expansion in the provision of goods and services. In fact, it is precisely due to the widespread expectation of redistribution – and hence the realization that their taxes are used to finance social spending – that they are more likely to support limits on government expenditures.

Particularly since the 1990s, another way in which DPOs can legitimate their property rights is by adopting practices that are not only desirable for society but also ultimately good for business; that is, practices that have come to fall under the notion of CSR (for details, see Chapter 6). Whereas the state under S_1 must demonstrate that it is adequately distributing the benefits of mineral wealth to the population, private owners must demonstrate that they are appropriately utilizing the country's mineral wealth. This includes increasing the productivity of the mineral in question and conversely reducing waste. Much of the controversy that transpired in Texas in the 1930s regarding the zealous production of "hot oil," for example, centered precisely on this question of reducing waste (Olien and Olien 2002, Yergin 1991). Adopting CSR can also extend to minimizing environmental damage caused by exploring for and producing the natural resource in question. Private oil companies have an incentive to demonstrate that they are protecting the environment in order to both improve their public image and to minimize future liabilities. As the record of Mexico's state-owned Pemex versus private U.S. oil companies in the Gulf of Mexico illustrates, they are more likely to be held accountable for damage caused by oil spills – both by governments that can fine them and NGOs that can publicize and protest their actions – than state-owned companies, where the government is more likely to be complicit in trying to hide the damage (see Riding 1979).

Because societal expectations regarding the benefits of mineral wealth are likely to be higher in those communities and regions where this wealth is actually extracted, yet another, quite complementary way for DPOs in the mineral sector to legitimize their property rights vis-à-vis society is to provide direct social and economic benefits to the population living in the regions of the country where they operate. Oilmen in Texas, for example, have a long history of philanthropy, ranging from large grants to health and educational facilities at the state level to building parks and swimming pools for local communities (see Presley 1983). Since the late 1980s, the notion that legitimating property rights requires providing public goods and social services to the local population has become increasingly prominent. DPOs are most likely to feel such pressure where property rights are not well institutionalized and there is a very low level of socioeconomic development. The latter in particular provides DPOs with a dual motivation for improving healthcare and educational opportunities at the local level, since it is the local population that will constitute the bulk of their labor force.

Beyond the domestic population, DPOs are also more likely to seek validation abroad and, since the 1990s, have several alternatives for doing so. For example, they may adopt international standards for accounting and extend public offerings to foreigners. They may also choose to bring in foreign advisors and hire foreign managers – an unlikely strategy under S_1 owing in part to the potential reluctance of Western businessmen to serve on NOC boards with tarnished reputations for corruption. Lastly, they may opt to create partnerships abroad with major foreign oil companies. While all of these may have the added benefit of increasing shareholder value, each of these strategies primarily serves to help secure property rights by deterring the state from arbitrary confiscation. Simply put, foreign shareholders and partners make it more difficult, albeit not impossible, for the government to seize property.

In sum, societal expectations under P_1 reinforce DPOs' incentives, stemming from high TCs, to support the emergence of a strong fiscal regime – in particular, a stable and explicit tax system and an effective NRF – and, since the 1990s, perhaps even to help finance socioeconomic development at the local level and to build financial linkages at the international level.

Booms and busts are likely to strengthen these incentives, because DPOs are more likely to take a cautious approach to export volatility and income fluctuation.[33] Just as DPOs are likely to make more rational and efficient use of oil revenues from commodity booms (Collier and Gunning 1996), they are also more likely to utilize the opportunity (or exigency) provided by a bust to restructure their companies. These tendencies are reinforced by the government's likely response to booms and busts. First, in order to avoid a windfall tax, DPOs may opt to publicly commit a significant portion of their profits during a boom not only to reinvesting in their companies and expanding their operations abroad, but also to making philanthropic contributions. Already during the oil boom of the 1920s, the "oil barons" in Tulsa, Oklahoma spent their extraordinary profits not only on the arts through their support for museums, ballets, orchestras, and the construction of Art Deco buildings, but also on expanding their businesses into other sectors of the economy (see Ervin 2007). Second, DPOs are better able to adjust to a shock because they do not have to contend with high societal expectations for widespread benefits in the form of universal subsidies and employment. Thus they are more likely than governments under S_1, for example, to undergo internal restructuring during a bust, which may include curtailing production, lowering the costs of operation, improving corporate governance, bringing in foreign partners, and forming mergers with other DPOs. Finally, both the likelihood that the government will seek to raise taxes in response to a boom and their own desire to restructure during a bust reinforces DPOs' preference for a stable tax regime.

POWER RELATIONS

While the level of TCs and societal expectations influence whether the main claimants to the proceeds from mineral wealth have an incentive to supply or demand strong fiscal institutions, power relations between these claimants affect how such institutions emerge and thereby the form they take and whether they persist. As discussed previously, there are two alternatives to the "contractarian" approach whereby institutional outcomes are merely a function of efforts to solve collective action problems: (1) bargaining, which can be either implicit or explicit; and (2) pure coercion (for details, see Knight 1992). The key difference is that bargaining results in distributional outcomes such that both sides incur gains and losses and institutions become harder to

---

[33] For example, private actors in low-income countries are more likely to save during busts than their governments (see Ross 1999, 310).

change, whereas coercion generates asymmetrical or zero-sum outcomes that can be reversed by a shift in the balance of power (Jones Luong 2002). Simply put, whether fiscal regimes emerge via bargaining or coercion depends on the form of ownership structure because each form produces a distinct set of power relations.

Power can be defined and operationalized in many different ways; it can refer to coercion, authority, or influence and can be relational or absolute (for details, see Baldwin 2002). Given our conceptualization of ownership structure as a set of relations among claimants, following both Baldwin (2002) and Zürn (2002) we adopt a relational approach to power that focuses on mutual dependency in achieving one's goals – that is, whether one party needs the other to maximize its utility. Utility maximization in this context refers to the main claimants' ability to realize the full potential of their ownership and control status vis-à-vis mineral rents. In other words, each wants to benefit as much as possible, subject to the type of claims they can make to the proceeds from mineral wealth. When the main claimants are interdependent – that is, when each side depends primarily on the other to enforce its access rights – institutions are more likely to emerge via bargaining. Conversely, when one side depends more on the other to maximize its claims to mineral rents – that is, when these actors are in a dependent relationship – institutions are more likely to emerge via coercion.

In the case of S_1 and P_1, both forms of ownership structure promote interdependent power relations between the main claimants and thus facilitate bargaining that produces distributional outcomes. Yet the mutual desire to hide information from the public under S_1 encourages *implicit* bargaining whereas the mutual desire to reveal information to the public under P_1 encourages *explicit* bargaining.[34] The degree of transparency and accountability in the bargaining process varies considerably under S_1 and P_1, which serves to reinforce the likelihood for the emergence and persistence of weak and strong fiscal regimes, respectively.

Power relations under S_1 are interdependent because, in their role as agents, governing elites and NOC managers need each other to enforce their direct claims vis-à-vis the principal whose interest they are ostensibly empowered to serve – that is, the population. Yet because they face both low TCs and societal expectations for widespread distribution, this is most readily achieved by concealing information from the public about the true level of mineral rents that the government extracts and how they are allocated, including, perhaps most importantly, what portion of the mineral rents actually flows into government coffers and the daily operations of the NOC.[35] The fact that direct taxation

---

[34] State ownership creates incentives for hiding information whereas private ownership creates incentives for sharing it, which parallels the argument in Whiting (2001) regarding rural industry in China.

[35] According to Madelin (1975), even in developed countries, "state [oil] companies often work in semi-secrecy," keeping their income and spending patterns hidden from the public, but

of the population is minimal (if not absent) both serves to justify and reinforce state elites' desire to hide information from the public. As one Aramco executive explained regarding public disclosure of mineral rents: "But what right do they have [to know] when they pay no taxes and when the government provides all the needed services" (Marcel 2006, 143). Governing elites and NOC managers thus find themselves locked into a situation of "mutual hostage taking" whereby a shift in strategy on the part of one actor would affect the ability of the other to maximize its utility.[36] For example, the ability of either governing elites or managers to plunder the NOC's coffers and procure patronage depends on each side's willingness not to expose the other. This understanding is embodied in the de facto self-regulation of the NOC, to which the petroleum ministry and parliament have historically deferred when it comes to monitoring the industry, allegedly because they lack the technical competence (see Marcel 2006, 87–90). The mutual desire to hide information from society about both their individual misconduct and that of the other, in turn, fosters implicit bargaining.

Why does implicit bargaining reinforce weak fiscal regimes? First and foremost, by definition, this type of bargaining undermines the development of formal institutions – particularly those that would impose rigid constraints. Secondly, because it occurs implicitly, the bargaining process itself lacks transparency. Not only does it occur behind closed doors and without public knowledge, the actors and interests involved are deliberately kept opaque. Third, implicit bargaining perpetuates the need to conceal the true nature of the NOC's finances in particular and the country's finances in general. This, in turn, has two separate effects on prospects for long-term economic growth. On the one hand, it undermines the collection of accurate financial information, and thus, reinforces both the government's and NOC managers' tendency to eschew the need for a clear economic rationale for its spending priorities. On the other, maintaining secrecy over financial transactions in the petroleum sector undermines the NOC's ability to gain access to capital markets to self-finance its operations (see Marcel 2006, 143). In sum, implicit bargaining serves to reinforce weak fiscal regimes not only because it reduces accountability and increases opportunities for corruption but also because it reinforces personalism as the basis for allocating resources. At the same time, it compromises the long-term viability of the NOC itself.

Similarly, under P_1, the main actors – DPOs and state elites – cannot realize the full potential of their status as direct and indirect claimants, respectively,

---

not the government. More recent research indicates that this observation continues to be valid (see Ascher 1999, Marcel 2006). Even those petroleum-rich states that acknowledge the need to increase transparency of the NOC's financial operations reject the idea that this must include "increasing public disclosure of information" (Marcel 2006, 142).

[36] For the application of "mutual hostage-taking" to other contexts, see Boylan (2001) and Kang (2002).

without the other's support. Simply put, state elites cannot maximize their share of the proceeds from mineral wealth unless DPOs pay taxes and DPOs cannot maximize their share unless the state protects their property rights. This also produces a form of "mutual hostage-taking." For example, the fact that DPOs have access to semilegal means of hiding their income and evading taxes, such as transfer pricing, makes the state vulnerable. These schemes, however, are not without considerable cost to the DPOs. Likewise, without the state's protection against expropriation, the DPOs cannot manage its assets in the mineral sector effectively; for example, they will have a greater incentive to engage in asset stripping rather than investing in their companies. Over time, however, asset mismanagement will undermine the companies' profitability and thereby reduce the mineral sector's fiscal contribution to the state budget.

In short, if DPOs and state elites fail to enforce each other's claims, they will suffer joint losses because neither can maximize its utility. Yet because they face both high TCs and societal expectations for redistribution, this is best achieved by revealing, not concealing, information – both to one another and to the public. On the one hand, maintaining their access rights to mineral rents requires that each can acquire private information – in other words, state elites need to know how much profit the private oil companies are actually generating and the rate at which the DPOs prefer to pay rather than evade taxes. On the other hand, both sets of actors want the general public to know that the DPOs are paying their "fair share" and profits are not "excessive." DPOs also have other audiences from which hiding information does not serve their financial interest, including current shareholders and future potential investors or partners. The ability to attract foreign investment, for example, requires public disclosure about the company's fundamentals. Likewise, a minimum requirement for selling American Depositary Shares on the New York Stock Exchange is adopting international accounting standards. The need to uncover hidden information and make the agreement public knowledge, in turn, fosters explicit bargaining.

Whereas implicit bargaining reinforces weak fiscal regimes, explicit bargaining contributes to the emergence and persistence of strong ones. First and foremost, it fosters a more transparent bargaining process because the actors and interests involved in making the bargain are clear rather than left to the imagination, and the process itself is more likely to occur in a public forum or at least to be covered by the news media. Second, precisely because of its public nature, those involved in making the explicit bargain can be more easily held accountable. At a minimum, there is likely to be some formal documentation of the negotiation process and hence the institutional decisions that are made. The mineral sector's tax burden, for example, will be a matter of public record for which both the DPOs and the governing elites are liable. Third, the public nature of the bargaining process also extends the life of the institutions it produces because it means that something equally public is required to revoke the terms of the agreement.

IMPLICATIONS

The contrasting cases of S_1 and P_1 provide a vivid demonstration of the main thrust of our argument – that the negative outcomes usually attributed to mineral wealth should instead be attributed to state ownership with control. In particular, we argue that weak fiscal regimes are not inevitable in mineral-rich states, but rather depend on who owns and controls the mineral sector. Thus, while our predicted outcomes for countries that adopt S_1 do not necessarily contradict the conventional literature on the resource curse, we provide a more complete explanation for why they emerge. First, we connect ownership structure to specific types of taxation and spending policies in mineral-rich states. In other words, we argue not only that S_1 fosters a fiscal regime that relies primarily on mineral sector taxation and lacks institutionalized limits on government spending – the standard prediction in the resource curse literature – but also that the fiscal regime under this form of ownership structure will consist of an unstable tax regime that is based largely on indirect and implicit taxation, and an expenditure system that emphasizes universal subsidies and implicit transfers.

Second, we argue that elites' preferences for building weak fiscal regimes are a rational response to the incentives that S_1 generates via low TCs and societal expectations for widespread distribution of the proceeds from mineral wealth. This contrasts sharply with the most common explanation for the lack of institution building found in the conventional resource curse literature – that is, that mineral wealth necessarily induces myopia and risk aversion among governing elites (see Anderson 1987, Beblawi and Luciani 1987, Chaudhry 1989, Karl 1997, Mahdavy 1970, Mitra 1994). In other words, governing elites and NOC managers under S_1 do not simply neglect institution building because their wealth makes them shortsighted or, to put it bluntly, giddy. Rather they deliberately forego creating strong institutions because both their mutual interest in maximizing discretion over the management of the mineral sector and their need to demonstrate that they are the "rightful" custodians of the nation's wealth are better served by relying primarily on QFAs.

Third, we take the demand side of institutional formation seriously both by placing greater emphasis on the role that societal expectations play in elites' decision-making calculus and by treating them systematically across different forms of ownership structure. The common tendency for state elites in mineral-rich countries to resist constraints on expenditures, for example, is not simply a function of either their desire to build and maintain patronage networks or to pacify the population, as is often assumed in the conventional resource curse literature (see Entelis 1976, Norton 1995, Shambayati 1994, Vandewalle 1998). Rather when the state owns and controls the mineral sector, it is also driven by the popular notion that the state should constitute both the country's primary source of revenue and economic activity.

More specifically, elite perceptions of societal expectations under S_1 are a crucial part of the story because they help explain not only why mineral-rich states are unlikely to tax their citizens directly and explicitly but also why such states tend to utilize indirect and implicit taxation across sectors coupled with targeted subsidies that only benefit some segments of the population alongside universal access to basic goods and services. Here, it is not merely that indirect and implicit taxes are invisible – because in fact they never really are – but rather that these forms of taxation are much less visible than expenditures. In other words, what is taken away from the general population is invisible compared to what it receives via universal subsidies. The government's predilection toward visible benefits relative to costs means that social welfare functions essentially as a populist gesture. High levels of spending, therefore, do not alleviate and may even exacerbate inequality and poverty, as the richer segments of the population are more likely to benefit disproportionately from fuel and food subsidies. Thus, another aspect of the curse associated with mineral wealth – high degrees of income inequality and endemic poverty (see Collier 2007, Ross 2001b) – should be attributed instead to S_1.

A more prominent role for elites' perceptions of societal expectations also helps explain why governing elites in mineral-rich states would ever prefer to constrain themselves – a possibility that the conventional resource curse literature does not even entertain. Under P_1, elites have two mutually reinforcing incentives to build institutions that effectively limit their ability to extract and distribute resources. One stems from the desire to lower TCs. The other stems from the reduced political risk of pursuing taxation and expenditure reform outside the mineral sector due to low societal expectations. For example, because they believe that society only expects to receive a portion of the proceeds from mineral sector development via redistribution, governing elites are more likely to institute not only an effective NRF but also a broad-based tax system.

More broadly, our analytical focus on ownership structure and the mechanisms through which it shapes elites' institutional incentives sheds new light on why even well-intentioned governments in mineral-rich states have so often failed to promote development. The conventional view, perhaps best articulated by Richard M. Auty (1997), is that resource abundance fosters governments that willingly distort the economy in the pursuit of rents whereas resource scarcity fosters governments that prioritize both the efficient allocation of economic resources and investment in human and social capital. As a result, mineral wealth has impeded the emergence of "developmental states," which are widely credited with achieving economic growth in other parts of the developing world since the 1950s, most notably East Asia (see Castells 1992, Johnson 1982, Wade 1990). That developmental states are a rare occurrence in mineral-rich countries is an incontrovertible fact. What is much less clear, however, is why. We suggest that the dearth of such states in petroleum-rich countries from roughly the late 1960s to the early 1990s is directly related to the prevalence of S_1 during this same period.

In short, both of the core features that have made developmental states a viable engine for achieving growth are at odds with governing elites' incentives under S_1. The first is the need to delegate economic decision making to a technocratic bureaucracy (see Johnson 1982, Wade 1990). Yet low TCs motivate elites to do precisely the opposite – that is, to create blurred rather than clear boundaries and to conflate economic with political goals. The second core feature is that the government's legitimacy is tied directly to achieving sustained economic growth (Castells 1992, Wade 1990). Because societal expectations are high under S_1, however, elites feel pressured to legitimize their rule not through long-term investment but rather through the immediate and widespread distribution of rents. High societal expectations also complicate the evolution of a cooperative relationship between the government and the private sector, which some describe as a third core feature (see Johnson 1982), because the view that the state should dominate the economy fosters entrepreneurs engaged in securing particularistic benefits rather than creating productive enterprises. That bankrupt NOCs are a pervasive feature across states that adopt S_1 is a poignant illustration of how these incentives combine to deter governments in mineral-rich states from pursuing a similar path to their mineral poor East Asian counterparts. In sum, in the context of low TCs and high societal expectations, it is politically rational for governments to systematically undermine their primary vehicle for extracting mineral rents and then distributing them via universal subsidies and large public works projects. The most recent example can be found in Venezuela, where PdVSA has not only experienced a decline in its oil-production capacity since the mid-2000s despite a sustained oil price boom, but also failed to serve as a vehicle for realizing President Chavez's populist agenda owing to "the demands of a growing web of political patronage" (Rodriguez 2008).

4

Two Versions of Rentierism

State Ownership with Control in Turkmenistan and Uzbekistan

> I'm becoming more and more convinced in the correctness of my decision to provide the population with such an inordinate degree of social protection, as its implementation has allowed every Turkmen to receive practically every day a guaranteed share of our national wealth, every hour to feel the support of the state. ...
>
> – Saparmurat Niyazov, President of Turkmenistan, explaining his decision to give free gas, electricity, and water to the population[1]

> Until recently, we were forced to import virtually all important oil products, mainly from Russia. But a lot has been done towards achieving energy self-sufficiency in the last two or three years ... . [Now we can reduce the amount of] cotton we sell to buy these products. We will sell cotton instead to satisfy people's needs; we will buy foodstuffs and consumer goods, build new factories and facilities.
>
> – Islam Karimov, President of Uzbekistan, September 1994

Turkmenistan and Uzbekistan stand alone among the petroleum-rich Soviet successor states in their decision to retain the ownership structure that they inherited from the Soviet Union – that is, state ownership with control (S_1), and thus to eschew direct foreign involvement. By 1992 – just one year after declaring their independence – the newly elected presidents[2] of both countries had publicly asserted that both petroleum resources and the right to develop them belonged solely to the state and began restructuring their respective oil and gas industries to reflect the "transfer" of property from the Soviet state to their own nations. Alongside newly empowered oil and gas ministries, therefore, emerged fully state-owned concerns or corporations, such as Turkmengaz,

---

[1] *Nezavisimaya Gazeta*, July 31, 1996.

[2] Saparmurat Niyazov, appointed president of the Turkmen Soviet Socialist Republic on October 27, 1990, was elected president of independent Turkmenistan on June 21, 1992. Islam Karimov was appointed first secretary of the Uzbek Soviet Socialist Republic in June 1989 and elected to the presidency in December 1991.

Turkmenneft, and Uzbekneftegaz, to perform the oversight and managerial functions previously usurped by the Soviet government (for details, see IEA 1998). "These new national concerns," according to von Hirschhausen and Engerer (1998, 1116), "simply inherited almost the entire exploration, production, transmission and some distribution activities, engineering and other elements of their respective republics, not to forget all 'social assets.'"

For those who emphasized institutional continuity with the Soviet system, S_1 may seem the most obvious choice. Indeed, neither country had a significant petroleum industry prior to Soviet rule. Although oil extraction began in both Turkmenistan and Uzbekistan prior to the Bolshevik Revolution, it was rather minimal and mined primarily for kerosene, which was then used in the cotton-processing factories and dairies (Sagers 1994). Yet, considering their mutual need for significant capital investment to build new and upgrade existing infrastructure, the decision to go it alone is not only surprising, it is quite counterintuitive (see Amuzegar 1998). Nor, as others have claimed, was S_1 the only choice due to the sheer dearth of interested foreign investors and – particularly in the case of Uzbekistan – the meagerness of estimated reserves. On the contrary, several foreign oil and gas companies were clamoring to buy into both countries' petroleum sectors immediately after the Soviet Union's demise. Enron's representative in Uzbekistan, who arrived in 1994, for example, underscored that this was "the only time that Enron has come into a country without a deal signed first," justifying this decision with the conviction that "more than half of the country contain[ed] undiscovered and untapped oil and gas reserves" (Authors' interview).[3] Moreover, although Uzbekistan did not have the same level of proven reserves as either of its Central Asian counterparts, the potential rents from its petroleum sector were believed to be "still higher than Indonesian oil rents during the 1974–78 and 1979–81 oil booms" (Auty 2003, 259).[4] Furthermore, although Uzbekistan's total potential rents as a percentage of its GDP were about half of both Azerbaijan's and Turkmenistan's in 2000, they certainly rivaled Kazakhstan's (see Table 4.1).

Despite having adopted the same ownership structure, Turkmenistan and Uzbekistan have not developed their respective petroleum sectors at the same pace or for the same purpose. Turkmenistan pursued the quintessential strategy according to proponents of the resource curse thesis: Less than two years after gaining independence from Soviet rule, "[t]he Turkmenistan government launched an ambitious ten-year development plan in 1993 which was designed to achieve the country's potential as a 'second Kuwait' as quickly as possible" based on the rapid exploitation of its oil and gas reserves for export

---

[3] The most important early foreign oil companies in Turkmenistan were Bridas (Argentina), Larmag (the Netherlands), and Unocal (United States), which are discussed in greater detail later in the Chapter. In Uzbekistan, other potentially large foreign investors included the self-ascribed "usually very cautious" Texaco (Authors' interview).

[4] In the 1990s, Uzbekistan claimed to have over 6 billion tons of oil and over 5 trillion cubic meters of gas (Hines and Sievers 2001).

TABLE 4.1. *Potential Energy Rents (selected Caspian Basin countries) 2000 (in percent of GDP)*

	Export rent	Domestic producer rent	Total rent	Domestic consumer subsidies
Azerbaijan	31.2	16.8	61.4	13.4
Kazakhstan	20.2	9.8	33.6	3.6
Turkmenistan	43.0	-5.2	65.3	27.5
Uzbekistan	6.3	26.2	36.4	3.0

Source: Auty (2003, 259) but originally from Esanov et al. (2001).

(Auty 1997c, 3).[5] Uzbekistan did not. In sharp contrast to Turkmenistan, in the early 1990s Uzbekistan focused its efforts on self-sufficiency in energy, which it achieved by 1995, prioritized oil and gas production from existing fields, alongside the increased use of hydropower,[6] to satisfy internal demand, and sought international financing to build or upgrade local refineries rather than to discover and exploit new reserves (Authors' interviews with Persheyev and with Karchenko and Tashpulatov). Thus for roughly a decade after independence, it deliberately limited both opportunities to expand the size of its proven reserves[7] and the overall contribution of the petroleum sector to its economy. While energy rents accruing directly to Turkmenistan's government between 1994 and 1999 are estimated to be between 33 percent and 64 percent of GDP, for example, during the same period Uzbekistan's government captured energy rents estimated at between 13 percent and 21 percent of GDP (Pomfret 2004, 9).

As noted in Chapter 3, S_1 can enable governments to delay the development of their mineral resources and to produce them primarily for domestic consumption rather than foreign markets – possibilities that the standard resource curse literature excludes – by virtue of the minimal role S_1 affords foreign investment, and hence the burden of self-financing, which may reinforce structural impediments such as access to external pipeline routes. Furthermore, as we argue in Chapter 9, countries are more likely to adopt S_1 when they have a viable source of revenue in the status quo and no additional claims on this revenue because they feel less immediate pressure to generate new sources of revenue, and hence to either develop and expand their mineral reserves rapidly or produce them primarily for export.

[5] See also "Kontseptsiia 'O razvitii neftianoi i gazovoi promyshlennosti Turkmenistana do 2020 goda,'" (Concept of Development of the Oil and Gas Industry in Turkmenistan until Year 2020.) *Interfax Oil and Gas Report* 1994, no. 24 (17 June), p. 7.

[6] Uzbekistan's NOC, Uzbekneftegaz, was initially under the direction of the Ministry of Energy as well as the Ministry of Water, both of which placed a high priority on developing hydropower (Authors' interview with Saifulin).

[7] Uzbekistan did not launch exploration initiatives in two areas believed to contain significant additional reserves – the Aral Sea Basin and Amu Darya Basin – until the mid-2000s. For details, see Ulmishek (2004).

It is precisely for such reasons that Uzbekistan was able to forego the immediate development of its petroleum for export. Although both countries were
the largest producers of natural gas in Soviet Central Asia, Turkmenistan's
gas sector benefited from a surge of investment into exploiting new fields in
the 1980s, which made it the second-largest supplier of gas within the Soviet
Union (Krasnov and Brada 1997) and the fourth-largest gas producer in the
world at independence (Pomfret 2004, 3). Uzbekistan, in contrast, "was a net
energy importer in the Soviet era, importing oil and hydroelectricity [from
other Soviet republics] and exporting small quantities of gas only to south-
eastern Kazakhstan and the Kyrgyz and Tajik republics" (Pomfret 2004, 8).
Instead, its main contribution to the Soviet economy was cotton; by the late
1980s, Uzbekistan accounted for two-thirds of all cotton produced in the
Soviet Union (Rumer 1989, 62) and with independence it became the world's
fourth-largest cotton producer (World Bank 1993c, xi). Turkmenistan produced the bulk of the remaining one-third (Gleason 1990), placing it among
the top ten producers in the world (World Bank 1994b, 30).

In short, the more established economic role of the cotton sector relative to
petroleum meant that the Uzbekistani government could rely on the former to
provide the bulk of its revenue during the transition to statehood while developing the latter primarily for internal consumption. This, in turn, mitigated
the effects of S_1 on societal expectations vis-à-vis the size and immediacy
of proceeds from mineral wealth. In particular, the reduced speed at which
petroleum rents were anticipated to flow into the country, as well as the source
of these rents, meant that, for most of the 1990s, the Uzbekistani government
could both continue to utilize direct and explicit forms of taxation across
sectors, namely agriculture, and avoid pledging an immediate and dramatic
expansion of preexisting public goods and social services. It also meant that
the government was less inclined to promote large public works or "national
prestige" projects as a way of demonstrating to its population that society at
large was indeed benefiting from the country's "newfound" wealth.

Thus, while it was clear by the mid-2000s that Turkmenistan and
Uzbekistan more closely resembled the OPEC nations that adopted S_1 from
the 1960s through the 1980s than the other petroleum-rich Soviet successor
states, they did so to varying degrees. In sum, they have not had the same level
of budgetary dependence on the petroleum sector; the relative share of the
petroleum sector's contribution to the government budget was much larger
in Turkmenistan than in Uzbekistan. Nor have they exhibited the same level
of extravagance when it comes to spending the proceeds from their mineral
wealth. Turkmenistan, which has employed substantial mineral rents to fill
its capital city, Ashgabat, with gold-plated statues and four-star hotels while
its largely rural population receives free gas, water, and salt but is deprived of
basic education and healthcare, embodies the classic model of the rentier state.
Uzbekistan, in contrast, has utilized its access to mineral rents primarily as a
means to increase its leverage over proceeds from cotton exports and thereby
to support the growth of state-owned industry via import substitution (ISI)

while engaging in only a modest expansion of the basic cradle-to-grave welfare system it inherited from the Soviet Union, and even attempting to target the delivery of social assistance.

Nonetheless, Uzbekistan's decision to consume rather than to export its petroleum wealth has neither engendered positive socioeconomic outcomes in the short term nor improved its long-term development prospects due to the broader negative impact that S_1 has on fiscal regimes. As predicted, due to the particular institutional incentives it generates via its effects on transaction costs (TCs), societal expectations, and power relations, S_1 has fostered the same core features of a weak fiscal regime in Uzbekistan as it did in Turkmenistan. These include an unstable tax system that increasingly relies on indirect and implicit taxation across sectors, unconstrained government expenditures in the form of universal subsidies, centralized investment aimed at promoting state-owned enterprises (SOEs) via ISI, and the pervasive use of quasi-fiscal activities (QFAs). Thus in both countries, an inefficient public sector persists at the expense of private sector development, and comparatively high levels of social spending have failed to either reach the poorest segments of the population or contribute to human capital formation. At the same time, their respective governments have eschewed the opportunity not only to build a more predictable source of revenue but also to develop the capacity for allocating this revenue more effectively.

RETAINING STATE OWNERSHIP WITH CONTROL

For both President Niyazov and President Karimov, independent statehood went hand-in-hand with full possession of the material and physical resources that had once been controlled from Moscow. Most importantly, this meant the ability "to dispose of [oil, gas, and cotton] at [their] own discretion" (Rumer 1992, 40). In hindsight, given what we now know about their distinct styles of authoritarian rule, perhaps it is not surprising that they found different ways to lay claim to this authority. Niyazov, who dubbed himself "Turkmenbashi" (father of all Turkmen), conferred various state prizes upon himself, and renamed collective farms, districts, and streets in the capital (Ashgabat) after himself following his reelection in 1992 (Anderson 1995, 512), has become notorious for establishing a cult of personality that is reminiscent of – albeit much more colorful than – Stalinism. Thus while both presidents oversaw the adoption of a constitution in the early 1990s that essentially vests all political power in their office and neither has tolerated political opposition in any form (Gleason 2003), Niyazov clearly relied more on charismatic authority to sustain his rule.

Accordingly, Niyazov signified his intention to retain S_1 over the petroleum sector largely by word and deed rather than merely through legislation. The sole mention of the country's natural resource wealth in the 1992 Constitution, for example, is in reference to the Cabinet of Ministers duty to "ensure the rational use of and protection of [these] resources" – a duty that was de facto delegated to the Ministry of Oil and Gas.[8] Yet, one of Niyazov's first major acts as president was to raise substantially the price of gas exports so that its former customers (namely Ukraine) could no longer afford to purchase Turkmenistan's gas (see Rumer 1992, 40), thereby paving the way for new, preferably foreign, buyers.[9] Even prior to this, he began pursuing alternative routes to deliver the country's gas to international markets. Niyazov's first state visit – less than two weeks after announcing the date for a referendum on independence – was to Iran to seek financial and political support to build a pipeline that would carry Turkmenistan's gas to Europe.[10]

At the same time Niyazov sought to broaden Turkmenistan's export options, he openly discouraged foreign investors in the petroleum sector and actively thwarted their operations. Thus, while Niyazov authorized the Ministry of Oil and Gas to sign joint venture (JV) contracts with a handful of foreign oil companies in the early 1990s, he did so with the express understanding that, "as commander and chief of the country's gas fields," they would be forced to follow his directives (Authors' interview with foreign consultant in the energy sector no. 1).[11] According to those who worked closely with him during this time, "he [wa]s innately suspicious of foreigners and their intensions" vis-à-vis the petroleum sector (Authors' interview with former government official no. 1). Not surprisingly, then, the only foreign companies that initially consented to invest in Turkmenistan's petroleum sector were two minor players in the international petroleum market – Bridas of Argentina and Larmag of the Netherlands.[12] Furthermore, Niyazov turned quickly against the country's first Oil and Gas Minister, Nazar Soiunov, who had been largely responsible for attracting such foreign investment, forcing him to resign in July 1994. Soiunov's replacement, Khekim Ishanov, was then "given a mandate to deliberately derail foreign investment" (ibid). Within months of his appointment, the new Oil and Gas Minister began unilaterally revising the terms of contracts signed under his predecessor – for example, introducing clauses that "allowed the government to divert oil from export markets at prices set by government officials" (Auty 1997c, 10). His first target was Bridas. The assault began in September 1994, when the company was informed that the JV had to send all of its recovered crude to refineries

---

[8] Turkmenistan's Law on the Subsurface (December 14, 1992), however, underscored the state's authority over its petroleum resources (Hines and Varanese 2001).

[9] As a result, on February 29, 1992, Turkmenistan officially suspended gas deliveries to Ukraine. They were resumed at the end of 1992 and then suspended again in February 1994 due to nonpayment.

[10] An agreement was signed in August 1992.

[11] The 1993 Law on Concessions is a testament to this. Not only was it originally intended for the industrial rather than petroleum sector, it was deliberately written to "allow ample room for negotiation and renegotiation" (Authors' interview with foreign consultant in the energy sector no. 2).

[12] Of the six tenders issued from 1991 to 1994, the winners of three others just walked away (*RPI* 1996d, 56).

in Turkmenistan and that its general director had to be a Turkmen national (*RPI* 1994a). It ended in May 1996 with Bridas seeking international arbitration to recover $225 million in investments (for details, see *RPI* 1996b, 54–7). The Ministry's response was simply: "If they want to leave, let them go" (ibid., 54).

Only several years later did Niyazov deem it necessary to codify his verbal and physical assertion of state ownership with control over the petroleum sector. In July 1996, a presidential decree disbanded the Ministry of Oil and Gas, replaced it with the Ministry of Oil and Gas Industry and Mineral Resources, and created five new state concerns: (1) Turkmenneft, responsible for the development of all the country's oil fields; (2) Turkmengaz, responsible for the development of all the country's gas fields; (3) Turkmenneftegazstroy, responsible for coordinating engineering and construction jobs in the petroleum sector; (4) Turkmenneftegaz, responsible for operating the country's refineries and wholesale facilities; and (5) Turkmengeologiya, responsible for exploring new mineral deposits.[13] These concerns were officially charged with managing the day-to-day operations of the petroleum sector and instructed to report directly to the president. Several months later (December 1996), President Niyazov signed into law the country's first and only piece of comprehensive legislation governing the petroleum sector (effective March 1997), the Law on Hydrocarbon Resources (or Petroleum Law of Turkmenistan). Article 3 declares hydrocarbon resources to be "the exclusive property of Turkmenistan" and grants management rights (including "exploitation and disposal of petroleum") to the Cabinet of Ministers, which Article 4 charges with developing an overall strategy for the development of hydrocarbon reserves, protecting the environment, and compiling "statistical reports on petroleum reserves." Importantly, the 1996 Petroleum Law was not designed to meet international standards for the protection of foreign direct investment (FDI); in fact, the foreign investor community scoffed at the inclusion of several articles that allowed the government "to annul a petroleum license unilaterally and to have the associated contract terminated and deemed invalid" (Hines and Varanese 2001, 48).[14] The general cynicism of foreign investors was echoed in an expert analysis of legislation in Turkmenistan's energy sector: "[t]his latest legislative package completes the framework for energy operations in Turkmenistan but, instead of helping Ashgabat increase Western investment and production in the republic, it is far more likely to discourage foreign investment" (*RPI* 1996a).

For most of the 1990s, therefore, Turkmenneft and Turkmengaz continued to produce the vast majority of oil and gas at the same time that President

---

[13] Presidential Decree on the "Efficient Oil and Gas Industry Administration and Rational Use of Mineral Resources," July 1, 1996. For more information, see Hines and Varanese (2001).

[14] Most glaring was the absence of any stability provisions and protections against expropriation as would be common under ownership structures where foreign investors have a prominent role (such as S_2 and P_2).

Niyazov has retained "full decision-making authority" over the petroleum sector (Authors' interview with representative of Texaco; see also, Gleason 2003, 106). Foreign companies only played a minimal role.[15] Regarding gas, for example, Turkmengaz operated 25 of the country's gas fields, including the two largest, Dauletabad and Malai, which are devoted to export, and accounted for over 90 percent of total production while Turkmenneft produced the remainder (Kamenev 2001, 163). Oil is only slightly different; Turkmenneft produced about 80 percent of the country's oil while the "four foreign companies … engaged in oil production in Turkmenistan … account[ed] for about 20 percent of all oil extracted in the country" (Kamenev 2001, 164).[16] More common was for the foreign investors' involvement to be restricted to service contracts. Since 1998, for example, Schlumberger has provided oil and gas services for Turkmenneft (*RFE/RL* April 15, 2004). Foreign involvement in Turkmenistan during this period also consisted of international loans to upgrade the outmoded infrastructure in the energy sector, including its refineries. For instance, in the late 1990s, Turkmenistan received several loans from Japan's Export-Import Bank to finance modernization projects for the Turkmenbashi Refinery.[17] While foreign investment increased in the late 1990s and early 2000s, particularly in the oil sector, it still remained so minimal that "Turkmenistan ha[d] one of the lowest private sector-to-GDP ratios in the [Central Asian] region, estimated by the European Bank for Reconstruction and Development (EBRD) to be 25 percent" (Sabonis-Helf 2004, 170). Indeed, Niyazov continued to declare emphatically on several occasions that privatization in the oil and gas sectors was banned (see *RFE/RL* October 17, 2002, *RFE/RL* September 23, 2003).

In addition, while the 1996 Petroleum Law authorized both JVs and production-sharing agreements (PSAs), the government not only continued to favor the former (*RPI* 1997), but also did so arbitrarily.[18] By 2001, the Turkmenistani government unilaterally decided that it would assume full responsibility for exploiting many of the fields where foreign oil and gas companies were actively part of JVs (Glych 2001). One official in the Ministry of Oil and Gas justified the decision thus: "the oil sector performance figures show that things develop successfully at fields where our [Turkmen] enterprises operate. Projects involving foreign companies do not yield good results" because they do not "vigorously develop their projects" (ibid, 43). This notion, however, largely reflects divergent production strategies during a bust: Whereas Turkmenneft's production climbed by 6 percent from 1999

---

[15] The IEA (1998) concluded that "[i]n Turkmenistan there are no large foreign equity investment projects for oil and gas production," although several PSAs had been signed for offshore development as of 1997.

[16] In 2000, for example, Turkmenneft produced 6.5 million tons of oil while foreign investors produced only 220,000 tons (Glych 2001).

[17] For details, see http://www.jbic.go.jp/english/base/release/exim/1996-e/A16/nr96–27.php

[18] The only PSAs to date are in the offshore oil sector (see Olcott 2004, 33) – and most focused on exploration activities (Glych 2001).

to 2000, the foreign oil companies' opted to cut production by more than 25 percent (ibid).[19]

In contrast, Uzbekistan officially declared the inviolability of S_1 over the petroleum sector in its first Constitution, adopted in December 1992, according to which mineral resources "constitute the national wealth" and thus are not only the exclusive property of the state, but also necessarily fall under its jurisdiction.[20] Shortly thereafter, the government began drafting legislation governing subsoil resources, approved in September 1994, which served to reaffirm the state's choice of ownership structure over the petroleum sector as well as to officially confer regulatory authority upon the Cabinet of Ministers.[21] The Uzbekistani government also launched the process to restructure the Soviet-era oil and gas industry much earlier than the Turkmenistani government. Similar to other petroleum-rich countries that adopt S_1, it immediately created a national oil company (NOC) to oversee oil exploration and production. In 1992, the primary units of its petroleum industry (that is, exploration, extraction, processing, transportation, and marketing) were united within one state-owned "concern" – Uzbekneftegaz – that was later transformed into the Uzbekneftegaz Corporation by presidential decree in 1993 (IEA 1998, Sagers 1994). In 1998, Uzbekneftegaz was reorganized as a national holding company in which the state holds 99.7 percent of the shares and that is comprised of eight joint-stock companies (Denisova 2006, Hines and Sievers 2001).[22]

When it came to the treatment of foreign investors, however, their approaches were strikingly similar. As in Turkmenistan, foreign investment in the petroleum sector was actively discouraged.[23] Throughout the 1990s, Uzbekistan refused to promulgate any domestic legislation to protect FDI that met international standards or to introduce any specific tax privileges that foreign investors in the petroleum sector desired (Authors' interviews with representatives of Agip and JNOC; for details, see Hines and Sievers 2001). For example, although Uzbekistan technically has allowed concessions since the early 1990s, the legislation to this effect "reserv[es] the exclusive right to dispose of the concession property" (Baker and McKenzie 2006, 40). Similarly, the 1994 version of the Law on Subsoil was seen to reflect Uzbekistan's preference for

---

[19] The marked increase in Turkmenneft's production also reflects the fact that production levels were so low during the preceding three years due to disputes with Ukraine.

[20] In many ways, this law merely extended the September 1990 "Law on Property," which conferred ownership and control of minerals upon the government of the Uzbek Soviet Socialist Republic, to the government of Uzbekistan.

[21] Zakon Republika Uzbekistan Sentiabria 23, 1994, "O Nedrakh."

[22] These are Uzgeoburneftegazdobycha (extraction), Uzburneftegaz (drilling), Uzneftegazpererabotka (processing and refining), Uzneftegazsnabzheniye (supply), Uzneftegazstroi (construction), Uznefteprodukt (marketing), Uzneftegazmash (equipment), and Uztransgaz (gas transportation).

[23] This was not the case in other sectors of the economy. Several foreign companies were active, including the Daewoo Corporation, Mercedes Benz, British-American Tobacco Plant, Newmont Mining, and Coca-Cola.

autarchy – that is, "relying on its own strengths" and not catering to foreign investor concerns (Nobatova 2003b, 63). At the same time, those investors who nonetheless showed interest were subjected to the whims of Karimov who "just ma[de] deals at will" (Authors' interview with representative of Agip) and could "issue a decree declaring your status and privileges" (Authors' interview with Barry). Thus by the end of 1990s, no major foreign companies had made any significant investments in the upstream sector. The absence of foreign involvement in Uzbekistan's petroleum sector is in sharp contrast to the high volume of FDI that flowed into Kazakhstan's petroleum sector in the 1990s. For example, in 1998, FDI per capita in Uzbekistan was only $7 compared to $74 in Kazakhstan (Alam and Banerji 2000, 8).

Also like Turkmenistan, the government's strategy envisaged that foreign investors would play only a minimal role in developing the petroleum sector while domestic sources and foreign loans would finance most upstream investment. Only rarely did government allow service contracts, albeit without any equity interest, to abet oil exploration (IEA 1998, 35). Rather, for the first decade after independence, Uzbekneftegaz conducted virtually all of the nation's oil and gas drilling (Authors' interview with representatives no. 2). It was able to achieve its goal of self-sufficiency in both oil and gas production in less than four years, moreover, by investing the revenue generated from cotton exports to both expand its production capacity and explore for new fields (Kotz 2003, 3). Oil production, for example, expanded into new areas, such as the Karshi Steppe in southwestern Uzbekistan, along with some additional discoveries in older producing regions in the Fergana Valley that included a major discovery at the Min-Bulak field in Namangan Oblast in 1992 (Sagers 1994). Meanwhile, Uzbekistan too relied on foreign loans to upgrade and expand its refining capacity. In 1997, Uzneftegazpererabotka, which is responsible for the processing and refining of petroleum products within Uzbekneftegaz, signed a $180 million loan agreement (combined) with the EBRD and Exim Bank of Japan to refurbish the Ferghana plant (Authors' interview with representative of TACIS).[24] During this same year, Uzbekistan also contracted with the French company, Technip, and the Japanese companies, Marubeni and JGC, to construct the Bukharan oil refinery, which was the first new refinery built in the Soviet successor states since independence (DOE-EIA 2005).[25]

The Uzbekistani government's policy toward foreign investment, however, changed abruptly in 2001 when it promulgated new legislation that allowed for PSAs alongside traditional JVs. In short, the PSA Law, along with a new Law on Subsoil, passed the following year (2002), granted foreign oil and gas companies the "exclusive rights to explore and extract minerals on specified subsoil land" (Saparov 2003, 53; for details, see also Hines and Sievers 2001). As was intended, this has spurred foreign investor activity in Uzbekistan's

[24] For details, see http://www.ebrd.com/new/pressrel/1997/03jan20x.htm
[25] With the building of the Bukharan refinery, Uzbekistan has a total of three. The Ferghana Oil Refinery began operation in 1958, and Altyarik refinery was established in 1906.

petroleum sector, though the most important project was not initiated until September 2005 when Uzbekneftegaz, China National Petroleum Corporation, Malaysia's Petronas Carigali Overseas, Russia's Lukoil Overseas, and Korea National Oil Corporation set up a consortium to develop the gas fields in the Aral Sea Basin, which is believed to contain over two billion tons of crude oil and around two trillion cubic meters of natural gas (*RFE/RL* September 14, 2005, Yakovleva 2005b).[26]

As of 2001 then, Turkmenistan and Uzbekistan had parted ways in one important respect: While Turkmenistan maintained S_1 from 1992 until 2005, Uzbekistan formally adopted S_2 in 2001. Both because the predicted effects of S_1 and S_2 are almost identical – except for the role of the foreign investors – and because there was no substantial foreign investment until 2005, however, there should be little discernible difference in outcomes regarding Uzbekistan's fiscal regime prior to 2005. Subsequently, the decisive factor in whether this change in ownership structure promotes fiscal reform depends on the foreign investors themselves – that is, whether they can effectively exert pressure on the state and whether they are committed to corporate social responsibility (CSR). (See Chapter 6 for details.) We leave the task of explaining Uzbekistan's change in ownership structure from S_1 to S_2 to Chapter 9.

THE EMERGENCE OF WEAK FISCAL REGIMES

During the 1990s and first half of the 2000s, Turkmenistan and Uzbekistan's fiscal regimes shared many core similarities that classify them as weak: Their tax systems were notoriously unstable and unreformed, they had no institutionalized limits on spending, and both taxation and expenditures relied heavily on QFAs. And yet, as aforementioned, this has not precluded some important differences concerning the scope of taxation and the level of expenditures. For example, Uzbekistan initially relied on cotton rather than the petroleum sector to provide the bulk of its tax revenue and has not shown the same proclivity as Turkmenistan toward making populist gestures and building national prestige projects.

Taxation

By all accounts, Turkmenistan and Uzbekistan have been the biggest laggards on tax reform – both among their petroleum-rich counterparts and other Soviet successor states.[27] With the exception of Belarus, they occupy the last place when it comes to drafting new tax codes and share the dubious honor of

[26] A PSA was signed in August 2006, granting each company a 20 percent stake in the consortium. The only other significant PSA was signed with Lukoil in June 2004 to produce natural gas in the Bukhara-Khiva region of southwestern Uzbekistan.

[27] Both countries actually initiated reforms in the early 1990s, alongside their former Soviet counterparts, but this process was derailed by the mid-1990s (see Cornia 2003, 3–4; EBRD 1996).

having the lowest overall levels of tax reform, including policy and administration (see, for example, Ebrill and Havrylyshyn 1999, Martinez-Vasquez and
McNab 2000, Stepanyan 2003).[28] Moreover, Turkmenistan and Uzbekistan
are notorious for having tax regimes that are highly unstable – that is, subject
to frequent change and arbitrary enforcement. In Turkmenistan, the fact that
new taxes and tax rates were introduced exclusively by presidential decree
until the end of the 1990s contributes to this perception (Authors' interview
with USIA officer; see also Begjanova 1998, IMF 1999).

Yet, Uzbekistan's tax system has actually been more plagued by constant
fluctuations and numerous privileges and exemptions that lack a clear economic rationale. According to one comprehensive analysis in the 1990s, it was
extremely difficult to keep track of the composition of Uzbekistan's tax system
because new taxes were routinely revoked almost immediately after they had
been introduced (Rosenberg et al. 1999, 5).[29] This instability has been most
evident concerning the value added tax (VAT). Uzbekistan introduced a VAT
in 1992 at a rate of 30 percent and then reduced it to 25 percent in 1993,
which was then reduced further to 18 percent in 1995, 17 percent in 1996,
and then raised to 18 percent in 1997 and to 20 percent in 1998 (IMF 2000b,
Stepanyan 2003). The unpredictability in the VAT's rate has made it a very
volatile source of government revenue despite its significant contribution to
the state budget (Rosenberg et al. 1999, 7). Uzbekistan's experience thus lies
in stark contrast to that of OECD countries and to other parts of the former
Soviet Union (hereafter, FSU), where the VAT is one of the most reliable contributors to the budget (ibid.). As a result of continued rate fluctuations and a
"myriad of exceptions, exemptions, [and] special treatments," this instability
and unpredictability has persisted despite supposed efforts at tax reform since
2000 (Cornia 2003, 9; see also World Bank 2005c, 6–7).

In addition to their instability, the tax systems in Turkmenistan and
Uzbekistan share a growing reliance on the mineral sector. Turkmenistan's
however, was much more immediate and pronounced. During the early 1990s,
for example, "taxes … from natural gas exports … accounted for 85 percent
of non-farm foreign exchange earnings" (Auty 1997c, 6). Because petroleum
(specifically gas) is both the country's main export and source of state revenue,
it has been subjected to a myriad of both explicit and implicit taxes since
independence. In addition to high excises on fuel production,[30] explicit taxes
include a requirement to surrender 50 percent of export proceeds directly to
the Turkmen Foreign Exchange Reserve Fund (FERF). After paying what

---

[28] At the end of the 1990s, for example, Turkmenistan was the only FSU country still to have an
excess wage tax and to lack a legal framework for tax administration (Ebrill and Havrylyshyn
1999, 26, Stepanyan 2003, 18).

[29] Since 1997, for example, there have been 250 changes and amendments to the Tax Code and
more than 1,300 regulatory acts related to taxation were introduced (UNDP 2005).

[30] One of the first decrees that President Niyazov issued concerning taxation extended excise
taxes "to include petroleum and petroleum products" and "raised [rates] significantly" (Ebrill
and Havrylyshyn 1999, 17).

TABLE 4.2. *Effective Tax Rates on Key Economic Sectors in Turkmenistan, 1998*

Gas exports	
Cash sales	
50 percent tax payable to the FERF	20
43 percent average taxation of remaining proceeds[31]	9
Non-cash sales	
43 percent average taxation	26
TOTAL	55
Oil and oil products	
Oil sales	
Oil proceeds allocated to the budget	6
35 percent average taxation of remaining proceeds	33
TOTAL	39
Cotton fiber	
Cotton sales	
33 percent payable to the FERF	33
32 percent average taxation of remaining proceeds	22
TOTAL	55

Source: IMF 1999, 74 (estimates based on government data).

amounts to an excessive export tax, Turkmenneftegaz is then required to pay VAT, profit tax, the natural resource tax, and property tax.[32] What this means is that petroleum export proceeds are essentially taxed twice (see Repkine 2004). Not surprisingly, then, the total effective tax rate on gas exceeds 50 percent of its output value while the effective tax rate on state-produced oil is around 40 percent (IMF 1999, 67). At the same time, Turkmenistan also heavily taxes the cotton sector; initially, the effective rate for cotton was as high as it is for gas (IMF 1999, 68; see Table 4.2 for details). Yet while cotton rents were significant during the 1990s, their import as a main source of government revenue waned in the 2000s (Pomfret 2008a, 3). Moreover, as the country has become increasingly dependent upon taxation from the petroleum sector, the government has freed up the agriculture sector from taxation. In 2003 in the midst of the oil price boom, Niyazov announced that farmers would not have to pay any taxes until 2010 (*RFE/RL* May 16, 2003).

Because cotton continued to serve as Uzbekistan's main export after independence – and to bring sizeable and reliable export earnings until 1998[33] – it extracted a similarly high level of explicit taxation from the cotton sector for

[31] Includes VAT, profit tax, natural resource tax, property tax, and excises.
[32] In the 1990s, gas contributed about 10 percent of VAT and 85 percent of the natural resource tax (IMF 1999, 66).
[33] For details, see EIU (2002), 38.

most of the 1990s, but deemphasized this form of taxation in the petroleum sector. For example, in 1992 excise taxes from cotton alone accounted for over 20 percent of the country's total tax revenue. Although the size of this tax's contribution to the state budget appeared to decrease dramatically by the mid-1990s, this was purely a function of the government's decision to "report" these earnings as "non-tax revenue" (Rosenberg et al. 1999, 8). In addition, Uzbekistan employed a similar double-taxation system as Turkmenistan whereby all exporters were required to surrender some portion of their foreign currency earnings but those exporting state-procured commodities (i.e., cotton and wheat) had to relinquish all of their hard currency earnings (see Jones Luong 2003b for details).

In contrast, Uzbekistan's main explicit tax on petroleum was the excise tax, which only gained increasing importance in the late 1990s as the government began to shift its emphasis toward the mineral sector.[34] When it was introduced in 1995, the excise tax on crude oil was 24 percent and 42.6 percent on natural gas. By 1998, the corresponding rates amounted to 53.8 percent and 53.7 percent respectively (Rosenberg et al. 1999, 8). By 2004, receipts from excise taxes on oil and gas alone amounted to "over 4 percent of GDP, or more than half of excise tax revenues" (World Bank 2005c, 6). As both the rates and revenue generated from fuel excises increased, moreover, fiscal dependence on the cotton excises decreased so that by 1998 they accounted for less than one percent of total revenue (Rosenberg et al. 1999, 8).

In both Turkmenistan and Uzbekistan, exports are also heavily taxed via implicit means. Regarding the agricultural sector in particular, this is largely tied to the fact that both countries have continued the Soviet-era practice of using production quotas and price controls via state-owned monopsonies for cotton (*Turkmenpagta* and *Uzpakhtasanoat*, respectively) as well as wheat.[35] Farmers working on state and collective farms, therefore, are not only forced to devote their land to growing so-called "strategic crops," but also to sell their cotton to the state at prices that have been consistently well below world market prices (for details see Weinthal 2002, Pomfret 2008b).[36] More generally, since the mid-1990s, both countries have employed a foreign exchange regime (FER) whereby the government sets artificially high exchange rates and strictly regulates both the supply and demand of foreign currency at these rates. Turkmenistan thus has two exchange rates: the official one set by the government and what is known as the "*kerb*" rate.[37] In Uzbekistan, there are

[34] According to Anoshkina (1997), Uzbekistan's second stage of tax "reform" (1995–1997) focused on increasing the contribution of mineral taxes to the state budget.

[35] In Uzbekistan, farmers are also subjected to the arbitrary confiscation of excess production (Jones Luong 2003b).

[36] Uzbekistan has undergone some farm restructuring (see Thurman and Lundell 2001). As of 2001, for example, private farmers are exempt from these production targets and price controls. However, this is not the case in practice (ICG 2005, 3–5).

[37] The official rate was often enshrined in the Turkmenbashi's ten-year development plans discussed below (see, for example, Kalyuzhnova and Kaser 2006, 169).

three: the auction rate and commercial rate, which are set by the central government, and the black market rate.[38] This arrangement operates as a sizeable implicit tax on exporters who are forced to surrender their foreign exchange earnings at the overvalued official rate. Exporters of state-procured commodities (or centralized exporters) are the hardest hit because, as mentioned above, they must surrender their hard currency at both a lower rate and a higher portion of their earnings (Jones Luong 2003b). As others have noted, this form of implicit taxation – which is in fact widely used in developing countries whose economies depend on agricultural exports – can pose an even greater burden on farmers than either trade barriers or direct taxes combined (Krueger et al. 1988). What is perhaps most striking about the FER in Turkmenistan and Uzbekistan, however, is that they are the only Soviet successor states to have utilized this particular policy tool except for Belarus, which is notorious for its lack of political and economic reform.

Thus, while the cotton sector in both countries is considered to be "excessively taxed" (Guadagni et al. 2005, 8; see also UNDP 2005), only Turkmenistan is widely regarded as taxing the energy sector excessively. For example, one group of international financial advisors concluded that Turkmenistan's tax system is deliberately based on "punitive taxation of energy and cotton" rather than on broad-based taxes (IMF 1999, 68). Yet this assessment does not give full consideration to the role of explicit taxation in Uzbekistan. By some estimates, the effective tax rate in the oil sector in the early 2000s was 80 percent (Cornia 2003, 8). Moreover, it does not take into account the high levels of explicit fuel subsidies (discussed more fully below), which function as an implicit tax on energy producers – most notably Uzbekneftegaz.

Finally, Turkmenistan and Uzbekistan's respective tax regimes are also strikingly similar in their composition. Both countries have increasingly emphasized indirect and implicit forms of taxation across sectors and deliberately neglected the development of direct forms. As in other parts of the FSU, the VAT quickly became the largest source of tax revenue after independence (Barbone and Sánchez 2003).[39] In Uzbekistan, for example, the VAT comprised approximately one-third of total government revenues as early as 1992 and the following year provided a larger share of tax revenue (25.7 percent) than either of the two other major taxes – the enterprise profit tax (EPT) (20.8 percent) and excise taxes (15.7 percent) (Anoshkina 1997).[40] The VAT's role in Uzbekistan, however, is even more pronounced than in other Soviet successor states partly because it has refused to grant credit

---

[38] The much-awaited April 2002 devaluation of the *som* applied only to the commercial exchange rate, which was lowered to approximately the black market rate. Access at both this rate and the auction rate remains restricted.

[39] Also like other parts of the FSU, the first phase of tax reform (1992–1994) in Uzbekistan focused on raising revenue from VAT (Anoshkina 1997).

[40] In Turkmenistan, the VAT made up almost half of the country's total tax revenue in 1994 (IMF 1999, 106).

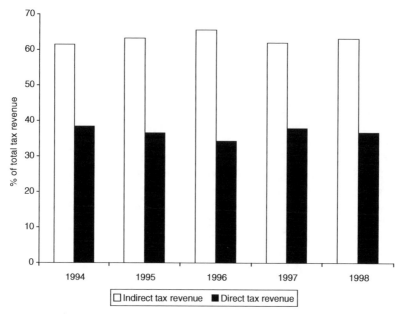

FIGURE 4.1. Indirect versus Direct Taxation in Turkmenistan (as a Percentage of Total Revenue).
Source: IMF 1999.

for purchases on capital goods, increasing their price by an additional 20 percent (Rosenberg and DeZeeuw 2001, 175, World Bank 2003b). During the period 2001–2005, for example, the VAT's contribution to total revenue was much greater than in any other transitional or high-income country – it averaged 51 percent as compared to 33 percent and 28 percent, respectively (Cornia 2003, 10).

As demonstrated in Figures 4.1 and 4.2, in both countries indirect taxes such as the VAT have also increased relative to direct taxes. Direct taxes – in particular, the EPT – actually made a substantial contribution to Turkmenistan's and Uzbekistan's respective state budgets in the 1990s (Barbone and Sánchez 2003); the EPT was second only to the VAT in the former (IMF 1999, 106) and larger than the VAT until 1997 in the latter (Cornia 2003, 6). In fact, with the exception of Ukraine, the contribution of EPT to Uzbekistan's state budget in the 1990s was by far the largest in the FSU (Stepanyan 2003, 18). The significance of this tax, however, is not a sign of how healthy the tax system was during this period, but rather a testament to the lack of tax reform that occurred in these two countries, as the EPT always makes up the bulk of government revenue in centrally planned economies (see Rosenberg et al. 1999, 4). Both countries opted to retain core features of the Soviet tax system, which was largely based upon turnover, payroll, and profit taxes imposed on state enterprises and deducted automatically from state-controlled bank accounts (Cornia 2003, IMF 1999, 66–7). While Turkmenistan appeared to receive less revenue from the EPT than

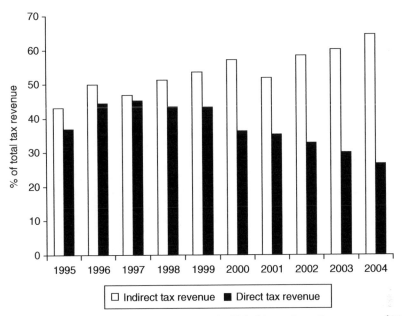

FIGURE 4.2. Indirect versus Direct Taxation in Uzbekistan (as a Percentage of Total Revenue).
Source: Authors' calculations based on World Bank (2005c), 5 and IMF (2007c), 21.

Uzbekistan, its increasing reliance on implicit taxation of state enterprises via canceling out government debt against unpaid taxes (offsets) actually increased its fiscal dependence on SOEs. By the mid-1990s, for example, offsets accounted for about 40–50 percent of revenue or 10–18 percent of GDP, "with an increasing trend after 1996" (Ebrill and Havrylyshyn 1999, 6).

Since 2000, however, direct taxes have represented a declining share of total revenue. This is also a function of the continued lack of tax reform – specifically, the absence of administrative reform aimed at raising collection rates and increasing compliance. Neither Turkmenistan nor Uzbekistan has established a large taxpayer unit or assigned taxpayer identification numbers, as was common elsewhere in the FSU (Ebrill and Havrylyshyn 1999, 11). Turkmenistan and Uzbekistan were also the last to institute legal provisions for the protection of taxpayers' rights (ibid., 26). Both governments, thus, opted to rely so heavily on the EPT precisely because it facilitated collection without requiring either a competent tax administration or acquiescent taxpayers. At the same time, they have also allowed this tax rate to fluctuate widely, inviting high levels of both bureaucratic discretion and enterprise evasion. The EPT rate in Uzbekistan, for example, changed six times between 1991 and 1999 (see Anoshkina 1997, IMF 2000b), leading some analysts to describe its evolution as a "deliberately complex and non-transparent system of business taxation" (Rosenberg et al. 1999, 7). This corresponds to the general picture of both countries' tax systems. Based on "the number of taxes and the average rates that are imposed on businesses," Turkmenistan and Uzbekistan (along with Belarus) had the most complex national tax systems in the CIS (Mitra and Stern 2003, 29).

Similarly low levels of reform account for the already low and declining contribution of direct taxes to total tax revenue since the late 1990s (IMF 1999, 106, World Bank 2005c, 5). Both countries also rank lowest among the FSU countries (along with Tajikistan and Belarus) when it comes to reforming the personal income tax (PIT) (see Stepanyan 2003, 17). Uzbekistan's 1997 Tax Code, for example, reduced the number of income brackets from seven to five and did little to unify the rates across sectors and enterprises (Stepanyan 2003). As a result, it fostered overzealous and corrupt tax authorities that used taxpayers' confusion to extract bribes and force them to pay unrecorded fines (see Jones Luong 2003b). Uzbekistan has also become notorious for increasing the rate for PIT at a time when the growing trend in the FSU and East Central Europe, following Russia, has been to reduce this rate and introduce a flat rate to simultaneously simplify this tax and raise collection rates (Zermeno 2008, 15). Not surprisingly, the relatively high tax rate for PIT has led not only to widespread evasion in the formal sector but also to the growth of the informal sector, which Uzbekistan has not built the capacity to tax effectively, and thus to the shrinking of its own tax base over time (see Anoshkina 1997, Cornia 2003, 8). The small and medium enterprise (SME) sector has been most affected by this particular lack of reform, which is consistent with the government's blatant disinterest in promoting the growth of the private sector (see Jones Luong 2003b).

While indirect and implicit forms of taxation have clearly come to dominate tax revenue in both countries, the shift over time is perhaps most noticeable in Uzbekistan. Part of the reason is that this change in the composition of Uzbekistan's tax structure was propelled by the government's conscious decision to decrease the tax burden on public enterprises in 1997, which led to falling tax receipts from the EPT (Anoshkina 1997). The expected decline in the proceeds from this tax were then "compensated by an increase in personal income tax and – especially by a rise in indirect taxes such as VAT and excises that ... account[ed] for 60 percent of the overall revenue" as of 2002 – compared to "an average of 33 percent in the economies in transition and 28 percent in the high income countries" (Cornia 2003, 10). By 2003, "indirect tax revenues ... accounted for 13 percent of GDP, the second highest level in the CIS" (World Bank 2005c, 6). Since the late 1990s, the government has also exhibited a clear desire to shift taxation from explicit to implicit across sectors. Although this trend has been widely noted in the cotton sector (see Guadagni et al. 2005, Rosenberg et al. 1999), it is not at all limited to cotton. As illustrated in Table 4.3, the importance of implicit taxation on foreign trade operations increased across sectors in the late 1990s, including energy (Rosenberg and Zeeuw 2000, 169). When implicit taxation is taken into account, "Uzbekistan has a fairly high overall tax ratio by international standards" (Cornia 2003, 7).

TABLE 4.3. *Implicit Taxes on Foreign Trade in Uzbekistan,*
1997–1999 (in percent of GDP)

	1997	1998	1999
Foreign exchange inflow	6.0	10.7	16.2
Centralized exports	5.2	8.1	11.8
Cotton	3.4	5.4	6.7
Gold	1.8	2.7	5.2
Other exports	0.9	2.6	5.4
Foreign exchange outflow	8.5	10.4	15.1
Centralized imports	7.0	6.3	7.1
Other imports	1.5	4.1	8.0

Sources: Auty 2003, 260, Rosenberg and Zeeuw 2000.

Expenditures

Government expenditures in Turkmenistan and Uzbekistan likewise share several core features. First and foremost, neither country endeavored to establish institutions that would place bona fide limits on government spending or borrowing, such as an effective natural resource fund (NRF). Aside from Moldova, for example, they are the only Soviet successor states to have retained central bank financing, which allows the government to spend without regard for either internal debt accumulation or external sources of funding (Andrews and Shatalov 2004, 14–15). In Uzbekistan, the ability to borrow from abroad with few restrictions and little oversight is extended to SOEs, for which "government guarantees have been issued liberally" (EIU 2002, 30). Turkmenistan and Uzbekistan have also undergone the least amount of reform to their treasury system, which would "[result] in better controls during budget execution and [enable the t]reasury to check whether budgetary expenditures are in accordance with the approved budget and within the spending limits and funds allocations, prior to approving an expenditure transaction" (Andrews and Shatalov 2004, 31–2).

This has enabled them not only to maintain the command economy they inherited from Soviet rule but also to orchestrate an expansion of the public sector. Thus they have countered the trend in other transition economies, where according to "[c]onventional measures of government size – aggregate government spending ... in relation to GDP and the share of public employment – ... there has been a widespread downsizing" (Gupta et al. 2003, 559). The size of the public sector in Turkmenistan, for example, was estimated at 75 percent of GDP in 2004 (Nichol 2004), while in most other Soviet successor states (including Russia) it was less than half this amount (see ADB 2005b, EBRD 2004). The level of overall public expenditure in Uzbekistan in the early 2000s was also "higher than in other economies in transition at the same level of development and only 3–5 GDP points below that of the economies in transition of Central Europe" (Cornia 2003, 17). Moreover, even after substantial reductions in the late 1990s, at close to 39 percent of GDP in 2003, public expenditure was still quite high for a country at Uzbekistan's income level. For example, it was "higher than in most countries at its per capita income level and many fast-growing countries of East Asia and Latin America" (World Bank 2005c, 7).

Turkmenistan and Uzbekistan also share the dubious honor of being the only Soviet successor states that still employ communist-style central planning. In the 1990s, for example, Niyazov promulgated two ten-year plans for achieving broad social and economic development. The first was unveiled in a well-known public address entitled "Ten Years of Prosperity" in 1993 and called for a gradual transition in which the initial phase would maintain Soviet central planning and social protection programs. The second was announced in 1999. Entitled "Strategy for the Social and Economic Transformation of Turkmenistan for 2000–2010," it comprised a much more ambitious development program, encompassing all sectors of the economy as well as the social sphere and setting targets for them to meet within a specified time frame.[41] An even more brazen program intended to raise Turkmenistan to the same levels of social and economic development as found in Western countries by 2020 (the "Strategy for Turkmenistan's Development to 2020") was subsequently issued in August 2003.

The continued reliance on central planning in both countries has gone hand-in-hand with an emphasis on centralized investment. From the mid- through the late 1990s, for example, Turkmenistan consciously "maintain[ed] a high investment to GDP ratio," averaging just over 45 percent of GDP for the years 1995–1999 (Pomfret 2001, 170). Similarly, in the late 1990s and early 2000s, approximately "one-fifth of [Uzbekistan's] state budget [was] absorbed by centralized investments" (Cornia 2003, 18). Although the average investment to GDP ratio was much lower in Uzbekistan during this period – approximately 12 percent of GDP from 1996–2003 – "[p]ublic investment … accounted for almost half of total investment in the economy" and "was still higher than in any other transitional economy, except for Belarus and Turkmenistan" (World Bank 2005c, 10).

A significant portion of public investment, moreover, has been devoted to supporting ISI. While this is the case in both countries,[42] it is particularly true for Uzbekistan, where the government has deliberately redirected resources from the country's traditional export sector (that is, cotton) toward

[41] For example, the plan called for increasing gas production to 120 billion cubic meters, mostly for export, doubling the figures for electricity generation, creating new sectors of the economy devoted to ferrous and nonferrous metallurgy, and increasing the amount of grain and cotton production.

[42] The bulk of public investment in Turkmenistan has been devoted to unproductive and infrastructure projects. What has been allocated toward industrial projects is concentrated in "upgrad[ing] … the Turkmenbashi oil refinery and development of petrochemicals there, and the creation of a cotton textile industry" (Pomfret 2001, 170–171).

the development of industries that reduce the need for imports, including automobile production, chemical and petrochemical plants, and oil refining, since the mid-1990s (Rosenberg et al. 1999, 3, World Bank 2005c, 11). Enterprises in these industries are given priority when it comes to both the import of capital goods and state guaranteed loans. They have also benefited from "[g]overnment budget financed jobs," which "account[ed] for most of the increase in formal sector employment in the second half of the 1990s" World Bank (2003b, 3). As in the classic model of ISI, in order to achieve these goals, "the Uzbek authorities [have] rel[ied] on many methods inherited from the central planning era, such as production targets, the centralized allocation of foreign exchange, and the control of selected producer and consumer prices" (Rosenberg et al. 1999, 3). In order to prop up these fledging industries, they have also relied heavily on protectionism (EIU 2002, 19).

Not surprisingly then, the public sector in both countries dwarfs the private sector. Part of the reason for this, of course, is the lack of private sector growth itself, which has been stunted by the aforementioned tax policies (see EBRD 2006b). At the end of the 1990s, Turkmenistan and Uzbekistan had the lowest levels of private sector contribution to GDP in the FSU except for Belarus and Tajikistan (World Bank 2002, 40). The participation of the private sector in production in the early 2000s continued to be low relative to their petroleum-rich counterparts: From 2001 to 2003, for example, it was just 45 and 25 percent, respectively, in Uzbekistan and Turkmenistan, compared to 60 percent in both Azerbaijan and Kazakhstan and 70 percent in Russia (EBRD 2002, Kalyuzhnova and Kaser 2006, 169). Yet the relative paltriness of the private sector in Turkmenistan and Uzbekistan is primarily due to the sheer size of the state, which not only owns the bulk of the economy, but also is the largest employer. Indeed, both countries have continued the Soviet practice of guaranteeing employment and "protecting" public sector wages (see ADB 2005a). Thus, while government employment and wages declined sharply in the 1990s throughout the FSU, they actually increased dramatically in Uzbekistan, where the percentage of the population employed by the government nearly tripled from 1995–1999 (Gupta et al. 2003, 562–3, 566). And salaries for public sector workers continued to rise faster than private sector wages in the early 2000s. In Uzbekistan, for example, "wages [for public sector workers] were raised on average by 45 percent in nominal terms" (World Bank 2005c, 9). This brought the government's wage bill to 6.6 percent of GDP in 2003 – higher than any other low-income CIS country (ibid.). Based on its ten-year development plan issued in 2003, which pledged to increase wages by 50 percent by 2005 and then to double them every five years up to 2020, Turkmenistan should experience an even steeper rise. Niyazov's creation of an indigenous textile industry as part of his own efforts at ISI is not only "grossly inefficient," but also serves to provide thousands of state jobs for the population (Pomfret 2008a, 5–6).

In order to maintain as well as to expand the state's dominant role in the economy, both countries have relied heavily on QFAs – the most significant of which include large fuel subsidies to households and enterprises, preferential credits and subsidized inputs for selected industries and producers of "strategic goods," and extrabudgetary funds (EBTs). While all of the Soviet successor states have utilized QFAs to some degree, especially in the early 1990s as they struggled to preserve some aspects of the Soviet social safety net in the face of a severe budgetary crisis (see Petri et al. 2002), Turkmenistan and Uzbekistan both lie conspicuously at the far end of the scale. The annual level of QFAs in Uzbekistan in the late 1990s and early 2000s, for example, was estimated at 20–25 percent of GDP in comparison to 5–10 percent in Moldova (Andrews and Shatalov 2004, 9). Another indication of the extent of QFAs in Uzbekistan's economy is that "if all *officially* reported extrabudgetary funds together with 'budgetary debt' and grant-financed expenditures are added to the State Budget, *consolidated budget* expenditures [as a percentage of GDP] would be over 10 points higher" (World Bank 2005c, 1).

As in all mineral states that adopt S_1, fuel subsidies have served as one of the primary means through which the government in both countries has simultaneously distributed the benefits of mineral wealth to the population and bolstered struggling state enterprises. In Turkmenistan, for example, every citizen has been entitled to a "substantial free gas quota" since independence (EIU 2003b, 21). The government has actively sought to expand this subsidy, doubling the number of citizens who are connected to gas in less than 10 years – from 40 percent in 1990 to over 90 percent in 1999 (ibid). Heavy fuel subsidies, moreover, are not limited to natural gas. In fact, "Turkmenistan has the most heavily subsidized gasoline and diesel in the world" (Morgan 2007). Household consumers are also heavily subsidized in Uzbekistan, where oil and natural gas, as well as coal, "are sold at a fraction of world market prices" (Sharma et al. 2003, i; see also EIU 2002, 18). In the mid-1990s, for example, households were charged only 0.12–0.15 US cents per cubic meter compared to 4.2 US cents in Kazakhstan, and enterprises were charged a mere 1.84 US cents per cubic meter compared to 8.37 US cents in Kazakhstan (Skagen 1997, 51–2). Likewise, the Uzbekistani government has sought to ensure that the entire population benefits from access to cheap energy; as of 2003, 95 percent of the households had access to piped gas (World Bank 2003b, 3).

These explicit subsidies, albeit substantial, are only one of the many QFAs that dominate the energy sector. Among the most significant is the toleration of payment arrears – for both households and enterprises in Turkmenistan (Petri and Taube 2003) and primarily for enterprises in Uzbekistan (Sharma et al. 2003, 7). These arrears serve as an additional *implicit* subsidy to consumers and a direct loss to the economy by depriving both the NOC and the government of revenue. Because repressed prices and chronic nonpayment amount to a rather hefty implicit tax on the NOC, they can severely reduce its income. This, in turn, undermines not only the NOC's ability to build up its own capital stock to make necessary investments, but also to pay its own *explicit* tax bill (see Petri et al. 2002). Indeed in both countries, SOEs in the energy sector are undercapitalized and have substantial tax arrears (see Sharma et al.

2003). Repressed fuel prices generate additional losses to the economy because they encourage overusage among consumers as well as theft. Energy intensity (that is, consumption per unit of GDP) in Turkmenistan, for example, was estimated to be 13 times the U.S. level at the end of 1990s (EIU 2003b) while in Uzbekistan it was "over three times as high as in countries like the USA or Malaysia, and far above the levels of Kazakhstan or Russia" (World Bank 2003b, 17; see also Sharma et al. 2003, 7). Gas distribution losses are also much higher than for comparator countries. In Uzbekistan, for example, they were "estimated at over 20 percent, at least 15–18 percent over the industry standard" (World Bank 2003b, 17). Heavy energy consumption, moreover, is compounded by high rates of smuggling – particularly of petroleum products that can either be sold on the black market or across the border at much higher rates (EIU 2002, 18).

Consequently, subsidies in the energy sector constitute a substantial portion of government expenditures in both countries. In 2000, "total domestic subsidies for the oil and gas sector alone were estimated at around US$600 million (21 percent of GDP) in Turkmenistan" (EIU 2003b, 21). Similarly, Uzbekistan's total quasi-fiscal deficit (QFD) and QFAs in the energy sector for 2002 alone were estimated at US$2.2 billion, or 19 percent of GDP (Sharma et al. 2003, 8). This is staggering when compared to other former Soviet republics, where estimates of energy sector QFD and QFAs average around 5 percent (Petri et al. 2002, 6). Yet the actual figure is probably even higher if the full nature of the energy sector's contribution to government spending is taken into account. Turkmenistan's fuel and energy complex, for example, "[has] help[ed] to alleviate the grave problem of unemployment and part-time employment" by "provid[ing] jobs for a sizeable segment of [the] population" (Kamenev 2001, 161).

At the same time, both Turkmenistan and Uzbekistan have combined universal fuel subsidies with those reserved for enterprises engaged in the production of particular industrial and agricultural goods. This is facilitated by the fact that the financial sector in both countries has been devoted to allocating government-directed credits since independence. Among the chief recipients of this implicit subsidy in Turkmenistan have been the textile industry (Pomfret 2001, 168) and producers of cotton and wheat, both of which are considered "strategic goods" (Kamenev 2002, 172). As part of its drive for rapid industrialization via ISI discussed above, preferential credits in Uzbekistan have primarily been directed to "traditional heavy industry" (EIU 2002, 30; see also World Bank 2003b, 10–11). Producers of agricultural goods – particularly cotton and wheat – have also been heavily subsidized since independence, although there is a general consensus that any gains farmers might receive from these subsidies are offset by the aforementioned high implicit taxes they pay in the form of price controls and production quotas (see Jones Luong 2003b, Rosenberg et al. 1999). In Turkmenistan, for example, "producers of cotton and wheat [have remained] exempt from [property and personal income] taxes, and 50 percent of their expenses on seeds, chemicals, mineral fertilizers and all kinds of technical services are [still] met by the government" (Kamenev 2002, 172). Cotton and wheat producers in Uzbekistan were also given access to free or cheap inputs, such as land and water, which were notably scarce (see Weinthal 2002). These subsidies constitute a significant portion of government expenditure. In 2001 alone, for example, they made up over half of Uzbekistan's GDP (World Bank 2003b, 6).

Finally, Turkmenistan and Uzbekistan have relied heavily on EBTs. In Turkmenistan, the most important ones include the Foreign Exchange Reserve Fund (FERF) and the State Fund for the Development of the Oil and Gas Industry and Mineral Resources (SFDOG), both of which were established in 1996, and the Agricultural Development Fund (ADF). Each has its own source of funding and (unofficially) designated purpose. Perhaps the most notorious of these is the FERF because the revenue it accumulates from compulsory foreign currency surrender requirements has allegedly been utilized to finance the President's pet construction projects (see EIU 2003b, 28). However, the SFDOG is the largest known EBT because it is considered the "official" repository of export revenues from the sale of oil and gas abroad.[43] Its nominal purpose is to finance investment in the energy sector; in the first nine months of 2000 alone, for example, the government set aside $78.8 million for petroleum sector development (Glych 2001, 46). Yet to date, it has largely served as a source of debt service payments for other sectors of the economy (see IMF 1999, 28). Thus, while SFDOG may be the closest thing Turkmenistan has to a NRF, it has been used neither to foster savings nor promote stabilization. Rather, like Kuwait's Reserve Fund, it serves largely as a personal slush fund for the President, especially since only the president can dispense the revenue, which is held offshore (Kaiser 2002). The ADF receives the bulk of the proceeds from the huge differential between the state-mandated domestic price of cotton and the world market price among the three official recipients – while the rest is siphoned off into "a myriad of off-budget funds controlled directly by the President" (Pomfret 2004, 12).[44] While there are no hard numbers indicating exactly how much money flows through these funds or their size relative to the state budget, the unreliability of the country's budgetary data, particularly since the late 1990s, has led many international experts to conclude that most government spending is done via EBTs, and yet, that only a fraction of the country's export earnings is actually spent inside the country (see EIU 2003b, 26, Global Witness 2006).

As part of its budgetary "reform" process in the early 1990s, Uzbekistan also created several independent EBTs, including the Mineral Resources Development Fund, the Road Fund, and the Pension Fund, which were

---

[43] In May 2007, suspicions were confirmed that gas revenues have long been deposited into the Turkmenistan Central Bank's account at Deutsche Bank before they are reallocated into this and other EBTs (Williamson 2007).

[44] The other two (minor) recipients are the cotton marketing agency and the state budget (Pomfret 2004, 12).

intended to "collect revenue directly from the relevant entities and activities and earmark these resources to specific uses" (Cornia 2003, 3; see also IMF 2000b). Although Uzbekistan's utilization of EBTs clearly has not been as extensive as Turkmenistan's, in addition to the "significant earmarked revenue" that these funds have continued to received (see Andrews and Shatalov 2004, 13), the latter two funds in particular have incurred continual deficits that had to be "covered by transfers from the State Budget" (Cornia 2003, 3). Several local economic analysts suspect that an increase in transfers to extrabudgetary accounts helps explain the decline in (official) budgetary expenditures after 1999 (Authors' interviews with CER analysts and World Bank representatives).

Despite all of these important similarities, including their pursuit of ISI and widespread use of QFAs, Turkmenistan and Uzbekistan exhibit some key differences in their respective spending patterns and apparent priorities. First of all, while the governments in both countries have emphasized spending on social protection, the provision of free goods and services has been much more extensive in Turkmenistan. If Niyazov's first major act as president was to signal his intention to redirect the sales of the country's gas from the CIS to Europe, then his second was to announce that the population of Turkmenistan would be supplied with gas, electricity, water, and salt free of charge as a part of the new government's policy for maintaining "social protection ... in the transition period" – a pledge that the national legislature (*Khalk Maslakhaty*) then "further extended to the year 2020" in August 2003 as part of its ten-year development plan (Dadabaev 2006, 124). Other substantial consumer subsidies consist of reduced fares for public transportation and low prices for a variety of staple foods, including bread and milk, as well as some fruits and vegetables (see, for example, Kamenev 2002, 177). In addition, the Turkmenistani government has not only continued the Soviet practice of providing guaranteed pensions at 57 for women and 62 for men, regardless of need, but also actively raised wages for persons of working age outside the "dominant state sector" (that is, oil, gas, and cotton) in order to impose uniformity "across all enterprises, despite wide variations in skill shortages" (Auty 1997b, 7). The ten-year development plan to 2020, moreover, pledges to raise pensions as well as grants to the population in order to increase general living standards by 8–8.5 times their level as of August 2003.

The greater emphasis on providing social protection for its citizens via free access to goods and services in Turkmenistan, however, has not been converted into a higher standard of living. Rather, the provision of these universal benefits has largely functioned as a "populist gesture." Despite guaranteed employment, for example, unemployment is quite high; by some estimates, it was as high as 70 percent in some regions of the country in the early 2000s (Kamenev 2002, 176). Similarly, despite Niyazov's steadfast public commitment to protect wages as way of "increasing the development of the social sphere," there has also been a decline in *real* wages due to high rates of inflation (ibid.). Perhaps most telling, however, is that Turkmenistan had among the highest levels of spending on health and education in the 1990s, and yet by the 2000s, citizens of Turkmenistan had the lowest life expectancy in the FSU (UNDP 2006).[45] Thus, while official figures put health and education expenditures at more than 10 percent of GDP, life expectancy for men and women in 2003 was only 58 and 65 years respectively (IMF 1999, 106; Pomfret 2006, 98). Since then, the government has reduced "some state services ... , most significantly in education. Compulsory schooling is now nine years, down from eleven, and free university education has been abolished" (Sabonis-Helf 2004, 166).

While Uzbekistan has also devoted a significant amount of its public expenditures to social protection, in contrast to Turkmenistan, it has relied less on *universal* subsidies. As in other parts of the FSU, in the first five years of the transition, Uzbekistan experienced "a sharp decline in outlays on social protection" (Cornia 2003, 14). Yet it continued to spend more than both "other economies in transition and ... developing countries at the same level of development" (ibid., 15). Government expenditures allocated to pensions, for example, have continued to be "much higher than in the other CIS countries" (ibid, 16). It has followed a similar trajectory to the other Soviet successor states (except for Turkmenistan and Belarus), however, in that this decline occurred mostly via a gradual reduction in consumer subsidies and public transfers. By 1995, for example, all food subsidies had been eliminated and by 2002, "only heating, public transport and housing charges remained partially subsidized" (ibid., 14).

More importantly, Uzbekistan stands out among many of its former Soviet counterparts – but especially Turkmenistan – in its efforts to provide social protection through *targeted* goods and services and its emphasis on human capital formation. In late 1994, Uzbekistan introduced what has been deemed "an innovative and reasonably successful targeting of delivery of social assistance" through residential community associations, or *mahallahs* (Pomfret 2003, 453). Among the many cited merits of this community-based social assistance delivery program (see Coudouel et al. 1999) is that it has enabled the government to reduce budgetary outlays for social protection since the mid-1990s. The Uzbekistani government has also displayed a noteworthy shift in spending toward human capital formation – particularly education – since the mid-1990s (see Cornia 2003, 16–18). Thus in the early 2000s, Uzbekistan "allocate[d] about 9 percent of GDP on education – a higher share than any other country in the region or indeed, any OECD country" (World Bank 2005c, iii) – and "close to a quarter of [its own] consolidated budget spending" (ibid., 8). Public expenditures on health, however, declined by 3.4 percent between 1991 and 2005 – more than in any other transition economy, including its petroleum-rich counterparts (Ahmedov et al. 2007, Chapter three).

---

[45] Turkmenistan also devotes a greater proportion of its *budgeted* spending on social programs and subsidies – 70 percent, according to the Economist Intelligence Unit's most recent estimates (EIU 2006c).

Although a far cry from Turkmenistan's populist-style spending that fails to deliver on exaggerated promises, Uzbekistan's approach toward social spending has nonetheless failed to meet its main goals. While it was primarily intended to alleviate poverty, particularly for families with children, targeted spending has disproportionately benefited high-income households (see, for example, Coudouel et al. 1999). In part, this is a function of design. As Marianne Kamp (2003) has expertly documented, the use of traditional structures (specifically, the mahallahs) often discriminates against those households that violate convention, including single mothers and divorcees. The program has also suffered from the absence of a regional targeting of subsidies, such that "even if the transfers administered by the *mahallahs* [were] well targeted by income group within each region, they tend[ed] to be proportional or worse by region" (Cornia 2003, 20). Yet the failure to relieve poverty is also directly related to larger problems generated by other features of Uzbekistan's fiscal regime, including its increased reliance on implicit taxation and continued preference for central planning, which inherently limits the government's ability to collect reliable economic information. As discussed in Chapter 2, without access to accurate information on employment and income, the state cannot develop the capacity to accurately target its citizens for social welfare provision. At the same time, "as a result of reduced funding [in the early 2000s], the number of beneficiaries of targeted social assistance [in Uzbekistan] is declining and the real benefits low and declining" (World Bank 2003b, 4).

Similarly, expenditure reforms allegedly aimed at building human capital have not necessarily translated into better social outcomes. Rather, they seem to have had a perverse effect on the availability of basic health care and primary education – that is, on the types of services that are most widely needed and utilized by the poor (for details, see World Bank 2005c). Reductions in public expenditures on healthcare, moreover, have placed an additional burden on the poorest segments of the population because they have increased the need for informal payments to access services (Ahmedov et al. 2007, Chapter 3).

Again, the failure of such efforts is partly a function of design. Education spending, for example, has deliberately prioritized "new programs of upper secondary education while acute funding shortages persisted in general education (grades 1–11)" (ibid, iii).[46] Like targeted social assistance, spending directed at human capital formation has also been handicapped by the lack of regional targeting. As a result, it does not necessarily reach either the segments of the population or areas of the country that need it most. Per capita spending on healthcare, for example, "is lower in regions with a higher incidence of poverty" (World Bank 2005c, ii). The rationale for these spending priorities, however, is linked to the country's broader development strategy – most notably ISI – as well as its need to provide particularistic benefits to the elite.

---

[46] A presidential decree issued in May 2004 pledged greater investment in primary education to rectify this imbalance (World Bank 2005c, iii), but the evidence to date suggests this has not been done (see Unicef 2008).

Simply put, the government placed a higher priority on secondary education because "the success of its industrialization program depend[ed] on generating a new cadre of well-trained professionals" who were loyal to the government (Authors' interview with Saifulin). At the same time, it was understood that most of the students "attracted to such institutions [would be] children of the elite" (ibid.). Viewed in this light, the emphasis on building new academic institutions rather than improving existing ones and providing stipends to all students regardless of household income can be understood as a direct subsidy to supporters of the incumbent regime. More generally, the "strong share of wages" in expenditures on education and healthcare from the late 1990s to the early 2000s suggests that the government maintained high levels of spending on these sectors due largely to the political difficulty in cutting wages (Cornia 2003, 16).[47] In the early 2000s, for example, wages in both education and healthcare remained high in comparison to other sectors, while budget cuts in these sectors entailed "non-salary recurrent expenditures, often vital materials and supplies, and maintenance expenditures" (World Bank 2005c, i).

Second, while the government in both countries has devoted a significant portion of its budgetary outlays to public investment, Turkmenistan has allocated much more to unproductive or national prestige projects than to infrastructure and industrial projects. Ashgabat (the country's capital) has been perhaps the greatest beneficiary of prestige projects with its new presidential palace, international airport, and numerous ornate monuments commemorating Turkmen history and the Turkmenbashi's family – including the grandiose "Monument to Independence" which features Niyazov, as the greatest figure in Turkmen history, surrounded by other famous historical figures. The most extravagant project is the "Arch of Neutrality" upon which a gold statue of Niyazov rotates in the direction of the sun. Outside of the capital city, perhaps the most ostentatious public display of Turkmenistan's petroleum wealth is the construction of a 1,300-square-mile artificial lake in the middle of the Karakum Desert "despite its huge cost and almost universal condemnation by external observers as unable to achieve the stated impact on agricultural output and as being an environmental disaster" (Pomfret 2001, 171). While the exact source is unknown, these projects are clearly financed via the use of aforementioned EBTs (Pomfret 2008a, 3), of which the FERF is the most likely candidate (EIU 2003b, 28).

In contrast, Uzbekistan's public investment program has clearly prioritized infrastructure and industrial projects. Over a quarter of "officially reported investment in 1995–99," for example, went to manufacturing and, aside from a few modest statues and a museum to Timurlane, as well as "upgrading the country's airports ... , the government has sponsored "few of the high-profile, prestige projects that are seen elsewhere in Central Asia" (EIU 2002, 31). While expenditure on public investment continued to increase over the course

---

[47] Sixty percent of healthcare expenditures, for example, went to "staff salaries and benefits" (World Bank 2005c, 10).

of the 1990s in Turkmenistan, in Uzbekistan it "remained stable at 6 percent of GDP between 1991 and 2002" and actually "fell to 3.8 percent in 2002," bringing it closer to "other countries at similar levels of development" (Cornia 2003, 17).

Causal Mechanisms

Above we demonstrate that, as predicted under S_1, both Turkmenistan and Uzbekistan adopted weak fiscal regimes. In order to further substantiate our claims, we now turn to the three causal mechanisms described in Chapter 3 whereby S_1 fosters weak fiscal regimes: low transaction costs (TCs), high societal expectations, and implicit bargaining. Specifically, we provide empirical evidence below to suggest first, that S_1 generated incentives for weak fiscal regimes via low TCs and high societal expectations; and second, that these fiscal regimes emerged via implicit bargaining due to elites' mutual desire to hide information from the public.

Transaction Costs
Low TCs under S_1 manifest themselves first and foremost in the daily interactions among cabinet ministers and NOC managers, which are deliberately structured to blur the boundaries between these two sets of actors. Thus, while we cannot provide direct evidence that cabinet ministers (or their functional equivalent) and NOC managers faced low TCs in Turkmenistan and Uzbekistan, what we can show is that the structure of their interactions fostered blurred boundaries between them.

First, Turkmenistan and Uzbekistan's respective NOCs have both conformed to the common model of NOCs in petroleum-rich states that adopt S_1 in which the board of directors is not only staffed but also chaired by government appointees, and government officials are periodically rotated with the NOC's top management. Although the corporate structure of their respective NOCs differ, in both countries the president has had sole authority to appoint the various bodies that are responsible for carrying out the NOC's principal operations (that is, production, sales, and distribution) and overseeing its finances. From the mid-1990s thru the early 2000s, for example, Uzbekneftegaz was governed by a board of directors and a "supervisory committee" to which the board reported. The board was comprised of nine of the NOC's senior managers – all of whom were presidential appointees – while the committee was chaired by the prime minister and included members of the cabinet and other government representatives (Authors' interviews with representatives no. 1 and no. 2). In addition, the company's head has always had the rank of minister and held a cabinet position, which further facilitates his ability to communicate directly with all the relevant parties (ibid.; see also Broadman 2000).

Both countries have also followed the well-established practice of rotating government officials and NOC managers periodically. In Turkmenistan, for example, it became customary by the late 1990s for a deputy within the Ministry of Oil, Gas and Natural Resources to replace the head of Turkmengaz or Turkmenneft and for the deputy head of one of these state companies to replace the Minister, who would then be appointed governor in one of the country's hydrocarbon-rich regions. Before he was selected to head the Ministry at the beginning of 2004, for example, Amangeldy Pudakov served as first deputy chairman of Turkmenneft, while the Minister he replaced (Tachberdy Tagiev) became governor of the petroleum-rich Balkan Oblast in western Turkmenistan (*RFE/RL* January 26, 2004). The terms of petroleum sector ministers and NOC managers were also extremely short during the period under study here – the former, for example, averaged about one year from 1994 to 2005 (see Table 4.4 for details). While some have been overtly demoted – most notably, Soiunov – the majority have actually been promoted for successfully fulfilling their "mandate ... to work together with [the relevant state company] to ensure that government policy is carried out" in the oil and gas sector (Authors' interview with former government official no. 2).[48]

Further evidence that boundaries between cabinet ministers and NOC managers have been blurred over time include the fact that, on the ground, these two sets of actors were effectively interchangeable. This is particularly evident in Turkmenistan. In the mid-1990s, for example, the Ministry of Oil, Gas, and Natural Resources convinced Niyazov to temporarily disband Turkmengaz because it "merely duplicated their efforts" (Authors' interview with former government official no. 2).[49] Since then, the two have operated in concert under the direction of the Competent Authority and the Cabinet of Ministers, both of which were directly subordinate to the President according to the 1997 Petroleum Law.[50] As one former government official explained, "the Minister [of Oil, Gas, and Natural Resources] and the Chairman of Turkmengaz are the same ... , they have the same interests, and they are on the same level ... both are under the authority of the Turkmenbashi and must ultimately answer to him" (ibid). In Turkmenistan as well as Uzbekistan, international consultants ostensibly hired to help restructure the oil and gas industry remarked that they could discern only a marginal difference between the various entities governing the sector (Authors' interview with foreign

---

[48] Only in 2005 did Niyazov shake up the oil and gas sector with the highly public dismissal of Deputy Prime Minster Yolly Gurbanmuradov on charges of "serious shortcomings" and "misappropriation of over $60 million in state funds" (*RFE/RL* May 23, 2005). He was replaced by the head of Turkmengaz, Guichnazar Tachnazarov. That same year Niyazov also removed Saparmamed Valiev as the head of Turkmenneft (*RFE/RL* August 15, 2005). In his place, Niyazov appointed Karyagdy Tashliev, first deputy director of Turkmenneft.

[49] The Ministry may have been motivated by other factors, of course. See, for example, Kamenev 2001, 164.

[50] The petroleum sector underwent a reorganization and series of purges from mid-2005 to mid-2006, arguably bringing managerial control even more directly under the president (for details, see ICG 2007, Appendix F).

TABLE 4.4. *Oil and Gas Ministers of Turkmenistan, 1994–2005*

Dates held Office	Minister	Length of Term in Office
To July 1994	Nazar Suyunov	
July 1994 to July 1996	Khekim Ishanov	2 years
July 1996 to April 1997	Gochmurad Nazdzhanov	1 year
April 1997 to May 1998	Batyr Sardzhayev	1 year
May 1998 to May 1999	Rejepbay Arazov	1 year
May 1999 to January 2001	Elly Kurbanmuradov	1½ years
January 2001 to January 2003	Kurbannazar Nazarov	2 years
January 2003 to January 2004	Tachberdy Tagiyev	1 year
January 2004 to September 2005	Amangeldy Pudakov	1 ½ years
September 2005 to October 2005	Guichnazar Tachnazarov	1 month
October 2005 to December 2005	Atamurad Berdiev	2 months

Source: Compiled by authors based on *RFE/RL*, *Alexander's Oil and Gas*, *RPI*, and various issues of *Netral'niy Turkmenistan*.

consultant in the energy sector no. 1). One legal expert purportedly advising the Turkmenistani government summarized his experience thus:

> We would schedule a meeting with the so-called 'relevant parties' about drafting a new [petroleum] law, but it was never clear who those parties were because we never knew who was going to show up. Sometimes we would meet with the Competent Authority. Sometimes the Minister of Oil and Gas would show up or just send his deputy. Other times we would meet with the head of Turkmengaz. ... (Authors' interview with foreign consultant in the energy sector no. 2).

Societal Expectations

Demonstrating that societal expectations were indeed high in Turkmenistan is especially difficult given that both the availability of survey data and access to government officials is extremely limited – even more so than in Uzbekistan. The evidence that is available, however, is consistent with the claim that the majority of the population expects the state to distribute the benefits of mineral wealth widely and that elites have internalized these expectations – in word if not deed. Turkmenistan has only participated in one independent public opinion survey to date – the Asia Barometer Survey, conducted in 2005.[51] Its questions are not ideally suited to gauging societal expectations and the results are somewhat suspect considering the high rate of "don't know" responses, which are strongly correlated with the political sensitivity of the question.[52]

[51] Turkmenistan was the only former Soviet republic to refuse to participate in the EBRD's 2005 "Life in Transition" Survey (LiTS).

[52] The questionnaire, along with the entire database, is available at https://www.asiabarometer.org/

However, what the survey results do tell us is that, in comparison to countries at a similar level of development, Turkmenistan's population not only supports slightly higher levels of government spending on education and health but also places a higher priority on the government's role in fighting inflation through subsidies and price controls than, for example, "maintaining public order."[53] As one survey administrator and analyst concludes, what they suggest in aggregate is that "there are strong public expectations of the government in terms of providing for their well-being and economic needs," and that these expectations "far exceed the government's ability and willingness to deal with the challenges of post-Soviet development" (Dadabaev 2006, 131).

Due to the difficulty in conducting systematic and extensive interviews with state elites in Turkmenistan, we rely primarily on public speeches to assess whether they were not only aware of societal expectations for widespread distribution but also felt compelled to at least appear to be fulfilling them. As discussed in Chapter 1, in order to ensure consistency across cases, our main source here is President Niyazov's annual speech to the Khalk Maslakhaty (hereafter *Address*). However, since the text of this speech is not available for every year, we supplement our analysis of these speeches with his published addresses to the Turkmenistani people on various important occasions such as national holidays and party congresses. Consistent across his speeches, we find a deliberate emphasis on showing that the country's petroleum wealth is being used widely for the benefit of society.[54] In his 2001 *Address* for example, Niyazov remarked,

Oil producers will produce 10 million tons of oil and the gas producers will sell 47 billion cubic meters of gas and in the future will sell even more. This way, our income only from gas will amount to over 2 billion dollars. Where will this money go? You will see that great construction is underway in this country; the well-being of the people is increasing. We don't hold back resources in fulfilling the needs of the people. Basically, money will be used as we decide. And I haven't even mentioned the creation of Turkmenistan's lake, and the construction of automobile roads and rail lines.

Evidence from other public speeches, interviews and official documents – particularly those outlining the government's development strategy – provide additional support for the contention that fiscal policies in Turkmenistan were driven by state elites' desire to demonstrate that society was indeed benefiting from the country's mineral wealth. The first and second long-term development plans mentioned above – "Ten Years of Prosperity" and "Strategy of Socio-Economic Development in Turkmenistan for the period until 2010" – provide

---

[53] Nearly half of Turkmenistan's population, for example, ranked the importance of the "fighting rising prices" above "maintaining public order." In the majority of other countries, including those that have experienced little civil unrest in recent years, this prioritization was reversed – that is, half the population or more ranked "maintaining public order" above "fighting rising prices."

[54] This was the case in all but 3 of the 17 speeches we were able to analyze between 1992 and 2006.

another strong indication. Issued by decree amidst much fanfare in 1993 and 1999, respectively, both stressed the need for the state not only to continue to improve the social welfare of its population but also to increase oil and gas production in order to achieve this goal. Most notably, in articulating his vision of "Ten Years of Prosperity" in 1992, Niyazov emphasized the extent of universal benefits that would be granted via the proceeds from petroleum exports:

My dream is to see a cow and a calf in every yard in five to ten years ... I strongly believe that in five to ten years every family will have its own house and car and will live much better than it does now. Beginning on January 1 1993, the population will receive gas, electric power, and water free of charge. Not a single house without natural gas, water, electricity, and a telephone by the year 2000.

Similarly, the development plan issued in 1999 repeatedly mentions the need to raise both the earning potential and overall quality of life for Turkmenistan's citizens commensurate with the country's own growing prosperity. Perhaps the most prominent indication of the desire to demonstrate that society is sharing the rewards from the country's mineral wealth is President Niyazov's continual proclamation that the state must continue to provide free gas, water, and salt, as a "way to ... share the enormous revenues from gas and oil with the people," which most local analysts recognize as "largely a populist gesture" (Dadabaev 2006, 124). Referring to this plan, Niyazov explained,

Why is it that in Turkmenistan social protection of the citizens has been raised to the rank of a special state policy? ... in no other country of the world will you find a practice whereby the population is provided with electricity, gas, and drinking water free of charge. But this practice has been in place here for five years now ... . We will not depart from this policy ... [which] depends on boosting gas exports.[55]

The commitment to and expansion of such spending, moreover, became exacerbated during the boom in the 2000s. In his 2003 *Address*, Niyazov once again extended these universal benefits for more than a decade (this time until 2020), stating emphatically that

Turkmenistan has enough power resources so as to offer them free to the country's population. Back in 1993, we settled this question, giving electricity, gas, salt and water to population for free use. We shall take a decision now that these boons for people will be extended and will be free. ... Today's decision is a noble act. Each family and each people can feel the state's care. (Kurbanova 2003)

At this same meeting, he also underscored that the country's "underground resources belong to the entire population" and that such policies ensure that "[e]very person possesses a share of these riches."

Finally, the government's accomplishments vis-à-vis raising living standards are deliberately exaggerated to the public, while its failures are

---

[55] Quoted in *Nezavisimaya Gazeta*, October 27, 1999.

disguised – further indication that the government is less committed to improving social welfare than to giving the impression that it is doing so (see, for example, Pomfret 2001, 166). As one close observer of Turkmenistani politics in the early 2000s[56] notes:

One gets the impression that some of the aspirations of the Turkmen authorities ... concerning the development of the social sphere either remain a mere declaration on paper and in the mass media or some positive shifts are blown up to such an extent as to invite the conclusion that the government's more or less only concern is to improve the people's living standards. (Kamenev 2002, 177)

Several local and foreign analysts alike have noted this tendency regarding growth and income levels in particular (see EIU 2003b, 24–5). According to one such analyst, while Niyazov claimed to have increased income per capita to somewhere between two and three thousand US dollars in the year 2000, it was actually much closer to less than two hundred US dollars (Authors' interview with former government official no. 2).

We have better evidence to assess whether this mechanism is at work in Uzbekistan because both the availability of survey data and the ability to conduct systematic and extensive interviews with state elites are greater. In addition to the Asia Barometer Survey, for example, Uzbekistan participated in the EBRD's 2005 Life in Transition Survey (LiTS) and one of the author's own mass survey conducted in October/November 2003, which attempts to assess popular attitudes toward first, the state's "proper" role in the economy, and second, the legitimacy of taxation as a source of revenue generation (hereafter, Jones Luong-McMann survey).[57] As in Turkmenistan, we expect to find that the population widely believes that the state should not only constitute the bulk of revenue, but also be the greatest source of economic activity. Societal expectations regarding widespread distribution and the general public's aversion to taxation, however, should be tempered by the mineral sector's relative underdevelopment.

Both surveys provide strong evidence that the majority of Uzbekistan's population expects the state to play a dominant role in the economy. First of all, there seems to be broader popular support for state ownership of industry in Uzbekistan than any other Soviet successor state. When asked "what should be done with most privatized companies," for example, 51.6 percent responded that they should be "renationalized and kept in state hands," as compared to 36.7 percent in Russia, and only 22.6 percent answered that these companies should be "left in the hands of current owners provided they pay the privatized assets' worth," as compared to 31.5 percent in Russia.[58] This

---

[56] Sergei Kamenev served as first secretary of the Russian Embassy in Turkmenistan from 1999–2001.

[57] The survey was conducted jointly by Pauline Jones Luong and Kelly McMann in Kazakhstan, Kyrgyzstan, and Uzbekistan with the financial support of the National Council for Eurasia and Eastern Europe Research (NCEEER).

[58] See Appendix for a full table of results on this and other relevant questions. The full dataset and questionnaire are available at http://www.ebrd.com/country/sector/econo/surveys/lits.htm

TABLE 4.5. *Support for State Ownership in Uzbekistan*

The state should retain ownership of scarce resources in the agricultural sector, such as land, water, fertilizer, and machinery

	Frequency	Percent	Cumulative
1 strongly agree	370	24.67	24.67
2 agree	538	35.87	60.53
3 somewhat agree, somewhat disagree	256	17.20	77.73
4 disagree	106	7.07	84.80
5 strongly disagree	29	1.93	86.73
6 difficult to answer	188	12,53.00	99.27
7 rejection	11	0.73	100.00
Total	1500	100.00	

Source: Jones Luong-McMann survey, October–November 2003.

support, moreover, is almost uniform across age groups in Uzbekistan but not in Russia, just as we predict. (See Appendix C for details.) In Uzbekistan, the difference between respondents 18–34 years of age and those over 65 regarding whether privatized companies should be renationalized was just over five percentage points (50.0 and 55.7 percent, respectively) whereas in Russia the difference was almost 25 percentage points (26.2 and 50.0 percent, respectively).

Second, there is also broad popular support for state ownership of key agricultural inputs. Over 60 percent of the population in Uzbekistan, for example, either strongly agreed or agreed that "the state should retain ownership of scarce resources in the agricultural sector, such as land, water, fertilizer, and machinery." (See Table 4.5 for details.) While this finding may not seem surprising in and of itself, when coupled with an equally broad recognition that privatizing these scarce resources would actually improve access to agricultural goods and increase their own income while decreasing the government's authority, it deserves some attention. (See Table 4.6 for details.) Over 60 percent, for example, responded that privatization would increase access to agricultural goods and nearly 50 percent responded that it would increase the national income as well as their own income. The support for state ownership, therefore, is somewhat paradoxical. In other words, it remains robust despite the broad recognition that privatization would yield significant economic improvements for both individuals and the country as a whole.

Finally, the Uzbekistani population also appears to be more supportive of the state playing a very direct role in the economy – even beyond ownership of industry and land – than its counterparts in the FSU. Nearly 90 percent of Uzbekistanis, for example, responded that the state should be "strongly involved" in guaranteeing employment. More importantly, in contrast to elsewhere in the FSU (most notably Russia and Kazakhstan), this sentiment was

TABLE 4.6. *Perceived Effects of Privatization in Uzbekistan*

	Increase	No effect	Decrease	Difficult to answer
Access to agricultural goods	630	300	204	366
The level of unemployment	434	210	482	374
Your own job security	257	441	174	628
The national income	495	217	198	590
Your own income	487	320	183	510

Source: Jones Luong-McMann survey, October–November 2003.

consistent across age groups, suggesting that neither the Soviet legacy nor culture can explain these attitudes. In Russia, for example, 73.2 percent of respondents 18–34 years of age responded that the state should be "strongly involved" in guaranteeing employment versus 82.0 percent over 65 – that is, a difference of almost 10 percentage points – whereas in Uzbekistan, these numbers were 87.6 percent versus 89.8 percent – that is, a difference of just over 2 percentage points. Our interviews further highlight that the population widely believes that the state should be the greatest source of economic activity. Several energy analysts underscored the expectation that the revenue from both the energy and cotton sectors would be directed toward developing public enterprises (Authors' interview with Karchenko and Tashpulatov).

The evidence concerning popular attitudes toward taxation is less conclusive because it provides some mixed evidence and is difficult to interpret. On the one hand, contrary to our predictions, the Jones Luong-McMann survey data suggests that the population in Uzbekistan is more accepting of taxation than it is in Kazakhstan, where the petroleum sector was privatized to foreign investors in the mid-1990s. (See Chapter 7 for details.) They are more likely, for example, to believe that their fellow citizens pay their taxes and as likely to claim that they either "completely" or "mostly" pay their own taxes. They are also more likely to view their tax system as "fair." On the other, Uzbekistani citizens are much more likely to believe that the government utilizes the revenue it generates from taxation to make everyone better off. For example, when asked "where do you think the taxes that you and others pay to the government actually go," 58.8 percent of the population in Uzbekistan responded that they "are used to provide social services to the general public," whereas only 8.6 percent believed that their taxes were "usurped by government officials to benefit particular groups or people," compared to 45.4 and 25.1 percent, respectively, in Kazakhstan. This suggests that citizens in Uzbekistan associate paying their taxes with contributing to the general welfare, which may also help explain the higher level of (reported) compliance. Their apparently greater willingness to pay taxes is also consistent with our prediction that citizens should not be as opposed to taxation as they are in Turkmenistan – particularly if they believe that these taxes are being used to supplement the state's efforts to provide social services. At the same time, there is a strong correlation between those who claimed to pay their taxes and those who are employed in state enterprises, suggesting that whether individuals actually pay (or claim to pay) their taxes depends on their perception of the state's ability to collect taxes rather than any willingness on the part of the citizen to pay them. In other words, compliance is neither voluntary nor quasi-voluntary.

The survey results are more conclusive when it comes to expenditures. In sum, they indicate that the population expects a high degree of social spending and access to low-priced goods and services commensurate with what it received under Soviet rule. According to the LiTS, for example, nearly 90 percent of Uzbekistanis responded that the state should be "strongly involved" in guaranteeing employment, and just over 80 percent responded that the state should be "strongly involved" in guaranteeing low prices for basic goods. These expectations, moreover, are not correlated with either the respondent's own socioeconomic circumstances or age group. The difference between those in the 18–34 years of age category and those in the 65 years of age category who responded that the state should be "strongly involved" in guaranteeing employment is a mere 2 percentage points (87.6 and 89.8 percent, respectively). The difference between respondents in these two age groups who believed the state should be "strongly involved" in guaranteeing low prices for basic goods and services is only slightly larger at 5 percentage points (79.1 and 84.1 percent, respectively).

Interviews conducted with government officials in various ministries, including energy and finance, as well as Uzbekneftegaz managers and local economic analysts during the spring of 1997 and 2002, lend further support to our claim that elites in Uzbekistan not only perceived societal expectations for widespread distribution but also formulated fiscal regimes with these expectations in mind. A close advisor to President Karimov on fiscal matters, for example, explained the persistence of universal subsidies for basic goods and services thus: "the people know that the state is wealthy ... , that it is capable of providing these things for them, and they are accustomed to this" (Authors' interview with Fazilova). Managers of Uzbekneftegaz similarly tied popular expectations to their "social obligation" to continue to provide subsidized oil and gas to the population: "the people will simply not pay for something they in fact already own" (Authors' interview with Persheyev).

Public speeches provide additional evidence that the state felt obligated to at least acknowledge societal expectations for widespread distribution, albeit to a much lesser extent than in Turkmenistan. Here, again, we rely primarily on the president's annual speech to the national legislature, or *Oliy Majlis* (hereafter, *Address*). When this is not available, we include presidential speeches or public addresses to commemorate Independence Day. In contrast to Turkmenistan, these speeches and addresses are striking for their lack of emphasis on the country's mineral wealth. Rather, until the early 2000s, President Karimov tends to emphasize cotton as the primary vehicle for financing Uzbekistan's social and economic development. For example, the quote at the beginning of the chapter from his 1994 *Address* emphasizes the importance of cotton sales for meeting the "people's needs," whereas the oil and gas sectors are only mentioned in the context of achieving self-sufficiency. Karimov's *Addresses* over the next several years (1995–2004) are also remarkable in this regard. The sole mention of the oil and gas sectors in his 1999 speech, for example, concerns the need for the Central Asian states to cooperate in constructing pipelines.

At the same time, his speeches highlight the extent to which governing elites believed that society expected a level of fairness when it comes to taxation and benefits, especially for pensioners. For example, in his 1995 *Address*, Karimov underscored,

The idea of fairness should envelop all spheres of public life. The formation of all fields of legislation – state and civil, labor and housing, pensioner and taxation, natural protection and criminal should begin and end with this idea.

Interestingly, it is not until 2005 – that is, just after Uzbekistan signs its first major PSA under its new ownership structure (S$_2$) and just before it announces what to date is its largest foreign investment project in the petroleum sector – that taxation of the mineral sector is mentioned in any of Karimov's *Addresses*. This is entirely consistent with what we would predict, since S$_2$ adds an entirely new dimension to societal expectations that directly affects perceptions of fairness regarding taxation (see Chapter 6 for details). In sum, the adoption of S$_2$ in Uzbekistan should heighten societal expectations not vis-à-vis the state but vis-à-vis foreign investors, making it imperative that the former demonstrate it is adequately extracting tax revenue from the latter in lieu of taxing the population. Karimov's 2005 *Address*, in which he first heralds the benefits that will accrue from increasing direct foreign investment in the oil and gas sector and then insists that "the main [fiscal] burden should lie on taxes on resources," seems aimed at doing exactly that.

Implicit Bargaining

Although it is difficult to find direct evidence that fiscal regimes in Turkmenistan and Uzbekistan emerged via implicit bargaining, there is substantial indirect evidence. The first type of evidence concerns the secret nature of the policymaking process itself. In both countries, there has been a virtual lack of publicity surrounding the formulation of taxation and spending policies – even in official government newspapers. So-called "drafts" of their respective tax codes, for example, were published preceding the legislature's approval that were almost identical to the final document, suggesting there was little room for open debate. As one former high-ranking official who participated in this process in Uzbekistan explained, "when it came to drafting tax legislation, a special committee was convened ... [and] it was not publicly released until we had the version the President wanted the deputies [in the Oliy Majilis] to approve" (Authors' interview). The process is equally opaque on the expenditure side. Not only does the formulation of the budget occur behind close doors in both countries, in Uzbekistan it also purposefully lacks a well-defined structure (see World Bank 2005c, Chapter four), whereas in Turkmenistan information about this procedure is simply not made available. Moreover, the increased reliance on EBTs that has occurred in both countries makes open discussions over spending priorities unnecessary.

The second involves the aforementioned interviews with elites, most of whom eschewed the need for a formal discussion of fiscal policies. Rather, the consensus was reflected in one former Uzbekistani government official's observation that "negotiations over issues of such great importance are, by necessity, on-going ... and they happen in various forms at various times" (Authors' interview). Managers of the NOC similarly emphasized the need for both the government and the NOC to be "flexible" when it came to "who owes whom ... and how much" (Authors' interview with Persheyev).

The third type of indirect evidence relates to the views of third parties to these informal "negotiations" – that is, the international consultants who tried to influence the formulation of fiscal policy. Of those we interviewed, the majority felt they were denied access to the *real* bargaining process. Some foreign advisors seeking to influence Uzbekistan's draft tax code, for example, expressed their frustration at participating in a series of one-on-one meetings with "a multitude of officials," but never together as a group "to hash out the details," while others complained bitterly that they were never even invited to attend a single meeting and felt "completely shunned" (Authors' interview with foreign economic consultant no. 1). Moreover, they conveyed a profound sense that the formal document on which they were concentrating their efforts "had already been trumped by an informal agreement" (Authors' interview with foreign economic consultant no. 2). Representatives of foreign oil and gas companies had a similar perspective. When trying to figure out the "rules of the game" for getting an exploration contract in Uzbekistan, for example, Enron's representative complained "there is no legislation on oil and gas here ... the chairman of Uzbekneftegaz just does as he pleases, the rules change at his whim" (Authors' interview with Berry).

Perhaps more importantly, there is also ample evidence to suggest that the key motivation for implicit bargaining – that is, elites' mutual desire to hide information from the public – was very much present in both countries. This desire for secrecy concerns not only the state's actual income and the general health of the economy but also how much the state is spending, as well as who is actually benefiting from state spending. In other words, it is not just a matter of governments withholding what they consider to be "state secrets," but the particular type of information that is being hidden. In order to conceal state income and the health of the economy, for example, both countries have sought to conceal the volume of oil and gas exports as well as other financial data. A dramatic example of this is Nizayov's decree in 2000 banning "the supply of any statistical data to unauthorized persons, especially foreigners" (Kamenev 2001, 162). Then, beginning in 2001, the government of Turkmenistan refused to disclose any data on oil and gas production and exports, as well as any financial data, to the international community, including data on foreign reserves.[59] While Uzbekistan also deliberately concealed information in the 1990s (see Broadman 2000), it displayed a similar degree of increasing secrecy in the late 1990s and early 2000s. In short, it placed new restrictions on access to, and the generation of, statistical data. This, combined with the scarcity of reliable sectoral data, made independent "[a]ssessments of [its] economic performance ... very difficult" (EIU 2002, 25). The concealment of reliable statistical data to both the domestic population and international community also extended to expenditure priorities. Turkmenistan, in particular, has not only refused to turn over data on basic health indicators to UN agencies, but also made it difficult for any "independent verification of expenditure and activity" in the health realm (Rechel and McKee 2007).

In order to conceal government spending, both governments have relied increasingly on EBTs. Turkmenistan had already become notorious by the late 1990s for the lack of transparency in its public finances due to "a large proportion [of its income and expenditures] not recorded in the state budget but passing through a number of funds, some of which are directly controlled by the President" (Pomfret 2001, 168). The two most significant EBTs (described above) – the SFDOG and the FERF – are known to be "under the personal control of the President and are not required to publish accounts" (Kalyuzhnova and Kaser 2006, 173). Similarly, the largest EBT in Uzbekistan – the Fund for Settlements for Agricultural Products Purchased for State Needs, which was established in 1998 to collect the proceeds from cotton sales – has also been shrouded in secrecy (Authors' interview with World Bank representatives; see also, World Bank 2005c, 3).

IMPLICATIONS

The fact that both Turkmenistan and Uzbekistan developed a fiscal regime that is neither constraining nor enabling provides strong evidence for one of this book's central claims: that is, that state ownership with control – rather than mineral wealth per se – is the driving force behind weak fiscal regimes in mineral-rich states. Some aspects of their respective fiscal regimes, such as a heavy reliance on mineral sector taxation and unrestrained government expenditures, are clearly consistent with what the conventional literature on the resource curse expects, and thus, the causal link to ownership structure may not be as apparent. Yet several others are not, including a highly unstable tax regime that is based largely on indirect and implicit taxation combined with an expenditure system that emphasizes universal subsidies and implicit

---

[59] As a result, "[t]he most reliable (but increasingly dated) indicator is an IMF estimate from mid-1999" (IMF 2007b, 40).

transfers. Moreover, we demonstrate that these outcomes are not the product of wealth-induced myopia and risk aversion among elites in mineral-rich states, as the resource curse literature assumes, but rather of rational decision making in response to the incentives fostered via low TCs and high societal expectations, and reinforced via implicit bargaining.

The emergence of weak fiscal regimes in Turkmenistan and Uzbekistan also has important empirical implications for these countries and their citizens in both the short and the long term. As discussed in Chapter 2, precisely because they fail to either constrain or enable state leaders, weak fiscal regimes tend to have two sets of adverse consequences.

First, they have a decisively negative impact on the quality of citizens' daily lives. In both countries, for example, the reliance on unstable and implicit forms of taxation and privileging of SOEs over the private sector has clearly fostered an unfriendly business environment and stunted the growth of SMEs. While the 2005 Business Environment and Enterprise Performance Survey (BEEPs)[60] compares Uzbekistan favorably to other CIS countries in several areas, it also indicates that a relatively higher and increasing percentage of firms continue to experience problems with unofficial payments when it comes to paying taxes, obtaining a license, and accessing public services.[61] Similarly, according to *Doing Business in 2005* – the second in a series of annual reports that assess the impact of regulations on business activity – Uzbekistan ranks among the most difficult countries concerning labor regulations (28), among the most complex when it comes to registering property (34–6), and was only one of two countries that actually made closing a business more difficult since 2004 (70–1). Consequently, for the majority of citizens there is no real alternative to pubic sector employment, which in Turkmenistan is very limited beyond the petroleum sector and in Uzbekistan has chronically low wages (see Abdurakhmanov and Marnie 2006). The expansion of the informal sector in Uzbekistan relative to other transition countries, for example, has been attributed to its onerous labor regulations, such as the difficulty of firing employees (*Doing Business in 2005*, 29).[62] At the same time, although both countries have engaged in higher-than-average public spending levels and enjoyed continued GDP growth – particularly

---

[60] BEEPs has been conducted jointly by the World Bank and the EBRD in transition countries since 1999 (for details, see Hellman et al. 2000; for access to data by country and year, see http://go.worldbank.org/RQQXYJ6210). All CIS countries are included except for Turkmenistan.

[61] Moreover, there is good reason to believe that in Uzbekistan as well as Belarus, the incidence of bribery and corruption is actually underreported (see Anderson and Gray 2006, Chapter 3).

[62] ADB (2005a, 3) reported that the "informal sector accounts for as much as 30–50% of the official reported GDP." This contrasts sharply with prior studies that found the share of Uzbekistan's informal sector in GDP to be "low" compared to that of other transition countries (Taube and Zettelmeyer 1998, 12).

Uzbekistan – this has not "contribut[ed] to [either] poverty reduction or income equality" (Abdurakhmanov and Marnie 2006; see also, Alam et al., 2005). Not surprisingly, then, it also has not translated into improvements in the overall level of human development. For example, whereas Turkmenistan was ranked 80th (out of 179 countries) on the UNDP's Human Development Index in 1994, by 2005 it had fallen to 105th. Uzbekistan has followed a similar path. Whereas in 1994 it was ranked 91st on the HDI, by 2005 it had fallen to 113th.

Second, and directly related, weak fiscal regimes are the key intervening variable between mineral wealth and the most pervasive negative social and economic outcomes associated with the resource curse – including weak administrative capacity, unbalanced economic growth, and authoritarian regimes. Here too Turkmenistan and Uzbekistan conform closely to the classic rentier model. After only a decade of state ownership with control over their respective petroleum sectors, they already exhibited several of the impediments to socioeconomic development that characterized the infamous OPEC countries at the end of the 1980s: bloated public sectors and inefficient industry, governments with notoriously high levels of corruption, and impoverished populations with little or no access to primary healthcare and basic education despite over a decade of overzealous social spending. At the same time, the centralized and nontransparent accrual of export rents facilitated the consolidation of authoritarian regimes in both countries. While much less blatant than Niyazov's abuse of the SFDOG in Turkmenistan to reward his allies, it is an open secret that Karimov has made the security apparatus one of the primary beneficiaries of Uzbekistan's proceeds from cotton and increasingly gas (Authors' interview with former government official; see also, ICG 2007). Thus, as of 2005, Turkmenistan and Uzbekistan were not only considered the most corrupt among the CIS,[63] but they were also considered the least free.[64]

Indeed, that these countries' developmental trajectories have clearly converged by the mid-2000s despite some important differences regarding expenditures is a testament to how formidable the negative effects of weak fiscal regimes are. As described above, Uzbekistan's efforts to provide social protection through targeted goods and services and its emphasis on human capital formation is a stark contrast to Turkmenistan's penchant for extravagant monuments and hotels. And yet, neither has produced its desired results owing to the deficiencies of the broader fiscal regime – specifically, the absence of real tax reform and the predominance of QFAs. Targeted social assistance,

---

[63] Turkmenistan and Uzbekistan were both at the bottom of Transparency International's Corruption Perception Index (CPI) in 2005–137 and 155, respectively, out of 158 countries. They both dropped to 166 (out of 180 countries) in 2008. See http://www.transparency.org/policy_research/surveys_indices/cpi for details.

[64] Although the gap has narrowed over time, both countries have also been consistently ranked below their petroleum-rich CIS counterparts on the Freedom House Index since the early 1990s. For details, see http://www.freedomhouse.org

for example, has not alleviated poverty or reduced income inequality largely because the government has used traditional structures to deliver this assistance rather than pursuing income tax reform or building a tax administration that could collect reliable information about individuals' income and employment. Attempts at building human capital via increased spending on education have been similarly marred by the government's priority on wage increases for public employees and using the educational system to fortify the dominance of SOEs and to reward children of the elite.

At the end of the 2000s, moreover, neither country had changed course. Although there was some hope that Niyazov's death in December 2006 would bring some reform, his anointed successor (Gurbanguly Berdimuhammedov) has maintained not only S_1 in the petroleum sector but also the bulk of Niyazov's detrimental socioeconomic policies (for details, see Kjaernet and Overland 2007). The direct connection between the two is eerily apparent in Berdimuhammedov's first annual New Year's address to the Turkmenistani people, wherein he reaffirms the state's commitment to using gas revenues to extend the universal provisions of free goods as well as to raise salaries and pensions for everyone.[65]

Uzbekistan's decision to adopt state ownership without control (S_2) was also cause for some (albeit guarded) optimism. And yet, this strategy is unlikely to improve the country's developmental prospects, as it has done, for example, in Azerbaijan (see Chapter 7 for details). Rather, the overwhelming evidence suggests that the government has continued to eschew real fiscal reform. While Uzbekistan has been more receptive to international institutions' efforts at improving its taxation system outside the mineral sector, for example, its business environment has actually deteriorated.[66] At the same time, the government has bolstered efforts to maintain the public sector as the primary source of employment.[67] Nor has the country seen any improvement in either its poverty rate or its human development indicators. As we argue in Chapter 6, this is directly related to the fact that the foreign investors with whom it has chosen to sign production-sharing contracts are not committed to CSR in Uzbekistan. Its largest and most influential investor in the petroleum sector, Lukoil Overseas Holding Ltd., does not cooperate with IFIs and INGOs pushing for broad tax reform and greater budgetary transparency. And when it comes to its own role, Lukoil Overseas prefers to engage in voluntary social spending and to focus its spending on charity and sponsorship at

[65] The speech took place on January 1, 2008. The full text is available at http://www.turkmenistan.ru/

[66] For example, according to *Doing Business 2006*, Uzbekistan is one of the few countries in the world where it actually became "more difficult for businesses to register property, get credit and trade across borders" as well as to pay their taxes from 2005 to 2006 (*Doing Business 2007*). Despite some tax reform in 2005–2006, it still ranked 159 (out of 178 countries) regarding the ease of paying taxes at the end of 2007 (Djankov and Symons 2007).

[67] For example, wages for public employees have become an increasing portion of state expenditures since 2006, which has contributed to strong inflationary pressures (IMF 2008, 11).

the national level rather than supporting local development initiatives (see Oil of Russia 2006). Its social contributions, therefore, have been minimal and limited to cultural events and institutions, such as the Navoi Opera and Ballet Theater, as well as various charities prioritized and controlled by President Karimov himself, such as the Fund for Children's Sports Development (see Lukoil Overseas 2006).

5

Petroleum Rents without Rentierism

Domestic Private Ownership in the Russian Federation

If the [Russian] state does not learn to collect taxes, it will cease to exist.
— Sergei Kiriyenko, Prime Minister, June 23, 1998

Competitiveness of the economy ... rests on stability and predictability, clearness and transparency of rules and procedures. Otherwise, we can hardly ever succeed. Capital is invested in areas where it is guaranteed best possible conditions, and love to Russia alone is not a sufficient motivator.
— Sergey Dimitrievich Shatalov, First Deputy Minister of Finance, July 5, 2002

The most important feature of the new Tax Code is its stability. Even if you don't like paying taxes, there are now rules that do not change. Even if it is not perfect, it is clear and predictable. This is good for business ... . It is good for the major oil companies. And what is good for the major oil companies is good for Russia. Just like Ford [Motor Co.] in America ... .
— Representative of Lukoil, June 25, 2002

Whereas Turkmenistan and Uzbekistan adopted one of the most common ownership structures among petroleum-rich states – state ownership with control (S_1) – from the early 1990s through the mid-2000s, the Russian Federation adopted one of the rarest over its oil sector – private domestic ownership (P_1). According to our research, over the course of the twentieth century, only a handful of developing countries – Brazil (1891–1937), Venezuela (1904–1906), Romania (1924–1944), and Guatemala (1949–1982) – have opted to privatize their petroleum sector to domestic actors. Russia officially joined this small group in 1993 when it created three vertically integrated joint-stock oil companies – Lukoil, Surgutneftegaz, and Yukos – to replace the state-owned Soviet oil monopoly. As a result, we predict that it is also more likely to enjoy a rare outcome across mineral-rich states: a strong fiscal regime – that is, one that encompasses a tax system that is stable, broad-based, and relies primarily on direct and explicit taxation and a system of expenditures that emphasizes budgetary stability and transparency. In this chapter, we demonstrate not only that Russia did indeed adopt a strong fiscal regime from 1999–2005 – contrary to what both scholars of Russia and the resource curse predicted – but also that this outcome was facilitated by its choice of ownership structure.

As we argue in Chapter 3, P_1 fosters strong fiscal regimes because – in contrast to S_1 – it provides both the direct claimants (here, domestic private owners) and indirect claimants (here, governing elites and the population) with an incentive to supply and demand institutions that set effective limits on the state's ability to extract and spend the proceeds from mineral wealth – incentives that are reinforced by the process through which these institutions emerge. More specifically, P_1 generates high transaction costs (TCs), societal expectations for limited redistribution, and interdependent power relations. The combination of high TCs and low societal expectations promotes a mutual desire for fiscal stability, more visible forms of taxation across sectors, and limited public spending, while interdependent power relations in the context of low TCs and high societal expectations serve to reinforce these incentives via an explicit bargaining process.

Russia serves as a critical test of our argument – not merely because it represents a very small number of cases of P_1, but more so because it lacks many of the presumed "fundamentals" of private domestic ownership. Thus, it has evoked a significant degree of pessimism about the potential benefits of privatization among casual observers and experts alike. First, similar to many of its counterparts both in the former Soviet Union (FSU) and the developing world, Russia has had little history of private entrepreneurship and a fledgling capitalist class. Second, many analysts argue that because the privatization process was carried out in an arbitrary manner that lacked transparency, the ownership rights it created will never be considered legitimate within Russia. Third, the domestic entrepreneurs who did emerge from privatization – particularly those in the oil sector – quickly earned a tarnished reputation as "oligarchs" and "robber barons" (see Hoffman 2002). They became notorious not only for amassing great personal fortune from siphoning off Russia's most prized national assets but also for their efforts to use personal ties with state leaders to block any fiscal, regulatory, or administrative reforms that might threaten their current and future economic gains (see Hellman 1998). Finally, the privatization of petroleum in Russia has not been complete. Contrary to the oil sector, the single entity that replaced the Ministry of Gas – Gazprom – successfully retained its monopoly structure by exploiting close links to the government. As a result, ownership structure in Russia's gas sector in the 1990s amounted to "private domestic ownership with state control." As we will discuss further below, the "partial privatization" of the gas sector has had many of the disadvantages of S_1 and few of the benefits of P_1 because it created a nominally private oil company with institutional incentives akin to an NOC.

Tax reform in Russia also provides a rather large hurdle to overcome in substantiating our argument that P_1 fosters a form of business – state relations that provides incentives for creating strong fiscal regimes in mineral-rich states. Pessimism about the prospects for building a viable tax system in

Russia has been as pervasive as the pessimism surrounding privatization (see Easter 2002, Pavlova 1999, Treisman 1998). And this is for good reason. Like its counterparts across the FSU, Russia inherited a completely dysfunctional tax system that was only exacerbated by hasty and ill-conceived attempts to replace this system in the first several months of its independence (Shatalov 2006, 778–9). Moreover, efforts to restructure the tax system in the 1990s were so feeble and ineffectual that tax reform was essentially abandoned by 1998. The government opted instead to set excessive tax rates arbitrarily by decree, which perpetuated high rates of evasion across sectors (Ivanenko 2005). The Russian oil companies (hereafter, ROCs) were no exception. During this period, they developed elaborate schemes to evade these exorbitant tax rates. As a result, the government was only able to collect approximately half of its projected tax revenues.

Yet despite all of these obstacles, Russia's experience is consistent with both the fiscal outcomes we predict and the causal mechanisms we identify as linking P_1 to these particular outcomes. As we demonstrate below, the mutual desire of government officials and private domestic owners in the oil sector to set formal limits on taxation and expenditures following the 1998 financial crisis enabled Russia not only to institute a relatively stable and increasingly effective broad-based tax regime but also to create one of the few functioning natural resource funds (hereafter NRFs) in the developing world and the only one in the FSU.[1] These dramatic improvements in the country's fiscal regime, moreover, occurred at a time when, according to the conventional literature on the resource curse, we should least expect them. In short, the Russian government initiated fiscal reform during a bust, when the leaders of mineral-rich states are said to be *least capable* of adopting and implementing structural reforms due primarily to political constraints, and then sustained during a boom, when these same leaders are assumed to be *least willing* to adopt such reforms due to cognitive ones. To clarify: our contention is not that P_1 made this outcome inevitable, but rather that it increased the likelihood this would occur because it laid the groundwork for mutual interests in fiscal reform to emerge among economic and political elites – even if these mutual interests could not be realized immediately. Russia's ownership structure, moreover, also helps explain the unexpected timing of this realization.

In sum, in sharp contrast to Turkmenistan and Uzbekistan, as of 2005, Russia represented a significant departure from the classic rentier state model. It had achieved fiscal stabilization, controlled inflation, repaid its debt, and sustained industrial growth, thus experiencing minimal Dutch Disease effects even during an unprecedented oil price boom (see Roland 2006).[2] That Russia

[1] To date, the only other functioning NRFs outside the OECD are in Botswana and Chile. As we describe in Chapters 7 and 8, respectively, Azerbaijan and Kazakhstan both created NRFs in the 1990s but neither can be considered "effective" according to the criteria laid out in Chapter 2.

[2] In fact, as of 2003, Russia was among the most diversified economies among petroleum-rich states, including Norway and the United States (Schubert 2007, 9).

was on the right track regarding fiscal reform is underscored by the partial derailing of these reforms since 2005, following Russia's decision to reassert state ownership and control over its entire petroleum sector.[3] Particularly worrisome is its dramatic turn away from fiscal stabilization. Government spending, for example, has increased by roughly 25 percent annually in accordance with the country's first three-year fiscal plan adopted in July 2007, which codifies an end to the budgetary surplus that Russia had accumulated since 2000 in what became the Oil Stabilization Fund (hereafter, OSF). As we demonstrate in the concluding section to this chapter, this is directly related to the country's shift from P_1 to S_1 as of 2005.

THE PRIVATIZATION OF PETROLEUM

The Soviet energy sector was part of a large state-owned conglomerate in which the central state had sole authority to direct oil and gas exploration, production, and distribution and to collect the proceeds from their sale abroad. As in the other petroleum-rich republics of the FSU, when the Soviet Union collapsed in 1991, this authority within the Russian Soviet Federated Socialist Republic (RSFSR) was transferred to the newly independent Russian state. At this time, the Soviet Oil Ministry was effectively replaced by the Rosneftegas Corporation, whereas the Soviet Gas Ministry had already been converted into the State Gas Concern Gazprom (GGK Gazprom) in 1989. Although the government set a clear course for privatization of the entire petroleum sector as early as 1992, the paths that oil and gas followed departed soon after. By the mid-1990s, the Russian government had radically restructured the oil industry by breaking up this natural monopoly into several private vertically integrated companies (VICs) and dramatically reducing state shares in all but one of these new VICs. Conversely, the gas sector retained its monopoly structure in the form of the Gazprom Joint Stock Company in which the government not only retained enough shares to maintain a controlling interest but also leveraged these shares to cement its close personal and political ties to this new private company. In both cases, however, insiders were the primary beneficiaries of the nontransparent process through which the Russian government relinquished all or part of its hold on the country's immense petroleum reserves.

For most of the 1990s, then, two forms of ownership structure over petroleum prevailed in Russia. While private domestic ownership (P_1) was firmly established over the oil sector by the end the 1990s, ownership structure over the gas sector is best described as private domestic ownership with state control, because the transfer of control to the new owners was incomplete. By the mid-2000s, however, the government's strategy vis-à-vis oil and gas seems to have converged again. Already in 1999 there were clear signs that the

---

[3] We offer a broader explanation for this change in ownership structure from P_1 to S_1 in Chapter 9.

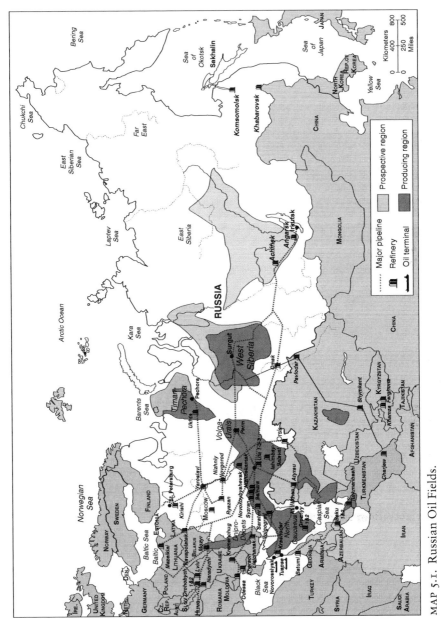

MAP 5.1. Russian Oil Fields.
Source: Russia Energy Survey, © OECD/IEA, 2002, map 1, page 11.

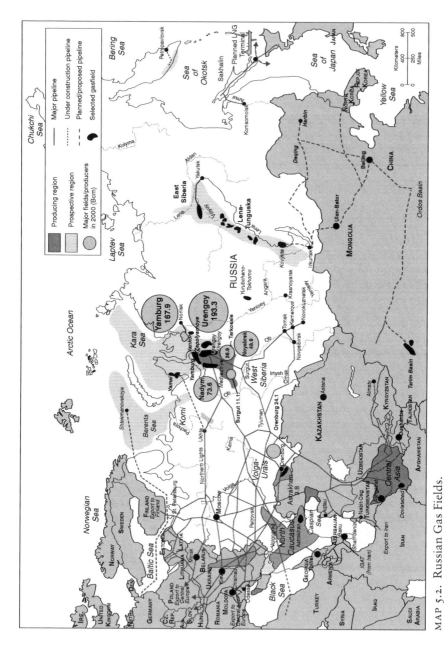

MAP 5.2. Russian Gas Fields.
Source: Russia Energy Survey, © OECD/IEA, 2002, map 4, page 14.

TABLE 5.1. *Stages of Reform in the Russian Oil Sector, 1992–1998*

STAGE I (1992–1993)	STAGE II (1995–1996)	STAGE III (1997–1998)
State Ownership Maintained	State Ownership Reduced	State Ownership Relinquished
Government held majority shares in holding companies and majority interest in VICs	Largest banks acquire state shares as collateral for loans Rosneft partially privatized shares in several VICs But several companies still protected from full privatization	By 1997, the government held majority shares in less than half and no shares in almost one-third Government issues tender for 75 percent of Rosneft shares but forced to withdraw due to sharp drop in oil prices Transneft partially privatized
Foreign Involvement Restricted	Foreign Involvement Restricted	Restrictions on Foreigners Loosened
Limited to between 5 and 15 percent	Limited to between 5 and 15 percent	Limit on foreign ownership abolished (to be determined by individual oil companies) Duma adopts limited PSA law in 1998

government sought to increase its formal stake in Gazprom with the aim of reestablishing ownership alongside control, which it had achieved by 2002. Although the government's efforts to (re)assert state ownership and control over the gas sector began several years earlier and with greater foresight, by the end of 2004 there was clearly a shift from P_1 to S_1 in the oil sector as well.

Oil Sector

The privatization of Russia's oil sector took place in three stages and was completed by the end of the 1990s. (See Table 5.1 for an overview.) The first stage began soon after Russia launched its official privatization program for large state enterprises when President Boris Yeltsin issued Presidential Decree #1403 in November 1992 calling for dissolving the Soviet oil monopoly and creating several holding companies (Moe and Kryukov 1994). It entailed breaking up the Soviet oil monopoly along geographical lines in which regional oil production associations were recombined with refineries and product distributors, resulting in the formation of three vertically integrated joint-stock companies: Lukoil, Surgutneftegaz, and Yukos (Sagers et al. 1995). In addition, the

Rosneftegas Corporation was transformed into the large state holding company, Rosneft, and officially charged with directing this process and temporarily managing the remaining state enterprises and shares.[4] In 1994, several additional VICs were carved out of Rosneft – including Slavneft, Sidanco, Vostochnaya Neftianaya Kompaniya (VNK), and Onaco – alongside two joint-stock companies – Tatneft and Bashneft. Presidential Decree #327 subsequently transformed Rosneft itself into a joint-stock company in April 1995. And then, a few months later (in August – September 1995), the number of enterprises remaining within Rosneft was reduced even further when two new VICs were formed – Tyumenskaya Neftyanaya Kompaniya (TNK) and Sibneft (Khartukov 2002).[5]

Similar to the privatization of state enterprises that took place in the early 1990s, during the first stage of oil sector privatization, shares were offered only to company employees and to Russian citizens.[6] This initial phase (a.k.a., voucher privatization) enabled a small number of individuals (many of whom were tied closely to the state – such as, Communist party officials and factory directors) to buy up the majority of shares in Russia's oil companies at a nominal price rather than through competitive bidding (Dienes 1996). Thus, from its inception, the privatization process in the Russian oil industry has been harshly criticized because it enabled "insiders" to consolidate their hold over state assets – much of which they had previously seized through semi-legal means (Lane 1999). Indeed, this process mirrored the "spontaneous" or unofficial privatization that took place throughout the entire economy (Solnick 1998).

Shortly afterward, in order to reduce its growing budget deficit and cut inflation, the Russian government found itself forced to borrow money from the newly formed commercial banks that had emerged in the early 1990s. Through its controversial "loans for shares" program in 1994–1995, the government put up for collateral some of the country's largest and most valuable enterprises as well as its controlling shares in the integrated oil companies in exchange for commercial bank loans. Thus, when the government failed to repay these loans, their remaining shares were transferred directly to the banks, allowing commercial bankers to acquire these coveted assets (for details, see Johnson 1997).[7] These included Russia's main producer of nickel, Norilsk Nickel, and three of Russia's most lucrative newly formed vertically-integrated

---

[4] Initially, the government planned to retain some control over the oil industry through maintaining substantial ownership of stocks in the holding companies for a period of three years (Lane 1999, Locatelli 1995).

[5] Thus, Rosneft was never intended to become the dominant player in the Russian oil industry, as a presidential decree (no. 872) signed on August 24, 1995 made clear (*RPI* 1995c, 11).

[6] For details concerning the privatization process in general, see Boycko et al. (1997).

[7] In some cases (such as, Surgutneftegas), the source of the loans came from within the company itself. Thus, company "insiders" rather than financial "outsiders" took over these companies (Lane 1999).

oil companies – Sidanco (Oneksimbank), Yukos (Menatep Bank), and Sibneft (Boris Berezovsky's National Oil Company with the help of Menatep and Stolichnyi Bank). According to numerous critics of the "loans for shares" program, the result was that these commercial bankers acted as "roving bandits," pursuing their own short-term economic interests by divvying up Russia's strategic oil resources through highly dubious means at the expense of Russia's economic recovery (see Dienes 1996, Goldman 1999).

The third stage, during which the government continued to relinquish ownership of oil sector assets, commenced in the late 1990s and persisted through the early 2000s. Since the first phase of privatization, the state's share in each company has declined dramatically except for a controlling interest in Rosneft (see Table 5.2 for details), which it tried in vain to privatize from mid-1996 through the end of 1998.[8] Perhaps most telling is that President Vladimir Putin, who succeeded Yeltsin in March 2000, continued privatizing Russia's oil sector during his first few years in office – despite the public's misgivings and hostile reaction from the Communists to his predecessor's policies in this regard. In September 2000, for example, the government sold its 85 percent stake in Onako (*RFE/RL* September 20, 2000). And in the fall of 2002 the Russian Fund for Federal Property (RFFI) put up 74.95 percent of its remaining shares in Slavneft for sale (*Kommersant* 2005). As of 2002, therefore, the oil sector comprised approximately a dozen private VICs, including VNK, Lukoil, Onako, Sibneft, Sidanco, Slavneft, Surgutneftegas, TNK, and YUKOS, Bashneft, Komitek, and Tatneft (Khartukov 2002). Between 1999 and 2004, these companies collectively produced more than 85 percent of the country's oil while state-owned entities produced less than 15 percent (Milov 2007).

The government's full divesture of ownership in the oil industry, however, has not translated into a substantial role for foreign investors. Until 1997, the official limit for foreign ownership was only 15 percent of each company (Rutland 1997a, 9).[9] Moreover, the government and the domestic private oil companies colluded to prevent foreign investors from taking part in subsequent auctions and to delay passage of PSA legislation that would provide foreign investors with stable tax guarantees.[10] According to the director of the Petroleum Advisory Forum, the strategy of the private ROCs was "to block out foreign investors from Russia" (Authors' interview with Konovalov). The relaxation of limits on foreign ownership in the late 1990s, however, did pave the way for British Petroleum to buy a 50 percent stake in

---

[8] The legislation stipulating the terms of Rosneft's privatization was approved in September 1997. Nearly a year later, the government had still not launched a successful tender.

[9] The regional authorities could impose their own restrictions on foreign bidders (*RPI* 1994b, 28).

[10] Only in May 2003 did the Duma approve new rules for PSAs, which permitted them only for deposits that no domestic company was willing to develop (*RFE/RL* May 15, 2003).

TABLE 5.2. *Percentage of Government Stake in Russian Oil Companies*

Company	Year Formed	1994	1995	1996	1997	1998	1999	2000	2001	2002	2003	2004	2005
Sidanco[a]	1994	–	100	85	51	0	0	0	0	0	0	0	0
Sibneft	1995	–	–	100	51.1	0	0	0	0	0	0	0	75[b]
TNK[c]	1995	–	–	100	91	51	49.8	0	0	0	0	0	0
SNG	1993	100	40.1	40.1	40.1	0.8	0.8	0.8	0	0	0	0	0
Onaco[d]	1994	–	100	85	85	85	85	85	0	0	0	0	0
Komitek[e]	1994	–	100	100	92	1.1	1.1	1.1	1.1	0	0	0	0
Yukos	1993	100	86	53	0.1	0.1	0.1	0.1	0.1	0.1	0.1	0.1	60[f]
VSNK[g]	1994	–	100	85	38	1.0	1.0	1.0	1.0	1.0	1.0	1.0	1.0
Lukoil	1993	90.8	80	54.9	33.1	26.9	26.6	23.7	14.1	7.6	7.6	7.6	7.6
Tatneft[h]	1994	–	46.6	46.6	30.3	30.3	30.3	30.3	30.3	30.3	30.3	30.3	30.3
VNK[i]	1994	–	100	85	85	36.8	36.8	36.8	36.8	36.8	36.8	36.8	36.8
Slavneft	1994	–	93.5	92	90	85.8	85.8	85.8	85.8	85.8	0	0	0
Rosneft	1995	–	100	100	100	100	100	100	100	100	100	100	100

Sources: Compiled by authors from Khartukov 2002, Locatelli 2006, and annual reports of various ROCs (available online)

[a] Controlled by TNK since mid-2001.

[b] The state-owned gas monopoly Gazprom bought 75 percent of Sibneft's shares in 2005.

[c] Became TNK-BP when British Petroleum bought 50 percent of TNK shares in 2003.

[d] Controlled by TNK since September 2000.

[e] Controlled by Lukoil since mid-1999.

[f] In December 2004, the government bought Yukos' largest subsidiary – Yuganskneftegaz. This is a rough estimate, since it is difficult to determine what percentage the other two subsidiaries – Tomskneft and Samaraneftegaz – constituted of Yukos.

[g] Controlled by Sibneft (since March 1997 until November 1999) and by Yukos (February 2001–December 2004).

[h] State's share refers to regional not federal government.

[i] Controlled by Yukos (December 1997–2004).

SNG – Surgutneftegaz

TNK – Tyumenskaya Neftyanaya Kompaniya

VNK – Vostochnaya Neftyanaya Kompaniya

VSNK – Vostochno-Sibirskaya Neftyanaya Kompaniya

TNK in 2003, creating TNK-BP – at the time, Russia's third-largest oil company in terms of reserves and crude oil production (see McAllen 2003).[11]

During this period, several key asset mergers also took place that laid the foundation for the consolidation of the industry around five major domestic private oil companies by the end of the 1990s: (1) Lukoil (acquired 100 percent of Komitek); (2) Yukos (acquired 54.2 percent of VNK); (3) TNK (acquired 100 percent of Sidanco and 37.48 percent of Slavneft); (4) Sibneft (acquired 37.48 percent of Slavneft), and (5) Surgutneftegaz (see Table 5.2.).

Some would argue that the Russian oil sector has undergone a fourth stage of transition in its ownership structure – away from rather than toward more privatization – in the mid-2000s under Putin. The strongest evidence to support this, of course, is the state's acquisition of a controlling stake in Yukos at the end of 2004 after the arrest of its CEO Mikhail Khodorkovsky in October 2003 and forced sale of its most valuable subsidiary and covetable asset – Yuganskneftegaz – in December 2004 in a government-controlled auction. The formal buyer was the firm OOO "Baikalfinansgroup," but the clear beneficiary was the state-owned company Rosneft.[12] Just nine months later, Gazprom purchased Sibneft. While these acquisitions are substantial – the portion of total Russian crude oil produced by state-owned companies rose to over a quarter in 2005[13] – they did not amount to the renationalization of the oil sector. Afterall, "[t]he total share of [Yuganskneftegas and Sibneft] in any segment of the country's oil sector [wa]s below 30 percent ... , which is very far from 'centralization' (Woodruff 2007). Nor did increased state ownership over the oil sector appear to have been part of the Putin administration's official energy strategy before 2005.[14] Yet, as discussed in the concluding section, the trend since 2005 has been firmly in the direction of reestablishing state ownership and control over the oil industry. In particular, there was much speculation in the years immediately following that the government planned to acquire both Surgutneftegaz and at least half of TNK-BP's shares, which would effectively transfer another 30 percent of total Russian crude oil production to state-owned companies, bringing the total to approximately 70 percent (Milov 2007). At the same time, a 2005 draft of the new subsoil law barred companies without majority Russian ownership (public or private) from developing oilfields with reserves of over a billion,

---

[11] Prior to this, the only significant project involving foreign investors was the Polar Lights Company, formed jointly by Conoco and Arkhangelskgeologia in 1992 to develop fields in the Timan-Pechora basin in Northwest Russia.

[12] While many expected Gazprom to sweep up the remains of Yukos, fears of lengthy litigation led the largely unknown entity, Baikalfinansgroup, to emerge as the victor (Belton and Faulconbridge 2004). Several days later, news surfaced that Rosneft had bought 100 percent of the Baikalfinansgroup and thus became the new owner of the main production assets of Yukos (Finn 2004).

[13] "In 2003, state-controlled companies accounted for about 16.0 percent of crude production. By the end of 2005, that figure had reached 33.5 percent" (OECD 2006).

[14] In fact, the government approved an official "Energy Strategy" in late 2003 for the period up to 2020 (Decree No.1234) that reaffirmed the role of private VICs.

thereby outlawing foreign ownership of the most productive oilfields (Aron 2006, Grigoryev 2007).

Gas Sector

The privatization process in the gas sector was initially designed to mimic that of the oil sector. It began with a proposal to establish several independent gas companies while preserving the unity and state ownership of the transportation network (Authors' interview with Eskin). A presidential decree (no. 1403) then officially transformed GGK Gazprom into the Joint Stock Society Gazprom (RAO Gazprom) on November 5, 1992, similar to the creation of Rosneft, and was expected to take on an analogous role vis-à-vis the gas industry – that is, to manage the enterprises that comprised production, transportation, and processing (Locatelli 1995). As in the oil sector, what was to constitute the first stage of voucher privatization involved cheaply selling off a portion of Gazprom shares (60 percent) to workers and Russian citizens in proportion to the value of Gazprom's assets on their territories (Sagers 1995). Gazprom employees were given the opportunity to purchase shares equivalent to about 15 percent of the company's equity while inhabitants of the krais, oblasts, and republics where various Gazprom enterprises operated could purchase shares equivalent to about 35 percent of the company's equity.[15] Gazprom itself purchased the remaining 10 percent. At this time, the government also retained a controlling interest (40 percent) in the holding company, which was to be auctioned off during the second stage of privatization.[16]

But that is where the similarities end. Even before privatization began, Gazprom's managers sought to maintain control over this process with the aim of avoiding the break-up that occurred in the oil industry. In particular, they exploited close links to the government via Prime Minister Viktor Chernomyrdin, who was not only the last Soviet Minister of the Gas Industry but also the company's founder and first chief executive,[17] in order to win two key exemptions that would enable Gazprom to maintain its monopoly structure. The first concerned the transferability of shares. While a key part of Russia's voucher privatization required (and indeed celebrated) that no restrictions could be placed on the ability of shareholders to transfer ownership, Gazprom was among a select group of enterprises that attained "a special status ... which required employees to obtain written permission from managers to sell shares to outside investors" (Appel 1997, 1436). In effect,

---

[15] Also similar to the oil sector, two presidential decrees in the 1990s restricted foreign-owned shares in the company to 14 percent (Stern 2005, 171).

[16] According to a September 1994 presidential decree, "some part of this remaining share [was to] be sold on an accelerated timetable" (IEA 1996, 164).

[17] Chernomyrdin served as the Soviet Gas Minister from 1989–1992 and Russia's first Prime Minister from 1992–98.

this gave Gazprom the first right of refusal to buy any shares that would otherwise be sold on the open market.[18] The second concerns the relationship between Gazprom and its subsidiaries. While subsidiaries in the oil sector were considered the "full owners of physical upstream or downstream assets," and thus had full control over these assets, most of Gazprom's subsidiaries became the company's "daughter enterprises" or "legal entities with restricted property rights," which meant that "they [could] not sell, pledge, or otherwise dispose of assets without consent of the owner, Gazprom" (Surovtsev 1996). This did not merely facilitate concentrated ownership over the gas sector but, more importantly, ensured the concentration of ownership in Gazprom's own hands.

The ability of Gazprom's managers to benefit from close links with the government in general and Chenomyrdin's political status in particular, however, did not come without costs. In exchange for preserving its monopoly, Gazprom conceded to a certain degree of continued state interference in its internal affairs. On the one hand, this was a conscious strategy, "codified" in a clandestine agreement between the Russian government and Rem Vyakhirev – Chernomyrdin's handpicked successor to head the gas giant he created.[19] Vyakhirev's first management contract, the full terms of which have never been made public, effectively transferred 35 percent of the government's shares in Gazprom to the company's management to hold "in trust," giving it the right to vote on behalf of the government.[20] Yet this agreement also came with the understanding that the government would reserve the right to exert influence on the company – both via formal mechanisms, such as selecting its CEO and being heavily represented on the Board of Directors, and informal channels via Chernomyrdin himself (Authors' interview with former high-ranking government official no. 1).[21] On the other hand, it was an inevitable (and perhaps, unforeseen) consequence of the fact that, by retaining Gazprom's monopoly, the privatization of the gas sector was effectively the wholesale privatization of a government ministry that generated the bulk of revenue for both the late Soviet and new Russian governments. This public

[18] It is largely for this reason that from 1993–2004, the division of shareholders in the company "changed remarkably little, with the Russian government holding 35–40 percent, Russian legal entities 35–40 percent, Russian individuals (including Gazprom employees) 15–20 percent, and foreigners 10–12 percent" (Stern 2005, 170).

[19] Vyakhirev, who served as Chernomyrdin's first deputy, was appointed Gazprom's CEO in 1992, when Chernomyrdin became Prime Minister. He held this post until 2001, when he was replaced by Alexei Miller.

[20] The agreement to transfer the government's share to Gazprom, signed in secrecy in 1993, was issued as a presidential decree in 1996 (Author's interview with Eskin; see also Stern 2005, 172). Yet the full text of the original agreement was reportedly kept in a location so secret that even First Deputy Prime Minister Nemstov could not locate a copy (Rutland, 1997b).

[21] Vyakhirev's second management contract, negotiated approximately four years later (1998), reinforced this exchange but with slightly better terms for the government.

ministry turned private company incorporated production, transportation, and distribution, sales, research, and even regulation for both domestic markets and, more importantly, international ones.[22]

Thus, in contrast to the oil sector, the main result of voucher privatization in the gas sector at the end of the 1990s was the nominal privatization of Gazprom as a single entity, and thus a cementing rather than severing of ties between this industry and the government. By the end of the 1990s, it was clear that the government wanted to strengthen these ties, for example, by increasing its de facto control over the company's Board of Directors,[23] with the expressed intension of recouping Gazprom's lost assets[24] and opening up the gas sector to greater competition (Authors' interview with Eskin). It was not until 2002, however, that the government formally became the company's majority shareholder via a combination of formally revoking the CEO's (then Vyakhirev) voting control over the existing treasury stocks and its own shares. Majority state ownership was firmly established in 2005 when it bought another 10 percent via the majority state-owned company Rosneftegaz (Gazprom 2006, 68).

THE EMERGENCE OF A STRONG FISCAL REGIME

For most of the 1990s Russia's fiscal regime experienced little substantive reform. On the taxation side, this amounted to an "actual tax burden [that] was stifling" (EIU 2007, 36) and a tax system that suffered from high levels of instability and rampant evasion. Yeltsin arbitrarily set tax rates for industry, which he often raised, and revenue sharing for regions by decree. Not surprisingly, these official tax rates were rarely, if ever, observed in practice, and tax collection receipts were abysmally low as a result (see Gustafson 1999, Chapter 9, Shleifer and Treisman 2000, Chapter 6).[25] Instead, enterprise owners and managers as well as regional leaders engaged in ongoing negotiations with the government to determine their respective tax burdens (see Easter 2002). Implicit subsidies via tax arrears and offsets thus became part of the natural terrain in the Russian economic landscape (see Mikesell and Mullins 2001, 559–60). The highly lucrative and concentrated industries in the energy sector also followed this pattern whereby arbitrary and excessive tax rates led to high rates of evasion. Nonetheless, the oil and gas sectors made up the bulk of the country's tax revenue; the former alone accounted for approximately one-fourth of all explicit tax revenues in 1998 (*Russian Economic Trends*

---

[22] Gazprom is not merely the world's largest natural gas company; it owns the world's largest gas pipeline network, totaling over 155,000 km.

[23] In 1999, the government demanded that its representatives on Gazprom's Board increase from 4 to 5 out of 11. In 2000, Putin replaced Chernomyrdin as the Chairman of the Board with Dmitry Medvedev.

[24] For example, Gazprom bought back Purgaz from Itera (*NewsBase*, March 1, 2002).

[25] According to the IMF (2000c, 69, 71), as of January 1, 2000, the value of unpaid taxes at the consolidated level (federal and regional governments) was 8.3 percent of GDP.

1998, 6) while the latter contributed the lion's share of implicit tax revenues via energy subsidies to consumers. At the same time, the Yeltsin administration expanded the extensive benefits in kind – a welfare system that Russia inherited from the Soviet period – a significant portion of which continued to be paid through extrabudgetary funds. In 1998, for example, "the pension fund, employment fund, social insurance fund, and medical insurance fund accounted for expenditures equaling 9 percent of GDP," or roughly "63 percent of direct general expenditures" (Mikesell and Mullins 2001, 552). As a result, by the end of the 1990s, the country had a huge budget deficit and was becoming more dependent on the energy sector to finance government spending.

This situation, however, changed dramatically after the financial crisis of 1998. Despite nearly a decade of failed tax reform, by 2002 Russia had adopted and enacted a new tax code that was designed to broaden the tax base by increasing quasi-voluntary compliance across sectors so as to reduce the country's fiscal reliance on indirect and implicit taxation as well as the oil sector.[26] As of 2005, this tax system was not only stable but also becoming increasingly effective. Alongside these dramatic improvements to its taxation system, Russia also underwent significant expenditure reform aimed at placing formal limits on government spending and increasing the transparency of budgetary operations, and thereby further reducing the size of the public sector and the prominence of quasi-fiscal activities (QFAs). Most notably, this included maintaining a budget surplus since 2000 – a practice that was codified in 2002 and then further institutionalized with the creation of its OSF in 2004 – and actively "dismantl[ing] the massive system of state-administered, untargeted social benefits and privileges to which more than a quarter of the population remained entitled" (Cook 2007b, 182).

The emergence of a strong fiscal regime in Russia from 1999–2005 generates two sets of interrelated empirical puzzles. First, what explains this radical shift in Russia's fiscal regime? We argue that this outcome can be attributed directly to the particular institutional incentives that private domestic ownership (P_1) generates via the mechanisms identified in Chapter 3: high transaction costs (TCs), low societal expectations, and explicit bargaining.

Second, why did Russia launch a significant reform agenda in the throes of an economic crisis brought on largely by a steep decline in world oil prices and how was it able to successfully implement and sustain these reforms during the unprecedented boom in oil prices that followed? The timing of fiscal

---

[26] This Tax Code consists of two parts. Part I, adopted in July 1998 and enacted in January 1999, covers administrative and procedural matters, including the introduction of new taxes and the protection of taxpayers' rights. Part II, adopted in August 2000, amended in November and December 2001, and enacted in 2001 and 2002, covers specifications on various taxes, including the value added tax (VAT), corporate profits tax (CIT), personal income tax (PIT), and social tax. (For an overview, see OECD 2001, 115–44.) Our analysis concerns Part II as well as subsequent changes to Part I.

reforms in Russia is particularly puzzling in light of the conventional resource curse literature, which tells us to expect precisely the opposite behavior. Busts are assumed to make leaders in mineral-rich states more inclined to eschew institution building, particularly concerning taxation, and to incur significant debt in order to sustain public spending rather than reduce expenditures (see Chaudhry 1989, Karl 1997, Shafer 1994). Yet, Russia not only responded swiftly and decisively to the commodity bust that triggered a financial crisis[27] at the end of 1998 by devaluing its currency, placing a moratorium on external debt payments, and reducing government spending rather than resorting to uncontrolled monetary expansion; it also "finally made a commitment to *real* tax reform" aimed at increasing quasi-voluntary compliance across sectors (Authors' interview with Shatalov). Commodity booms are assumed to be equally bad for institution building because they simultaneously reinforce the myopia endemic to leaders of mineral-rich states and make it impossible for them to resist overextending the state, largely via a bloated and ineffective bureaucracy whose primary function is to distribute the windfalls from high prices (see Karl 1997, Robinson et al. 2004). Yet when oil prices began to recover in 1999, jumped by over $10/barrel in 2000, and then continued to rise steadily from 2001–2005,[28] the Russian government not only continued to pursue its timeline for comprehensive tax reform but also expanded its fiscal reform agenda to include placing formal limits on its ability to spend its oil-induced bonanza.

The combination of high TCs, low societal expectations, and explicit bargaining under P_1 again serves to illuminate why such unexpected outcomes occurred. First, high TCs meant that the bust presented an opportunity for changing a suboptimal status quo. As alluded to above, Russia's tax system during the first decade of independence amounted to a series of informal exchanges from which both the government and the private domestic oil companies incurred significant losses in time, effort, and revenue. Yet neither set of actors seemed willing or able to escape this vicious cycle and embrace reform. This situation changed almost immediately after the financial crisis hit, reflected in the protracted formal negotiations over a new tax code that began in the fall of 1998. Second, low societal expectations made it politically feasible for the Russian government both to institute a broad-based tax regime and to institutionalize reductions in public spending, even as the oil sector experienced a sustained boom. In contrast, as we demonstrate in Chapter 4, its FSU counterparts that adopted S_1 (i.e., Turkmenistan and Uzbekistan) felt greater societal pressure to reduce taxation and increase public spending during this period. Finally, the public nature of negotiations over tax reform and the creation of a stabilization fund meant that reversing course was more difficult – because it required an equally public process.

---

[27] The 1998 financial crisis was also precipitated by the recession that spread across Asia in 1997.

[28] According to IMF (2006b, 6), the oil boom began in 2000.

Taxation

In sharp contrast to the 1990s, the tax regime that emerged in Russia at the beginning of the 2000s was thus clearly designed to broaden the government's tax base and to decrease its reliance on the mineral sector. Most importantly, in contrast to its counterparts in the other petroleum-rich countries of the FSU, the Russian government produced a unified Tax Code – that is, one that integrated the mineral sector with all other economic sectors.

Among the central features of the new Russian Tax Code were flat rates for personal (13 percent) and corporate income tax (reduced from 35 to 24 percent), a unified social tax (UST) on employers[29] (capped at 35 percent), and a simplified tax system for small and medium enterprises (SMEs) that allows them to pay the lesser of 6 percent of gross sales or 15 percent of profits. Corporate income tax (hereafter, CIT) rate reductions were accompanied by the "abolition of numerous loopholes" as well as "improved provisions for the deductibility of regular business expenses" (EIU 2007, 36). At the same time, individuals previously exempted from paying personal income tax (hereafter, PIT) (for example, military and law enforcement officials) lost their exempt status, and tax concessions for corporate entities (which had proliferated under Yeltsin in the 1990s) were eliminated. All these reforms are primarily aimed at bolstering government revenue from taxation in the long run by increasing both the rate of compliance among existing taxpayers and the number of new taxpayers over time.[30] Rates for both PIT and CIT, for example, were deliberately set at the highest rate that experts deemed individuals or entities would be willing to pay, which in turn corresponded to the "effective tax rate," or what the Tax Ministry was able to collect in the status quo (Author's interview with Shatalov; see also, for example, Stepanyan 2003, 17). Both the Tax Ministry and the newly created Ministry of Economic Development and Trade (MEDT),[31] moreover, anticipated that this would lead to a decline in revenue from the CIT in the short term (Authors' interviews with Dvorkovich, with Reznikov, and with Vyugin). Similarly, both the UST and the simplified tax system for SMEs were part of a conscious strategy to give employers a greater incentive not only to hire additional workers, but also to reduce the number of employees paid "off the books" so as to avoid payroll taxes (Authors' interview with Shatalov).

These core features were accompanied by similar efforts to reduce reliance on both indirect and mineral sector taxation over time. As in other parts of the FSU, the two largest sources of indirect taxation in Russia prior to the new Tax Code were turnover taxes and the value added tax (VAT) – each of

---

[29] Formerly, employers were required to contribute to four types of social funds on behalf of each employee: pension, social insurance, medical, and unemployment.

[30] Regarding CIT, the Tax Code contains several additional benefits, such as clarifying the definition of profit and the rules governing both depreciation and transfer pricing (see IMF 2006b, 14).

[31] The MEDT was created in 2000.

which played a critical role in tax collection and government revenues during the first decade of independence at the subnational (local and regional) and federal levels, respectively (see Mertens and Tesche 2002, Struyk et al. 1996). And yet, both underwent reform at the beginning of the Russian Federation's second decade of independence that significantly jeopardized the size of their contribution. By 2003, all turnover taxes were eliminated, including the two most important ones in terms of their contribution to the local, particularly municipal, budgets – the social infrastructure maintenance tax (1.5 percent) and road users' tax (2.5 percent).[32] The standard VAT rate (initially set at 28 percent and then lowered to 20 percent in 1993) was reduced from 20 to 18 percent in January 2004.

Again the government was motivated by a desire to expand the tax base and increase the rate of taxpayers' compliance, even if it suffered a fiscal loss in the short-term. The turnover tax is widely recognized – both within Russia and more generally – as a disincentive to business growth and innovation, particularly in manufacturing, because it deliberately subjects more sophisticated products to heavier taxation. By eliminating it, the government sought instead to create a further incentive for business growth and innovation, thereby diversifying the economy (Author's interview with Dvorkovich). In addition, the MEDT openly acknowledged that many existing businesses hid their activities from the government because the turnover tax was too high (ibid). Lowering the VAT rate was similarly seen as a mechanism for stimulating business growth and investment – domestic as well as foreign – across sectors (ibid.). More generally, Chapter 25 of the Tax Code was aimed at broadening the tax base over the long term by promoting private investment (for details, see World Bank 2003d, 10).

The final relevant – and for some, most important – aspect of Russian tax reform we must consider is mineral sector taxation. Unlike most mineral-rich states, including its counterparts in the FSU, Russia has never created a stand-alone tax system for the mineral sector.[33] Thus, the aforementioned changes in tax rates also apply to corporate and individual entities in the petroleum sector. Nonetheless, by necessity there are also specific sectoral taxes (such as for extraction and export). Here, efforts have been directed less at lowering the mineral sector's tax burden or increasing compliance (which is already addressed by changes to CIT and VAT), and more at reducing Russia's budgetary dependence on the energy sector, and hence its instability, in both the short and long term (Authors' interview with former deputy minister of finance). On the taxation side, these efforts are embodied in the introduction of the natural resources extraction tax (TENR) and, on the spending side, by the continued commitment to maintaining a budget surplus, which we discuss in the subsequent section.

---

[32] In 2001, the social infrastructure maintenance tax was abolished and the road users' tax was reduced to 1 percent.

[33] For example, it has also strongly resisted instituting a PSA regime, in stark contrast to both Kazakhstan and Azerbaijan (for details, see Bayulgen 2003, Chapter 5).

As outlined in Chapter 26 of the Russian Tax Code, on January 1, 2002, the TENR (a.k.a., the mineral extraction tax, MET) replaced three existing taxes: the use of subsoil resources, the mineral replacement tax, and the excise tax on oil and gas condensate (for details, see Borodin and Smirnov 2003). This new tax is noteworthy not merely because it streamlined tax payments for the mineral sector, but also because it is calculated based on a fixed tax rate (in Russian rubles) per ton of extracted mineral and then this rate is multiplied by a coefficient reflecting changes in the world market price (adjusted quarterly) for the mineral in question. This had three intended effects (Authors' interview with Dvorkovich). First, by reducing the number of taxes and setting a flat rate at approximately the same level that current taxpayers were actually paying (i.e., "adopting the *de facto* rather than the *de jure* collection rate"), it would increase compliance. Second, by changing the basis of mineral taxation from trade to actual production, it would eliminate the ability of companies to utilize transfer pricing to reduce their tax payments. Third, by pegging this tax payment to the world market price, it would both reduce the impact of market volatility on the government's budget and enable the government to capture a larger share of the industry's profits when its rents were excessive.[34]

Perhaps even more significant than the intended effect of the Russian government's tax reform efforts since the late 1990s is that it has largely achieved its lofty goals. The results as of 2005 indicate that the Tax Code has been stable and – perhaps largely for this reason – has both boosted government revenue from direct taxes and increased compliance since its adoption. As several analysts pointed out, the success of the Tax Code was predicated on individuals and companies taking these new rules of the game as given, and "in Russia three years is sufficient to create such a perception" (Authors' interview with Ustinov). Otherwise, they would have little incentive to comply. Unless they believe their payroll and profits tax rates will remain stable, for example, most SMEs are probably better off leaving some of their activities in the shadow economy. And yet, the evidence suggests that tax reform had an immediate and rather dramatic effect on reducing the size of the shadow economy that appears to have been sustained over time.[35]

The stability of Russia's tax regime can be measured not just in terms of whether or how much the new Tax Code has changed, but whether these changes have moved fiscal reform in the same direction. In contrast to the 1990s, during which tax rates constantly fluctuated, there is no question that the new Tax Code was stable in the early- to mid-2000s. Since

---

[34] This latter goal is also served by changes to the export tariffs levied on oil (effective since August 2004), which set a rate of 35 percent for the excess over $15–20/barrel, 45 percent for the excess over $20–25/barrel and 65 percent for the excess over $25/barrel (IMF 2006b, 14).

[35] Already in 2002, the Aton investment group attributed the shrinking of the shadow economy from 45 percent in 1998 to 37 percent in 2002 to tax reform (Levinsky 2002). Another estimate finds that the shadow economy declined from approximately 50 percent of GDP in the mid-1990s to about 25 percent in 2008 (Lissovolik 2008).

its adoption (1998–2000) and implementation (2001–2002), the initial flat rates it set for PIT, CIT, and SMEs have remained unchanged. VAT rates have also remained steady – particularly in contrast to the other parts of the FSU, whether petroleum-rich or poor. In addition, the UST rate was reduced in 2005 from 35.6 percent to 26 percent to further lower the tax burden on employers – particularly in the SME sector – and thereby increase their incentive to both hire more workers and pay higher salaries (Authors' interview with Dvorkovich). While several amendments have been made to the new Tax Code, there is no comparison to the 1990s when "one journalist compared early Russian tax legislation to a weekly newspaper, so often were amendments introduced" (Samoylenko 2003, 21). These amendments, more-over, have been directed at either "work[ing] out the bugs out in the Code," as the government promised at the start of the reform process (Authors' interview with Ustinov),[36] or restricting the tax administration's authority by bolstering taxpayers' rights (see Samoylenko 2006, 1). The nature of these changes thus underscores the government's commitment to fostering a stable tax regime. As one technical advisor who has worked closely on the development of the Tax Code recounted, "proposals that either revoke prior reforms or which hamper the potential for future reform are being aggres-sively resisted" (Conrad 2005).

The fact that these changes have been directed primarily toward safeguard-ing taxpayers' rights further bolsters our contention that Russia is more likely to build a tax regime that is based on quasi-voluntary compliance. In the early 1990s, the only tax law that remained stable was the one that "provided unreasonable and overly broad powers to the tax authorities, virtually depriv-ing taxpayers of the right to defend themselves" (Samoylenko 2003, 20). Not surprisingly, this contributed to a great deal of arbitrariness in the tax police's enforcement of various tax laws and high levels of tax evasion because it was often more cost-effective to pay bribes than taxes (ibid). By the end of 2005, however, the Russian Parliament (Duma) had approved several amendments to Part I of the Tax Code that shifted the balance of power decisively in the taxpayers' favor (for details, see Samoylenko 2006, 1).

Assessing the effectiveness of Russia's tax regime is somewhat more com-plicated. The clearest measure is whether tax collection rates have actually increased. Yet, there are several problems with using this metric: (1) the expectation that revenues would actually fall during the first 1–2 years; (2) it only provides a short-term indicator whereas the Tax Code is part of a long-term strategy; and (3) economic prosperity in first half of 2000s makes it difficult to establish that the new Tax Code itself is primarily responsible for increased tax collection. With these caveats in mind, therefore, we look not just at revenue from direct and indirect taxes in absolute terms, but their growth relative to their own previous share of total tax revenue and to one

---

[36] Amendments were made to both the CIT and VAT in the summer of 2005, for example, to "eliminate certain gaps in this legislation" (Zaitseva and Nikolaeva 2005).

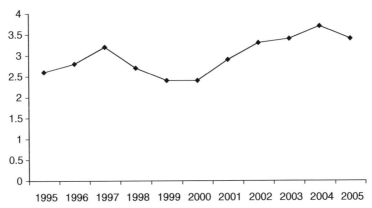

FIGURE 5.1. PIT as a Percentage of GDP, 1995–2005.
Source: Ministry of Finance.

another's. We also attempt to tie these shifts in sources of government revenue to an increase in both the rate of taxpayers' compliance and the number of taxpayers.

We start with direct taxes because one of our main predictions is that Russia should be building a Tax Code that relies on a combination of direct and indirect taxes across sectors. Since Russia's tax regime previously relied primarily on indirect taxes, this necessitates a shift both away from indirect taxes (i.e., VAT) and toward direct taxes (i.e., PIT and CIT). The empirical evidence generally supports this expectation. First, the contribution of direct taxes to total government revenue and GDP increased steadily between 2000 (when the new Tax Code was introduced) and 2005. Changes in the contribution of PIT have been perhaps the most dramatic and surprising. Tax receipts from PIT increased by just over 25 percent in 2001 – the first year after the new Tax Code went into effect – by 24.6 percent in 2002, 15.2 percent in 2003, and 26.1 percent in 2004 (Rabushka 2005) – and its contribution increased from 2.6 percent of GDP in 1995 to 3.7 percent in 2004 (see Figure 5.1). Second, the share of both PIT and CIT has increased relative to that of the VAT. While the contribution of VAT did not decrease dramatically, it also did not increase; rather, it stabilized at approximately 7 percent of GDP. As some have argued, the fact that it has remained steady should be interpreted as a sign that Russia's VAT has reached a comparable level of efficiency and stability to that of OECD countries with established VAT (Mertens and Tesche 2002, 93).[37]

The relative rise in the share of direct taxes, moreover, has occurred alongside a significant improvement in the rate of compliance. A 2005 IMF study estimates that the compliance rate for the top two income brackets

[37] By contrast, in the 1990s the VAT as a percentage of GDP fluctuated widely – from 12.4 percent in 1992 to 5.9 percent in 1995 – which some attribute directly to the lack of administrative reform concerning tax collection during this period (Mertens and Tesche 2002, 91).

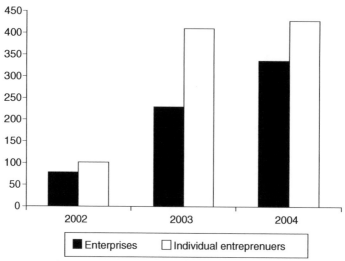

FIGURE 5.2. Number of SMEs Using Simplified Tax System.
Source: Ministry of Finance.

rose considerably – by 17 percentage points – between 2000 and 2001 while remaining constant for the bottom income bracket (Ivanova et al. 2005).[38] This occurred despite the fact that during this period, "gross incomes for this group in fact fell quite strongly" (ibid., 431). Subsequent studies have confirmed these earlier findings – that is, that flat tax reform has been instrumental in decreasing tax evasion in Russia and that greater fiscal revenues since 2001 are linked to increased voluntary tax compliance and reporting (Gorodnichenko et al. 2008).

The growth of SMEs since 2001 has also been much greater than many of the Tax Code's designers anticipated. On the one hand, this is clearly a response to the simplified tax regime and reduced tax burden. In short, the number of businesses actually utilizing the simplified tax system has expanded exponentially since 2002 (see Figure 5.2), causing an explosive growth in budget revenues from this sector of the economy.[39] As a result, the share of SMEs' contribution to Russia's GDP doubled in just three years – rising from less than 6 percent in 2002 to 12 percent in 2005. SMEs received an additional boost from the lowering and then elimination of turnover taxes, which stimulated growth by "reduc[ing] the tax burden by 8 percent of added value in the industrial sector, 7.3 percent in construction, and 5.8 percent in transportation" (Vasilieva et al. 2003, 13). Yet, it is also a product of the government's

[38] This is not surprising since compliance rates were already quite high (over 70 percent) for this group. Arguably, this was also not the group that the tax reforms were targeting to increase the overall rate of compliance.

[39] According to the Ministry of Finance, federal budget revenues rose from 7.9 billion RUB in 2002 to 30.7 billion RUB in 2005.

deliberate attempts to improve the business environment for SMEs. In 2003, for example, Russia was the only FSU country (aside from Moldova) that ranked among the top 20 reformers in terms of making it easier to start a business by reducing the number of procedures (*Doing Business in 2005*, 18–20) and "creating single access points for entrepreneurs" (ibid., 21) – both of which contributed directly to a rise in the number of SME registrations (ibid., 23). It also ranked alongside the U.S. as among the easiest countries with regard to procedures for hiring, which has contributed to the rise in employment for existing SMEs (ibid., 28). And in 2004, Russia was among only nine countries – none of them in the FSU – that significantly "eased business entry" for the second year in a row (*Doing Business in 2006*, 10).

Not everyone, however, is convinced that these positive results can be attributed to the new Tax Code. Critics are particularly skeptical that the flat tax on personal and corporate income has actually contributed to the rise in government revenue – largely because, due to high rates of evasion, the majority of taxpayers were already paying taxes at the lowest rate (13 percent and 24 percent, respectively) before the reform (see Vasilieva et al. 2003) and because this revenue boost occurred in the context of robust economic growth and high oil prices (see Gaddy and Gale 2005). Yet this line of criticism ignores two important facts: first, that the new flat rates were deliberately set at the effective rate in order to expand the tax base (as discussed earlier); and second, that a rise in GDP alone cannot account for the documented increase in taxpayers' compliance (see above). It also fails to account for the continued rise in PIT in 2003 despite the decline in other revenue sources (Ivanova et al. 2005, 412). Moreover, these same critics also acknowledge that the tax base of both PIT and CIT has indeed expanded due to other fiscally related reforms, including increased wages due to the UST and improvements in tax collection efforts via better enforcement mechanisms and the protection of taxpayers' rights (see Gaddy and Gale 2005, Vasilieva et al. 2003; see also Ivanova et al. 2005).

Another central component of assessing the effectiveness of Russia's new tax regime is the degree to which it has undergone administrative reform since 2001. By all accounts, Russia has indeed endeavored to institute the fundamental features of a modern tax system. Among these are "the introduction of a common taxpayers ID number," withholding "all taxes on income paid to private individuals ... at the source," and the authorization of "tax audits when sufficient evidence of a tax or nontax crime was available" (Gaddy and Gale 2005, 986). And there is some evidence that it is working. The aforementioned 2005 IMF study, for example, also included survey data suggesting that one of the factors motivating the increase in taxpayers' compliance since 2000 is the *perception* that others are also paying their taxes, which may in turn be related to the *reality* that enforcement has improved (Ivanova et al. 2003, 431).[40]

---

[40] Over 60 percent of those surveyed responded that "the perception that no one else pays taxes" was either important or very important in their own decision to comply.

Our other principal expectation regarding the direction of tax reform is that Russia should be reducing its reliance on the mineral sector over time. On the face of it, this expectation is clearly unrealized. There is little doubt that the contribution of the oil sector to the federal budget increased during the first half of the 2000s – especially given the reduced percentage of mineral taxes going to regional budgets since 2002[41] and the unprecedented rise in oil prices since 1999. The newly introduced TENR is by far the largest contributor of all the natural resource taxes – comprising almost 10 percent of the total budget in 2003[42] – and, although this tax includes all commercial minerals (that is, not just hydrocarbons), oil companies pay the lion's share (Borodin and Smirnov 2003). The windfall tax in particular has resulted in a steep rise in fiscal revenue from the oil sector since 1999. The taxation of the oil sector, however, is by no means excessive by international standards (Ahrend 2006). Moreover, while "the sensitivity of revenues with respect to changes in the oil prices has increased ... for prices above US$24 per barrel ... , the sensitivity of revenues to oil prices below US$24 has decreased substantially" (IMF 2006b, 50). Thus, while the new tax has enabled the government to capture excess rent from the oil industry in good times, it was also designed to help insulate the government in bad times. The initial rationale for reducing the regional government's share of mineral taxes, for example, was to avoid inflationary pressures by transferring this "windfall" to the OSF (Kurlyandskaya 2007).

Expenditure

The system of expenditures in Russia also underwent a transformation after 1998 aimed at establishing fiscal stability and increasing transparency. Thus, although Russia's budget system in the 1990s was already considered to have undergone significantly more reform than that of its energy-rich counterparts in Uzbekistan and Turkmenistan (see, for example, Ebrill and Havrylyshyn 1999, Mikesell and Mullins 2001), by 2005 there was no comparison.

First and foremost, the government not only adopted an explicit policy of budgetary surplus, but sought to codify and institutionalize this practice. To enforce fiscal discipline, for example, the 1999 Federal Budget Law stipulated "that contracts signed by spending units that exceed budgetary limits [would] not be considered legal obligations of the government" (Mikesell and Mullins 2001, 562). At this time, Russia also began to establish an effective system to monitor the budgetary process, which included introducing an independent audit procedure and elevating the Ministry of Finance's authority over spending ministries, as well as making the budget available to the legislature for

---

[41] Until 2002 mining regions received 60 percent of revenue from taxes on "mining operations" but the percentage going to regional budgets has been decreased each year since then (Kurlyandskaya 2007).

[42] Compare this to the taxes it replaced, which provided 5.65 percent of the federal budget (Borodin and Smirnov 2003).

review and approval (Jarmuzek et al. 2006, 15–16; see also IMF 2004c). To gain a sense of the significance of these reforms, one only needs to compare Russia to its former Soviet counterparts. For example, aside from its obvious contributions to fiscal stability and transparency, assigning supervisory power to the finance ministry is noteworthy because, as of mid-2005, Russia was the only country in the FSU (other than Moldova) to have done this.[43] Russia is also unique in being the only FSU country, as of 2006, in which the legislature had any real budgetary oversight (see, for example, IBP 2008, 22, 26).

The 2002 Federal Budget Law – the first to "[envision] a surplus in the history of the Russian Federation" (EIU 2001b, 5) – went even further toward institutionalizing these fiscal policies by providing for the creation of a financial reserve fund (*Rezervny Fond*) into which this surplus would be placed and stipulating its use for "financing the federal budget deficit and repaying external debt" (Authors' interview with Vyugin). This was followed roughly two years later by the establishment of the OSF, which was intended to "sterilize the economy" from the impact of booming oil prices while also "provid[ing] another layer of protection" against the surplus being spent "in an arbitrary or superfluous manner" (Authors' interview with Illarionov). Indeed, explicit rules governing the OSF were designed precisely to restrict the government's use of the budgetary surplus generated from high oil prices to pay off external debt (ibid.; see also, OECD 2004). As several government officials remarked during the period leading up to its formal establishment, the OSF was also intended to constrain the Duma from controlling how the proceeds from the boom were spent, based on the perception that otherwise "the deputies ... [would] direct extra funds from the budget for their own populist goals" (*Izvestiya* 2003).

Until the end of 2005, these formal limits on government spending and borrowing were very effective. A clear indication of this is that, despite the broad economic recovery that occurred across the FSU after 1999, Russia was the only country with a budgetary surplus from 2000–2004 (OECD 2005, 60). As a result, public debt as a share of GDP declined substantially beginning in 1999 (IMF 2005d, 48). In addition, from 2002–2004 Russia took full advantage of its improved fiscal position "not only to remain current on its debt ... , but also to start buying back debt head of schedule" such that by 2005 Russia could pay off all of its outstanding debt to the International Monetary Fund (EIU 2007, 55). Thus, both the commitment to maintaining a fiscal surplus and to using windfall revenues to manage debt "since 2000 have drastically improved Russia's debt profile and have practically eliminated the debt sustainability problem that was a major macroeconomic and fiscal problem for Russia in the 1990s" (World Bank 2005d, 3). At the same time, it has kept expenditures under control. "Despite windfall revenues, federal government spending since 1999 has remained in the range of 16–18 percent

---

[43] It is also noteworthy because in the Soviet Union, the Ministry of Finance played a passive role in this regard (Diamond 2002, 8–9).

TABLE 5.3. *Government Finances, 2001–2005 (percent of GDP)*

	2001	2002	2003	2004	2005
Federal Budget					
Expenditure	14.8	18.9	17.1	15.5	16.2
Revenue	17.9	20.5	19.5	20.3	23.7
Balance	3.1	1.7	2.4	4.9	7.5
Consolidated Budget					
Expenditure	27.1	31.6	29.9	27.5	27.4
Revenue	30.0	32.5	31.2	31.9	35.1
Balance	3.0	0.9	1.3	4.5	7.7

Source: EIU 2006b, 66.

of GDP" (World Bank 2005e, 9) and actually declined from 2002–2004. (See Table 5.3 for details.)

In this regard, Russia's OSF deserves particular emphasis. Although not the first legal expression of Russia's commitment to fiscal discipline since 2000, it has most overtly and effectively institutionalized the Russian government's practice of responding to oil export windfalls by saving the unexpected revenue gains rather than by decreasing nonoil revenue or increasing expenditures, as is commonly the case in mineral-rich states (IMF 2005d, 58). By the end of 2005, the OSF had accumulated more than double its target of 500 billion RUB (including the unspent surplus from 2003 – transferred to the Fund in 2004 – and unspent surplus from 2004),[44] and had spent only a tiny fraction of this toward anything other than servicing its foreign debt (IMF 2006b, 15).[45] As a result, the OSF – along with its predecessor, the *Rezervny Fond* – has played a key role in stabilizing the federal budget, controlling inflation, and thereby, sustaining economic growth. According to the World Bank (2005e, 8), for example, "[t]he Stabilization Fund continues to be far and away the most important economic policy instrument for limiting [inflationary] pressures." Russia's initial success at establishing an effective NRF, moreover, makes it an anomaly among mineral-rich states – both in the FSU and throughout the developing world (Weinthal and Jones Luong 2006b).

A large part of the OSF's effectiveness is due to its structure. As we argue in Chapter 2, the degree to which stabilization funds actually serve their intended purpose depends on several factors, including most importantly whether they are subjected to a formal oversight mechanism, clearly demarcate spending priorities, and are integrated into the formal budget process. Prior to its transformation at the end of 2007, Russia's OSF met all of these requirements. It

[44] The OSF reached 832 billion RUB (4.0 percent of GDP) by the end of August 2005 (World Bank 2005e, 8).
[45] 30 million RUB was transferred to the Pension Fund.

automatically accumulated all "surplus revenues" – that is, tax revenue from the aforementioned mineral sector taxes (TENR and export tariffs) – "above that which would accrue at an oil price of USD 20/barrel (Urals)" and by law could only be used "to finance the federal deficit arising as a result of oil prices below the baseline USD 20 level" until it had amassed 500 billion RUB (OECD 2004). The legislation that created the OSF also stipulated that its revenues could only "be invested [in the] government securities" of foreign states that met certain criteria, such that doing so would serve to stabilize the exchange rate (ibid.).[46] In addition, the executive body charged with managing the Fund – the Ministry of Finance – was required to report to the Duma on both a quarterly and annual basis (IMF 2006b).

Yet, perhaps the most striking feature of the OSF was its relative transparency. In contrast to most other mineral-rich states, where the establishment of an NRF has led to the creation of a "dual budget" (Davis et al. 2003), Russia's stabilization fund was an explicit part of the government's annual budget. This means that it has been subjected to the same rigorous budgetary process described above, which also includes a relatively high degree of public scrutiny (for details, see IBP 2008). Russia ranked higher than any of its FSU counterparts, for example, on the Open Budget Index for 2006 (ibid., 30).

Second, the Russian government's reform policy agenda after 1998 included reducing further the size of the public sector in the economic as well as the social sphere while continuing to expand the role of the private sector in both. Along with most other transition economies (except for Turkmenistan and Uzbekistan), in the 1990s Russia's public sector underwent a significant downsizing according to "[c]onventional measures of government size – aggregate government spending ... in relation to GDP and the share of public employment" (Gupta et al. 2003, 559). This is largely due to the fact that Russia is among a handful of countries in the FSU wherein the reduction of public expenditures during this period was actually accompanied by a decline in public employment (Mikesell and Mullins 2001, 551). Public employment declined, in short, because it became increasingly less attractive relative to the private sector. Rather than guaranteeing state jobs and continuously increasing salaries for state employees, as occurred in Turkmenistan and Uzbekistan, the Russian government allowed labor markets to emerge in the 1990s (see, for example, Foley 1997, Kapeliouchnikov 1999) that facilitated the reallocation of labor from less productive sectors (such as, agriculture) to more productive sectors (such as, manufacturing and services) after 1998. As we will elaborate upon later in this chapter, this is one of the main reasons why the manufacturing sector – against all odds – contributed to Russia's sustained economic growth in the first half of the 2000s (see Desai and Goldberg 2007, World Bank 2007).

---

[46] For more detail, see "On Amendments and Addenda to the Budget Code of the Russian Federation in regard to the Creation of the Stabilization Fund of the Russian Federation," December 2003.

The size of the public sector has also shrunk owing to some fundamental changes in the Russian government's approach to public investment. In the mid-1990s, the Yeltsin government made significant progress in contracting the scope of government activity – both by reducing overall size of government spending and by limiting the federal government's role as a source of public financing (see World Bank 2001, 8). At approximately 40 percent of GDP, for example, average general government outlays in Russia from 1995–2000 were "virtually the same as OECD average expenditure" from 1965–2000 (Sharipova 2001, 29). After 1999, the Putin administration began to deepen these reforms. It actively sought to cut total public expenditures by more than half as well as to further reduce the federal government's contribution to public investment and was largely successful in doing both (Authors' interview with Illarionov). Expenditures declined by almost 10 percentage points between 1998 and 2002 (see Table 5.3 for details) and the federal government's contribution to public investment "fell sharply from 35 percent in 1997 to 22 percent in 2000" (World Bank 2001, 8). From 2001–2004, public investment averaged around 18 percent of GDP, "which is significantly below the shares found in other fast-growing countries in Eastern Europe or Asia and well below the OECD average of around 22 percent" (Ahrend 2006, 99–100). During this period, the Russian government also focused its efforts on improving the efficiency of public investment so as to minimize government outlays, which included some of the aforementioned changes to the budgetary process (see Sharipova 2001). Perhaps most indicative of the government's approach to public investment, however, is the virtual absence of federally-financed large public works or national prestige projects, even after oil prices rebounded in 2000. In fact, this makes Russia noteworthy not only among its petroleum-rich counterparts in the FSU, particularly Turkmenistan and Uzbekistan, but also among petroleum-rich countries throughout the developing world, where such investment projects are commonplace (see Chapter 3 for details).

As the public sector continued to shrink, moreover, the size of the private sector continued to grow. At the end of the 1990s, Russia already had the largest private sector in the FSU at 70 percent of GDP (Gupta et al. 2003, 568).[47] In addition to the tax reforms described above, continued growth in the first half of the 2000s was the product of several deliberate macroeconomic policies designed to promote the private sector. At the top of the list was stimulating private sector investment by deregulating the business environment. Indeed, data from business surveys suggests that the investment environment improved substantially between 1999 and 2002 (for details, see World Bank 2003c, 15–16).[48] An independent (and perhaps more compelling) indicator of

---

[47] Next highest were Kazakhstan and Ukraine at 60 percent, and the lowest was Turkmenistan (Gupta et al. 2003, 568).

[48] Thus is not to say that there is no need for further improvement. At the end of 2005, for example, "[t]he Russian business environment was significantly worse than in the most developed benchmark countries (South Korea, Spain, Germany)" (Desai and Goldberg 2007, 34).

this is the fact that actual rates of private investment, which "fell continuously" from 1990–1998, increased sharply from 2000–2005 (Ahrend 2006, 109), though the initial spike in 2000–2001 is obviously related to the devaluation of the ruble in 1999 as well. The Russian government also vigorously pursued financial sector reform aimed at strengthening the banking system (Authors' interview with Vyugin; see also, World Bank 2003c, 17–18) – particularly to provide the private sector with greater access to credit (see Berglof and Lehmann 2008). In short, over the long term, the Putin administration was committed "to develop[ing] all aspects of the economy in partnership with private businesses," which underscored the necessity of building a robust private sector (Authors' interview with Illarionov). As of 2008, these efforts seemed to be paying off. Increased access to bank-issued credit, for example, which was virtually absent outside Moscow prior to 2000, has proven to be "an important engine of growth" at the regional level (Berkowitz and DeJong 2008).

Shrinking the size of the state while supporting private sector growth also contributed to the Russian government's efforts to reduce the use of QFAs. In the 1990s, Russia's economy was famously described as "virtual" because it relied so heavily on noncash transactions (that is, promissory notes, tax offsets, and the accumulation of arrears) that acted as hefty implicit subsidies for enterprises that did not produce any real value (Gaddy and Ickes 1998).[49] By some estimates, these implicit subsidies accounted for approximately 40 percent of GDP in 1998 (Gupta et al. 2003, 565). Sure enough, "the primary source of QFAs in the Russian economy" prior to 1998 was the state-owned electricity and state-controlled gas sector (IMF 2004c, 6). Explicit subsidies to enterprises were also high during the first decade after independence. For example, enterprises' subsidies were the only economic category of government spending for which Russia departed significantly from the OECD average in 2000 (Sharipova 2001, 29). At the end of the 1990s, the government began to reduce these subsidies but enterprises were compensated by currency devaluation in 1998, which enabled them to avoid the hard task of restructuring. As energy subsidies were further reduced in the early 2000s (see World Bank 2003c, vii, IMF 2004c, 6) and once the so-called "easy gains from devaluation [were] exhausted," however, a "large number of enterprises finally began restructuring with a view to improving [labor] productivity" (Ahrend 2006, 104). As a result, from 2002–2005, "industrial output [grew] relatively strongly while industrial employment [fell]" across all major sectors (ibid). The Putin administration has had less success in reducing subsidies in the agricultural sector, where "farms still enjoy a wide range of tax breaks and direct subsidies, as well as access to budget-financed soft loans" (EIU 2007, 43).

Expenditure reform in the social sphere mirrored these changes in the economic sphere. Broadly speaking, despite an increase in its tax revenue from 2000–2005 the Russian government sought to contract the state's role in

---

[49] For a critique of this view, see Woodruff (1999).

providing social welfare. More specifically, this included the adoption of targeted (that is, income-tested) spending in lieu of a wide range of universal subsidies, as outlined in the strategic plan approved by the government in the spring of 2000.[50] The first Putin administration (2000–2004) began to develop targeted spending in earnest in three areas: child allowances, housing and utility allowances, and regional programs for the poor (for details, see World Bank 2005d). As part of its efforts to reduce poverty by developing "a standardized system of means-tested state social assistance," the Putin administration also introduced monetarized benefits to replace "the massive system of in-kind social benefits and privileges that had been inherited form the Soviet period, and expanded by the patronage politics of 1994–1999" (Cook 2007b, 219). The monetarization of benefits has not only "been a key step towards rationalising public expenditure," but it has also increased the transparency of social transfers (EIU 2007, 36).

At the same time, the government actively sought to expand the private sector's role in the social sphere. As one scholarly expert describes, social welfare reform was part of "a comprehensive plan to move Russia toward a social model in which markets and private actors would play the major role and the state a limited one" (Cook 2007b, 190). This included movement toward the establishment of private medical insurance and pension funds, also outlined in the strategic plan adopted in 2000. In conjunction with delegating more to the private sector the government also sought to improve state regulations – for example, by creating institutional mechanisms to monitor financial services for pension investment and setting a minimum wage (ibid.).

Thus, Russia has undergone significant expenditure reform at the national level aimed at limiting the public sector's role in providing public goods and social services. Yet, as discussed in Chapter 3, in those subnational units where petroleum is being developed, a very different picture should emerge; that is, we should see not only a higher level of public goods and social service provision but also a greater role for private oil companies in providing these goods and services. To some extent, this effect should be magnified in Russia because most regions continued to rely on local firms to perform such a role long after the collapse of the Soviet Union (see Haaparanta et al. 2003). Indeed, as is well-documented, there are significant social and economic disparities across Russia's regions that are highly correlated with regional GDP, and consequently, the ability of regional governments to meet their expenditure requirements (see Benini and Czyzewski 2007, UNDP 2006/2007). While the Russian system of fiscal federalism employs mechanisms that are theoretically

---

[50] For details, see "Programma Pravitelstva Rossii: Osnovnyi napravleniia sotsial'no-ekonomicheskoi politiki Pravitel'stva Rossiiskoi Federatsii na dolgosrochnuiu perspectivy." (Russian Government Program: Main Directions of the Socioeconomic Policies of the Government of the Russian Federation for the Long Term.) This strategic plan is based on a document drafted by German Gref's think tank – Center for Strategic Planning. According to Cook (2007b, 190), "[t]he Center's documents were to set the intended directions of social and economic development over the following decade."

designed to ameliorate these disparities, moreover, this has not occurred in practice (see Desai et al. 2005, 819). The system of fiscal equalization, for example, is only minimally redistributive and, to the extent that income is transferred from wealthier to poorer regions, it is the medium-income regions that bear the burden of this income transfer (Thiessen 2006).

Not surprisingly, the oil and gas-producing regions are among the primary beneficiaries of such a system. Tyumen Oblast, for example, which contains the bulk of Russia's oil and gas reserves[51] and has hosted all of the largest private ROCs, has prospered due to both the enormous tax revenue that ROCs have contributed directly to the regional budget and the plethora of targeted social programs they have financed. Under Sergei Semyonovich Sobyanin's leadership, who served as governor from 2001 to 2005, the region was considered "a leader in providing affordable access to upgraded housing structures, communal services, and healthcare" (Authors' interview with Zotikova). At the end of 2005, Tyumen ranked second in the Human Development Index (HDI) among regions in the Russia Federation and its "oil producing autonomous districts [had] the lowest poverty rate in the country" (UNDP 2006/2007, 12, 70).[52] It is also in Russia's oil- and gas-producing regions where we see the tendency for regional administrations to support large public investment projects, particularly those that are highly visible to the local population, though nothing on the scale of the national prestige projects we have seen in Turkmenistan. The governor of Khanty-Mansi, for example, has become notorious for building an ornate shopping emporium and other architectural monuments in the autonomous district's capital city to showcase his efforts to distribute the benefits of the region's petroleum wealth (see Starobin 2008).

The impact of expenditure reform in the short term has been arguably less impressive than tax reform. Poverty, for example, has declined overall since 1999 largely as a result of economic growth. According to the most recent data available using a consistent national poverty standard, between 1999 and 2002 "Russia succeeded in cutting poverty in half, from about 42 percent in 1999 to 20 percent in 2002" (Alam et al. 2005, 53). Yet growth in Russia (as well as Kazakhstan) has had a bigger impact on poverty reduction precisely because, due to the aforementioned prudent fiscal policies, it translated into more employment opportunities and real increases in wages (ibid, Chapter 2). It is also for these reasons that, with the exception of Moldova, Russia is the only country in the CIS where "the poor benefited proportionately more than the rich from the growth rebound" (ibid., 84). Yet the fact that poverty remains a significant problem – particularly at the regional level, where there are large discrepancies (UNDP 2006/2007) – is also linked to the limited timeframe for some of these policies to be effective. For example, at the end of 2004,

---

[51] Tyumen Oblast includes both Yamal-Nenets and Khanty-Mantsi Autonomous Okrugs, which contain the country's largest-producing fields.

[52] At the same time, however, it had among the highest levels of income inequality – along with Moscow, St. Petersburg, and other oil-producing regions (UNDP 2006/07, 28).

targeted spending had reached only a fraction of the poor in comparison to other countries using a similar means-tested program, including Kazakhstan (World Bank 2005f, 98–100) – and by the end of 2005, the monetarization of social benefits had simply become "impossible to implement" at the regional level (Thiessen 2006, 214).

Causal Mechanisms

As described above, the fact that Russia adopted a strong fiscal regime from 1999–2005 is particularly puzzling not only because it represents a radical shift from the 1990s but also because significant taxation and expenditure reforms were initiated during a bust and then sustained during the first several years of a boom. In short, we argue that this outcome is a direct result of the institutional incentives generated by private domestic ownership (P_1) via three causal mechanisms: (1) high transaction costs (TCs), (2) low societal expectations, and (3) explicit bargaining. While high TCs and low societal expectations explain why governing elites and domestic private owners prefer strong fiscal regimes, explicit bargaining tells us how these institutions come about and why they are more likely to be sustained over time. To further substantiate our claims, in this section we demonstrate that each of these causal mechanisms is indeed at work.

Transaction Costs

That TCs were high in the 1990s is evident in the type of interactions that characterized the relationship between the Russian government and the ROCs. In short, the information asymmetries they faced as a result of divergent interests vis-à-vis the management of the oil sector were reinforced by structures that served to clarify the boundaries between them. In contrast to Uzbekistan and Turkmenistan (both of which adopted S_1), where mutual interests in promoting discretion were reinforced over time by structures, such as government representatives on the NOC's board of directors and periodic rotation of NOC managers and government employees, that deliberately blurred the boundaries between governing elite and NOC managers, the ROCs retained control over their internal affairs and daily operations. Their main interface with the government, moreover, was not the Ministry of Oil and Gas, which not only tends to gain prominence under S_1 but also to facilitate (if not embody) the conflation of the sector's economic interests with the government's political priorities. Rather, it was the Ministry of Finance.

The interactions between the ROCs and the Ministry of Finance, which was charged with extracting the government's share of rents via taxation, provide a vivid illustration of the relationship between high TCs and clear boundaries. From the latter's perspective, the magnitude of information asymmetries it faced vis-à-vis the ROCs meant that setting arbitrarily high tax rates was the best way to replenish the budget (Authors' interview with Dvorkovich; see also, Samoylenko 1998). As one deputy minister explained, "the attitude was simply this: we could not know their *real* profits unless they revealed them to us, and they had no reason to tell us the truth, so we had to assume they were lying to us ... , that they would not pay all of what they *really* owed" (Authors' interview with Dvorkovich). Yet this strategy only exacerbated the problem of noncompliance by creating a greater incentive for the ROCs to conceal their profits. By the mid-1990s, they had developed a series of legal and semilegal schemes in order to evade excessive taxation. Transfer pricing was the most common form through which, by some estimates, the ROCs were able to hide at least 25 percent of their export proceeds (Authors' interview with Yermakov). The prevalence of such tax evasion schemes, in turn, greatly diminished the Finance Ministry's ability to ascertain a close estimate of what the ROCs' actual profits were via the mechanisms it had developed to serve this purpose – that is, export quotas and yearly audits – and made it extremely costly to catch or to sanction the ROCs for tax evasion (Authors' interview with representatives of ROCs, and with Former Deputy Minister of Finance).

Thus, by the end of the 1990s the Russian government and the ROCs were locked in a vicious cycle in which exorbitant tax rates encouraged evasion and evasion encouraged even higher tax rates and threats of expropriation, leading to more elaborate and time-consuming schemes to hide profits. As a result, both sides incurred heavy costs in the form of unreliable revenue streams and lower productivity. The government was only able to collect between 33–35 percent of the ROCs' revenues based on a statutory tax rate of 53 percent (Authors' interviews with Yermakov and with Dvorkovich)[53] – or approximately half of its projected tax revenues – and kept only a small portion of windfall revenues. In 2000, for example, it received 22 percent of the approximately USD 30 billion in rent from natural resource sales while 78 percent remained in the hands of oil and gas exporters (Authors' interview with Yermakov). At the same time, devising and executing tax evasion schemes were costly for the ROCs because these efforts diverted attention and resources away from building their companies. Transfer pricing, for example, involved creating trading subsidiaries (often located in a low tax zone within Russia) from which the ROCs' parent companies purchased oil at below market prices and then resold this oil at equally low prices to offshore Russian intermediaries (often located in a free-trade zone). Other forms of tax evasion that detracted from profit-making activities included the development of intricate schemes to avoid payroll taxes.[54] Here, parent companies would create offshore subsidiaries to pay their employees, arranging for insurance companies to pay their employees under the guise of large monthly payouts from life insurance policies, and paying higher corporate banking fees so that employees would earn higher

[53] Actual (versus statutory) tax rates on oil were not only lower than they should have been, but also differed markedly from company to company (see, Stolyarov 2000).
[54] One ROC representative estimated the cost of such schemes at 15 percent of their profits (Authors' interview with Sibneft representative).

interest rates than the market rate on their checking accounts (Authors' interview with Reinhardt).

The extent of these costs, however, was not fully realized until the financial crisis hit in August of 1998. In short, the crisis, which resulted in enormous revenue losses for both the Russian government and ROCs, revealed their mutual vulnerability to global markets and the need to insulate themselves from the effects of future crises. According to the IMF (2000c, 60, 63), government revenues dropped in the third quarter of 1998 to just 7 percent of GDP from 10.5 percent of GDP in the first half of 1998, and spending fell in the third quarter to 11 percent of GDP from 16 percent of GDP in the first half of 1998. As its income plummeted, the government began to recognize the inherent limitations of increasing its reliance on the oil sector for budgetary revenue and, more importantly, the consequences of a fluctuating tax rate. Sergei Dimitrievich Shatalov, First Deputy Minister of Finance, who had been a strong (but lonely) advocate of tax reform since the mid-1990s, summarized the collective sentiment thus: "the August 1998 crisis created the ... realization that we needed to change the [current] system of securing [government] revenue" (Authors' interview).

Similarly, several representatives of the ROCs described the crisis as "sobering" because it "forced [them] to acknowledge the cumulative negative effects of their previous behavior" (Authors' interviews). Many ROCs, including YUKOS, Sibneft, and TNK, faced bankruptcy and lacked cash flow to service their short-term secured bank debt (Authors' interviews; see also, Tanguy 2002). Because many of them acquired substantial foreign debt, the Russian government's decision to devalue the ruble made it even more expensive for the ROCs to repay these loans. Over the first nine months of 1999, for example, the indebtedness of the five major ROCs went up 54 percent (Kommersant 1999). As a result, many of them were unable to pay salaries and some were forced either to shut down their operations for several months or to radically downsize their operations and decrease expenditures (Authors' interviews). Moreover, due to their reduced cash flow, combined with the lack of prior strategic planning and domestic investment to boost productive capacity, they could not immediately reap the benefits of the ruble's devaluation by increasing production (ibid).

The August 1998 financial crisis also made it painstakingly clear to both sides that achieving economic recovery in the short term and insulating themselves from the effects of future crises over the long term required stable rules. For the ROCs, at a minimum, "recovery" required investing in modernization, for which they also needed both greater fiscal predictability and more secure property rights. Part of ensuring fiscal predictability, as they understood it, was instituting a stable tax regime not just for the oil sector but for the economy as a whole. As several ROC representatives argued, this, would ensure that the state "could generate tax revenue from its citizens and not just from the oil companies," thereby insulating the oil companies from future fluctuations in their tax rates (Authors' interviews). They also appeared to realize that tax stability and secure property rights are integrally linked. As a representative of Sidanco explained: "we may never have fully secure property rights as you have in the U.S., but if we can pressure the government to enact a stable tax code, this can be a way of protecting our property" (Authors' interview).

At a maximum, the ROCs' "recovery" required attracting Western partners in order to improve their assets at home and expand their operations abroad, which in turn required increasing transparency (for example, disclosing information about profits and providing accurate information about profitability to shareholders) and establishing corporate governance. Specifically, the ROCs recognized that strategic partnerships with Western companies would give them access to foreign capital and technology, thereby enabling them to engage in long-term strategic planning and domestic investment that were clearly so vital after the August 1998 crisis.[55] At both ends of the spectrum, then, the ROCs could not recover without obtaining formal guarantees from the government that it would not arbitrarily expropriate their assets or the proceeds from these assets through indiscriminate taxation (Authors' interviews with ROC representatives and with domestic and foreign oil and gas analysts). Tax legislation, moreover, would both enhance predictability and require increased transparency, thus providing them with the stability to invest in their assets at home and the credibility to attract Western partners to expand their operations abroad. As one former high-ranking government official summarized: "This was not an act of charity. The [private domestic] oil companies wanted to improve the country's tax system as a means to improve the country's reputation, and hence to improve their own capitalization" (Authors' interview no. 2).

"Recovery" for the Russian government required, at a minimum, budgetary stability. In order to regain their budgetary losses in the short term and to stabilize the flow of tax revenue from the oil sector, the Russian government needed to give the ROCs a greater incentive to pay their taxes voluntarily. This, in turn, required "setting a tax rate that would encourage ROCs to reveal their *real* income" (Authors' interview with Dvorkovich). As aforementioned, throughout the 1990s, the Russian government relied heavily on taxing the oil sector to fill its coffers. In addition to exorbitant CIT rates, oil producers were subject to a fixed excise tax rate and stiff export tariffs. Yet by August 1998, it became clear that this strategy was leading to the ROCs' insolvency and creating an unreliable revenue stream. The fixed excise tax rate, for example, meant that oil producers paid approximately 55 rubles per ton (or about USD 9) regardless of the price of oil. Thus, when oil prices plummeted in 1998, "many of the companies [were driven] to the verge of bankruptcy"

---

[55] The desire for strategic partnerships does not mean that the ROCs sought foreign direct investment or that they were willing to share equity in the Russian energy sector with Western companies, but rather that they were willing to make Western companies minority shareholders in order to gain access to foreign markets.

(Samoylenko 1998, 3). At the same time, cumbersome bankruptcy procedures hampered the Russian government's ability to seize private assets in order to induce tax compliance.[56]

The government's "recovery" at a maximum required expanding the tax base and increasing compliance overall so as to reduce the budget's dependence on the oil sector for revenue. This, in turn, created an opening for advocates like Shatalov to resurrect efforts to pass a comprehensive tax code.[57] Following the crisis, structural reform aimed at promoting real growth across sectors became a top priority for the government, and establishing a stable, broad-based tax regime was a central component of this strategy (Authors' interviews with Dvorkovich and Shatalov; see also, Vasiliev 2000). In particular, Prime Minister Yevgeni Primakov sought to reduce the overall tax burden (that is, lower the profit tax and VAT) and to introduce a package of basic laws in the Duma concerning fiscal reform (see *RFE/RL* October 14, 1998, Vasiliev 2000). Alongside the Finance Ministry, his efforts were supported by the Ministry of Energy and Fuel, and later, by the Ministry of Economic Development and Trade in 2000, both of which viewed lowering the overall tax rates for PIT and CIT and tying export tariffs directly to the price of oil as promoting long-term recovery and growth in the oil sector while also serving to stabilize the government's revenue stream, broaden the tax base, and improve the rate of compliance (Authors' interviews with Dvorkovich and Shatalov).

By 2000, the Russian government's fiscal reform agenda also came to encompass public expenditures. This was motivated by both short- and long-term concerns. In the short term, governing elites – particularly those in the Finance Ministry, including Alexei Kudrin himself – considered spending cuts necessary to cushion the budget from the initial reduction in revenue due to tax reform (Authors' interview with Shatalov). Over the long term, however, governing elites viewed reducing entitlements and shifting the burden of social service provision to the individual and the private sector as necessary to ameliorate the budget's future vulnerability. "We were working together to find a way to insulate the budget from future shocks ... [and] we recognized early on that tax reform was only one half of the equation" (Authors' interview with Dvorkovich). It was also at this time that debates over the establishment of a stabilization fund began in earnest. While most agreed that maintaining a budgetary surplus "made good fiscal sense," there was still no consensus over how best to institutionalize this practice (Authors' interview with Deputy Minister of Finance).

---

[56] Russia has introduced several versions of insolvency laws since independence (such as the 1992 insolvency law and the 1998 insolvency law), which has resulted in many ambiguities, making implementation an extremely difficult process (for details, see OECD, 1995). In 2002, Putin vetoed the latest version (*Pravda*, August 7, 2002).

[57] Shatalov tried to push through tax reform in the early 1990s but resigned in frustration because "the Yeltsin administration's was not committed to real tax reform" (Authors' interview). According to another high-ranking government official under Yeltsin, by December 1997, "tax reform was practically dead" (Authors' interview).

Societal Expectations

To assess popular attitudes toward taxation, government spending, and the role of the private sector, we consult a variety of mass surveys and public opinion polls available in Russia,[58] but rely primarily on the EBRD's 2005 Life in Transition Survey (LiTS). Among the FSU (excluding the Baltic States), Russia stands out for having the lowest percentage of the population that favors renationalization of privatized property. When asked "what should be done with most privatized companies," for example, only 36.7 percent responded that it should be "renationalized and kept in state hands," as compared to 51.6 percent in Uzbekistan. And conversely, Russia had the highest percentage of respondents that favored leaving this property "in the hands of current owners provided they pay the privatized assets' worth" – 31.5 percent as compared to 22.6 percent in Uzbekistan. It is noteworthy that the majority of Russian respondents (63.3 percent) preferred some form of private ownership to state ownership.[59] Just as we predict, moreover, assuming that the expectations of those with the longest history of living under the Soviet system will be the least affected by a change in ownership structure, this support varies across age groups in Russia, whereas in most other FSU countries, particularly Uzbekistan, it is virtually uniform. The difference between respondents 18–34 years of age and those over 65 regarding whether privatized companies should be renationalized, for example, was almost 25 percentage points (26.2 and 50.0 percent, respectively) in Russia, whereas in Uzbekistan the difference was just over five percentage points (50.0 and 55.7 percent, respectively).

In sum, these survey results suggest both that the population widely accepts private ownership of large companies and that it does not do so unconditionally. Rather, its support is tied to the state's ability to make private owners fairly compensate the public. Other mass surveys of the Russian population provide corroborating evidence for this broad popular sentiment. A national survey conducted in January and February 2005, for example, suggests that Russians are willing to overlook misdeeds of the privatization process if the beneficiaries of this process (that is, the private owners or companies) engage in some form of public good provision (Frye 2006). It also suggests that the population accepts and appreciates private sources of public goods. The author finds that when a private company provides public goods to the local population, its approval rating improves by just over 10 percentage points when the asset in question is put to "bad use" and by over 20 percentage points when this asset is put to "good use" (ibid., 491).

The form of compensation most widely expected of private owners – particularly the owners of large profitable companies (or "big business") – however,

---

[58] The public opinon polls consulted in this chapter were conducted by the Public Opinion Foundation. For more information on this organization and access to the data, see http://bd.english.fom.ru/

[59] Perhaps even more striking, the vast majority of Russians also view the privatization process itself as having been "dishonest" or "conducted with major [legal] violations" (Frye 2006).

appears to have been paying their taxes. According to public opinion polls, for example, what seems to have angered average citizens most about the tax system under Yeltsin was the "great deal of loopholes ... allowing big businessmen to dodge taxes" (*Taxes and Justice*, 1). Public reaction to the arrest and trial of Mikhail Khodorkovsky, the former CEO of the now defunct privately owned and operated Russian oil company Yukos, in October 2003 on charges of tax evasion (hereafter: the "Yukos affair"), is a good case in point. National public opinion polls conducted at the end of June 2004 (eight months later) and in October 2004 (a year later) suggest that the majority of Russians believe the government's primary motivation for Khodorkovsky's arrest and the assault on Yukos more generally is directly related to "disregard of the tax law," and therefore consider the government's actions to be legitimate.[60] As one political commentator explained, "the informed public" viewed this conflict as "an open and shut case of the government going after tax evaders who must be made to pay what they owe" rather than as an attempt to either "collectively punish the oligarchs" or "confiscate their property" (Authors' interview with Urnov 2004). Others concurred that the public supported the government not because they disliked Khodorkovsky himself, but because he failed to fulfill "the main responsibility of business towards society ... [,which is] to pay their taxes fully and in a timely manner" (Authors' interview with Makarenko 2004).[61] A further indication of this sentiment is that the population's tendency to side with the government versus Yukos was also linked to its presumption that Khodorkovsky was, in fact, guilty of these charges, and thus that forcing him to pay would actually raise the state's tax revenue.

The notion that paying taxes is a social obligation (or "necessary evil") among Russians, moreover, seems to extend beyond "big business" to oneself and one's fellow citizens. A national public opinion poll conducted in April 2002, for example, suggests that a large majority of respondents (54 percent) would voluntarily "share some part of their income with the state" (*Taxes and Justice*, 11) and that a only slight majority of respondents (37 percent) considered the income taxes they currently paid to be too high, as compared to 34 percent for whom "this amount [was] acceptable" (ibid., 3). The fact that compliance rates have increased markedly since 2001, moreover, suggests that the willingness to pay taxes is not simply hypothetical. The results of this poll also indicate that the vast majority of Russians (86 percent) "think the authorities [should] toughen measures against tax dodgers." While previous polls have also shown strong popular support for punishing tax evasion, there has been a marked increase since the new Tax Code was implemented alongside an increase in the perception that the tax system is fair (*Taxes and Justice*, 11–13). This does not mean, however, that Russians associate a citizen's obligation to

[60] For a detailed analysis, see *The Yukos Case* and *Yukos and the State*.
[61] The survey data supports this view. Most respondents were indifferent toward Khodorkovsky, and even those who had a positive impression of him and/or his company nonetheless sided with the government.

pay taxes with the tax system's fairness. A series of public opinion surveys conducted by the same organization in 2004 and 2005, for example, shows that 71 percent of Russian respondents believe that everyone must "follow all the tax laws even if he or she considers them to be unfair" and 53 percent claim that they personally would comply with tax laws taxes even if they did not consider them to be fair (Berenson 2007, 5).[62]

Finally, the Russian population also appears to favor a reduced role for the state in both the economic and social spheres more than its counterparts in the FSU, particularly Uzbekistan. On a general level, public opinion polls indicate that a majority of the Russian population (57 percent) favors spending limits (*Taxes and Justice*, 12–13). More specifically, according to the LiTS, less than 80 percent of Russians, for example, responded that the state should be "strongly involved" in guaranteeing employment, compared to nearly 90 percent of Uzbekistanis. And there was a considerable gap across age groups in Russia, but not in Uzbekistan, lending support to our argument that ownership structure affects these attitudes. In Russia, for example, 73.2 percent of respondents 18–34 years of age responded that the state should be "strongly involved" in guaranteeing employment, versus 82.0 percent over 65 – that is, a difference of almost 10 percentage points – whereas in Uzbekistan, these numbers were 87.6 percent versus 89.8 percent – that is, a difference of just only 2 percentage points. Polling data also suggests that – with the exception of eliminating housing subsidies (Cook 2007b) and monetarizing benefits (see *Benefits Reform*) – many of Putin's social reforms have gained broad support. The privatization of pensions in particular has been viewed rather positively, with 45 percent approving of "the accumulation of pension funds in an employee's individual account" (*Pension Reform*; see also *Reforms: Popular and Unpopular*). After two years in office, moreover, the majority of those who responded (29 percent) viewed "social policy" as Putin's greatest achievement in office, but largely because he paid pension and wage arrears. And, after six years in office, 53 percent of Russians included "social protection of the poor" among Putin's greatest achievements as president (Rose 2007, 34).

At the same time, there appears to be a favorable attitude toward private ownership more broadly and policies that support the growth of the private sector. One indication of this is widespread support for private ownership of land – specifically, the right to buy and sell land without restrictions – particularly among youth. Although public opinion in general was "sharply divided" over this issue with 48 percent of Russians strongly endorsing this reform while 45 percent vehemently opposing it – the corresponding numbers for those respondents between 18 and 35 years of age were 63 percent and 28 percent (Aron 2001). Another is broad support for tax reductions for small businesses. Public opinion polls indicate not only that the majority of Russians

---

[62] Compare this to 79 and 83 percent of Polish respondents and 57 and 36 percent of Ukrainians (ibid.).

(58 percent) supported this reform, but also that they did so precisely because they believed that it would stimulate the growth of SMEs, and thereby, reduce unemployment and poverty as well as tax evasion (see *Business is Small but the Taxes are Big, Great Expectations for Small Business*, 3).

In sum, there is a considerable amount of evidence to suggest that societal expectations in Russia were for limited redistribution of the proceeds from mineral wealth via taxation, and thus, contrasted sharply with societal expectations for widespread distribution in Turkmenistan and Uzbekistan. And yet, in seeking to demonstrate that both the substance and timing of fiscal reform in Russia were also facilitated by low societal expectations, our aim is less to prove that the population actually held these beliefs than it is to demonstrate that governing elites were motivated by the conviction that the population held these beliefs. In order to assess this, we rely on a combination of systematic and extensive interviews with governing elites as well as domestic political analysts conducted primarily during the fall of 2001 and the summer of 2002[63] and the president's annual address to the Duma (or "State of the Nation," hereafter *Address*) from 1995–2005.

These interviews and speeches share two striking features. First, there is a collective emphasis on taxation and regulation as the government's primary role – both vis-à-vis the energy sector and the economy more broadly. When asked to compare government – business relations in the 1990s with the 2000s, for example, the majority of our interviewees described the former as a "constant battle for tax revenue" and attributed "these difficult times" to the Yeltsin administration's failure to either effectively collect taxes from the private sector or regulate its activities (Authors' interviews with Former Deputy Minister of Finance and Ustinov). As one government official who was particularly close to the battles over taxation in the 1990s lamented, "this was more than a failure to tax … it was a failure to govern" (Authors' interview with Shatalov). The main casualty, they seemed to agree, was the loss of public confidence that, some argued, reduced tax compliance more broadly. The Putin years, in contrast, were commonly depicted as a time in which the government began to live up to its expected role as "chief tax collector," particularly vis-à-vis the private oil companies (Authors' interviews with First Deputy Minister of Finance and Vyugin). The standard characterization of the aforementioned Yukos affair as "showing both [the oligarchs and the public] who is in charge" and "making an example out of tax dodgers" encapsulates this image (Authors' interview with former high-ranking government official no. 3). This interpretation was shared by the ROCs themselves, who considered it "not mere chance" that the main charge brought against Khodorkovsky was tax fraud (Authors' interview with Yukos representative no. 2).

Similarly, in their *Addresses*, both Yeltsin and Putin have consistently emphasized the need to improve tax collection, but they have not done so

---

[63] We conducted follow-up interviews with political analysts and ROC representatives from 2004–2005 and with current and former government officials from 2006–08.

exclusively in the context of the mineral sector.[64] Rather, the focus is on broad-based tax reform and compliance across sectors. In Yeltsin's 1997 *Address*, for example, the problem of tax evasion is one of the central themes, and yet, there is no mention of the mineral sector. In fact, the energy sector itself is rarely mentioned at all in the annual *Addresses* from 1995–2005. And when it is mentioned, it has little rhetorical importance. Concerning tax reform specifically, the only explicit reference to the mineral sector is in Putin's 2001 *Address* in which he remarks that it is a "strategic priority to ensure fair and rational taxation of natural resources."

At the same time, government officials did not seem to be concerned with the popularity or social acceptability of taxation itself. While they acknowledged the need to overcome a "Soviet mentality" whereby individuals "were not accustomed to pay taxes [but rather] … to receive benefits," they viewed this as a matter that could be addressed by eliminating the "key obstacles" to tax compliance in the 1990s – the complexity of the tax system and lack of confidence in the government (Authors' interviews with Dvorkovich and Former Deputy Minister of Finance). In the words of one prominent government official working on tax reform: "the Russian people are not afraid of taxes, they are afraid of overzealous tax collectors … and [the] Byzantine bureaucratic procedures [of the Yeltsin administration]" (Authors' interview with Shatalov). Not surprisingly, then, the improvement in compliance rates since 2001 was commonly invoked as evidence to support such claims. Yet it was also viewed as an indication of the widespread recognition that "reform was unavoidable" in the wake of the 1998 financial crisis. As one Deputy Minister insisted: "it was not just the government that wanted [tax] reform [after the Crisis]. No one was happy with the tax situation in 1999. Everyone came to view the tax system as a break on economic development.… It changed the psychology of the government, business interests, and the [Russian] people …" (Authors' interview with Dvorkovich).

The second feature that our interviews and these public speeches have in common is a disconnect between the country's vast mineral wealth and government spending, particularly in the social sphere. In marked contrast to Turkmenistan and Uzbekistan, where natural resource wealth is routinely credited for the population's alleged higher standards of living, the two are rarely mentioned in tandem. In short, while the link between the petroleum sector and taxation in the *Addresses* from 1995 to 2005 is weak at best, the link between government spending and the petroleum sector is nonexistent.

Rather, the tendency has been to discuss petroleum wealth in the context of the need to develop other sectors so as to avoid relying on natural resources as the basis for Russia's economy. In his 1999 *Address*, for example, Yeltsin attributed the downfall of the Soviet Union to its budgetary reliance on natural resources rather than "high technology and those sectors whose products can be competitive on the world market of the 21st century." Similarly, in his

---

[64] They have also emphasized the need to regulate the natural monopolies.

2001 *Address*, Putin laments the large amount of private investment going into the petroleum sector, and then, in his 2002 *Address*, praises the growth of Russia's nonraw material exports as evidence of the country's improved economy. Despite this emphasis on diversifying the economy, the proceeds from petroleum wealth were never invoked as the source of diversification. Nor was government investment viewed as the primary vehicle. In fact, the consensus among governing elites, especially those in the MEDT, seemed to be that "state led development [would be] disastrous" (Authors' interview with Dvorkovich) and that the best way to stimulate economic growth was through "pursuing tax reform" and "developing the private sector," which were of course "mutually reinforcing" (Authors' interview with Deputy Minister, MEDT). Again the recent experience of the Soviet Union served as a foil for justifying such views. In emphasizing the need to expand the role of the private sector, for example, one official explained: "we have all lived under the Soviet system, [so] we all know the disadvantages of such a system ... of course, there is public distrust for the private sector but there is also great hope in its potential to achieve what the state cannot" (Authors' interview with Deputy Finance Minister).

The consensus regarding a reduced role for the state in economic development also extended to the social sphere. Public opinion polls to the contrary, governing elites espoused the belief that the population had a "more realistic understanding" of their relationship to the government, meaning that they did not expect a continuation of a Soviet-style cradle-to-grave social welfare system (Authors' interviews with Former Deputy Minister of Finance). There was also a tendency for elites to discount popular protest to social welfare reform because they equated this with "Communist influence" and "old thinking" and not the "will of rational people" (Authors' interview with First Deputy Minister of Finance) Thus, their perception was that the government had a green light not only to limit its own role in providing goods and services but also to delegate more to the private sector.[65] The lack of emphasis on improving the social sphere or raising living standards relative to tax reform in both Yeltsin's and Putin's annual presidential addresses reflect this. What is even more telling is that the lengthiest discussions of living conditions in their respective *Addresses* focus on the need to expand employment opportunities in the private sector and the role of economic growth outside the petroleum sector in order to make this possible. In his May 2003 *Address*, for example, Putin boasts:

Thanks to [broad] economic growth, almost four million people have left the ranks of the unemployed and found new jobs over these last years. ... Real personal incomes have increased by 32 percent. [P]er capita consumption rose by almost a third over the

[65] This (mis)perception ultimately backfired. While Putin was able to push through most of his social welfare reform agenda after his reelection in March 2004, due to popular opposition he was forced to compromise on some key aspects such as housing reform. For details, see Cook 2007b, Chapter 4.

last three years. ... Finally, there can be no opposition between a policy of pursuing economic growth and a social welfare policy. I would like to emphasize that we need economic growth above all in order to improve the living standards of our people.

Debates surrounding the establishment of the OSF also serve to illustrate these elite perceptions regarding social policy. Although there was a clear consensus that placing limits on government spending would bolster budgetary stability, there was no consensus as to how this could best be achieved beyond reforms to the budgetary process itself. While some promoted the idea of institutionalizing the budgetary surplus via the establishment of an NRF as early as 1999, "the idea of creating a permanent stabilization fund was still very contentious at this point" (Authors' interview with Illarionov). As it was originally conceived, the stabilization fund would serve a dual purpose: first, to "combat the negative affects associated with Dutch Disease, particularly the rise of the real exchange rate and inflationary pressures; and second, to "enable Russia to repay its foreign debt" (ibid.). Those who initially opposed the idea did so either because they thought a smaller portion of the projected surplus should be set aside in the fund or because they thought the amount exceeding this portion should be spent differently. Some argued, for example, that taking too much of the windfall revenue out of the economy would deprive the private sector of deciding how it should be used (Authors' interview with Zadornov; see also, *Izvestiya* 2002). Others insisted that the money set aside in the fund should only be spent during an economic crisis akin to 1998 to make up for budgetary shortfalls. But no one who objected to the stabilization fund in the early 2000s did so on the grounds that the government should use the windfall revenue to increase social welfare spending or build massive public works projects. Nor did they object on the grounds that the idea itself would be unpopular. In fact, the main proponents of the stabilization fund were so certain that the population would support the idea that they deliberately "took the debate public" in order to bolster support for their position within the government (Authors' interview with Illarionov).

Societal expectations also played an important role in shaping the attitudes of the ROCs toward taxation and social spending. Our own surveys of these companies' activities and follow-up interviews with their representatives suggest that most were not only acutely aware of the need to "show the population that they [were] behav[ing] responsibly" in order to secure their assets, but also willing to do so (Authors' interview with Yukos representative no. 1).[66] While this centered primarily on a general recognition that paying taxes is "perhaps [their] main obligation to society," it also included a willingness to provide social services and public goods – particularly at the local level in the regions where their companies and its subsidiaries operate (Authors'

---

[66] This is by no means limited to the ROCs. In fact, successful tycoons across sectors and companies of all sizes have taken on an increasing degree of social responsibility, at least partly (if not mostly) due to the recognition that this would help secure their property rights (see Europe's Top 50 2006, Frye 2006, Khodorova 2006).

interview with Alexeeva; see also Kuznetsov et al. 2009).[67] Since 2000, most have explicitly incorporated social investment into their corporate profile at both the national and regional level, albeit spending the bulk of their profits allocated to "charitable activities" on the latter (see, for example, Lukoil 2001).[68] Yukos is a case in point. While the company sponsored a variety of educational and cultural projects at the national level, it deliberately focused its efforts on "improving the social and economic prospects of the inhabitants of Russia's oil-producing regions" since 1996 (Authors' interview with Yukos representative no. 1).[69] Like most other ROCs, its rationale was twofold. On the one hand, there was a perception that, because it was profiting from what is viewed not just as a public but a local resource, the company had a special duty to devote some of its profits to raising the standard of living for the population in the areas most affected by its operations. As explicitly stated in its 2002 Annual Report: "our primary mission is to contribute to economic prosperity and social progress in the regions where the Company does business" (Yukos 2003). On the other hand, there is a keen understanding that "promoting a healthy and educated [local] population ... simply makes good business sense," for example, because this is the company's primary source of labor (Authors' interview with Yukos representative no. 1).

In the post-Soviet context, these sentiments are compounded by the fact that the state-owned predecessors of the private ROCs were responsible for financing entire cities.[70] While this practice ended officially in 1992, it has created a dependent relationship between these private companies and the subnational (that is, local and regional) governments to which these so-called "social assets" were transferred (at least on paper). Thus, for some companies, like Lukoil, the costs of maintaining these assets are deliberately calculated as part of their annual social contribution (Authors' interview with Lukoil representative; see also the company's annual reports from 2000 to 2005) while for others, like Yukos and BP-TNK, they are treated as "just another cost of doing business in Russia" (Authors' interview with Bigman).

The ROCs' response to real and perceived societal expectations at the subnational level thus helps to explain the regional disparities described earlier. Yet, it is only part of the story. These disparities also stem from the effects

---

[67] The fact that "Russian law does not provide [nor has it provided] any tax incentives or other benefits to companies spending money for charitable purposes" (Khodorova 2006, 14) is yet another indication that ROCs (and Russian entrepreneurs in general) view these expenditures as an extension of their tax burden.

[68] "Experts estimate that more than 80 [percent] of corporate funds are distributed in regions" (Khodorova 2006, 14).

[69] In 1996, the company launched its first educational program in Russia's oil-producing regions, "New Civilization," with the expressed intention of training the country's youth in the principles of democracy, market economics, and civic responsibility.

[70] This, of course, was the case for the majority of Soviet-era enterprises. Yet in the case of the oil and gas industry, particularly in Siberia, these towns were often created by the industry itself. Urai and Surgut in Western Siberia, for example, both began as oilmen's settlements in 1964.

of societal expectations on officials at the local and regional level versus the national (that is, federal) level. In short, subnational leaders feel a greater obligation to at least appear to be spending the revenue they derive from oil and gas production in a way that benefits the local population, which translates into both utilizing the funds they have to improve local standards of living and reinforcing the pressures that ROCs feel to help provide the means for doing so beyond their tax burden. Thus, not surprisingly, the majority of ROCs surveyed indicated that they developed their investment priorities in cooperation with the local government and, where possible, with local NGOs. One representative described this relationship as "mutually beneficial" because "the governors want to show the people that they have not been left out in the cold" and "we want to spend our money where it is most needed, where it can do the most good" (Authors' interview with Bigman). In other words, the quality of life for citizens living in Tyumen has vastly improved since 1999 not just because local and regional governments have had the financial means to provide better public goods and social services, but more so, because they have had an incentive to utilize their capacity in such a way. This practice was facilitated, moreover, by the relative lack of interest on the part of the federal government in rectifying regional social and economic disparities resulting from the sustained oil boom. Rather, as we predict, federal officials seemed to support a minimal degree of redistribution from oil-rich to oil-poor regions. One First Deputy Minister of Finance expressed the sentiments of the Putin administration thus: "we have an obligation to help the most vulnerable [segments of society], nothing more, nothing less" (Authors' interview).

Explicit Bargaining

There is ample evidence to suggest not only that both government officials and the ROCs preferred to uncover hidden information and make their negotiations public knowledge but also that, as a result, fiscal reform in Russia emerged via an explicit bargain. First, in sharp contrast to Turkmenistan and Uzbekistan, for example, government officials in the relevant ministries acknowledged the need to make reliable macro and microeconomic level data available to both the general public and the international community. Against all odds, as of 2002, Russia's national statistics collection bureau – Goskomstat – was considered to be fully compliant with the International System of National Accounts, which sets standards for the quality as well as dissemination of economic data (Herrera 2006). Moreover, Russia is among a handful of countries in the FSU that has made some effort to comply with international reporting standards regarding government statistics (Jarmuzek et al. 2006, 13). In July 2003, the government went further, issuing new standards for improving corporate governance that focused on stringent requirements for financial disclosure (Kostikov 2003). The Russian government under Putin has also displayed a high level of openness when it comes to its domestic population regarding budgetary matters. Several officials involved in the budgetary reform process, for example, argued that making government finances part of the public record was another key factor motivating these reforms (Authors' interviews with Kovalevskaya, Shatalov, and Zadornov). Concerning the energy sector in particular, public disclosure was also a crucial reason why the Rezervny Fond and then the OSF were made part of the official budget. "Only in this way," asserted one senior official close to the deliberations, "could we reassure the public that the tax revenue from oil exports was not simply going into our own pockets" (Authors' interview with Illarionov).

The ROCs' approach to sharing information has been similar. In terms of international standards, they willingly adopted and successfully implemented generally accepted accounting principles (GAAP) after 1999. One of the primary motivations for doing so, of course, is market pressure: "if you want to increase your profits, you have to be listed on the NYSE," explained one company executive, "but if you want to be listed on the NYSE then you have to reveal your assets ... and not just to your shareholders, but to everyone" (Authors' interview with Fossum).[71] Yet, the managers of private oil companies in Russia also claimed to be motivated by the desire to "show off their success" in order to demonstrate to the public that they are in fact "better managers of oil wealth" than the state (Authors' interview with Yukos representative no. 1). These same managers also insist that, although the government initially "encouraged" them to do so, they eventually embraced corporate governance both as a way to attract foreign investment and, perhaps more importantly, "to build public trust" (ibid; see also Yakovlev 2004). Domestically, in the late 1990s the ROCs also became more emphatic about "publicizing their tax bill" so as to increase their standing vis-à-vis both the government and the general public (Authors' interview with Lukoil representative). The arrest of Yukos' CEO (Khodorkovsky) on charges of tax fraud merely served to reinforce the value of "regularly disclosing [ones] tax payments" (Authors' interview with Yukos representative no. 2).

Second, the nature of the negotiations between government officials and the ROCs over tax reform was deliberately explicit, taking place via formal meetings and organized interests. The initiative to overhaul Russia's taxation system came from within the government itself. One of Putin's first acts after being elected to the presidency in the spring of 2000 was to invite Shatalov to return to the Ministry of Finance and begin drafting what became Part II of the new Tax Code. At this initial stage, the discussion over tax reform was primarily among the relevant ministries (that is, the Ministry of Finance, the MEDT, the Ministry of Taxation, and the Ministry of Energy and Fuel) and Duma committees (that is, the Budget Committee and Subcommittee on Tax Legislation), but "business interests were involved from the start," and chief among them were the ROCs (Authors' interviews with Shatalov and Dvorkovich). One of the primary vehicles through which the ROCs participated actively in this process was a consortium they created in 1999 in order

---

[71] The Securities and Exchange Commission (SEC) requires that all public companies listed on the New York Stock Exchange (NYSE) adhere to the GAAP.

to lobby the Duma more effectively for their mutual interests regarding tax reform, which enabled them to successfully push for a strong advocate of the oil industry (Vladimir Dubov) to head the Subcommittee on Tax Legislation (Authors' interview with high-ranking official no. 2). Then, at the end of 2000, the government and the ROCs started to work together more closely in the form of an official "working group" that Putin commissioned to discuss several remaining aspects of the Tax Code, especially those that were of special concern for the ROCs, such as the CIT and the TENR (Authors' interviews with Shatalov and Dvorkovich).

These deliberations were also characterized by a willingness to accept the distributional consequences that a negotiated solution would produce. Because both sides "agreed on the basic framework of the new Tax Code" – that is, that it should increase compliance and encourage investment across sectors so as to expand the tax base – they were able to "work as a joint team" (Authors' interview with former high-ranking official no. 2). Nonetheless, they engaged in heated debates before they could reach a satisfactory compromise (Authors' interview with Dvorkovich). For example, the ROCs were initially opposed to adopting a flat rate for CIT because they had previously been able to significantly reduce this tax by making capital investments, which they had been actively doing since 1999. They were eventually persuaded to support the flat tax, however, in part because the government offered to reduce the proposed rate to 24 percent (ibid). In the end, both sides benefited from creating formal rules that increased the reliability of their revenue streams. Yet, they also had to incur losses. The ROCs paid for these benefits not only by agreeing to full disclosure and stricter governmental controls but also accepting a higher tax burden overall. The 24 percent flat rate for CIT, for example, was in some cases a higher tax rate because it eliminated the tax benefits of transfer pricing and capital expenditure deductions (Authors' interview with Yermakov; see also, Mazalov 2001, 2). Similarly, by agreeing to the new Tax Code the Russian government forfeited its advantage vis-à-vis the ROCs – not only could it no longer raise tax rates arbitrarily, but it also risked a deficit in its budget revenue if the ROCs failed to comply with the new (significantly lower) tax rates.

Third, the reform process itself has been heavily publicized. Regarding tax reform, Putin launched the formal negotiation process by holding a very public meeting with the infamous oligarchs – most of whom owned large stakes in the oil industry – on July 28, 2000, at which he reportedly pledged that he would stay out of business if they stayed out of politics (Authors' interviews with representatives of ROCs). According to public opinion polls, over half of the population knew something about this meeting between Putin and the Oligarchs (see *Power and Big Business*). The deliberations over the Tax Code that ensued were similarly part of the public domain, albeit with less drama and intrigue (Authors' interview with Zadornov). On the expenditure side, two other prominent examples of this are the establishment of the OSF and social welfare reform. From Andrei Illarionov's deliberate strategy to "take the debate public" in the fall of 2000 until Putin's formal announcement of the OSF at the end of 2003, hundreds of articles were devoted to explaining the government's rationale for creating the Fund in three of the top national publications alone.[72] Social welfare reform was also highly publicized, thus providing an opportunity for multiple actors outside the government to contest the most controversial of these reforms – in particular, the end of housing subsidies (for details, see Cook 2007, Chapter 5). As a result, the Putin administration was able to adopt most but not all of its desired reforms.

There is also evidence to suggest that the emergence of Russia's fiscal regime via explicit bargaining has affected its longevity – particularly, it's ability to survive during an unprecedented boom in international oil prices. Even after the government reversed course on the expenditure side in response to rising societal expectations following the adoption of S_1 in 2005, the comprehensive Tax Code passed in 2000 and the budgetary reforms enacted since 1999 remained relatively intact. In fact, administrative changes introduced subsequently suggest that Russia was continuing to make the necessary improvements to enforce the new Tax Code (Ernst and Young 2006b, 1). As the oil price slumped in the late 2000s, moreover, the Ministry of Finance remained committed to maintaining "the basic tax structure and rates ... [as] the best course of action" (with the exception of social taxes) and the MEDT planned to introduce further tax incentives to stimulate the economy (Conrad 2009).

Yet while the public nature of negotiations over fiscal reform meant that reversing course was more difficult, it did not make this impossible. Rather, it meant that doing so required an equally public process. The fate of the OSF serves to illustrate. Controversial from its inception, codifying the role of the OSF as a mechanism to repay foreign debt in the short term and sterilize surplus energy revenues over the long term nonetheless won the full support of Putin and most of the executive branch by 2002 (Authors' interview with Illarionov). As this support started to wane at the end of 2005 for reasons we elaborate upon below, there was also a consensus that "any changes [to the rules governing the Fund] that would loosen spending restrictions had to be made through the legislative process" (ibid.). In order to accomplish this, in late 2006 the government began openly soliciting and discussing proposals for reorganizing the OSF (ibid). The winning proposal, not coincidentally submitted by former Prime Minister Yegor Gaidar, became part of the 2008 Federal Budget Law.

A TALE OF TWO SECTORS: OIL VERSUS GAS

Still another challenge presented by the Russia case is the partial privatization of the gas sector until 2002. As described above, because Gazprom was able to retain its monopoly, ownership structure in Russia's gas sector in the 1990s amounted to private domestic ownership with state control, and then,

---

[72] Based on authors' survey of *Izvestiya*, *Kommersant*, and *Pravda*.

in 2002 reverted to state ownership with control (S_1). Yet this also presents us with an additional opportunity to test our hypotheses concerning the linkages between P_1 and strong fiscal regimes, as well as to further explore the empirical implications of our argument. The blurring of boundaries between the main claimants to the proceeds from Russia's gas wealth (here, governing elites and Gazprom's managers) due to low TCs, for example, points to the key role that high TCs, and hence clear boundaries, play in determining whether domestic privatization promotes the incentives that produce positive fiscal outcomes. At the same time, the fact that Russia established a strong fiscal regime from 1995–2005 despite the divergence in ownership structure between the oil and gas sector suggests that domestic privatization of even one part of a country's mineral wealth – albeit a significant one – may be sufficient to promote fiscal reform. Russia's experience after 2004 also suggests, however, that it may not be sufficient to sustain domestic privatization itself.

In sum, concerning its impact on the fiscal regime, we predict that Russia's initial choice of ownership structure in the gas sector had many of the disadvantages of S_1 and few of the benefits of P_1. On the one hand, as under S_1, TCs were low because governing elites and Gazprom's managers shared a mutual interest in maximizing their discretion over the management of the company's assets. On the other hand, as under P_1, societal expectations were low due to Gazprom's nominal status as a private company. Finally, interdependent power relations in the context of low TCs fostered implicit bargaining between Gazprom's managers and governing elites. Thus we should find a tacit agreement whereby the former could utilize their privileged position to enrich themselves personally in exchange for meeting the latter's basic political requirements via huge gas subsidies to domestic consumers. At the same time, low societal expectations both reduced the government's incentive to utilize Gazprom as a vehicle for building large public works projects and encouraged the government to impose a hefty explicit tax burden on the company alongside its implicit one. We should also find that, in contrast to the ROCs, Gazprom's managers have not only shown little interest in promoting broad fiscal reform but also that, along with the government, they knowingly pursued fiscal policies that left the company undercapitalized. This behavior, moreover, should be exacerbated by commodity busts and booms. Following the 1998 financial crisis, for example, we should find that they used their political clout to lobby for lowering their implicit rather than their explicit tax burden and to resist pressures for internal restructuring.

Throughout the 1990s, the Russian government imposed both an equally heavy explicit tax burden on Gazprom as it did on the oil sector[73] and a much heavier implicit tax burden. Similar to state-owned companies in petroleum-rich countries that adopt S_1, its implicit tax burden included providing implicit and explicit fuel subsidies (gas as well as electricity) for households and

---

[73] By the middle of 1998, Gazprom's payments to the State Tax Service accounted for one-quarter of Federal tax receipts (Stern 2005, 56).

industrial consumers. In particular, Gazprom was subjected to price controls and delivery requirements for nonpaying domestic customers,[74] forcing it to sell most of the gas it produced (roughly 70 percent) on the domestic market for approximately 15 percent of the price it would have received on the global market (Weinthal and Jones Luong 2006a). The fully privatized ROCs, in contrast, were no longer bound by either price or export controls as of 1995 and were legally empowered to cut off delinquent customers via a 1994 presidential decree (ibid). Because roughly 60 percent of Russia's electricity is generated from natural gas, Unified Energy Systems (UES), the centralized electricity-generating monolith, has been one of Gazprom's largest customers and greatest beneficiaries of subsidized fuel. And because UES, which is majority state-owned, was required to supply electricity to nonpaying domestic customers during this period, including the federal government, it has also been responsible for a significant portion of Gazprom's payment arrears. Thus, needless to say, gas and electricity were the largest source of QFAs in the Russian economy prior to 1998 (IMF 2004c, 6). According to World Bank estimates, for example, payment arrears to both Gazprom and UES alone "provid[ed the Russian] economy with an annual implicit subsidy equal to 4 percent of GDP" in the 1990s (Pinto et al. 2000, 14).[75] Consequently, the Russian economy has remained highly energy-intensive because household and industrial consumers alike have little, if any, incentive to conserve their usage or, for the latter in particular, to develop or adopt technologies that make their usage more efficient (IEA 2002). For example, "[e]nergy consumption per dollar of GDP in 2003 was estimated to be 2.3 times the world average and 3.1 times the European average" (Ahrend and Tompson 2005, 810) and "at the end of the twentieth century, industrial use accounted for a third of total energy consumption in the United States, but for three-quarters in Russia" (Kuz'min et al. 2008, 62).

By the early 2000s, the combination of Gazprom's explicit and implicit tax burden earned it the dubious honor of becoming Russia's largest taxpayer (see Agafonov 2003). Similar to other petroleum-rich states under S$_s$, this was designed to enable governing elites to satisfy societal expectations by supplying cheap fuel to households across the country while also "rewarding" their particular constituencies.[76] Yet, in contrast to *fully* state-owned and controlled NOCs operating in other parts of the developing world, Gazprom's hefty tax burden was not aimed at enabling the government either to furnish

---

[74] This included "household utilities – such as water and electricity suppliers, hospitals, military and state telecommunications organisations and other consumers whose activities were held to be vital to national security and environmental safety" (Stern 2005, 49).

[75] When combined with the low price subsidy, this estimate rises to 5.5 percent of GDP (OECD 2002, 121–32).

[76] While fuel subsidies are more or less guaranteed for households, annual quotas (which can be adjusted quarterly) are arbitrarily set for other consumers through an opaque bidding process between the government, Gazprom, and industrial consumers (Authors' interview with Eskin).

the population with numerous free or heavily discounted goods and services or to build large public works projects. Rather, as we describe in Chapter 3, its purpose was to provide the bare minimum that consumers have come to expect in petroleum-rich states – direct subsidies for fuel and electricity.

As is the case with the oil sector, to the extent that proceeds from the gas sector were used to expand social services and public goods provision prior to 2002, this has been most prominent in those regions where Gazprom (and its subsidiaries) operate. Since the 1980s, three major gas fields located in the Nadym-Pur-Taz region of the Yamal-Nenets Autonomous Area of Western Siberia and the large enterprises that developed them – Urengoigazprom, Yamburggazprom, and Nadymgazprom – have dominated gas production in Russia. (Refer to Map 5.2) As was customary during the Soviet period, these enterprises provided their employees and the surrounding community with a plethora of social and economic benefits, including subsidized housing, free healthcare, and all-expense paid vacations. Hence, just like the ROCs, when Gazprom absorbed these enterprises as its subsidiaries, it also inherited the costs of their respective social welfare obligations. Technicians employed by Urengoigazprom, for example, earn over 10 times what the average Russian worker earns and have access to heavily subsidized childcare, free medical services, and interest-free housing loans (Authors' interview with Gazprom representative no. 1). At the same time, the company boasts that in addition to supplying the town where its headquarters reside – Novy Urengoi – with low-cost electricity, heat, and water as well as maintaining its infrastructure, it also sponsors a variety of cultural and sporting events for the city's residents (ibid). Unlike the ROCs, however, Gazprom did not actively attempt to divest itself of these so-called "social assets," but rather, agreed to absorb these costs as part of its tacit exchange with the government to retain its monopoly status (Authors' interview with former high-ranking official no. 1). These costs have represented a significant portion of Gazprom's budget. In the early 2000s, for example, over 40 percent of Gazprom's total personnel was occupied with providing services unrelated to gas production and transit, including health-care, transportation, and even catering (for details, see the company's annual reports from 2000 to 2003).

Until 2002, Gazprom also mimicked the oil sector in sponsoring educational programs and cultural activities at both the national and subnational levels as part of its attempt to meet its perceived social obligation. In addition to financing institutes that train oil and gas professionals throughout the country, for example, it has contributed to the restoration of important national monuments such as the historic building housing the State University of Economy and Finance in St. Petersburg (for details, see the company's annual reports from 2000 to 2002). The company also placed "special emphasis" on promoting social and economic development in "those regions in which [it] has a presence" (Authors' interview with Gazprom representative no. 1). Similar to the ROCs, this included, but was not limited to, paying a "substantial amount of [explicit] taxes" (ibid.). Its subsidiary Yamburggazprom, which is licensed to develop the Yamburg and Zapolyarnoye fields in Yamal, for example, "actively supports [the local government in] the implementation of priority national projects" including affordable housing and healthcare (ibid). Yet even at the regional level, the company's social contribution, technically speaking, did not match that of the ROCs, which Gazprom's management justified by pointing to the huge fuel subsidies it provides. Rem Viakhirev, who served as the company's CEO until 2001, for example, referred to the chronic nonpayments problem as "interest free credit" to the Russian economy (Viakhirev 1999).

Despite some similarities, Gazprom's experience amounts to a significant departure from the ROCs in that it has suffered from many of the same pathologies as NOCs in other parts of the developing world. These include, first and foremost, undercapitalization and gross mismanagement. Due to pervasive asset stripping equal to approximately 10 percent of the company's total reserves in the 1990s, as of the summer of 2002, the market capitalization of Gazprom [wa]s so small that it was described as "a national embarrassment" (Browder 2002b). In 2002, for example, "Gazprom's reserves trade[d] at 10 cents for energy equivalent to one barrel of oil" compared to "Exxon Mobil's reserves, [which] trade[d] at $13.80 per barrel" (Browder 2002a). This contrasts starkly with the experience of the oil sector, in which private owners and managers have exercised a much greater degree of oversight over their subordinates, for example, by carrying out annual audits since the mid-1990s and basing employment decisions on performance (Weinthal and Jones Luong 2006a). Gazprom has also been involved in an accounting scandal on par with Enron in the United States, which has scared off already reluctant investors, and thus, lowered its market valuation further. Specifically, minority investors suggest that Gazprom's stock was undervalued in the late 1990s and early 2000s owing to lax financial audits carried out by Pricewaterhouse Coopers that deliberately "overlooked" the above-mentioned murky asset transfers (ibid.). Moreover, due to its high tax burden combined with its low market capitalization, Gazprom suffered from an acute shortage of investment capital in the 1990s. While, in contrast to the oil sector, Gazprom received directed credits from the government, due to low domestic prices and the chronic problem of payment arrears, these were "never sufficient to recoup our current costs of production, let alone leave us any capital to expand production" (Authors' interview with Gazprom representative no. 2). The inability to invest adequately in acquiring production technologies for existing fields and exploring new fields has had lasting repercussions: acute financial and debt problems that have been exacerbated by declining production levels since 1999 (see Ahrend and Tompson 2005, IEA 2002).

Where the gas sector departs most starkly from the oil sector, however, is in its reaction to the commodity bust that triggered the 1998 financial crisis, which exacerbated many of these pathologies. Rather than serving as an impetus for embracing reform, when the crisis first hit, Gazprom's managers immediately sought protection from the government and showed no interest in overhauling Russia's weak fiscal regime. Instead, they used their political clout to lobby for lowering their implicit rather than their explicit tax burden and to resist internal restructuring aimed at improving the company's performance (Authors' interview with former high-ranking government official no. 1). In the first few months following the crisis, Gazprom's managers began actively pressuring the government to increase the domestic price for gas and to allow the company to cut off delinquent customers. But its efforts were met with strong resistance from a government desperate to limit the commodity bust's economic, and hence political, damage. And when governing elites attempted to turn the discussion toward structural reforms, including regular internal audits to increase transparency and giving small producers access to pipelines to introduce some competition into the gas sector,[77] Gazprom's managers focused their efforts on avoiding such reforms, either by using their control over the Board of Directors to stall the reform process indefinitely, dominating commissions designed for this very purpose, or insisting that it must protect the national interest in maintaining a secure domestic gas supply (Weinthal and Jones Luong 2006a).

Conversely, in addition to pursuing broad fiscal reform (discussed above), the ROCs responded to the "bust" by embracing the need for internal restructuring.[78] Whereas Gazprom continued to operate with a high level of secrecy over its financial records and "interactions with its subsidiaries" in the first half of the 2000s (Ahrend and Tompson 2005, 813), shortly after the crisis, the ROCs either created or expanded their existing oversight mechanisms for internal monitoring through the adoption of corporate governance measures, which included new international accounting procedures (that is, GAAP standards) and the formation of an independent board of directors empowered to conduct regular audits (Authors' interviews with Adshead and O'Sullivan). Oil companies like Sidanco that had failed to institute effective monitoring mechanisms in the 1990s, for example, made "eliminating leakage [of assets] ..., controlling internal costs ..., [and] gaining complete control over [its] cash flow" a focus of their post-crisis reform efforts (Authors' interview with Fossum). The oil sector also made substantial progress toward establishing corporate governance in several other areas, including making a formal commitment to protect shareholders rights (see Yakovlev 2004), for example, by increasing transparency and "reduc[ing] the risk of shareholder dilution" (Youssef-Martinek et al. 2003, 4), and even adopting international standards on environmental management (see Tkatchenko 2002, 17). Furthermore, the ROCs have restructured their internal management through hiring internationally. By 2001, foreigners comprised approximately 25 percent of top-level

[77] Due to Gazprom's integrated monopoly structure, which includes transportation, neither independent gas producers nor the private oil companies can transport the gas they produce without the company's authorization.

[78] Admittedly, they did so to varying degrees. Generally speaking, there was a greater degree of restructuring and reinvestment in bank-owned (such as Sidanco and Yukos) than insider-owned (such as Tatneft and Lukoil) oil companies.

management in Yukos. As intended, these changes in company strategy have signaled to both shareholders and potential strategic partners that the ROCs are concerned about improving their profitability and operating under hard budget constraints (Authors' interview with O'Sullivan).

The divergence in reactions of the gas versus the oil sector, moreover, has had important consequences for their subsequent trajectories. In the oil industry, production growth rose dramatically from 1999–2004, particularly among those companies that underwent the most vigorous internal restructuring,[79] making it the primary contributor to Russia's own dramatic economic recovery in the first half of the 2000s (see Ahrend 2004). Meanwhile, Gazprom continued to experience a sharp decline in production while small independent gas companies extracting deeper-lying gas deposits sustained an increase in production (see Ahrend and Tompson 2005, 811–2). Similarly, while the ROCs made substantial gains in market capitalization and attracting foreign investors and partners, Gazprom remained undercapitalized and scorned internationally (see Epstein and Berezanskaja 2002). As noted above, a shortage of investment capital undoubtedly exacerbated its production decline by undermining its ability to finance the investment needed to address the underlying causes of this decline. In addition to the aforementioned imperative to explore new fields, investment is needed even more acutely in the transportation and distribution system, which already "consumes far more of Gazprom's capital investment than its production activities do" (Ahrend and Tompson 2005, 805). Another indication of the oil sector's marked rebound compared to the gas sector is that by 2003, the major ROCs were paying more than 20 percent of net profits by way of dividends, whereas Gazprom paid less than 9 percent (Weinthal and Jones Luong 2006a).

Why, then, did Gazprom fail to restructure? Given the obvious benefits of embracing reform, already apparent in the oil sector's impressive performance by the early 2000s, why this divergence in responses to the 1998 financial crisis? For a compelling answer we must return to the divergence in their ownership structure – specifically, the fact that whereas full privatization in the oil sector fostered high TCs, and thus, clear boundaries between governing elites and the ROCs, partial privatization in the gas sector fostered low TCs, and thus, blurred boundaries between governing elites and Gazprom's managers. Simply put: in contrast to the oil sector, it is difficult to distinguish the management from the government in the gas sector. As described above, for most of the 1990s, Gazprom's President and Board of Directors not only controlled their own shares but also were entrusted with the government's shares. Thus, they openly ran the company as if they owned it. Moreover, Gazprom's CEO has always been a presidential appointee and its managers and government representatives have consistently formed a majority on the Board of Directors.

---

[79] Yukos had the greatest growth in production: in 2001, it "increased [its] volume of oil production by 17.5 percent, which its twice the average of the industry," enabling it to surpass Lukoil (Tkatchenko 2002, 13).

It is perhaps this more than anything else that led many close observers to conclude that it is hard to determine where "Gazprom ends and the Russian state begins" (Rutland 1997a, 8). Similar to an NOC under S_1, therefore, this gave the company's managers both a greater opportunity to steal from the company and a greater incentive to do so because, as de facto government employees, they were not compensated for performance. Rather, Gazprom's managers reaped direct benefits by engaging in pervasive asset stripping.

While this difference was present throughout the 1990s, it was made painstakingly clear following the 1998 financial crisis. In short, because the ROCs faced hard budget constraints, they knew that "only [they] were responsible" for [their] recovery and "only [they] would pay the consequences" if they failed to do so (Author's interview with Sidanco representative no. 2). This served as a strong motivating force, not only to support the government's efforts to institute a stable tax code, but also to fundamentally change the way they did business. For example, as mentioned previously, many ROC managers understood that increasing production and profitability over the long term required attracting Western partners, which in turn required adopting the principles of corporate governance. Thus, many ROCs viewed the crisis as a "second chance," an opportunity to focus their efforts on "the business of doing business" (Authors' interview with O'Sullivan). From this perspective, some welcomed Putin's well-publicized meeting with the oligarchs on July 28, 2000 because they considered it a deliberate attempt to "establish a clearer separation between business and the state" (Author's interview with Bigman).

Conversely, private discussions between the Putin administration and Gazprom's managers just after the crisis seemed to bring the company "[back] into the state's arms" (Authors' interview with former high-ranking official no. 1). Because of its close ties to the state, Gazprom lacked not only the incentive to undergo the type of restructuring that the ROCs actively pursued in the early 2000s, but also the capacity to do so. In short, due to their Faustian bargain with the government whereby Gazprom preserved its monopoly in exchange for subsidizing the domestic gas market, the company's managers created the greatest single obstacle to its financial health. Simply put, artificially low domestic prices and chronic nonpayments have prevented Gazprom from accumulating investment capital necessary to reverse its production decline and forced it to amass substantial foreign debt by borrowing to fund new projects. According to the company's own managers, "the [domestic] price of gas [was] too low to recoup outlays on its production" (Kuz'min et al. 2008, 61) and revenue from domestic sales was "insufficient even to cover short-run costs" (Ahrend and Tompson 2005, 803). Compounding this, since 2000, domestic demand has been growing while production has been declining, which further limited the company's ability to generate capital via exports.[80] Yet the government refused to change its policy, "demonstrat[ing]

---

[80] Gazprom could only export about one-third of its total production after meeting domestic demand.

the considerable degree to which Gazprom's interests [have been continuously] subordinated to the solution of ... state problems" (Kuz'min et al. 2008, 62).

Both the nature of Gazprom's relationship with the state and its accompanying financial problems, moreover, have been exacerbated by the government's reassertion of state ownership with control (S_1) over the gas sector in 2002. First and foremost, Putin has shown an increasing willingness to exploit the government's close ties to Gazprom to serve his own political ends. Certainly, Putin exploited these links early on, dipping into the gas monopoly's coffers to bankroll his initial presidential election campaign in 2000, and then later, to debilitate the oligarchs who had amassed media empires, which they used both to support Yeltsin's reelection in 1996 and to sustain their own political influence over the previous regime (see, for example, Belin 2004). His primary target became Vladimir Gusinsky – not merely because his media holding company owned the highly popular private television channel NTV but more so because his media outlets (including NTV) became notorious for criticizing the conduct of the war in Chechnya and questioning Putin's credentials (ibid). In 2001, Putin used Gazprom to finance the forced takeover of NTV and to buy out Gusinsky's remaining shares in other Russian media companies (for details, see Hoffman 2002, Chapter 16).

By mid-2003, however, the notion that Gazprom could be a powerful tool for eliminating those who represented a serious threat to the regime (a.k.a., the oligarchs) became more prominent within the Putin administration (Authors' interview with former high-ranking official no. 3).[81] And this time the oligarch of choice was Khodorkovsky, who sought to bolster his political influence not by accumulating TV stations and newspapers but rather by vigorously supporting liberal opposition political parties and, perhaps most detrimental from the Kremlin's perspective, by building diplomatic links in preparation to expand his oil company (Yukos) beyond Russia (see Sakwa 2009). The primary target for a Gazprom buyout, therefore, became Yukos itself. In late 2004, Khodorkovsky was forced to sell the company's most valuable subsidiary and covetable asset – Yuganskneftegaz – to cover tax claims exceeding the company's revenue. When international banks withdrew their financial support for Gazprom's bid after the company's shareholders contested the forced sale, however, the Russian government had to come up with an elaborate scheme to find another (albeit, temporary) Kremlin-friendly buyer (ibid). This buyer turned out to be another state-owned company in the petroleum sector – Rosneft – a small and fairly insignificant oil company (prior to this purchase) whose planned merger with Gazprom was already under way.[82]

---

[81] At the same time, Gazprom-Media's acquisition of prominent TV stations and newspapers continued; by 2007, it had become Russia's leading media group (for details, see Reporters without Borders 2007).

[82] Although the merger failed, the intended goal was for Gazprom to eventually acquire Yuganskneftegaz.

Second, Gazprom has been under greater pressure to ramp up spending on social services and "national prestige" projects. Only in 2002 did the company begin to take a real interest in its public image and to make an earnest attempt to design, implement, and publicize comprehensive social programs (Author's interview with Gazprom representative no. 2; see also the company's annual reports from 2002 to 2005). Since 2004, moreover, not only have gas subsidies to consumers persisted, but also there has been a concerted effort to expand "gasification." Gazprom's chairman from 2002 until he was elected president of the country in 2008, Dmitri Medvedev, publicly pledged to bring gas to 1,120 towns and villages between 2005 and 2007, increasing the number of Russians whose homes were directly hooked up to gas from 53 percent to 60 percent. At the same time, the company has actively financed the erection of monuments to "showcase its success," including, for example, its new national headquarters in Saint Petersburg, which it boasts will be higher than the Eiffel Tower, the Peter and Paul Cathedral, and Smolny Cathedral (see Gazprom 2008).

Finally, particularly since 2005, Gazprom has played a central role in the expansion of the state's direct role in the economy. Along with Rosneft, it has been the primary vehicle for buying controlling state shares in industrial giants – both within and outside the petroleum sector (for details, see OECD 2006, Tompson 2008). At the end of 2005, for example, Gazprom purchased a 69.66 percent stake in the private oil company Sibneft and a 75 percent stake in the heavy machinery company United Heavy Machinery (OMZ). A year later, via government pressure on Royal Dutch Shell, Gazprom acquired a 50 percent stake plus one share in the Sakhalin Energy Investment Company Ltd. (SEIC), making it the leading shareholder in the Sakhalin II oil project. This has contributed to both the company's and the country's growing external indebtedness; together with Rosneft, Gazprom is responsible for about one-fifth of total corporate foreign debt (OECD 2006). And yet, because the bulk of the capital that Gazprom has raised abroad has been devoted to bringing more assets under its control, it has been deliberately foregoing desperately needed investments in new fields.

Thus, whereas prior to 2002 Gazprom exhibited some of the features of a typical NOC, after 2002 it started to behave exactly like one.

IMPLICATIONS

In sum, because it adopted what has historically been a rare form of ownership structure – private domestic ownership (P_1) – from 1993–2004, Russia was able to achieve what few mineral-rich states have – a strong fiscal regime. It accomplished this, moreover, when proponents of the resource curse thesis would least expect it – that is, during a sustained oil price boom. As an IMF study (2005d, 47) concluded,

The Russian economy has made impressive progress since the 1998 crisis. This rebound has clearly been facilitated by a high oil price ... but it has also been supported by improved economic policies, not least fiscal policy. After the crisis, fiscal policy increasingly became a tool for promoting macroeconomic stabilization and long-term growth.

As a result, at the end of 2005, Russia's fiscal policy bore little resemblance either to the classic rentier model or to its petroleum-rich FSU counterparts, Turkmenistan and Uzbekistan, who adopted state ownership with control (S_1). Indeed, by many accounts, owing to the government's successful efforts at controlling inflation, repaying debt, and amassing foreign reserves,[83] Russia seemed poised to avoid the counterproductive development trajectory so prominent among OPEC members (Authors' interview with Illarionov; see also World Bank 2005e).

By the end of 2006, however, the situation had clearly changed. On the one hand, the Putin administration remained committed to the tax and budgetary reforms it enacted since 1999, as well as to furthering the positive economic effects of these and other reforms. In 2005 and 2006, for example, Russia continued to strengthen the aforementioned reforms aimed at reducing the size of the informal economy and facilitating the growth of SMEs (for details, see *Doing Business in 2007*).[84] On the other hand, Russia's fiscal reform efforts on the expenditure side were clearly being derailed.

In what seemed to be a complete reversal of its conservative fiscal stance, the 2007 Federal Budget Law (submitted to the Duma in August 2006 and approved in November) authorized a 25 percent increase in government spending, primarily for raising public-sector salaries, pensions, and public financing for social services.[85] Spending on education and healthcare alone, for example, was to increase by 60 and 30 percent, respectively, relative to the previous year's already expanded budget. That this upward trend in government spending would continue was made clear in the 2008 Federal Budget Law, which created a three-year federal budget for the first time, and included another 25 percent increase in spending by 2010, aimed largely at expanding social service provision and bolstering salaries for state employees and especially military personnel. The most dramatic changes enacted by this law, however, are the end of the government's commitment to maintaining a fiscal surplus, which is slated to disappear altogether by 2010, and the relaxation of rules governing the OSF, which affords the government much greater flexibility in allocating the surplus that accrues in the fund (for details, see World Bank 2007).[86] Regarding the latter, the greatest cause for

---

[83] Not including the $65 billion in its OSF, "Russia's foreign reserves totaled $258 billion" in mid 2006. When compared to under $8 billion and falling" in mid-1999, this is staggering (Gaddy 2007, 38).

[84] Stimulating SME growth continued to be a priority under Putin's successor, Medvedev (see, for example, BOFIT 2008).

[85] For details, see "O federal'nom budzhete na 2007 god." (On the Federal Budget for the Year 2007.)

[86] The OSF was divided into two separate funds: (1) the "Reserve Fund," which would hold surplus revenues up to 10 percent of GDP in order to shield the budget from fluctuations in world

concern comes from the establishment of the National Welfare Fund, which will be used to invest in unspecified longer terms assets and has the potential not only to negate the intended purpose of the OSF's creators but also to "open Pandora's box" when it comes to government spending (Authors' interview with Illarionov).

What accounts for this dramatic turnaround? We argue that it can be explained by Russia's equally dramatic shift from private domestic ownership (P_1) to state ownership with control (S_1) as of 2005. Consistent with our expectations, the state's acquisition of a controlling stake in Yukos in December 2004, followed by its open support for legislation that would pave the way for expanding state ownership over the oil sector, triggered a perceived (if not real) rise in societal expectations. As we discuss at length in Chapter 3 and demonstrate in Chapter 4 in the cases of Turkmenistan and Uzbekistan, S_1 fosters weak fiscal regimes in part because it generates high societal expectations for the widespread distribution of benefits from mineral wealth – or, more correctly, elite perceptions that this is the case. In Russia, this effect was in some ways more immediate than we might have anticipated because it changed not only governing elites' perceptions of societal expectations but also the balance of power among liberals and conservatives (a.k.a., the *siloviki*) within the Putin administration, and thus the direct influence of the latter over the former.[87]

The appreciable effect that S_1 can have on elite perceptions of societal expectations is already evident in the aforementioned change in Gazprom's spending patterns and priorities since 2002, which the company's own managers viewed as a direct consequence of its change in ownership structure: "we are no longer a private company that can do mostly what we please with our profits … we now have some very serious social commitments" (Authors' interview with Gazprom representative no. 2). Yet, this has been magnified since 2005.

Generally speaking, sustained calls within the administration for Putin to ramp up social spending commensurate with Russia's massive petroleum wealth began to manifest themselves only in mid-2005. And, not coincidentally, this pressure came directly from the siloviki, who had been not only opposed to the oligarchs' influence over the development of what they considered a "strategic state asset" but also much less committed to fiscal reform during the first Putin administration (Authors' interviews with Illarionov and Shatalov). While not the original intention of Putin's assault on Khodorkovsky, it was they who seized this opportunity to expand state ownership over the entire oil sector. It was also they who most prominently advocated the view that the shift to S_1 should coincide with greater and expanded role for the state

oil prices; and (2) the "Fund for Future Generations" (later called the "National Welfare Fund"), which would accrue the additional surplus revenues.

[87] For a discussion of the various factions within the Putin administration, see, for example, Bremmer and Charap (2006–07).

in the economy as well as in the provision of public goods and social services (Authors' interviews with Illarionov and former high-ranking government official no. 3).

One prominent illustration of their newfound influence and its effect is the significant increase in the rhetorical importance of the petroleum sector in Putin's annual public addresses. Whereas there had been little if any mention of Russia's petroleum wealth prior to 2005, particularly in the context of its relationship to the general welfare, by 2007 its role in raising living standards had become a central focus. In justifying the expanded role of the state outlined in the new budget, for example, Putin states:

> To be frank, our policy ... is not to everyone's taste. Some ... would like to return us to the recent past, ... to once again plunder the nation's resources with impunity and rob the people and the state. ... We are taking a different route. ... We began implementing the priority national projects eighteen months ago. The primary aim of these projects is to invest in people and improve their quality of life.

More specifically, pressure to spend the funds accumulated in the OSF – from both within and outside the executive branch – began in early 2005 but escalated rapidly in early 2006 to such an extent that the government believed it "was forced to act ... [or] face the public's outrage" (Authors' interview with former high-ranking official no. 3). In fact, Putin gave special emphasis to the creation of the National Welfare Fund in his 2007 *Address*, declaring that

> the money in this Fund should be spent on raising the quality of life of our citizens and developing our economy. This Fund should help bring greater prosperity for our people both now and in the future. In this respect, it would be more correct to call it the National Prosperity Fund.

While a full treatment of the causal mechanisms whereby the shift from P_1 to S_1 weakened Russia's fiscal regime is not possible here, there is ample evidence to suggest that the adoption of S_1 at least partially derailed Russia's fiscal reforms because it triggered a perceived (if not real) rise in societal expectations. Indeed, it suggests how rapidly a change in ownership structure can have such an effect. This serves to bolster our central claim that ownership structure – not petroleum wealth – is responsible for the so-called resource curse. The shift from P_1 to S_1, moreover, provides an additional opportunity to test our explanation for why mineral-rich countries choose different ownership structures. We turn to this subject in Chapter 9.

6

State Ownership without Control versus
Private Foreign Ownership

> We need to use transparency in revenue and financial management to allow people to hold government to account and build public trust ... but companies have an interest in promoting transparency too. Transparency should help companies to reduce reputational risk, to address the concerns of shareholders and to help manage risks of long-term investments. And transparency is a positive contribution to development as it increases the likelihood that revenues will be used for poverty reduction.
>
> – Prime Minister Tony Blair commenting on EITI, London, 2003

> Corporations ... are increasingly being asked to step into roles that were once the domain of governments or international bodies such as the UN.
>
> – Jim Buckee, CEO Talisman Energy, cited in Kobrin (2004, 455)

In the preceding chapters we make a general case for the importance of ownership structure in understanding the relationship between mineral wealth and fiscal regimes over time. To recap, we argue that a country's choice of ownership structure over mineral wealth rather than mineral wealth per se is responsible for the negative outcomes that are so prevalent in mineral-rich states. Ownership structure, however, does not exist in a historical vacuum, but rather, within a specific international context. Because petroleum is such an important international commodity, the influence of actors and norms outside the domestic arena is often unavoidable. This is most apparent where foreign investors (hereafter, FIs) are directly involved in the exploitation of mineral reserves; that is, when governments adopt the two remaining ideal types of ownership structure – state ownership without control (S_2) and private foreign ownership (P_2).

Indeed, the heightened role of FIs sets S_2 and P_2 apart from the other two ideal types discussed in Chapter 3 (S_1 and P_1) in two equally important ways. First, they can only produce fiscal regimes that are partially constraining and enabling – or what we call "hybrid" – because their primary influence is within the mineral sector – that is, on the size, stability, composition, and degree of transparency of the FIs' fiscal burden, which, in turn, can affect both the quality of citizens' daily lives and the long-term developmental prospects of mineral-rich states. Second, their effect on fiscal regimes is dynamic. As different actors gain and lose prominence in this sector at the international level, they can transform the impact of ownership structure itself on the triadic relationship between the primary direct claimants to the proceeds from mineral wealth (here, FIs) and the primary indirect claimants (here, governing elites and their societies). More specifically, changes at the international level mediate the direct effects of ownership structure on the three mechanisms we identify in Chapter 3: (1) transaction costs (hereafter, TCs), (2) societal expectations, and (3) power relations. The purpose of this chapter is both to enumerate the distinct effects of S_2 and P_2 on fiscal outcomes in mineral-rich states and to elucidate how their effects vary over the course of the twentieth century with particular emphasis on the most recent time period (1990–2005).

In contrast to P_1, which is the rarest form of ownership structure, FIs have been involved in the exploitation of petroleum in almost every petroleum-rich country since the late-nineteenth century and throughout the twentieth century, making S_2 and P_2 some of the more ubiquitous forms of ownership structure (Appendix B).[1] The extent of their involvement, however, has varied over the twentieth century. During the first part of the twentieth century, P_2 was unmistakably the most prevalent form of ownership structure – often associated with the rise of such global giants as the Standard Oil of New Jersey, Royal Dutch Shell, and the British Petroleum Company (see Bamberg 1994, Gibb and Knowlton 1956, Larson et al. 1971). Then, from about 1970 until the mid-1990s, the number of countries that adopted S_2 surpassed P_2 for the first time, although S_1 was the predominant form of ownership structure during this period (Appendix B).[2] Since the mid-1990s, P_2 has made a comeback such that it surpassed S_1 and rivaled S_2 as the most common ownership structure among petroleum-rich countries by 2000.[3]

Despite its historical "popularity," P_2 is perhaps the least desirable form of ownership structure from the perspective of the governing elites because full decision-making authority over the development of the country's mineral wealth is transferred to foreign private companies with headquarters normally located in their home countries. P_2 essentially entails the granting of wide-ranging concession contracts to these FIs. Consequently, FIs are the sole direct claimants to the proceeds generated from the exploitation of the mineral wealth, and similar to P_1, the primary role of governing elites is to tax and regulate the mineral sector on behalf of the population. In contrast to S_2 (below), however, this role is usually not performed by a national oil company (hereafter, NOC) because one is usually not created, but rather by a "competent authority."[4] As a result, P_2 creates a triadic relationship whereby there are two sets of indirect claimants to

---

[1] The few exceptions include Chile, China, and the Soviet Union.

[2] In 1970, 17 countries adopted S_1 while 12 adopted S_2 and 7 adopted P_2.

[3] By 1995, only 12 petroleum-rich countries had adopted S_1 whereas 17 had adopted S_2 and 15 had adopted P_2.

[4] The competent authority can also take the form of the Ministry of Petroleum, the Ministry of Taxation, or the Environmental Ministry.

the proceeds from mineral wealth – governing elites and the population – who can make demands on the direct claimants – FIs.

S_2 differs from P_2 in that FIs are only involved in the exploitation of mineral wealth as managers on behalf of the state rather than as owners. It is a more desirable strategy than P_2 from the perspective of the state, then, because the state retains some direct claim due to its ownership status, which is most often realized through a NOC. As under S_1, the NOC plays a key role under S_2. It not only serves as a nominal partner to any major venture in the mineral sector and, in some cases, operates a few small fields on its own, but also is usually charged with negotiating the contracts and collecting the royalties, income taxes, and bonuses that FIs owe to the state (Bindemann 1999).[5] Thus, the triadic relationship under S_2 consists of the same set of actors as under P_2 – that is, FIs are the main direct claimants to the proceeds from the mineral wealth and both governing elites and the domestic population serve as the indirect claimants. Yet because the state retains some direct access to the proceeds generated from the exploitation of some of its mineral wealth, the governing elites under S_2 also serve as a direct claimant.

The international context has experienced two major shifts over the course of the twentieth century in terms of which actors and norms dominated the petroleum industry, split into three distinct time periods. The first time period (1900–1960), which corresponds to the first half of the twentieth century, was characterized by a small number of large FIs (the "Majors") that dominated the international petroleum market.[6] The second (1960–1990) came about with the proliferation of smaller FIs that eroded the Majors' control over the global supply of oil and facilitated the foundation of the Organization of Petroleum Exporting Countries (OPEC); combined, they effectively toppled the Majors' oligopoly pricing structure (see Keohane and Ooms 1972, Morse 1999).[7] The third (1990–2005) begins with the emergence of new norms regarding the way that businesses should conduct their operations abroad accompanied by the entrance of another new set of actors. Specifically, since the 1990s, international nongovernmental organizations (hereafter, INGOs) and international financial institutions (hereafter, IFIs) have sought to play a more pronounced role in the sphere of petroleum revenue management globally through their indirect and direct influence on the contractual relations between the FIs and the host governments.

As we elaborate upon below and summarize in Table 6.1, each time period has a profound effect on the hybrid fiscal regimes that S_2 and P_2 tend to generate

[5] For example, it is likely to be part of a consortium selected to develop an oil and gas field, which often requires it to provide some of its profits as "share capital" (Radon 2005, 68). For more details on the NOC's evolution, see Baker Institute (2007).

[6] Known as the Seven Sisters, they included Standard Oil of New Jersey (Exxon), Royal Dutch Shell, Socony-Vacuum (Mobil), Texaco, Gulf Oil, Standard Oil of California (Chevron), and British Petroleum.

[7] Most notorious among these new entrants were ENI/AGIP (Italy), Arabian Oil Company (Japan), and Occidental Petroleum (U.S.).

TABLE 6.1. *Predicted Fiscal Outcomes under P₂ and S₂, 1900–2005, by Time Period*

Time Period	Taxation		Expenditures	
1) 1900–1960	**Within the mineral sector:**	**Outside the mineral sector:**	**Within the mineral sector:**	**Outside the mineral sector:**
S₂ and P₂	FIs' taxation minimal and stable	Government relies primarily on mineral sector taxation	FIs' spending minimal and stable	Formal limits unlikely but government spending minimal
2) 1960–1990	**Within the mineral sector:**	**Outside the mineral sector:**	**Within the mineral sector:**	**Outside the mineral sector:**
S₂	FIs' taxation higher and unstable	Broad-based tax reform unlikely	FIs' spending largely symbolic, limited to regions of operation	Budgetary reform unlikely
	NOC's taxation high and unstable		NOC's spending unconstrained	
P₂	FIs' taxation higher and unstable	Some potential for broad-based tax reform	FIs' spending largely symbolic, limited to regions of operation	Some potential for budgetary reform

3) 1990–2005	Within the mineral sector:	Outside the mineral sector:	Within the mineral sector:	Outside the mineral sector:
S_2	FIs' taxation higher; may be stable or unstable NOC's fiscal burden high and unstable	Broad-based tax reform unlikely	FIs' engage in social spending at subnational & national levels; has potential to alleviate poverty & promote development NOC's spending unconstrained Stable NRF unlikely but potentially transparent	Budgetary reform unlikely
P_2	FIs' taxation higher; may be stable or unstable	Greater potential for broad-based tax reform	FIs' fiscal burden includes social spending at subnational level; has potential to alleviate poverty & promote development Potential for stable and transparent NRF	Greater potential for budgetary reform

in the states that adopt them. During the first time period (1900–1960), the predicted fiscal regimes under S_2 and P_2 look very similar because the effects on TCs, societal expectations, and power relations are virtually identical. In sum, TCs are universally negligible due to the widespread use of a global template for contractual relations between FIs and host governments (a.k.a. "model contract"), societal expectations are low vis-à-vis both the state and FIs, and power relations decisively favor the FIs, who are thus able to enforce unilaterally their access rights to the proceeds from mineral wealth. The meaning of "low" societal expectations during this period, moreover, is shaped by an international context in which the state does not yet perform much more than its "traditional" functions (that is, maintaining order and securing borders), and the development of the petroleum sector is carried out under immense secrecy, reinforcing its enclave nature. As a result, both governing elites and FIs have a strong incentive to build a tax regime that relies primarily on the mineral sector, remains stable in accordance with the preferences of FIs, and eschews broad social spending. This translates into a minimal and stable fiscal burden for FIs within the mineral sector and the absence of broad-based taxation and unbridled government expenditures outside the mineral sector.

Beginning with the second time period (1960–1990), the expected fiscal regimes under S_2 and P_2 start to diverge both within and outside the mineral sector. While TCs remain negligible due to the persistence of the model contract, societal expectations are universally elevated after 1960, with the heightened publicity surrounding petroleum in the developing world and the changing international norms concerning the role of FIs, and power relations shift decisively in favor of the state. Within the mineral sector, then, we are likely to find both a higher and much less stable fiscal burden for FIs under both S_2 and P_2. Not only do governing elites have a greater incentive to retroactively increase tax rates or impose new taxes to meet their augmented spending needs – that is, to unilaterally change the initial terms of contracts with FIs – consistent with the so-called "obsolescing bargain" (see Vernon 1971), they also have a greater ability to do so. FIs' spending under S_2 and P_2 is also indistinguishable during this period because the prevailing international norms do not require much beyond symbolic spending within the regions where their operations lie.

Yet, owing to the difference in societal expectations vis-à-vis the state, the similarities end there. Under S_2, societal expectations are high because, as under S_1, the state is the self-designated owner (and hence, caretaker) of the country's mineral wealth. We thus expect to find both a high and unstable fiscal burden for the state within the mineral sector, which it exercises via the NOC, and unconstrained state spending outside the mineral sector in the form of universal subsidies and large public works projects. Under P_2, societal expectations vis-à-vis the state remain low. However, due to the greater visibility of the FIs' role in petroleum production after 1960, they have a slightly different meaning. Rather than feeling pressure to distribute the benefits of mineral wealth widely, as is the case under S_1 and S_2, governing elites feel pressure to address the disparities that arise from the geographical distribution of petroleum wealth. Government spending outside the mineral sector, therefore, should largely encompass policies aimed at redistributing wealth from oil-rich to oil-poor regions, such as nationally mandated social transfers. Low societal expectations under P_2 are also important because they create *some* potential for broad-based taxation and budgetary reform outside the mineral sector by reducing governing elites' disincentives for doing so, whereas high societal expectations under S_2 foster strong incentives against pursuing such reforms. Because favorable power relations ease the state's ability to extract increasing amounts from FIs, however, the likelihood that elites will pursue this option even under P_2 is low.

The greatest divergence in the hybrid fiscal regimes generated under S_2 and P_2 is in the third time period (1990–2005). Largely owing to fundamental changes in the international context, these two forms of ownership structure bear little resemblance either to S_2 and P_2 in the previous time periods or to one another during this time period. Their contrast to earlier time periods is starkest within the mineral sector. First, although TCs remain negligible due to the existence of a model contract, direct pressure from INGOs and IFIs for these contracts to incorporate new norms regarding corporate social responsibility (hereafter, CSR) formally expands the FIs' fiscal burden to include some form of broad social spending. Second, INGOs and IFIs also elevate the meaning of high societal expectations vis-à-vis FIs, both by contributing to the greater visibility of foreign investment in the mineral sector and by encouraging domestic populations in mineral-rich countries to demand that FIs do more in exchange for access to the country's natural resource wealth. Thus FIs are often taking on social obligations that exceed the terms specified in their contracts. The pressure to go "beyond compliance" also fosters a greater interest among FIs in supporting institutions for the mineral sector that both set limits on government spending and channel it toward more productive and socially desirable outcomes, such as building human capital and alleviating poverty. In particular, FIs are more likely to support IFI and INGO efforts to establish an effective natural resource fund (hereafter, NRF) in order to increase governmental accountability regarding the mineral rents it accrues and how these are spent. Third, because societal expectations vis-à-vis the state under S_2 and P_2 continue to diverge, both the prospects for creating an effective NRF and the scope of FIs' spending also diverge. *Ceteris paribus* high societal expectations under S_2 mean that governing elites are unlikely to support an effective NRF and that FIs' social obligations are more likely to encompass the national level, whereas low societal expectations under P_2 mean that governing elites are more likely to support an effective NRF and that FIs' social obligations are more likely to be directed primarily at the regions in which they operate. It is also due to these contrasting levels of societal expectations vis-à-vis the state that the key difference between S_2 and P_2 continues to be the potential for fiscal reform outside the mineral sector. Yet, IFIs' willingness to pressure mineral-rich states to adopt broad-based taxation and improve budgetary stability and transparency, combined with FIs' greater interest in supporting these efforts, can magnify this difference because it increases the likelihood that the potential for reform under P_2 will be realized.

What makes the third time period most unique, however, is that because the FIs' fiscal burden can vary considerably in terms of its size, stability, composition, and degree of transparency, so too can their potential to improve both the quality of citizens' daily lives and the long-term developmental prospects of mineral-rich states. Two key factors account for this variation. The first concerns whether power relations favor the FIs or the state. In the first two time periods, the dominant actor could be identified *ex ante*. Simply put, gunboat diplomacy secured the predominance of FIs in the first half of the twentieth century when only a few large FIs effectively exploited the world's oil fields, while the intense competition from new entrants after 1960 inevitably shifted power to host governments via the aforementioned obsolescing bargain. By the end of the 1980s, however, this was no longer the case, as some FIs began to develop strategies to counter the inevitability of the obsolescing bargain. In particular, where they could overcome the collective action problem (CAP), they could prevent the state from reneging on the terms of their contracts. The second key factor concerns how committed FIs are to the norms embodied in CSR. While most FIs have at least acknowledged CSR, FIs have also displayed different levels of commitment to CSR.

The best-case scenario for mineral-rich states that adopt either S_2 or P_2, then, is in which power relations decisively favor FIs that are strongly committed to CSR. Within the mineral sector, this would yield a stable and transparent fiscal burden for FIs, and a high likelihood for their spending to be aimed at alleviating poverty and promoting development, albeit at the national level under S_2 and primarily at the subnational level under P_2. It would also foster a transparent NRF. Outside the mineral sector, this would increase the prospects for governing elites to adopt broad-based tax reform.

And yet the respective best-case scenarios under S_2 and P_2 are not equally desirable. Within the mineral sector under S_2, it remains unlikely that the NOC will match the FIs' fiscal burden in terms of its stability, transparency, or intended socioeconomic impact. There is also less likelihood that the NRF will be aimed at alleviating poverty and promoting development as compared to P_2. Outside the mineral sector, the prospects for both taxation and expenditure reform are also greater under P_2.

In sum, while all fiscal regimes in mineral-rich states that adopt S_2 and P_2 are only partially constraining and enabling, they should look qualitatively different in those that have adopted S_2 and P_2 since the 1990s. This is because the most recent time period offers the greatest potential for S_2 and P_2 to constrain and enable the state both within and outside the mineral sector. The best-case scenarios under S_2 and P_2 in the 1990s, however, also reveal the inherent limitations of the fiscal regimes that emerge where FIs play a dominant role in developing the petroleum sector, and hence why they remain "second best" outcomes. Even if they produce more desirable short- and long-term outcomes for mineral-rich states than the weak fiscal regime that emerges under S_1, they nonetheless fall short of the outcomes generated by the strong fiscal regime that emerges under P_1. Part of the reason for this is that hybrid fiscal regimes, by definition, exert their primary influence within the mineral sector and thus taxation and expenditure policies outside the mineral sector often counteract and even undermine the stability and transparency achieved within the mineral sector. The other, more pernicious reason, however, is that the expanded role of FIs alongside IFIs and INGOs has fostered the emergence of what we term a "proxy state," whereby international actors become de facto mediators between the state and society in lieu of various forms of local organization (see, for example, Migdal et al. 1994). We explore this theme in more detail in the concluding section.

TRANSACTION COSTS

The one constant across the three time periods is that TCs are negligible under both S_2 and P_2. Consequently, neither the direct nor indirect claimants has an incentive to build strong fiscal institutions in the form of a broad-based tax system. At first glance, this is counterintuitive because, as under P_1, the direct claimant to the proceeds from mineral exploitation – FIs – is also the residual claimant, while the other main actor – governing elites – is primarily an indirect claimant. Thus, like domestic private owners (DPOs), the FIs' primary interest concerning the management of the mineral wealth is to maximize their profit, which requires a stable fiscal regime that locks in their fiscal burden; this, however, deviates from the governing elites' primary interest, which is to maximize their discretion over the revenue that accrues to the state budget. Accordingly, given their divergent interests regarding how the mineral sector should be managed, TCs would be high, and they would face mutual incentives to build strong fiscal institutions. However, once we consider the international context in which these FIs operate, it becomes evident that any information asymmetries that arise from their divergent interests are effectively neutralized by the existence of the "model contract" – a contractual template that has standardized the way in which FIs and host governments conduct business throughout the twentieth century.[8]

In sum, the model contract has dictated the terms of exchange between FIs and governing elites in host countries since oil exploration in the developing world began in earnest. Its main purpose has been to establish the rights and duties of both parties with regard to the revenue generated from the exploitation of mineral wealth, such that FIs can both recoup their initial investments and retain a certain level of profits while the state can expect a certain level of income. As one veteran of the international oil industry described, "we have always started and ended our negotiations by taking the model contract off

[8] For North (1981, 26), standardization plays a key role in minimizing the influence of TCs.

the shelf and just using it" (Authors' interview with representative of Amerada Hess).

To say that the model contract sets the terms of exchange between the governing elites and FIs, however, is not to say that these terms have not changed over time. Rather, the precise form the model contract has taken corresponds to the three major time periods we identify above: (1) 1900–1960; (2) 1960–1990; and (3) 1990–2005.[9]

During the first time period (1900–1960), it was possible to describe the model contract as a truly international template because its terms were universal; that is, one version applied to everyone. Beginning with the D'Arcy Concession with the Shah of Persia in 1901, the FIs carried out their business operations with oil producers in the developing world according to an internationally recognized system of isomorphic concession contracts that grossly favored the FIs' preferences over those of the host governments.[10] These concession contracts granted the FIs huge tracts of land (sometimes the whole country) for extremely long periods of time (fifty or more years) wherein the FIs not only acquired the rights to develop the petroleum in the ground but had full control over production schedules; the host governments, in turn, only received payment upon actual production (Bindemann 1999, 9, Smith and Dzienkowski 1989, 2). The 1948 concession between the government of Kuwait and the American Independent Oil Company (AMINOL), for example, was intended to last for 60 years (Bantekas 2005) and only granted the host government a fixed royalty on the amount of oil produced, either per ton or barrel of oil, and not a share of the profits (Hartshorn 1967, 149).[11] Similarly, the original contract between Saudi Arabia and Aramco promised the government 21 cents per barrel of oil at a time when oil was selling for over $2 per barrel (Bindemann 1999, 9).

The terms remained virtually unchanged until 1950, when Aramco agreed to split the profits 50/50 with the Saudi Arabian government, and this became the predominant formula for profit sharing (Odell 1968, Wells 1971).[12] The model contract nonetheless continued to favor disproportionately the FIs (see Tanzer 1969).[13] Simply put, during the first half of the twentieth century, the

[9] The power asymmetries that undergird each version of the model contract will be discussed at length in the subsequent section on power relations.

[10] The Shah granted D'Arcy the right to explore 500,000 square miles of land for a period of 60 years; in return, the Shah received a $100,000 bonus, a 16 percent royalty, and a share in the company worth $100,000 (Bindemann 1999, 9, Smith and Dzienkowski 1989).

[11] The IPC contract (the 1931 Principal Agreement) has been signalled out, as it not only granted the IPC 32,000 square miles of Iraqi territory, but also did not impose any taxes (Watts 2005, 381).

[12] In part for this reason, some scholars (such as Karl 1997) offer a different breakdown for classifying changes in the international petroleum industry: (1) from the discovery of oil until the 1950s – Majors dominate; (2) from the mid-1950s to early 1970s – Majors begin to lose control; and (3) after 1973 – host governments gain control.

[13] As Mira Wilkins surmised in Latin America, the end result was that the FIs "did not pay high taxes" (1974, 127).

model contract granted companies such as Sarawak Shell in Malaysia "complete freedom in the management of oil resources. ... The foreign oil giants only had to pay taxes and royalties. Malaysia, like other governments of the region, operated merely as the tax collector" (Gale 1981, 1131).

During the second time period (1960–1990), however, contractual relations between the FIs and governing elites have largely been defined by the standardization of a new model contract – the production-sharing agreement (PSA) – the specific terms of which have varied from country to country, and sometimes even within a country, over time (Bindemann 1999, Johnston 1994). In many petroleum-rich countries, there is a readily available physical document in government offices that lays out the "basic terms of an agreement" and serves in some ways as a "first offer" (Bindemann 1999, 7).

Generally speaking, under a PSA the host government contracts an FI to undertake exploration and production, and in return for carrying the initial risk, the FI receives a share of the oil produced as payment (Bindemann 1999, Johnston 1994).[14] The first major PSA was signed in Indonesia in 1966, and since then has become the predominant template in all oil-producing regions except North America and Western Europe (excluding Malta) (Bindemann 1999). It was based on a 65/35 split of profit oil in the government's favor until 1976, when Indonesia negotiated the second generation of PSAs, which introduced an 85/15 split in the government's favor (ibid, 68).[15] Yet, contrary to the uniformity in the prior concessionary system, there has been and remains more variation among PSAs, largely depending on how quickly the FIs' costs are recouped and how the profits are divided between the FIs and the government (Bindemann 1999, Johnston 1994, 5).[16] According to one comprehensive study, between 1966 and 1998, 74 countries had signed 268 PSAs; approximately one-third of these were identical versions of the model contract used in another country (Bindemann 1999, 47).

The catalyst for change in the terms of the model contract was the foundation of OPEC in 1960, which was itself a response to the opportunity created by the Majors' weakened position in the international marketplace due to the emergence of several new smaller producers. Thus, it is no coincidence that the 1966 PSA with Indonesia is seen as the turning point in the shift to an international template that deliberately favored the host governments (ibid.). Such

[14] In contrast, under a concession, the FI is entitled to all the reward for carrying all the risk (in other words, all the production belongs to the FI) and the government's share is only a function of production and price (i.e., royalties) (Bindemann 1999, 11).

[15] Indonesia introduced a third generation of PSAs in 1988 that pioneered tranche payments whereby the government's take increases as production increases (Bindemann 1999, 18).

[16] PSAs have four main properties: (1) a pre-specified *royalty* that FIs pays on gross production; (2) a pre-specified share of production for cost recovery, or *cost oil*, that FIs are entitled to after the royalty is deducted; (3) a pre-specified split in *profit oil*, or the remainder of the production shared between the host country and the FI; and (4) a prespecified *corporate income tax* that the FI pays on its share of the profit oil. In addition, some PSAs require FIs to pay signature and production *bonuses*.

contracts were qualitatively different from the prior concessions not only in that the level of taxation and royalties were increasingly more generous to the host governments, but also in that some began to include nominal spending provisions for the FIs known in the industry as "local content." For the most part, local content entailed requirements for FIs to reserve a portion of fuel production for the local economy, to employ a certain share of the local work-force, and to purchase locally made goods and services (Bindemann 1999, Smith and Wells 1975).[17] The Indonesian PSAs, for example, were the first to require FIs to provide a share of their profit oil to the NOC at a price well below the market rate (Bindemann 1999, 68). For countries that adopted S_2, it was also increasingly common for the NOC to stipulate *ex ante* the terms of the country's model contract.[18] In short, as one study of oil contracts across different time periods found, "the forms and substance of oil contracts negoti-ated in the 1970s are, almost without exception, dramatically different from those negotiated in the 1950s" (Smith and Wells 1975, 4).

During the most recent time period (1990–2005), the model contract under-went two critical changes. First, it became increasingly common for some countries to offer several versions of the model contract from which an FI could select. Second, the terms of the model contract underwent a qualitative transformation. While the model contract has continued to retain its basic form as either a PSA or concessionary agreement that largely advantages the host governments regarding taxation, as of the 1990s it automatically incor-porates "stability" and "international arbitration" clauses to protect the FIs against expropriation (Smith and Dzienkowski 1989), as well as explicit spend-ing provisions for the FIs that solidify the local content requirements that were only sometimes specified in their contracts during the 1970s and 1980s. In contrast to the preceding time period, these spending provisions have not only gone beyond token or charitable spending, instead requiring FIs to encompass broad social spending, but also become standard fare (that is, rather than ad hoc), as both sides came to anticipate the inclusion of such provisions either in their contracts or as a verbal or written appendage to these contracts (Radon 2007, 107). For example, according to one account of the contractual process in Angola, the NOC, Sonangol, made it very clear to the FIs from the outset that it expected them to make philanthropic contributions to local communi-ties that have amounted to spending approximately $1 million per year on social programs for every 100,000 barrels of oil per day extracted from the ground (Ball 2006).

---

[17] While we focus on local content as primarily a form of FIs' expenditures, it also provides a source of increased taxation for the state since the state may be able to extract taxes from local suppliers tied to the energy sector at the same time that the FIs are exempted from cer-tain taxation via their contracts.

[18] For example, between 1966–71, Pertamina, Indonesia's NOC, had negotiated PSAs with thir-ty-six foreign oil and gas companies that not only specified their tax obligations but included pricing provisions for sales to third parties (Smith and Wells 1975, 50).

Thus, despite the waning influence of OPEC from the late 1980s onward (Amuzegar 2001), by the last decade of the twentieth century, the terms of the model contract had become even more auspicious to host governments. From the start of the negotiations it is presumed that host governments can require FIs not merely to pay royalties, taxes, and bonuses but also fines for violating stringent environmental, health, and safety regulations and the costs associated with providing training, jobs, and basic public goods and social services to the communities where they operate (Radon 2007).[19] In the deliberations over the 2007 Iraqi Draft Oil and Gas Law, for example, there was a strong consensus that contracts with FIs must stipulate spending provisions for the training of Iraqi personnel, environmental protection, and local development projects.[20] As in the shift from the first to the second time period, this transformation in the terms of the model contract is tied to the emergence of new actors – here, the proliferation of INGOs and IFIs. These actors have fostered norms whereby FIs in the mineral sector should be expected not only to improve their own business practices vis-à-vis host governments but also to vastly increase the scope of their social and economic activities so as to improve the conditions in host countries – that is, to engage in CSR.[21]

Their differences notwithstanding, the model contract has fostered the same basic outcome across the three time periods – a fiscal regime in which the government relies primarily on taxation within the mineral sector for revenue. In short, because it creates a stand-alone tax regime for each FI, by virtue of its existence and widespread use, the model contract provides little or no incentive for either the state to supply or FIs to demand tax reform outside the mineral sector. Governing elites have little incentive to supply broad-based tax regimes because of the relative ease with which they can tax FIs. Under the first version of the model contract that privileged their interests, the FIs were more willing to meet their tax burden because the tax laws in their home countries often allowed them to write off some portion of their overseas taxation (Hartshorn 1967, 195–6, Tanzer 1969, 62). Even during the second time period when the preferred PSA advantaged the host governments, because this contract exempted FIs from other domestic tax laws, they did not have an incentive to encourage governing elites to pursue tax reform outside the mineral sector. This continues to be the case in the third time period because the PSA and the concessionary agreement have remained the predominant contractual templates. Yet it has not precluded FIs from supporting IFIs' efforts

---

[19] Regarding taxation, new provisions often call for a "windfall tax" such that when oil prices are high, the government's take increases disproportionately (Stiglitz 2007).

[20] For example, visit http://web.krg.org/uploads/documents/Draft%20Iraq%20Oil%20and%20 Gas%20Law%20English2007.pdf. The PSA signed with Nigeria-Sao Tome and Principe Joint Development Authority (JDA) in 2005 included similar provisions (JDA treaty available at http://www.nigeriasaotomejda.com/). Yet this contract has moved beyond prior contracts by including a "transparency clause" that stipulates that every signature and production bonus should be published on the JDA's website (Save the Children 2005, 21).

[21] The origins of CSR can be traced to Bowen (1953).

to push for tax reform since the 1990s. Whether these efforts actually produce a viable broad-based tax code, however, hinges upon the cooperation of governing elites, which, *ceteris paribus*, face a higher barrier to taxing their own populations under S_2 than P_2 due to differences in societal expectations vis-à-vis the state. We discuss this in greater detail in the subsequent section on "Societal Expectations."

The likelihood that the fiscal regime that emerges under S_2 and P_2 will include some limits on the expenditure side, however, varies across the three time periods. Until the third time period, the model contract had virtually no effect on the spending side of the fiscal regime. Because their social spending obligations are essentially absent and quite minimal in the first and second time periods, respectively, FIs have little or no incentive to support effective limits on government expenditures either within or outside the mineral sector. That the model contract has come to include explicit and substantial spending requirements in the third time period, however, has meant both that the state's reliance on the mineral sector has been expanded to include FI spending and that there is greater potential for limits on government expenditures within the mineral sector to emerge because the FIs have a greater incentive to support such limits. In particular, there is a much greater likelihood for FIs to support INGOs and IFIs in pressuring governments to adopt an effective NRF. Similar to tax reform, whether this actually materializes depends on the governing elites' incentives, which are greatly influenced by the differences in societal expectations under S_2 and P_2.

Lastly, while the terms of the model contract have become more favorable to the host governments over time, whether the contract is stable depends upon whether the FIs can enforce the contract, which also varies by the international context. Simply put, *ceteris paribus*, FIs and governing elites have different preferences regarding contractual stability. Whereas FIs view contracts as a means of locking in their fiscal burden *ex ante*, and thus providing some guarantee against arbitrary extraction, governing elites want to be able to alter the terms of these contracts as their fiscal needs change. Thus, during the first time period when the state was more dependent on FIs who could unilaterally enforce their contracts, fiscal regimes were stable; yet when dependency shifted in favor of the state during the second time period, contracts became more "flexible," changing at the whims of governing elites, and fiscal regimes were thus unstable. The stability of the fiscal regime in the third time period is less straightforward despite the inclusion of stability clauses, because the international context does not necessarily favor one side over the other.[22] We discuss this in more detail in the section on "Power Relations."

---

[22] Indeed, the increased attention to host governments' interests has not meant that the FIs' interests are completely disregarded, but owing to what Eden et al. (2004) describes as the inclusion of more "red carpet" than "red tape" treatment has cultivated a more nuanced model contract at the end of the twentieth century such that broader social spending provisions now coexist with stabilization clauses.

SOCIETAL EXPECTATIONS

In contrast to TCs, where there is little difference between S_2 and P_2, these two forms of ownership have divergent effects on societal expectations. There are two reasons for this. First, although societal expectations vis-à-vis FIs are the same under both S_2 and P_2 in each time period, they are not the same across time periods due to changes in the international context. As explicated in Chapter 3, societal expectations of the state's role have been elevated in the latter half of the twentieth century throughout the developing world, but particularly in petroleum-rich countries. The presence of FIs, however, makes this both more complicated and dynamic because the international context also shapes the population's sense of entitlement vis-à-vis the foreign companies that are exploiting their country's mineral wealth.[23] The heightened publicity surrounding petroleum production in the developing world, especially as the contracts with the FIs have become more visible to the public, has further elevated societal expectations vis-à-vis the FIs. Most importantly, since the early 1990s societal expectations have been heavily influenced by the emergence of INGOs and IFIs that have encouraged local populations and governments in petroleum-rich states to demand that FIs take on a direct role in fostering development.[24] Societal expectations vis-à-vis FIs, therefore, have ranged from muted in the first half of the twentieth century to high in the latter part of the twentieth century.

The second reason that societal expectations diverge under S_2 and P_2 is that the state has a dual claimant status under the former (but not the latter) due to the existence of a vested NOC. Simply put, while FIs are the direct claimants and governing elites are the primary indirect claimant under both S_2 and P_2, governing elites can also serve as a direct claimant under S_2 but not P_2. Under the latter form of ownership structure, then, the state is primarily charged with ensuring that the population receives a share of the proceeds from its mineral wealth through extracting revenue from the FIs who are exploiting this wealth, albeit not the full amount of these proceeds. As under P_1, privatization to FIs sends a strong signal to the population that there will be disparity in the allocation of benefits accruing from mineral wealth. In contrast, that the state is the ultimate owner under S_2 (as under S_1) – and in most cases retains full control over a small share of the country's oil fields – means that its need to demonstrate that it is adequately fulfilling its role as the guardian of the public's interest goes beyond taxing and regulating FIs. Thus, whereas

---

[23] Venezuela's President, Eleazar López Contreras (1935–40) memorable proclamation, "Sow the Petroleum," is one of the first statements to capture this sentiment, which, according to Wilkins (1974, 224), alluded "to spread[ing] the earnings of the oil enterprises throughout the Venezuelan economy, so that the nation as well as the foreigners would profit from oil developments."

[24] One of the first instances where INGOs allied with local communities to exert pressure on governments and the international petroleum industry was the "Amazon for Life" campaign in Ecuador in the early 1990s (Treakle 1998).

societal expectations vis-à-vis the state under P_2 are more likely to resemble P_1 – that is, that the state should redistribute the proceeds from mineral wealth in order to ameliorate the disparities arising from its development and export (in this case, via foreign investment) – under S_2 they are more likely to resemble S_1 – that is, that the state should distribute the benefits widely so as to prevent such disparities.

Yet because the primary direct claimants under both forms of ownership are foreign rather than domestic investors, societal expectations also remain distinct from those under S_1 and P_1 across the three time periods. First, both S_2 and P_2 are likely to face a much higher barrier to attaining societal acceptance than either S_1 or P_1, respectively. This sentiment has been consistent over the course of the twentieth century. For example, those opposed to granting Standard Oil a concession in Romania in the 1920s clamored that the Romanian people were "selling their heritage for a mess of potage and would give themselves over into the hands of a monopolistic combination which would endanger their economic independence" (Quoted in Wilkins 1974, 221). Thus, although the population expects some disparity in the allocation of benefits accruing from mineral wealth under P_2, that the primary beneficiaries are foreigners makes this disparity more egregious. Second, inspired by the emergence of new international norms described in the preceding section, since 1960 both the domestic population and the state have increasingly come to view FIs not just as an additional source of revenue, but also as another means for distributing benefits and providing public goods. FIs can also serve as a convenient scapegoat for persistent poverty and other ills associated with inadequate levels of social spending. Societal expectations under both S_2 and P_2, therefore, have created an incentive for governing elites to make extraction from FIs in the mineral sector as visible as possible, even if it merely takes the form of public pronouncements and veiled threats, while keeping the actual amount of revenue it receives from mineral extraction a well-guarded secret.

Only during the first time period do S_2 and P_2 generate similar societal expectations vis-à-vis both the FIs and the state. This is primarily due to the fact that – beyond the immediate area in which they were operating – foreign activities in the petroleum sector were essentially hidden from public view. Owing to the enclave nature of the petroleum industry, which is often geographically isolated, the FIs' tendency to reinvest their profits elsewhere (see Ross 1999), and the host government's desire to restrict contact between FIs and the local population, strong linkages to both the domestic economy and the local population were absent (UNCTAD 1999). In many instances, the enclaves were "closed towns" with gates at the entrance of the camp and restrictions on who could enter or live in the camps (Wilkins 1974, 125). Aramco's operations in Saudi Arabia epitomized this model (see Vernon 1971). At the same time, there was little publicity surrounding foreign investment in the petroleum industry at either the domestic or the international level. In contrast to the subsequent two time periods, there were also no INGOs or IFIs actively encouraging the citizens of petroleum-rich states to demand more from either their governments or FIs. Thus societal expectations were low vis-à-vis both FIs and the state concerning the degree to which mineral rents should be disseminated among the population, as well as the scope. This was reinforced by the fact that the state's requirements for FIs were minimalist. While FIs were expected to provide for their employees by paying higher salaries and at times even providing housing and a clinic for their workers, largely as an "economic necessity," their responsibilities did not extend beyond these "workers' camps" to the community or region as a whole (Vernon 1971, Wilkins 1974, 123–4). Simply put, the FIs did not face either domestic or international pressures to be "concerned with solving the social problems" of the local communities (Wilkins 1974, 127).

It is in the 1960s that societal expectations under S_2 and P_2 begin to diverge. As described in Chapter 3, in the second half of the twentieth century, societal expectations vis-à-vis the state were elevated across developing countries due to the emergence of international norms concerning the state's role in promoting social and economic development. At the same time, greater public awareness surrounding petroleum production and its immense potential to fuel development made this more acute in petroleum-rich states. Thus, the petroleum sector easily became the focal point for fulfilling these elevated popular expectations. For those states that adopted S_2 and P_2, the public's heightened awareness also pertained to the role of foreign investment. In sharp contrast to the first half of the twentieth century, for example, it became common for host governments to ratify mineral exploration and production contracts with foreign companies as a government decree or act of parliament with tremendous fanfare (McKern 1996, 332). Yet, consistent with our argument that each form of ownership structure has a unique effect on societal expectations and that these effects are filtered through the international context where FIs are actively involved, societal expectations under S_2 and P_2 take on different meanings during the second and third time periods, as well as across these two subsequent time periods. During both the second and third time periods, societal expectations under S_2 and P_2 are distinguished by whether society looked primarily to the state or to FIs to fulfill its expectations. In each of these two time periods, however, societal expectations are moderated by the same set of international norms concerning the appropriate role and responsibilities of FIs. Thus, while they are high vis-à-vis FIs during both the second and third time periods, particularly in comparison to the first time period, the meaning of "high" is shaped by the prevailing global standards governing FIs' behavior.

In states that adopted S_2 during the second time period, the onus for fulfilling societal expectations was primarily on the state. Similar to S_1, because the state owes its status as direct claimant to its role as owner on behalf of the population, and hence society's agent, governing elites faced societal expectations for widespread distribution of the proceeds from mineral wealth. When it comes to what form taxation and government spending should take, therefore, we would expect governing elites' preferences to be analogous to those under S_1. Governing elites should not only be reluctant to tax the population directly and explicitly, thereby favoring indirect and implicit forms of taxation, they should exhibit a strong tendency to engage in populist-style spending at the national level, consisting largely of universal subsidies on goods and services, and to build large public works projects. In other words, they are unlikely to support broad-based taxation or spending limits outside the mineral sector. As under S_1, we should also expect to see a central role for the NOC in facilitating the state's ability to spend in this manner. Because the state often retains control over some of its reserves via the NOC under S_2, we are likely to see the NOC engaged in noncommercial tasks and an energy sector dominated by quasi-fiscal arrangements (QFAs), including the provision of universal fuel subsidies. Generally speaking, due to pressures to spend (rather than to save) the proceeds from mineral wealth in response to high societal expectations, governing elites under S_2 are also inclined to resist setting any limits on government spending within the mineral sector, and thus are unlikely to support the establishment of an effective NRF that would force them to set aside their share of mineral rents.

At the same time, due to FIs' greater visibility and the emergence of international norms governing their behavior, societal expectations were also high vis-à-vis FIs during this second time period. The main thrust of these norms, however, was that FIs should both accept a much larger tax burden at the national level and assume some limited responsibilities for spending beyond their enclaves at the local level. The state's dual claimant status under S_2 complicates things further because governing elites are driven by the need to demonstrate to society that they are not only extracting a sufficiently large share of mineral rents from the FIs, but also utilizing this revenue to benefit the country as a whole. This has two empirical implications. The first is that the NOC will also serve a dual role; in addition to producing oil on behalf of the state and fulfilling the state's spending obligations, it will be charged with ensuring that the FIs are paying their taxes and meeting the new local content obligations stipulated in their contracts. The second is that societal expectations will reinforce both FIs' preferences for a stable fiscal regime within the mineral sector and governing elites' preferences for an unstable one. Governing elites will find it particularly attractive to have the "flexibility" to extract more from FIs, when needed, in order to either sustain or augment government spending. Hence, when the obsolescing bargain does ensue, we would expect the contractual changes to be focused more on increasing FIs' tax burden than their spending requirements.

In states that adopted P_2 during the second time period, the onus was instead on the FIs to fulfill societal expectations, albeit with the state as the chief intermediary. Similar to P_1, society looked primarily to the state to ameliorate the disparities generated by privatization of the petroleum sector via limited redistribution. Low societal expectations vis-à-vis the state enabled governing elites to fulfill their role as indirect claimant by extracting an appropriate (or "fair") share of the FIs' profits via taxation and then redistributing this tax revenue, for example, through nationally mandated social transfers from the oil-rich to the oil-poor regions. Thus governing elites have much less incentive to engage in populist-style spending outside the mineral sector. For this very reason, low societal expectations also increase the likelihood that governing elites will support spending limits within the mineral sector in the form of a stable (but not necessarily transparent) NRF, whereby revenue flowing into the fund is saved for use during commodity busts and directed toward long-term investment programs. When it comes to taxation outside the mineral sector, low societal expectations reduce the political costs of taxing the population directly and explicitly, and thus governing elites do not have the same disincentive to pursue broad-based tax reform. Yet, unlike P_1 where governing elites and the private oil companies have a mutual incentive to support such reform – that is, where a nonstate actor with a vested interest is advocating tax reform – in this case, it is not until the 1990s that such an actor emerges (namely IFIs).

Because FIs were widely perceived to be a limitless source of revenue during this period – a perception that was routinely fostered by governing elites themselves[25] – high societal expectations vis-à-vis the FIs also reinforce governing elites' preferences, stemming from low TCs, for an unstable fiscal regime within the mineral sector. Thus, as under S_2, what constitutes FIs' "fair share" is shaped by the international context – specifically the emerging norms governing foreign investment. We expect to find that FIs accept not only a larger tax burden but also a direct role in spending beyond the "company town," for example, in the form of providing on-the-job training for employees, infrastructure, and educational scholarships, while continuing symbolic forms of philanthropy to benefit the local community.[26] At the same time, these elevated societal expectations regarding the FIs' responsibilities should reinforce FIs' preferences for a stable tax regime within the mineral sector.

The differences between S_2 and P_2 are magnified in the 1990s due to the pronounced role of INGOs and IFIs in the contractual process combined with new international norms regarding CSR that have set new and higher standards for what society should expect from both FIs and its own government. In general, various INGOs in the mid-1980s joined forces and launched a crusade to persuade multinational corporations (MNCs) to adhere to a new code of conduct regarding the way they carry out business abroad (see Gereffi et al. 2001). Their goal has been to encourage FIs not only to improve the transparency of their fiscal transactions with the host government but also

---

[25] Maintaining this perception is one of the main reasons that host governments did not publicize the actual terms of their agreements with FIs under both S_2 and P_2 during this period.

[26] FIs' obligations to the regions where they operated would often entail, for example, the "rerouting of roads and rail lines" to correspond to the region's infrastructure plans and token investments in community services that could entail building a school or hospital (Smith and Wells 1975, 107). Aramco's local expenditures in Saudi Arabia in the 1960s included the provision of free medical services, voluntary employee training, technical assistance to local enterprises, and the construction and maintenance of publicly used roads (Wells 1971, 232).

to engage in activities that would better promote economic development, social welfare, and conflict prevention in the countries where they operate (see Bennett 2002).

Specifically with regard to mineral-rich states, since the 1990s INGOs and IFIs have elevated societal expectations by contributing to both the greater visibility of foreign investment and the more active involvement of local communities.[27] Above all, their role has entailed influencing the contractual process between FIs and host governments to ensure that revenue flows within the mineral sector are not only more transparent to the population, but also channeled into savings funds that put aside some revenue for future generations and directed toward poverty reduction at the local level (Gary and Karl 2003, Haufler 2006, Tsalik 2003).

INGOs have promoted greater visibility largely through their focus on transparency. Global Witness, Oxfam, Save the Children, and the Open Society Institute (OSI), for example, have targeted fiscal transactions within the mineral sector, scrutinizing the way that royalties, income taxes, and bonuses are paid to host governments through such prominent campaigns such as "Publish What You Pay," "Revenue Watch," and the "Extractive Industries Transparency Initiative" (EITI).[28] Their initial focus on improving transparency was also aimed at providing the citizens of host countries with better information about how their "national wealth" was being used and for whose benefit. According to Global Witness (2004, 4), absent such international initiatives "ordinary citizens, who often own a country's resources under its constitution, are ... left without the information to call their governments to account over the management of their revenues."

Concerning the empowerment of local communities, INGOs have contributed in multiple ways. First and foremost, they have actively and publicly pressured FIs to improve their business practices and expand the scope of their social and economic activities in host countries in accordance with CSR. In particular, they have emphasized FIs' responsibility toward local communities where they operate, for example, by raising international awareness of the plight and protests of those most affected by the negative externalities of oil exploration and production (see Ikelegbe 2001). Second, in this regard, INGOs have also enlisted the support of IFIs, pressuring them to use their financial leverage to help persuade FIs to invest locally in social welfare and environmental protection (see Watters 2006). The "Boycott Shell" campaign in the mid-1990s, followed by the World Bank's (2004b) *Extractive Industries Review*, for example, set the stage for FIs to be more attuned to environmental and social concerns in their host countries (see Shankelmen 2006). Finally,

---

[27] For instance, the World Bank's (2004b) *Extractive Industries Review* recommended better coordination with local stakeholders to ensure that communities benefit from the exploitation of mineral resources.

[28] Publish What You Pay is a consortium of over 300 NGOs. For more information on these campaigns, see http://www.publishwhatyoupay.org/english/; http://www.eitransparency.org/; http://www.revenuewatch.org/

they have encouraged FIs to build transnational alliances with local activists in the regions where they operate in order to make their spending programs more responsive to local needs (see Jordan and Van Tuijl 2000).

Thus societal expectations vis-à-vis FIs remained high under both S_2 and P_2 in the third time period (1990–2005). Yet, this does not convey the same meaning as it did during the previous time period. According to the international norms of the time, a higher tax burden ensuring that "foreign oil companies ... get only a fair rate of return" (Stiglitz 2007, 44) was only part of the equation when it came to extracting "society's due" from FIs. In addition, it was considered reasonable not only to require FIs to engage in broad social spending at both the national and the local level in their contracts, but also to assume social obligations at the local level that went beyond these explicit *ex ante* requirements. Since the 1990s, therefore, both local populations and host governments have come to expect FIs to provide an array of public goods and social services for the benefit of entire communities that surround their operations, which may include building roads, hospitals, and schools along with providing subsidized fuel to local consumers. Indeed, it is quite customary for local populations to view the FIs not just as a source of unlimited tax revenue, but also as a constant source of public goods provision. One citizen in Angola in 2006, for example, described Exxon as a "father. A father who likes to give is a father we're going to ask a lot" (Ball 2006).

The pressure to go "beyond compliance," in turn, should expand the preferences of FIs regarding fiscal reform. Rather than merely seeking to secure a stable tax regime within the mineral sector, as in previous periods, FIs should also have a greater interest in supporting INGOs' and IFIs' efforts to enhance both the transparency and effectiveness of fiscal transactions within as well as outside the mineral sector.

FIs will be more likely to support fiscal transparency initiatives, for example, not only because such campaigns have the potential to tarnish their reputation and ultimately hurt their bottom line, but because, similar to the DPOs under P_1, they want society in the host countries to know that they are meeting their fiscal burden – in terms of both paying their fair share of taxes and financing public goods and social services. This is precisely why such transparency initiatives have largely been aimed at the FIs, obliging them to provide information regarding the state's share of the profits (see Haufler 2006). Thus whereas it was inconceivable for the general population to know precisely how much the host governments were receiving in payments from the FIs for most of the twentieth century[29] – despite the increasing visibility of contract ratification in the mid-twentieth century – since the 1990s it has become more common for FIs to make this kind of information publicly available. One of the first FIs to yield to this pressure was British Petroleum. Following Global Witness's 1999 exposé on the links between foreign investment in the petroleum sector and

---

[29] For example, in 1922, the IPC secretly paid the Peruvian government a bonus or "gift" of one million dollars as "precondition to settlement" (Wilkins 1974).

the Angolan civil war, it made a commitment to fiscal transparency, beginning with its operations in Angola (Christiansen 2002).

Much for the same reason, FIs should also want their own spending commitments to be both stable and more transparent. They desire firm limits on how much they are expected to spend and increasingly detailed specification on what they are expected to spend. This is reflected in the contracts that FIs have signed with the new oil and gas producers that emerged following the discovery of huge petroleum reserves in parts of Africa, Southeast Asia, and the former Soviet Union during this period. One common feature is a social contribution fund that can either be part of the contract or outside their contractual obligations, whereby FIs are required to allocate a portion of their profits to local development projects.[30] For instance, Exxon anticipated that it would spend $2.7 million on social projects in Angola along with another $4 million designated for largely fighting malaria (Ball 2006). BP stands out among the FIs for its commitment to social spending; in 2000 it spent $81.6 million dollars on social investments that include community development, education, and the environment (Christiansen 2002, 25).

There is also a greater likelihood that FIs will see it in their interest to place constraints on government spending within the mineral sector so as to reduce wasteful spending. Simply put, channeling the government's share of mineral rents to more productive uses relieves some of the spending pressure that FIs face from both the domestic population in host countries and international actors. They are thus more likely to join INGOs and IFIs in encouraging governing elites to establish an effective NRF than in previous periods. In addition to specifying how much of its income from mineral rents the government can spend and on what this revenue should be spent, an effective NRF has the additional advantage of being another means to raise society's awareness concerning how much revenue the state actually has at its disposal as a result of foreign investment in the mineral sector.

Beyond stability and transparency, similar to DPOs under P_1, FIs should view both directing their spending toward the local community where they operate and building links with local activists as cost-effective ways of achieving at least tacit popular approval for their status as owners and managers of the lucrative mineral sector. This is particularly true under P_2 because, as previously mentioned, foreign ownership creates a greater hurdle to achieving this approval. In short, the lessons learned from being disconnected from the local population in the prior periods have made many FIs realize that the benefits of being a good corporate citizen greatly outweigh the economic costs of incurring public protests and disruptions to their operations. ARCO's

---

[30] According to the authors' own surveys of FIs operating (or hoping to operate) in the petroleum sector in Azerbaijan, Kazakhstan, the Russian Federation, Turkmenistan, and Uzbekistan, conducted from 1999–2003, this was a common expectation. As the case studies will demonstrate, however, it was particularly pronounced in Azerbaijan and Kazakhstan (in other words, under S_2 and P_2).

experience in Ecuador is a case in point; in response to the popular protests it confronted in the late 1980s, when it embarked upon seismic exploratory work in the Ecuadorian Amazon, it did not initiate its operations in a subsequent project (in Villano) until it had negotiated the provision of specific public works projects in each community, including building schoolhouses and medical facilities (Sawyer 2004, 64–8).[31]

It goes without saying that while they should all have a greater incentive to comply with new international norms regarding CSR, not all MNCs will internalize these new international norms and embrace CSR to the same degree. While elevated societal expectations increase the likelihood that FIs will adjust their spending commitments to accommodate these expectations and even support INGO and IFIs efforts in building a stable and transparent fiscal system within the mineral sector, it does not guarantee that they will adopt the spirit rather than the letter of CSR. Indeed, some have argued quite forcefully that MNCs merely pay lip service to CSR (see Bakan 2004, Litvan 2003). There are also examples of FIs, most notably Chinese companies in Sudan (specifically the Chinese National Petroleum Company and PetroChina) that have not even bothered to acknowledge CSR (Human Rights Watch 2003). As we will discuss in the next section on "Power Relations," whether FIs embrace CSR is a variable that helps explain why we see such diverse outcomes in petroleum-rich countries that adopt S_2 and P_2 in the 1990s.

Elevated societal expectations vis-à-vis FIs also have some important effects on governing elites' preferences. First, they reinforce governing elites' preference for secrecy concerning fiscal transactions within the mineral sector under both S_2 and P_2 so that they can not only line their own pockets, but also blame FIs for inadequate levels of social spending. Even when governments agree to join transparency initiatives such as EITI, it is unlikely to reduce secrecy regarding financial flows both within and outside the mineral sector aside from what the FIs who have also joined are willing to reveal. Second, they both reinforce governing elites' preference for an unstable fiscal regime within the mineral sector and, given the expanded role of FIs in financing public goods provision and social services, expand this predilection for instability to include the expenditure side of the FIs' fiscal burden. Thus whereas during the second time period we predicted that the state's tendency to renege on contracts (the obsolescing bargain) would be focused only on increasing FIs' tax burden, in the third time period it should also include ramping up their spending requirements. Third, because they face high societal expectations vis-à-vis the state, governing elites under S_2 will be more inclined to utilize FIs' expanded role in social spending to supplement expenditures at the national level, whereas under P_2 governing elites are more likely to encourage FIs to direct their spending toward the areas in which they operate. Thus under S_2 we expect to find FIs engaged in development

[31] The provision of public goods has also enabled ARCO to avoid the international criticism that cast a shadow on its previous operations in Ecuador (see Kimerlang 1991).

projects at both the national and subnational levels but primarily at the sub-national level under P_2.

Differences in societal expectations vis-à-vis the state under S_2 and P_2 also affect the prospects for reform both within and outside mineral sector. While we expect the pronounced role of INGOs and IFIs alongside the emergence of new norms regarding CSR since the 1990s to augment FIs' interest in broad fiscal reform under both S_2 and P_2, these changes have a greater likelihood of actually resulting in reform under P_2 due to low societal expectations. Regarding taxation, the fact that the population does not expect the mineral sector to make up the bulk of state income creates an opportunity for IFIs to convince governing elites that they can benefit from broadening the tax base without incurring significant political costs. Regarding expenditures, govern-ing elites under P_2 should be more receptive to setting formal limits than under S_2 because they do not feel the same pressure to distribute the proceeds from mineral rents widely (or rather, to create the impression that they are doing so). This facilitates IFIs' and INGOs' efforts to promote the establishment of an effective NRF, in which mineral rents are not only saved but also utilized for long-term investment, as well as the adoption of budgetary reform such as better accounting practices and the targeting of benefits.

POWER RELATIONS

Similar to TCs, because of the heavy influence of the international context, power relations are virtually the same across the three time periods and the two ownership structures, but there is an important qualitative difference in the 1990s. As detailed in Chapter 3, whether fiscal regimes emerge via bar-gaining or coercion depends on the form of ownership structure, because each form produces a distinct set of power relations. They are more likely to emerge via coercion under S_2 and P_2 because both forms of ownership foster depen-dent power relations – that is, an asymmetrical relationship in which one of the main claimants to the proceeds from mineral wealth (here, FIs and govern-ing elites) can unilaterally enforce its claims. These claims are embodied in the model contract discussed above. Enforcing one's claims, therefore, is synony-mous with dictating the terms of this contract – most importantly – whether it remains stable. Just as the model contract changes over time in response to the three major shifts in the international context we identify, so too does which of the main claimants is predominant, and thus, both the content and stability of the fiscal regime that emerges.

During the first time period (1900–1960), the international context – in which seven major oil companies dominated the petroleum market – clearly privileged FIs over governing elites in the host countries. One way in which FIs determined the amount of tax revenue that the state could extract from the mineral sector was by de facto controlling the world market price for oil, which was deliberately based on the price of crude from the Gulf of Mexico despite its lower production costs.[32] Their ability to limit the amount of rents accruing to the state was also facilitated by the international oil market's vertically integrated structure, which allowed FIs to hide their true income and thus to artificially reduce their tax burden (Tanzer 1969). Most importantly, the FIs were able to rely on the international system to enforce unilaterally the model contract via two mechanisms, which essentially freed them from worrying about whether the host government was committed to enforcing their claims (see Krasner 1978, Lipson 1985, Mommer 2002, Moran 1996).

The first was the solidarity among the FIs who, in an environment of limited competition, had a direct interest in securing the contracts of their peers. Their ability to ensure that these contracts were universally respected was reinforced both by the existence of "constraint mechanisms" that championed each other's market share (Moran 1987)[33] and the intricate web of joint ventures that defined many of their operations (Adelman 1972, Penrose 1968, Vernon 1971). The overlapping membership in joint ventures especially facilitated the sharing of information regarding production plans, allowing the companies to guarantee that the host governments would not be able to strike a better deal regarding the price of crude.[34] Thus it was not uncommon in the Persian Gulf for British Petroleum to know about the production plans of its partner, Gulf Oil, and to divulge this information to its partners in a different consortium (IPC that included Esso and Mobil); the result was that SoCal and Texaco were also fully aware of these production plans, as all the companies were involved in the same consortium in Iran (Adelman 1972, 88). Consequently, host countries that objected to the terms of the model contract could not simply turn to another FI to negotiate better terms. Rather, the Majors could rely upon this solidarity to "enforce private, collective sanctions" (Lipson 1985, 113) against host countries whose governments sought to revoke contracts they found unfavorable. When Iran abrogated the Anglo-Iranian Oil Company's (AIOC) contract in 1951, for example, AIOC could easily obtain the approbation of the other Majors to shut down Iranian output (Krasner 1978, Rodman 1988, Smith and Wells 1975).

The second, and perhaps more common, mechanism was the "support" of their home governments, which could range from diplomatic pressure to influence the outcome of the negotiations between FIs and host countries[35] to

---

[32] Much has been written about this "Gulf-plus formula" (Hartshorn 1967, Moran 1987, Penrose 1968). Basically, because the price of crude from the Persian Gulf was set according to that of the U.S. Gulf, where production costs were much lower, the actual profit margin was much lower.

[33] Examples of these "supra-sovereign constraints" include the Red Line Agreement of 1928, the Achnacarry Agreement ("As Is" system), and the Gulf-plus formula (Moran 1987).

[34] Access to this information also enabled them to monitor whether others were adhering to strict limits on output (Smith and Wells 1975).

[35] The U.S. government used its diplomatic influence to ensure that no monopolistic concession would be granted in Iraq so that all of the Majors could be involved (Mommer 2002),

direct military intervention, particularly when the FIs were threatened with expropriation. As Theodore Moran (1996, 424–5) writes: "there is an impressive record of cases in which the parent authorities have intervened against host countries whose domestic agendas included strong nationalistic policies toward [transnational corporations]."[36]

The fiscal regime that emerged under both S_2 and P_2 in the first half of the twentieth century, therefore, was likely not only to limit the fiscal contribution of the FIs but also to be very stable. In short, that FIs could unilaterally enforce the model contract reinforced the effects of negligible TCs and low societal expectations vis-à-vis both the FIs and the state on the minimalist terms of the model contract and enabled the FIs to impose their preference for contractual stability. As a result, the model contract served as the functional equivalent of an NRF during this period because it both shielded the state from the volatility of the international oil price that became so prominent in the second half of the twentieth century and contributed to limited government expenditures. While the negative effects of this have been enumerated and emphasized elsewhere (see Penrose 1968, Vernon 1971), the positive benefits include a fiscal regime that generates a stable, albeit highly skewed, revenue stream and ameliorates the dependency of government expenditures on the mineral sector.

During the second time period (1960–1990), the emergence of both new actors and norms at the international level shifted the balance of power to the state as FIs came to rely increasingly on the governing elites in host countries to enforce the terms of the model contract. First and foremost, the entrance of several new FIs onto the international scene (a.k.a. the "independents") not only created more competition for the Majors but also more options for host governments. Specifically, they could now select among FIs based on which one would agree to more favorable contract terms (Tanzer 1969). Italy's Ente Nazionale Idrocarburi (ENI), for example, was able to obtain a concession in the tightly controlled Iranian market in 1956–1957 by offering to exceed the traditional 50/50 profit-sharing formula (ibid., 75). The increased competition was also felt in Libya during the mid-1960s when some oil companies were pressured to pay the government more taxes than required in their original concession agreements, especially if they hoped to be considered for future concessions (Hartshorn 1967, 18). The independents also undermined the solidarity of the FIs to enforce each other's claims. When the independent French company, Entreprise de Recherches et d'Activités Pétrolières (ERAP), took over the confiscated concession in Iraq in 1967, for example, this move was described as "br[eaking] faith with other consuming nations which had

---

    while the British government offered direct financial assistance to both the Royal Dutch/Shell Group and the AIOC during the interwar period (Jones 1977).

[36] Rodman (1988) maintains that intervention in socialist-leaning governments during the first half of the twentieth century was more likely to be based on principle (that is, politico-ideological objectives) rather than pragmatism.

previously refused to support similar seizures by producing governments" (Quoted in Tanzer 1969, 76–7).

These changes in the competitive environment culminated in the creation of OPEC in 1960, which host governments used to wrest away control over the price of oil from the FIs. Initially, this meant that the FIs were prevented from making any cuts in the posted price of crude (Amuzegar 2001). But subsequently, they were forced to concede to a set of regionally based agreements that essentially reflected host governments' demands for more revenue via the corporate income tax (Yergin 1991). The first was the Tehran Agreement on February 14, 1971 whereby the posted price for crude in the Persian Gulf was tied to Arabian light crude. The Tripoli Agreement between Libya and the FIs, which raised the posted price of Libyan crude, followed a few months later.[37]

The rise of the independents also coincided with a shift in international norms. By the end of the 1970s, FIs were no longer able to rely on their home governments to intervene on their behalf so as to prevent host governments from unilaterally changing the terms of their contracts (Rodman 1988). While partly a function of declining U.S. economic hegemony, the increasing reluctance of home governments to intervene can largely be attributed to the emergence of international norms against direct involvement in the affairs of Third World countries (Rodman 1988, Smith and Wells 1975). The formation of the G-77 and the push for a New International Economic Order in the UN General Assembly in 1974 helped redefine relations between advanced industrialized countries and developing countries (Hart 1983). The failure of the U.S. to intervene on behalf of Occidental Petroleum Co. when Libya forcibly changed the price of oil – and thereby increased the company's tax burden – is a testament to this (Adelman 1972). The Majors were also unable to persuade the U.S. government to take diplomatic action against the nationalization of the International Petroleum Company in Peru in 1968 (Krasner 1978, Lipson 1985, Rodman 1988).

These changes ushered in an era characterized by the obsolescing bargain, whereby host governments automatically gain leverage in their contractual relations with FIs once the latter's costs are sunk (Vernon 1971).[38] Although it is widely recognized that FIs seek to protect themselves against uncertainty and the risk involved in their operations, according to obsolescing bargain theory, once a company has incurred a large fixed investment (sunk costs), it becomes inevitable for the terms of the contract to be subjected to renegotiation so that the host government can capture a greater share of the rents – either directly in the form of higher royalties and income taxes or indirectly

[37] The negotiations had the full backing of other oil-exporting countries that transported crude to the Mediterranean, including Algeria, Saudi Arabia, and Iraq. Thus, on the same day that the price of Libyan crude rose, so did Algerian crude (Yergin 1991).

[38] Thus, another way to distinguish forms of ownership structure during this time period in which FIs are involved from S_1 and P_1 is that whereas S_1 and P_1 both create "mutual hostages" among the actors involved, S_2 and P_2 have the potential to transform FIs' assets into hostages (Eden et al. 2004).

in the form of public goods provision. As Raymond Vernon (1971, 47), the architect of obsolescing bargain theory, wrote: "almost from the moment that the signatures have dried on the document, powerful forces go to work that quickly render the agreements obsolete in the eyes of the government." This is wholly consistent with the state's need to respond to mounting societal pressure "to raise the demands on the foreign investor," which starts to increase as soon as a project begins to yield income (ibid., 53).

Similar to the first time period, then, the ability of governing elites to enforce unilaterally the model contract serves to reinforce the effects of TCs and societal expectations on both the substance and stability of fiscal arrangements in the mineral sector. During the second period, TCs remain negligible due to the existence of the model contract, but the terms of this contract include both an increase in the FIs' tax payments and an expansion of their spending commitments, albeit still largely restricted to the vicinity of their operations. Thus the contract that governing elites are enforcing is one that advantages them since it substantially increases the government's share of the proceeds from mineral wealth. Because governing elites prefer the "flexibility" to alter the fiscal contributions required of FIs as political and economic circumstances dictate, their ability to enforce unilaterally this contract will amount to frequent and arbitrary changes in its terms, and hence a highly unstable fiscal regime within the mineral sector.

Many of the advantages that stemmed from the direct involvement of FIs under S_2 and P_2 during the first time period, therefore, are eroded after 1960, as the FIs can no longer shield the domestic economy from the impact of boom and bust cycles endemic to mineral exports or limit government expenditures. Rather, the FIs become a potential source of unfettered taxation and state spending, and thus budgetary instability. This is exacerbated under S_2 due to the state's dual status as direct claimant. The shift to greater host governments' control over the price of oil particularly benefited those states that adopted S_2 because their dual status as direct and indirect claimants meant that they could also reap the benefits of higher oil prices directly through producing and exporting oil from their own fields.

Once again, the third time period marks a dramatic change from the previous two time periods. Whereas the international context clearly favored one side over the other for most of the twentieth century, by the 1990s, whether FIs or the host governments were empowered to enforce the model contract was no longer apparent. The main impetus for this change was twofold. First, among the new set of norms that IFIs and INGOs promoted toward the end of the twentieth century was the notion that the state was not necessarily the most appropriate agent for managing mineral wealth. Disappointed by decades of wasteful spending, corrupt governments, and failed ISI programs ostensibly aimed at diversifying mineral-dependent economies, the international donor community began to question the premise that had guided their unwavering support for FIs to turn over the bulk of mineral rents directly to the state. While it is still widely taken for granted that the mineral wealth belongs to the state and that the contracts should provide the host governments with a disproportionate share of the wealth (see Stiglitz 2007), a large number of scholars and practitioners have put forth alternatives to state-led development such as direct distribution schemes (Birdsall and Subramanian 2004, Palley 2003, Sala-I-Martin and Subramanian 2003). Moreover, as detailed in the previous section, INGOs began to engage FIs directly in their efforts to promote greater transparency, the protection of human rights, and other best practices concerning labor and the environment – that is, to view them as potential allies rather than adversaries. EITI and the UN Global Compact, in particular, stand out for their commitment to a multistakeholder approach to development that brings together the corporate sector, nonstate actors, and governments.[39]

Second, alongside the new standards of corporate behavior that IFIs and INGOs fostered beginning in the late 1980s, FIs began changing their own behavior vis-à-vis one another, which opened the door for more cooperative relationships. In short, by the 1990s, sufficient learning had taken place among FIs that their interests were better served if they viewed each other as potential partners rather than solely as competitors. This newfound predilection toward cooperation, reminiscent of the amity among the Majors in the first part of the twentieth century, was facilitated by several other related factors. First and foremost, FIs' eagerness to devise strategies to counter the so-called "inevitability" of the obsolescing bargain – in other words, when FIs could operate as a united force, they could prevent the state from unilaterally reneging on the terms of their contracts. Second, new discoveries increased the FIs' leverage. Specifically, the discovery of significant petroleum reserves outside of the traditional exporting countries (i.e., OPEC members), including the Gulf of Guinea in Africa, Timor Sea in Southeast Asia, and the Caspian Basin within the former Soviet Union, created alternative exploration options (and thus a potential for new partners) for FIs that faced unfavorable or fluctuating contract terms. Finally, the bust in the international petroleum market in the late 1990s set off a wave of mergers among the big oil companies, thus allowing them to pool their resources once again vis-à-vis the host governments.[40]

The absence of a clear unilateral enforcer from the 1990s onward, therefore, has coincided with more influence for IFIs and INGOs in mineral-rich states. On the one hand, this has been an expansion of their role in the previous period. At the same time that they continued to shape the content of contracts indirectly via their influence on societal expectations, IFIs and INGOs have assumed a more direct role in negotiating the specific means whereby FIs meet their fiscal and social obligations. For example, INGOs have feverishly sought to "teach" host governments how better to deal with FIs, especially when it

---

[39] For details, see http://www.unglobalcompact.org/ and http://eitransparency.org/

[40] The first of the big mergers was between British Petroleum and Amoco in 1998, culminating in BP. In late 1999, Exxon and Mobil merged into ExxonMobil, and in 2001, Chevron and Texaco completed their merger into ChevronTexaco.

comes to negotiating and evaluating the fiscal terms of a contract in order to ensure that host governments fully benefit from foreign exploitation of their mineral wealth.[41] Similarly, IFIs have published primers on how to design a fiscal regime for the mineral sector so as to ensure that the host government receives an "appropriate" share of the revenue (see, for example, Baunsgaard 2001), reinforcing the notion that the terms of the model contract should favor the host governments. As a result, the FIs' increasing ability to counter the obsolescing bargain has not translated into an ability to turn back the clock to the first half of the twentieth century regarding their spending commitments. As the contracts signed with new producers in the Caspian Basin and Africa demonstrate, it remains patently clear to both the host governments and the FIs at the outset of negotiations that the latter's contractual obligations include a plethora of social and economic responsibilities beyond the mineral sector linked to CSR. Indeed, the basic terms of the model contract from the 1990s onward have continued to advantage host governments vis-à-vis FIs.

On the other hand, there has been a qualitative change in the role of IFIs and INGOs. They have exhibited a much greater interest in pressuring governments to adopt specific institutional forms – especially when it comes to fiscal institutions both within and outside the mineral sector. Since the 1990s, IFIs and INGOs have not only promoted new norms of "petroleum revenue management" but also utilized their power to ascribe meaning to these new norms (see Barnett and Finnemore 1999). They have exerted considerable influence on the creation of NRFs, for example, as a means of both promoting transparency and stabilizing budgets. *Ceteris paribus*, countries that are either directly targeted by INGOs or recipients of assistance from IFIs are more likely to adopt NRFs in the late-twentieth century. Under certain conditions (discussed below), these INGOs and IFIs are able to influence the exact terms of the NRF and, more importantly, whether it is actually effective. Yet NRFs are only one of the many fiscal institutions on which IFIs and INGOs have attempted to exert their influence in the 1990s. IFIs in particular have sought to influence the broader fiscal regime through the diffusion of another isomorphic template – that is, a standardized tax code at the domestic level.

In sum, the uncertainty surrounding who will enforce the model contract, combined with the expanded and more direct influence of IFIs and INGOs, means that there is much greater variation in the types of fiscal regimes that will emerge in mineral-rich states that adopt S_2 and P_2 during the 1990s than in either of the two preceding time periods. While we still expect S_2 and P_2 to produce hybrid fiscal regimes, there is greater uncertainty concerning the precise features of this hybrid fiscal regime and, perhaps more importantly, the social and economic outcomes that it is likely to generate. In particular, all should entail an expansion in the state's reliance on the mineral sector to include direct social spending on the part of FIs, and yet the extent of this

[41] The Revenue Watch Program at OSI has supported studies to help host governments negotiate with FIs and manage their revenue (see Humphreys et al. 2007).

reliance and the degree as well as nature of this spending will vary depending on two key factors. The first concerns which of the two main direct claimants – governing elites or FIs – enforces the contract. Which set of actors enforces, in turn, hinges upon whether the FIs can effectively form a united front vis-à-vis the state – that is, whether they are able to overcome the collective action problem (CAP). Briefly, this is because when FIs are able to form an alliance, they can more effectively resist the state's tendency to continually "renegotiate" the terms of their contracts, and instead impose their own preference for stable contractual relations. It has become quite common in countries that adopt S_2 or P_2, such as Indonesia and Kazakhstan, for FIs to form petroleum associations to lobby government agencies for the harmonization of laws and regulations or "a level-playing field" (see Prattini 2007). While we do not attempt to explain why some FIs are able to overcome the CAP and others are not, several factors can certainly facilitate the FIs' ability to work collectively, such as the composition of the FIs in a given country, the size of the country in which they are operating, and type of fields. Thus, for example, FIs are less likely to overcome the CAP if they are large in number with operations widely dispersed both onshore and offshore; in contrast, they are more likely to overcome the CAP if they are small in number and working offshore.[42]

The second variable concerns whether the FIs are committed to CSR. As noted previously, although most FIs have acknowledged CSR to some degree by the end of the twentieth century, they have displayed different levels of commitment to the norms embodied in CSR. The Goldman-Sachs Energy Environmental and Social Index provides a good benchmark for assessing these differing levels of commitment. Those companies that rank high on the Index and endorse wholeheartedly the principles espoused by EITI and "Publish What You Pay" are more likely to push for transparency measures, including an effective NRF, and even to go "beyond compliance" with their social spending and environmental commitments. Indeed, the foreign oil companies that are ranked as "leaders" according to this Index – such as British Petroleum (BP), RD/Shell, Statoil, ExxonMobil – are known to fully comply with and exceed their social welfare and environmental commitments (for details, see Goldman Sachs 2004). BP, in particular, has been singled out for commendation both for its high level of commitment to protecting the environment and for embracing the spirit of CSR more broadly (Christiansen 2002). Conversely, those considered "laggard" companies – such as CNOOC, PetroChina, MOL, Sinopec, Lukoil, and CEPSA – are less likely either to promote transparency or to implement environmental and social welfare programs.

---

[42] This is consistent with the notion that a hegemon is necessary to pay the costs of collective action (Keohane 1984). While some (for example, Shafer 1994) equate solving the CAP in the mineral sector with collusion, such that firms operate according to an oligopoly management structure, we contend that the sector does not overly determine whether collusion will transpire.

The various combinations of these two variables yield four different possible types of hybrid fiscal regimes under both forms of ownership structure. (For details, see Tables 6.2 and 6.3.) The best-case scenario for both S_2 and P_2 is when FIs who are fully committed to CSR can unilaterally enforce their contracts because the state is most constrained and potentially enabled – albeit primarily within the mineral sector. When these two factors are present, there is a greater likelihood not only that FIs' tax rates and spending commitments will be stable, but also that what they do spend will be more transparent and effective – for example, because it is deliberately aimed at reaching the poorest segments of society. Moreover, where FIs who embrace CSR are the enforcers, social spending programs are more likely to be devised in cooperation with INGOs and IFIs, as well as local activists, which increases the likelihood that they will adequately address the economic and social needs of those communities most affected by mineral extraction. There is also a greater likelihood that the NRF will be transparent, as the FIs are more inclined to make their revenue payments public. Yet even under the best-case scenario for S_2, the potential for fiscal reform within the mineral sector remains low. In short, high societal expectations vis-à-vis the state make it difficult for the governing elites to stabilize the NOC's tax burden and the NRF's expenditures. Thus, while INGOs, IFIs, and the FIs might convince governing elites to establish an NRF, it is likely to be only semieffective, because governing elites will still have an incentive to either raid the funds held in the NRF or fail to transfer sufficient funds into it when they deem it necessary to increase public spending.

Although the influence of hybrid fiscal regimes outside the mineral sector is inherently limited, we also expect this to be greatest under the best-case scenario for P_2, which thus most closely approximates a strong fiscal regime (that is, both constraining and enabling). Combined with their support for IFIs' and INGOs' efforts, the ability of FIs to essentially freeze their fiscal burden reinforces governing elites' incentives to adopt broad-based tax reform. High societal expectations vis-à-vis the state under S_2 instead dampen such incentives. Likewise, the FIs' ability to maintain stable and transparent expenditures that are directed toward reducing poverty and promoting socioeconomic development is more likely to foster budgetary reform under P_2 than S_2 owing to differing levels of societal expectations vis-à-vis the state. Indeed, high societal expectations under S_2 make it more likely that, even when external actors are successful in convincing governing elites to direct spending within the mineral sector at alleviating poverty and promoting development, the effects will be counteracted by unconstrained spending outside the mineral sector.

Conversely, the worst-case scenario under both S_2 and P_2 is when governing elites can unilaterally renege on the contracts of FIs who are not committed to CSR. Under these conditions, the fiscal regime that emerges within the mineral sector is most likely to reflect the preferences of governing elites – that is, to consist of a tax regime for the FIs that is unstable and nontransparent, and a system of expenditures for the FIs that is neither stable, transparent, nor

TABLE 6.2. *Hybrid Fiscal Regimes under S₂ from 1990–2005*

	State Enforces	Foreign Investors (FIs) Enforce
FIs +CSR	**Within the Mineral Sector:**	**Within the Mineral Sector:**
	FIs: taxation transparent but unstable; spending transparent but unstable with some likelihood that aimed at alleviating poverty and promoting development	FIs: taxation stable and transparent; spending stable and transparent with high likelihood that will be aimed at alleviating poverty and promoting development
	NOC: unlikely for taxation and spending to be stable or transparent	NOC: low likelihood for taxation and spending to be stable or transparent
	NRF: unlikely to be stable but some likelihood to be transparent; low likelihood that aimed at alleviating poverty and promoting development	NRF: unlikely to be stable, but high likelihood to be transparent; some likelihood that aimed at alleviating poverty and promoting development
	Outside the Mineral Sector:	**Outside the Mineral Sector:**
	Low likelihood for broad-based tax reform	Some likelihood for broad-based tax reform
	Expenditure reform unlikely	Expenditure reform unlikely
FIs -CSR	**Within Mineral Sector:**	**Within the Mineral Sector:**
	FIs: taxation neither stable nor transparent; spending neither stable or transparent and unlikely to be aimed at alleviating poverty and promoting development	FIs: taxation stable but not transparent; spending stable but not transparent with low likelihood that will be aimed at alleviating poverty and promoting development
	NOC: unlikely for taxation and spending to be stable or transparent	NOC: unlikely for taxation and spending to be stable or transparent
	NRF: unlikely to be stable or transparent; unlikely to be aimed at alleviating poverty and promoting development	NRF: unlikely to be stable or transparent; unlikely to be aimed at alleviating poverty and promoting development
	Outside the Mineral Sector:	**Outside the Mineral Sector:**
	Broad-based tax reform unlikely	Some likelihood for broad-based tax reform
	Expenditure reform unlikely	Expenditure reform unlikely

TABLE 6.3. *Hybrid Fiscal Regimes under* P_2 *from 1990–2005*

	State Enforces	Foreign Investors (FIs) Enforce
	Within the Mineral Sector:	**Within the Mineral Sector:**
FIs +CSR	FIs: taxation unstable but transparent; spending unstable but transparent with some likelihood that aimed at alleviating poverty and promoting development at subnational level	FIs: taxation stable and transparent; spending stable and transparent with high likelihood that will be aimed at alleviating poverty and promoting development at subnational level
	NRF: some likelihood to be stable, transparent, and aimed at alleviating poverty and promoting development	NRF: high likelihood to be stable, transparent, and aimed at alleviating poverty and promoting development
	Outside the Mineral Sector:	**Outside the Mineral Sector:**
	Some likelihood for broad-based tax reform	High likelihood for broad-based tax reform
	Some likelihood for expenditure reform	High likelihood for expenditure reform
	Within the Mineral Sector:	**Within the Mineral Sector:**
FIs -CSR	FIs: taxation neither stable nor transparent; spending neither stable or transparent and unlikely to be aimed at alleviating poverty and promoting development	FIIs: taxation stable but not transparent; spending stable but not transparent and unlikely to be aimed at alleviating poverty and promoting development
	NRF: unlikely to be stable, transparent, and aimed at alleviating poverty and promoting development	NRF: some likelihood to be stable but not transparent; unlikely to be aimed at alleviating poverty and promoting development
	Outside the Mineral Sector:	**Outside the Mineral Sector:**
	Some likelihood for broad-based tax reform	High likelihood for broad-based reform
	Some likelihood for expenditure reform	High likelihood for expenditure reform

aimed at poverty alleviation and socioeconomic development. More so, governing elites are likely to direct FIs' spending toward their own pet projects, whether at the national level (under S_2) or at the subnational level (under P_2). The predicted fiscal outcomes, however, are still more desirable under P_2 than S_2 owing to differing levels of societal expectations vis-à-vis the state. High societal expectations under S_2, for example, will continue to generate perverse incentives among governing elites to adopt a fiscal regime within the mineral sector in which both the NOC's fiscal burden and the NRF are unstable and nontransparent and in which the NRF is not aimed at addressing real social and economic problems. Outside the mineral sector, they will continue to generate strong incentives for governing elites to emphasize indirect and implicit forms of taxation and to reject spending limits so as to sustain widespread distribution via universal subsidies. In sharp contrast to the best-case scenario under P_2, then, the worst-case scenario under S_2 comes closest to fostering a weak fiscal regime (that is, neither constraining nor enabling).

In sum, in the 1990s S_2 and P_2 produce a range of fiscal outcomes that can have varying effects on the host country's social and economic development trajectory in general and society's welfare in particular. For instance, even though a best-case scenario under S_2 is not as constraining or enabling as under P_2, when the FIs' social spending emphasizes development, this can foster better short- and long-term outcomes. In fact, if the positive influence of either the FIs or the INGOs and IFIs can contribute to governing elites embracing CSR such that they would not only require greater transparency from the FIs but also from their own financial transactions within the mineral sector (via the NOC and the NRF), the best-case scenario under S_2 would more closely resemble that under P_2.[43] Yet if FIs who are fully committed to CSR cannot enforce their contracts – whether under S_2 or P_2 – their efforts to establish a fiscal regime that generates socioeconomic benefits over the long term are likely to fail. For instance, although widely hailed as a new paradigm for petroleum revenue management in developing countries in the early 2000s, the unprecedented bargain hammered out between the Chadian government, IFIs, and FIs to promote transparent spending directed at poverty alleviation as part of the Chad-Cameroon Oil Pipeline deal[44] had completely unraveled by 2008 because the government simply reneged on its promise (for details, see Polgreen 2008).

IMPLICATIONS

By incorporating the influence of changes at the international level on ownership structure, this chapter offers a dynamic explanation for institutional emergence in mineral-rich states. Simply put, where FIs play a substantial role in developing the mineral sector, the effects of ownership structure on fiscal regimes are filtered through the international context. More specifically, we argue that, owing to two major shifts in the international actors and norms that dominated the petroleum industry, P_2 and S_2 foster distinct types of fiscal

---

[43] One indicator of this would be signing onto EITI and carrying out its commitments fully so as to achieve "Compliant Status." For details, see http://eitransparency.org/compliantcountries

[44] In 2000, the World Bank agreed to help finance the $4.2 billion construction of a pipeline that would transport oil from Chad to the port of Kribi in Cameroon.

regimes in each of the three main time periods we identify: (1) 1900–1960; (2) 1960–1990; and (3) 1990–2005. While we classify all of these fiscal regimes as "hybrid" because they only serve to partially constrain and enable the state across time periods, those that emerge during the third are capable of doing so to a much greater extent. In the first half of the twentieth century, for example, mineral-rich states were minimally constrained and enabled by FIs' ability to impose a fixed tax rate on host governments and to reinvest their profits abroad, thereby shielding the domestic economy from a huge influx of rents and lowering the threshold for acceptable levels of government spending. As a result, states had some capacity to curb inflation, but their populations remained impoverished. By the 1990s, however, FIs have become capable not only of stabilizing their fiscal burden, which has been expanded considerably in size and scope since the 1960s, but also of ensuring that their tax payments are transparent and their expenditures are directed toward alleviating poverty and promoting socioeconomic development. Moreover, they have the opportunity to utilize their expanded influence both to pressure host governments to establish effective NRFs and to encourage them to pursue broad-based taxation and adopt budgetary reform.

In sum, it is during the third time period that P_2 and S_2 have the greatest potential to foster stability and transparency not only within the mineral sector but also outside the mineral sector, and thus to improve citizens' daily lives and the developmental prospects of mineral-rich states. This is no coincidence. Rather, it is due to the efforts of INGOs and IFIs to play a more pronounced and global role in petroleum revenue management. On the one hand, these efforts have largely focused on promoting CSR and local community involvement, which has required FIs to expand their role to include providing public goods and social services as well as facilitating public participation. On the other, INGOs and IFIs have sought to galvanize FIs' support in promoting stability and transparency not only of their own fiscal burden but also of the state's.

That we have witnessed an upward trend in both P_2 and S_2 in the 1990s and 2000s, then, should be grounds for optimism (see Appendix B). And yet even during this period, there is considerable variation when it comes to the size, stability, composition, and degree of transparency of FIs' fiscal burden, and hence its potential to have a positive impact in either the short or the long term. As discussed at length above, two key factors account for this variation: first, whether power relations favor the FIs or the state; and second, how committed FIs are to the norms embodied in CSR. The best-case scenario for mineral-rich states that adopt either S_2 or P_2, then, would be one in which power relations decisively favor FIs that are strongly committed to CSR. Within the mineral sector, this would yield a stable and transparent fiscal burden for FIs and a high likelihood that their spending would be aimed at alleviating poverty and promoting development. It would also foster a transparent NRF. Outside the mineral sector, this would increase the prospects for governing elites to adopt broad-based tax reform. Both within and outside the mineral sector, however, the likelihood that host governments would pursue taxation and expenditure reform is greater under P_2. Thus we should be particularly sanguine that, while S_2 has been increasing steadily since the 1970s, the number of countries that adopted P_2 has almost doubled since the 1980s (ibid.).

The increasing popularity of both P_2 and S_2, however, should also give us cause for concern due to the inherent danger that the expanded role of FIs in alleviating poverty and promoting socioeconomic development will lead to the emergence of what we term "proxy states." Simply put, a proxy state is one in which international actors become de facto mediators between the state and society in lieu of "local strongmen" whose authority is often based on traditional forms of organization (see Migdal 1988) or more modern alternatives such as political parties (see Aldrich 1995). This, again, is no historical accident but rather connected directly to the particular international context. First and foremost, the emergence of new norms and actors actively engaged in their promotion in the 1990s and 2000s was accompanied by a change in attitude toward the "rightful" agent of development. In other words, promoting CSR has not only involved placing greater responsibility on FIs for the social and economic well-being of the domestic population in mineral-rich countries, but also placing less emphasis on the role of the state. Whereas in the 1960s and 1970s, the focus was on ensuring that host governments captured a larger share of the rents from FIs, which they then could harness for their own economic developmental priorities, by the 1990s it became widely recognized not only that this approach was insufficient to achieve desirable outcomes, but also that mineral rents might actually be better spent by socially responsible FIs than states that lacked Weberian bureaucracies (see, for example, de Soto 1989). Secondly, since the 1990s INGOs and IFIs have actively encouraged FIs to incorporate local community organizations in determining how they allocate these rents.

Thus, the irony is that the very norms and actors that are responsible for increasing the propensity for foreign investment to improve citizens' daily lives and the developmental prospects of mineral-rich states are also responsible for generating this perverse outcome. Proxy states are an unintended, and yet direct, consequence of empowering both FIs and local communities because this serves to enervate the state. For example, while it might be more conducive to raising the transparency and efficacy of expenditures, diverting money that would otherwise go into state coffers to funds that are controlled by FIs also contradicts one of the basic tenets of modern statehood: the generation and control of revenue. Similarly, incorporating local nonstate actors is more likely to guarantee that those most affected by the extraction of mineral resources are involved in the decision-making process concerning the distribution of its benefits, and yet, it serves primarily to increase popular accountability vis-à-vis FIs rather than government officials. The promotion of FIs as mediators, therefore, presents a serious trade-off for developing countries: While this strategy has significant social and economic advantages, it also has serious political disadvantages. The most vivid illustration of this is that it impedes the emergence of what is perhaps the sole (if not most widely recognized) alternative vehicle for simultaneously achieving legitimacy and sustained development: the "developmental state" (see Castells 1992, Johnson 1982). As we argue in Chapter 3, such states were a rare occurrence in mineral-rich countries from the 1960s through the 1980s owing to the prevalence of state ownership with control (S_1) during this period. Here, we suggest the likelihood for their emergence is also diminished in the 1990s owing to the prominent role of international norms and actors under P_2 and S_2 that have transformed the traditional suppliers of capital (i.e., the FIs) into the legitimate drivers of state development.

7

Eluding the Obsolescing Bargain

State Ownership without Control in Azerbaijan

> Oil incomes serve the people, it is an integral part of the oil strategy, oil incomes should effectively serve the Azerbaijani people. With this aim, the State Oil Fund of Azerbaijan has been set up. The creation of this Oil Fund is a very significant event in the modern history of Azerbaijan. This fund meets all the international standards and its activity is transparent.
>
> – President Ilham Aliev, inauguration ceremony (October 31, 2003).

> Unless people feel they are benefiting from our presence then it's not going to be a sustainable environment for us to do business.... We need to be here not just for a few years, but for the next few decades.
>
> – David Woodward, President of BP Azerbaijan, speaking on the day of the opening of the BTC pipeline (May 25, 2005, *The Times*)

While both Uzbekistan and the Russian Federation rebuffed prospective foreign investors (FIs) after the demise of the Soviet Union, Azerbaijan's decision to involve FIs in the exploitation of its petroleum sector through state ownership without control (S_2) in the early 1990s denoted a significant departure from the ownership structure it inherited from the Soviet Union – state ownership with control (S_1) – that since the abolition of Lenin's New Economic Policy in the 1920s shunned "foreign capitalists."[1] Azerbaijan's decision to pursue S_2 after achieving independence, furthermore, coincided with a worldwide resurgence in foreign investment in the exploration for and production of petroleum at the end of the twentieth century. According to our research, in the year 2000, approximately 75 percent of 47 petroleum-rich countries in the developing world had opted for direct foreign involvement in their petroleum sector either in the form of S_2 (~38%) or P_2 (~36%).[2]

---

[1] On May 24, 1924, the Azerbaijan oil industry was nationalized by decree (for details, see Mir-Babayev 2004).

[2] S_2 became common only beginning in 1970. In 1975, 18 petroleum-rich countries had adopted S_1 whereas 13 had adopted S_2. By 1990, S_2 had surpassed S_1 as the preferred form of ownership structure. (See Appendix B for details.)

As we show in Chapter 6, ownership structures where FIs are actively involved do not operate in a historical vacuum but rather within a specific international context. Because Azerbaijan adopted S_2 in the 1990s, it offers an opportunity to test its effects on fiscal outcomes during what we designate as the third time period (1990–2005), which commenced with the emergence of new norms regarding the way that businesses conduct their operations abroad, accompanied by new actors (INGOs and IFIs) seeking to diffuse these norms. This particular international context mediates the direct effects of S_2 on our three causal mechanisms, generating negligible transaction costs (TCs), high societal expectations vis-à-vis both the FIs and governing elites, and power relations that can favor either the FIs or the host government. Although each of these three mechanisms is at work in promoting incentives for hybrid fiscal regimes – that is, fiscal regimes that are only partially constraining and enabling – due to the uncertainty surrounding which set of actors will ultimately enforce the model contract in the 1990s, coercion takes on greater significance in determining which of the four potential hybrid fiscal regimes depicted in Chapter 6 is most likely to emerge in Azerbaijan.

As predicted, because its FIs have both been fully committed to CSR and able to unilaterally enforce their contracts, Azerbaijan adopted what we describe as the "best-case" hybrid fiscal regime under S_2. Within the mineral sector, foreign oil companies (hereafter, FOCs) have enjoyed a stable and transparent fiscal burden. They have also been successful at directing the bulk of their spending at both the national and subnational levels toward improving people's lives in the short term and contributing to social and economic development over the long term. In order to achieve these dual goals, moreover, FOCs have not only been willing to commit to expenditures beyond those stipulated in their contracts but also to pressure the government to introduce an NRF through which it could publicize its share of petroleum rents and explicitly target some of them at poverty alleviation programs. Yet while this has increased transparency over the revenue flowing into the NRF, and thus created some degree of popular accountability, it has not stabilized the government's use of this revenue. Likewise, governing elites have continued to use the NOC as both a source of unstable and nontransparent revenue generation and unbridled state spending via quasi-fiscal activities (QFAs). Outside the mineral sector, the FOCs' impact has also been somewhat positive, albeit less expansive. Although Azerbaijan's budgetary dependence on the petroleum sector has swelled, the stability of the FOCs' taxation has mitigated governing elites' disincentives from high societal expectations to initiate broad-based taxation. Thus, in conjunction with the FOCs' support of IFI and INGO efforts, some tax reform outside the mineral sector has transpired. Nonetheless, high societal expectations vis-à-vis the state have made budgetary reform outside the mineral sector more difficult, resulting in the persistence of a bloated and inefficient welfare system.

This chapter and the next demonstrate that the hybrid fiscal regimes that emerge under ownership structures with foreign involvement at the turn of the twenty-first century, on balance, look much better from the perspective of both governing elites and the general population than those that existed during the preceding two time periods (that is, 1900–1960 and 1960–1990). Azerbaijan is an especially poignant case on which to test the hypothesized effects of these changes at the international level on fiscal regimes, not only because Azerbaijan inherited the oldest petroleum industry in the world, but also because FOCs were actively involved in its early development at the turn of the twentieth century. Indeed, the world's first successful oil well was drilled at Bibi-Heybat in the Absheron Peninsula in 1848 – a decade prior to the discovery of commercial oil in Titusville, Pennsylvania in 1859 (Bagirov 2008, 167). From the legalization of the sale of land in 1872 to private investors (McKay 1984, 607) until the Bolshevik Revolution in 1917, FOCs obtained a prominent place in Azerbaijan's petroleum sector, such that by 1910, three major ones – Royal Dutch Shell, the Nobel Brothers Petroleum Company, and the Russian General Oil Society – operated more than 60 percent of the oil fields around Baku (Bagirov 1996). Largely owing to the pioneering innovations and pecuniary means of the Nobel Brothers' Petroleum Company, by the start of the twentieth century Azerbaijan's oil fields were responsible for one-half of the world's production of crude oil (McKay 1984, Sagers 1994).[3]

How qualitatively different then was Azerbaijan's fiscal regime at the turn of the twentieth century for both the direct claimants (here, FIs) and the indirect claimants (here, governing elites and the domestic population)? As predicted in Chapter 6, FOCs incurred a much lower tax burden; for instance, in July 1877 in order to support innovation, the State Council "freed the petroleum industry from any special taxation" (McKay 1984, 607). Also consistent with our predictions, their fiscal obligations did not include any local content provisions such as for labor and the environment; as a consequence, their operations generated tremendous waste whereby the residual oil from the refining process was "simply burned or dumped in the sea" (ibid., 609). Rather, whatever social spending the FOCs did undertake was a function of their own limited goodwill and economic necessity; even the now celebrated philanthropist Ludwig Nobel confined charitable spending to his enclave operations, which amounted to the construction of a workers' compound known as Villa Petrolea (LeVine 2007, 15).[4]

Although any of the four possible hybrid fiscal regimes at the end of the twentieth century is preferable to Azerbaijan's fiscal regime in the first part of the twentieth century, they are nonetheless "second best" outcomes because unlike strong fiscal regimes, their ability to constrain and enable the state is very limited – particularly when it comes to taxation and spending outside the mineral sector. Yet as the case of Azerbaijan makes clear, being the "best" of these second best outcomes still has its virtues. In particular, while the theory of the "obsolescing bargain" (Vernon 1971) assumes that governments will

---

[3] For an early history, see Marvin (1884).
[4] Villa Petrolea became the home of BP in the 1990s.

inevitability renege on the terms specified in FOCs' contracts, this chapter provides evidence that since the 1990s FOCs can elude the obsolescing bargain. It also shows that, where these FOCs are pro-CSR, the resulting hybrid fiscal regime is more likely not only to constrain and enable the state within the mineral sector, but also to improve citizens' lives in the short term and foster social and economic development over the long term. The likelihood for such an outcome increases, moreover, when the FOCs in conjunction with IFIs and INGOs can also effectively pressure the state to embrace fiscal reform outside the mineral sector.

ADOPTING STATE OWNERSHIP WITHOUT CONTROL

As discussed in the preceding chapter, there are several features that distinguish state ownership without control (S_2) from both private foreign ownership (P_2) and state ownership with control (S_1). Perhaps the clearest sign that Azerbaijan adopted S_2 rather than P_2 or S_1 is the role of the FIs. In contrast to P_2, FOCs are involved in the exploitation of petroleum reserves as managers on behalf of the state rather than as owners. As under S_1, the state retains ownership of the resources; and yet, it invites FOCs to participate in the petroleum sector through very permissive contracts such as the PSA, which affords them both managerial and operational control.

Among its petroleum-rich counterparts in the FSU, Azerbaijan stands out as having signed the largest number of PSAs; by 2005, it had concluded approximately 26 PSAs with approximately 30 foreign oil and gas companies.[5] Most notably, on September 20, 1994, President Heydar Aliyev signed what is widely referred to in the popular press as the "Contract of the Century." This historic PSA was reached with a consortium of major foreign oil and gas companies known as the Azerbaijan International Operating Company (AIOC)[6] to open up the Azeri, Chirag, and deep-water portion of the Guneshli oil fields (ACG) for exploration and production.[7] The other monumental PSA signed was for the Shah Deniz giant natural gas and condensate field in June 1996.[8] This field is considered to be one of the world's largest natural gas field discoveries in the last 20 years. The government's indirect claimant status vis-à-vis the revenue generated from the exploitation of its petroleum reserves thus comes from

[5] For details, see the website of Azerbaijan's NOC (meaning SOCAR) (http://www.socar.az/oilstrategy-en.html).

[6] The AIOC partners include BP, ChevronTexaco, SOCAR, Inpex, Statoil, ExxonMobil, TPAO, Devon Energy, Itochu, Delta/Hess). The initial configuration was SOCAR (20%), BP (17.127 %), Amoco (17.01%), Lukoil (10%), Pennzoil (9.82%), Unocal (9.52%), Statoil (8.563%), McDermott International (2.45%), Ramco (2.08%), Turkish State Oil Company (1.75%), and Delta-Nimir (1.68%) (Sagheb and Javadi 1994).

[7] This agreement was ratified by Parliament on December 2, 1994 and went into effect on December 12, 1994.

[8] This consortium consists of BP, Statoil, SOCAR, Lukoil, National Oil Company Iran (NICO), Elf, and Turkish Petroleum Overseas (TPAO).

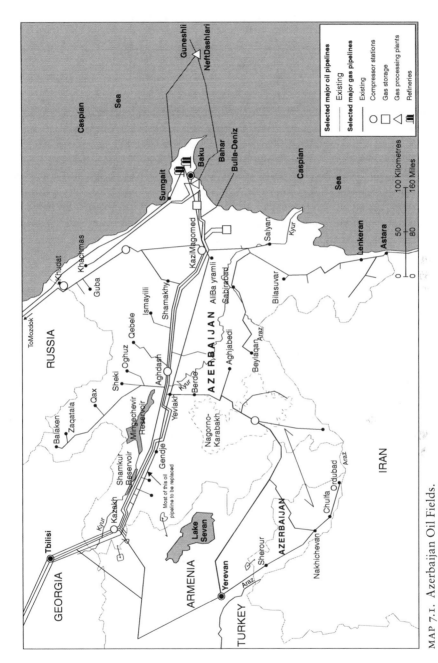

MAP 7.1. Azerbaijan Oil Fields.

Source: Caspian Oil and Gas ©OECD/IEA, 1998, map 2, page 22.

the fact that it has relinquished its operational control and decision-making authority over production decisions in its most lucrative and abundant fields.

Second, the prominent role of the NOC distinguishes S_2 from P_2. Under S_2, the NOC both manages the older and less lucrative oil and gas fields that the state retains under its own control and acts as a nominal partner in any major venture with FOCs. Soon after attaining independence, the Azerbaijani government set up two state concerns (Azerineft and Azneftkimiya) to manage its oil exploration and extraction from its residual fields and to provide transportation and refining, respectively (Hoffman 2000b). On September 13, 1992, Azerbaijan's second president, Abulfez Elchibey, issued a presidential decree to merge Azerineft with Azneftkimya into a new NOC (hereafter, SOCAR).[9] Like Uzbekneftegaz in Uzbekistan, SOCAR is a state-owned producer and derives its direct claimant status from its own production. According to the first head of SOCAR, Sabit Bagirov, SOCAR inherited 6,800 wells onshore and nearly 1,400 wells offshore, two major refineries, an 1,150-km oil pipeline network, 12 pumping states, and four research institutes along with 80,000 employees (Bagirov 1996).

As common under S_2, SOCAR serves as a nominal partner in almost all of the country's PSAs. For example, SOCAR holds a 10 percent interest in both the AIOC and the Shah Deniz consortia, which obligates it to contribute some of its profits as "share capital" (Radon 2005). Its responsibilities also include collecting the taxes that the FOCs pay from their PSAs. Most of its own production since 1991, however, is derived from the "shallow-water Guneshli" field that came online in 1981 and referred to as the "28th of April Field" during the Soviet era (DOE-EIA 2007, Sagers 1994). SOCAR also operates another 40 older fields, both onshore and offshore (DOE-EIA 2007). The *Neft Dashlari* field (Oily Rocks) that was discovered in 1949 with production commencing in 1951 is the most famous (Sagers 1994).[10] Estimates of its remaining reserves hover around 1.3 billion barrels of oil (DOE-EIA 2007). In contrast, British Petroleum (hereafter, BP) – the operator of the AIOC consortium – reckons that just the ACG fields contain approximately 5.4 billion barrels.[11] While in most cases under S_2, the NOC is only responsible for managing a small amount of the country's petroleum production, this, however, has not been the case in Azerbaijan for most of the 1990s; until 2005, SOCAR was still producing approximately half of the country's oil production (World Bank 2005a, 38). That SOCAR has remained a significant producer despite production declining by 1 percent annually (DOE-EIA 2007) should not obscure the

---

[9] Elchibey was in the office of the Presidency from June 1992 until June 1993. Former First Secretary of the Azerbaijan Communist Party, Ayaz Mutallibov, ruled Azerbaijan upon gaining independence.

[10] SOCAR has either retained sole ownership and control over the development of these older fields or encouraged joint ventures (JVs), in which FOCs initially could hold no more than 49 percent of shares (Nobatova 2002).

[11] See http://www.bp.com/genericarticle.do?categoryId=9006615&contentId=7014620. DOE-EIA (2007) has estimated that ACG contains 6.5 billion barrels of estimated reserves,

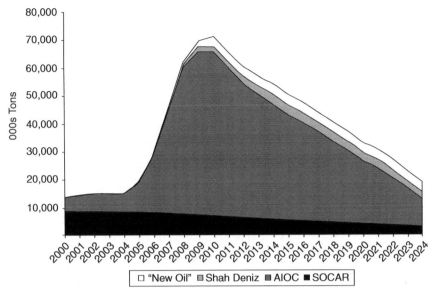

FIGURE 7.1. Azerbaijan Oil Production (Actual and Projected), 2000–2024.
Source: World Bank 2005a.

fact that since 1997, the resources under the FOCs' managerial control have steadily been coming online. As significant production and transportation costs were required to bring these new fields into operation, only in 2005 did the FOCs' production outstrip SOCAR's (see Figure 7.1).[12]

SOCAR also plays a prominent role during the contract negotiation process. In fact, it has become known among potential FIs as a "one-stop shop," because it represents the government in the PSA negotiations for oil and gas development projects and is also responsible for their implementation (Baker & McKenzie, 2003, Matthews 2001).[13] Within SOCAR, the Division of Foreign Investment is responsible for all legal and commercial transactions with the FOCs. In fact, everyone we interviewed made clear that *the* person to meet at SOCAR was Valekh Aleskerov – the General Manager in the Foreign Investments Division, as he oversaw *all* such transactions. As the "competent authority," SOCAR is also responsible for regulating the mineral sector (World Bank 2005a, 5).

Third, S_2 is distinct from S_1 in that it requires a particular legislative framework. Similar to Uzbekistan, which adopted S_1, Azerbaijan's constitution explicitly affirms that "natural resources belong to the Azerbaijan Republic." Yet, because PSAs in Azerbaijan are considered to have the "status of law,"

---

[12] By 2007 FOC production (i.e., AIOC) soared to approximately 80 percent of total production (EIA-DOE 2007).

[13] On February 4, 1994, President Aliyev issued a presidential decree sanctifying this role for SOCAR (Aliyev 1994).

the government has also vested in developing a legislative framework to support the operations of the FOCs. Thus, similar to Kazakhstan, which adopted P_2, it introduced a Law on the Protection of Foreign Investments in 1992 that provides the FOCs with the necessary rights to explore and develop the country's natural resources (World Bank 2005a, 83). Moreover, the Law on Subsoil Reserves (1998) and the Law on Energy (1998) specify the system of permits, licenses and contracts used in the exploration and production of petroleum reserves in Azerbaijan (Luecke and Trofimenko 2008, 136).

THE EMERGENCE OF A HYBRID FISCAL REGIME

Azerbaijan's hybrid fiscal regime from the mid-1990s to 2005 is largely consistent with what we expect to find under our best-case scenario for S_2: (1) a tax system within the mineral sector that is stable for the FOCs but not the NOC and has only undergone some reform outside the mineral sector; and (2) an expenditure system within the mineral sector that is transparent and stable for the FOCs but not the state and has undergone minimal reform outside of the mineral sector. On the one hand, while the FOCs have incurred a much heavier fiscal burden than they did in prior time periods, their taxation and spending obligations have remained remarkably stable and they have directed the latter toward poverty alleviation programs at both the national and local levels. On the other hand, the governing elites have frequently utilized the NOC as a source of QFAs rather than seeking to broaden the tax base outside of the mineral sector. The duality of Azerbaijan's fiscal regime is reflected in the creation of a partially effective NRF within the mineral sector that has increased transparency and stability vis-à-vis the revenue that the government collects from FOCs but not how it spends this revenue, as is the case with expenditures from the state's formal budget outside the mineral sector.

Taxation within the Mineral Sector: FOCs and the NOC

By all accounts, since the early 1990s, the focus of governing elites in Azerbaijan has been on taxing the FOCs via a specialized tax regime solely for the petroleum sector rather than the country's general tax code. Unlike Russia, where elites and domestic oil companies worked together to produce a unified Tax Code, they have deliberately sought not to integrate the mineral sector with all other economic sectors. In fact, a foreign tax consultant underscored that the Azerbaijani government has relied upon "stand alone tax regime[s]" for each individual investor (Authors' interview). In the case of a consortium such as AIOC, therefore, the FOCs' tax obligations are defined solely within their contracts, specifying the financial commitments of each member for each stage of field development.[14] For instance, some of the FOCs' tax regimes

---

[14] Many of Azerbaijan's PSAs are available in the public domain. For the AIOC PSA, see subsites.bp.com/caspian/ACG/Eng/agmt1/agmt1.pdf

include large bonus payments to the state that are essentially "one-off payments" for licenses and for reaching production targets (Gulbrandsen and Moe 2007, 821).[15]

On balance, as expected, the content of the FOCs' specialized tax regimes favors the government to a greater extent than it would during either of our prior time periods. According to the former head of SOCAR, Azerbaijan is expected to receive approximately 80 percent of the profit oil (or what is also referred to as the "Government Take") over the duration of the contract with AIOC (Bagirov 1996).[16] More favorable terms for the government, however, are accompanied by stability clauses to reassure FOCs so that they are willing to undertake the substantial upfront capital investments. All the contracts also contain explicit provisions for international arbitration in the case that a dispute arises between the host government and investor (see, for example, Bayulgen 2005).

In the case of Azerbaijan, this has contributed to stable tax commitments for the FOCs. Indeed, our interviews confirm that their contracts have remained fixed unlike in Kazakhstan where the rules of the game have constantly changed so that the government can relentlessly extract more revenue from the FOCs than what is laid out in their original contracts. One BP representative in Azerbaijan emphasized that even though they had already fully paid their bonus, the "government ha[d] not placed pressure on [the company] for additional bonuses and funds" (Authors' interview with Hedarov). Likewise, the General Manager at SOCAR for Foreign Investment underscored that when President Aliyev met with the FOCs (in 2002), David Woodward of BP informed him that the "foreigners are facing no problems in Azerbaijan ... [and] that there are no legalistic and bureaucratic problems" (Authors' interview with Aleskerov). A stable tax burden for the FOCs has also facilitated their compliance. In 2000, for example, AIOC drew attention to having obtained its first "Tax Milestone;" it had reached $100 million in payments to the state budget between 1995 and 2000 that included taxes for foreign employees, national employees, pension and employment funds, and withholding tax on foreign subcontractors (Bayatly 2000).

Also consistent with our expectations, the state's budgetary reliance on the petroleum sector has increased dramatically in Azerbaijan since the mid-1990s. The petroleum sector has provided not only the largest percentage of its total exports (90 percent as of 2005) but also the bulk of its fiscal revenue (Cohen 2006, DOE-EIA 2007). Whereas in 2001, the oil sector accounted for one-third of its fiscal revenue (EIU 2001a, 22), as of 2005, it made up 54 percent of total fiscal revenue (Cohen 2006, 13). With the increase in production from the FOCs from the ACG fields in 2005, the government has received a

[15] AIOC agreed in its contract to pay SOCAR $300 million in three installments (Sagheb and Javadi 1994). The Ashrafi/Dan-Ulduzu contract included bonus payments of up to $75 million depending on production thresholds (Bindemann 1999, 72).

[16] Regarding other projects, see (Bagirov 2006).

significant increase in personal and corporate income tax from the FOCs and their subcontractors, both of which flow into the state budget and are discussed in greater detail further in this Chapter (for details, see Bagirov 2006). In addition, the government began receiving profit oil in 2005 from the PSAs, which, as discussed under the subsequent section on expenditures, has flowed into the NRF known as the State Oil Fund of the Azerbaijan Republic (hereafter, SOFAZ) along with bonus payments, rental fees from state property used in oil projects, acreage fees for land use (or royalties), and government earnings from the transport of oil and gas through the Baku-Tbilisi-Ceyhan (BTC) and Baku-Tbilisi-Erzurum (BTE) pipelines.[17]

The single largest source of income to the state budget from the petroleum sector during the 1990s, however, has come from SOCAR (EIU 2001a, IMF 2000a, 2003b). Unlike the FOCs' specialized tax regimes, SOCAR is taxed according to the domestic statutory tax regime. SOCAR receives revenue from its own onshore and offshore shallow-water fields shipped via pipeline to the Russian port of Novorossiysk, revenue from petroleum products shipped by rail to the Georgian port of Batumi, and tariffs collected by the state railway company, by the port of Baku, and from the use of its oil terminals by foreign companies transporting oil by rail from Turkmenistan and Kazakhstan (Bagirov et al. 2003). In 2002, tax payments from SOCAR to the state budget amounted to $340 million, which was, in fact, about $100 million higher than the revenue that accrued to SOFAZ from the FOCs' tax payments (Wakeman-Linn et al. 2004, 10).

Moreover, because the revenue SOCAR generates from its equity interests in its PSAs and joint ventures are accumulated in SOFAZ (Authors' interview with Sharifov; see also IMF 2003b, Wakeman-Linn et al. 2004), the tax side of the state budget up until 2005 has remained highly dependent upon income tax revenue, VAT, and royalties generated from SOCAR's own fields. Royalties, which were introduced at the end of 1995, are an especially important component of the state's tax regime for SOCAR and its production subsidiaries (EIU 1999). In short, one analyst pointed out that while one-half of the country's tax revenue is derived directly from the oil and gas sector, one-third of the budget revenue comes from SOCAR (Karimli 2006; see also EIU 2003a). Lastly, because the FOCs' specialized contracts have remained stable, it is not surprising that in an effort to increase government revenue, the governing elites have sought to force large taxpayers such as SOCAR to pay their taxes in advance (Umurzakov 2003).

Like an NOC under S_1, SOCAR has incurred an even heavier implicit tax burden consisting of fuel subsidies for households and industry and quasi-fiscal payments, which are discussed in detail in the section about expenditures. In part for this reason, the government has been more flexible when it comes to SOCAR's explicit tax payments. For example, in 2001 when the government ended negotiated tax payments for state-owned enterprises (SOEs),

---

[17] For details, see www.oilfund.az

which led to a decline in tax receipts from other SOEs, SOCAR was still allowed to continue negotiating its formal tax burden with the Ministry of Taxation in order to take its informal tax payments into account (Authors' interview with Rudy; see also, Petri et al. 2002, World Bank 2003a, 12). But this is not the sole reason. As one foreign advisor to the Ministry of Finance emphasized, because it can comfortably rely on corporate income tax (CIT) from the FOCs for revenue, it prefers not to tax SOCAR at its statutory rate and allows SOCAR to treat its taxes as "fungible" (Authors' interview with Rudy). As a result, SOCAR's explicit tax burden is much less stable than the FOCs. It is also much less transparent, due in part to the fact that SOCAR does not have to comply with international financial reporting standards for its own operations. This has led the World Bank to conclude: "it is very difficult for the government to get a clear picture of SOCAR's financial performance and of its associated tax obligations" (2005a, 18).

Taxation outside the Mineral Sector

When it comes to tax reform, Azerbaijan closely resembled the laggard countries of the FSU during its first decade of independent statehood (Ebrill and Havrylyshyn 1999). State elites preserved a Soviet-style tax regime in which taxes were addressed in legislative acts (for example, the civil code and labor law) rather than initiating tax reform (Authors' interview with foreign tax consultant). Yet by July 2000, the Azerbaijani government achieved some tax reform when it introduced a new Tax Code (that came into force on January 1, 2001) that was ostensibly designed to broaden the government's tax base to include both indirect and direct taxation. Through consolidating Azerbaijan's taxes into a single "Western style" law (IMF 2003b, 58), it was able to achieve a Tax Code that was "comparable to other tax systems elsewhere" (Authors' interview with Mered). Specifically, the 2001 Tax Code was comprised of two parts (general and special); the general part describes the tax system, the power and duties of the tax authorities and the basic rules for taxpayers. The special part covers the particular taxes levied on tax payers that include personal income tax (PIT), corporate income tax (CIT), value added tax (VAT), property tax, land tax, highway tax, mining tax, and the simplified tax.

Overall, the Tax Code has had more success in expanding the tax base than in both Uzbekistan and Turkmenistan, but nowhere to the extent that it has reduced the government's fiscal reliance on the mineral sector as in Russia. Prior to introducing the new Tax Code, the PIT's contribution to the state budget had already declined from 30.1 percent of total tax revenue in 1996 to 15.8 percent in 2001 (World Bank 2003a, 12). Although PIT rebounded slightly in the 2000s, reaching 16.5 percent of total tax revenue as of 2005, the IMF emphasized that this increase was still way "below potential" (IMF 2007c, 17). One of the reasons for this has to do with the retention of "multiple personal and capital income tax rates" that have ranged from 14 percent up to 35 percent (Authors' interview with foreign tax consultant; see also Baker and McKenzie 2003, 45). Because PIT rates were not only "relatively high" (Zermeno 2008, 14) but also were compounded by similarly high employer contribution rates (29 percent) for the social protection fund, these combined changes to the Tax Code made "it extremely hard to hire people" and expand private sector employment (Authors' interview with Rudy).

Thus increases in the contribution of PIT to the state budget could not be interpreted as a sign that Azerbaijan was broadening the tax base. According to a foreign tax consultant, the reason for the increase in PIT had to do with the fact that most employed Azerbaijanis who pay taxes are in the energy sector, and thus in the higher tax brackets (Authors' interview with foreign tax consultant). Although expatriates are taxed differently in their respective PSAs, most still end up paying a rate of 35 percent, which is the equivalent of the highest tax bracket for the nonoil sector PIT. Expatriates are also subject to tax on their worldwide income as tax-resident individuals, while non-residents are subject to tax only on their income from sources in Azerbaijan (Baker and McKenzie 2003). An additional reason for the marginal increase in PIT as a percentage of tax revenue in 2005 is linked to an increase in public sector wages (discussed in more detail below under government expenditures); that the government's withholding system for state employees also allows for PIT to be directly deducted from paychecks has further facilitated this rise in PIT (Zermeno 2008).

When it comes to CIT, there has been some success in expanding the tax base such that the amount of CIT as a percentage of non-oil GDP grew from 3.6 percent in 2003 to 3.8 percent in 2004 and to 5.1 percent in 2005 (IMF 2007c, 27).[18] Yet the bulk (approximately 85 percent) of this revenue comes directly from large companies rather than individual entrepreneurs or small and medium enterprises (SMEs) owing to a deliberate government policy to focus its efforts on improving tax compliance from the largest taxpayers (Authors' interview with Mered). Indeed, according to a financial consultant, the Tax Code had, for the most part, only abetted the operations of large companies working in areas related to the petroleum sector since the CIT rate introduced in 2001 was relatively common as in other countries (27 percent), and these companies could claim back any VAT expenses (Authors' interview with Rudy). Moreover, at the same time, the government has increased its focus on large companies, its decision to introduce numerous tax discounts for certain regions and industries outside the mineral sector not only obstructed the Tax Code's ability to expand the tax base, but drew IMF criticism for affecting "'the integrity' of the country's tax code" (Wall 2003). Specifically, the government had granted the mountainous regions a 40 percent discount on their CIT; other tax breaks existed for tourism activities (80 percent) and for handicraft (e.g., carpet weaving) and woodwork activities (40 percent of the regular tax rate) (Asadov and Hadiyev 2002).

---

[18] For comparison purposes, CIT was 4.9 percent of nonoil GDP in Kazakhstan in 2003 (World Bank 2008, 20).

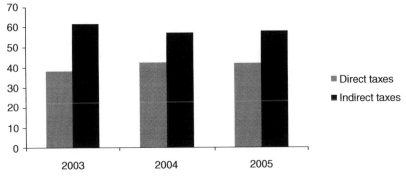

FIGURE 7.2. Indirect versus Direct Taxation in Percent of Total Non-Oil Tax Revenues.
Source: Zermeno 2008.

The one area in which the Tax Code was deliberately designed to increase reliance was indirect taxes such as the VAT and excises. Indeed, largely because the FOCs are exempt from VAT (Bagirov 2008, 41), we do not anticipate that they will make up the bulk of the VAT, especially when they can enforce their contracts. Whereas since 1996, the percentage of VAT's contribution to GDP has gradually increased (IMF 2000), this trend has continued with the implementation of the new Tax Code in 2001. Simply, the VAT has become the "main source of tax revenue for the state budget," jumping from 15.8 percent of total tax revenue in 1995 to 32.5 percent in 2003 (World Bank 2003a, 11–12). Although there was a small drop in the contribution of the VAT to total non-oil revenues between 2003 and 2005 from approximately 42.8 percent to 38 percent, this has not amounted to a decreased reliance on indirect taxes, especially in relation to direct taxation (see Figure 7.2). Rather, the contribution of excise taxes has increased from 6.8 percent of total non-oil revenues in 2003 to 8.5 percent in 2005 (Zermeno 2008). Moreover, this decline in the VAT has been attributed to the lack of administrative reform, which has facilitated fraud and evasion (ibid).

While we would expect indirect taxes to make up the lion's share of taxation under S_2 (as under S_1), reliance on the VAT has also come at the expense of SME development. Paradoxically, while FOCs' specialized tax regimes grant them and their local subcontractors VAT exemptions, the lack of the same VAT exemptions for SMEs has obstructed small business development (Authors' interview with Rudy). The Association of Local Entrepreneurs is painfully aware of this inequitable treatment and the counterproductive effects of the new tax code on the development of SMEs. According to its General Secretary, the number of small businesses had declined by three times (Authors' interview). Yet the results of the Association's efforts to make this clear to government representatives in the Ministry of Taxation, the Ministry of Economic Development and Trade, or even the Parliament have been "discouraging ... [because] they simply don't seem to care whether we survive"

(Authors' interview with Rzaeyeva). One member of the Association described their plight thus: "the more we complain, the higher the taxation and the more audits we face" (Authors' interview).

Furthermore, the persistence of a "large informal economy" has "significantly undermine[d] non-oil tax collection" in Azerbaijan (Zermeno 2008, 8). Already at independence, the unofficial economy accounted for 50.3 percent of GDP; by 1997, it had increased to 61 percent of GDP and as of 2000, it remained the second-largest unofficial economy among all 23 transition countries – still accounting for approximately 61 percent of GDP (Schneider 2005, 610, Umurzakov 2003, 70). Even in spite of the introduction of a simplified tax system, the government has been unable to shrink the size of Azerbaijan's shadow economy, foster the growth of SMEs, and hence broaden the tax base, as was the case in Russia. Under the simplified tax system, entrepreneurs are only taxed 2–4 percent of their gross proceeds and are, moreover, exempt from the VAT, PIT and CIT (IFC 2009). Yet, the persistence of high VAT and income tax rates outside the simplified tax has fostered disincentives for individuals to grow their businesses. This is potentially troublesome given that about "90 percent of all the labor force within the entrepreneurship community is employed by individual entrepreneurs" (IFC 2009, 34). While the majority of these individual entrepreneurs use the simplified tax, for companies that, in fact, want to hire additional workers, they have to forfeit these low tax rates and exemptions and move to the standard tax regime (see IFC 2009). As a result, the simplified tax system has pushed many of these individual entrepreneurs into the informal economy and encouraged "tax evasion and corruption" (ibid., 111).[19] That non-oil revenues in 2005 remained below potential, according to the IMF, was accordingly "due to the importance of the informal economy" (IMF 2007c, 17).[20]

Lastly, the instability and nontransparency of the Tax Code has further hampered its effectiveness to broaden the tax base. While on paper the Tax Code is considered to be "very transparent" (Authors' interview with Mered), its implementation has been mired in nontransparency and instability.[21] Specifically, the governing elites have "refused to introduce instructions because they did not want clarity"; rather, they wanted the flexibility "to send out the tax inspectors to continue to negotiate tax payments" (Authors' interviews with foreign tax consultant). Thus, while the 2001 Tax Code was "very Western" in its form, it still lacked "sophistication" precisely because the lack of instructions left "many things open to interpretation" for the tax inspectors (ibid). As such, the "inability to know what you will end up paying in taxes" has also further deterred the development of private sector investment (ibid).

[19] Analysts have attributed the decline in VAT contributions to pervasive tax evasion for similar reasons (Zermeno 2008).

[20] UNDP (2005) also concluded that approximately 50 percent of money circulation continues to be in the shadow economy (http://www.un-az.org/undp/bulnews25/inflation.php).

[21] Between 2001 and 2008, the Tax Code was amended 19 times (IFC 2009, 110).

Specifically, the government did not simultaneously take measures to ease the tax environment for SMEs and individual entrepreneurs. A 2005 World Bank study showed that one-fourth of Azerbaijani firms reported the taxation regime as the main constraint for carrying out business (IFC 2009, 110). Furthermore, according to the results of *Doing Business in 2006* – the first time that it included an assessment of "paying taxes" for business – Azerbaijan was ranked well behind Russia and Kazakhstan, yet still above Uzbekistan, for countries that made it most difficult to pay taxes in 2005. When it came to the amount of hours a business could expect to devote to making tax payments, Azerbaijani businesses could expect to spend approximately 756 hours annually on their tax payments in comparison to 156 in Kazakhstan (*Doing Business in 2006*). In sum, in contrast to the stability of the FOCs' tax payments that eases their compliance, the constant fluctuations in the Tax Code has made it increasingly difficult for Azerbaijani citizens to pay their taxes and further increases the incentives for a business to "hide or 'adjust' its turnover" (IFC 2009, 116).

Expenditures within the Mineral Sector (FOCs)

The empirical evidence also suggests that, as expected, the FOCs in Azerbaijan have spending obligations enumerated in their contracts at the subnational level that both make these obligations explicit and exceed requirements from previous periods. Thus, alongside an increased tax burden, the aforementioned contracts stipulate local content provisions that cover environmental regulations, local hires, and training of the workforce (ACG PSA article 6 and 26). For example, ACG not only committed to investing $8–10 billion over a 30-year period, but its contract lays out provisions for spending on public health, safety, and environmental protection in order to safeguard the natural environment of the Caspian and the workforce (Adams 1995b, Bagirov 1996). Terry Adams, the first president of AIOC, in elucidating their obligations pertaining to local content, emphasized that the consortium members would use Azerbaijani companies and organizations for the provision of goods and services (Adams 1995b). AIOC, for instance, signed contracts with the State Committee on Hydrometerology for support vehicles. In order to meet its local content obligations, AIOC has organized training courses for the National Oil Academy (Bayatly 2003a). AIOC has also invested in projects to create opportunities for local businesses to serve as major suppliers of goods and services (ibid). For example, in cooperation with the shareholders from the Shah Deniz consortium and the BTC pipeline consortium, AIOC in 2002 helped establish an Enterprise Center in Baku that according to Karen St. John, BP's Director of Social Performance, would "build up small and medium businesses" so that they could serve as "suppliers to local businesses" (Authors' interview).[22] Through

---

[22] Likewise, they were one of the steering members of the Business Development Alliance led by the NGO, International Alert, to support local business development (Killick 2006).

helping small companies develop strategic business plans, the Enterprise Center has, in fact, nurtured new entrants into BP's supply chain, shifting its dependence away from SOEs to SMEs (BP 2007, 51).

FOCs in Azerbaijan, moreover, have engaged in spending over and above the local content obligations specified in their contracts, such that they are providing public goods and services "beyond compliance" at the subnational level. Consider BP's spending patterns, which have focused on both social welfare and human development. BP has routinely volunteered to renovate schools and drill wells for water in order to improve local development prospects. As part of the Early Oil Project, for example, BP supported local communities in Sangachal and Supsa areas through the refurbishment of local schools and improvements to water supply systems to expand access to potable drinking water. Similarly, near the Shah Deniz project, BP refurbished a school heating system in order to increase attendance (BP 2005, 45).

BP has also willingly expanded its spending on local development projects to help "improve livelihoods and economic opportunities for the population living in the communities" along its pipeline corridor (BP 2003, 119). Thus, during the construction phase of the BTC pipeline, which serves as the main export pipeline from the ACG oil fields to international markets, BP along with its AIOC partners carried out an expansive "Community Investment Program," which entailed spending on health and education (Authors' interview with Mehdiyeva).[23] Overall, BP planned to spend "$8 million in community investment and an additional $2 million in environmental investment in Azerbaijan through 2006" (Bayatly 2003b).[24] One such project was the Human Development Program associated with AIOC's Sangachal Terminal Expansion Program (STEP) wherein as of 2003, AIOC supported 36 projects in the Garadagh district aimed at improving the health, economic development prospects, and educational opportunities in most of the local communities in the district (Bayatly 2003c).

Yet as we predict under S_2, a large share of the FOCs' spending in Azerbaijan is also directed toward the national level in compliance with their contracts. For example, the AIOC contract includes an "interruption clause" that ensures enough oil production to meet domestic requirements even if exports are halted (Adams 1995b, 40). Whereas FOCs have traditionally opted to flare rather than develop the gas from their oil fields, the domestic market obligations for the AIOC consortium also require that the associated gas from AIOC's operations be delivered "free of charge" to SOCAR to help meet Azerbaijan's energy needs (BP 2003, 131, World Bank 2005a, 50 and article 15.1 of the PSA).

---

[23] Projects included a new gym and first aid station for the secondary school at Bibi-Heybat and spending on health and education in the Garadagh District through its Community Assistance Program (for details, see Bayatly 2005).

[24] In 2003, BP allocated $2.72 million to social spending in Azerbaijan (*RPI* 2004, 62). By 2006, BP and its partners invested approximately $6.7 million in the social sector, of which $3.2 million was spent on "community development investment projects" (BP 2006).

Likewise, at the national level the FOCs have engaged in spending outside of their contractual obligations such that they are also providing essential public goods and services "beyond compliance." In fact, they voluntarily chose to do so right from the moment the ink dried on their contracts. For example, in 1994, BP bequeathed $5 million for President Aliyev's Hospital Fund in addition to more than $50 million designated for the Government Social Fund (Adams 1995b, 40, Sagheb and Javadi 1994). The shortage of education materials in the Azerbaijani language was endemic after the government adopted the Latin alphabet at independence and government spending on education plummeted in the early 1990s (AEU and UNICEF 2008). In response, Exxon has voluntarily developed dictionaries and encyclopedias in the new Latin alphabet to facilitate the transition away from the Cyrillic alphabet (*Azerbaijan International* 2003, 76). According to Statoil's Corporate Social Responsibility Advisor, Statoil has also explicitly directed its social investments at the "country level," selecting projects that support the Millennium Development Goals (MDGs) and Azerbaijan's poverty reduction program (Authors' interview with Mehdiyeva). Even Lukoil, whose corporate giving in Russia is largely confined to the regions where it and its subsidiaries operate, has explicitly focused its social expenditures at the national level in Azerbaijan with the creation of the Azerbaijani Charity Fund in 1996 (*Azerbaijan International* 2000).

To enhance the social and economic impact of its spending in both the short and the long term, BP established an independent, external advisory board – the Caspian Development Advisory Panel (CDAP) (for details, see CDAP 2003). Thus, rather than deciding its spending priorities solely in-house, BP fully embraced a recommendation by the CDAP in 2003 that the consortium should "'invest in sustainable development in the Caspian region as a whole' for the full lifespan of the projects" (BP 2005, 40).[25] As a result, BP committed $20 million annually to a new initiative – the Regional Development Initiative (RDI) (BP 2005) – which according to Gulbrandsen and Moe (2007, 824) was conceived in 2003 to focus on "macro-level issues and large-scale, country-wide and cross-regional programmes."[26] BP also recruited international staff with developmental expertise from outside the oil sector to manage its programs (Authors' interview with St. John). As one BP representative proudly summarized, "it's an investment approach to development rather than the old philanthropy" (quoted in Gulbrandsen and Moe 2007, 824).

In addition, FOCs have been developing vibrant collaborative partnerships with INGOs and local activists in those communities most affected by petroleum extraction to determine their spending priorities, as well as to ensure that their spending will actually address the specific economic and social needs of those areas (for details, see BP 2003, 119). According to a specialist on corporate social investment, these "partnerships with non-profit associations"

[25] In drafting its recommendations, the Panel sought input from government officials, NGOs, and academics, and any other interested party. See http://www.caspsea.com.
[26] "In the 2006–08 period, BTC expects to spend some $41 million across the region under the auspices of RDI" (CDAP Final Report 2007, 18).

have allowed companies to take into account "the long-term impact" of their spending (Authors' interview with Kazimov). Through partnering with the International Rescue Committee (IRC), for example, BP has directed its funding toward the "rehabilitation of the electricity supply system, renovation of a secondary school, rehabilitation of a culture centre, rehabilitation of the electricity system of an Internally Displaced Persons settlement, and construction of a health care facility" in the Bibi-Heybat area (BP 2006, 51–2). Similarly, working with the local NGO, UMID, BP has financed the installation of water purification units in a number of communities (BP 2006).[27] Here, because UMID designed a proposal that was "adaptive to local conditions," these collaborations, according to the head of UMID, have allowed for the implementation of "significant and effective projects" (Authors' interview with Iskendorov).

In order to create alternative income-generating opportunities, partnering with local NGOs has also allowed BP to exploit "good, old-fashioned traditions" of vocational training for young people (ibid). Again working with UMID has allowed BP to successfully "provide apprenticeship training for several hundred young people in which the majority found jobs in the process, generating much-needed income for their families" (ibid.). The creation of the aforementioned Enterprise Center also entailed working with an alliance of NGOs, local business, and development agencies. Prior to its creation, BP actively participated in a multistakeholder dialogue initiated by the British NGO, International Alert, to support the development of local businesses through the Business Development Alliance (BDA) (Authors' interview with St. John; see also Killick 2006).[28] According to one of the architects of the BDA, "[t]he Azerbaijan multi-stakeholder dialogue was conceived in the belief that the companies investing in Azerbaijan could be engaged not in the socially responsible management of their own operations but also in tackling some of the underlying, structural causes of the conflict in the region" (Killick 2006, 100). Overall, these efforts have deliberately bypassed public sector institutions to promote the private sector and to provide "private skill training" (UNDP 2006/2007, 61).

Lastly, the extent to which the government has influenced any of the FOCs' spending priorities "beyond compliance" at the national level has been limited to the refugee and internally displaced persons (hereafter IDP) populations that comprise approximately 12 percent of the total population.[29] For

---

[27] UMID works with "marginalized" segments of the population on social problems, including education, basic needs, and employment opportunities. See, http://www.umid-hsdm.com/index.htm.

[28] Other members of the steering committee included Citizen's Democracy Corps, Azerbaijan Entrepreneur's Confederation, Eurasia Foundation, Kosia-Smeda, and the American Chamber of Commerce.

[29] The bloody war with Armenia over Nagorno-Karabakh from 1988–1994 resulted in approximately 1 million people becoming refugees or internally displaced persons (IDPs). See http://www.adb.org/Documents/Policies/Azerbaijan/AZB.pdf.

example, in 2001 BP funded the construction of a library and kindergarten for refugee children in Sabirabad, and then in 2004 it funded several income-generating activities for internally displaced persons in Khirdalan near Baku that included the building of several greenhouses and a sewing workshop (Bayatly 2004). The AIOC consortium helped build a water pipeline to bring water from the Kur River in Sabirabad to the refugee camp in Saatli and has worked with the State Committee on the Problems of Refugees to ensure that the population will have enough water for domestic uses and agricultural purposes (Bayatly 2001). Likewise, Exxon's social spending (more than $3 million) has gone to the construction of schools, community centers, medical clinics, and provision of clean water supplies for the refugee and IDP populations in Bilasuvar, Saatli, and Sabirabad and other regions of Azerbaijan (*Azerbaijan International* 2003, 76). Yet here too, to ensure that their spending will actually address the specific economic and social needs of the refugee and IDP populations, the FOCs have directed much of their spending toward supporting the work of major relief agencies such as International Federation of Red Cross and Red Crescent Societies, CARE, and Relief International with experience in providing medical and educational assistance to such populations (*Azerbaijan International* 2004, 133). FOCs such as StatoilHydro, therefore, have worked with the Norwegian Refugee Council, the Danish Refugee Council, and UNHCR to design income-generating programs and support SME development specifically for the refugee population (Authors' interview with Mehdiyeva).

Expenditures within the Mineral Sector: SOCAR and SOFAZ

When it comes to the government expenditures within the mineral sector (that is, via SOCAR and SOFAZ), we find a different picture in terms of both stability and transparency. In sharp contrast to the FOCs, SOCAR's expenditures are characterized by extreme instability and nontransparency. This is because the high level of fuel subsidies to households and SOEs that SOCAR must provide are a major component of government expenditures and have remained largely unreformed since independence. Similar to countries with S_1, subsidizing energy consumption via the NOC has served as the primary mechanism for the government to distribute the benefits of its petroleum wealth widely and visibly to the population. In Azerbaijan, the government thus not only explicitly taxes SOCAR through royalties and income taxes, but because SOCAR serves as the "the 'single buyer' of gas for the domestic market" (World Bank 2005a, 8), the government relies upon it to subsidize domestic energy consumption. In particular, SOCAR is expected to provide free gas to agriculture during the planting and harvesting seasons and to provide underpriced energy to households and other domestic customers such as Azerenergy and Azerigaz (Authors' interview with Bagirov; see also Petri et al. 2002, World Bank 2005a, 38). Azerbaijan has the dubious honor of being among the least successful of the FSU countries in reducing its fuel subsidies; only Uzbekistan has recovered a lower portion of its gas production costs (World Bank 2005a, 9). As of 2005, fuel subsidies have hovered around 12.7 percent of the country's GDP; in contrast in 2005 fuel subsidies only comprised 3.1 percent of the GDP in Bolivia and 3.6 percent in Ecuador or 3.2 percent in Indonesia (Coady et al. 2006, 3).[30] Furthermore, while Turkmenistan ranks number one worldwide for having the most heavily subsidized gasoline and diesel, out of 171 countries surveyed by the German development agency, GTZ, Azerbaijan ranks number 46 and 41, respectively, which places it in the same league as Ecuador and Indonesia (Morgan 2007). As is often the case with nontargeted subsidies, underpriced energy in Azerbaijan has benefited disproportionately the "richest 20 percent of population of the capital city Baku" that "consume[s] 5 percent more electricity per month than the poorest 20 percent in 2002" (IMF 2005a, 8). Likewise, because poor families have "limited or no services," the IMF concluded that these subsidies "as a form of social protection is neither pro-poor, nor cost-effective" (2003a, 94).

Azerbaijan, moreover, stands out among the FSU states as having the largest energy QFAs – estimated at over 20 percent of GDP (Petri et al. 2002, 5). These QFAs are manifested through the high toleration for payment arrears and noncash arrangements (IMF 2005a, 4). SOCAR bears the brunt of these QFAs because it is forced to accept nonpayment from Azerenergy and Azerigas, and yet is obligated to provide them with a sufficient supply of fuel (EIU 2001a, IMF 2005a, 20). High payment arrears, in turn, are responsible for SOCAR's high tax arrears, which by the end of 1999 totaled 23 percent of GDP (IMF 2000a).

Perhaps what most distinguishes expenditures within the mineral sector under S_2 from under P_2 – and hence, Azerbaijan from Kazakhstan – is the ability of the governing elites to rely upon the NOC to finance their spending priorities at both the subnational and national levels. Such expenditures, moreover, are not reflected in the state budget, which contributes to their lack of stability and transparency in part because they are not subjected to an independent audit (Lorie 2003, Makhmutova 2007). As a result, there are no limits on the degree to which SOCAR is utilized as a vehicle for providing not only basic welfare to its own employees, but also to the broader population. Providing for the welfare of its own employees is no small task, given that SOCAR is such a large source of public employment and excessively so. While figures for the number of people SOCAR employs range anywhere from 60,000 to 78,000 persons (EIU 2000, World Bank 2005a), according to an IMF representative in Azerbaijan, SOCAR is well-overstaffed and "probably only needs 5,000" (Authors' interview with Mered). A comparison with ChevronTexaco demonstrates just how irrational the size of SOCAR's workforce is: As the second-largest U.S.-based oil company with operations in more than 180 countries and assets valued over $80 billion, it only employs 51,000 people

[30] Earlier these were even higher – around 22 percent of GDP in 2000 (IMF 2005a, 9).

(World Bank 2005a, 39).[31] What is even more telling is that many of SOCAR's employees are not based near its oil-producing fields in the Baku area. One reason for this is clearly the huge socioeconomic benefits that one is entitled to as a SOCAR employee. As was the case for all SOEs during the Soviet period, SOCAR is responsible for furnishing its workforce with kindergartens, housing, health care, and a living fund (Authors' interview with Aleskerov; see also Gorst 2008, Habibov and Lida Fan 2006). It is also responsible, however, for providing such benefits to nonemployees. If SOCAR wants to build housing for its employees, for example, it is obliged to provide housing for a certain percentage of the population elsewhere (Authors' interview with Aleskerov). Beyond this, SOCAR's largest spending obligation concerns the unspecified monies it must allocate regularly to the refugee population from the brutal Nagorno-Karabakh conflict with Armenia that ended with a ceasefire in 1994 (Authors' interview with Sharifov).[32] In short, while SOCAR has been commended for "spending a lot" on the population, it is obvious that unlike the FOCs, there is "nothing strategic" about the way it spends: "It is unclear why [SOCAR] is picking to spend on one hospital in one region versus another; it may just be that it received a call from the government to do this" (Authors' interview with Kazimov).

When it comes to SOFAZ, there is much greater transparency of fiscal transactions. Azerbaijan was applauded for being the first among the petroleum-rich FSU states to introduce a NRF. President Aliyev established SOFAZ by decree on December 29, 1999 as an extrabudgetary fund to collect the oil and gas proceeds that would normally accrue to the state from the PSAs, and to invest these assets abroad (Bacon and Tordo 2006, 72, World Bank 2005a, 21). The justification underlying the creation of SOFAZ was to establish an institutionalized means both to save revenue generated from the exploitation of its natural resource wealth for future generations and to use this revenue to support investment projects for education, poverty reduction, and raising rural living standards (IMF 2003b, Wakeman-Linn et al. 2003). According to its official statement, SOFAZ is to "ensure intergenerational equality of benefit with regard to the country's oil wealth, whilst improving the economic well-being of the population today and safeguarding economic security for future generations."[33]

Yet SOFAZ has only partially lived up to these expectations. On the one hand, it has made a good deal of progress in increasing fiscal transparency – albeit only regarding revenue collection from the FOCs. While SOFAZ was supposed to accrue revenue from both the FOCs' profit oil and SOCAR's earnings from its equity interest in the PSAs, the NRF has only reliably received

[31] McPherson (2003) made a similar comparison between SOCAR and Mobil. Both companies employ 65,000 people, but Mobil produces approximately 1.6 million barrels of crude per day whereas SOCAR only produces 100,000 barrels.

[32] Since 1998 SOCAR has supported 6,000 refugees in the "Golden Moon" tent town in the Barda region (http://www.socar.az/11-social-view-en.html).

[33] See http://www.oilfund.az/en/content/21/85.

funds from the FOCs, which are then deposited in "highly reputable financial institutions" rather than remaining in the National Bank (Petersen and Budina 2002). The government has redirected SOCAR's funds into a separate escrow account to support its borrowing for its share of investment in Shah Deniz and its pipeline investments (World Bank 2005a). In order to foster transparency regarding the FOCs' payments, SOFAZ has made them available in its annual reports and on its website (Author's interview with Sharifov). SOFAZ's Executive Director, Samir Sharifov, also took additional steps to increase transparency through meeting intermittently with journalists (ibid). Furthermore, since Azerbaijan volunteered to be a pilot case of the Extractive Industries Transparency Initiative (EITI) in 2003 in which both the government and the FOCs must produce reports on their revenue flows from the petroleum sector and submit them to an internationally reputable accounting firm, it is widely agreed that when it comes to the FOCs' revenue flows, SOFAZ has become "the most transparent government body in Azerbaijan" (EIU 2006a, 26).[34]

On the other hand, despite these gains in public accountability, the government has deliberately avoided bolstering SOFAZ's transparency when it comes how the revenue it accumulates is actually disbursed by continuing to transfer funds out of SOFAZ to the state budget to finance public investments. In 2003, for instance, the government transferred 500 billion manats ($115 million) to the state budget for such purposes (IMF 2004a, 14).[35] This practice not only undermines efforts to improve transparency, but also hampers the effectiveness of the fund to increase budgetary stability and maximize savings, especially during the boom because, as discussed below, Azerbaijan has undergone minimal budgetary reform outside the mineral sector (see Usui 2007, 7).

SOFAZ, however, has been less effective at fostering predictability regarding its spending priorities because it does not include a mechanism (such as parliamentary oversight) to constrain state spending. Ultimate authority over spending decisions rests solely with the President who can "liquidate and reestablish the fund, approve the fund's regulations, identify its management structure, etc." (Petersen and Budina 2002). Moreover, its Executive Director is appointed directly by the President and only reports to the President. Although in December 2001, a Supervisory Board was introduced to oversee the "composition of the fund's assets and compliance to the expenditure rules (ibid), this board's ten members (two of which are members of Parliament,

---

[34] Azerbaijan volunteered to be a pilot case of EITI, which means that FOCs and state must agree to certain reporting and auditing requirements in order to be compliant; on March 15, 2005 it achieved the honor of becoming the first oil-producing country to publish EITI reports and have them scrutinized by an international audit firm. For details, see http://eitransparency.org/Azerbaijan.

[35] There are indications that this practice has continued to an increasing degree; in first half of 2006, for example, over $200 million was transferred to the state budget (Luecke and Trofimenko 2008).

government officials from key economic ministries, head of the National Bank, and from academia) are also all presidential appointees. Thus, while the Executive Director is responsible for its day-to-day functions, all decisions regarding how the revenue in the NRF is spent lies with the President. A foreign advisor to the Ministry of Finance commented that SOFAZ "is set up well institutionally and is indeed very transparent, but ... puts a lot of faith in the President" (Authors' interview with Rudy). Another tax consultant echoed this concern: "Azerbaijan and Kazakhstan can show that they can [create a NRF].... The real issue is how the money is spent and who controls it" (Authors' interview).

While the potential upside is that the President has the autonomy to explicitly channel funds into poverty alleviation programs, the more likely downside is that without any formal oversight mechanisms, the President can arbitrarily and surreptitiously utilize the funds for special pet projects and to achieve certain political ends. SOFAZ's increasingly unfettered spending suggests that the latter is more common and that it is therefore unable to either promote savings or foster budgetary stability. According to its official rules, the government could not access SOFAZ's funds for the first five years, but this has not stopped the government from making numerous exceptions almost as soon as the first influx of revenue was deposited in the NRF (Kalyuzhnova, 2006). Specifically, in 2001 President Aliyev personally diverted funds through presidential decree from SOFAZ to finance refugee housing (Authors' interview with Sharifov) and to cover SOCAR's participation in the BTC oil pipeline (IMF 2004a, 13).[36] The World Bank anticipated a similar level of discreet expenditures from SOFAZ in 2002; yet, whereas President Aliyev's discretionary spending in 2001 amounted to a mere $3.6 million, at the first meeting of SOFAZ's Supervisory Board in July 2002 he ratcheted up this amount to approximately $69 million (World Bank 2003a). By 2005, four presidential decrees have called for spending from the fund – three for social spending to improve living conditions of refugees and IDPs and one for financing SOCAR's share of BTC costs (Cohen 2006).

Although the primary focus of this chapter is on the period 1991–2005, subsequent spending patterns indicate that as production levels and oil prices rose in tandem during the mid-2000s, expenditures from SOFAZ have also escalated, as we would anticipate during a boom under S_2. By the first half of 2006, for example, expenditures from SOFAZ amounted to $357.3 million, of which $40 million went to construction of housing for refugees and IDPs (Luecke and Trofimenko 2008; see also, Bagirov 2006). Thus, unlike Russia and Kazakhstan that have managed to save more than half of their windfall from 2003–2007 in their oil funds, Azerbaijan has saved only less than one-tenth of its total oil revenues (CASE 2008, 121).

---

[36] Presidential decree no. 592 of Oct. 2001 authorized 3.6 million to construct housing and other infrastructure to improve living conditions of IDPs and refugees (Petersen and Budina 2002, World Bank 2003a, 29).

In sum, that SOFAZ has allowed Azerbaijan to sterilize some of the oil revenue from its budget has kept inflation rates low since its introduction, ranging from 1.8 percent in 2000 (IMF 2002, 42) to 2.2 percent in 2003 (IMF 2004a, 13). Yet, as Azerbaijan has expanded the use of revenue from SOFAZ, inflation, which is an initial sign of Dutch disease, has also begun to rise such that by 2005 it was 5.5 percent (IMF 2007c). Compounding the potential for Dutch disease is the Azerbaijani government's lack of support for private sector growth; unlike Kazakhstan, which introduced a clear development strategy for fostering diversification of the economy, SOFAZ has explicitly banned credits to private businesses (Kalyuzhnova and Kaser 2006, 175).

Expenditures outside the Mineral Sector

Outside the mineral sector, Azerbaijan's system of expenditures has undergone minimal reform aimed at promoting transparency and fiscal stability. In short, the budgetary process has largely remained opaque while government spending has remained essentially unconstrained.

The government's efforts to establish an effective system to monitor the budgetary process have been fairly lackluster. While making the budget available to the legislature for review, budgetary experts have underscored that the Azerbaijani Parliament (*Milli Majlis*) is not granted sufficient time to consider the draft budget (Makhmutova 2007, 56). Even though it can pass along recommendations to the Cabinet of Ministers, its role in the budgetary process is further limited by the fact that the Cabinet of Ministers can reject any or all of its recommendations (ibid). Efforts by Parliament to constitute a Counting Chamber in 2001 for carrying out independent audits of the budget have also not improved transparency and hence public accountability, as these reports are not made accessible to the general public (ibid., 53). More so, the government has not made any attempts to open its budget up for public scrutiny by publishing a "citizen's budget" or holding consultations with its citizens when developing its budgetary priorities (ibid., 57). As a result, when it comes to fiscal transparency, Azerbaijan ranks well behind Russia and Kazakhstan, yet still above Uzbekistan (Jarmuzek 2006, IBP 2006).

As in the Soviet successor states that have adopted S_1, the Azerbaijani government has not sought to contract its expenditures but rather to expand the state's influential role in the economic and social spheres. Thus, despite an aggregate decline in its public spending in the early 1990s, as occurred throughout the FSU, Azerbaijan actually increased the size of the public sector "substantially" during this period (Gupta et al. 2003, 563). Government employment increased from 9.5 percent of the population in 1990 to 13.5 percent of the population in 1995 (ibid, 566) and remains a hefty recipient of public expenditures in Azerbaijan. For example, the government has sought to create employment in such sectors as education by simply enlarging the numbers on the state payroll (EIU 2001a). According to the World Bank (2003a, 16), teachers in Azerbaijan account for approximately 25 percent of all general government employment in 2000, but a full-time teacher is only required to work 12 hours a week. As a result, 84 percent of public expenditures in the education sector were devoted to paying wages rather than to improving human capital (ibid). Azerbaijan has similarly high levels of spending on employment in the health sector despite having the lowest public health expenditures among the CIS as a percentage of GDP (0.9 percent) in 2005 (AEU and UNICEF 2008, 33, 39). More so, in the midst of the oil price and production boom in 2003, the government introduced "significant and widespread wage increases" (IMF 2004a, 7).

On what Azerbaijan's governing elites spend is similar to Turkmenistan's with its focus on maintaining some of the widespread distribution programs associated with the Soviet safety net rather than introducing targeted spending. Because social assistance programs in Azerbaijan are based on "categorical" classifications inherited from the Soviet Union, which do not assess income or consumption, they are not designed to identify the most vulnerable populations so as to alleviate poverty (Habibov and Fan 2006). In particular, the largest portion of its social welfare expenditures go to providing support for large numbers of persons, such as pensioners, and for an array of programs designated for broad groups, such as pregnant women and new mothers (ibid, World Bank 2003a, 9). As a result, these benefits are actually very meager and too insignificant to assist those who need them most (ibid, 222, 73). Other universal subsidies that remain in place include funeral fees and sanatorium vouchers – the latter of which are widely viewed as "subsidized vacations" since the government covers 85 percent of the cost of the visit (World Bank 2003a, 76). Not surprisingly, then, despite such a large percentage of expenditures going toward social protection, "the money is spent very poorly" and thus "if one is poor, then [these expenditures] do not really help" (Authors' interview with Rudy).

Yet there has been some reform in the delivery of social assistance in the 2000s. Similar to Turkmenistan and Uzbekistan, the Azerbaijani government maintained large extrabudgetary funds in which little oversight over their operations existed. The Social Protection Fund (SPF), for example, is responsible for paying social insurance benefits such as old age pensions and social assistance allowances (World Bank 2003a, 74). In 1998, it received funds equal to 11.1 percent of total budget revenue and 9 percent of expenditures (Mikesell and Mullins 2001, 553). In order to improve its execution of payments, in 2002 it was brought under the authority of the Treasury; yet this has not resolved the problem that its payments "do not vary according to needs" (World Bank 2003a, 74). Likewise, since 2005, the government has introduced a poverty reduction program that has shifted substantial spending toward social protection (see GoA 2005, Luecke and Trofimenko 2008 for details). This, however, came after a decade and a half during which Azerbaijan lagged behind most of the FSU in its spending on social assistance programs (Habibov and Fan 2006).

Yet a large share of the government expenditures targeted for poverty alleviation programs in the mid-2000s have come from an unmistakable shift in policy to borrow from IFIs rather than to direct SOFAZ funds toward social assistance programs. Several analysts have questioned the economic wisdom of such a strategy (Kalyuzhnova 2006, 83, Usui 2007, 5). Norio Usui, an economist with the Asian Development Bank, commented, for example, that "[i]t is clearly inconsistent to build up funds in [SOFAZ] and, on the other hand, borrow abroad. Given the relatively low return to investments from [SOFAZ] (at around 3–4% in nominal dollar terms during the past few years), the government bore financial costs to fill the gap between the interest rate for external borrowing and investment returns to [SOFAZ]" (2007, 5). And yet the political rationale is clear: financing government spending via international loans has allowed the government to loosen its fiscal policy and accelerate public spending outside the mineral sector during the mid-2000s oil price and production boom despite the introduction of an NRF within the mineral sector (Koeda and Kramarenko 2008, Usui 2007, 4). The result is that while the FOCs' spending obligations have remained remarkably stable, the non-oil primary deficit has swelled from 13 percent of non-oil GDP in 2005 to 33 percent in 2006 with the increase is oil revenue (IMF 2007c, 7). In this sense, Azerbaijan fits the classic pattern of the rentier state, which tends to become increasingly indebted during a boom.

Lastly, that the president retains sole discretionary power to transfer funds from SOFAZ to the state budget [as described above] has further exacerbated budgetary instability. Specifically, the use of open-ended transfers into the state budget ends up simply being "dissolved in the rest of the budget resources and impossible to keep track of" (Bagirov 2006, 9). Such transfers, moreover, hamper the government's ability to channel these rents to productive uses (Usui 2007, 7). In fact, some analysts have suggested that the increase in revenue from the petroleum sector into the state budget accounts for the dramatic jump in the government's expenditures on the defense industry (Cohen 2006).

Causal Mechanisms

In sum, the hybrid fiscal regime that emerged in Azerbaijan approximates our best-case scenario under S_2, as we predict. To be sure that this occurred for the reasons we put forward in Chapter 6, here we seek to demonstrate not only that TCs were negligible and societal expectations were high vis-à-vis both FOCs and the state, but more so that power relations decisively favored FOCs who are strongly committed to CSR.

Transaction Costs

Our argument that TCs are negligible is premised on the understanding that both host governments and FOCs regard the post-1990 model contract as the appropriate global template for structuring their negotiations. Thus, we should find that both FOCs and governing elites in Azerbaijan presumed not only that the model contract would serve as the starting point for their negotiations, but also that this contract would include a heavier tax burden and some degree of social spending for the FOCs alongside stability provisions.

Indeed, ever since the first set of formal negotiations commenced between the Elchibey government and a consortium of FOCs led by BP and Amoco in 1992, both sides have recognized that the PSA would serve as the prevailing contractual template. That both the FOCs and the governing elites assumed they would utilize this model contract for the negotiations over the ACG fields was confirmed by the first head of SOCAR – Sabit Bagirov – who referred to Azerbaijan's monumental 1994 contract with the consortium of FOCs (that is, AIOC) as "modeled on a production-sharing form, which is accepted universally throughout the world" (Bagirov 1996, 10). Likewise, BP stated that the PSAs are "the legal arrangements under which international petroleum companies operate in Azerbaijan" (BP 2003, 29). Terry Adams, the first President of AIOC, underscored that the prevailing contractual template for the ACG fields not only "favors the country," but also "compl[ies] with international standards for such negotiations" (Adams 1995b, 40). Even IFIs such as the World Bank have concurred that the PSA adopted in Azerbaijan is "consistent with best industry practice" (World Bank 2005a, 24).

Further evidence confirms that both the FOCs and the governing elites emphatically understood that significant spending obligations for the FOCs were required if a deal was to be struck. SOCAR emphasized that as a minimum baseline for any deal, local training and employment would be mandatory (Authors' interview). One BP representative remarked that the company understood from the outset that social spending was to be part of their "normal operational procedures" (Authors' interview with BP representative no. 1). Indeed, Terry Adams, the first president of BP in Azerbaijan, emphasized in a speech to the Royal Society for Asian Affairs that "[e]ach contract would include significant financial commitments, that would become the basis for economic revival in the Republic as a whole" (1999, 15).

Likewise, the inclusion of stability clauses to protect the FOCs from arbitrary changes to the terms of their contracts was widely agreed upon by the parties. FOCs, according to Terry Adams, would not have embarked upon exploration and production of petroleum in Azerbaijan if their contracts were not "based on well-defined oil production sharing contracts that clearly recognized and protected investor needs" (1999, 15). More importantly, there is also ample evidence that Azerbaijan's government fully endorsed the inclusion of such provisions in their contract with FOCs. Valeh Aleskerov, SOCAR's chief negotiator, for example, acknowledged that from the outset the Azerbaijani government was acutely aware that it needed to "establish a system that would encourage and protect foreign investment" (Authors' interview). The PSA coupled with Parliamentary ratification, he continued, was designed to "reassure the international companies that we were not going to change their contracts. They would be valid for 25 to 30 years, and nobody would be able to change them, even if new laws were adopted in Azerbaijan. Any changes to their contracts would have to be carried out with the consent of both sides."

Societal Expectations

Both the state and the FOCs confront high societal expectations under S_2. Because they feel pressured to at least appear to be distributing the benefits of the country's petroleum wealth widely, we should find that high societal expectations reinforce governing elites disincentives to adopt limits on spending both within and outside the mineral sector and to pursue broad-based tax reform outside the mineral sector. Likewise, we argue that high societal expectations foster the perception among FOCs that they must overcome a high barrier to attaining social acceptance for their access rights to petroleum rents. As a result, we should find that FOCs have an incentive not only to go "beyond compliance" regarding their own spending but also to encourage governing elites to establish an effective NRF within the mineral sector and promote tax and budgetary reform outside the mineral sector. Moreover, we should find evidence that INGOs and IFIs have played a direct role in elevating societal expectations in Azerbaijan.

As in the other case studies included in this book, we rely primarily on the EBRD 2005 Life in Transition Survey (LiTS) to assess whether societal expectations vis-à-vis the state are consistent with our expectations in Azerbaijan. The results should be very similar to those in Uzbekistan, since societal expectations vis-à-vis the state are also high under S_1. Indeed, the survey results indicate that the vast majority of the population expects that the state should assume a strong role for alleviating inequalities and a dominant role on the economy. An overwhelming 87 percent, for example, responded that the state should be "strongly involved" in "reducing the gap between the rich and the poor." Likewise, 85 percent of those surveyed responded that the state should be strongly involved in guaranteeing employment. These responses, moreover, are fairly uniform across age groups, as they are in Uzbekistan, and just as we predict. For example, the difference between those 18–34 years of age and those over 65 who responded that the state should be strongly involved in reducing the gap between the rich and the poor was seven percentage points, and the difference between these two groups of respondents regarding whether the state should be involved in the ownership of large companies was less than four percentage points (50.4 and 53.6 percent, respectively). (See Appendix C for details.)

In contrast to the other case studies included in this book, there are several additional surveys conducted by NGOs and scholars that we can utilize to assess societal expectations concerning what the role petroleum wealth and the FOCs involved in exploiting this wealth should play in the future development of Azerbaijan.[37] Consistent with the LiTS survey results, for example, a survey carried out by Shannon O'Lear (2007, 218) found that 94 percent of the respondents believed that they were fully, significantly, or a little dependent on the national government; moreover, this survey also found that 47 percent of the respondents believed that the FOCs were to some extent responsible

[37] The AsiaBarometer, however, was not carried out in Azerbaijan.

for their well-being (ibid). Similarly, according to a survey conducted by the Entrepreneurship Development Foundation (EDF)[38] in Azerbaijan, 43.5 percent of the respondents believed that "oil revenues will help the progress of Azerbaijan, solve many of the existing problems and lead to an increase in my personal welfare," whereas another 38.9 percent were still optimistic about the benefits of oil for the development of the country though somewhat less optimistic about their own personal welfare (EDF 2006, 3). The survey also found that approximately 54 percent of the population was optimistic about the future of the country, and of those with a positive orientation toward the future, more than half believed that the use of oil revenues would bring about decisive improvements in the country (ibid, 6). These findings were corroborated in another survey, which found that 66.8 percent of the respondents were "optimistic" regarding their "expectations of [the] benefits from [the] oil contracts and agreements" – that is, how much the contracts will contribute to the economy and how widely and fairly the benefits will be distributed (Faradov 2003). In fact, those skeptical regarding the benefits of the contracts declined from 18.9 percent in 2001/2002 to 5 percent in 2002/2003 as the level of optimism rose from 63 percent in 2001/2002 to 70.6 percent in 2002/2003 (ibid.).

More importantly, the public statements of FOCs and governing elites, especially surrounding the signing of the contracts and the presentation of these agreements with great fanfare to the public, provide strong support for our contention that both sets of actors not only believed that society held high expectations but also took them into consideration in their decision-making calculus. From the outset, both parties desired to communicate to the public that the FOCs were not stealing the nation's resource wealth but rather exploiting it for the enhancement of society's welfare. For example, when Azerbaijan concluded the "Contract of the Century" on September 20, 1994 – approximately 150 years after the world's first oil well was drilled in Azerbaijan – President Aliyev chose to welcome back FOCs in a lavish ceremony at Baku's Gulistan Palace where he hailed the petroleum sector as "the main and richest national wealth of the Azerbaijan Republic and Azerbaijani people" (quoted in Sagheb and Javadi 1994).[39] BP's Managing Director, John Browne, boasted that the agreement would transform Azerbaijan's economy and standard of living of its population. "The investments will open new possibilities for Azerbaijan and will ensure thousands of occupations for all people. It will be one of the greatest projects in the history of Azerbaijan," he said (ibid). For their part, FOCs, utilized these ceremonies as an opportunity to showcase the presentation of gifts to the people of Azerbaijan; oil company presidents, for example, presented checks to the government that were to be

---

[38] The Entrepreneurship Development Foundation (EDF) was founded in 1994 by Sabit Bagirov. See http://edf-syf.org/ts_general/eng/about/about.htm. This 2006 survey polled 1000 people in 15 districts and 12 cities.

[39] Subsequent contracts were signed with similar fanfare, involving heads of states along with FOC representatives (for details, see Mir-Babayev 2003).

spent on improving the general public's social welfare (ibid). In fact, they readily admitted that the purpose of these public speeches and ceremonies was to ensure that "the Azerbaijani population kn[ew] that [they were] contributing to their social welfare" from the moment the contracts were signed (Authors' interview with AIOC representative no. 1).

Consistent across our interviews, moreover, was the belief that the governing elites felt obligated to fulfill these expectations that the petroleum sector should provide the bulk of government revenue and be distributed widely. First of all, the consensus among government officials was that SOCAR should be the primary source of domestic taxation [rather than the population]. As the head of SOFAZ emphasized, taxing SOCAR is the "appropriate" strategy because "otherwise it would send a wrong signal to the public" (Authors' interview). The "right" signal, according to the Ministry of Finance, was that the government relied on the petroleum sector for income, which in turn entailed a strategy focused on taxing the largest oil companies, including SOCAR (Authors' interview with foreign tax consultant). Second, governing elites emphasized the need to maintain large subsidies for basic goods in order to "satisfy the people's need to reap the benefits of their own wealth" (Authors' interview with government representative no. 1). Popular expectations for widespread state spending were echoed in our interviews with local NGOs. One member of the aforementioned Association of Local Entrepreneurs, for example, emphasized that "taxing small business was unnecessary," because SOFAZ should be sufficient to finance most of government spending while the income generated from the FOCs could be used to provide additional subsidies such as "directing loans to small businesses" and "underwrit[ing] credits to the farmers" (Authors' interview).

Evidence from public speeches that include both the President's annual addresses (hereafter, *Address*) and those regarding the government's development strategy, along with statements by SOCAR itself, further substantiate our claim that fiscal policies were influenced by the state's desire to demonstrate to society that the proceeds from foreign investment in the petroleum sector are being widely distributed. Indeed, governing elites have consistently sought to show that the FOCs are contributing to both the country's social welfare and economic potential. For example, in his 1996 *Address*, President Aliyev spoke at lengths about the development of the country's petroleum wealth and the "concrete results" that would ensue from the contracts signed with FOCs; in particular, he emphasized that "happy good days" are in store for Azerbaijan when society would experience higher living standards due to the exploitation of its petroleum wealth. Likewise, in his 1997 *Address*, President Aliyev further drew attention to how foreign investment in petroleum would contribute directly to the social welfare of Azerbaijan's citizens, placing special emphasis on public wage increases:

Agreements signed with foreign companies on the joint use of natural resources and the economic potential of our republic, especially in the joint development of oil and gas reserves, ... are already yielding concrete results. We will be witnesses of these concrete results in 1997. All of this will establish conditions for fast-paced economic development in our country and will offer the opportunity to raise the well-being of the nation from day to day. I believe that the state budget, approved for the next year, will make it possible to raise salaries for the population in 1997, and I will take the necessary measures in connection with this. In one word, our primary goal is to provide stability and peace in the country and to establish all conditions for the improvement of the nation's welfare.

Across his public speeches, President Aliyev relentlessly championed the widespread benefits of his "oil strategy" that would bring about a "positive shift" for the population at large (Kuliev 2000, 96).[40] Ilham Aliyev, who succeeded his father as President in 2003 following his death, actively reinforced this sentiment. Ten years after the Contract of the Century was signed, for example, he boasted:

When marking the 10th anniversary of Heydar Aliyev's oil strategy this year, we stated that this strategy, this policy and strict line will be continued. Azerbaijan's oil potential will serve the Azerbaijani people and will continue to bring more currency reserves to Azerbaijan and to its treasury in the future as well. Regions will develop, new jobs will open, social welfare will improve. ... Over the past year, more than 110,000 new jobs have opened. ... Social tasks were carried out properly. Salaries, pensions and other social allowances were increased and paid timely. A minimum wage increased as well ... . I would like to add that well-being of the Azerbaijani people will improve on a yearly basis.

Indeed, the focus on using the tax revenue collected from FOCs to improve living conditions was a central component in many speeches. During his inauguration speech, Ilham Aliyev vowed that SOFAZ would "effectively serve the Azerbaijani people" and "promised 'great works' would be carried out to improve social conditions, pledging that 60 percent of Azerbaijan's 2004 budget would be devoted to social spending" (Eurasia Insight 2003).

Moreover, as revenue to the NRF has rapidly accumulated, the Azerbaijani government has consistently sought to convince society that SOFAZ is being harnessed for its long-term benefit. In his 2005 *Address*, for example, Ilham Aliyev stated:

Another important task we have to solve is an effective use of the oil revenues for them to be spent on improvement of the welfare of the Azerbaijani people, and development of the non-oil sector in the country. There is a very good mechanism to do so. [SOFAZ] ... is playing a key role in this work. The oil revenues are transparently accumulated ... , and are used for realization of necessary projects.

While high societal expectations vis-à-vis the state under S_2 generate incentives for widespread distribution, on what the Azerbaijani government has focused its expenditures at the national level is also very much a function of

---

[40] This was the case in 7 out of 10 speeches we analyzed between 1993 and 2002.

the country's particular domestic situation since the mid-1990s. Because the conflict with Armenia over Nagorno-Karabakh imprinted an indelible mark upon the national consciousness of both the governing elites and the population, every one of our interviews with members of the Azerbaijani government began with a short homily about the plight of the refugees and displaced persons and the need to regain the territory of Nagorno-Karabakh. Moreover, it was common for governing elites to begin almost every public speech with a direct reference to the conflict with Armenia and the refugee problem, which consistently has been deemed the country's most pressing national problem. Survey evidence available also indicates that the most important problem facing the country is "the settlement of Nagorno-Karabakh conflict," even more than the economic situation and social welfare of the citizenry (Faradov 2003). A survey carried out by O'Lear and Gray (2006), for example, found that Nagorno-Karabakh consistently ranked among the populations' top concern.

Thus, where the majority of the population expects the state to distribute the benefits widely, in contrast to the large prestige projects that are also so prevalent in many countries with S_2, for the general population in Azerbaijan, the "building of housing and improvement of socioeconomic conditions for refugees and internally displaced persons" has been a national priority.[41] When discussing the government's priorities for the fund accumulated in SOFAZ, Ilham Aliyev in his 2004 *Address* stressed that "the first revenues of the State Oil Fund will go to creating conditions for refugees and displaced persons."

High societal expectations also clearly motivated FOCs' behavior. In their private statements, FOCs made it clear that they understood the "public euphoria" surrounding oil and gas development in general and the role of FOCs in particular. "The people of Azerbaijan rightly assume that petroleum should improve their lives ... [and] their children's lives. ... We are in an especially difficult position because, rightly or wrongly, we are going to be held responsible for whether petroleum turns out to live up to these expectations ... [and] we don't want to be the scapegoat for their disappointment" (Authors' interview with BP representative no. 2). As Sheyda Mehdiyeva underscored, "people see a lot of wealth in the country" and as a result, "companies can be easily criticized if they do not do something for the population" (Authors' interview). Indeed, it is widely understood that the population expects "these big businesses [to] provide for [them]" (Authors' interview with Kazimov).

FOCs' efforts to survey the local population along with our interviews provide additional evidence that their spending patterns were influenced by high societal expectations. For example, BP sponsored its own survey of NGOs in Azerbaijan to gauge "civil society expectations" (BP 2006, 14).[42] The survey results led BP to conclude that "expectations of BP are very high – in some cases beyond the scope of our business. Sometimes these expectations do not match our remit as an oil and gas business. For example the company is

---

[41] See http://www.azerbaijan.az/_Economy/_OilStrategy/oilStrategy_07_e.html.
[42] BP surveyed 37 local NGOs.

regarded by some as a potential provider of such services as children's summer camps and family resorts" (BP 2006, 14). Similarly, many FOCs have carried out Environmental and Social Impact Assessments (ESIA). BP again stands as case in point. As part of its ESIAs in Azerbaijan, the company conducted baseline surveys and consultations with various communities to understand their concerns and found that "access to energy [was] a major concern for the communities living near the pipeline routes and facilities" (BP 2003, 130). As Karen St. John explained, there was a "clear rationale" behind this: "[since] the Azerbaijani people assume that the big energy companies can fix all their problems, we have to know what these problems are" (Authors' interview). In short, BP ascertained that "there are high expectations that the project sponsors, as major international firms, will make available their resources, either through engagement in government planning, technical assistance or direct investment, to help address these challenges" (BP 2003, 130).

Furthermore, that high societal expectations influenced FOCs' interests is clear in how they articulated their rationale for supporting INGOs' and IFIs' efforts to establish an effective NRF in Azerbaijan. Our interviews with FOCs indicate a universal commitment not only to increasing the transparency of their own payments to the state but also to placing constraints on how the state could spend this revenue. This commitment, moreover, is predicated on the understanding that their interests are better served by doing so: "if what comes out does not make a sufficient impact on society's well-being, then they will begin to suspect that what goes in is not sufficient" (Authors' interview with AIOC representative no. 2). At a National NGO Forum in November 2002, David Woodward provided a public endorsement of this sentiment: "[w]e are looking at ways to help facilitate responsible and imaginative stewardship of [SOFAZ] for the benefit of all Azerbaijani people."[43]

Lastly, what is also clear is that the pronounced role of INGOs and IFIs in Azerbaijan's oil sector helped promote these high societal expectations. First, we find numerous instances in which INGOs and IFIs are exerting pressure on the FOCs to adopt "best practices" in Azerbaijan. Second, we are able to establish that transnational alliances exist between INGOs and local NGOs such that together they are simultaneously working to persuade the FOCs operating in Azerbaijan to embrace CSR and empowering local communities.

Since the mid-1990s, INGOs have been actively involved in encouraging both direct public participation in the development of the country's petroleum wealth and FOCs operating in the Caspian Basin to be more socially engaged and attuned to environmental conditions (Weinthal 2003). In the late 1990s, these efforts were given a potent boost when ISAR – a U.S.-based NGO with offices throughout the FSU – received funding from USAID to launch a three-year program to strengthen cooperation among local NGOs to increase public awareness and participation in the decision-making process regarding oil and gas development (Watters 2000). Most notably, in April 1999, ISAR organized

---

[43] See http://www.azerweb.com/en/report.php?id=464.

a conference for local NGOs in Baku (capital of Azerbaijan) in which approximately 50 environmental NGO representatives took part, which was then followed by a subsequent seminar in Baku in March 2000 to promote "public monitoring" of the FOCs' operations. One important area of concern was the environment, especially as the companies began to explore offshore.

Another prominent INGO – the Open Society Institute (hereafter OSI) – also began to fund programs in Azerbaijan to strengthen the role of local NGOs and civil society more broadly (Authors' interview with Asadov). Specifically, through its Caspian Revenue Watch program, OSI has advocated for the FOCs to "respond to civic demands for accountability in the region" so that the oil and gas revenue will "be invested and expended for the benefit of the public, such as poverty reduction, education, and public health."[44] In doing so, it has fostered transnational alliances that contribute to demands on the FOCs not only for greater transparency but also for better social spending programs (ibid). Azerbaijan OSI, for instance, has established an NGO Monitoring and Audit program.[45] Through publishing reports and generating information for the broader public about the state of the country's oil wealth and revenue streams accruing to the foreign oil and gas companies, they have established a formal grammar to help local NGOs articulate societal expectations. Indeed, the motto of one NGO campaign in Azerbaijan is simply: "Oil revenues belong to all" (Bagirov 2006).

Coercion

The final causal mechanism we invoke is coercion – specifically, whether power relations decisively favor the governing elites or the FOCs. In the 1990s, moreover, it is equally important to determine whether the FOCs are committed to CSR. Here, we show both that the FOCs could enforce their contracts and that they were pro-CSR. As a result, they sought to implement spending programs that not only improved living standards for the population in the short term but improved socioeconomic development prospects over the long term, while also seeking to promote this type of spending on the part of the state.

In short, the FOCs operating in Azerbaijan have avoided the obsolescing bargain because they were able to overcome the collective action problem (CAP). In this case, what facilitated this outcome is simply the existence of a hegemon. Without a doubt, BP is the predominant FOC in exploration and production in Azerbaijan with the highest participation rate of all the FOCs. Already by 1998, BP had signed 5 PSAs with the Azerbaijani government (for details, see Bindemann 1999, 71–2). Its merger with Amoco in 1998 further strengthened its ability to present a united front vis-à-vis the state through expanding the percentage of its participation shares in the contracts. This

---

[44] See http://www.osi-az.org/crw.shtml.
[45] Other organizations, such as the Eurasia Partnership Foundation (EPF), have since begun to focus on corporate social investments and community empowerment. For details see, http://www.epfound.az/.

merger also helped to mitigate the effects of competition from other smaller FOCs seeking to gain a foothold in Azerbaijan in the 1990s. Many of the smaller companies, such as Ramco, moreover, sought to be included in the consortium agreements with BP and other "Majors" rather than go it alone as so many did in Kazakhstan (Klebnikov 1994). Compounding its dominant position is the fact that BP is the operator of the most important projects producing petroleum (i.e., ACG and Shah Deniz) as well as the BTC pipeline.[46]

Furthermore, as was common in the early part of the twentieth century, many of the consortia operating in Azerbaijan in the 1990s included companies with overlapping memberships in the other consortia. For example, BP, Statoil, and TPAO were involved in both the AIOC and Shah Deniz consortia. This proliferation in cooperation among the FOCs solidified BP's position as the single hegemon who could not only unify their interests and negotiation strategies, but also act as their unanimously recognized chief negotiator; this then served as a way for them to hedge against the obsolescing bargain. The FOCs clearly realized early on the power of a unified front. As David Woodward explained, "[f]ollowing the merger of BP Amoco [in 1999], it was recognized that BP Amoco had, by far, the largest shareholding in AIOC (34 percent). The partners saw the value of having a single company responsible for the operation rather than having it managed by the consortium and agreed that BP Amoco should take on this role commencing in June 1999" (Blair 1999).

BP's unique dominance in Azerbaijan has also been buttressed by the failure of several other foreign investor projects to find commercially viable oil and gas deposits (IMF 2003b, 10, Sultanova 2001). According to one study, since 1994, the government of Azerbaijan had signed 25 PSAs of which 8 had been stopped due to exploratory failures (Bagirov 2006). This includes the Caspian International Petroleum Company (formed in 1995) on the Karabakh offshore block and the North Apsheron Operating Company (NAOC) (formed in 1996) on the Ashrafi/Dan-Ulduzu offshore block (Grigoryev 2001).[47] Only the AIOC consortium has reported that their oil deposits were higher than originally anticipated. More so, the increase in the rate of oil production in Azerbaijan since 1997 was derived entirely from this consortium, which began producing "early oil" in 1997 at the Chirag oil field (part of the ACG fields).[48] The subsequent spike in production since 2005 is a result of the central portion of the Azeri field coming online with the completion of Phase one of AIOC's field development project.

---

[46] It is also the operator of two other potentially substantial fields (Inam and Araz, Alov and Sharg). Although it is not the commercial operator of the other major pipeline – the South Caucasus Pipeline (SCP), it is the technical operator and, along with Statoil, the largest investor with each holding 25.5 percent.

[47] As of April 1999, NAOC was no longer in operation. Several other projects ended with similarly disappointing results in the late 1990s/early 2000s (see, e.g., Wakeman-Linn et al. 2004, 9).

[48] http://www.eia.doe.gov/cabs/Azerbaijan/Oil.html

The united front that the FOCs in Azerbaijan formed with BP at the helm enabled them both to direct their spending priorities and to maintain a stable rate of taxation even after their costs were sunk in the late 1990s – that is, when the obsolescing bargain is presumed to take effect.[49] During the bust in 1998, when the price of oil fell below $10 a barrel, for example, the FOCs were able to cut back dramatically their investment expenditures and reduce their operational budget for 1999 rather than having to increase production to make up for budgetary shortfalls (see, e.g., Auty 2006, 61, Khanlou 1998). When oil prices began to rise in the early 2000s, foreign tax analysts commented with astonishment: "On the positive side, Baku – unlike Astana – has not (yet?) attacked the tax provisions of PSAs and reform of the tax administration under IMF auspices continues to edge forward" (Townsend 2002).

Our interviews with representatives of several FOCs, moreover, provide compelling evidence that they were able to withstand pressure at both the national and subnational level for funding that did not accord with their own spending priorities. BP led the charge early on in resisting such pressures from local leaders or community groups. According to one company representative, "previously local NGOs would come in and ask for money and BP would just write out a check from [its] charitable contribution fund" ... "for a local chess club or to sponsor a jazz festival," but once BP employees recognized that local NGOs were "diverting" and "misusing" BP's charitable giving, they were able to put a decisive end to such "abuse." BP instead rewrote the rules of its social contributions so that they would be used to invest in "capacity building and small and medium businesses" (Authors' interview).

Because BP has embraced CSR, moreover, its dominance also accounts for the actual form that social spending has taken – both within and beyond the terms specified in these contracts. According to the Goldman-Sachs Energy Environmental and Social Index, BP was the "outright winner," topping the list of FOCs when it comes to supporting transparency.[50] BP was also one of the first companies to endorse wholeheartedly the principles espoused by EITI and "Publish What You Pay." As early as 1995, Terry Adams pledged, "We're committed to making sure our business process is transparent to the industry at large" (Adams 1995a). One BP representative in Azerbaijan conveyed to us that the company is actively "engaging in the policy debate for revenue management" (Authors' interview with St. John). Regarding their community development initiative that began in 2001, she continued, "This is the first time that any company has tried anything like this – thinking about what corporate social responsibility means in the Caspian." As a result, BP and its partners in the AIOC consortium have, according to David Woodward,

---

[49] By 1999 AIOC had channeled over $2 billion in investments into ACG (*RPI* 2000). As of 2004, its capital costs reached $2.36 billion – a 10 percent increase from 2003 levels (Denisova and Grigoryev 2004).

[50] Statoil – the second largest investor in Azerbaijan – was also ranked in the first tier behind BP and RD/Shell.

sought to ensure "that everyone in Azerbaijan benefits from the oil income" (quoted in *Azadliq*, August 20, 2002).

BP's commitment to CSR is also evident in its willingness to design their programs with full public involvement. AIOC, for example, has institutionalized regular public meetings with communities to allow the public to voice their demands and concerns. Beginning early in its operations in 1996, the public was able "to participate in open dialogue about the environmental impact" of AIOC (Bergh 1996). Regarding the BTC project, one account recorded that BP as the operator of the consortium had met with "each of the 450 villages along the route and the 30,000 landowners and land users .... discussed issues extensively with the host governments, local governments, local and international NGOs, local and international media and the international community" (Bayatly 2003c). In its Sustainability Report for 2005, BP counted that it held 42 public meetings with local communities in the 4th quarter alone. This commitment to expanding the stakeholder base has allowed "communities to realize the benefits from such partnerships" (Authors' interview with Kazimov).

In fact, BP is so concerned about what the population thinks of its spending programs that it has carried out a survey of local NGOs to gauge their satisfaction. While some might contest that such as survey is heavily biased and not representative of the population as a whole, given that the NGOs are often the most vocal critics of the FOCs' operations, their responses are actually quite illuminating. The results indicate that local NGO representatives "regarded BP's performance in the country as good overall" and viewed favorably its "capacity-building projects, community development initiatives and the contributions [it] make[s] to the economy" (BP 2006, 14). They also indicate, however, that the NGOs were dissatisfied with "a perceived lack of BP focus on national education and educational institutions," which according to BP "may reflect a lack of awareness of our educational activities in Azerbaijan" (BP 2006, 14). What this dissatisfaction underscores is our contention that there is a broad popular expectation, albeit unfulfilled, that FOCs should spend broadly on national development such as education. At the same time, there is evidence to suggest that BP's strategy is generally working, especially in contrast to other FOCs in countries under S_2 during our third time period (such as Nigeria) whose operations have been attacked by angry members of the local population. Outside assessments indicate that communities along the pipeline viewed the CSR activities of BP and its partners in a positive light (Jordan and Schleifer 2008). In the words of a local farmer: "[w]e have felt some positive benefits from BP, so, of course, we must show them the same" (ibid).

Additional survey results also corroborate that the FOCs are fully committed to CSR and care what happens to the oil and gas revenue once it reaches the government coffers. A survey of 20 FOCs carried out in 2006 by the Baku-based Economic Research Centre (ERC) found that the major companies operating in Azerbaijan, in particular BP, Shell Azerbaijan, and Statoil, desire to make broader information on their activities available to the public (ERC 2006, 9–10). All the FOCs who responded also indicated a belief that their tax payments to the government should be made publicly available and its use monitored (ibid, 12). Many companies, including BP, Shell, Statoil, and Lukoil, for example, responded affirmatively to the question "[are you interested in] obtaining complete information on the targeted/correct use of funds your company has paid to the government" (ibid, 14).

Moreover, FOCs were able to impose their preference for transparency on SOCAR. By unilaterally deciding to make public its PSA and how much revenue it transfers to the government, BP compelled not only the other partners of the consortia (AIOC) to move toward greater transparency, but also SOCAR to agree to publish all the PSAs online (Gulbrandsen and Moe 2007, 821).[51] The FOCs' positive influence also extended to Azerbaijan's decision to join EITI, making it part of the first tranche of petroleum-rich countries to do so.[52] On November 24, 2004 the National Committee on EITI, foreign and local extractive industry companies, and the NGO Coalition to Improve Transparency in the Extractive Industries (with over 40 members) signed a Memorandum of Understanding to implement EITI in Azerbaijan (for details, see ERC 2006). With BP as the unilateral enforcer, it has encouraged the government to be more "open to disclosure of revenue payments (Save the Children 2005, 24). According to Save the Children's report on measuring revenue transparency, BP "leads the way with a full score" on anti-corruption and whistle-blowing (ibid., 18). This view was also confirmed in the aforementioned ERC survey, which found that among local NGOs there was clear recognition that "BP leads the companies surveyed in the context of ensuring greater transparency" (ERC 2006, 18). Moreover, a Transparency International report on revenue transparency of FOCs concluded that Azerbaijan is a case of "company disclosure effort in restrictive environments that challenge the view that restrictions in host countries are impossible to overcome" (2008, 22). According to Gulbrandsen and Moe, "It is safe to conclude, then, that BP, on its own and through EITI, has contributed to enhancing oil revenue transparency in Azerbaijan" (2007, 822). Indeed, this may account for why SOCAR responded in the 2005 ERC survey that it too has "made a commitment to ensure transparency of its operations" (ERC 2006, 10).

IMPLICATIONS

In sum, that Azerbaijan adopted a hybrid fiscal regime supports the central claim of this book that ownership structure rather than mineral wealth per se is responsible for institutional outcomes. The fact that its hybrid fiscal

---

[51] FOCs have had an impact on SOCAR's operations in other areas. Statoil, for example, has conducted workshops, resulting in some very "positive trends" concerning environmental clean-up (Authors' interview with Mehdiyev).

[52] BP, Shell, and Statoil, in particular, have propelled EITI forward in Azerbaijan.

regime is not only more effectively constraining and enabling the state within the mineral sector but also fostering broader social and economic development than during prior time periods also corroborates our contention that the effects of ownership structure in which FIs are directly involved (i.e., S_2 and P_2) are dynamic due to changes at the international level. Specifically, Azerbaijan demonstrates the uncertainty of power relations between host governments and FOCs since the 1990s. While others have insisted that the obsolescing bargain is still "alive and well" in the twenty-first century (Gould and Winters 2007, 2), FOCs in Azerbaijan were quite successful in eluding it as of the late 2000s. Most importantly, we demonstrate that because its hybrid fiscal regime comes closest to our best-case scenario under S_2, Azerbaijan is in a better position to avoid the development trajectory of other petroleum-rich countries that adopted S_2 during the 1970s and 1980s, in which states were able to revoke the terms of FOCs' contracts, engage in a feeding frenzy, and spend these windfalls without improving the lives of their citizens.

Thus, the development of Azerbaijan's petroleum sector under S_2 promises to have a much more positive social and economic impact in both the short and long term. Regarding the short term, the most important impact to date has been poverty reduction. Unlike Turkmenistan, where populist gestures have not resulted in any improvements in social welfare, Azerbaijan has made significant progress in reducing the level of poverty; most notably, the percentage of the population living in poverty was halved between 2003 and 2008 (World Bank 2009). While 22.1 percent of the population lived in extreme poverty in 2003, this number dropped to 9.2 percent in 2005 (IMF 2007c, 7). Likewise, Azerbaijan has begun to experience significant declines in the level of infant and child mortality (IMF 2007c, 25). There is also independent confirmation that the government has been directing more of its oil revenue "for truly poor segments of the population" through the introduction of its State Program on Poverty Reduction and Economic Development (Luecke and Trofimenko 2008, 151; see also UNDP 2007, 20). Thus, in contrast to Uzbekistan, which was deemed "unlikely" to achieve its Millennium Development Goal (MDG) target to reduce poverty, the World Bank concluded that Azerbaijan "likely" is to achieve its MDG target (Alam et al. 2005, 200).

FOCs' spending has both contributed to these short-term successes by improving citizens' daily lives and gone beyond them by promoting long-term development. Through explicitly linking poverty alleviation to employment generation in its regional development program (BP 2006, 49), for example, BP has helped foster local business development both within and outside of its supply chain. In part owing to such efforts to support the Enterprise Center, in 2006 alone, BP's direct spending on SMEs increased 44 percent while declining 28 percent on SOEs, as more new local companies were able to meet its standards (BP 2007, 52). These efforts are ongoing and extend beyond its operations; for example, in 2006, BP joined with the EBRD to support SME development and microfinance lending programs (ibid., 44). At the same time, FOCs have consciously supported programs that promise to promote long-term socioeconomic development. In order to ensure this, in 2007 BP carried out its "biggest tax audit in [its] history and the largest ever done in Azerbaijan" to evaluate whether its spending ($8 billion) on projects carried out from 2004 to 2006 would contribute to such outcomes (BP 2007, 50). It also established an independent commission – Azerbaijan Social Review Commission – comprised of nonindustry personnel, including NGOs and students to advise its Strategic Performance Unit (ASRC 2007).

FOCs have also continued to help the Azerbaijani government improve its budgetary process and capacity to engage in long-term strategic planning. Since 2005, for example, BP has provided an independent economic consultancy from the United Kingdom to work with SOFAZ to develop a model for managing the impact of oil revenues on the Azerbaijani economy and worked closely with the Ministry of Economic Development to build its macroeconomic policy-making capability (BP 2007, 50). As a result, Azerbaijan has been singled out for having made "significant progress" when it comes to transparency concerning its proceeds from the mineral wealth (Global Witness 2007, 2) and for having made "good progress in both development and poverty reduction" since joining EITI in 2003 (ibid., 11). In similar fashion, Statoil has partnered with the Eurasia Partnership Foundation to enhance budgetary transparency and strengthen administrative capacity in twenty municipalities in ten regions of Azerbaijan (Authors' interview with Kazimov). Owing to these efforts, for "the first time ever, the head of Kish Municipality has agreed to publicize [the city's] entire estimated budget for 2010 in the newspaper, including costs for electricity and phone calls" (Authors' interview with Mehdiyeva).

While these positive effects should not be discounted, they nonetheless come at a price. On the one hand, the progress that Azerbaijan has made in fiscal reform has been tempered by high societal expectations vis-à-vis the state, which generate strong incentives for the government to dominate the economy and engage in unconstrained spending. Not surprisingly, Azerbaijan has continued to increase its public expenditures by a cumulative 160 percent in nominal terms from 2005 to 2007, with most going to infrastructural investments and salary increases that are unlikely to have long-term economic benefits (Koeda and Kramarenko 2008, 3). On the other hand, societal actors have not only increasingly come to expect FOCs to provide public goods and social services, but also viewed FOCs as the preferred supplier. Simply put, Azerbaijan's significant gains in improving its administrative capacity should be credited to the efforts of FOCs who are both able to enforce their contracts and pro-CSR rather than to the state's efforts to build closer ties with its society. Thus, Azerbaijan also supports our contention that even under the best-case scenario under S_2, the hybrid fiscal regimes that emerge are both very limited in their ability to foster taxation and expenditure reform outside the mineral sector and have a strong tendency to promote the emergence of a proxy state (see Chapter 6 for details).

8

Revisiting the Obsolescing Bargain

Foreign Private Ownership in Kazakhstan

> Russia makes western oil companies fret and fume. Kazakhstan, by comparison, makes them feel rather secure.
> — Economist 1992

> If I had to describe the investment climate [in Kazakhstan] in one word it would be – unpredictable.
> — FOC representative 2000 (Authors' interview)

> The Kazakhs see the foreigners coming with boat loads of money that is easy cash and taxes for the government.
> — USAID representative 2000 (Authors' interview)

In 1999, Kazakhstan marked the centennial of the first major oil gusher discovered on its territory – in Karashungul, Western Kazakhstan (Khusainov and Turkeeva 2003, Tasmagambetov 1999). The celebration that ensued in Atyrau region heralded Kazakhstan's long history of indigenous petroleum exploration and production. In reality, however, by the end of the 1990s, Kazakhstan's oil and gas industry no longer reflected its indigenous roots. Only a few years after its independence from Soviet rule, the country's leadership chose to forge ahead with private foreign ownership (P_2). By choosing to sell off the majority of shares (>50 percent) in its production, refining and export facilities to a large number of foreign investors (FIs) in the mid-1990s, Kazakhstan veered 180 degrees away from the ownership structure that it inherited from the Soviet Union – state ownership with control (S_1). As a result, in the 1990s the dominance of foreign oil and gas companies in the development of its petroleum industry had to be reconciled with the mirage of "Kazakhstani Oil."

That its leadership would agree to bequeath both ownership and control over its petroleum industry to foreign oil companies (hereafter, FOCs) took many observers by surprise. At first glance, it did not seem that this newly independent state, which possessed some of the most prized oil fields in the Soviet Union such as the gigantic Tengiz field, and an indigenous cadre of *neftyaniki* or oilmen, was in dire need of foreign investment. Moreover, oil production had begun to climb in the 1970s in Kazakhstan such that it ranked second only to Russia among the Soviet successor states, which sharply contrasted with Azerbaijan's dwindling production after having peaked in 1941 (Raballand and Genté 2008, 10–11, Sagers 1994, 271). It was also well known that the Minister of Oil and Gas, Nurlan Balgimbayev, opposed the privatization plan introduced under Prime Minister Akezhan Kazhegeldin in 1995 (Peck 2004, 150).[1] Yet, owing to the domestic constraints that Kazakhstan's governing elites faced at independence (discussed in Chapter 9), they were unable either to retain S_1 or to adopt state ownership without control (S_2), and instead, opted to pursue what is arguably the least preferred ownership structure from the state's perspective – private foreign ownership (P_2).

Despite the transfer of decision-making authority over its most coveted assets to FOCs, the Kazakhstani government retained the upper hand in determining the size, stability, composition, and degree of transparency of the FOCs' fiscal burden. Simply put: FOCs in Kazakhstan failed to form a united front so as to prevent the government from arbitrarily increasing their taxation and spending obligations. Unlike their counterparts in Azerbaijan, therefore, they have fallen prey to the obsolescing bargain. At the same time, because the majority of these FOCs were only weakly committed to corporate social responsibility (hereafter, CSR), if at all, they have taken little interest in the broader social and economic impact of either the government's expenditures or their own.

Thus, while Azerbaijan allows us to test our hypotheses concerning the "best-case" scenario under S_2 in the 1990s and 2000s, Kazakhstan provides an opportunity to test them concerning the "worst-case" scenario under P_2. As expected, we find that within the mineral sector, the FOCs' fiscal burden has not only expanded, but is increasingly unstable and nontransparent. Their spending, moreover, is directed toward indiscriminate charitable giving at the subnational level rather than broader socioeconomic development at the national and subnational levels as is the case in Azerbaijan. We also find that, while Kazakhstan has indeed created an NRF – the Natural Resource Fund of Kazakhstan (hereafter, NRFK) – the FOCs have played no active role in promoting transparency in its operations or influencing how the proceeds that are deposited into it are used. Largely as a result, unlike SOFAZ in Azerbaijan, the NRFK has not been an effective tool for increasing public accountability.

At the same time, however, Kazakhstan demonstrates that even under the worst-case scenario, P_2 is in some ways still preferable to S_2 because it offers greater prospects for fiscal reform outside the mineral sector. The key to understanding why lies in one of the three mechanisms that we argue in Chapter 6 links ownership structure to fiscal regimes. Under both P_2 and S_2

---

[1] Many oilmen believed that the energy sector should be treated as a strategic sector (Authors' interview with representative of Kazakhoil; see also *RPI* 1995a).

during the third time period (1990–2005), transaction costs (TCs) are negligible, societal expectations are high vis-à-vis FIs, and power relations can favor either the FIs or the host government. Yet they diverge when it comes to societal expectations vis-à-vis the state, which are low and high, respectively. In short, low societal expectations created a political opening for governing elites in Kazakhstan not only to create a relatively stable NRF but also to pursue broad-based taxation and budgetary reform. Thus, while the NRFK is much less transparent than SOFAZ, it has been better able to contribute to budgetary predictability due to its relative stability. Moreover, in contrast to Azerbaijan, where a bloated and inefficient welfare system persists despite government efforts to channel some of the benefits of foreign investment toward poverty alleviation programs, we find that Kazakhstan has managed both to redistribute the benefits of foreign investment from the petroleum-rich to the petroleum-poor regions and to institutionalize limits on expenditures that has at least created the possibility for the government to make better spending decisions.

EMBRACING FOREIGN PRIVATE OWNERSHIP

The main oil production enterprises inherited from the Soviet Union were largely concentrated in the western regions of Atyrau, Aktobe, and Mangistau – most notable were Embamunaigas, Mangistaumunaigas, Aktobemunaigas, Tengiz, Karazhanbasmunai – but also extended into Kyzlorda region (Yuzhneftegaz).[2] As an intermediary step right after independence, the Kazakhstani government established a state holding company – Kazakhstanmunaigas – to oversee temporarily these oil enterprises along with its refineries and pipelines until the legislative and regulatory framework was in place to facilitate foreign investment (Peck 2004, 149, Sagers 1994, 271).[3] The state retained a 90 percent interest in most of these enterprises while the remaining 10 percent of nonvoting shares were distributed among the employees (Peck 2004, 149). Its main gas field, Karachaganak, was located in Uralsk and was similarly administered initially by a national gas concern, Kazakhgazprom, which was constituted in 1991 (Sagers 1994, 272).

In contrast to Azerbaijan's decision to fortify its NOC (SOCAR), the Kazakhstani government chose not to rehabilitate its own proven reserves and convert Kazakhstanmunaigas into a full-fledged NOC. Rather, it initiated an all-encompassing sell-off of Kazakhstanmunaigas' assets to FOCs, and thereby, relinquished any direct claimant status to the proceeds from its petroleum wealth. In fact, while Azerbaijan retained some significant ownership

---

[2] Previously these companies were referred to by the Russian version of their names – for example, Aktyubneft and Karazhanbastermneft.

[3] The creation of a holding company was similar to Russia's creation of Rosneft. In Kazakhstan, the initial consolidation into a holding company facilitated the privatization of its petroleum reserves, as the government could assess the entirety of its reserves.

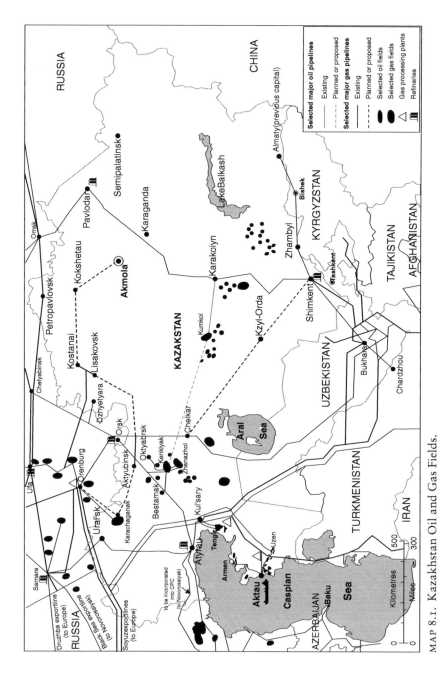

MAP 8.1. Kazakhstan Oil and Gas Fields.

Sources: Caspian Oil and Gas (c) OECD/IEA, 1998, page 24, figure 4.

and control over its brown fields,[4] Kazakhstan opened up these older fields immediately for far-reaching foreign investment.[5]

One of the first major FOCs courted was the U.S. oil company Chevron, which had already been negotiating with the Soviet regime since 1990 to develop the giant Tengiz oil field that was discovered in 1979 (ibid, 275). Already toward the end of the Soviet period it was widely recognized that the Tengiz field was one of the most important oil discoveries for ramping up production in western Kazakhstan. In April 1993, the Kazakhstani government concluded a 40-year joint venture (JV) agreement with Chevron under which it would operate the Tengiz field – by then Kazakhstan's largest active field and the fifth largest in the world with 6–9 billion barrels of recoverable reserves (IMF 2003c, 8). Then in April 1996, the government sold Mobil half of its share (25 percent) in TengizChevroil (TCO) for approximately $1 billion.[6]

While Kazakhstan initiated a sweeping privatization program in 1991 (Kalyuzhnova 1998, 69), the conclusion of the TCO deal in 1993 hailed FOCs' first foray into the petroleum sector. Full-blown privatization of the petroleum sector followed in June 1995 with Kazhegeldin's announcement to offer FOCs a chance to acquire 90 percent equity in two oil production associations (Yuzhneftegaz and Aktobemunaigas) and one refinery (Shymkent) while the employees and management would still retain the remaining ten percent (*RPI* 1995a, *Petroleum* 2001, 8–9).

To bolster its attractiveness to FOCs, many of which were cautious about investing in a politically risky and unfamiliar environment, in the mid-1990s the Kazakhstani government set in place a legislative framework that would support their operations. More importantly, this also had the effect of distinguishing Kazakhstan's investment climate from that of Russia (P_1) on the one hand and Turkmenistan and Uzbekistan (S_1) on the other – all of which adopted ownership structures that minimized FOCs' involvement. The first major piece of legislation introduced was the 1994 Law on Foreign Investment, which provided FOCs with several important guarantees, including mechanisms for dispute resolution and contractual stability (for details, see Slone and Lain 1995).

Following the 1995 dissolution of the Kazakhstani Parliament (*Majilis*), President Nursultan Nazarbayev capitalized on a nine-month hiatus to introduce a bundle of legislation via presidential decree that expedited the realization

---

[4] A brown field is one that has already been producing. It differs from a green field that has yet to be exploited.

[5] Although Kazakhstan retained a small number of its own fields, they were largely insignificant in comparison to what it sold off to the FOCs. One FOC representative remarked that he would be "scared" to see the fields where Kazakhoil (the Kazakhstanmunaigas' successor) is producing because it is not a "fully-fledged company" whereas "SOCAR is a real oil company" (Authors' interview with Total representative no. 1).

[6] As of 2005, Tengizchevroil consists of 50% Chevron; 25% ExxonMobil; 20% KazMunaiGas; 5% LUKArco (Russia/US).

of P_2.[7] On June 28, 1995, he signed a presidential decree that put into place the Law on Petroleum, which laid out the competitive tender process in which petroleum exploration and production rights were to be awarded (ibid.).[8] Such decrees, de facto, had the rule of law. The Law on Petroleum, most importantly, provided the legislative basis for "private ownership of petroleum once it has been lifted to the surface" (ibid.).[9] In contrast to the Russian Federation that shunned foreign investment in its petroleum sector, Kazhegeldin's reformist government was positively regarded by the foreign investor community as having "mov[ed] full speed ahead with passing the comprehensive set of energy laws it need[ed] to unleash foreign investment" (*RPI* 1995b). In addition, the September 1995 Constitution reaffirmed a place for private ownership over the country's natural resources (Article 6).

Thus, with an investment climate primed for foreign investment, the Kazakhstani government managed to complete in August 1996 its first full privatization of a petroleum enterprise with the sale of 89.5 percent of shares in Yuzhneftegaz to a small and largely unknown Canadian company – Hurricane Hydrocarbons – for $120 million. Most of Yuzhneftegaz's production comes from the Kumkol field in Kyzlorda that was discovered in 1984 (Sagers 1994, 277). The sale of Yuzhneftegaz was the first time the government sold its entire share of an oil enterprise (Peck 2004, 159).[10] Prior to the conclusion of this first tender, the government announced a second tender on June 28, 1996 when Kazhegeldin signed Resolution No. 830 on the privatization of the joint-stock company Mangistaumunaigas (*Oil & Gas of Kazakhstan* 1996, 23), which led to the sale of a 60 percent stake to an Indonesian petroleum company, Central Asia Petroleum in 1997 for a reportable $4.35 billion (*New York Times*, May 13, 1997, Peck 2004, 166). In June 1997, the government then sold a 60 percent stake in Aktobemunaigas to the Chinese National Petroleum Corporation (CNPC), and later that year, the CNPC won the tender to develop the Uzen oil field.[11] In 1997 another small Canadian oil company, Triton-Vuko (later renamed Nations Energy), purchased 94.5 percent of shares of the oil and gas enterprise Karazhanbasmunai for $45 million.

The privatization process essentially eliminated the role of the NOC, Kazakhstanmunaigas, in exploiting petroleum and the Ministry of Oil and Gas in cutting the deals with the FOCs. Instead, the government established in November 1996 the State Investment Committee (SIC) to bolster P_2 by

---

[7] Prior to the dissolution of Parliament in March 1995, Nazarbayev faced a vociferous opposition from within the new Parliament that was elected in December 1994.

[8] Edict No. 2350 of the President of the Republic of Kazakhstan having the force of Law "Concerning Petroleum" of June 28, 1995.

[9] The other major piece of legislation introduced was Law No. 2828 "Concerning the Subsurface and Subsurface Use" on January 27, 1996 (Ernst and Young 2008).

[10] The block of shares held by employees, however, was not sold.

[11] Later, CNPC chose not to go forward with the project, returning responsibility for developing the Uzen field to Uzenmunaigas (http://www.eia.doe.gov/emeu/cabs/kazapriv.html).

fostering a "one-stop" shop for FOCs.[12] This contrasts sharply with S₂ in Azerbaijan that privileged SOCAR as the main intermediary with the FOCs. Rather, the residual shares in these former state enterprises were transferred to a new company – Kazakhoil – that would only be responsible for managing the remaining government interest (Peck 2004, 150).[13]

In like manner to other countries (e.g., Guatemala) that have utilized PSAs under P_2 (Radon 2005), the Kazakhstani government also recruited FOCs' participation in its oil and gas sector in 1997 through a few PSAs. The first was with British Gas (32.5 percent), Agip (32.5 percent), Texaco (20 percent), and Lukhoil (15 percent) to exploit the giant Karachaganak oil and gas condensate field located onshore in Western Kazakhstan.[14] The second PSA was with another international consortium – the Offshore Kazakhstan International Operating Company (OKIOC, then later called Agip KCO – Agip Kazakhstan North Caspian Operating Company) – to develop the Kashagan deposit in the Caspian Sea shelf.[15] These PSAs are clearly distinguishable from those under S_2, precisely because they did not specify any role for the NOC (i.e., either for Kazakhstanmunaigas or Kazakhgazprom) as was common in Azerbaijan.

By the end of 1997, Kazakhstan had fully embraced P_2 (see Table 8.1 for details). While some rumored that P_2 would be reversed that year following the replacement of Kazhegeldin with Balgimbayev as Prime Minister, it remained in place. Although further privatization was temporally put on hold, Balgimbayev subsequently supported the sale of an additional five percent of the state's share in TCO in 1999, leaving the state with only a 20 percent interest (Peck 2004, 150–51).[16] According to one estimate, by 2002 FOCs controlled 75 percent of geological reserves of oil and 79 percent of gas reserves (Kusainov 2002).

THE EMERGENCE OF A HYBRID FISCAL REGIME

In the decade that followed the adoption of P_2, the fiscal regime that emerged in Kazakhstan is consistent with what we describe as a worst-case scenario

---

[12] See Decree No. 3203 of the President of the Republic of Kazakhstan on the Formation of the State Investment Committee of the Republic of Kazakhstan. November 8, 1996. Published in a joint publication of ITIC and Faxinform at the order of the State Committee on Investments of the Republic of Kazakhstan. Almaty 1997.

[13] On May 19, 1998 the government issued Ordinance No. 452, which transferred the state's shares in the Pavlodar oil refinery, Aktobemunaigas, Mangistaumunaigas, Uzenmunaigas, and the Tengizchevroil JV into Kazakhoil's ownership. Balgimbayev was appointed as the head.

[14] For details, see http://www.eia.doe.gov/emeu/cabs/kazaproj.html

[15] Exploration initially began in 1993 with the establishment of the Kazakhstancaspishelf Consortium. For details, see http://www.eia.doe.gov/emeu/cabs/kazaproj.html. Although discovered in 2000, production is, nonetheless, unlikely to commence before 2011 (ICG 2007, 7).

[16] At times, the use of the term JV is a misnomer in Kazakhstan because it did not necessarily necessitate a 50–50 split. Indeed, the state only retained a 25 percent share in TCO.

TABLE 8.1. *Overview of Most Prominent Early Deals with FOCs*

Field or Enterprise	Date	Foreign Participants' Share (percent)
TengizChevroil	April 1993	Chevron 50%
(TCO)	April 1996	Chevron 50%, ExxonMobil 25%
Shymkent Oil Refinery	July 1996	Vitol Munay 85%
Yuzhneftegaz	August 1996	Hurricane Hydrocarbons 89.5%
Karazhanbasmunai	March 1997	Triton-Vuko Energy Group 94.5%
Aktobemunaigas	June 1997	Chinese National Petroleum Co. 60%
Uzenmunaigas	July 1997	Chinese National Petroleum Co. 60%
Mangistaumunaigas	January 1998	Central Asia Petroleum (60%)
Karachaganak (PSA)	1997	British Gas (32.5%), Agip (32.5%), Texaco (20%), Lukoil (15%)
Northern Section of the Caspian – Kashagan (PSA)	November 1997	Offshore Kazakhstan International Operating Company (OKIOC) – Agip (14.3%), BP/Statoil (14.3%), BG (14.3%), Mobil (14.3%), Total (14.3%), Shell (14.3%)

under this ownership structure in the 1990s and 2000s. Within the mineral sector, we find a tax regime for the FOCs that is unstable and a system of expenditures for the FOCs that is neither stable, transparent, nor aimed at poverty alleviation and socioeconomic development. Like Azerbaijan, the FOCs' fiscal burden is heavier in comparison to prior time periods; and yet, unlike Azerbaijan, their spending has taken the form of conventional charity at the subnational level. As expected, while Kazakhstan's governing elites have used their ability to extract increasing amounts from the FOCs to engage in some savings via the NRF, they have also frequently directed the FOCs' spending toward their own pet projects at the subnational level. Outside the mineral sector, we find that Kazakhstan's governing elites have indeed pursued some tax and expenditure reform, such as a prefabricated tax code allegedly aimed at broad-based taxation and formal limits on government spending.

Taxation within the Mineral Sector: FOCs

As in other petroleum-rich countries that have pursued P_2 over the course of the 20th century, the Kazakhstani governing elites' focus has been on taxing the FOCs via a separate tax regime. One tax consultant underscored that the foreign oil and gas companies have "negotiated their own tax incentives" and that "these are not part of the code and not published anywhere" (Authors' interview with Minnehan). For example, Nations Energy negotiated a three-year grace period wherein it initially paid royalties of three percent before they gradually increased to five percent, which was far below what Chevron and

Hurricane Hydrocarbons were purported to pay (Authors' interview with representative of Nations Energy). OKIOC and British Gas (BG)/Agip, likewise, negotiated specialized tax regimes to develop the Caspian Sea shelf and the Karagachagank oil and gas condensate field, respectively (Authors' interviews with representatives of Total no. 1 and BG no. 1).

That the terms of such contracts have become more favorable to the host governments in the 1990s is evident in the larger upfront bonuses that FOCs were required to pay and the higher profits that would accrue to the state over the life-span of the project. For instance, from the TCO deal, the government would receive 80 percent of the profits (Authors' interview with representative of TengizChevroil). These contracts have also included advanced forms of taxation – in particular, bonuses. For example, Hurricane Hydrocarbons agreed to pay a bonus of $120 million (Authors' interviews; see also Peck 2004, 159) and CNPC agreed to pay a bonus amounting to $320 million and a subscription bonus of $5 million for Aktobemunaigas (Ostrowski 2007, 90). Likewise, the Kashagan PSA is expected to reap $600 billion in profits of which 80 percent will flow to the government and 20 percent will be divided among the FOCs (*RPI* 1997/1998, 41–2, *Petroleum* 2001, 10).

Although the terms of these contracts clearly favored the Kazakhstani government, they included several protections for the FOCs that have become increasingly common in the 1990s. In particular, they offered stability assurances against fluctuations in the general tax code even though at times the country's tax legislation served as the baseline. Thus, Chevron's contract for TCO not only defined its tax commitments, but also specified that its contract would supersede any changes to the general tax code. Moreover, its contract stipulated that the government would receive almost no revenue until the FOC had recouped its initial investments; this was supposed to allow Chevron to safeguard its revenue stream so that it could prudently plan its investments and protect itself from the uncertainty of available export routes (Matzke 1994).

Nonetheless, the terms of the FOCs' contracts have been deliberately and repeatedly violated. In many instances, the governing elites backpedaled on the FOCs' tax privileges only a few years after they signed contracts. The most common of these were exemptions from the value added tax (VAT) and custom duties. It was not unusual for FOCs to be exempt from VAT by contract, but then be forced to pay VAT "due to budgetary shortfalls" during the late 1990s (Authors' interviews with representatives of Preussage Energie, BG no. 2, and Mobil). One company that was planning to invest about $100 million found the VAT to be highly problematic three years into its operations because it was forced to pay before production, which was "like giving away 20 percent or $20 million free to the state" (Authors' interview with representative of Preussage Energie). Even the large FOCs such as those involved in the Agip KCO consortium have not been immune; in 2003 the Kazakhstan government withdrew its 20 percent VAT exemption (*Nefte Compass*, May 21, 2003).

Moreover, despite having tax obligations clearly stated in their contracts, the FOCs were frequently subjected to hefty fines for noncompliance and penalties for late payments. In an interview, Marlo Thomas, President of Hurricane Hydrocarbons, complained bitterly:

> ... the local and national tax environment in the Republic of Kazakhstan is constantly changing and subject to inconsistent application, interpretation and enforcement. There have been many new tax and foreign currency laws and related regulations introduced in recent years which are not always clearly written and whose interpretation is subject to the opinions of the local tax inspectorate. (*Petroleum* 2000b, 16)

Another tactic frequently employed by subnational authorities in the late 1990s to extract additional taxation and hence violate the stability of the FOCs' contracts was the use of environmental fines (Authors' interview with representatives of BG no. 2 and Nations Energy). The case that has, however, received the most international coverage concerns the decision by Kazakhstan's Supreme Court in March 2002 to uphold a $72 million fine for environmental damage resulting from the storage of sulphur in Atyrau region that TCO claimed was a byproduct of the way it processes its crude and not a "waste" (Lelyveld 2002). Their use has remained popular: according to one study, environmental fines increased by approximately 400 percent in 2004 compared to 2003 (Najman et al. 2008, 119).

The growing instability in the country's general Tax Code in the early 2000s (discussed below) also exacerbated the instability concerning the FOCs' tax obligations. In particular, revisions to the Tax Code in 2002 allowed for contracts to be amended if the position of the FOC improves due to changes in the tax law (Pearce 2003, 62, Slater 2002). Subsequent amendments in 2004 reaffirmed that for new contracts, FOCs would lose their stability guarantees found in the older contracts (Shyngyssov 2004).[17]

It is no surprise then that the FOCs have complained relentlessly about "Astana's non-stop lawmaking" and "[t]he continuing changing of the rules of the game" (Nezhina 2000, 32). The constant fluctuations in the general Tax Code that apply to the FOC' operations has, moreover, forced them to maintain a full-time staff to stay abreast of tax issues and hire professional tax consultants, who are most often former employees of the government's tax administration. In order to keep up with the changes in the Tax Code so as to avoid fines and penalties, one FOC representative remarked that "taxes is the area where [we] have spent more time working and researching than others" (Authors' interview with BG representative no. 2). Because the tax laws are constantly changing and "go into effect immediately after they are written ... before either the company or the tax office knows that they have changed and how" (Authors' interview with Eriksen), most companies

---

[17] See The Law on Introducing Changes and Additions to Some Legislative Acts on Taxation Issues of the Republic of Kazakhstan (in effect January 1, 2004). For details, see Denisova (2004).

experience frequent audits, ranging from 6–15 times a year to several times a week (Authors' interviews with Page, Minnehan, and with representatives of Amerada Hess, Oryx, Nations Energy, and BG no. 2).

Obviously, this interferes greatly with the company's daily operations, so they are often willing to offer some "concessions" to the local tax inspectorate or "negotiate" with the central tax authority to decrease the number of audits (Authors' interview with Fast). In fact, it is a common tactic for both the central and local government to use tax audits as a way to extract other concessions from the FOCs or to bring them back to the bargaining table on an unrelated issue. Most often, however, the purpose of frequent tax audits is to find a mistake so that companies can be charged a fine or penalty. Because the tax authorities are not required to formally issue a statement affirming that the audit has been completed, moreover, the audit can "remain open indefinitely" (Witt 2006, 298).

Lastly, the fact that FOCs' tax payments have been extremely opaque has contributed to the lack of transparency within the mineral sector. Many of the initial bonuses the government received, for example, were placed in offshore bank accounts and not formally reported in the state budget, "undermining the validity of fiscal data" (Ramamurthy and Tandberg 2002, 12). Only in 2002 did Prime Minster Imangaly Tasmagambetov reveal that in 1996, a \$1 billion "bonus" payment from an oil contract was surreptitiously siphoned off into a "top-secret Swiss [bank] account under Nazarbayev's direct control" that was created for this very purpose (Global Witness 2004, 15–16).

Taxation outside the Mineral Sector

Similar to many other Soviet successor states, Kazakhstan initiated tax reform shortly after the Soviet Union's collapse by replacing the turnover tax in 1992 with the VAT (ADB 1999 Chapter 1, Witt and McLure 2001). General tax reform then followed, with Vice President Yerik Asanbayev (1991–1996) appointing a Working Group in 1994 to prepare a new tax code for Kazakhstan (See McLure, 1998 for details, ADB 1999 Chapter 3, Witt and McLure 2001). The ensuing 1995 Tax Code dramatically reduced the number of taxes from 50 different taxes to only 11, of which the most important remaining were the income tax for individuals and enterprises, VAT, and excises (ADB 1999). In comparison to the dearth of tax reform in Uzbekistan and Turkmenistan in the early 1990s, Kazakhstan's Tax Code was judged to be "the most comprehensive, most systematic, most modern, and most investor-friendly of any in the FSU" (ADB, 1999, 84). Since then, attempts to reform further its tax regime have both solidified a separate tax regime for the mineral sector and created a potential basis for broadening the domestic tax base, which served to reduce the country's fiscal reliance on the mineral sector more so than in Azerbaijan but still less so than in Russia.

The conspicuous absence of the petroleum sector in the 1995 Tax Code was thus the first legal step toward congealing a tax regime that was narrow in

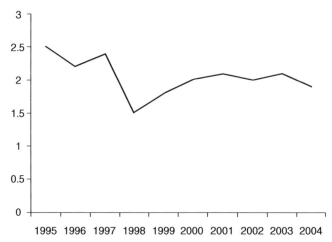

FIGURE 8.1. PIT as a Percentage of GDP.
Sources: IMF 2005c, Ministry of Finance.

scope. The government's subsequent revisions to the Tax Code in 1997 explic-itly reinforced the maintenance of separate tax provisions for the petroleum sector rather than its integration with other economic sectors, as in Russia (*RPI* 1996c).[18] Simply, Kazakhstan's tax regime during the period in which most companies were negotiating their contracts consisted of two separate tax codes – a general tax code for the Kazakhstani population and a petroleum-specific tax regime for the FOCs.

Like Russia, Kazakhstan's tax reform outside the mineral sector was report-edly aimed at broadening the tax base, and yet this goal has not been achieved to the same extent. The main reason is the retention of high rates for per-sonal income tax (PIT); Kazakhstan maintained multiple marginal tax brack-ets on PIT ranging from 5 to 30 percent (World Bank 2008). Thus, whereas Russia enjoyed increasing revenue from PIT shortly after introducing a flat tax, Kazakhstan faced a sharp drop in revenue from PIT immediately follow-ing its introduction (see Figure 8.1). An IMF representative in Kazakhstan underscored that, in contrast to Russia, there was "a decline in people pay-ing personal income taxes" (Authors' interview with Ross). Figure 8.1 serves to illustrate further that only after a decade of tax reform did PIT begin to rebound to its 1995 levels.

Increased revenue from the PIT, moreover, is largely coming from two sources connected to the petroleum sector. The first is Kazakhstani citizens who work for either foreign companies or large enterprises because their employers pay all their taxes and social benefits directly to the tax authorities whereas other individuals are required to file directly with the tax administration (World

[18] Law on Amendments to the Decree of the President of Kazakhstan, Having the Power of Law, on Taxes and Other Mandatory Payments to the Budget, April 24, 1995, No. 2235.

Bank 2008, 1). The second is foreign nationals, whose income tax falls outside the companies' fiscal burden protected by their contracts and is subjected to the general tax code. According to one tax expert, because "[t]he government has a broad definition of what is Kazakhstan[i] employment" the government has also been able to increase its PIT from the energy sector through its taxation of expatriate salaries that are based on their worldwide income rather than just the income remitted in Kazakhstan (Authors' interview with Page). The payroll tax, furthermore, is "quite hefty" since it is mostly based on gross, and not net income (ibid.), and as a result the petroleum sector has ended up being the main contributor to the PIT.

Unlike Russia that slashed its corporate income tax (CIT) with the introduction of a flat tax rate of 24 percent, Kazakhstan has also maintained a high CIT rate of 30 percent (World Bank 2008, 20). Contrary to most OECD countries where the PIT provides a greater share of tax revenue than the CIT, the CIT plays a large role in the composition of Kazakhstan's tax system (Berdalina and Mustapaeva 2003) because the largest share comes from the profit taxes that the FOCs are required to pay directly to the government budget (also see World Bank 2008). For the few years of data (1999–2003) that we have on the breakdown of CIT between oil and nonoil revenue as a percentage of GDP, we found that CIT from oil revenue has made up approximately 40 percent of overall CIT (see Figure 8.2 below). The IMF, moreover, found that even when oil prices ranged from $25 to $28 a barrel in the early 2000s, Kazakhstan's projected revenue from CIT and royalties would reach more than a billion dollars per year (IMF 2001, 8). Besides collecting revenue from

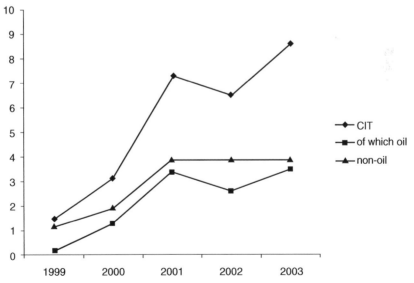

FIGURE 8.2. Breakdown of CIT as a Percentage of GDP.
Source: IMF 2005c.

the FOCs, the contracts' local content provisions have bolstered local production companies affiliated with the petroleum sector and as a result they also account for an increasingly important share of the CIT (Pulsipher and Kaiser 2006). In fact, the revenue collected from the taxation of these enterprises dwarfs the tax revenue from small and medium enterprises (SMEs) (Berdalina and Mustapaeva 2003).

Moreover, at the same time that CIT from the petroleum sector has steadily increased, the government has granted numerous discretionary tax exemptions for failing domestic enterprises and industries outside the petroleum sector such as the food industry (Authors' interview with Tatem, World Bank 2000, 11). Likewise, the Tax Code allows for an 80 percent discount on CIT for agricultural enterprises, which essentially amounts to a "non-transparent means of subsidizing agriculture" (World Bank 2008, ii).

Thus, when it comes to expanding the tax base, the World Bank (2000, 4) adduced that "the state revenue collection system has under-performed" in comparison to Russia; indeed, average tax collection in Kazakhstan from 1997–2000 was only 18 percent of GDP in comparison to 23 percent in Russia (ibid.). Because of numerous tax exemptions and holidays, another tax consultant similarly suggested the tax reforms had gone "off-track," leaving a tax code in place that "should have been simpler than it was" (Authors' interview with McLure).

Kazakhstan's reforms have had some success in broadening the tax base concerning indirect taxes. In particular, the VAT and excises have been used to overcome the poor performance of PIT outside of the energy sector (World Bank 2000, 4) (See Figure 8.3). Even as the government has reduced the VAT in 2002 from 20 percent to 16 percent and then again in 2004 to 15 percent,

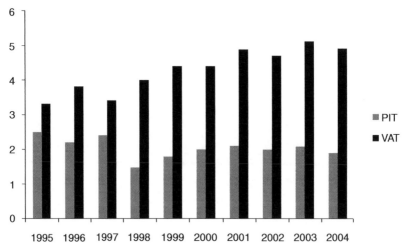

FIGURE 8.3. PIT Relative to VAT (Percentage of GDP).
Source: IMF 2005c, Ministry of Finance.

the VAT has consistently been a main source of revenue (Author's interview with Page; see also, World Bank 2008, 42–3). In 2005, the VAT was the second largest source of government revenue (after CIT), "accounting for 26 percent of total non-oil tax revenue or 4.6 percent of GDP in 2005" (World Bank 2008, 42). And yet, the government has also focused on the VAT from the FOCs' operations (described above) because it "made perfect sense" to tax expenses rather than just profits given that many of the FOCs were spending more money than they were making initially (Authors' interview with McLure).

Since the late 1990s, moreover, the government has pursued tax reforms that have increased its budgetary reliance on the petroleum sector. As the price of oil skyrocketed in the 2000s, for example, it reduced the amount of non-oil taxes "across the board" (IMF 2005b, 12). Revisions to the Tax Code in 2002 included decreases in the rates of the VAT and social tax[19] accompanied by increases in the rates of petroleum sector taxes such as royalties; in particular, it increased the minimum royalty rate from 0.5 percent to 2 percent (Abayev 2004).[20] Because many companies had reached production levels that required raising royalty rates, from 2000 to 2001, royalty payments to government coffers actually doubled (Berdalina and Mustapaeva 2003). The government also shifted its attention to the excess profit tax (EPT) and increased the maximum EPT rate from 30 percent to 60 percent (Abayev 2004). In 2004, as part of the amendments to the Tax Code, the government introduced a new oil export tax (also called a "rent tax" on exports) in which the amount of tax increases as oil prices rise (Anderson 2003, Abayev 2004).[21] Combined, these changes to the Tax Code have raised the state's share on oil company earnings from 55 to 85 percent (*Nefte Compass* 2004). By 2004, total government revenues from the oil sector had thus jumped to 30 percent from 6 percent in 1999 (IMF 2005b, 12).

Lastly, our interviews corroborate that Kazakhstan's tax regime outside the mineral sector has also been increasingly fraught with fluctuations and arbitrariness, which has further undermined its potential to broaden the tax base. A USAID representative counted that between 1994 and 2000, approximately 250 amendments were introduced to the tax code, producing "a very messy document" (Authors' interview with Tatem). According to another tax consultant, "in 1999 they were issuing changes every quarter to the tax code and then they would go back and change the changes" (Authors' interview with Minnehan). Others have remarked "that the tax code is amended in one form or [other] every six weeks a trend that is generally destabilizing to tax policy on the whole" (Lianguong and Kuleshova 1999, 36). Simply, as one

[19] The latter declined from 26 to 21 percent.

[20] Royalties are on a sliding scale depending upon the volume of accumulated oil production for each year – range from 2% to 6% (Ernst & Young 2006a).

[21] The Parliament adopted this law on 27 November 2003 and Nazarbaev signed it on December 1, 2003 (*RFE/RL* December 2, 2003).

tax consultant surmised, "there is lots of information about the rights of the tax authorities and very little about the taxpayer's rights" (Authors' interview with Page). In sharp contrast to Russia where tax reform bolstered protections for taxpayers, it is not surprising then that the absence of such safeguards for taxpayers' rights in Kazakhstan has also contributed to its tax regime's instability and hence inability to broaden the tax base.

Thus, by 2000 the World Bank (2000, 12) concluded, "the tax policy itself should be revisited, since the Tax Code that was adopted in 1995 has been amended so many times ... that a new one is needed."[22] The instability of the tax code compounded by "high nominal tax rates" and a "narrow tax basis" has not only resulted in low collection rates and limited success in broadening the tax base (World Bank 2000, 11, World Bank 2008), but also hindered the development of SMEs. Results from recurring surveys carried out by the Economic Research Institute in Kazakhstan show that the main issue raised by SMEs is the instability of the tax code (Engelschalk 2005, 14). More so, as it became easier to squeeze the FOCs for more taxation vis-à-vis the VAT and EPT, Kazakhstan's government has focused less and less on reining in the informal economy. The size of the informal economy had grown from about 25 percent of GDP in 1998 (Alam and Banerji 2000) to approximately 43 percent of GDP by 2000 (Toxanova 2007, also see Kalyuzhnova and Kaser 2005). Others have noted a widespread perception among both local and Western observers that the informal economy was continuing to expand, especially in the rural areas (Authors' interview with Ross).

Expenditures within the Mineral Sector: (FOCs)

As in Azerbaijan, the FOCs' contracts in Kazakhstan include extensive stipulations regarding their spending obligations that cover local content, domestic market obligations, the environment, and social welfare. Yet as we predict under P_2, a large share of this spending is directed toward the regions in which they operate. For example, Hurricane Hydrocarbon's contract required they would spend 2 percent on training the local staff, and to buy all products locally and to use local specialists "whenever possible" (Authors' interview with former director). Moreover, FOC spending in Kazakhstan often takes the form of a social contribution fund at the subnational level, whereby the FOCs are required to allocate a portion of their profits to local development projects. According to our interview with a representative from the OKOIC consortium, its contract stipulates that it will pay a certain amount annually for social contribution (approximately $5 million), which is split somewhat unevenly between Mangistau Oblast and Atyrau Oblast – the two regions where they operate. Likewise, in its contract for the Tulpar field, Mobil agreed to pay approximately $750,000 to each of the two regions in which it operates

---

[22] The World Bank (2008) Tax Strategy Report echoed this sentiment.

for three years (Authors' interview). Nations Energy, in similar manner, agreed to invest $5 million over five years for "social enhancement" (Authors' interview), and BG and its partners at Karachaganak agreed to allocate $10 million each year for 40 years for social development projects (Authors' interview with representative no. 2). Kazgermunai's contract stipulated that it would allocate DM 50 million for social infrastructure projects (*Petroleum* 2000a, 26).

When the FOCs bought former state-owned enterprises (SOEs), they often would just graft their social expenditures at the subnational level upon prior spending priorities that were already well-ensconced under the Soviet system (Authors' interviews with BG representative no. 2 and Fast; see also, Carlson 2009). As was the case of many older producing fields, Yuzhneftegaz consisted of a medical center, road building company, a farm that contained numerous livestock to feed the workers, a catering company, a transportation company to move the workers back and forth to the town of Kyzylorda, and a construction company (Authors' interview with former Hurricane Hydrocarbons' manager; see also Peck 2004, 159). Thus, it was quite common for SOEs such as Yuzhneftegaz to sponsor summer camps in the regions where their operations were based, build housing for their employees and provide the employees with vouchers to the local sanatorium for a holiday. As one expatriate employee of Hurricane Hydrocarbons quickly realized, "Hurricane did not buy an oilfield, it bought a community" (Authors' interview). For FOCs such as Hurricane Hydrocarbons, this has meant that they have ended up taking over many of the responsibilities of the prior SOEs, which ultimately has cost the company "hundreds of thousands of dollars" (ibid.).

TCO's spending in Atyrau, furthermore, showcases the subnational nature of expenditures we expect under P_2 in Kazakhstan that sharply contrasts with BP's focus on broader national-level spending in Azerbaijan under S_2. In 1993, in conjunction with signing its contract, TCO initiated its Atyrau Bonus Fund Program that set out to address some of the social and economic problems in Atyrau Oblast through "community outreach and social infrastructure projects in the oblast" (Adamson 2001). The majority of the projects took place either in Atyrau or in Kulsary – the latter is the closest town to the TCO field. Some of the early projects included the construction of 20 cottages for flood victims in Kulsary, an emergency hospital in Kulsary, and a boiler-house plant in Atyrau (*Kazakhstan International Business Magazine* 2003, Adamson 2001). Other expenditures were directed toward the building of a regional hospital for tuberculosis patients in 1995, a new bakery in Atyrau in 1996, and a modern diagnostic center in 1998 (ibid.). By the end of the five-year Bonus Fund Atyrau Program in 1998, TCO had allotted approximately $50 million for the provision of social goods and services in Atyrau (ibid.).

Other companies' social contribution funds have also focused on the subnational level, helping to finance community schools, playgrounds, hospitals, and the arts (Authors' interviews with representatives of Oryx, Nations

Energy, Preussage Energie, Mobil, and BG no. 2). As part of its "we build our future together" program, for example, Hurricane Hydrocarbons sponsored two orphanages and an elementary school in Kyzylorda, built a regional hospital, and provided funds for a local artists' works exposition, Hurricane Cup basketball and football tournaments for children, and entertainment for children for the New Year and *Nauryz* holidays (*Petroleum* 2000b, 19).[23] One of the most common expenditures reported to us was for the building of a local soccer stadium or sports complex (Authors' interview with representative of Oryx). These expenditures not only replicate many of the spending practices of the former Soviet SOEs, but they, moreover, end up providing a significant share of what otherwise would be derived from the regional government budgets. For instance, one study found that in 1998, KazGerMunai donated $4 million for the construction of the regional hospital when the region's total budget for health care only amounted to $11 million (Carlson 2009, 19).

As in Azerbaijan, FOCs' spending in Kazakhstan has intensified over time, but in contrast to Azerbaijan has focused solely on the subnational level. Indeed, if we look at the trajectory of TCO's spending, the unbridled provision of public goods at the subnational level has continued with the introduction of the Igilik social program in 1999 that not only replaced the Bonus Fund Atyrau program, but also augmented the funds available for social expenditures.[24] According to Chevron, this program has already provided $59 million "to meet community health, education and social infrastructure needs, including hospitals, university buildings, schools, gasification and power lines, upgrading of sewage systems, water supply, resurfacing of roads, and the beautification of buildings within the Atyrau and Zhylyoi region (home of the Tengiz Field)."[25] FOCs' spending programs are also focused on highly visible projects in the main urban areas or in close proximately to their production fields. Specific examples of such expenditures on infrastructure include the renovation of the Central Bridge across the Ural River, construction of a new building for Atyrau University, and reinforcement of the river embankment along the Ural River to prevent flooding and mudslides (*Kazakhstan International Business Magazine* 2003, Adamson 2001).[26]

Also in contrast to Azerbaijan, FOCs' spending in Kazakhstan has been less directed toward achieving specific developmental goals such as poverty alleviation. One oil company representative stressed from the outset that "oil and gas companies should not [be a] substitute for government obligations," as "[they] are not the Red Cross" (Authors' interview with Total representative

---

[23] For a detailed discussion of PetroKazakshtan's (i.e., the successor to Hurricane Hydrocarbons) subsequent expenditures, see Carlson 2009.

[24] Igilik means "benefit" in Kazakh.

[25] http://www.chevron.com/countries/kazakhstan/?view=3 (last accessed May 8, 2008).

[26] Tengiz is located in Zhylyoi region. In 2003 and 2004, $8 million was allocated for infrastructure to these two regions (*Kazakhstan International Business Magazine* 2005).

no. 1). Because the FOCs are often responding to spending requests at the sub-national level, there is a great likelihood that their spending will be less likely to foster broader social and economic development. Indeed, one company agreed to give $50,000 to support a regional football team (ibid). A development worker tied to Chevron's funded programs, furthermore, highlighted the ineffective nature of this spending. After $5 million of the $10 million promised by Chevron for local development had been spent, he commented, "If you looked around Atyrau [Oblast], you would hardly be able to notice this. In the opinion of many the money has been wasted on inane projects; for example, [they] used the money to build a huge bread factory that could feed half of Kazakhstan but it only operates at 12 percent capacity because there is no one to buy the bread and it is not cost-efficient to transport outside the oblast" (Authors' interview with Compy).

Where FOCs' expenditures in Kazakhstan further diverge from Azerbaijan is the level of instability and arbitrariness. While the FOCs generally desire stability in their spending obligations as well as their tax burden to protect their revenue stream, our interviews with the FOCs and survey of trade journals show that their ability to determine how much to spend and on what was severely limited and their actual contributions were highly unstable. One of the members of the OKIOC consortium commented that they were continuously approached by the *oblast akim* (governor) for additional funds outside of their normal expenditures. One such request (that was granted in the sum of $2 million) was support for the millennium celebrations (Authors' interview with Total representative no. 2). The instability in expenditures has also been the result of various district akims' requests to embark upon infrastructure projects to mollify particular constituents. For instance, Aktobemunaigas ended up building a gas pipeline to supply the local population (Authors' interview with representative of CNPC). Not only are expenditures arbitrary, but increasingly the FOCs have been asked to do things that a traditional NOC would do under S_1 or S_2. For example, a law signed by President Nazarbayev in August 1999 required subsoil users to include a gas utilization program in their project plans rather than being allowed to flare it (*RPI* 1999, 24–5). During September 2000 at a special session of the Majilis, the Minister of Agriculture, Sauat Mynbaev, requested that the FOCs provide an additional 50 thousand tons of subsidized diesel fuel for the harvest season (Authors' interview with representative of CNPC; see also Babak 2001, 40).

Lastly, that FOCs' social spending obligations in Kazakhstan are also non-transparent is suggested by the fact that many companies opted to just make a lump sum contribution to the regional budget each year that could be used at the sole discretion of the *oblast* akim (Authors' interview with representative of Mobil). It was often the case when companies gave money directly to the *akimiyat* (regional administration), the funds "essentially disappeared" (Authors' interview with Kurbanova). Others have agreed to pay subcontractors directly for projects that district and *oblast* akims commissioned autonomously (Authors' interview with BG representative no. 2).

Not surprisingly then, unstable and nontransparent FOC expenditures have spawned poor results for poverty alleviation in the oil-rich regions; these contrast sharply with the tremendous strides Kazakhstan, as a whole, has made toward poverty reductions (see Agrawal 2008). In 2004, while the overall poverty headcount was approximately 16 percent of the population, the government's Statistics Agency found that in the oil-rich regions of Mangistau, Atyrau, and Kyzylorda, the poverty rates still exceeded 20 percent, with 29.1 percent recorded in Atyrau (UNDP 2005a, 19, 28). The rates are especially high in the rural areas that have, for the most part, not reaped the full benefits of the FOCs' spending (Najman et al. 2008, 114). In fact, Najman et al. concluded that "in the midst of an oil boom, being located in the oil-producing western region is not associated with higher living standards, and indeed the relative position of households in those regions were worse than in 1996" (2008, 113). More so, the jump in per capita GDP in the oil-rich provinces has not been accompanied by improvements in life expectancy and infant mortality. Indeed, some of the highest infant and mortality rates among all the Central Asian countries are still found in Kyzylorda province despite the FOCs' construction of new medical facilities and schools (Makhmoutova 2006).

Expenditures within the Mineral Sector: NFRK

Until the creation of an NRF in 2001, the Kazakhstani government's own spending within the mineral sector also lacked transparency; similarly opaque as taxation, it often resulted in the imprudent use of these funds. Even after Tasmagambetov's aforementioned revelation to the Majilis in 2002 that the country's leaders had created a secret offshore bank account for oil bonuses, the government never divulged how these funds were spent (Global Witness 2004, 15–16). Some have, however, suggested that these funds went to pay for the President's daughter's boarding school fees in Switzerland (ibid., 13).

Perhaps the most prominent illustration of the ambiguous way in which revenue from within the mineral sector was spent is the construction of Kazakhstan's new capital city – Astana – in the barren steppe in the center of the country in the late 1990s (World Bank 2000, 35). While the related expenditures on lavish government buildings can be likened to a "national prestige project," what is crucial is that, despite the high degree of discretion over mineral sector revenues that governing elites enjoyed, this has been the exception rather than the rule in Kazakhstan (as compared to those made in Turkmenistan, for example). And as we have argued elsewhere, the construction of a new capital can be considered an essential part of Kazakhstan's "nation building" project (Jones Luong and Weinthal 2001; see also, Schatz 2004, Wolfrel 2002). The government's lack of involvement in large construction projects in Astana (and elsewhere) following the sharp rise in oil prices in the early 2000s, moreover, corroborates its broader reform agenda to restrict its own spending from within the mineral sector, and instead, to delegate such activities to the private sector.

Since 2000, the Kazkhstani government has moved rather quickly to improve budgetary stability and transparency within the mineral sector – most notably with the introduction of its NRF, the National Fund of the Republic of Kazakhstan (hereafter, NFRK). The NFRK was set up in 2001 to act as both a stabilization fund and as a savings fund (see Chapter 2 for details), though in contrast to Azerbaijan, it places more emphasis on the former (Wakeman-Linn et al. 2003). Revenue flowing into the fund is divided into two separate portfolios. Following the establishment of a reference price for oil, which as of 2006 still was $19 a barrel, every dollar over this benchmark flows into the stabilization account while 90 percent of every dollar up to the benchmark is budgeted for government spending and deficits with the remaining 10 percent of the income under the benchmark is transferred to the savings account (Bacon and Tordo 2006, 84). The NFRK received its first payment in 2001 from the government's 2000 sale of a 5 percent share in TCO and a related bonus payment (ibid., 85).

As in Russia, Kazakhstan's NRF has played a vital role in fostering budgetary predictability, controlling inflation, and sustaining economic growth. Like Russia's OSF and in sharp contrast to Azerbaijan's SOFAZ, the NFRK stands out in its ability to save rather than spend oil export windfalls and curtail increasing public expenditures from within the mineral sector. Table 8.2 illustrates how fast the fund has managed to accumulate revenues. In 2001, the government received $1.1 billion in revenue from the foreign oil and gas companies of which $576 million went to the NFRK and $500 million went to national and local budgets (about 40 percent of government revenues) (ibid, 85). By 2005, the fund had accumulated $8 billion or the equivalent to about 5 percent of GDP. Its ability to stabilize the government's budget can be seen in how well it has performed in comparison to Azerbaijan. According to an economist with the ADB (Usui 2007, 3), from 2003 to 2006, "Kazakhstan saved more than 60% of the increased oil export receipts in its oil fund, while Azerbaijan saved only 12%." The World Bank (2005b, 20) applauded Kazakhstan for its "remarkably prudent fiscal stance" and found that between 2001 and 2003, its public spending decisions were also characterized by "frugality" and were "cautious" (see also, IMF 2004b).

TABLE 8.2. *Budget Revenue from Oil and the NFRK (current US$ millions)*

	1999	2000	2001	2002	2003	2004
Budget revenue from oil[a]	158	604	1,430	1,075	1,900	N/A
NFRK assets	0	0	1,240	1,915	3,663	5,131
Return	–	–	2.86	-0.43	8.69	7.61

[a] Excludes bonuses, privatization receipts and other exceptional payments
Source: Bacon and Tordo (2006, 86).

Indeed, the sterilization of the budget via the NFRK has simultaneously helped keep inflation relatively low since its introduction, ranging from 8.3 percent in 2001 (IMF 2005b) to 6.9 percent in 2004 (IMF 2006a, 4), and precluded a rise in the real exchange rate – both of which are signs of Dutch Disease. The IMF underscored that the NFRK "has played a crucial role in easing the burden on monetary policy and reducing pressure for an appreciation of the exchange rate".[27] To reinforce these policies aimed at reducing Dutch Disease effects, the Kazakhstani government has taken further steps to use its earnings to invest in economic diversification. Specifically, in 2003 Nazarbayev introduced his "Innovative Industrial Development Strategy," which aimed to promote the development of the non-oil sectors of the economy by stimulating the private sector (ICG 2007, 25, Pomfret 2006, 57).[28]

The NFRK has not been as effective as Russia's OSF, however, in reducing the government's ability to borrow, especially during the early 2000s when oil export windfalls were abundant. A clear indication of this is that, despite achieving the status of being the first country in the FSU to repay back all its debt to the IMF in 2000 – seven years ahead of schedule – (USAID 2005, 15) the government increased its borrowing at the same time that it was accumulating funds in the NFRK. Although Kazakhstan actually experienced a decline in its external public debt during this period, according to the World Bank (2005b, 33), "issuing debt while contributing an equal amount to the NFRK deteriorates the position of the budget even when it does not increase net debt."

Moreover, while the NFRK has been better able to contribute to budgetary predictability than SOFAZ in the short term due to its relative stability, the fund still has numerous design flaws that could hamper its ability to improve the quality of managing its budget over the long term, especially those pertaining to transparency. First, like SOFAZ, the NFRK was established by presidential decree with the President retaining exclusive decision-making authority regarding how the funds are spent (Tsalik 2003). The Majilis only gets to vote on the recommendations made by the President. Second, contrary to the government's broader budgetary reforms (discussed in greater detail below), which aimed to reduce the negative impact of extrabudgetary funds on the state budget, the NFRK was set up as an off-budget account held at and managed by the national bank, and hence deliberately not integrated into the larger budgetary process (Bacon and Tordo 2006, 87; IMF 2005b, 14; Ramamurthy and Tandberg 2002).

The lack of oversight mechanisms, such as formal checks on the president, also provides an opportunity for the President to usurp the fund for discretionary spending, especially since the Majilis's role in managing the NFRK is only "nominal;" it does not, for example, "approve reports on implementation

---

[27] IMF 2004 public consultancy (available at: http://www.imf.org/external/np/sec/pn/2004/pn04106.htm)

[28] For details, see http://en.government.kz/resources/docs/doc3

and auditors' reports" (Makhmutova 2007, 44). Nor does the Accounting Chamber possess any authority to conduct its own audit of the NFRK (ibid, 52). That information about the internal workings of the fund is not made readily available to the public is still another indicator that the NFRK has yet to improve accountability (Makhmutova 2007). Thus, although the NFRK has not been raided to finance discretionary projects, the possibility, nevertheless, remains as the President retains sole authority to change the rules and procedures governing the fund (Bacon and Tordo 2006, 87).

The limited transparency concerning the mineral sector revenue that flows into the NFRK has also been affected by Kazakhstan's reluctance to sign onto the "Extractive Industries Transparency Initiative" (EITI). In contrast to Azerbaijan, which did so immediately, Kazakhstan joined only in 2005, and thus has only made minimal efforts to harmonize its legislation with the international principles and criteria of EITI (ICG 2007, 25).

Expenditures outside the Mineral Sector

Outside the mineral sector, Kazakhstan has made greater strides toward institutionalizing limits on public expenditures than Azerbaijan and less progress in improving the transparency of its budgetary process than Russia. First and foremost, alongside several of its FSU counterparts, Kazakhstan adopted a new national budget code in 1996 (amended again in 1998 and 2005) that required it to prepare an annual budget and obtain legislative approval (Makhumutova 2007, Mikesell and Mullins 2001, 522). Second, in order to improve its budgetary execution, the government also introduced an Accounting Chamber on Monitoring of Republic Budget Implementation in 1996 (Makhumutova 2007, 27).[29] Third, in 1998, the government consolidated several extrabudgetary funds (such as the Pension Fund and Medical Insurance Fund) into the state budget, which was considered to be "a substantial step in the right direction of presenting a transparent, fully integrated budget document" (Edmiston 2001, 17; also see Potter and Diamond, 2000, Ramamurthy and Tandberg 2002, 10). As a result, a comparative study of fiscal transparency among the Soviet successor states found that while Kazakhstan falls slightly behind Russia, it ranks well ahead of Azerbaijan and Uzbekistan (Jarmuzek 2006).

Kazakhstan has also made significant progress in improving budgetary predictability by institutionalizing limits on public expenditures. As in many other transition countries, in the 1990s, government spending was "substantially cut" from approximately 30 percent of GDP at independence to approximately 23 percent of GDP by 1999 (World Bank 2000, 4). Moreover, similar

[29] In contrast to Russia, the Accounting Chamber is still "not entirely independent" and the Ministry of Finance does not have same level of authority over the spending ministries in the budgetary process (Jarmuzek et al. 2006, 15). This is partially due to the fact that the Accounting Chamber is comprised of nine members, three of which are appointed by the President (including the Chair) (Makhmutova 2007, 52).

to Russia in the late 1990s and in contrast to Azerbaijan, the Kazakhstani government succeeded in introducing measures to reduce the overall size of the public sector (ibid., 1). The percentage of the population employed in the public sector, for example, fell from an average of 6.9 percent of GDP between 1990 and 1995 to 5.6 percent from 1995 to 1999 (Gupta et al. 2003, 566). In short, as in Russia, these efforts to reduce the scope of government activity were consistent with the Kazakhstani government's overall strategy to achieve a balanced budget (Edmiston 2001, 5).

Also similar to Russia, Kazakhstan's reform agenda has included shrinking government spending within the social sphere. Indeed, by the mid-1990s Kazakhstan had "implemented deep expenditure cuts and radical liberalization" in the social sphere (Cook 2007a, 41). Spending on social protection dropped by approximately 60 percent from 11.2 percent of GDP in 1992 to 6.6 percent in 1996 (World Bank 1998, 30). Even as government revenues began to rebound, the share of social expenditures as a percent of total expenditures continued to decline from 62 percent in 1999 to 47.5 percent in 2002 (Agrawal 2008, 105).

Consider first fuel subsidies. Like the rest of the petroleum-rich FSU countries, energy resources in Kazakhstan were underpriced throughout most of 1990s such that if the true costs of its energy subsidies were taken into account in 1998, they would have amounted to 26 percent of government expenditures (IEA 1999, 9). In sharp contrast to Azerbaijan (as well as Uzbekistan and Turkmenistan) that maintained universal energy subsidies, however, Kazakhstan managed to slash these subsidies. By 2000, "energy prices [were] closest to opportunity costs and domestic subsidies [had become] relatively small" (Esanov et al. 2003, 5). Interestingly, in the agricultural sector, these cuts were facilitated by the government's ability to require FOCs to deliver essentially free fuel during the planting seasons.

Other significant reforms in the social sphere concern pension reform, which was designed precisely to "limit the government's social obligations" and ultimately to shift the burden for saving for retirement onto society (Becker et al. 2009, 120). Here, Kazakhstan has actually gone beyond Russia by not only contracting the state's role but also expanding the private sector's role. In early 1998, the Kazakhstani government eliminated overnight its entire pay-as-you-go (PAYGO) pension system and introduced a privately funded system based on mandatory individual contributions (see Andrews 2001, Hinz et al. 2005, Orenstein 2008).[30] Prior to this reform, public pensions in 1997 had accounted for 90 percent of all social protection expenditures (World Bank 1998, 29). By 2000, private pension funds made up 45 percent of all contributions (Alam and Banerji 2000, 11). The establishment of these private pension funds has also had a broader impact upon the economy through

---

[30] In contrast, PAYGO was funded exclusively by mandatory employer contributions. Workers received the equivalent of 60 percent of their final salary if they had worked at least 25 years for men and 20 years for women (ADB 2000, 1).

both contributing to the growth in capital markets and administrative organs responsible for regulating these new private pension funds (Akimov and Dollery 2008, Andrews 2001, Orenstein 2008). By 2004, these pension funds had generated $2.5 billion in capital for investment (Akimov and Dollery 2008, 86).

Kazakhstan's efforts have been less successful in other aspects of social reform. In the late 1990s, the government cut the number of entitlements inherited from the Soviet Union dramatically – from 47 to 14 benefit categories and introduced cash allowances instead of subsidies (World Bank 2000, 38). Yet it seems such reforms have not been sufficient to produce their intended outcomes. For instance, many of the remaining categorical benefits, such as for veterans of wars and holders of extraordinary service, were not reformed to target directly the poor (World Bank 2000, 38). Similarly, Kazakhstan has systematically introduced means-tested social assistance for children's allowances, and yet, the World Bank (1998, 38) has found that this improvement on paper "performs quite poorly" in practice. In particular, when it comes to "directing benefits toward the poor ... [for] the bottom quintile, the Kazakhstan scheme performs worse than the *mahalla* scheme in Uzbekistan" (ibid.).

Kazakhstan has been successful, however, in reallocating government spending toward human capital formation. In comparison with other middle-income countries, for example, Kazakhstan spends "relatively less on mostly unproductive military expenditures and relatively more on growth-enhancing education and health sectors" (ibid., 6). Concerning education in particular, Kazakhstan has shifted some of its funding of preschool and university education to primary and secondary education – two areas, "which have been show internationally to have greater returns" for the development of human capital (Edmiston 2001, 9). This shift at least partly explains why Kazakhstan has been able to recoup some of the losses it incurred in its overall HDI ranking following the Soviet Union's collapse. In the educational sphere, as of 2004, it had "managed to return to its 1990 level in terms of per capita GDP and the share of people between [the ages of] 5 and 24" enrolled in school (Makhmutova 2006, 19).[31]

A clear sign that the aforementioned spending limits were institutionalized is that the government did not significantly increase its spending following during the oil boom of the early 2000s. Indeed, from 2003 until 2005, Kazakhstan's "total spending in relation to GDP has risen only modestly" (IMF 2005b, 14). The rationale for this increase, moreover, was the need to address the shortcomings of its pension reform, which had inadvertently left a large number of retired women and elderly citizens with insufficient income (Hinz et al. 2005, Orenstein 2008, 131). Thus, the greatest increase was in

---

[31] In fact, Kazakhstan lagged significantly behind its 1990 HDI levels on only one indicator by 2004: average life expectancy (Makhmutova 2006, 19).

social security expenditures, which rose from 5.4 percent of GDP in 2002 to 11.5 percent in 2003 (Agrawal 2003, 105).

Lastly, as expected under P_2, in lieu of the widespread distribution we found in Azerbaijan, the Kazakhstani government has engaged in redistribution of the proceeds from foreign investment in the petroleum-rich regions to those poor in petroleum reserves.[32] Although taxes are accumulated in the center, following budgetary reform in 1998 with the Law on the Budget System, Kazakhstan has largely decentralized its expenditures through direct transfers to subnational governments (Makhmutova 2001, Ostrowski 2007). Thus regional and local officials have received increased authority, albeit often in the form of an unfunded mandate, to determine expenditures on education and health care, social protection, support of employment, water supply, and construction, for example (Jones Luong 2003a). Not surprisingly, the petroleum-poor regions' budgets depend greatly on official transfers from the center. A recent study, for example, found that the "the share of official transfers in regional revenue is higher in most [petroleum] poor regions" (Najman et al. 2008, 120). That the petroleum-rich regions provide the bulk of these funds is clear: only an estimated 15 percent of revenues remain in the country's petroleum-rich Western regions (ICG 2007, 29). In particular, the petroleum industry in Atyrau region is widely viewed as providing "the lion's share of earnings to the Kazakhstan budget" (*Petroleum* 2002, 12). This, of course, does not mean that the petroleum-poor regions have benefited equally or can be considered as well off as the petroleum-rich regions, but rather, that there should be less inequality in budget revenue at the subnational level than there would be if all the benefits of foreign investments remained in the oil-producing regions. It is telling that Kazakhstan's efforts at redistribution have been attributed to the overall decline in poverty incidence in Kazakhstan in 2004 (UNDP 2005a).

Causal Mechanisms

That Kazakhstan's fiscal regime is clearly distinct not only from Russia's strong fiscal regime and Uzbekistan's and Turkmenistan's weak fiscal regimes but also Azerbaijan's lends further support to our argument that fiscal regimes are a product of ownership structure rather than mineral wealth. As predicted, the hybrid fiscal regime that emerged in Kazakhstan comes closest to our worst-case scenario under P_2. To assess whether it materialized for the reasons we posit in Chapter 6, here we seek to demonstrate that TCs were negligible, societal expectations were high vis-à-vis FOCs and low vis-à-vis the state, and that power relations decisively favored the state at the same time the FOCs were not strongly committed to CSR.

[32] As of the mid-1990s, Kazakhstan is divided into 14 provinces (*oblasts/oblystar*) two cities with special status, and 160 districts (*awdandar*). For an overview of subnational government in Kazakhstan, see Makhmutova 2001.

Transaction Costs

Our contention that TCs are negligible is based on the understanding that both host governments and FOCs viewed the global model contract as the appropriate template for their negotiations. Thus, to demonstrate the causal link between negligible TCs and Kazakhstan's hybrid fiscal regime, we should find not only that both the FOCs and governing elites assumed and indeed accepted that the model contract would serve as the starting point for setting the tax rate and determining the profit split but also that both parties understood that the contract would include some degree of social obligations and stability provision for the FOCs.

Our interviews with the FOCs provide evidence that it was widely accepted that the negotiations would begin with the taking the model contract "off the shelf and just us[ing] it" (Authors' interview with representative of Amerada Hess). As one investor remarked, "the model contract – that is, consistent with international standards – is used as a basis for drafting all contracts on Kazakhstan" (Authors' interview with Leonard). The formation of the State Investment Committee (SIC), moreover, further formalized the adoption of the model contract since all negotiations were then required to adhere to the same contractual process. This entailed:

using the Model Contract to put together a draft and submit it to the [SIC], which then breaks it into several parts and gives it to the relevant agency or ministry to look over and approve. After the relevant ministries review the draft and send it back to the [SIC] with comments, the company and the [SIC] would meet again to discuss any changes that must be made to the draft. (ibid.)

The establishment of a foreign investor-friendly legal environment provided the appropriate signal to the FOCs that the governing elites had also assumed the use of a model contract as a specialized tax regime for the FOCs. Specifically, the government introduced a decree in early 1997 that upheld the primacy of the model contract for subsurface operations.[33]

The influence of the international context on the model contract used in the 1990s is manifested in the level of social spending specified in the contracts of the FOCs. In Kazakhstan, the governing elites bought into these new norms that the contractual template would not just be restricted to taxation. Thus, for a deal to be struck, the model contract had to specify significant spending for the FOCs. The 1996 Subsurface Law, moreover, reinforced such spending obligations through its stipulation that local content provisions be required for FOCs' participation in the mineral sector (see Chentsova 2004).[34]

Our interviews with the FOCs also confirm that all the contracts were expected to include a stability clause that would fix their tax regime to a

[33] RK Government Decree dated January 27, 1997 on "Approval of the Model Contract for subsurface operations in the Republic of Kazakhstan" (Chentsova 2004, 126).

[34] This law replaced the 1992 Mining & Mineral Code that opened the doors for foreign investors in the mineral sector (Bassin 2004, 116).

certain date to protect their operations against any fluctuations in the tax code (Authors' interviews with representatives of Mobil and Amerada Hess, and with Page). In short, their contracts were intended to supersede changes to the general tax code, and a stability clause implied that any terms of the Tax Code that were applicable to the operations of the foreign oil and gas companies at the time the contracts were negotiated would remain valid for the full term of the contract (Arthur Anderson 1999, 23).

Given these negligible TCs that have provided disincentives for the FOCs and the governing elites to actively pursue broad-based tax reform outside of the mineral sector, why did Kazakhstan end up with a formal tax code allegedly aimed at broad-based taxation? If we are right, then it is a function not only of low societal expectations vis-à-vis the state (discussed below), but also of the international context in which IFIs and INGOs promote the creation of an internationally isomorphic tax code on paper.

Indeed, international tax consultants were intimately involved in the drafting of Kazakhstan's general tax code (Authors' interviews with McLure and Townsend). For instance, the ITIC, a Western tax advisory group, agreed to help prepare a "Concepts Paper" in 1994 that would outline the basic objectives and principles of a fiscal regime (ADB 1999, Chapter 2). Besides ITIC contributing to the writing of the first tax code were also consultants from the OECD, IMF, EU-TACIS, USAID, and the U.S. Treasury (ADB 1999). The Western tax advisors not only sought to foster a "simple tax code with low tax rates," but preferred a separation of general taxes from energy taxes as a means to keep the tax code "relatively clean" by not providing special treatment for selected sectors or regions and hence encouraged deferring both the issues of the natural resources sector and intergovernmental fiscal relations (Authors' interview with McLure). They shared the presumption, in short, that "any country [like Kazakhstan] with oil will have a separate tax regime for oil" (ibid).

Societal Expectations

In contrast to Azerbaijan, societal expectations vis-à-vis the state are low. This, we argue, fosters the perception among governing elites that they can demonstrate that they are managing mineral wealth in society's best interest by extracting an appropriate share of the FOCs' profits and redistributing them from the oil-rich regions to the oil-poor regions. They should also consider it is less costly to pursue some tax reform outside the mineral sector. Likewise, low societal expectations vis-à-vis the state should make the governing elites more amenable to setting some formal limits on their own spending both within and outside the mineral sector. Yet as in Azerbaijan, FOCs in Kazakhstan under P_2 confront high societal expectations. Thus, their spending patterns should reflect their perception that they face high barriers to attaining social acceptance of their access rights to the proceeds from the mineral sector. This perception, in turn, should encourage the FOCs to engage in highly visible forms of spending that go beyond the terms specified in their contracts – albeit primarily at the subnational level. Lastly, we should find evidence that INGOs and IFIs are directly involved in shaping societal expectations, and thus, the nature of fiscal pressures on the FOCs in Kazakhstan.

As in the other case studies included in this book, we rely primarily on the EBRD 2005 Life in Transition Survey (LiTS) to assess whether societal expectations vis-à-vis the state are consistent with our expectations. In the case of Kazakhstan, we expect the results to be very similar to those in Russia since, as under P_1, they are low under P_2, and therefore, distinct from Azerbaijan, since they are high under S_2. Indeed, the survey results indicate that the population in Kazakhstan is as likely as the population in Russia and less likely than in Azerbaijan to expect the state to assume a strong role for alleviating inequalities and a dominant role in the economy. For example, only 62.5 percent responded that the state should be "strongly involved" in "reducing the gap between the rich and the poor" in Kazakhstan and 67.3 percent in Russia versus 87 percent in Azerbaijan. While a slightly higher percentage of respondents in Kazakhstan agreed that the state should be "strongly involved" in "the ownership of large companies in the country" than in Azerbaijan (86.5 and 84.7, respectively), in the former (as in Russia) there is significant variation across age groups while in the latter this is fairly uniform. The difference between those 18–34 years of age and those over 65 who responded in this manner was just under 13 percentage points compared to just over 3 percentage points in Azerbaijan. (See Appendix C for details.) This is consistent with our expectation that those with the longest history of living under the Soviet system will be the slowest to change their attitudes toward the state's role in response to a change in ownership structure.

The 2003 Jones Luong-McMann survey also helps us assess popular attitudes toward the state's role in the social sphere. As in Russia, the Kazakhstani population appears to support a reduced role for the state in the social sphere. While during the Soviet period, approximately 90 percent of the respondents in Kazakhstan and 86 percent of the respondents in Uzbekistan were found to use state resources such as medical services and education, by 2003 only 28 percent of the population in Kazakhstan sought out these resources in contrast to 51 percent in Uzbekistan (for details, see McMann 2009). Pertaining to the government's decision to reform its pension program, results from an ADB survey carried out in its aftermath were consistent with our predictions regarding support for this reduced state role in the social sphere. The survey found that there was a "15 percent decrease in the number who believe[d] that the Government should be responsible for their retirement" (ADB 2000, 18).

More importantly, governing elites have consistently emphasized their role as tax collectors – both within and outside the mineral sector. In his annual "State of the Nation" address, for example, Nazarbayev has highlighted the necessity for the country to undergo tax reform and to strengthen the tax administration to increase state revenue. In our interviews, governing elites also consistently expressed the sentiment that Kazakhstani society was more accepting of taxation outside the mineral sector than many of its neighbors. One such elite, for example, remarked that although the population "understood that the oilmen would pay the largest share of taxes," this did not mean that they "considered themselves exempt from paying taxes" (Authors' interview with Vice Minister). As discussed further below, however, tax reform outside the mineral sector has received less attention over time owing to the onset of the obsolescing bargain. One indicator of this is the noticeable shift in focus in Nazarbayev's speeches to taxation within the mineral sector and the government's efforts to extract more revenue from the FOCs.

The LiTS survey is also somewhat helpful in assessing societal expectations toward the FOCs. Among the FSU, Kazakhstan stands out for having the lowest percentage of the population (with the exception of Ukraine) that favors retaining the "current owners with no change" from privatization. Even among the youngest respondents (18–34 years of age), only 16.1 percentage preferred leaving the assets in the hands of the current owners with no changes, in contrast to 26.5 percent of the same age group in Russia. Likewise, in contrast to 31.5 percent of the respondents in Russia that preferred leaving this property "in the hands of current owners provided they pay the privatized assets' worth," only 26.5 percent preferred doing so in Kazakhstan. These survey results can be interpreted in two different ways, both of which are consistent with our expectations. On the one hand, they suggest that the FOCs in Kazakhstan face a much higher barrier to attaining societal acceptance than domestic private owners in Russia under P_1. On the other, they suggest that FOCs in Kazakhstan are not meeting these expectations because their spending, while visible, has not been effectively directed at addressing the social and economic problems that plague society.

More importantly, that society viewed FOCs as an unlimited source of taxation and spending in the regions where they operate is evident in the FOCs' private and public statements. Shortly after the major exploration contracts were signed, one company representative remarked, "people are waiting for development of the Caspian to bring health and wealth" (Authors' interview with Starukhin). In our own survey of the FOCs operating in Kazakhstan, conducted between 1999 and 2000, the respondents consistently underscored the high level of individual and collective demands on them at the regional level for public goods and social service provisions. For instance, one FOC representative remarked that in early 1995, they were visited nearly every week with requests for social assistance, varying from paying an individual's hospital bill to refurbishing a neighborhood school (Authors' interview with representative of Preussage Energie). Another commented that he was asked "at least twice a day for something," usually by a family or community representative, but also by a member of the regional government (Authors' interview with representative of Mobil). They also uniformly expressed the sentiment that these demands were not unexpected, but rather, a "natural artifact of our presence here." Moreover, a former Hurricane Hydrocarbons' manager described the overwhelming burden the company faced at the regional level: "the oblast depended upon [Hurricane] for everything because Hurricane was the only game in town ... from employment to social assistance" (Authors' interview).

Not only were the FOCs cognizant of these heightened individual and collective demands, but our interviews demonstrate that, in fact, the FOCs were clearly motivated by them and hence took them into consideration in their strategic decision-making. As one foreign investor remarked: "[We] have a social obligation to the region in which [we] operate. This is all part of being a good citizen" (Authors' interview with representative of Oryx). Likewise, this meant that companies like Hurricane Hydrocarbons did not refuse "the constant stream of requests for aid from both the oblast akim and its residents" because "providing social assistance to the people of Kyzlorda was part of [its] public relations strategy" (Authors' interview with former manager). One representative from the Human Resources department of one of the oil companies commented that they "literally received a pile of applications everyday from people wanting some kind of aid" that ranged from people wanting money to help to bury a loved one to a local artist requesting monetary supplements." That these demands influenced their decision-making was evident by the fact that 90 percent of this company's expenditures ended up being based on these local expectations whereas only 10 percent was based on what was actually written into their contract (Authors' interview). The overwhelming pressure felt by the FOCs to spend led one company's representative to sardonically point out that their social contributions have not only included building playgrounds, refurbishing schools with computers, upgrading plumbing systems, but have extended to "shoot[ing] wild dogs" to free the region of rabies and plague (Authors' interview with representative of Nations Energy). Thus, often even in anticipation of such expectations, the FOCs would provide their managers with a special sponsorship budget for discretionary use so that they could fund highly visible projects to enhance their company's public relations image locally. According to another foreign investor, this was crucial because the company needed it to maintain "a high profile" (Authors' interview with representative of Chevron Munaigas Inc.).

What these surveys also suggest is that INGOs and IFIs have been directly involved in shaping such spending pressures on the FOCs. The majority of our respondents, for example, acknowledged that their spending priorities were often influenced by INGO activities that have served to empower local communities. When asked about the activity of local NGOs in the regions where their operations take place, one foreign investor remarked that he was not aware of any local NGO activity in of itself. Rather in the realm of the environment, for example, he commented that INGOs are trying to "bring environmentalism from abroad to an inhospitable [domestic] environment" (Authors' interview with BG representative no. 2). Indeed, international NGOs have served as the conduit through raising awareness of the plight of local populations affected by the negative externalities of oil and gas exploration and production. For instance, Western NGOs such as Crude Accountability have worked with local citizens in the town of Berezovka to demand compensation, entailing the resettlement of the populations residing in close proximately to the Karachaganak oil and gas fields (Akhmediarov 2006).

At the same time that the FOCs were motivated by these high societal expectations, evidence from presidential speeches and interviews with governing elites provides additional support for the contention that fiscal policies in Kazakhstan were also spurred by the governing elites' desire to demonstrate to society that the FOCs were paying their fair share for society's benefit. Here too, we primarily rely upon the annual "State of the Nation" address (hereafter *Address*), wherein the President lays out the main budget priorities for the upcoming year.[35]

Beginning with his most prominent *Address* in 1997 that outlined his vision for "Kazakhstan 2030," Nazarbayev identified the development of the energy sector with foreign investment as one of the long-term priorities that, economically, would transform the country into a Central Asian Snow Leopard, and socially would improve the citizenry's living standards. He also made a pledge to ensure that the FOCs would serve this role:

> We are in search of partners for long-term outlook, whose challenges coincide with our challenges. In contracts we shall strictly and reasonably stand up for interests of Kazakhstan, ecology, employment and labor training, the necessity of settling a number of social tasks. Finally the strategy stipulates efficient and expedient utilization of future profits drawn out of these resources.

Several years later, in a television interview, he echoed this sentiment, publicly calling upon the FOCs to increase their local content expenditures:

> I am once again calling on all investors operating in Kazakhstan to fully help Kazakh enterprises, otherwise why have we invited you here Kazakhstan? As soon as you face problems with oil transportation and quotas and as soon as you need to tackle some issues you run to the government and I step in and help. And I have the right to expect you all to be attentive to the requests of the Kazakh head of state. (BBC October 30, 2001)

In his *Addresses*, Nazarbayev has also increasingly emphasized that the FOCs should provide the bulk of taxation. In 2000, for example, he argued that the government should develop mechanisms to "seize exceeding incomes of companies working with raw materials" since the government "cannot be satisfied with low level of collection on excises and some other taxes." The need to demonstrate to the population that the FOCs are being made to pay became even more acute with the post-1999 oil price boom (Author's interview with Vice Minister). Thus, while the 2004 amendments to the tax code appeared to target the FOCs' profits with the introduction of a "rent tax" on exports, they were "largely cosmetic and only serve[d] to appease public opinion, largely

---

[35] Until 2001, these annual addresses were presented in the fall. Since 2002, they have been presented in the spring "in order to integrate the goals set in the *Address* into the draft budget for the coming year" (Makhmutova 2007, 31).

because the "contracts for developing most fields ha[d] already been signed" (Khusainov and Brentaev 2004).

At the same time that Nazarbayev has publicly championed increased taxation and spending from the FOCs, he has also reiterated that the proceeds from mineral wealth would not be distributed broadly, but rather, used to alleviate disparities. For example, in his 1997 *Address*, Nazarbayev stated that by 2000 the energy sector would allow "the most needy layers of our society [to] receive state aid thus providing 150 thousand people through microcredits and more than 3.5 million people (including pensioners) through social insurance systems." Similarly, in a speech on Independence Day in 2003 he stated that Kazakhstan's energy is capable of "support[ing] the improvement of villages, industrialization, and social growth."

Lastly, published interviews in the popular press with regional leaders provide additional evidence that, especially at the subnational level, leaders felt obliged to show that the FOCs were making significant financial contributions to improving local infrastructure and services that went beyond their contractual obligations. As Tasmagambetov, who served as the akim of Atyrau Oblast from 1999 until he became prime minister in 2002, emphasized:

Today in Atyrau Oblast, construction work worth 3.5 million tenge is being carried out. (I remind you that our budget is only 5.6 million). To accumulate such means for the construction of roads, bridges, [and] housing is very expensive! Where is such money from? Of course, from the oilmen: large investors, punctually fulfill their obligations to the budget, [they] must meet the local government halfway to resolve the most pressing problems of the region. (*Biznes Klass* 1999, 2)

Because many of these projects were both highly visible and accessible to the local population, he quickly won a reputation for extracting social contributions from the FOCs – a reputation he was "very pleased" to have (Authors' interview).

Coercion

The final causal mechanism we invoke to explain how a hybrid regime that approximates our worst-case scenario emerged in Kazakhstan is coercion. In contrast to Azerbaijan, where power relations decisively favored the FOCs, here we need to show that the governing elites in Kazakhstan were the unilateral enforcers of the contracts because the FOCs were unable to overcome the collective action problem (CAP), and hence avoid the obsolescing bargain. Here, it is also essential to show that, unlike Azerbaijan, the FOCs were not committed to CSR.

To demonstrate that the governing elites were the unilateral enforcers, we first provide evidence that the companies were unable to evade government demands for higher tax payments, which was exacerbated during the oil price boom in the early 2000s. Here too, we rely upon our interviews with the FOCs and trade journals to show that the FOCs were increasingly forced to acquiesce or risk having their contracts revoked and operations hampered. For instance, in 2000 the Kazakhstani government made it clear to the FOCs that they would undertake "a compulsory review of all contracts" to see if they were in compliance with country's tax legislation (Authors' interview with Page). In a meeting with the Foreign Investors Council (FIC),[36] Nazarbayev backed this aggressive move to exercise greater leverage over the FOCs' fiscal burden. He explained, "[s]ome conditions [of projects' operation] have changed, i.e. prices, taxes. We are talking of the need for a balance of interests" (Denisova 2002, 30). While the FOCs perceived this as an outright attempt to remove their investor privileges, the mere threat to review contracts resulted in numerous contract revisions in 2001 in which the FOCs arranged to increase their tax payments to the budget "voluntarily." In particular, Hurricane Kumkol Munai, Mangistaumunaigas, and CNPS-Aktobemunaigas petitioned the Ministry of Finance to change the tax regime applied to their previously signed contracts and hence to increase the amount of royalties paid to the government (ibid., 29). As a result, in 2001 Nazarbayev was able to announce publicly that 33 of 47 companies approached by the government had agreed in private talks with the Kazakhstani leadership to increase their royalty payments following a session of the FIC (*RFE/RL* December 17, 2001).

Although the FIC was established to resolve foreign investors' grievances and provide direct access to the President, its efforts have essentially failed to protect their stability guarantees because it has failed to form a united front. Many FOC representatives have utilized "their own resources" to negotiate with the President while others have come to believe that their survival depends solely on their own actions (Authors' interviews). One foreign consultant observed that because the FOCs "have not banded together and each company [has tried] to cut its own deals, [they] have a collective action problem" (Authors' interview with Rowley). The chronic breach in the FOCs' contracts regarding VAT payments (discussed above) serves to illustrate. As one company representative underscored, "it was simply impossible to get the other companies' support on this issue" (Authors' interview with representative of Preussage Energie). Another described the inefficacy of the FIC more bluntly: "[it] offers us an opportunity to pop our heads up so that the government can hit it with a sledge hammer" (Author's interview with representative of Nations Energy).

Even the largest and presumably most powerful FOCs were not immune to coercion. In particular, in 2002 TCO's stability guarantees also came under fire. When TCO sought to reinvest its profits to fund a $3.5 billion expansion project as was allowed in its contract and that would ultimately increase the profitability of the project over the long term, the government immediately rejected this plan since it would reduce their tax payments over the next four years (Pala 2003).[37] Because the government was determined not to relinquish

---

[36] Established in 1998, the FIC is composed of 13 of the largest foreign companies operating in Kazakhstan along with the EBRD.

[37] The original JV agreement required financing of new projects to come from oil revenues rather than external sources (Peck 2004, 158).

almost $200 million a year in profits taxes, it successfully forced TCO to finance the project with loans (Lelyveld 2003, Pala 2002). The governing elites argued that the tax breaks TCO had received in its initial contract were "too generous" (Nobatova 2003a). After heated negotiations in which TCO suspended the projects, it was evident the extent to which the governing elites were the unilateral enforcers since not only did TCO agree to continue its tax payments, which account for 15 percent of the state revenue, but also agreed to pay an additional $810 million in taxes and take out an additional loan to cover the government's share of the expansion (Pala 2003).

The inability of the FOCs to enforce their contracts further surfaced in 2004 when BG was unable to sell its share (16.67 percent) in the Kashagan field first to the China National Offshore Oil Corporation and Sinopec for $1.23 billion and then to its partners (Pulsipher and Kaiser 2006). While the consortium partners had made it public that they opposed the sale to the government, especially since the terms of their contract provided for no such first refusal on the part of the state, they ultimately were forced to concede half of BG's share (8.33 percent) to the newly created NOC – KazMunaiGaz (KMG) (Pala 2004, Pulsipher and Kaiser 2006). The introduction of the December 2004 Law "On Certain Amendments and Changes into the Legislative Acts of the Republic of Kazakhstan Concerning Subsoil Use and Oil Operations in the Republic of Kazakshtan" that provided the government with a pre-emptive right to buy up first any subsoil use right or equity interest that a foreign oil and gas company would want to sell, in essence, cemented the governing elites as the unilateral enforcer of contracts (Pulsipher and Kaiser 2006, Yakovleva 2005a, 13).[38] This move also provided a legal basis for the government's decision to intervene in the anticipated sale of PetroKazakhstan (previously Hurricane Hydrocarbons) to CNPC and its eventual purchase of a 33 percent share in PetroKazakhstan (Ritchie 2005).

That coercion on the part of the governing elites was the mechanism at work when the FOCs incurred expenditures outside of their contractual obligations was repeatedly emphasized in our interviews. One FOC representative confided to us that they considered supplying subsidized fuel to the agricultural sector during the harvest and planting seasons as a form of "confiscation" rather than "national assistance" (Authors' interview with representative of Nations Energy). Another example of the FOCs' inability to enforce their contracts is the government's ability to introduce export restrictions at will so that Kazakhstan's domestic refineries would work at full capacity and to ensure adequate reserves for domestic consumption (Authors' interviews with representatives of Preussage Energie and Mobil). According to one FOC representative, the government "forced the companies to make individual agreements with the refineries" that goes "against all the[ir] contracts" (Authors'

---

[38] For details surrounding the controversy of PetroKazakshtan's sale, see Yakovleva (2005a). KMG then purchased a 33 percent share. In 2002 Kazakhoil was merged with state pipeline company to form KMG.

interview). The decree that mandated these quotas, explained another investor, was "a ploy to pressure people to sign supply contracts" (Authors' interview with representative of Mobil). In reacting to export restrictions imposed on the FOCs in February 2000, Hurricane Hydrocabons' president remarked, "this contradicts the agreements that were signed by Hurricane and the Government when the Government privatized Yuzhneftegas ... . I feel that our Company is being discriminated against" (*Petroleum* 2000, 17–8). In both instances, companies are forced to sell surplus crude at below world market prices – hence, impeding their ability to maximize their profits. Although the FOCs had formed their own association – the Kazakhstan Petroleum Association (KPA)[39] – in 1997 to lobby government agencies for a level playing field, what became remarkably clear during the "export quota crisis" was that the companies were simply unable to overcome the CAP. According to one FOC representative, while this was "the first time that the KPA acted as a body ... some [FOCs] broke ranks. So, in the end, the Kazakhs got what they wanted" (Authors' interview with representative of Preussage Energie).

The ability of the governing elites to coerce was especially evident during times of busts. When oil prices plummeted in the late 1990s, many of the foreign oil and gas companies such as CNPC sought to cut expenditures by reducing the number of employees on their payroll (Authors' interview with representative of CNPC, *RFE/RL* January 31, 2000). Yet in the face of mounting pressure from these disgruntled former employees and regional leaders, the governing elites directly interfered with the companies restructuring plans to ensure that contractual obligations were met. In the case of Aktobemunaigas, the CNPC was then forced to establish several new JV companies in Aktobe Oblast that would serve as local subcontractors for their operations, allowing them to reabsorb these redundant employees (Authors' interview with representative of CNPC).

The inability of the FOCs to rebuke demands from the regional leaders for more munificent social spending further corroborates that the governing elites were the unilateral enforcers. In Atyrau, for example, the akim was able to increase the amount of social contributions to the region by halting the operation of several of Tengiz's wells ostensibly for violating oil recovery regulations (Ostrowski 2008, 158; also see *Petroleum* 2002). A representative from Hurricane Hydrocarbons, likewise, commented that there was "constant pressure from the akim's office" to fulfill the oblast's social and economic needs. This pressure came in the form of interfering with the progress of [our] daily operations" and included "threaten[ing] and prevent[ing] them from getting licenses and permits" (Authors' interview). More so, the greatest irony about the restoration of Atyrau leading up to the "100th Year Celebration of Kazakhstani Oil" is that it was funded in part by the major FOCs operating there. Atyrau's regional akim at the time boasted that he was personally able

---

[39] The KPA consists of 62 companies from 20 countries that are engaged in the exploration and/ or production of hydrocarbons and the service sector in Kazakhstan.

to persuade TCO to double its original $2 million contribution for the jubilee (Authors' interview).

Lastly, the FOCs in Kazakhstan have exhibited few signs of being pro-CSR. Their lack of commitment to transparency and public disclosure regarding their own projects came to light in 2003 with the "Kazakhgate" scandal. Companies such as Mobil were accused of rendering unlawful payments to President Nazarbayev and the former Oil Minister Balgimbayev through the middleman James Giffen between 1995 and 1999 for contract deals – some of which ended up in the previously mentioned offshore bank accounts (Global Witness 2007, Hersh 2001). Companies such as TCO are notorious for their blatant disregard for CSR (Yessenova 2008, 195). In sharp contrast to BP in Azerbaijan, TCO does not even maintain a website to divulge the names of its contractors or the value of its domestic contracts (ibid.).

The FOCs' weak commitment to CSR is also manifested in their lukewarm approach to international transparency initiatives such as EITI. Unlike the situation in Azerbaijan, where FOCs who were both the unilateral enforcers and committed to CSR pushed the governing elites to become more pro-CSR, Kazakhstan only reluctantly joined EITI in June 2005, largely in response to pressures from INGOs, such as the Open Society Institute, and IFIs, such as the World Bank and EBRD (EBRD 2006a, Oil Revenues – Under Public Oversight! 2007,). Moreover, whereas "all extractive industry companies operating in Azerbaijan are engaged in the implementation of the EITI" (Coffey International Development 2009, 2), Kazakhstan's largest FOCs (e.g., TCO and Agip, the operator of the Kashagan project) have been conspicuously absent from the EITI implementation process (Oil Revenues – Under Public Oversight! 2007).[40] In fact, of the 48 companies that were selected for EITI implementation, only 24 fully endorsed the memorandum (Makhmutova 2005).

More broadly, that FOCs in Kazakhstan are not pro-CSR is apparent in their minimal concern for the broader impact of their activities on the local communities where they operate. In contrast to FOCs in Azerbaijan, for example, they have not shown any interest in discussing "what many might regard as the key issues – that is, the spending of oil revenues, the economic and social development of the population at large and transparency – either in this forum [the KPA], or indeed at any other venue involving IOCs [international oil companies] and the government" (Gulbrandsen and Moe 2005, 61). Indeed, according to one company's representative, what really matters when it comes to FOCs' spending is that "the projects [are] beneficial to the akim" (Authors' interview with BG representative no. 2).

Furthermore, in contrast to Azerbaijan, where AIOC has made a concerted effort to hold regular public meetings with local communities, the Karachaganak consortium, for example, has refused to respond to local community concerns that they have both been denied access to basic information

---

[40] However, some of the stakeholders in TCO and Agip KCO have joined EITI individually.

on the field operations and environmental impacts and redress for widespread illnesses among the local population in the village of Berezovka that is situated five kilometers from the field, which according to Kazakhstani law should be free of inhabitants in such close proximity (Authors' interview with Watters). It is even more telling that they have seldom sought to develop any partnerships with INGOs and local NGOs in order to inquire about what would be beneficial for the villagers (ibid.). Thus, their lack of concern for the social impact of their investments has "without a doubt meant that the community that feels the impact the most from their operations has ended up benefiting the least" (ibid.).

IMPLICATIONS

The case of Kazakhstan provides an opportunity not only to test our hypotheses concerning the worst-case scenario under P_2 but also to assess the validity of our claim that, even under the worst-case scenario, P_2 is still preferable to S_2 under the best-case scenario, which we find in Azerbaijan. As the former has already received sufficient attention in this Chapter, here we shift our focus to the latter. It is motivated by the insight that, despite its overall negative impact within the mineral sector when power relations decisively favor the state and FOCs are not pro-CSR, P_2 is more likely to promote taxation and expenditure reform outside the mineral sector. Kazakhstan's experience to date both validates this claim and demonstrates the inherent limitations and dangers of hybrid fiscal regimes when it comes to a mineral rich state's prospects for short- and long-term development.

On the one hand, in the decade since it adopted P_2, Kazakhstan has made notable achievements in fiscal policy compared to Azerbaijan. Alongside the creation of a relatively stable NRF, Kazakhstan's governing elites have managed both to redistribute the benefits of foreign investment from the oil-rich to the oil-poor regions and to institutionalize limits on expenditures, which at least has created the possibility for the government to make better spending decisions. In the educational sphere, for example, this has resulted in the reallocation of funds to support those areas most likely to contribute to human capital formation – primary and secondary education.

On the other hand, Kazakhstan has not been able to fully realize the promise of such reforms. This can largely be attributed to the countervailing effects of its deleterious fiscal policies within the mineral sector. Governing elites have placed less of a priority on achieving viable broad-based tax reform over time, for example, because of their increasing ability to impose a greater fiscal burden on the FOCs. Similarly, the lack of transparency regarding the FOCs' taxation and spending has facilitated politically, rather than economically, motivated allocation decisions. One indicator of this is the increasing level of perceived corruption in Kazakhstan; its CPI score dropped from a high of 3 in 2000 to 2.2 by 2004 and remained roughly at that level through 2008.[41] This

---

[41] For details, see: http://www.transparencykazakhstan.org/eng/content/8.html

is compounded by the fact that the FOCs in Kazakhstan are only weakly committed to the principles of CSR. Among other things, the "hands-off" nature of FOC spending has exacerbated corruption and patronage in the allocation of contracts at the subnational level to such an extent that the oblast akimiyat's own construction department was responsible for administering the largest share of TCOs social projects (Carlson 2009).

Kazakhstan's experience under P_2 also illustrates the tendency for hybrid fiscal regimes to foster an even more pernicious long-term outcome – the development of a proxy state. Particularly in the oil-rich regions, societal actors have come to expect that FOCs will finance the provision of essential public goods and social services. Accordingly, they have increasingly opted to approach the FOCs directly to make requests rather than their local governments. At the same time, the national government's increasing reliance on the FOCs for tax revenue and social expenditures has deprived it of an opportunity to build closer linkages with society via direct taxation as well as its own administrative capacity.

Kazakhstan's decision to change its ownership structure to S_2 in 2005, moreover, has already shown clear signs of both further undermining its prudent fiscal policies and reinforcing its descent into a proxy state. In a few short years since the ratification of its new PSA law that required the reinvigorated NOC – KMG – to hold a 50 percent stake in all new deals, Kazakhstan has both transformed KMG into a source of implicit taxation and spending within the mineral sector and reversed many of its fiscal reforms outside the mineral sector.

KMG has been required not only to supply consumers with subsidized fuel throughout the country but also to sell petroleum products to the agricultural sector at well below market price (Kalyuzhnova and Nygaard 2008, 1832) and subsidize fuel in the domestic market through providing oil to the Atyrau Refinery (Olcott 2007, 41). Similar to SOFAZ in Azerbaijan, KMG is increasingly expected to provide social benefits at the national level that have included sponsoring sports tournaments and constructing swimming pools and stadiums throughout the country.[42] At the same time, since 2006, the government has altered the rules of its NRF in order to transfer more funds into the state budget to allegedly diversify the economy without specifying how the money will actually be spent (ICG 2007, 26).

Outside the mineral sector, the government has dramatically increased government spending in the social sphere and declared its intention to expand the size and role of government. In his 2007 *Address*, for example, Nazarbayev declared that the government would increase salaries of civil and public servants, provide larger child allowances and special state allowances to mothers in large families, and raise the level of the basic pension rate. Since 2006, the Kazakhstani government has also played a much greater role in the economic sphere. Most notably, it has increasingly relied upon two state holding

---

[42] For details, see: http://www.kmg.kz/page.php?page_id=1171&lang=2

companies – Samruk and Kazyna – to implement its "Industrial-Innovation Development Strategy" (EBRD 2006a)[43] and has redirected funding from SME development to support large SOEs (Kalyuzhnova and Nygaard 2009, 8).

This has coincided with an increased reliance on the petroleum sector as a source of revenue and an expansion of FOCs' spending at *both* the subnational and national level. In his March 2006 *Address*, for example, Nazarbaev proposed the establishment of a special department in the Tax Committee of the Ministry of Finance to audit the largest taxpayers (the FOCs). A year later, Prime Minister Karim Masimov announced that the government would carry out an audit of all energy and mineral resources contracts (Nurshayeva 2007). In response, companies such as PetroKazakhstan have acquiesced to signing memorandums of cooperation to provide "constant social support" to local communities – in this case, to Kyzylorda Oblast (Abdykalykov 2007). At the national level, FOCs have been called upon to participate in the country's new development strategy. As Nazarbayev underscored in his 2007 *Address*: "We should insist that our partners working on exploration of Kazakhstan's richest subsoil resources turn to the needs of the country and take active participation in diversifying our economy."

[43] Samruk was created to manage the assets of large SOEs such as KEGOC (the national electricity transmission monopoly), KMG, Kazakhstan Temir Zholy (national railway company), KazPost (national post), and Kazakhtelecom (national telecom operator) (for details, see Kalyuzhnova and Nygaard 2009).

9

Taking Domestic Politics Seriously

Explaining the Structure of Ownership over Mineral Resources

For reasons elaborated upon in Chapter 1, the literature on the resource curse has heretofore viewed ownership structure as a constant rather than a variable. In particular, this literature is characterized by a prevailing assumption that mineral wealth is always and necessarily state-owned and centrally controlled. Consequently, it has not invoked ownership structure as either a possible explanation for the empirical correlation between mineral abundance and a myriad of negative social, political and economic outcomes – poor economic performance, unbalanced growth, impoverished populations, weak states, and authoritarian regimes – or a possible remedy.

Yet the empirical reality is that ownership structure varies considerably both within and across mineral-rich states over time. If one takes a broader and more nuanced view, it becomes clear – at least regarding petroleum-rich states – not only that state ownership is not inevitable but also that it is accompanied by different degrees of state control. We provide such a view in Chapter 1 (see Figure 1.1) based on an original database of ownership structure in petroleum-rich states in the developing world from the late 1800s through 2005 (see Appendix B for details).

The variation in ownership structure over petroleum resources over the course of the twentieth century that we have identified not only bolsters our case for exploring the effects of ownership structure in the preceding chapters, but also demands an explanation. Why has private domestic ownership been so rare for the past century – particularly if we are correct that it offers a way for mineral-rich states to escape the alleged curse of their resource wealth? Conversely, why did private foreign ownership predominate during the first half of the twentieth century, and why did state ownership with and without control predominate during the second half?

Given the temporal trends in the data, the most obvious conclusion might be that this variation is due to international factors – namely, the structure of the international oil market and policy convergence via diffusion. Indeed, these are the standard explanations for the predominance of private foreign ownership during the first half of the twentieth century and its replacement with state ownership during the second half of the twentieth century. As many have argued, the 1960s ushered in a new era for petroleum-rich states in the developing world (see Klapp 1987, Philip 1994, Yergin 1991). Until then, a few major foreign oil companies (known as the "Majors" or the "Seven Sisters" – Royal Dutch Shell, Esso, Mobil, Texaco, Standard Oil of California, British Petroleum, and Gulf) dominated the international oil market, leaving petroleum-rich states little choice but to accept foreign ownership and control over their reserves. The emergence of several independent oil companies (such as Occidental in Libya) that were willing to cede more revenue and managerial control in order to wrest some market share away from the Majors, however, enabled developing countries to design more favorable contracts with foreign investors. This trend, combined with the establishment of the Organization of Petroleum Exporting Countries (OPEC) in 1960, created renewed pressures for policy convergence – albeit this time for nationalization of the petroleum sector. At the same time, international experts encouraged resource-rich states to adopt state ownership, both to gain independence from foreign oil companies (see Cardoso and Faletto 1979) and to better harness their export revenue for domestic economic development (see Baldwin 1966, Hirschman 1958).

Yet, while the leaders of developing countries are undoubtedly subjected to enormous international constraints, they must also contend with some significant constraints at the domestic level. The above arguments are based on the premise that international constraints are more formidable and influential than domestic ones. But there is no a priori reason to assume this. And, in fact, the divergence in petroleum development strategies among the Soviet successor states in the early 1990s directly challenges the presumption that an international environment with similar constraints will lead to policy convergence. As documented in the preceding chapters: for a decade or more following their independence Uzbekistan and Turkmenistan opted for state ownership with control (S_1); Azerbaijan chose state ownership without control (S_2); Russia pursued private domestic ownership (P_1); and Kazakhstan adopted private foreign ownership (P_2).

In contrast, we contend that one cannot understand this variation without taking domestic politics seriously. The conventional wisdom that emphasizes the role of international factors has led us to dismiss the ability of state leaders to make conscious choices, and thereby, to overlook the effect of *domestic* political and economic constraints on their decision-making calculus. More specifically, we argue that leaders in mineral-rich states choose ownership structure based on the interaction between two such constraints: (1) the degree to which they can access alternative revenue sources; and (2) the level of distributional conflict that they face.

Although a few scholars' explanations have invoked domestic-level variables, they are either too deterministic or limited in scope. Sectoralists, for example, argue that the main characteristics of the mineral sector, such as capital intensity and concentration, inevitably lead to state ownership (see

Gelb and Associates 1988, Karl 1997, Shafer 1994). Thus, they cannot account for either domestic or foreign private ownership, both of which have become more popular since the late 1980s. A slightly different version of this argument links resource endowments in general (including labor) to centralized, extractive institutions erected by European colonizers, but then assumes that these institutional legacies persisted (see Acemoglu et al. 2002). Nationalism is another plausible explanation for why countries adopt state ownership (see Klapp 1987), and yet it can explain only a fraction of the variation in ownership structures over the mineral sector across time and space. Nationalist sentiments may be entirely appropriate, for example, to explain Mexico's efforts to nationalize its oil industry after the 1911 Mexican Revolution (although it did not actually do so until 1938) or the nationalization of oil throughout the Middle East following the 1967 Arab – Israeli war. Nationalism does not, however, account for the trend toward private domestic ownership (P_1) and private foreign ownership (P_2) in the late 1980s and early 1990s or, for that matter, the predominance of state ownership without control (S_2) rather than state ownership with control (S_1). If nationalism was indeed the primary motivation behind the change in development strategies in the 1950s and 1960s, then we would expect to find the reverse, given the greater influence of foreign investors under S_2.

The purpose of this chapter is to provide an additional – and much broader – empirical test of our explanation for the variation in ownership structure over the course of the twentieth century. Elsewhere, we test our hypotheses by analyzing the initial choice of ownership structure across the five petroleum-rich Soviet successor states based on our own field research and other primary sources (Jones Luong and Weinthal 2001). Such a test enabled us to hold several factors constant and thus to dismiss the most important alternative explanations for these five cases (see Chapter 1). Here, we explore the external validity of these findings based on an original, cross-sectional dataset that includes all petroleum-rich countries from the dawn of the international petroleum market (that is, roughly the late 1800s) through 2005 based on secondary sources. In short, the results provide strong support for our contention that ownership structure is as much, if not more, a product of domestic constraints as it is international ones.

TAKING DOMESTIC POLITICS SERIOUSLY

Our explanation for the choice of mineral development strategies begins with two basic assumptions. First, we assume that all state leaders are sovereignty maximizers.[1] *Ceteris paribus*, state leaders prefer more rather than less sovereignty, which translates into more rather than less control over their natural resources – both because it can become an important source of revenue and

---

[1] We view sovereignty as equivalent to independent decision-making authority (Thomson 1995).

as a matter of national pride. This is particularly acute in postcolonial states, wherein leaders aim to preserve their recently acquired ability to make independent decisions concerning their natural resource wealth. Accordingly, they will prefer to adopt an ownership structure that grants the state the greatest amount of concentrated authority over both the daily operations of and rents accruing from the mineral sector, and thus, the least amount of uncertainty over capturing these rents. We can thus derive their preference rankings over the available set of policy choices:

1) State ownership with control (S_1)
2) State ownership without control (S_2)
3) Private domestic ownership (P_1)
4) Private foreign ownership (P_2)

These preferences, however, are secondary to their desire to remain in power. This is consistent with the widely accepted assumption that state leaders are concerned primarily with staying in office, and that in order to do so, they must satisfy those interests that support their rule and appease or defeat those that oppose it. In short, they must continue to satisfy their primary constituencies in the status quo. What this entails precisely will vary according to the particular system of patronage and the particular cleavage structure on which patronage is dispensed in a given country. In most developing countries, however, it amounts to incumbents directing a disproportionate share of political and economic benefits toward their supporters. Under the Soviet system, for example, regionalism – or identity with and loyalty to the region in which one studied, worked, and resided – served as the primary basis for the dispensation of political power and economic resources.[2]

Leaders in mineral-rich states, then, will choose a form of ownership structure that enables them to achieve a maximum level of sovereignty over their mineral resources without threatening their continued rule. Put more starkly, they will sacrifice sovereignty to consolidate their power; thus, where they face a trade-off between maximizing sovereignty and consolidating their power, they will opt for the latter.

The ability of such leaders to stay in power is based on the relationship between resources (R) to costs (C), where R is a function of the availability of alternative sources of revenue (that is, other than the development of mineral reserves) and C is a function of the level of distributional conflict that they face (that is, conflict over the basis for dispensing political and economic patronage). The availability of alternative revenue sources determines whether or not the leadership can maintain current levels of domestic spending without exploiting their oil and gas reserves and can range from "high" to "low". We consider this to be "high" when: (1) it has already developed a commodity

---

[2] Patronage networks based on regional affiliation developed over time and became institutionalized in the late 1960s and 1970s under Leonid Brezhnev (Jones Luong 2002).

or product for export that is viable without either immediate or substantial capital investment; and (2) the export of this commodity or product is capable of providing a disproportionate share of total revenue in the status quo. When either of these conditions is not met, it is considered "low". The level of distributional conflict determines the amount of resources that current leaders need to maintain their hold on power. We measure this by recording whether or not: (1) there exists a cleavage structure that could function as a viable alternative to the current basis for dispensing patronage; (2) political parties or social movements based on such an alternative cleavage have emerged and gained some popular support; and (3) these parties or movements have in fact made demands for greater resources, including secessionist attempts or claims for greater autonomy. All three criteria must be met in order for a country to be considered "high"; otherwise it is considered "low".

Simply put, leaders can safely maintain their hold on power when they possess the revenue necessary to dispense the required amount of patronage; that is, when they have sufficient resources (R) to meet their costs (C) in the status quo and these costs are not rising, or their access to alternative revenue sources is "high" and their level of distributional conflict is "low". Because their hold on power is most secure, these leaders face the least constraint on their strategic choices and thus are most likely to adopt their first rank order preference – state ownership with control (S_1). S_1 enables state leaders to maximize their sovereignty over the development of the mineral sector, because it concentrates both managerial decisions and the accumulation of rents in their hands. Yet it also decelerates the development of this sector in comparison, for example, to S_2 and especially P_2 due to the more restricted flow of foreign capital and technology. In adopting this ownership structure, therefore, state leaders forego the more immediate financial rewards they would receive, for example, via extracting large contract bonuses and royalties from foreign investors. Furthermore, as described in Chapter 3, because it affords a minimal role to foreign investors, under S_1 the state also takes on the burden of providing capital investment to the mineral sector, which contributes to the slower pace of exploration and production as well as the development of export capacity. Having the financial resources to maintain their status quo support from the dominant cleavage without the added cost of overcoming a challenge to their rule from a rival cleavage, therefore, affords state leaders the luxury to postpone mineral sector development and the inflow of export rents. Because the dominant cleavage is likely to be closely tied to the sector that provides the state with its alternative source of revenue, the state actually incurs less political risk by postponing mineral sector development.

In Uzbekistan, for example, substantial revenue from cotton exports for the first decade following independence, alongside the persistence of regionally based patronage networks, meant that state leaders felt no pressing need to develop petroleum reserves, and thus could adopt S_1. Uzbekistan provided the bulk of the Soviet Union's cotton supply and, at independence, easily became the world's fourth-largest producer of cotton (World Bank 1993c).[3] It also experienced a low level of distributional conflict since no alternatives emerged to challenge regionalism as the basis for political and economic patronage (Jones Luong 2002). Moreover, a gradual approach to petroleum sector development ensured the continued economic dominance of the cotton sector, which is integrally tied to the regionally based patronage system. Under the Soviet system, cotton production served as the crucial economic and political link between republic-level and regional-level elites on the one hand, and between regional elites and their local constituencies on the other (Weinthal 2002). In fact, for this very reason, government officials in the 1990s were convinced that it behooved them *not* to actively pursue the development of the petroleum reserves because it would have been potentially destabilizing (Authors' interviews with Saifulin and Fazilova). They pointed, for example, to the strong resistance they encountered from both the Ministry of Agriculture and governors of cotton-producing regions after independence (ibid).

State leaders' power becomes threatened when R decreases relative to C, C increases relative to R, or both occur simultaneously. Under any of these scenarios, state leaders' ability to choose their preferred form of ownership structure is constrained because they must generate additional resources with which to consolidate their power, and hence face a more pressing need to utilize their mineral wealth in order to do so. Yet how they utilize their mineral wealth – that is, which form of ownership structure they choose – will vary according to the degree and form of this pressure, which depends on the interaction between the degree of access to alternative revenue sources and the level of distributional conflict. These hypothesized relationships are summarized in Table 9.1.

State leaders feel most pressured to develop their mineral reserves when they have insufficient resources (R) to meet their costs (C) in the status quo and these costs are rising; in other words, their access to alternative revenue sources is "low" and their level of distributional conflict is "high". In addition to a contraction in resources, they face domestic pressures to generate revenue

TABLE 9.1. *Domestic Determinants of Ownership Structure*

		Level of Distributional Conflict	
		LOW	HIGH
Degree of Alternative Revenue	HIGH	S_1	P_1
	LOW	S_2	P_2

---

[3] Uzbekistan's cotton sector produced more than 65 percent of its gross output, consumed 60 percent of all resources, and employed approximately 40 percent of the labor force in the mid-1980s. It also accounted for about two-thirds of all cotton produced in the Soviet Union (Rumer 1989, 62).

immediately so as to both maintain status quo support from the dominant cleavage and diffuse a potent challenge to their continued rule. Because their hold on power is the least secure, these leaders face the greatest constraint on their strategic choices and thus are most likely to adopt their last rank order preference – private foreign ownership (P_2). Adopting P_2 minimizes central state leaders' sovereignty over the development of the mineral sector because, as described in Chapter 6, it transfers full decision-making authority to foreign private companies with their headquarters located abroad. Particularly where mineral wealth is dispersed geographically, it also increases the potential for subnational leaders to assert more regulatory control over this sector. And yet, this ownership structure maximizes central state leaders' ability to consolidate their power because it enables them to quickly gain access to the revenue they desperately need. Lured by the wide-ranging concession contracts that characterize P_2, foreign investors will not only pay the purchase price for shares in the mineral sector upfront but also offer huge royalties before the production process even begins and then slowly recover their costs.[4] The immediate access to a sizeable amount of cash, in short, enables state leaders not only to bolster their existing support base, but also to appease or defeat potential opponents from an emerging cleavage. At the same time, the threat to their continued rule posed by an acute lack of resources to meet their rising costs outweighs any political risk that incumbents might incur from the rapid and decentralized development of the mineral sector. In fact, by severing the direct link between these economic resources and the central state, privatization to foreign investors also provides incumbents with the means to establish their economic independence from the dominant cleavage, if they so choose, while preventing their opponents from gaining control over this lucrative resource.

In contrast to Uzbekistan, for the first decade after independence, state leaders in Kazakhstan faced both a low degree of alternative revenue and a high level of distributional conflict. At independence, Kazakhstan did not produce either an agricultural crop or manufactured good that could provide a viable alternative to petroleum as a primary source of export revenue. Agricultural products in the early 1990s, for example, accounted for only between 8 and 10 percent of total export revenues, ranking far behind projected income from petroleum exports (World Bank 1994a, 20, 1993b, 106). Also at this time, the country witnessed the emergence of several social movements and political parties based on nationality that explicitly challenged the continuation of its regionally based patronage system (see Jones Luong 2002 for details). Some Russian "nationalist" parties and movements, for example, called for the annexation of Kazakhstan's northern and eastern oblasts to Russia, or demanded outright secession; others claimed

---

[4] As foreign investors recover their costs through "cost oil," governments receive greater amounts of "profit oil" over time.

their right to greater political and economic autonomy within Kazakhstan. Meanwhile, Kazakh "nationalist" parties and movements called for greater linguistic and institutional privileges for Kazakhs, such as elevating the status of the Kazakh language over Russian and filling governmental posts with Kazakhs. Government officials thus felt immense pressure to utilize their mineral sector in order to generate sufficient resources to simultaneously bolster regionalism and adequately respond to new claims on state resources, and thus opted for P_2. A substantial amount of the funds generated from selling off their highly coveted petroleum reserves to foreign investors was used to counter nationalist forces, for example, by financing the construction of a new capital in Astana in order to block secessionist movements in the Russian-dominated North and East (Jones Luong 2000b). At the same time, by decentralizing managerial control over the petroleum sector, Kazakhstan's central government deliberately empowered subnational leaders in the oil-rich regions, giving them a continued stake in the regionally based distribution of benefits (ibid).

In between these two extremes – that is, where the degree of alternative revenue and the level of distributional conflict are either both "low" or both "high" – state leaders face a moderate degree of constraint. While the degree of pressure they face is roughly the same, the type of pressure they face is not. Where their access to alternative revenue sources and their level of distributional conflict are both "low," the source of this pressure is the lack of sufficient resources to meet current costs (that is, a decrease in R relative to C). In other words, incumbents are secure in their support base but not their revenue base. State leaders who want to consolidate their power, then, have a strong incentive to utilize their mineral resources to generate resources to bolster their existing support base. They are thus most likely to adopt their second most preferred policy outcome – state ownership without control (S_2). S_2 allows leaders to reap large and immediate benefits from the development of the mineral sector, albeit not on the same scale as under P_2, while also retaining a relatively high degree of sovereignty. Because their revenue needs are neither as large or as acute as state leaders (described above) who face both a decrease in R relative to C and an increase in C relative to R, these leaders can safely forego the larger upfront cash payments that privatization to foreign investors would yield in exchange for exercising more decision-making authority over exploration, production, and exports. At the same time, because they do not face a challenge from an emerging cleavage, there is no risk in developing the mineral sector. Nor is there any need to fear that opponents will capture the state and gain control of these resources. On the contrary, by concentrating the immediate rents accrued from foreign investment in the central government's hands, S_2 provides them with the easiest way to ensure that the benefits of mineral sector development are directed toward their supporters, whether these rents serve to reinforce existing political and economic ties or to create a new basis for cementing ties between the incumbent regime and the dominant cleavage.

Azerbaijan shares with Kazakhstan a low degree of alternative revenue and with Uzbekistan a low level of distributional conflict in the first decade after independence. Aside from oil, Azerbaijan contributed little to the Soviet economy, and after independence, both its small agricultural and industrial sectors required large capital investments and significant restructuring before either could compete on the world market (see Hoffman 2000b).[5] These economic problems were compounded by a prolonged war with neighboring Armenia, which caused a virtual halt in production and drained any potential investment revenue. Yet Azerbaijan's leadership did not face any direct or significant challenges to regionalism as the basis for political and economic patronage. While it did witness the emergence of a Popular Front that called for revitalizing the Azeri language and a secessionist movement in the Armenian enclave of Nagorno-Karabakh in the late 1980s, neither one competed with or threatened regionalism. President Heydar Aliev, who ruled the country from 1993 to 2003, continued to draw his primary support from his "regional 'tribe' composed of Azeris from Armenia (Yeraz) and the Azerbaijani enclave of Nakhichevan"(Hoffman 2000b, 15) as well as several semidemocratic movements based on regional affiliation (see Curtis 1995). Moreover, similar to cotton in Uzbekistan, oil production has historically been closely intertwined with political and economic influence in Azerbaijan such that the regional group that controls the oil also controls the state (see Hoffman 2000b). S_2 was thus the optimal strategy for the country's leaders because it required them to give up only a minimal amount of sovereignty over the mineral sector while both ensuring that traditional regionally based patronage networks were not disrupted and providing the central government with the financial means to continue to dispense political and economic rewards accordingly.

Where their access to alternative revenue sources and their level of distributional conflict are both "high," the pressure that state leaders feel to develop their mineral resources stems from an increase in C relative to R. In other words, incumbents are secure in their revenue base but not in their support base. State leaders who want to consolidate their power, then, have a strong incentive to utilize their mineral sector to generate resources to appease or defeat opponents from an emerging cleavage. Yet they must do so in such a way that does not undermine the dominant cleavage that provides their primary base of support. They are thus most likely to adopt their third most preferred policy outcome – private domestic ownership (P_1) – because it enables them to accomplish both. On the one hand, by selling off the mineral sector to their primary supporters, incumbents ensure not only their continued support but also that these resources will not fall into the hands of their opponents if, in fact, they succeed in capturing the state. On the other hand, by selling off the mineral sector to those who are challenging the dominant cleavage in exchange for their support, state leaders can silence some of its otherwise most

---

[5] Its primary agricultural product since the 1970s was grapes, the production of which declined dramatically in the 1980s under Gorbachev's antialcoholism campaigns.

vocal opponents. Excluding foreign investors from the bidding process greatly facilitates both of these strategies because it affords incumbents the luxury to handpick the beneficiaries of privatization by enabling them to price these lucrative assets well below their market value.

Like Uzbekistan, Russia inherited a high degree of alternative revenue; yet, like Kazakhstan, with independence from Soviet rule came a high level of distributional conflict. In the late 1980s, Russia alone accounted for more than half of the Soviet Union's total industrial output, which included the largest republican production volume of metallurgy, machinery, chemicals, and construction materials, as well as fuels and electric power (Kaufman and Hardt 1993, 91). Due to its sheer size and diversity, this sector alone served as a viable source of additional revenue from exports following the Soviet Union's collapse (see Dabrowski and Antczak 1996). Indeed, although Russia's industrial production fell sharply in the first few years after independence, its exports of metals, chemicals, and other manufactured goods to non-CIS countries grew dramatically after 1993 (see Ofer 1999). By 1994, metals and chemicals alone made up approximately 40 percent of all non-CIS exports – nearly the same percentage as mineral products (Goskomstat 1996). At the same time, Russia's leaders were confronted with two types of challenges. The first came from the emergence of separatist groups that launched a drive for secession or greater autonomy based on ethnic and territorial claims (see Gorenburg 1999). Many such movements, moreover, were in those areas that possess significant oil and gas reserves, such as the Republics of Bashkortostan, Chechnya, Komi, and Tatarstan, Tyumen Oblast, and Khanty-Mansi Autonomous Okrug, wherein regional- and district-level governments demanded a greater degree of control over these reserves and used their petroleum wealth as a basis for threatening secession (see Rutland 1997, 13). The second stemmed from the Communists' continued control over the national legislature (Russian Duma) following independence until it was disbanded in September 1993, triggering a state of emergency (for details, see Remington 2001, Chapter 4).

Under these conditions, P_1 was the optimal strategy because it allowed the Russian government under President Boris Yeltsin to effectively address both of these challenges. On the one hand, Yeltsin could reward its closest supporters and thwart the Communists' attempts to reassert influence over the economy by transferring ownership and control over the country's petroleum wealth to neoliberal "insiders." Indeed, the very absence of foreign competition for the purchase of previously state-owned shares in oil and gas enterprises, not to mention the lack of transparency in this process, enabled the central government to do so, despite limited domestic capital, because petroleum reserves could be significantly undervalued. On the other hand, Yeltsin could reinforce the dominant cleavage by providing nationalist regional governors with greater control over their petroleum reserves. The central state's divestiture in the petroleum sector made it possible for the central government to transfer ownership to regional governments, and thus, to guarantee them privileged access to revenue from oil production within and export from the territory under their administration. In short, although foreign involvement would have undoubtedly increased the selling price of Russia's oil and gas industry and improved its productive capacity through the immediate introduction of new technologies, state leaders opted to forgo a greater financial payoff for political gain.

EXPLAINING OWNERSHIP STRUCTURE IN
PETROLEUM-RICH COUNTRIES

Elsewhere, we test the propositions developed in the preceding section by analyzing the initial choice of ownership structure across the five petroleum-rich Soviet successor states based on our own field research and other primary sources (Jones Luong and Weinthal 2001). While this provides compelling evidence to support our claim that ownership structure is the product of the interaction between the degree of alternative revenue and the level of distributional conflict that state leaders face, it is not a sufficient test of our hypotheses. First and foremost, despite the fact that these five states share several important similarities, they do not allow us to adequately control for all the alternative explanations. For example, because Azerbaijan, Kazakhstan, Russia, Turkmenistan, and Uzbekistan chose their respective ownership structure within the same international context, we can control for the influence of the international environment and diffusion for these five cases, but not beyond. A more robust test requires looking across various types of international environments. It may be, for example, that the post-Cold War context is fundamentally different from other historical periods because it promotes policy divergence whereas other contexts (such as the period just after OPEC is founded) are more likely to promote convergence. Second, while the small number of cases is conducive to establishing a high degree of *internal* validity for our argument through the use of field research, other primary sources, and careful process tracing, it is not very helpful in establishing *external* validity. In order to address such concerns, we constructed an original, cross-sectional dataset that includes the universe of cases – that is, all petroleum-rich countries in the developing world from the time they first adopted an ownership structure over their petroleum sector through 2005 – based on secondary sources. We present our empirical results in the following sections.

The Dataset

To claim that our dataset includes the universe of cases, of course, demands some clarification, since which countries are included depends on both what constitutes a "petroleum-rich country" and what determines when a country first adopts an ownership structure vis-à-vis petroleum, or its "initial development strategy."

The standard and largely uncontested measure for petroleum (as well as mineral) wealth is exports as a percentage of total exports and government revenue. Once countries reach the 40 percent benchmark – that is, once oil (or any other mineral) makes up 40 percent or more of either their total exports or total government revenues – they are deemed "resource rich." We do not use this measure, in short, because it conflates resource abundance with resource dependence. Yet, the two are distinct – the former is pure chance while the latter is a policy outcome. Treating them otherwise creates an inherent bias toward the presumption that there is a "resource curse," since analytically most problems associated with resource wealth actually stem from the hegemony of the mineral sector and its consequent influence on a given country's economy and political system (see Chapter 10 for details). This, in turn, limits the number of cases and precludes the incorporation of developed countries alongside developing ones. As a result, there are automatically less "exceptions" or "success stories" in most databases of mineral-rich countries.

We use a measure of "petroleum-rich" that deliberately distinguishes *wealth* from *dependence*. Thus, our database includes a country based on the size of its estimated petroleum reserves over time relative to other countries with estimated petroleum reserves.[6] In order to do this, we created three different lists utilizing the *Oil and Gas Journal Database*[7]: (1) country's position from averaging world rankings; (2) country's position from averaging quantities; and (3) country's position from weighting quantities.[8] (See Appendix D for details.) We then included those developing countries that were within the top 50 on two of these three lists. This enabled us to include several countries that are not usually considered petroleum-rich because they are not oil dependent, as well as to exclude countries that are usually considered petroleum-rich solely because of their dependence on oil. We used estimated rather than proven reserves so as *not* to exclude those cases in which reserves might be sizable but little exploration has been undertaken. We also do this in order to avoid privileging any one form of ownership structure. For example, it allows us to separate the level of exploration, which is often highly correlated with the level of foreign involvement, from our measure of resource wealth.

---

[6] We considered using the average size of reserves per capita based on DOE estimates, but decided against this for two reasons: (1) these data are only available from 1980, thus biasing our sample towards the latter half of the 20th century, and (2) during this period, population growth rates skyrocketed, thus biasing our sample toward countries with lower than average population growth. For example, by this criterion, Nigeria, Indonesia, and China would be considered petroleum-poor while Belarus, Chile, and New Zealand would be considered petroleum-rich.

[7] This database is preferable to the other available sources, including the Department of Energy (DOE) database, because it extends the furthest back historically (to 1952) and is widely accepted in the industry as authoritative.

[8] The averages either by reserve or rank are simple averages. The weighted averages take into account that fact that different countries discovered their oil at different times and hence the numbers of years that we use to average them are different. Thus, the number of years is used as a weight.

As described in Chapter 1, we disaggregate the dependent variable (that is, ownership structure) into four discrete categories – state ownership with control (S_1), state ownership without control (S_2), private domestic ownership (P_1), and private foreign ownership (P_2) – in order to capture the variation in both ownership rights over petroleum resources and the actual locus of decision-making power over the development and export of these resources. To code each country's ownership structure, we rely on their respective constitutions, official laws and regulations governing the mineral sector, and (where available) mineral contracts between the state and corporate entities (foreign and domestic) operating in the petroleum sector.

But how do we determine when a country first chooses ownership structure over their petroleum resources – that is, its initial development strategy? In other words, what determines the start date for each country included in the dataset? Considering the fact that many of these countries were under colonial rule when they began to explore for petroleum, first discovered their wealth, or both, this is not always self-evident. It often requires deeper probing than simply recognizing the first mineral sector law adopted after gaining independence, which might also have the disadvantage of privileging path dependency as an explanation. Indonesia – where the Dutch had produced oil since the founding of the Royal Dutch Company in 1890 – is a prime example. Although Indonesia officially became independent in 1949[9] and then maintained existing concessions until they expired by the mid-1950s, President Sukarno did not sign a new oil and mining law establishing state ownership without control until 1960 (Carlson 1977, 11–12).[10] There might also be a lag between independence and the adoption of an initial development strategy due, for example, to the exigencies of civil war, as was the case in Angola.[11] Determining the starting point for those countries that were not colonies when they either began to explore for petroleum or first discovered their wealth can also be tricky. In many of these cases (such as Argentina, Peru, and Venezuela), states had broad laws governing concessions that were never intended to apply to petroleum (see Lieuwen 1954, Thompson 1921, Wilkins 1974). In others (such as Brazil, Ecuador, and Equatorial Guinea), no laws were actually formulated, but licenses for petroleum exploration were issued and then remained inactive for years and sometimes decades (see Bates 1975, Frynas 2004, and Martz 1987).

To address these issues, we determine a country's initial development strategy vis-à-vis petroleum based on two criteria: the decision must be made both independently and deliberately. In other words, countries must be free of direct external interference in their policymaking process, and their leaders must be

---

[9] Indonesia claimed independence from the Dutch in 1945, but sovereignty was not transferred until 1949.

[10] Sukarno appointed a commission to draft an oil and mining law in 1951 (ibid.).

[11] Angola became independent in 1975, but did not have an oil development strategy (S_2) until 1978.

conscious that they are, in fact, instituting such a policy. A key indicator of the latter, for example, is that when concessions are issued, they are actually monitored and there is some penalty for inactivity after a certain period of time. This criterion also applies to a change in strategy (that is, in ownership structure). At the same time, we want to avoid conflating a policy that is made deliberately with one that is immediately or successfully implemented.[12] Amending the constitution or passing a new law that signals the intent to alter current policy toward establishing one of the other three possible ownership structures, therefore, is sufficient to be considered a change in strategy. For example, we code 1951 as a change from P_2 to S_1 in Iran because the parliament, under the guidance of newly-appointed Prime Minister Muhammad Mosaddeq, passed legislation that nationalized the country's petroleum reserves – even though the Iranian government could never fully enforce this legislation (see Daniel 2001, 150–1). Similarly, Mexico declared nationalization of its petroleum reserves in 1938, but it was not until 1951 that the state oil company (Petromex) was able to acquire the properties of the last foreign company (Gulf Oil Co.) still in operation (Meyer and Morales 1990).

The criteria for coding our main explanatory variables – the degree of alternative revenue and the level of distributional conflict – in the dataset are the same as the criteria we outlined in the previous section. Both are dummy variables, receiving a value of "1" for "high" and "0" for low. The degree of alternative revenue is coded "high" (that is, given a value of "1") if: (a) it has already developed a commodity or product for export that is viable without either immediate or substantial capital investment; and (b) the export of this commodity or product is capable of providing a disproportionate share of total revenue in the status quo. The level of distributional conflict is coded as "high" (that is, given a value of "1") if: (a) there exists a cleavage structure that could function as a viable alternative to the current basis for dispensing patronage; (b) political parties or social movements based on such an alternative cleavage have emerged and gained popular support; and (c) these parties or movements have, in fact, made demands for a larger share of resources, including secessionist attempts or claims for greater autonomy. In all other cases, both variables are coded "low" (that is, given a value of "0").

In coding both variables, we rely on secondary rather than primary sources and make inferences where there was insufficient information or hard data was simply not available. Where we needed information regarding export potential at the end of the nineteenth or beginning of the twentieth century, for example, we could not rely on standardized indicators or data-gathering institutions (such as the IMF and World Bank), so we had to rely upon country data that was often based on self-reporting and given in local currencies, as documented by historians. Nonetheless, we made every effort to apply these

---

[12] In other words, we are interested in explaining leaders' *choice* of ownership structure, rather than their ability to enforce this decision.

TABLE 9.2. *Control Variables*

Alternative Explanation	Control Variable	Source(s)
Diffusion		
⇨ International	Dummy for whether adopted strategy before or after the formation of OPEC	Authors' original case studies
⇨ Regional	Two dummies: one for whether or not located in the MENA and one for whether or not in Latin America	N/A
International market conditions		
⇨ Oil price	Oil price	WTRG Economics (www.wtrg.com)
⇨ Technology and Difficulty of extraction	Oil price	
Path dependency		
⇨ Colonialism	Dummy for whether or not a former colony	Authors' original case studies
⇨ Policy inertia	Previous ownership structure	N/A
Economic development strategy	Dummy for whether or not pursued a "statist" economic development strategy	Authors' original case studies
Regime type	Normalized Index from 0 to 1	Polity IV Project dataset (2008)

criteria consistently across cases and across time. To ensure that our data was as accurate as possible, we cross-checked it with several secondary sources (when available) rather than relying on any one source. Our efforts resulted in 50 separate original "case studies" – one for each country included in the dataset.

To take into account the most salient alternative explanations, we included eight different control variables. (See Table 9.2 for a summary.) Three of these serve as proxies for international level explanations: (1) international demonstration effect, (2) regional demonstration effect, and (3) international market conditions. The remaining five are designed to capture explanations that emphasize path dependence, the country's overall economic development strategy, and regime type, respectively. In each case, we attempted to code the variable so as to most accurately represent the explanation within the constraints of doing regression analysis with a relatively modest sample size (n=2449). Some details concerning our rationale for including and coding each control variable follow.

International Diffusion Effect (OPEC)

To control for the role of policy diffusion at the international level, we created a dummy variable that assigns countries a value of "0" if they adopted an initial development strategy *before* the formulation of OPEC in 1960 and "1" if they did so *after* the formulation of OPEC. This serves as a good proxy for two related arguments that are often found (implicitly or explicitly) in the literature: first, that OPEC emboldened developing countries to nationalize their petroleum resources; and second, that state ownership is more prominent in the second half of the twentieth century, whereas private foreign ownership is more prominent in the first half, because power shifted away from the foreign oil companies and toward the oil-exporting countries (see, Morse 1999, Tanzer 1969, Vernon 1971).[13] Another possible way to capture policy diffusion would have been to use the number of years between a given country's first strategy and that of the country that most recently adopted its first strategy before this particular country. But the temporal gap between the two countries' strategies would indicate the *level* of international policy diffusion and not the *effect* per se.

Regional Diffusion Effect

Policy diffusion occurs not only at the international level but also at the regional level. And, in fact, a more compelling case can be made for a regional demonstration effect – particularly when it comes to foreign investment strategies and privatization (see Brune and Garrett 2002). Therefore, we also include a control for regional demonstration effect. Each country was assigned to one of six regions: Africa, Asia, Europe, Latin and South America, the Middle East and North Africa (MENA), and North America. This index was then broken into three dummy variables: one for the MENA countries; one for Latin America; and one for everything else. We use the MENA and Latin America dummies in all the regressions because these are the two regions in which we see the strongest evidence of regional policy diffusion.

International Market Conditions (Oil Price)

There are two features of the international marketplace for petroleum that are presumed to have an effect on ownership structure and, perhaps not surprisingly, they are closely related: the price of oil and the availability of technology. There are also two lines of argument concerning how each of these features affects state versus private (foreign) ownership. On the one hand, higher oil prices enable countries to nationalize or maintain state ownership over their oil resources – not only because the increased demand gives them greater leverage over foreign oil companies, but also because they can make the necessary investments (including purchasing advanced technology) without direct foreign involvement (see Friedman 2006, Philip 1994). On the other hand, high oil prices are thought to signal that world oil supply has peaked, and hence the

---

[13] The founding of OPEC is viewed as emblematic of this power shift.

need to develop more difficult fields that require the very technology to which only foreign oil companies have access, thus forcing petroleum-rich countries to relinquish greater control to foreign investors (see Yergin 2006).[14] Given the close relationship between the price of oil and technology, we use the variable *Oil Price* (in 2005 US dollars) to control for both.[15] In addition, oil price can serve as a proxy for the difficulty of extraction because, as the price of oil rises, so does the incentive to develop more problematic oil fields.

Path Dependency (Colony and Ownership Structure t-1)

Another probable alternative explanation is that ownership structure is path dependent. A country's initial development strategy, in particular, is likely to be influenced greatly by the colonial (or pre-independence) strategy. Since all colonial governments imposed the same ownership structure on their petroleum-rich subjects – private foreign ownership (P_2) – to control for this, we include a simple dummy variable *Colony* that takes on a value of "1" if the country in question was a former colony and "0" if it was not.[16] This variable also helps to control for the constraints imposed by colonial economic structures. To take into account the argument that policies and institutions, like ownership structure, are reticent to change (or "sticky") more generally (see Pierson 2000, Thelen 1999), we also include a lag of the dependent variable (Ownership Structure t-1).[17]

Economic Development Strategy

Ownership structure might also be determined by the country's general economic development strategy. We would expect, for example, that countries that adopt a statist economic policy would also want to nationalize the petroleum sector – either because it is consistent with their ideology of state-led development or because it is deemed necessary to fuel (quite literally) industrial growth. This variable is also a dummy, for which a value of "1" indicates that the country had a statist economic development strategy and a value of "0" indicates that the country did not have a statist economic development strategy. In coding this variable, we used whether a country's government

---

[14] This line of argument is premised on the worldview (based on Hubbert's 1956 prediction of "peak oil") that there is only very limited potential oil remaining and that this oil is much more expensive to exploit.

[15] This was widely suggested by experts we consulted at the DOE. We feel justified in doing this, moreover, because technology has actually changed very little whereas oil price has fluctuated widely. The technology that is used to conduct seismic surveys and drill offshore wells, for example, has been around since the 1960s and 1970s.

[16] Protectorates and mandates were treated as former colonies. North and South Yemen were treated as former colonies, but not unified Yemen.

[17] Including the lagged dependent variable also has an econometric rational; it enables us to control for serial correlation. Previously, we also included a variable (*Continuous Years*) to capture the effect of the number of years that a given country has had a particular ownership structure in place but omitted it because we were effectively "overcontrolling" for path dependency.

adopted import substitution industrialization policies (ISI) as an initial proxy for a statist economic development strategy but also considered whether it nationalized major parts of the economy outside the petroleum sector. Since adopting ISI is highly correlated with having a closed economy, we then cross-checked our codings with an updated and expanded version of Sachs and Warners (1995) trade liberalization data (Wacziarg and Horn Welch 2008). However, they are not equivalent. Governments can engage in state-led development strategies without either adopting ISI or closing their economies. They can also continue to engage in state-led development after disbanding ISI and opening their economies, to which the examples of the East Asian "tigers" clearly attest. Indeed, because we are most interested in testing whether a statist *ideology* is driving the decisions to adopt state versus private ownership over petroleum reserves, we also coded countries in which governments espouse state-led development as "statist."

Regime Type (Polity)

Finally, we control for regime type by including a continuous variable based on the Polity IV (2008) dataset.[18] There are two main reasons for doing so. First, authoritarian regimes may be better positioned to impose state ownership and centralize control over mineral reserves, assuming they have much lower levels of transparency and accountability. Second, one of our two main explanatory variables – distributional conflict – might be highly correlated with regime type. It is widely accepted, for example, that democracies are likely to experience higher levels of popular mobilization.

The Model and Results

We estimate the following model to test our hypotheses concerning the impact of alternative sources of export revenue and distributional conflict on ownership structure, using ordinary least squares (OLS) regression. Following Angrist and Pischke (2008), we estimate the coefficients with OLS because it offers the most efficient estimators and it allows for more intuitive interpretations than non-linear models.[19]

$$OS_{i,t} = \alpha + \beta_1 * Alt\,Re\,venue_{i,t} + \beta_2 * DistrConflict_{i,t} + \beta_3 * OS_{i,t-1} + \beta_4 * OPEC_{i,t} +$$
$$\beta_5 * EconomicDevelopmentStrategy_{i,t-1} + \beta_6 * Polity_{i,t-1} + \beta_7 * MENA_i +$$
$$\beta_8 * LatinAmerica_i + \beta_9 * Oil\,Pr\,ice_{i,t-1} + \beta_{10} * Colony_i + \epsilon_{i,t}$$

---

[18] Polity rates countries on a scale from -10 (most authoritarian) to +10 (most democratic). To preserve the information this scale provides while avoiding the difficulty in interpreting negative numbers, we created a normalized index from 0 to 1.

[19] Because our dependent variable is categorical with ordered properties, we are expected to run a multinomial and ordinal logistic regression. Following this expectation and also for robustness checks, we also estimate the coefficients using both mlogit and oprobit. The results confirm our findings using OLS (available upon request).

TABLE 9.3. *Descriptive Statistics*

	Range	Mean	Standard deviation
Ownership structure	0–3	1.439	1.294
Alternative revenue	0–1	0.412	0.492
Distributional conflict	0–1	0.451	0.498
International diffusion effect (OPEC)	0–1	0.664	0.472
Economic development strategy	0–1	0.600	0.490
Polity	0–1	0.341	0.307
Dummy Middle East	0–1	0.280	0.449
Dummy Latin America	0–1	0.381	0.486
Oil price	7.05–70.07	22.876	13.009
Colony	0–1	0.741	0.438

Overall, the results from this model specification lend strong statistical support to our main contention that domestic factors have equal if not greater influence on the choice of ownership structure in mineral-rich states – at least for the case of petroleum. In particular, we find that our two primary variables of interest – degree of alternative revenue and level of distributional conflict – are consistently in the right direction and statistically significant. They also appear to have a stronger effect than all of the alternative explanations, with the exception of path dependency. (For descriptive statistics, see Table 9.3.)

Let's begin with the second linear model (OLS (2)). Here, it is clear that whether or not we include fixed effects (OLS (3)),[20] the results are consistent with our expectations: first, that politicians are more likely to adopt their preferred ownership structure, S_1, when they face a "high" degree of alternative revenue and a "low" level of distributional conflict (and visa-versa); and second, that these two domestic factors are at least as important as – if not more important than – international factors in predicting which ownership structure a country will adopt. (See Table 9.4 for details.) A change in the degree of alternative revenue from low to high implies a change in the direction of state ownership; that is, that under these conditions politicians are more likely to choose S_1. Conversely, a change in the level of distributional conflict from low to high implies a change in the direction of private ownership; that is, that under these conditions politicians are more likely to choose P_2. While the

[20] Because they are highly correlated, we do not include the lagged dependent variable and fixed effects in the same model. See Angrist and Pischke (2008, 127–9) for details.

TABLE 9.4. *OLS Estimates*

Dependent variable: Ownership structure

	(1)	(2)	(3)
	OLS	OLS	OLS
Alternative revenue	-0.113***	-0.088***	-0.076***
	(0.302)	(0.020)	(0.022)
Distributional conflict	1.528***	0.117***	0.125***
	(0.294)	(0.023)	(0.028)
Ownership structure (t-1)		0.933***	0.911***
		(0.011)	(0.016)
International diffusion	0.061	-0.047***	-0.082***
effect (OPEC)	0.333	(0.017)	(0.026)
Economic development	-0.169	-0.016	-0.029
strategy (t-1)	(0.332)	(0.015)	(0.020)
Polity (t-1)	-0.481	-0.028	0.019
	(0.342)	(0.029)	(0.037)
Dummy Middle East		-0.027	
		(0.017)	
Dummy Latin America		0.013	
		(0.019)	
Oil price (t-1)	-0.020**	0.00003	-0.0002
	(0.007)	(0.0004)	(0.0004)
Colony	0.480	-0.004	0.130***
	(0.325)	(0.017)	(0.046)
Constant	1.488	0.123	0.066
	(0.629)	(0.033)	(0.027)
Country fixed effects	No	No	Yes
R-squared	0.503	0.942	0.940
Number of Countries	48	50	50
Number of Observations	48	2449	2449

Note: Robust standard errors in parentheses:** significant at 5 percent; *** significant at 1 percent.

size of the coefficients for both alternative revenue and distributional conflict indicates that the magnitude of the effect is not quantitatively large,[21] when we test the joint hypothesis that both of these variables are equal to zero we are given a value such that we can reject the hypothesis that they are not important in the model.

Only two other variables in the model are statistically significant – one that captures the effects of path dependency and the other that captures the effects

---

[21] In other words, the coefficient for alternative revenue suggests that a change from low to high will only affect a change in ownership structure by 10 percent.

of international policy diffusion. The magnitudes of their effects, however, are very different. A country's previous ownership structure clearly has the largest effect on leaders' subsequent policy choices, while whether a country adopts its ownership structure before or after the foundation of OPEC has the smallest effect on whether its leaders choose to adopt state versus private ownership. That the effect of previous ownership structure is so strong is neither entirely unexpected nor unwelcome. Indeed, our first instinct was that it made the most sense to look at country's initial development strategy vis-à-vis petroleum not merely because policies and institutions in general tend to be "sticky," but more so because we found empirical evidence to support this in the specific case of ownership structure over petroleum reserves. The global pattern we identify suggests that countries seldom change their ownership structure; there are often not just several years but several decades between such a policy change.

The fact that our two variables of interest are nonetheless important in the model, however, gives us good reason to believe that path dependency alone is not a sufficient explanation for the variation in ownership structure we document across time and space. Moreover, as the first linear model in the table (OLS (1)) illustrates, when we limit the dependent variable to the initial choice of ownership structure, not only are our two main explanatory variables the only significant ones but also the magnitude of the effect for both of these variables increases considerably.

IMPLICATIONS

The preceding chapters are dedicated to formulating and testing our argument that mineral-rich states are "cursed" not by their wealth per se, but by the structure of ownership they choose to manage their mineral wealth. In this chapter, we shift focus to the prior question of where ownership structure itself comes from. We offer an alternative explanation for the variation in ownership structure over petroleum wealth over the course of the twentieth century that emphasizes the role of agency and domestic conditions. We then utilize an original cross-sectional dataset that includes all petroleum-rich countries in the developing world from the late 1800s through 2005 to test our explanation against competing hypotheses. As such, this chapter serves two crucial purposes: first, to demonstrate that ownership structure is not endogenous to fiscal regimes; and second, to add further credibility to our central claim that ownership structure cannot be taken for granted across time and space, but rather, must be treated as a variable in our analysis of the development prospects for mineral-rich states.

In sum, we find robust empirical support for our hypothesis that the interaction between the degree of alternative export potential and the level of distributional conflict influences the choice of ownership structure in mineral-rich states. This explanation also departs from the conventional resource curse literature in several ways.

By elevating the role of the domestic political economy in influencing a developing country's choice over how (and indeed, whether) to develop its mineral wealth, we challenge both the popular notions that international pressures necessarily trump domestic ones, and that these countries have little or no choice when it comes to managing their mineral wealth. The two are integrally linked because the emphasis on factors at the international level is based on the perception that such pressures are so strong that they are in fact determinative. Yet our findings suggest that the global trends we have witnessed in the structure of ownership over time may be more accurately attributed to the coincidence of domestic processes across mineral-rich countries than to international pressures for policy convergence.

Assigning sufficient causal weight to domestic politics when it comes to governing elites' decision-making calculus also gives agency to leaders of mineral-rich states, lending further credence to our contention that what has become known as the "resource curse" is not inevitable. We find, for example, that private domestic ownership, which is most likely to foster strong fiscal regimes, is such a rare strategy because the domestic conditions that encourage governing elites to adopt this strategy – that is, a high degree of access to alternative revenue and a high level of distributional conflict – have also been rare in mineral-rich countries in the developing world. Our findings also suggest that the initial choice of ownership structure is crucial and that this choice is heavily influenced by how domestic economic and political conditions at the time affect state leaders' strategies for consolidating power. The paramount importance of which ownership structure these elites adopt when the country first has the opportunity to do so is clearly demonstrated by the strong statistical support for the path dependency argument in all the regression models. That this initial choice, in turn, can be best explained by our two variables of interest – that is, the degree of access to alternative revenue and the level of distributional conflict – is made apparent by a comparison between the results from our second and third linear regression models (OLS (2)) and (OLS (3)), with those from our first (OLS (1)), which limits the dependent variable (ownership structure) to the first year each country enters the dataset. (See Table 9.4 for details.)

Finally, whereas the resource curse literature has treated ownership structure as essentially fixed across time or space, our explanation offers a much more dynamic view. Simply put, as depicted in Table 9.1, our theory predicts that, *ceteris paribus*, a change in the degree of access to alternative revenue, the level of distributional conflict, or both increases the likelihood that there will be a subsequent change in ownership structure. Broadly speaking, the crossnational statistical results support this prediction. They clearly indicate that, even taking into account the strong effect of previous ownership structure, our two variables of interest continue to have an influence on whether a given country changes its ownership structure in the direction we predict.

The petroleum-rich Soviet successor states provide some additional evidence that this is the case. Contra the strength of path dependency effects in our statistical results, by 2005 (the end of our study), the majority had actually adopted a new ownership structure: Uzbekistan changed from S_1 to S_2 in 2001; Russia changed from P_1 to S_1 in 2005; and Kazakhstan changed from P_2 to S_2 in 2005. Consistent with our predictions, in each case, the government's decision to make this change followed a shift in one of our two variables of interest. Uzbekistan's decision to adopt S_2 followed a sharp decline in world market prices for cotton and a series of poor harvests that greatly reduced its access to what had been its primary source of revenue (for details, see EIU 2002, 38). As one former deputy minister of finance summed up: "cotton was becoming too unreliable... there was a fear that [the sector] would collapse... [and] create an economic crisis" (Authors' interview with former high-ranking official). Thus, opening up the petroleum sector to foreign investment was a direct response to a shift in the degree of its access to alternative revenue from high to low. In both Russia and Kazakhstan, the relevant shift occurred in the level of distributional conflict. By the mid-2000s, the social movements and political parties that generated a high level of distributional conflict in the 1990s had all but disappeared from the political scene. In short, having effectively consolidated their power, the respective governing elites in each country could adopt state ownership over their petroleum sector without fearing that opponents would capture the state and gain control of these resources. In the Russian case, this was clearly facilitated by the particularities of ownership structure over the gas sector – that is, the "partial privatization" of Gazprom in the 1990s followed by the reassertion of state ownership with control in 2002 (see Chapter 5 for details). Whereas the former enabled President Putin to buy up media outlets so as to effectively silence one of his chief critics in the early 2000s (media magnate Vladimir Gusinsky), the latter enabled him to orchestrate a forced buyout of one of his primary political opponents in the mid-2000s (Yukos CEO Mikhail Khodorkovsky).

The Myth of the Resource Curse

The resource curse is a reasonably solid fact.

– Jeffrey Sachs 2001

The link between mineral resource extraction and child development is a paradoxical one. This 'resource curse' is both unjust and unnecessary.

– Save the Children 2003

The first Law of Petropolitics posits the following: The price of oil and the pace
of freedom always move in opposite directions in oil-rich petrolist states.

– Thomas Friedman 2006

This book provides compelling evidence that one of the core assumptions of
the conventional literature on the resource curse – namely that ownership
structure does not vary and thus cannot hold any explanatory power – is
not only unfounded but also has impeded our understanding of the relationship between mineral wealth and institutions. More specifically, we utilize the
experience of the Soviet successor states to demonstrate first, that ownership
structure can vary even across countries that share the same institutional legacy; and second, that this variation helps explain the divergence in their fiscal
regimes, and hence developmental trajectories, from the early 1990s through
the mid-2000s. By documenting the variation in ownership structure over the
course of the twentieth century, moreover, we show conclusively that treating
ownership structure as a constant not only deprives us of a key explanatory
variable but also cannot be substantiated empirically.

Our findings thus also make a strong case for broadening our historical
perspective. As we describe in Chapter 1, both the assumption that mineral
wealth is always and necessarily state-owned and the conflation of state ownership with control have gone unquestioned for so long precisely because they
reflected the empirical reality of the narrow time period under study – that is,
from roughly the late 1960s to early 1990s. During this period, there was a
clear convergence toward state ownership due to the nationalization wave that
swept across mineral-rich states in the developing world beginning in the early

1960s. Less than a decade later, more than three-quarters of petroleum sectors in the developing world were state-owned. (See Appendix B for details). It is also during this period that the locus of bargaining power shifted from foreign investors to host governments via the onset of the obsolescing bargain. As a result, the fiscal regimes fostered under state ownership *with* control (S_1) and state ownership *without* control (S_2) were virtually indistinguishable – as were their negative social, political, and economic consequences (see Chapter 6 for details).

A closer look further reveals that the faulty assumption of state ownership with control is only one of several that have contributed to the myth of the resource curse. And they all share a common root – the conventional literature's focus on a truncated time frame. In this chapter, we review the most significant of these assumptions. Because they concern the link between mineral wealth, poor economic growth, and authoritarian regimes, a reappraisal suggests that the entire notion that mineral-rich countries are cursed by virtue of their wealth is bounded temporally. It also highlights why ownership structure is the crucial missing link. In other words, the key to understanding why this particular period lends such strong statistical support to the resource curse hypothesis is that there was, in fact, little variation in ownership structure in the 1970s and 1980s.

In sum, the consensus that has emerged over the past two decades among highly respected academics, international organizations (INGOs as well as IFIs), and even representatives of the popular media that oil is a curse is based on a narrow view of history. Proponents of the resource curse hypothesis have drawn general conclusions about the relationship between petroleum wealth, economic growth, state capacity, and democracy from what is actually a fairly unique historical time period without acknowledging its uniqueness.

THE WRONG COUNTERFACTUAL

The central premise for the notion that mineral wealth is a curse is the apparent paradox that richer countries are at a disadvantage when it comes to both economic and political development. This paradox, however, is based on a counterfactual that is rooted in a particular historical context. The approximately three decades between the late 1960s and early 1990s produced two striking empirical puzzles that led scholars to reconsider some of their prior assumptions about the relationship between resource abundance, economic growth, and democracy. First, why was resource-poor East Asia able to industrialize so rapidly and successfully, while resource-rich Latin America slowly went bankrupt? The sharp divergence in growth rates between petroleum-rich and petroleum-poor countries was considered to be especially baffling given that it occurred during an unprecedented mineral price boom. Second, why did resource-rich countries in general and petroleum-rich in particular seem to be immune to the third wave of democratization that swept the globe between 1974 and 1990 (Huntington 1991)? Among the 49 countries that democratized during this period, for example, only two (Indonesia and Nigeria) were major oil-producing countries.

Attempts to explain these related puzzles generated an impressive body of scholarly literature from which the contention quickly emerged that the problem was wealth itself: in other words, had resource-rich countries not exploited their wealth in the 1970s and 1980s, they would look much more like their resource-poor counterparts in the 1990s. This literature laid the groundwork for subsequent scholarship, which took as given the negative relationship between resource abundance, economic growth, and democracy, and sought to illuminate the causal mechanisms through which what has become commonly known as the "resource curse" operated. Most importantly, it fostered the perception that the early 1970s is the appropriate starting point for a comparison between resource-rich and resource-poor countries. The seminal paper that often serves as the takeoff point for explaining why resource abundance is more often a curse than a blessing (Sachs and Warner 1995), for example, is based on a dataset that was limited to a 20-year period (1970–1990). Similarly, the article credited with establishing the link between resource abundance and authoritarian regimes beyond the Middle East (Ross 2001a) bases its findings on a dataset that covers the years 1971–1997. Although both have since been expanded to include the 2000s, the availability of such datasets has reinforced this perception.

In sum, whether explicit or implicit, the counterfactual commonly invoked to gauge the probable development trajectory of resource-rich countries – had they not discovered their wealth – is the economic and political trajectory of their resource-poor counterparts since the late 1960s. The reason this is so problematic is twofold. First, it ignores the path-dependent effects associated with both economic development and regime type. In other words, using the early 1970s as the starting point treats resource-rich countries as if their economic and political histories begin when they discover commercial oil. And yet we have good reason to believe that the factors that promote or inhibit democracy have much deeper historical roots. As Horiuchi and Waglé (2008) rightly point out, one of the first things you notice when you look at the distribution of democracies and autocracies across oil-rich states in the 1990s is that it has not changed much since the 1900s (see Figure 10.1).[1] The classic cases of petroleum-rich countries with democratic regimes (those in the upper left-hand corner) were already more democratic *before* they started to generate windfalls from petroleum. And conversely, the petroleum-rich states that are authoritarian *after* they begin developing their petroleum wealth (those in the bottom right-hand corner) were already more authoritarian before they became fiscally dependent on oil. Interestingly, the Soviet Union and the Russian Federation as its primary successor provide a clear illustration of the former and the latter, respectively (see Figure 10.2). The strength of path dependency effects, furthermore, appears to remain as true for more recent

[1] This is, however, consistent with the notion that mineral rents "lock-in" preexisting regime type (see Karl 1997).

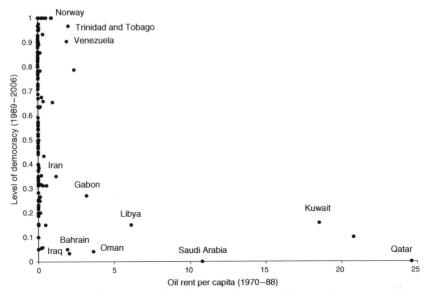

FIGURE 10.1. Distribution of Oil-Rich Democracies and Autocracies.
Source: Level of democracy is authors' calculations based on the Polity IV dataset.[2]
Oil rents per Capita are calculated by Michael Ross (see Ross 2008 for details).

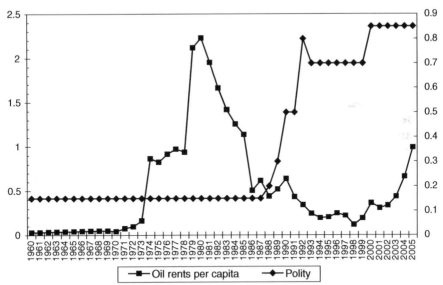

FIGURE 10.2. Petroleum Wealth and Level of Democracy in the Soviet Union and Russian Federation, 1960–2005.
Source: Same as above.[3]

---

[2] We utilize the Polity IV dataset throughout both because it is the most commonly used and because it provides consistent indicators over time rather than a snapshot view of regime type.

[3] Polity scores for Russia are higher on average than other indicators (see Freedom House, Voice and Accountability) but the trends are very similar.

history as it was for the past. The best predictor of a country's democracy score from 1989–2005 – whether oil-rich or oil-poor – is its democracy score from 1979–1988 (Horiuchi and Waglé 2008).

Second, as others have noted, a truncated dataset cannot adequately control for cultural, historical, and geographical factors that do not vary over time (in other words, fixed effects). And yet previous research also suggests that these factors, proxied by region, influence either a country's level of economic development or its propensity for democratization (see Przeworski et al. 2000). It is not mere coincidence, for example, that the majority of the democratic success stories among petroleum-rich states – that is, those countries that were authoritarian before they began to develop their petroleum sector, and yet democratized – are in Latin America.[4] From this perspective, what is surprising about Russia's regime transition is not its post-2004 descent into authoritarianism, but that it resisted the regional trend for so long. For most of the 1990s and early 2000s, Russia was considered to be more democratic than the majority of its neighbors – both petroleum-rich and petroleum-poor – scoring well above the CIS average on various indexes.[5] (See Table 10.1 for details.)

The limitations of the conventional approach become clear when we consider an alternative set of counterfactuals, such as those proposed in more recent work questioning the widely held view that mineral wealth necessarily undermines democracy. Both Michael Herb (2005) and Stephen Haber and Victor Menaldo (2008), for example, suggest that in order to gauge the impact of petroleum wealth on democracy in a given country, it is more appropriate to consider what that country's regime type would have been if it had never discovered oil – that is, to compare it to itself with and without oil rents. Although their approaches differ, both reach similar conclusions. Herb creates a counterfactual GDP in order to simulate a world in which countries heavily dependent on petroleum rents do not have access to those rents. His results indicate not only that there is no "consistent support for the thesis that rentierism has a harmful effect on democracy scores," but also that it has much less of a substantive effect in either direction than do other variables such as "region, Muslim share of the population, and income" (310). Whereas Herb's innovation enables him to utilize data corresponding to a similarly truncated timeline (here, 1972–2000) much more effectively, Haber and Menaldo engage in an explicitly longitudinal approach by extending their dataset to include the period before oil or minerals dominate a country's economy so that they can analyze long-term relationships between mineral sector reliance and regime type within countries over time. Based on a meticulous time-series analysis of

---

[4] These include Argentina (1983), Bolivia (1982), Ecuador (1979), Mexico (2000), and Venezuela (1958).

[5] Conversely, Central Asia has been a particularly inhospitable neighborhood for democracies; and yet, the two petroleum-rich states that chose state ownership (Turkmenistan and Uzbekistan) have the lowest average scores.

TABLE 10.1. *Average Democracy Scores: Voice and Accountability, 1996–2005, and Freedom House, 1991–2005*

Country	Voice and Accountability[a]	Freedom House[b]
Armenia	−0.58	4.1
Azerbaijan	−0.96	5.43
Belarus	−1.37	5.47
Georgia	−0.36	4.1
Kazakhstan	−0.96	5.37
Kyrgyzstan	−0.93	4.67
Moldova	−0.34	3.7
Russia	−0.54	4.23
Tajikistan	−1.39	5.93
Turkmenistan	−1.84	6.87
Ukraine	−0.5	5.53
Uzbekistan	−1.68	6.53
CIS	−0.95	5.16

Source: Freedom House scores are calculated from http://www.freedom-house.org/. Voice and Accountability scores are calculated from http://info.worldbank.org/governance/wgi/).

[a] Scores range from -2.5 (lowest) to 2.5 (highest). Average does not includes years 1997, 1999, and 2001 because they are not available.

[b] Scores range from 1 (highest) to 7 (lowest).

164 countries, they conclude that mineral wealth neither undermines democracy nor prevents democratic transitions.

These studies also address the second aforementioned shortcoming. In calculating hypothetical GDPs for resource-rich countries, for example, Herb (2005, 302) explicitly takes cultural and geographical factors into account by selecting comparator countries from within the same region, if not neighboring states. Similarly, Haber and Menaldo (2008) construct an alternative measure of the dependent variable to operationalize the counterfactual that oil-rich countries would have attained a similar level of democracy to that of other countries in their "geographic/cultural region" had they not discovered oil or mineral wealth. The fact that both their findings are at odds with the conventional wisdom underscores the importance of including fixed effects.

CONFLATION OF WEALTH AND DEPENDENCE

Another set of assumptions that undergirds the verdict that resource wealth is a curse concerns the relationship between wealth and dependence on the one hand, and between dependence and economic growth on the other. In sum, mineral wealth promotes slower and unbalanced growth precisely because it inevitably leads to export dependence on a single commodity, which makes economies vulnerable to fluctuations in world market prices. While market volatility in general creates unpredictable revenue streams that impede sustained investment (see Mikesell 1997) and promote excessive borrowing (see Katz et al. 2004), rapid price booms in particular generate Dutch Disease – that is, undermine manufacturing and agricultural sectors by shifting production inputs to the mineral and nontradable sectors (see Auty 2001b). This perspective is also linked directly to the literature's narrow temporal focus and the truncated datasets that such a vantage point has generated.

First, conflating mineral wealth with export dependence is seemingly unproblematic for the 1970s and 1980s given that they were highly correlated during this period. The vast majority of petroleum-rich states in the developing world, for example, opted to produce their wealth for export rather than for internal consumption, which was the norm in the eighteenth and nineteenth centuries. This is no historical accident. In the 1950s and 1960s, many development economists advised mineral-rich countries to export their natural resources in order to finance industrialization and thereby diversify their exports to shield their economies from price shocks (see Baldwin 1966, Hirschman 1958).[6] Indeed, the widespread conviction that this strategy would enable these countries to grow much faster than their resource-poor counterparts is the source of the initial optimism regarding their development prospects.[7] However, it is also the source of subsequent disappointment. Although most mineral-rich states made considerable investments in promoting other economic sectors from the late 1960s through the early 1980s, few actually succeeded in diversifying their economies (see Lewis 1984). Tunisia is the only mineral economy in 1970 that was no longer ranked as a mineral economy in 1991 (Davis 1995).

Until very recently, therefore, the preferred measure for natural resource wealth has been the ratio of primary product exports to GDP based on one of the most extensive datasets available at the time – World Data 1995, produced by the World Bank. This became the gold standard for measuring wealth with the publication of the aforementioned seminal 1995 Sachs and Warner article, which not only utilized this indicator but also demonstrated why it was superior to the existing alternatives. Because it disaggregates natural resource exports into "fuel" and "non-fuel" primary products, the World Bank data also proved to be a convenient source for studies that sought to isolate the effects of mineral and petroleum wealth on growth (see Auty, 2001b, Mikesell 1997) as well as regime type (see Jensen and Watchekon 2004, Ross 2001a).

Second, relating wealth to slower and unbalanced growth via dependence was also consistent with the experience of the majority of mineral-rich states from roughly 1970–1990. Not only did these states exhibit a strong tendency to become fiscally dependent on mineral exports during this time period, as

---

[6] This strategy was also widely endorsed by international organizations (for details, see Davis 1995).

[7] There were, of course, notable dissenters, such as Raúl Prebisch (1950).

noted above, they also encountered one of the most volatile international markets in history. This is particularly true for petroleum. As we describe in Chapter 6, the 1960s marked both the end of the major foreign oil companies' ability to impose price stability in the international oil market and the beginning of oil-producing countries' ability to utilize oil as a political weapon. It is perhaps not surprising, then, that when compared to the preceding two centuries, this was also a highly unusual period concerning economic growth – both in terms of its turbulence and slower rates of growth among resource-rich countries (Maloney 2002).

A broader historical view reveals that these assumptions are not merely untenable. Even more egregious is the fact that they have led us to wrongly malign mineral wealth itself – particularly petroleum – for the prevalence of poor and unbalanced growth as well as authoritarian regimes. First, the conflation of wealth with dependence has biased our findings toward failure in both respects. As Wright (2001, 2) and others have pointed out, because poorer countries are more likely to export their wealth, export dependence should be considered a cause rather than an indicator of underdevelopment. This is consistent with our own findings that a large number of the countries that qualify as "petroleum-rich" according to this measure, either first discovered or gained sovereignty over their wealth at a time when their traditional export sector was already in decline (see Chapter 9). Thus, mineral wealth quickly dominated exports not because it depleted other sectors but because it was the only viable source of revenue. Conversely, those countries that do not qualify – including Australia, Canada, Germany, the United States, United Kingdom, and New Zealand – managed to harness their natural resources for development precisely because they were able to consume them internally (see Wright and Czelusta 2003). Many of these same countries that are resource-rich, and yet excluded from conventional accounts of the resource curse because they are not dependent, are also democracies.

Perhaps the clearest indication that measuring resource wealth as dependence produces biased results, however, is that when alternative measures that actually measure abundance are employed, the negative relationships between resource wealth and economic growth on the one hand and resource wealth and democracy on the other simply do not hold.[8] Since the mid-2000s, a number of scholars have effectively challenged the resource curse hypothesis based on several such alternatives, including reserves per capita, production, and rents per capita (see Stijns 2005). Christa N. Brunnschweiler (2008), for example, utilizes per capita subsoil wealth (or "resource stock") based on a new set of indicators recently published by the World Bank and concludes that "natural resources, and in particular mineral resources, have a positive direct association with real GDP growth over the period 1970–2000" (412). Similarly, the aforementioned scholars who reject the claim that natural resource wealth

---

[8] This is also the case if a different time frame is used (see, for example, De Ferranti et al. 2002).

impedes democracy utilize rents per capita in their respective analyses (Haber and Menaldo 2008, Herb 2005).

Second, the tendency to assume that mineral-rich countries necessarily become economically dependent on export rents dismisses the possibility of natural resource-based growth. As noted above, one of the primary paths whereby this has occurred in countries such as Australia, Canada, and the United States is via the internal consumption of minerals (including petroleum) to fuel both industrial and technological development (Wright and Czelusta 2003). Resource intensity, then, did not undermine but rather contributed to sustained economic growth. Its role has been downplayed largely owing to a longstanding bias toward manufacturing-led growth, which is associated with knowledge accumulation and technological progress – a bias that slower growth rates for resource-rich countries from the late 1960s to the early 1990s seemed to confirm, and thus reinforced. And yet, more recent research indicates not only that "learning by doing" is not restricted to the manufacturing sector, but also that it can be achieved via the development of the mineral sector (see Maloney 2002, Wright 2001).

Third, the focus on the deficiencies associated with resource-based economies has diverted our attention away from the real problem, which is policy failure. As some scholars have recognized, because policy solutions exist to combat the effects of volatility in general and Dutch Disease in particular, the real question is why they have rarely been tried and, when tried, why they have rarely worked (see Ascher 1999, Ross 2001c). Their explanations, however, have largely centered around mineral wealth itself, attributing policy failure to its negative impact on leaders' ability to formulate and implement long-term development goals. Mineral wealth, in short, is incompatible with the emergence of a developmental state because it both induces myopic thinking and undermines the emergence of an insulated and autonomous technocracy committed to achieving long-term economic growth (see Auty 1997b).[9] Yet as we demonstrate throughout this book, policy failure should be attributed instead to ownership structure, because each form fosters incentives not only to create particular types of taxation and spending policies but also to follow a certain type of development strategy. And these are mutually reinforcing. The aforementioned common failure of petroleum-rich states in the 1970s and 1980s to realize their ambitious economic diversification programs, for example, can best be explained by the predominance of state ownership. Under both S_1 and S_2 during this period, the national oil company (NOC) quickly became both the primary source of implicit taxation and the main vehicle for achieving economic development (see Chapter 3). This had the dual effect of exacerbating the tendency for governments to make politically motivated investment decisions and undermining the NOC's long-term viability by depleting it of capital for reinvestment.

---

[9] Botswana's ability to avert both of these tendencies is the dominant explanation for why it has achieved fiscal discipline and avoided Dutch Disease effects (see Eifert et al. 2003, Gelb and Associates 1988).

ALL MINERAL-RICH STATES ARE RENTIER STATES

Negative political outcomes attributed to resource wealth are also based on the presumption that the tendency for the mineral sector to become the dominant source of government income is unavoidable. In particular, the prevalence of authoritarian regimes across mineral-rich states since the late 1960s is linked to the notion that all mineral-rich states will inevitably become rentier states (see Beblawi and Luciani 1987, Karl 1997, Vandewalle 1998). This can be summarized as the "rentier effect," the crux of which is that by liberating the state from the need to tax the domestic population and concentrating wealth in the hands of the central government, mineral wealth both suppresses (if not eliminates) demand for democracy from below and reduces incentives to supply democracy from above.

Underlying this mechanism is an additional set of assumptions that have been obscured by the resource curse literature's focus on a single narrow time period. The first is that the central government has direct and unrestricted access to both the accumulation and distribution of mineral sector rents. While this was largely the case from the late 1960s until the 1990s, it is not necessarily so. As we demonstrate throughout this book, the state's access to mineral sector rents is not unfettered but rather mediated by both the form of ownership structure it adopts and the international context in which it pursues this particular ownership structure. The 1970s and 1980s were characterized by the prevalence of state ownership in an international context in which host governments could unilaterally revise their contracts with foreign oil companies in order to extract an increasing share of the rents (a.k.a. the "obsolescing bargain") and transparency norms were essentially nonexistent. Mineral-rich states could thus effortlessly capture and distribute production and export rents with full discretion via their respective NOCs. Conversely, private domestic ownership can present a significant obstacle to tax collection. The high rate of tax evasion across the Russian oil industry for most of the 1990s documented in Chapter 5 provides a vivid illustration.[10] Changes in the international context since the 1990s have also limited the state's ability to either accumulate or allocate mineral sector rents directly and opaquely. As described in Chapter 6, in response to pressures from INGOs and IFIs, foreign investors have not only engaged in direct social spending as an increasing part of their overall fiscal burden, but also adopted corporate social responsibility (CSR). Under certain conditions, this has translated into both greater transparency over the mineral sector revenues that flow into state coffers and less autonomy over how this revenue is spent. Foreign oil companies have successfully pressured the Azerbaijani government, for example, to establish a natural resource fund (NRF) through which they publicize their tax payments (see Chapter 7). As this case demonstrates, the increasing tendency for

---

[10] The failed attempts of the Bolivian government to increase taxes on the privately owned tin sector in the 1940s provides another striking example from an earlier historical period (see Contreras 1993).

foreign investors to develop their own spending priorities in conjunction with community organizations in the regions where they operate has also limited the degree to which central governments can dictate how mineral sector rents are allocated.

The second set of assumptions follows directly from the first: the ease with which the central government can extract and spend mineral sector rents makes it both unwilling to tax beyond the mineral sector and eager to distribute these rents to the population in large quantities. In other words, mineral-rich states satisfy when it comes to tax revenue, and yet maximize when it comes to expenditures. This notion has also been bolstered by the literature's focus on the late 1960s to the 1990s during which these taxation and spending patterns appeared to be the norm.

It is well documented that over these approximately three decades, mineral-rich states received a much lower share of income from direct taxation than mineral-poor states. This finding is simply not robust, however, for the subsequent period. Concerning petroleum-rich states in particular, more recent data suggests that there is only a weak negative relationship between non-hydrocarbon sector taxation and hydrocarbon revenue. It also suggests two important outliers – one of which is Russia (see Figure 10.3). Moreover, there is good reason to believe that the presumed negative effect of mineral wealth on taxation does not hold even for the 1970s and 1980s. According to John Waterbury (1997a), once indirect taxation is taken into account, it turns out

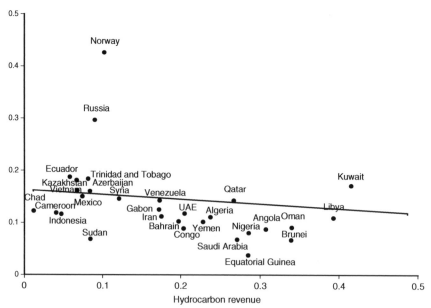

FIGURE 10.3 Non–Hydrocarbon Sector Revenue as a Function of Hydrocarbon Sector Revenue, 1992–2005.

Source: Bornhorst, Gupta, and Thornton 2008.

that the overall tax burden in the petroleum-rich Middle East and North Africa (MENA) is not much lower than it is in other regions of the world. The key difference is in the composition of taxation: the ratio of indirect to direct taxes in MENA is 2 to 1. And it is even higher for petroleum-rich states, in which even as the overall tax burden decreases, the ratio of indirect to direct taxes increases (ibid). Again, this is no coincidence but rather directly related to the prevalence of state ownership during this time period. As we argue in Chapter 3, when the mineral sector is state-owned, governments prefer to rely on less visible forms of taxation, such as sales and excise taxes, because it is more politically feasible given societal expectations that the mineral sector should be sufficient to finance the state.

The predominance of state ownership during this period had a similar effect on spending patterns because it exacerbated the distributional imperative in developing countries. Although the expectation that the state would play a leading role in the "transformation" of their economies and societies was pervasive throughout the 1970s and 1980s (Rueschemeyer and Evans 1985), mineral-rich states actually had the financial capacity to do so. State ownership coupled with the obsolescing bargain across petroleum-rich states, for example, granted them direct and unfettered access to rents, while the 1970s price booms generated an unprecedented windfall. At the same time, by fostering societal expectations that the public at large will receive the lion's share of benefits from the exploitation of its mineral wealth in the form of improved living standards, state ownership also generated strong disincentives to limit government spending. It is perhaps not surprising, then, that spending levels in petroleum-rich countries were much higher than in petroleum-poor countries from the 1960s to 1980s. This does not appear to be the case, however, for subsequent periods. As Figure 10.4 demonstrates, spending levels start to

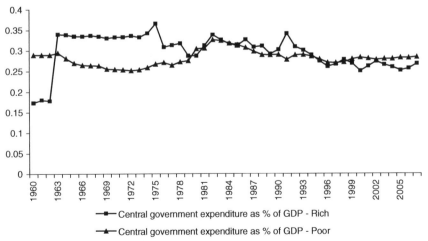

FIGURE 10.4. Spending Levels, 1960–2005.
Source: World Economic Outlook (WEO).

converge in the 1990s, and petroleum-poor countries overtake petroleum-rich countries by the 2000s.

Conversely, private forms of ownership structure (i.e., P_1 and P_2) create the potential for mineral-rich states to willingly adopt restrictions on government spending – albeit to varying degrees. In short, they are more likely first to constrain the state's ability to extract revenue from the mineral sector and second to lower societal expectations vis-à-vis the state. Both Russia and Kazakhstan, for example, could enact significant cuts in expenditures in comparison to the other three petroleum-rich Soviet successor states because their respective governments believed these actions were consistent with popular sentiments regarding how widely the benefits of mineral wealth should be distributed (see Chapters 5 and 8, respectively). Russia went even further. The bargain with the private oil companies that led to the adoption of a stable Tax Code, combined with the belief that expenditures could be limited without popular backlash, even during a boom, paved the way for the Russian government to establish the only effective NRF in the FSU (and one of the few in the developing world).

The final assumption underlying the widely held notion that rentierism necessarily leads to authoritarianism is that the absence of taxation in such states, combined with high levels of government spending, quells popular demands for representation and accountability (see Anderson 1987). The preceding discussion has already suggested why no single pattern of taxation and expenditures can be presumed to hold either across mineral-rich states or over time. Yet even if we could, there are still several very good reasons to doubt this causal mechanism. First the hypothesized relationship between taxing the domestic population and popular mobilization in support of democratization does not even seem to hold for the West European countries that serve as the basis for the popular adage "no representation without taxation" (see Herb 2003, Waterbury 1997b). Second, taxation is not necessarily the only or the main link between rulers and ruled. Rather, as the aforementioned third wave of democratization clearly demonstrates, citizens can and do mobilize for a variety of other reasons and via other means.[11] Third, it turns out that rentierism has not, in fact, created a docile population in the MENA, but rather one that has readily mobilized in response to the failure of the state to fulfill its economic promises (see Brynen 1992, Waterbury 1997a).

Despite these shortcomings, the "rentier effect" has received not only the most attention but also the most empirical support to date (see Ross 2001a). As a result, the literature has emphasized fiscal independence from the population as the critical link between mineral wealth and authoritarian regimes. This, in turn, has led us both to overlook the potentially positive relationship between oil and democracy and to focus our attention on the wrong causal mechanism. Simply put, because mineral wealth does not necessarily translate into dependence on the mineral sector, it also does not preclude the emergence

---

[11] As Herb (2003, 25) notes, the fact that a discussion of taxation is absent from the literature on this wave is striking.

of an economic elite outside this sector that is capable of exerting political influence – even in a rentier state. As Thad Dunning (2008) has shown, where such an elite exists, their interests are pivotal in determining whether a resource boom facilitates or impedes democratization. More specifically, by reducing elites' fear of redistribution, under high levels of inequality a resource boom can either facilitate an authoritarian regime's transition to democracy or contribute to a democratic regime's durability. This is a significant step forward not only because Dunning provides a compelling explanation for the supposed anomaly of rentier states with democratic regimes throughout Latin America, but also because he arrives at this explanation by highlighting the role of distribution rather than the absence of taxation. In other words, what is crucial here is not the state's fiscal independence but rather its ability to ameliorate redistributive conflict by distributing windfalls to the poor rather than taxing the rich.

The distributional power of the state regarding mineral sector rents, however, cannot be taken for granted. Rather, it depends on the degree of discretion that, in turn, is a function of societal pressures and the level of transparency. And yet both factors are largely absent from the conventional story of the resource curse. Societal pressures have been mostly ignored because societies in rentier states are presumed to react uniformly to their mineral wealth. In short, mineral wealth breeds "rentier societies" – that is, domestic populations that expect "easy access" to the proceeds from mineral wealth and thus are "idle and feckless" (Stevens 2003, 17). One of the key insights of this book, however, is that societal expectations in mineral-rich states vary across countries and over time. Just as the state's access to mineral rents is mediated by its choice of ownership structure and changes in international norms concerning the allocation of these rents, so too is society's.[12] Similarly, the role of transparency has been downplayed in the resource curse literature because transactions within the mineral sector are presumed to be necessarily opaque. As the experience of the petroleum-rich Soviet successor states demonstrates, however, the level of transparency can and does vary owing to these same two factors. The influence of ownership structure in particular is apparent in the growing ease with which the Putin administration utilized rents for political purposes once it asserted full state ownership and control over the gas sector.

A CONDITIONAL APPROACH

In sum, the conclusions you draw are highly dependent on the timeframe and scope of your analysis. As Alexander Gershenkron wrote in 1962 when seeking to understand the problem of late developers by examining the patterns of industrialization across Europe: "the quality of our understanding of current problems depends largely on the broadness of our frame of reference."

---

[12] The degree to which society is independently organized is another potential source of mediation (see Smith 2007).

The resource curse is no exception. Its focus on a truncated time period has led to a series of faulty assumptions and generalizations that have impeded our understanding about the actual relationship between mineral wealth, economic growth, state capacity, and democracy. Conversely, a much broader historical view, as we provide here, reveals that oil in and of itself is not a curse. Petroleum wealth can, however, become an impediment to both political and economic development under certain conditions, including, most importantly, when it is state-owned and -controlled. As such, this book is part of a new wave of research that adopts a conditional approach to the resource curse. It goes beyond this body of work, however, both by invoking ownership structure as an intervening variable and by exploiting a new set of cases. Our analysis of the Soviet successor states also demonstrates the need for continuing to broaden the study of mineral wealth geographically.

Appendix A

List of Authors' Interviews

1) Valekh F. Aleskerov, General Manager, Foreign Investments Division, SOCAR, Baku, May 23, 2002
2) Farda Asadov, Executive Director, Open Society Institute – Azerbaijan, Baku, May 20, 2002
3) Araz Azimov, Deputy Foreign Minister, Baku, May 20, 2002
4) Sabit A. Bagirov, President, Entrepreneurship Development Foundation, Baku, May 22, 2002
5) Foreign Tax Consultant based in Azerbaijan, name withheld, Baku, May 24, 2002
6) General Secretary, Association of Local Entrepreneurs, Baku, May 22, 2002
7) Vafa Guluzade, Foreign Policy Advisor to the President, Baku, May 23 2002
8) Government representative no. 1, name withheld, Embassy of Azerbaijan, Washington D.C., February 18, 2002
9) Murat Heydarov, Senior Advisor, Security & Political Risk Analysis, British Petroleum (BP) Group, Baku, May 21, 2002
10) Israil Iskenderov, Executive Director, UMID Humanitarian and Social Support Center, phone interview, December 3, 2009
11) Ahad Kazimov, Eurasia Partnership Foundation, phone interview, December 8, 2009
12) Erjan Kurbanov, Associate Director, US – Azerbaijan Council, February 20, 2002
13) Sheyda Mehdiyeva, Corporate Social Responsibility Advisor, Statoil Apsheron, phone interview, December 10, 2009
14) Member no. 1, Association of Local Entrepreneurs, name withheld, Baku, May 22, 2002
15) Member no. 2, Association of Local Entrepreneurs, name withheld, Baku, May 22, 2002

16) Michael Mered, IMF, Resident Representative in Azerbaijan, Baku, May 24, 2002

17) Doug Norlen, Pacific Environment, phone interview, October 28, 2009

18) Representative no. 1, BP Group, name withheld, Baku, May 21, 2002

19) Representative no. 2, BP Group, name withheld, Baku, May 21, 2002

20) Representative no. 1, Azerbaijan International Operating Company (AIOC), name withheld, May 25, 2002

21) Representative no. 2, AIOC, name withheld, May 25, 2002

22) Robert Rudy, Foreign Advisor to the Ministry of Finance, Baku, May 23, 2002

23) Gyulshan Rzayeva, Deputy Secretary General, Association of Local Entrepreneurs, Baku, May 22, 2002

24) Samir Sharifov, Executive Director, State Oil Fund of the Republic of Azerbaijan (SOFAZ), Baku, May 21, 2002

25) Karen St. John, Director of Social Performance, BP Group, Baku May 24, 2002

KAZAKHSTAN

1) Agip Caspian Sea representative, name withheld, Almaty, June 2000

2) Amerada Hess/CA Oil representative, name withheld, Almaty, June 9, 2000

3) Mike Biddision, Hagler Bailly, Almaty, June 16, 2000

4) British Gas (BG) representative no. 1, name withheld, Almaty, December 11, 1997

5) British Gas (BG) representative no. 2, name withheld, Almaty, June 16, 2000

6) Jason Compy, Atyrau USAID Regional Initiative (ARI) Coordinator, Atyrau, October 15, 1999

7) Chevron Munaigas Inc. representative, name withheld, Almaty, June 16, 2000

8) Chinese National Petroleum Company (CNPC) representative, name withheld, Almaty, June 20, 2000

9) Victor Eriksen, Financial Director, FIOC, Almaty, November 3, 1999

10) Steve Fast, Hurricane Hydrocarbons, Almaty, March 10, 1997

11) Megan Flavely, ISAR representative, Almaty, December 6, 1997

12) Former Director of Environment, Health, & Safety for Hurricane Hydrocarbons, Almaty, October 18, 1999

13) Former Human Resources and Public Relations Manager for Hurricane Hydrocarbons, Almaty, November 5, 1999

14) Kenzhebek Ibrashev, President, Kazkhstancaspishelf (KCS), Joint-Stock Company, Almaty, December 10, 1997.

15) Japan National Oil Corporation (JNOC) representative, name withheld, Almaty, Kazakhstan, June 19, 2000

16) Kairgeldy Kabyldin, Vice-President, KazTransOil, Almaty, December 8, 1997

17) Kazakh Turk Petroleum, Ltd. representative, name withheld, Almaty, December 9, 1997

18) Kerr-McGee Oil and Gas Corporation representative, name withheld, Almaty, June 2000

19) Gulnara Kurbanova, National Programme Officer, UNDP, Almaty, November 1999

20) Ray Leonard, VP, Exploration, First International Oil Company (FIOC), Almaty, October 20, 1999

21) Ruslan Mamishev, Operations Officer for Infrastructure, World Bank, Almaty, March 11, 1997

22) Charles McLure, Hoover Institution, Stanford University, Palo Alto, CA, December 8, 2003

23) Tom Minnehan, Deloitte & Touche, Almaty, June 12, 2000

24) Mobil representative, name withheld, Almaty, June 6, 2000

25) Nations Energy representative, name withheld, Almaty, June 9, 2000 and June 12, 2000

26) Marcia Occomy, resident advisor, USAID Fiscal Reform Project, Washington DC, August 2000

27) Oryx representative, name withheld, Almaty, June 9, 2000

28) Bill Page, Ernst & Young, Almaty, June 8, 2000

29) Preussage Energie representative, name withheld, Almaty June 13, 2000

30) Paul Ross, IMF, Almaty, June 15, 2000

31) Art Rowley, Hagler Bailly Consulting, Almaty, December 6, 1997

32) Azamat Sarsembayev, Director of the Permanent Secretariat of the Foreign Investors' Council, Almaty, June 11, 2000

33) Schlumberger representative, name withheld, Almaty, June 16, 2000

34) Oleg Starukhin, KCS and North Caspian Project representative, Almaty, December 12, 1997

35) Imangali N. Tasmagambetov, Akim (Governor) of Atyrau Oblast, Atyrau, October 1, 1999

36) Lewis Tatem, USAID, Almaty, June 7, 2000

37) TengizChevroil (TCO) representative, name withheld, Almaty, December 12, 1997

38) Texaco representative, name withheld, Almaty, June 13, 2000

39) Total representative no. 1, name withheld, Almaty, December 10, 1997

40) Total representative no. 2, name withheld, Almaty, June 12, 2000

41) Doug Townsend, ITIC Advisor, phone interview, January 19, 2004

42) Vice Minister of the Republic of Kazakhstan, name withheld, Washington, D.C., August 2000.

43) Kate Watters, Crude Accountability, phone interview, September 29, 2009

RUSSIA

1) Tom Adshead, Troika Dialog, Moscow, July 1, 2002
2) Olga Alexeeva, Charities Aid Foundation (CAF), Moscow, June 26, 2002
3) Alan Bigman, Vice President, Director of Corporate Finance, TNK, Moscow, July 2, 2002
4) Yekaterina Georgievna Bogatyreva, Chief Specialist of Geological Administration, Yukos Oil Company, Moscow, July 1, 2002
5) Deputy Minister, Ministry of Finance, name withheld, Moscow, July 5, 2002
6) Deputy Minister, Ministry of Economic Development and Trade (MEDT), name withheld, Moscow, July 5, 2002
7) Arkady Dvorkovich, Deputy Minister, MEDT, Moscow, July 5, 2002
8) Dr. Vadim Eskin, Cambridge Energy Research Associates (CERA), Moscow, September 12, 2001
9) Former Deputy Minister of Finance, name withheld, Moscow, July 6, 2002
10) Former Deputy Minister, (MEDT), name withheld, Boston, MA, November 14, 2006
11) Former high-ranking government official no. 1, name withheld, Moscow, September 24, 2001
12) Former high-ranking government official no. 2, name withheld, Durham, NC, February 6, 2006
13) Former high-ranking government official no. 3, name withheld, New York, NY, April 26, 2007
14) Martin Fossum, Sidanco Oil Company, Vice-President for Strategic Development and Business Development, Moscow, June 27, 2002
15) Gazprom representative no. 1, name withheld, Moscow, June 24, 2002
16) Gazprom representative no. 2, name withheld, Moscow, June 24, 2002
17) Andrei Illarionov, Former Economic Advisor to President Putin, New York, NY, May 15, 2008
18) Vladimir Konovalov, Director, Petroleum Advisory Forum, Moscow, September 14, 2001
19) Elena Valentinovna Korzun, General Director, Association of Small and Medium Oil Producers, Moscow, July 1, 2002
20) Antonia Kovalevskaya, Director for Business Development, Center for Fiscal Policy, Moscow, July 2, 2002
21) Mike Kubena, Partner, Tax Services, Global Energy and Mining, Price Waterhouse Coopers, Moscow Office, September 11, 2001
22) Lukoil representative, name withheld, Moscow, July 25, 2002
23) Boris Makarenko no. 1, Deputy Director General, Center for Political Technologies (CPT), Moscow, September 19, 2001

24) Boris Makarenko no. 2, Deputy Director General, CPT, phone interview, December 5, 2004
25) Anders Morland, President, BP Russia, TNK-BP representative, Moscow, September 17, 2001
26) Anne Nivat, Moscow correspondent for *Libération* (France), Cambridge, MA, June 29, 2000
27) Stephen O'Sullivan, United Financial Group, Moscow, July 2, 2002
28) Peter I. Reinhardt, Principle, Ernst & Young, Moscow, September 20, 2001
29) Konstantin Reznikov, Alfa Bank, Senior Oil and Gas Analyst, Moscow, September 19, 2001
30) Gerald Rohan, Price Waterhouse, Energy Committee American Chamber of Commerce, Moscow, September 20, 2001
31) Sergei Dimitrievich Shatalov, First Deputy Minister of Finance, Moscow, July 5, 2002
32) Sibneft representative no. 1, name withheld, Moscow, July 1, 2002
33) Sidanco representative no. 2, name withheld, Moscow, June 27, 2002
34) Mark Yurevich Urnov no. 1, Chairman of *Expertiza* Analytical Programmes Fund, Russia, Moscow, September 19, 2001
35) Mark Yurevich Urnov no. 2, Chairman of *Expertiza*, phone interview, December 5, 2004
36) Alexander Ustinov, Economic Expert Group, Moscow, June 26, 2002
37) Oleg Vyugin, Chief Economist, Troika Dialogue, Moscow, September 17, 2001
38) Glen Waller, Exxon, Moscow, September 21, 2001
39) Valery Yazev, Chairman of Subcommittee on Gas, State Duma, Moscow, June 24, 2002
40) Vitaly Yermakov, Research Associate, CERA, Moscow, June 27, 2002
41) Yukos representative no. 1 (vice president), name withheld, Moscow, June 23, 2002
42) Yukos representative no. 2 (former vice president), name withheld, phone interview, April 12, 2005
43) Mikhail Zadornov, Deputy and Member of the Budget and Taxation Committee, Russian Duma, Moscow, September 18, 2001
44) Victoria Zotikova, Communications Officer, United Nations Development Program (UNDP) Russia, phone interview, December 5, 2004

TURKMENISTAN

1) Foreign consultant in the energy sector no. 1, name withheld, Ashgabat, December 2, 1997
2) Foreign consultant in the energy sector no. 2, name withheld, Ashgabat, December 3, 1997

3) Former high-ranking government official no. 1, Washington D.C., February 19, 2002

4) Former high-ranking government official no. 2, Washington D.C., February 19, 2002

5) Representative of Delta Oil, name withheld, Ashgabat, December 1, 1997

6) Representative of Mobil, name withheld, Ashgabat, December 2, 1997

7) Representative of Unocal, name withheld, Ashgabat, December 3, 1997

8) Hail Ugur, Turkmenistan Ambassador to the U.S., Washington D.C., February 20, 2002

9) United States Information Agency (USIA) officer, name withheld, Ashgabat, December 1, 1997

UZBEKISTAN

1) Analysts, Center for Economic Research (CER), names withheld, Tashkent, May 10, 2002

2) Turson Akhmedov, Center for Effective Economic Policy, Ministry of Macroeconomics and Statistics, Tashkent, May 13, 2002

3) Bob Berry, Representative of Enron Oil and Gas Company International (EOGI), Tashkent, March 20, 1997

4) Energy Specialist, Technical Assistance to the Commonwealth of Independent States (TACIS), name withheld, Tashkent, February 28, 1997

5) Matluba Fazilova, Chief Economist, Strategic Institute under the President, Tashkent, February 27, 1997

6) Foreign economic consultant no. 1, name withheld, Tashkent, March 18, 1997

7) Foreign economic consultant no. 2, name withheld, Tashkent, March 18, 1997

8) Former high-ranking government official, Tashkent, May 4, 2002

9) Valery Vladimirovich Karchenko and Marat Sadikovich Tashpulatov, Energy Center, Tashkent, February 28, 1997

10) Saifulla Persheyev, Manager, National Oil and Gas Company Uzbekneftegaz, Tashkent, March 19, 1997

11) Representative of Agip Oil, name withheld, Tashkent, February 27, 1997

12) Representative of Texaco Oil and Gas Company, name withheld, Tashkent, February 27, 1997

13) Representative of Japan National Oil Corporation (JNOC), name withheld, Tashkent, March 20, 1997

14) Representatives of Uzbekneftegaz no. 1, names withheld, Tashkent, March 21, 1997

15) Representatives of Uzbekneftegaz no. 2, names withheld, Tashkent, May 16, 2002
16) Rafik Saifulin, Director, Strategic Institute under the President, Tashkent, February 25, 1997
17) World Bank representatives, Uzbekistan office, names withheld, Tashkent, May 5, 2002

Appendix B

Variation in Ownership Structure in Developing Countries

Time Period	Strategy	Countries
1900 –	S_1 (0)	
	S_2 (0)	
	P_1 (3)	Brazil (1891), Imperial Russia (1872), Venezuela (1904)
	P_2 (3)	Iran (1901), Mexico (1901), Romania (1895)
1905 –	S_1 (1)	Argentina (1907)
	S_2 (0)	
	P_1 (2)	Brazil, Imperial Russia,
	P_2 (4)	Iran, Mexico, Romania, Venezuela (1907)
1910 –	S_1 (1)	Argentina
	S_2 (0)	
	P_1 (2)	Brazil, Imperial Russia,
	P_2 (5)	Ecuador (1909), Iran, Mexico, Romania, Venezuela
1915-	S_1 (2)	Argentina, Soviet Union (1918)
	S_2 (0)	
	P_1 (2)	Brazil, Imperial Russia (ends 1917),
	P_2 (6)	Colombia (1915), Ecuador, Iran, Mexico, Romania, Venezuela
1920 –	S_1 (2)	Argentina, Soviet Union
	S_2 (0)	
	P_1 (2)	Brazil, Romania (1924)
	P_2 (7)	Bolivia (1916), Colombia, Ecuador, Iran, Mexico, Peru (1922), Venezuela
1925 –	S_1 (3)	Argentina, Chile (1926), Soviet Union
	S_2 (0)	
	P_1 (2)	Brazil, Romania
	P_2 (7)	Bolivia, Colombia, Ecuador, Iran, Mexico, Peru, Venezuela

Time Period	Strategy	Countries
1930 –	S_1 (3)	Argentina, Chile, Soviet Union
	S_2 (0)	
	P_1 (2)	Brazil, Romania
	P_2 (8)	Bolivia, Colombia, Ecuador, Iran, Mexico, Peru, Saudi Arabia (1933), Venezuela
1935 –	S_1 (6)	Argentina, Brazil (1938), Chile, Mexico (1938), Soviet Union, Bolivia (1937)
	S_2 (0)	
	P_1 (1)	Romania
	P_2 (6)	Colombia, Ecuador, Iran, Peru, Saudi Arabia, Venezuela
1940 –	S_1 (6)	Argentina, Bolivia, Brazil, Chile, Mexico, Soviet Union
	S_2 (0)	
	P_1 (1)	Romania
	P_2 (6)	Colombia, Ecuador, Iran, Peru, Saudi Arabia, Venezuela
1945 –	S_1 (7)	Argentina, Bolivia, Brazil, Chile, Mexico, Romania (1945), Soviet Union
	S_2 (0)	
	P_1 (1)	Guatemala (1949)
	P_2 (6)	Colombia, Ecuador, Iran, Peru, Saudi Arabia, Venezuela
1950 –	S_1 (9)	Argentina, Brazil, Chile, China (1950), Colombia (1951), Iran (1951), Mexico, Romania, Soviet Union
	S_2 (1)	Iran (1954)
	P_1 (1)	Guatemala
	P_2 (9)	Bolivia (1953), Ecuador, Egypt (1952), India (1953), Iraq (1952), Peru, Saudi Arabia, Syria (1954), Venezuela
1955 –	S_1 (8)	Brazil, Chile, China, Colombia, Mexico, Romania, Soviet Union, Tunisia (1958)
	S_2 (2)	Argentina (1955), Iran
	P_1 (1)	Guatemala
	P_2 (10)	Bolivia, Ecuador, Egypt, India, Iraq, Libya (1955), Peru, Saudi Arabia, Syria, Venezuela
1960 –	S_1 (13)	Argentina (1963), Brazil, Chile, China, Colombia, Egypt (1961), India (1961), Iraq (1961), Mexico, Romania, Soviet Union, Syria (1964), Tunisia
	S_2 (2)	Indonesia (1960), Iran
	P_1 (1)	Guatemala
	P_2 (14)	Algeria (1963), Bolivia, Cameroon (1964) Chad (1962), Ecuador, Gabon (1962), Iraq (1964), Kuwait (1961), Libya, Nigeria (1962), Peru, Saudi Arabia, Trinidad & Tobago (1962), Venezuela

Time Period	Strategy	Countries
1965 –	S$_1$ (13)	Bolivia (1969), Brazil, Chile, China, Colombia, Egypt, India, Mexico, Nigeria (1969), Romania, Soviet Union, Syria, Tunisia
	S$_2$ (4)	Argentina (1967), Indonesia, Iran, Peru (1968)
	P$_1$ (1)	Guatemala
	P$_2$ (13)	Algeria, Cameroon, Chad, Congo (1965), Ecuador, Gabon, Iraq, Kuwait, Libya, Malaysia (1966), Saudi Arabia, Trinidad & Tobago, Venezuela
1970 –	S$_1$ (17)	Algeria (1971), Brazil, Chile, China, Colombia, Ecuador (1972), India, Iran (1973), Iraq (1972), Kuwait (1974), Mexico, Nigeria, Romania, Saudi Arabia (1974), Soviet Union, Syria, Tunisia
	S$_2$ (12)	Argentina, Bahrain (1974), Bolivia (1972), Egypt (1974), Indonesia, Libya (1971), Malaysia (1974), Oman (1974), Peru, Qatar (1974), South Yemen, United Arab Emirates (1974)
	P$_1$ (1)	Guatemala
	P$_2$ (7)	Cameroon, Chad, Congo, Gabon, North Yemen (1974), Trinidad & Tobago, Venezuela
1975–	S$_1$ (18)	Algeria, Brazil, Chile, China, Colombia, Ecuador, India, Iran, Iraq, Kuwait, Mexico, Nigeria, Romania, Saudi Arabia, Soviet Union, Syria, Tunisia, Venezuela (1975)
	S$_2$ (13)	Angola (1978), Argentina, Bahrain, Bolivia, Egypt, Indonesia, Libya, Malaysia, Oman, Peru, Qatar, South Yemen (1976), United Arab Emirates
	P$_1$ (1)	Guatemala
	P$_2$ (7)	Cameroon, Congo, Chad, Gabon, North Yemen, Sudan (1975), Trinidad & Tobago
1980 –	S$_1$ (18)	Algeria, Brazil, Chile, China, Colombia, India, Iran, Iraq, Kuwait, Mexico, Nigeria, Romania, Saudi Arabia, Soviet Union, Syria, Tunisia, Venezuela, Vietnam (1981)
	S$_2$ (15)	Angola, Argentina, Bahrain, Bolivia, Brunei (1984), Ecuador (1983), Egypt, Indonesia, Libya, Malaysia, Oman, Peru, Qatar, South Yemen, United Arab Emirates
	P$_1$ (0)	
	P$_2$ (10)	Cameroon, Chad, Congo, Equatorial Guinea (1980), Gabon, Guatemala (1983), North Yemen, Sudan, Trinidad & Tobago, United Arab Emirates
1985 –	S$_1$ (15)	Brazil, Chile, China, Colombia, India, Iraq, Kuwait, Mexico, Nigeria, Romania, Saudi Arabia, Soviet Union, Syria, Tunisia, Venezuela

Time Period	Strategy	Countries
	S_2 (17)	Algeria (1986), Angola, Bahrain, Bolivia, Brunei, Ecuador, Egypt, Indonesia, Iran (1987), Libya, Malaysia, Oman, Peru, Qatar, South Yemen, United Arab Emirates, Vietnam (1989)
	P_1 (0)	
	P_2 (10)	Argentina (1989), Cameroon, Chad, Congo, Equatorial Guinea, Gabon, Guatemala, North Yemen, Sudan, Trinidad & Tobago
1990 –	S_1 (15)	Brazil, Chile, China, Colombia, Ecuador (1990), India, Iraq, Kuwait, Mexico, Saudi Arabia, Soviet Union (until 1991), Syria, Turkmenistan (1992), Uzbekistan (1993), Venezuela
	S_2 (17)	Algeria, Angola, Azerbaijan (1993), Bahrain, Bolivia, Brunei, Egypt, Indonesia, Iran, Libya, Malaysia, Nigeria (1991), Oman, Qatar, Tunisia (1990), United Arab Emirates, Vietnam
	P_1 (1)	Russian Federation (1993)
	P_2 (12)	Argentina, Cameroon, Chad, Congo, Equatorial Guinea, Gabon, Guatemala, Peru (1993), Romania (1992), Sudan, Trinidad & Tobago, Yemen (1990)
1995 –	S_1 (12)	Brazil, Chile, China, Ecuador, India, Iraq, Kuwait, Mexico, Saudi Arabia, Syria, Turkmenistan, Uzbekistan
	S_2 (17)	Algeria, Angola, Azerbaijan, Bahrain, Brunei, Egypt, Indonesia, Iran, Libya, Malaysia, Nigeria, Oman, Qatar, Venezuela (1995), Tunisia, United Arab Emirates, Vietnam
	P_1 (1)	Russian Federation
	P_2 (15)	Argentina, Bolivia (1996), Cameroon, Chad, Colombia (1999), Congo, Equatorial Guinea, Gabon, Guatemala, Kazakhstan (1995), Peru, Romania, Sudan, Trinidad & Tobago, Yemen
2000 –	S_1 (11)	Brazil, Chile, China, Ecuador, India, Iraq (until 2003), Kuwait, Mexico, Saudi Arabia, Turkmenistan, Venezuela (2001)
	S_2 (18)	Angola, Algeria, Azerbaijan, Bahrain, Brunei, East Timor (2002), Egypt, Iran, Libya, Malaysia, Nigeria, Oman, Qatar, Syria (2002), Tunisia, United Arab Emirates, Uzbekistan (2001), Vietnam
	P_1 (1)	Russian Federation
	P_2 (16)	Argentina, Bolivia, Cameroon, Chad, Colombia, Congo, Equatorial Guinea, Gabon, Guatemala, Indonesia (2001), Kazakhstan, Peru, Romania, Sudan, Trinidad & Tobago, Yemen.

Time Period	Strategy	Countries
2005 –	S_1 (11)	Brazil, Chile, China, Ecuador, India, Kuwait, Mexico, Saudi Arabia, Russian Federation (2005), Turkmenistan, Venezuela
	S_2 (18)	Angola, Azerbaijan, Bahrain, Brunei, East Timor, Egypt, Iran, Kazakhstan (2005), Libya, Malaysia, Nigeria, Oman, Qatar, Syria, Tunisia, United Arab Emirates, Uzbekistan, Vietnam
	P_1 (0)	
	P_2 (16)	Algeria (2005), Argentina, Bolivia, Cameroon, Chad, Colombia, Congo, Equatorial Guinea, Gabon, Guatemala, Indonesia, Peru, Romania, Sudan, Trinidad & Tobago, Yemen

Appendix C

**Responses to Select Life in Transition Survey (LiTS)
Questions by Age Group**

Question	Response categories (%)	Azerbaijan				Kazakhstan			
Should the state be involved in:		18–34	35–49	50–64	65+	18–34	35–49	50–64	65+
Reducing gap between rich and poor?	Not involved	3.4	4.1	4.5	7.2	5.4	3.3	4.6	1.3
	Moderately involved	11.1	4.8	6.8	14.4	38.9	33.4	26.9	29.5
	Strongly involved	85.4	91.1	88.6	78.4	55.8	63.2	68.5	69.1
	Total	100	100	100	100	100	100	100	100
		18–34	35–49	50–64	65+	18–34	35–49	50–64	65+
Guaranteeing employment?	Not involved	1.6	1.0	2.3	3.1	2.8	1.7	1.0	0.0
	Moderately involved	13.8	11.7	12.1	23.7	12.7	12.0	11.2	10.1
	Strongly involved	84.6	87.3	85.6	73.2	84.5	86.3	87.8	89.9
	Total	100	100	100	100	100	100	100	100
		18–34	35–49	50–64	65+	18–34	35–49	50–64	65+
Guaranteeing low prices for electricity and gas?	Not involved	6.4	6.1	7.6	7.2	1.7	0.7	1.5	0.0
	Moderately involved	31.6	29.7	25.0	33.0	19.7	20.1	13.2	14.8
	Strongly involved	62.1	64.2	67.4	59.8	78.6	79.3	85.3	85.2
	Total	100	100	100	100	100	100	100	100
		18–34	35–49	50–64	65+	18–34	35–49	50–64	65+
Guaranteeing low prices for basic goods and food?	Not involved	8.0	5.3	6.8	8.2	3.7	1.3	2.5	1.3
	Moderately involved	21.0	23.9	18.9	22.7	17.5	14.4	8.1	10.7
	Strongly involved	71.1	70.8	74.2	69.1	78.9	84.3	89.3	87.9
	Total	100	100	100	100	100	100	100	100
		18–34	35–49	50–64	65+	18–34	35–49	50–64	65+
Ownership of gas & electricity companies?	Not involved	8.0	8.1	7.6	11.3	3.4	4.0	1.0	2.0
	Moderately involved	38.5	33.0	31.8	34.0	33.2	27.1	26.9	16.8
	Strongly involved	53.6	58.9	60.6	54.6	63.4	68.9	72.1	81.2
	Total	100	100	100	100	100	100	100	100
		18–34	35–49	50–64	65+	18–34	35–49	50–64	65+
Ownership of large companies?	Not involved	9.3	9.6	16.7	8.2	6.8	6.0	3.6	0.7
	Moderately involved	40.3	36.0	35.6	38.1	25.6	30.1	33.0	18.8
	Strongly involved	50.4	54.3	47.7	53.6	67.6	63.9	63.5	80.5
	Total	100	100	100	100	100	100	100	100

Russia				Uzbekistan			
18–34	35–49	50–64	65+	18–34	35–49	50–64	65+
7.3	2.5	2.0	3.0	8.3	5.1	2.7	2.3
40.9	30.3	20.7	15.5	33.0	32.8	38.4	27.3
51.8	67.3	77.3	81.5	58.7	62.1	58.9	70.5
100	100	100	100	100	100	100	100
18–34	35–49	50–64	65+	18–34	35–49	50–64	65+
3.5	2.1	3.0	2.0	0.5	0.6	0.0	1.1
23.3	18.7	14.8	16.0	11.9	10.5	6.2	9.1
73.2	79.2	82.3	82.0	87.6	89.0	93.8	89.8
100	100	100	100	100	100	100	100
18–34	35–49	50–64	65+	18–34	35–49	50–64	65+
2.9	0.4	2.5	2.0	0.5	1.1	0.7	0.0
26.8	22.5	16.3	12.0	20.4	21.2	20.5	18.2
70.3	77.1	81.3	86.0	79.1	77.7	78.8	81.8
100	100	100	100	100	100	100	100
18–34	35–49	50–64	65+	18–34	35–49	50–64	65+
6.1	2.5	5.4	1.5	0.5	0.0	0.0	0.0
23.0	24.6	17.2	17.5	21.6	17.2	18.5	15.9
70.9	72.9	77.3	81.0	77.9	82.8	81.5	84.1
100	100	100	100	100	100	100	100
18–34	35–49	50–64	65+	18–34	35–49	50–64	65+
9.3	4.9	5.4	3.5	4.9	3.4	2.7	4.5
33.9	29.6	25.1	29.0	32.3	28.5	37.0	28.4
56.9	65.5	69.5	67.5	62.9	68.1	60.3	67.0
100	100	100	100	100	100	100	100
18–34	35–49	50–64	65+	18–34	35–49	50–64	65+
13.1	9.2	10.3	5.5	9.0	6.5	6.8	4.5
40.9	35.6	27.6	33.0	34.0	31.1	39.7	29.5
46.0	55.3	62.1	61.5	57.0	62.4	53.4	65.9
100	100	100	100	100	100	100	100

Question	Response categories (%)	Azerbaijan				Kazakhstan			
		18–34	35–49	50–64	65+	18–34	35–49	50–64	65+
What should be done with most privatized companies?	No change	28.6	22.3	17.4	28.9	16.1	9.7	11.2	11.4
	Current owners with compensation	7.4	8.9	12.1	6.2	27.0	28.4	24.9	20.8
	Renationalize/ kept by state	38.5	42.6	43.9	44.3	36.9	48.2	54.3	61.7
	Nationalize & re-privatize	25.5	26.1	26.5	20.6	20.0	13.7	9.6	6.0
	Total	100	100	100	100	100	100	100	100

Russia				Uzbekistan			
18–34	35–49	50–64	65+	18–34	35–49	50–64	65+
26.5	18.3	12.3	13.5	17.5	17.2	9.6	10.2
33.9	33.8	27.1	27.0	22.6	19.8	14.4	20.5
26.2	32.7	47.8	50.0	50.0	52.3	65.8	55.7
13.4	15.1	12.8	9.5	10.0	10.7	10.3	13.6
100	100	100	100	100	100	100	100

Appendix D

Ranking Basis for Determining which Countries are Included in Our Database[1]

Position from averaging world ranks	Position from averaging quantities	Position from weighting quantities
Saudi Arabia	Saudi Arabia	Saudi Arabia
Kuwait	Kuwait	Kuwait
Iran	Iran	Iran
Iraq	Iraq	Iraq
Soviet Union	Russia	United Arab Emirates
Venezuela	Soviet Union	Venezuela
Russia	United Arab Emirates	United States
United Arab Emirates	Venezuela	Mexico
United States	United States	Canada
Libya	Libya	Libya
Mexico	Mexico	Nigeria
Canada	Canada	Soviet Union
Indonesia	Nigeria	Algeria
Nigeria	Chile	Indonesia
Algeria	Algeria	United Kingdom
Norway	Norway	Qatar
Kazakhstan	Indonesia	Chile
Qatar	Kazakhstan	China
Oman	China	Norway
Egypt	United Kingdom	India
India	Qatar	Egypt
Argentina	Oman	Brazil
Malaysia	Azerbaijan	Oman
Brazil	Yemen	Argentina
Colombia	Malaysia	Russia
Chile	India	Angola
Yemen	Egypt	Syria

[1] Information compiled from the *Oil and Gas Journal Database*, based on the years 1952 to 2006. (Database begins in 1952.)

Position from averaging world ranks	Position from averaging quantities	Position from weighting quantities
Brunei	Brazil	Ecuador
Syria	Argentina	Colombia
Angola	Angola	Australia
United Kingdom	Syria	Brunei
Azerbaijan	Ecuador	Malaysia
Australia	Australia	Gabon
Ecuador	Colombia	Congo, Republic of
Trinidad & Tobago	Romania	Trinidad & Tobago
Gabon	Brunei	Tunisia
Peru	Gabon	Peru
Italy	Tunisia	Yemen
Yugoslavia	Congo, Republic of	Italy
Germany	Denmark	Germany
Tunisia	Trinidad & Tobago	Turkey
Romania	Uzbekistan	Denmark
Congo, Republic of	Vietnam	Kazakhstan
Turkey	Turkmenistan	Bahrain
Denmark	Peru	Bolivia
Viet Nam	Italy	Netherlands
Bahrain	Germany	Austria
Bolivia	Ukraine	France
Uzbekistan	Cameroon	Taiwan
Netherlands	Yugoslavia	Pakistan
Senegal	Sudan	Azerbaijan
Papua, New Guinea	Turkey	Romania
Cameroon	Bahrain	Cameroon
Afghanistan	Bolivia	Congo (formerly Zaire)
Turkmenistan	Guatemala	Thailand
France	Belarus	Yugoslavia
Ukraine	Senegal	New Zealand
Pakistan	Netherlands	Guatemala
Austria	Taiwan	Sudan
Sudan	Congo (formerly Zaire)	Papua, New Guinea
Cuba	Albania	Cuba
Congo (formerly Zaire)	Papua, New Guinea	Spain
Japan	Austria	Myanmar (Burma)
China	Cuba	Vietnam
Myanmar (Burma)	Thailand	Japan
New Zealand	France	Philippines
Honduras	New Zealand	Ivory Coast
Taiwan	Pakistan	Uzbekistan
Thailand	Hungary	Turkmenistan
Guatemala	Ivory Coast	Greece
Philippines	Croatia	Albania
Belarus	Serbia (Yugoslavia)	Benin

Position from averaging world ranks	Position from averaging quantities	Position from weighting quantities
Albania	Philippines	Suriname
Spain	Spain	Israel
Ivory Coast	Afghanistan	Hungary
Morocco	Poland	Serbia (Yugoslavia)
Israel	Suriname	Belarus
Hungary	Myanmar (Burma)	Croatia
Serbia (Yugoslavia)	Japan	Poland
Croatia	South Africa	Morocco
Suriname	Greece	Afghanistan
Greece	Kyrgyzstan	Ukraine
Benin	Benin	South Africa
Poland	Georgia	Bangladesh
Barbados	Bangladesh	Ghana
Ghana	Bulgaria	Barbados
South Africa	Czech Republic	Kyrgyzstan
Kyrgyzstan	Lithuania	Georgia
Bangladesh	Tajikistan	Bulgaria
Georgia	Equatorial Guinea	Senegal
Bulgaria	Israel	Czech Republic
Czech Republic	Slovakia	Equatorial Guinea
Equatorial Guinea	Ghana	Lithuania
Jordan	Morocco	Tajikistan
Lithuania	Jordan	Jordan
Tajikistan	Barbados	Slovakia
Slovakia	Honduras	Ethiopia
Ethiopia	Ethiopia	Honduras

Works Cited

Abayev, S. (2004). Legal tradeoff: Kazakhstan working on PSA legislation to clarify the shelf's rules of the game. *Russian Petroleum Investor* (February) 63–6.

Abdurakhmanov, U., and Marnie, S. (2006). Poverty and inequality in Uzbekistan. *Development and Transition* 5 (December), 16–8.

Abdykalykov, A. (2007). Striving for harmony through responsibility. *Kazakhstan International Business Magazine*, no. 3. http://investkz.com/en/journals/53/427.html

Acemoglu, D., Johnson, S., and Robinson, J.A. (2003). An African success story: Botswana, in *In Search of Prosperity: Analytic Narratives on Economic Growth*, ed. D. Rodrik (Princeton University Press, Princeton NJ), 80–119.

(2002). Reversal of fortune: geography and institutions in the making of the modern world income distribution, *Quart. J. Econ.* 117 (4), 1231–94.

Adams, T. (1999). Oil and geopolitical strategy in the Caucasus, *Asian Affairs* 30 (1), 11–20.

(1995a). Historical beginnings: the AIOC-Azerbaijan International Operating Company. *Azerbaijan International* 3 (2), 33–8.

(1995b). Will Azerbaijan really benefit from the consortium contract? *Azerbaijan International* 3 (2), 40.

Adamson, J. (2001). Tengizchevroil lists its commitments to community and social development, *Give and Take* (Winter), 36–7.

Adelman, M.A. (1972). *The World Petroleum Market* (Resources for the Future and Johns Hopkins University Press, Baltimore).

Agafonov, A. (2003). Restructuring of Gazprom: political rationale prevails. *New Energy Group Online*. April 24. http://www.newenergyanalytics.com/reports/index.phtml?234

Agbeibor, Jr., W. (2006). Pro-poor economic growth: role of small and medium sized enterprises. *J. Asian Econ.* 17, 35–40.

Agrawal, P. (2008). Economic growth and poverty reduction: evidence from Kazakhstan. *Asian Devel. Rev.* 24 (2), 90–115.

Ahmed, E. (1992). Social safety nets, in *Fiscal Policies in Economies in Transition*, ed. V. Tanzi (IMF, Washington, DC), 312–29.

Ahmedov, M. , Azimov, R. , Alimova, V., and Rechel, B. (2007). Uzbekistan health system review, *Health Systems in Transition* 9 (3), 1–210.

Ahrend, R. (2006). Russia's economic expansion 1999–2005, in *Return to Growth in CIS Countries*, ed. L. Vinhas de Souza and O. Havrylyshyn (Springer, New York), 9–121.

Ahrend, R. and Tompson, W. (2005). Unnatural monopoly: the endless wait for gas sector reform in Russia. *Europe-Asia Stud.* 57 (6), 801–21.

Akhmediarov, L. (2006). KPO listens and corrupts the air. *Uralsk Weekly*, (June 1).

Akimov, A. and Dollery, B. (2008). Financial system reform in Kazakhstan from 1993 to 2006 and its socioeconomic effects. *Emerging Markets, Finance & Trade* 44 (3), 81–97.

Alam, A., Murthi, M., Yemtsov, R., Murrugarra, E., Dudwick, N., Hamilton, E., and Tiongson, E. (2005). *Growth, Poverty, and Inequality: Eastern Europe and the Former Soviet Union* (World Bank, Washington DC).

Alam, A. and Banerji, A. (2000). *Uzbekistan and Kazakhstan: a tale of two transition paths?* Policy Research Working Paper 2472, (World Bank, Washington DC).

Alarcon, D. and McKinley, T. (1992). Beyond import substitution: the restructuring projects of Brazil and Mexico. *Latin Amer. Perspect.* 19 (2), 72–87.

Alchian, A. and Demsetz, H. (1972). Production, information costs, and economic organization. *Amer. Econ. Rev.* 62 (5), 777–95.

Aldrich, J.H. (1995). *Why Parties?* (University of Chicago Press, Chicago).

Alesina, A. and Drazen, A. (1991). Why are stabilizations delayed? *Amer. Econ. Rev.* 81, 1170–88.

Aleskerov, V. (2002). How far we've come: evaluating the progress of Azerbaijan's oil industry, *Azerbaijan International* 10 (Summer), 72–4.

Aliyev, N. (1994). The contract: anticipating the future. *Azerbaijan International* 2 (4), 25.

Alt, J.E. (1983). The evolution of tax structures, *Public Choice* 41, 181–222.

Amuzegar, J. (2001). *Managing the Oil Wealth: OPECs Windfalls and Pitfalls* (I. B. Tauris, London).

(1998). OPEC as omen. *Foreign Aff.* 77 (Nov/Dec), 95–111.

Anderson, G. (2003). The prospective tax regime for subsurface users in Kazakhstan, *International Tax and Investment Center Special Report* (November), 4–7.

Anderson, J. (1995). Authoritarian political development in Central Asia: the case of Turkmenistan. *Central Asian Survey* 14 (4), 509–27.

Anderson, J. and Gray, C. (2006). *Anti-Corruption in Transition 3: Who is Succeeding... and Why* (World Bank, Washington DC).

Anderson, L. (1992). Liberalization in the Arab world. Discussion paper for the Mellon Seminar, Near East Studies Department, Princeton University, February 14 (cited in Waterbury 1997, 149).

(1987). The state in the Middle East and North Africa, *Comp. Polit.* 20 (1), 1–18.

Andersson, K. (1992). Efficiency considerations in tax policy, in *Fiscal Policies in Economies in Transition*, ed. V. Tanzi (IMF, Washington DC), 101–19.

Andrews, E.S. (2001). Kazakhstan: an ambitious pension reform, *Social Protection Discussion Paper Series. No. 0104*, (World Bank, Washington DC).

Andrews, E.S. and Ringold, D. (1999). *Safety Nets in Transition Economies: Toward a Reform Strategy* (World Bank, Washington DC).

Andrews, M. and Shatalov, S. (2004). Public Expenditure Management in the CIS-7: Recent Developments and Prospects, A background paper for the CIS-7 Initiative, World Bank, Washington DC, (30 June).

Angrist, J.D. and Pischke, J.S. (2008). *Mostly Harmless Econometrics: An Empiricist's Companion* (MIT University Press, Cambridge MA).

Anoshkina, V. (1997). *Evolution of Tax System and Its Influence on Industrial Activity in the Republic of Uzbekistan after Independence.* Report 1997/05. Prepared under the auspices of UNDP Macroeconomic Policy Analysis and Training Project.

Appel, H. (1997). Voucher privatization in Russia. *Europe-Asia Stud.* 49 (8), 1433–49.

Aron, L. (2006). Russia's oil: natural abundance and political shortages. *Russian Outlook Online* (Spring). http://www.aei.org/outlook/24251

(2001). Land privatization: the beginning of the end. *Russian Outlook Online* (June). http://www.aei.org/outlook/12966

Arthur Andersen. (1999). *Kazakhstan Oil and Gas Tax Guide* (Arthur Andersen, Almaty, Kazakhstan).

Asadov, A. (1999). Azerbaijan modernizes its oil and gas legal framework. *Russia/ Central Europe Executive Guide* (May 15).

Asadov, A. and Hadiyev, K. (2002). *Tax regime refined to bolster business and prevent tax evasion.* Baker & McKenzie.

Ascher, W. (1999). *Why Governments Waste Natural Resources: Policy Failures in Developing Countries* (Johns Hopkins University Press, Baltimore/London).

Asian Development Bank (ADB). (2005a). *Asian Development Outlook 2005* (ADB, Hong Kong).

(2005b). *Private Sector Assessment for Uzbekistan* http://www.adb.org/Documents/Reports/PSA/UZB/default.asp

(2000). *Program Completion Report on the Pension Reform Program (Loan 1589-KAZ) in the Republic of Kazakhstan* (ADB, Manila, Philippines).

(1999). *Fiscal Transition in Kazakhstan* (ADB, Manila, Philippines).

Aslund A. (2001). Russia, *For. Policy* 125 (July/August), 20–5.

Auty, R.M. (2006). Optimistic and pessimistic energy rent deployment scenarios for Azerbaijan and Kazakhstan, in *Energy, Wealth and Governance in the Caspian Sea Region*, ed. R. Auty and I. deSoysa (Routledge, London), 57–76.

(2003). Natural resources and 'gradual' reform in Uzbekistan and Turkmenistan. *Natural Resources Forum* 27, 255–66.

(2001a). The political state and the management of mineral rents in capital surplus economies: Botswana and Saudi Arabia. *Resources Pol.* 27, 77–86.

(2001b). *Resource Abundance and Economic Development* (Oxford University Press, Oxford).

(1997a). Does Kazakhstan oil wealth help or hinder the transition? *Development Discussion Paper No. 615*, Harvard Institute for International Development, December.

(1997b). Natural resources, the state and development strategy. *J. Int. Devel.* 9 (4), 651–63.

(1997c). Sustainable mineral-driven development in Turkmenistan. *Environment Discussion Paper No. 36*, Harvard Institute for International Development, December.

(1993). *Sustaining Development in Mineral Economies: The Resource Curse Thesis* (Routledge, London/New York).

(1990). *Resource-Based Industrialization: Sowing the Oil in Eight Developing Countries* (Oxford University Press, New York).

Auty, R.M. and Gelb, A.H. (2001). Political economy of resource abundant states, in *Resource Abundance and Economic Development*, ed. R.M. Auty (Oxford University Press, Oxford), 126–44.

Azerbaijan Economists' Union (AEU) and UNICEF. (2008). *Budget Investments in Health and Education of Azerbaijani Children.* (AEU and UNICEF, Baku, Azerbaijan).

Azerbaijan International. (2004). Exxon Azerbaijan: involvement with education and refugees in Azerbaijan, 12 (Spring), 133.

(2003). Exxon Azerbaijan: philanthropic program in Azerbaijan, 11 (Autumn), 76.

(2000). SOCAR Section: LUKoil Ceremony, 8 (Spring), 89.

Azerbaijan Social Review Commission. (2007). Azerbaijan Social Review Commission First Report. June. Online: http://www.bp.com/genericarticle.do?categoryId=90 06625&contentId=7037156

Babak, V. (2001). Kazakh oil: economic booster or dead weight? *Central Asia and the Caucasus* 3 (9), 35–45.

Bacon, R. and Tordo, S. (2006). *Experiences with Oil Funds: Institutional and Financial Aspects*, Report 321/06, World Bank Energy Sector Management Assistance Program.

Baer, W. (1972). Import substitution and industrialization in Latin America: experience and interpretations. *Latin Amer. Res. Rev.* 7 (1), 95–111.

Bagachi, A. (1991). Perspectives on tax reform and agenda for future research, in *Tax Policy in Developing Countries: A World Bank Symposium*, ed. J. Khalilzadeh-Shirazi and A. Shah (World Bank, Washington DC), 246–7.

Bagirov, S. (2008). *Azerbaijani Oil: Revenues, Expenses, and Risks (View from 2007)* (Yeni Nesil Publishing House, Baku).

(2006). *Azerbaijan's Oil Revenues: Ways of Reducing the Risk of Ineffective Use*, Policy Paper, Central European University Center for Policy Studies/OSI, January.

(1996). Azerbaijani oil: glimpses of a long history. *Perceptions* 1 (2), 22–51.

Bagirov, S., Akhmedov, I., and Tsalik, S. (2003). State oil fund of the Azerbaijan Republic, in *Caspian Oil Windfalls: Who Will Benefit?*, ed. Svetlana Tsalik (Open Society Institute, Caspian Revenue Watch, New York), 89–125.

Bakan, J. (2004). *The Corporation: The Pathological Pursuit of Profits and Power* (Penguin Books, Toronto).

Baker Institute. (2007). The changing role of national oil companies in international energy markets. http://www.rice.edu/energy/publications/PolicyReports/BI_Study_35-1.pdf

Baker & McKenzie. (2006). *Doing Business in Uzbekistan* (Baker & McKenzie, Almaty).

(2003). *Doing Business in Azerbaijan* (Baker & McKenzie, Baku).

Baldwin, D. (2002). Power and international relations, in *Handbook of International Relations*, ed. W. Carlsnaes, T. Risse, and B.A. Simmons (Sage, London), 177–91.

Baldwin, R.E. (1966). *Economic Development and Export Growth* (University of California Press, Berkeley).

Ball, J. (2006). Digging deep: As Exxon pursues African oil, charity becomes political issue. *The Wall Street Journal* (January 10), A1.

Bamberg, J.H. (1994). *The History of the British Petroleum Company, Vol. 2: The Anglo Iranian Years, 1928–1954* (Cambridge University Press, Cambridge).

Bank of Finland Institute for Economies in Transition (BOFIT). (2008). Russia. *BOFIT Weekly* 34, 1.

Bantekas, I. (2005). Natural resource revenue sharing schemes (trust funds) in international law. *Netherlands Int. Law Rev.*, 31–56.

(2003). The 2003 investment law: its impact and compatibility with international foreign investment law, in *Oil and Gas Law in Kazakhstan: National and International Perspectives*, ed. I. Bantekas, J. Paterson, and M. Suleimenov (Kluwer Law International, The Hague), 171–85.

Barbone, L. and Sánchez, L.A. (2003). The political economy of taxation in CIS countries. Unpublished paper.

Barnett, M.N. and Finnemore, M. (1999). The politics, power, and pathologies of international organizations. *Int. Organ.* 54 (Autumn), 699–732.

Bassin, Y. (2004). Subsurface use legislation in Kazakhstan, in *Oil and Gas Law in Kazakhstan: National and International Perspectives*, ed. I. Bantekas, J. Paterson, and M. Suleimenov (Kluwer Law International, The Hague), 115–21.

Barzel, Y. (1977). Some fallacies in the interpretation of information costs. *J. Law Econ.* 20, 291–307.

Bates, L.W. (1975). *The Petroleum Industry in Brazil* (University of Texas at Austin, Austin TX).

Bates, R.H. (1988). Contra contractarianism: some reflections on the new institutionalism. *Politic. Soc.* 16 (June–September), 387–401.

(1981). *Markets and States in Tropical Africa* (University of California Press, Berkeley and Los Angeles).

Bates, R.H. and Da-Hsing, D.L. (1985). A note on taxation, development, and representative government. *Politic. Soc.* 14 (1), 53–70.

Bati, S.A. and Bayramov, J. (2002). Azerbaijan introduces changes to its tax code, in *Tax Issues for the Energy Sector in Russia and the Caspian Region* (World Trade Executive, Concord).

Baunsgaard, T. (2001). *A Primer on Mineral Taxation*. IMF Working Paper, WP/01/139 (IMF, Washington DC).

Bayulgen O. (2005). Foreign investment, oil curse, and democratization: a comparison of Azerbaijan and Russia. *Bus. Politic.* 7 (1), 1–37.

Bayulgen, O. (2003). *Polarizing Effects of Globalization: Political Regimes That Attract Oil Investments*. Ph.D. dissertation, University of Texas at Austin, Texas.

Bayatly, T. (2005). BP current developments: tap opened for the BTC pipeline. *Azerbaijan International* 13 (2), 92–5.

(2004). BP current developments: BTC pipeline moves ahead. *Azerbaijan International* 12 (3), 92–4.

(2003a). BP current developments: enlarging the terminal at Sangachal. *Azerbaijan International* 11 (2), 70–1.

(2003b). BP current developments: BTC pipelaying begins. *Azerbaijan International* 11 (3), 78–9.

(2001). BP current developments. *Azerbaijan International* 9 (1), 86–7.

(2000). BP current developments. *Azerbaijan International* 8 (Autumn), 100–3.

Beblawi, H. (1987). The rentier state in the Arab world, in *Nation, State and Integration in the Arab World. Vol. 2, The Rentier State*, ed. H. Beblawi and G. Luciani (Croom Helm, London), 49–62.

Beblawi, H., and Luciani, G., ed. (1987). *Nation, State and Integration in the Arab World. Vol. 2, The Rentier State* (Croom Helm, London).

Becker, C.M., Marchenko, G.A., Khakimzhanov, S., Seitenova, A.S., and Ivliev, V. (2009). *Social Security Reform in Transition Economies: Lessons from Kazakhstan* (Palgrave MacMillan, New York).

Bejanova, I. (1998). Turkmenistan's tax system. *BISNIS* (June). http://permanent. access.gpo.gov/lps3997/9806turk.htm

Belin, L. (2004). Politics and the mass media under Putin, in *Russian Politics under Putin*, ed. C. Ross (Manchester University Press, Manchester), 133–54.

Belton, C. and Faulconbridge, G. (2004). Mystery bidder wins Yugansk for $9.4Bln. *Moscow Times* (December 20), 1.

Benini, R. and Czyzewski, A. (2007). Regional disparities and economic growth in Russia, *Economic Change and Restructuring* 40 (1–2), 91–135.

Bennett, J. (2002). Multinational corporations, social responsibility, and conflict. *J. Int. Affairs* 55 (2), 393–410.

Bentham, R.W. and Smith, W.G.R. (1986). *State Petroleum Corporations: Corporate Forms, Power and Control*. The Centre for Petroleum Law and Mineral Studies (University of Dundee, Dundee).

Berdalina, J. and Mustapaeva, A. (2003). Tax burden in Kazakhstan. *Kazakhstan International Business Magazine* 1. http://www.investkz.com/en/journals/34/229. html

Berenson, M. (2007). *Becoming Citizens: Attitudes toward Tax Compliance in Poland Russia, and Ukraine*. Paper delivered at the Annual Bank Conference on Development Economics, May 17–18, Bled, Slovenia.

Bergh, E. (1996). AIOC current developments. *Azerbaijan International* 4 (2), 40.

Berglof, E. and Lehmann, A. (2008). *Sustaining Russia's Growth: The Role of Financial Reform*. European Bank for Reconstruction and Development.

Berkowitz, D. and DeJong, D.N. (2008). *Growth in Post-Soviet Russia: A Tale of Two Transitions*. Manuscript, Department of Economics, University of Pittsburgh.

Besley, T. (1990). Means testing versus universal provision in poverty alleviation programmes, *Economica* 57 (225), 119–29.

Bindemann, K. (1999). Production-sharing agreements: An economic analysis. *WPM* 25, Oxford Institute for Energy Studies.

Bird, R.M. and Gendron, P.P. (2007). *The VAT in Developing Countries and Transitional Countries* (Cambridge University Press, Cambridge).

Bird, R.M. and Zolt, E.M. (2005). Redistribution via taxation: The limited role of the personal income tax in developing countries, *UCLA Law Review* 52, 1627–95.

Birdsall, N. and Subramanian A. (2004). Saving Iraq from its oil. *For. Aff.* 83 (4), 77–89.

Biznes Klass. (1999). Interview with Akim of Atyrau Oblast. 11 (August), 2.

Bjorvatn, K. and Selvik, K. (2007). Destructive competition: Factionalism and rent-seeking in Iran, Discussion Paper, Norwegian School of Economics and Business Administration, February 14.

Blackmon, P. (2005). Back to the USSR: why the past does matter in explaining differences in the economic reform processes of Kazakhstan and Uzbekistan. *Central Asian Survey* 24 (4), 391–404.

Blair, B. (1996). Ilham Aliyev, SOCAR VP, Foreign Economic Relations (Interview). *Azerbaijan International* (Winter), 48–51.

Boix, C. (2003). *Democracy and Redistribution* (Cambridge University Press, Cambridge).

Bornhorst, F., Gupta, S., and Thornton, J. (2008). *Natural Resource Endowments, Governance, and the Domestic Revenue Effort: Evidence from a Panel of Countries*. IMF Working Paper 08/170 (IMF, Washington DC).

Bowen, H.R. (1953). *Social Responsibilities of the Businessman* (Harper and Row, New York).

Boycko, M., Shleifer, A., and Vishny, R. (1997). *Privatizing Russia* (MIT Press, Cambridge MA).

(1996). A theory of privatization. *The Economic Journal* 106, 309–19.

Boylan, D.M. (2001). *Defusing Democracy: Central Bank Autonomy and the Transition from Authoritarian Rule* (University of Michigan Press, Ann Arbor).

Bremmer, I. and Charap, S. (2006–07). The Siloviki in Putin's Russia: who they are and what they want. *The Washington Quarterly* 30 (1), 83–92.

Brennan, G. and Buchanan, J.M. (1980). *The Power to Tax: Analytical Foundations of a Fiscal Constitution* (Cambridge University Press, New York).

Bridgman, B., Gomes, V., and Teixeria. A. (2009). *Threatening to Increase Productivity.* Unpublished draft (October 16).

British Petroleum (BP). (2006). *BP in Azerbaijan Sustainability Report 2006.*

(2005). *BP in Azerbaijan Sustainability Report 2005.*

(2004). *BP in Azerbaijan Sustainability Report 2004.*

(2003). *Regional Review.*

Broadman, H.G. (2000). *Competition, Corporate Governance and Regulation in Central Asia: Uzbekistan's Structural Reform Challenges* (World Bank, Washington DC).

Bromley, D. (2006). *Sufficient Reason: Volitional Pragmatism and the Meaning of Economic Institutions* (Princeton University Press, Princeton NJ).

(1989). *Economic Interests and Institutions: The Conceptual Foundations of Public Policy* (Basil Blackwell: Oxford).

Browder, W. (2002a). *Gazprom and Itera: A Case Study in Russian Corporate Misgovernance.* Speech at the Carnegie Foundation, Washington DC, March 18.

(2002b). It is time to fix a national embarrassment. *St. Petersburg Times* 781 (47), June 28.

Brune, N. and Garrett, G. (2000). *The Diffusion of Privatization in the Developing World.* Paper presented at the annual meeting of the American Political Science Association, Boston, August 31–September 3.

Brunnschweiler, C.N. (2008). Cursing the blessings? Natural resource abundance, institutions, and economic growth. *World Devel.* 36 (3), 399–419.

Brunnschweiler, C.N. and Bulte, E.H. (2008). The resource curse revisited and revised: a tale of paradoxes and red herrings. *J. Environ. Econ. Manage.* 55 (3), 248–64.

Brynen, R. (1992). Economic crisis and post-rentier democratization in the Arab world: the case of Jordan. *Can. J. Polit. Sci.* 25 (1), 69–97.

Bulte, E., Damania, R., and Deacon, R. (2003). Resource abundance, poverty and development. http://www.econ.ucsb.edu/papers/wp21–03.pdf

Burgess, R. and Stern, N. (1993). Taxation and development. *J. Econ. Lit.* (June), 762–830.

Callaghy, T. (1984). *The State-Society Struggle: Zaire in Comparative Perspective* (Columbia University Press, New York).

Campbell, J.L. (1993). The state and fiscal sociology. *Annual Review of Sociology* 19, 163–85.

Cardoso, F.H. and Faletto, E. (1979). *Dependency and Development in Latin America* (University of California Press, Berkeley).

Carlson, E.V. (2009). *Managing Society: The Politics of Social Provision in Kazakhstan's Oil Industry*. Working Paper for Presentation at the Business and Society Workshop, University of Cambridge.

Carlson, S. (1977). *Indonesia's Oil* (Westview Press, Boulder).

Cashore, B. (2004). *Governing through Markets: Forest Certification and the Emergence of Non-state Authority* (Yale University Press, New Haven CT).

Caspian Development Advisory Panel (CDAP). (2003). Interim Report.

Castells, M. (1992). Four Asian tigers with a dragon head: A comparative analysis of the state, economy, and society in the Asian Pacific Rim, in *States and Development in the Asian Pacific Rim*, ed. R. Appelbaum and J. Henderson (Sage, Newbury Park), 33–70.

Center for Social and Economic Research (CASE). (2008). *The Economic Aspects of the Energy Sector in CIS Countries*. Economic Papers 327, European Commission, Brussels.

CER. (1996). *The State Budget of the Republic of Uzbekistan, 1991 to 1995*. CER Working Paper 96/3 (September), Tashkent.

Chaudhry K.A. (1997). *The Price of Wealth: Economies and Institutions in the Middle East* (Cornell University Press, Ithaca NY).

Chaudhry, K.A. (1993). The myths of the market and the common history of late developers. *Politic. Soc.* 21 (3), 245–74.

  (1989). The price of wealth: business and state in labor remittance and oil economies. *Int. Organ.* 43, 101–45.

Chentsova, O. (2004). Kazakh legislation on subsurface use: historical background and present status, in *Oil and Gas Law in Kazakhstan: National and International Perspectives*, ed. I. Bantekas, J. Paterson, and M. Suleimenov (Kluwer Law International, The Hague), 123–31.

Cheung, S. (1969). Transaction costs, risk aversion, and the choice of contractual arrangements. *J. Law Econ.* 12, 23–42.

Christiansen, A.C. (2002). *Beyond Petroleum: Can BP Deliver?* Fridtjog Nansens Institutt. FNI Report 6/2002.

Coady, D., El-Said, M., Gillingham, R., Kpodar, K., Medas, P., and Newhouse, D. (2006). *The Magnitude and Distribution of Fuel Subsidies: Evidence from Bolivia, Ghana, Jordan, Mali, and Sri Lanka*. IMF Working Paper WP/06/247 (IMF, Washington DC).

Coase, R.H. (1937). The nature of the firm. *Economica* (November), 386–405.

Coffey International Development. (2009). *Validation of the Extractive Industries Transparency Initiative (EITI) in the Republic of Azerbaijan* (Berkshire, UK).

Cohen, M. (2006). The effect of oil revenues on transitional economics: the case of Azerbaijan, *Geopolitics of Energy* 28 (6), 12–20.

Collier, P. (2007). *The Bottom Billion: Why the Poorest Countries are Failing and What Can Be Done About It* (Oxford University Press, Oxford).

Collier, P. and Gunning, J.W. (1996). *Policy towards Commodity Shocks in Developing Countries*. IMF Working Paper 96/84 (IMF, Washington DC).

Collier P., and Hoeffler, A. (2004). Greed and grievance in civil war. *Oxford Econ. Pap.* 56, 563–95.

Conrad, R. (2009). Memorandum. *Trip Report: Russia* (March 25), 1–4.

  (2005). Memorandum. *Trip Report: Russia* (December 18), 1–6.

Contreras, M.E. (1993). *The Bolivian Tin Mining Industry in the First Half of the 20th Century* (Institute of Latin American Studies, London).

Cook, L.J. (2007a). Negotiating welfare in postcommunist states. *Comp. Polit.* 40(1), 41–62.

(2007b). *Postcommunist Welfare States: Reform Politics in Russia and Eastern Europe* (Cornell University Press, Ithaca NY).

Cornia, G.A. (2003). *Taxation, Public Expenditure and Poverty Reduction.* UNDP Poverty Report Draft, chapter 7.

Costello, C., Gaines, S.D., and Lynham, J. (2008). Can catch shares prevent fisheries collapse? *Science* 321, 1678–81.

Coudouel, A., Marnie, S., and Micklewright, J. (1998). *Targeting Social Assistance in a Transition Economy: The Mahallas in Uzbekistan.* Innocenti Occasional Papers, Economic and Social Policy Series, No. 63 (UNICEF International Child Development Centre, Firenze).

Cremer, H., Pestieau P., and Rochet, J.C. (2001). Direct versus indirect taxation: the design of the tax structure revisited. *Int. Econ. Rev.* 42 (3), 781–800.

Curtis, G.E., ed. (1995). *Armenia, Azerbaijan, and Georgia Country Studies* (United States Library of Congress, Washington DC).

Dabrowski, M. and Antczak, R. (1996). Economic transition in Russia, Ukraine, and Belarus: Comparative perspective, in *Economic Transition in Russia and the New States of Eurasia*, ed. B. Kaminski (M.E. Sharpe, New York), 42–80.

Dadabaev, T. (2006). Living conditions, intra-societal trust, and public concerns in post-socialist Turkmenistan, *Central Asia and the Caucasus* 4 (40), 122–32.

Daniel, E.L. (2001). *The History of Iran* (Greenwood Press, Westport CT).

Davis, G. (1995). Learning to love the Dutch disease: evidence from the mineral economies. *World Dev.* 23 (10), 1765–79.

Davis, J., Ossowski R., Daniel J.A., and Barnett S. (2003). Stabilization and savings funds for nonrenewable resource experience and fiscal policy implications, in *Fiscal Policy Formulation and Implementation in Oil-Producing Countries*, ed. J. Davis, R. Ossowski, and A. Fedelino (IMF, Washington DC), 273–315.

de Ferranti, D., Perry, G.E., Lederman, D., and Maloney, W.F. (2002). *From Natural Resources to the Knowledge Economic: Trade and Job Quality* (World Bank, Washington DC).

de Soto, H. (1989). *The Other Path* (Harper and Row, New York).

Delacroix, J. (1980). The distributive state in the world-system. *Stud. Comp. Int. Dev.* 15(3), 3–1.

Deloitte & Touche. (2004). *Kazakhstan Oil and Gas Guide* (Deloitte & Touche, Kazakhstan).

Demsetz, H. (1967). Toward a theory of property rights. *Amer. Econ. Rev.* 57, 347–59.

Denisova, I. (2006). Uzbekistan attempts another sale of oil and gas companies: a second try, *Caspian Investor* (September), 22–5.

(2004). Kazakhs alter taxation rules: Kazakhstan increases tax burden on oilmen, especially participants in new projects, *Caspian Investor* (February), 11–13.

(2002). Astana's offer to foreign investors: let's exchange old taxes for new concessions, in *Tax Issues for the Energy Sector in Russia and the Caspian Region*, World Trade Executive, Inc., 29–34.

Denisova, I. and Grigoryev, I. (2004). Price of progress: project to develop Azeri-Chyrag Gyuneshli fields making progress–but at higher cost, *Russian Petroleum Investor* (June/July), 52–4.

Department of Energy-Energy Information Administration (DOE-EIA). (2007). *Country Analysis Briefs: Azerbaijan.*

(2005). *Country Analysis Briefs: Uzbekistan.*

Desai, R.M. and Goldberg, I. (2007). *Enhancing Russia's Competitiveness and Innovative Capacity* (World Bank, Washington DC).

Deutsch, K.W. (1961). Social mobilization and political development. *Amer. Polit. Sci. Rev.* 55 (3), 493–514.

Dienes, L. (1996). *Corporate Russia: Privatization and Prospects in the Oil and Gas Sector.* The Donald W. Treadgold Papers, No. 5.

Di John, J. (2006). *The Political Economy of Taxation and Tax Reform in Developing Countries.* UNU-WIDER Research Paper No. 2006/74.

Djankov, S. and Symons, S. (2007). *Paying Taxes 2008: The Global Picture* (World Bank Group and PricewaterhouseCoopers, Washington DC).

Doing Business in 2007: How to Reform. (2007). The International Bank for Reconstruction and Development and The World Bank, Washington DC.

Doing Business in 2006: Creating Jobs. (2006). The International Bank for Reconstruction and Development and The World Bank, Washington DC.

Doing Business in 2005: Removing Obstacles to Growth. (2005). The International Bank for Reconstruction and Development and The World Bank, Washington DC.

Dunning, T. (2008). *Crude Democracy: Natural Resource Wealth and Political Regimes* (Cambridge University Press, New York).

Duran, E. (1985). Pemex: The trajectory of a national oil policy, in *The Oil Business in Latin America*, ed. J.D. Wirth (Beard Books, Washington DC), 145–88.

Duwaji G. (1967). *Economic Development in Tunisia: The Impact and Course of Government Planning* (Praeger, New York).

Easter, G. (2002). Politics of revenue extraction in post-communist states: Poland and Russia compared. *Politic. Soc.* 30 (December), 599–627.

Ebrill, L. and Havrylyshyn, O. (1999). *Tax Reform in the Baltics, Russia, and the Other Countries of the Former Soviet Union.* Occasional Paper 182 (IMF, Washington DC).

Ebrill, L., Keen, M., Bodin, J.P., and Summers, V. (2001). *The Modern VAT* (IMF, Washington D.C).

Economic Research Center (ERC). (2006). *Three Views on EITI Implementation in Azerbaijan* (Economic Research Center, Baku).

Economist. (1992). Kazakhstan's oil industry: tomorrow's gusher. (July 25), 72.

Economist Intelligence Unit (EIU). (2007). *Russia Country Profile.* London.

(2006a). *Azerbaijan Country Profile.* London.

(2006b). *Russia Country Profile.* London.

(2006c). *Turkmenistan Country Profile.* London.

(2003a). *Azerbaijan Country Profile.* London.

(2003b). *Turkmenistan Country Profile.* London.

(2002). *Uzbekistan Country Profile.* London.

(2001a). *Azerbaijan Country Profile.* London.

(2001b). *Russia Country Profile.* London.

(1999). *Azerbaijan Country Report. 4th Quarter.* London.

Eden, L., Lenway, S., and Schuler, D. (2004). *From the Obsolescing Bargain to the Political Bargaining Model.* Bush School Working Paper #403 Texas A&M University, The Bush School of Government and Public Service.

Edmiston, K. (2001). *Expenditure Management and Fiscal Restraint: Lessons from Kazakhstan 1997–2000*. Working Paper 01–09. Georgia State University, Andrew Young School of Policy Studies.

Eggertson, T. (1990). *Economic Behavior and Institutions* (Cambridge University Press, New York).

Eifert, B., Gelb, A., and Tallroth, N.B. (2003). The political economy of fiscal policy and economic management in oil-exporting countries, in *Fiscal Policy Formulation and Implementation in Oil-Producing Countries*, ed. J. Davis, R. Ossowski, and A. Fedelino (IMF, Washington DC), 82–122.

Eller, S.L., Hartley, P., and Medlock, K.B. III. (2007). *Empirical Evidence on the Operational Efficiency of National Oil Companies*. The James Baker III Institute for Public Policy, Rice University.

Emran, M.S. and Stigltiz, J.E. (2005). On selective indirect tax reform in developing countries. *J. Public Econ.* 89, 599–623.

Engelschalk, M. (2005). *Creating a Favorable Tax Environment for Small Business Development in Transition Countries* (World Bank, Washington DC).

Entrepreneurship Development Foundation (EDF). (2006). Azerbaijan: The population's expectations from oil revenues and their spending. (On file with the authors).

Entelis, J.P. (1999). Sonatrach: the political economy of an Algerian state institution. *Middle East J.* 53 (1), 9–27.

(1976). Oil wealth and the prospects for democratization in the Arabian Peninsula: the case of Saudi Arabia, in *Arab Oil: Impact on the Arab Countries and Global Implications*, ed. N.A. Sherbiny and M.A. Tessler (Praeger, New York), 77–111.

Epstein, E. and Berezanskaja, E. (2002). Morgan Stanley priznal "Yukos" dostoinim investirovanija. (Morgan Stanley Found Yukos Worthy of Investment. *Vedomosti* (April), 15.

Ernst & Young. (2008). *Kazakhstan Oil and Tax Guide.*

(2006a). *Kazakhstan Oil and Tax Guide.*

(2006b). *Russian Tax Brief* (October).

(2004). *Oil and Gas Guide to Azerbaijan.*

Ervin, B. (2007). The new oil barons. *Urban Tulsa Weekly* (August 1).

Esanov, A., Raiser, M., and Buiter, W. (2003). *Nature's Blessing or Nature's Curse: The Political Economy of Transition in Resource-Based Economies*. National Bank of Poland (October 23–24).

Esanov, A., Raiser, M., and Buiter, W. (2001). *Nature's Blessing or Nature's Curse: The Political Economy of Transition in Resource-Based Economies*. EBRD Working Paper No. 65.

Eshag, E. (1983). *Fiscal and Monetary Problems in Developing Countries* (Cambridge University Press, Cambridge).

Eurasia Insight. (2003). Azerbaijan's new president expresses belief in 'lucky future' as crackdown on opposition continues. November 3. http://www.eurasianet.org/departments/insight/articles/eav110303a.shtml

Europe's Top 50: Russian philanthropy hits the big time. (2006). *Philanthropy in Europe* 25, 12.

European Bank for Reconstruction and Development (EBRD). (2008). *Financial Reform and Growth in Russia* (EBRD, London).

(2006a). *Strategy for Kazakhstan* (EBRD, London).

(2006b). *Transition Report: Finance in Transition* (EBRD, London).

(2004). *Transition Report: Infrastructure* (EBRD, London).

(2002). *Transition Report: Agriculture and Rural Transition* (EBRD, London).

(1996). *Transition Report: Building an Infrastructure for Transition and Promoting Savings* (EBRD, London).

Evans, P. (1992). The state as problem and solution: Predation, embedded autonomy, and structural change, in *The Politics of Economic Adjustment: International Constraints, Distributive Conflicts, and the State*, ed. S. Haggard and R.R. Kaufman (Princeton University Press, Princeton NJ), 139–81.

Faradov, T. (2003). *Foreign Policy Orientations in Azerbaijan: Public and Elite Opinion*. NATO-EAPC Fellowships Program (2001/2003).

Fauvelle-Aymar, C. (1999). The political and tax capacity of government in developing countries. *Kyklos* 52 (3), 391–413.

Fierman, W.K. (1997). Political development in Uzbekistan: Democratization? in *Conflict, Cleavage and Change in Central Asia and the Caucuses*, ed K. Dawish and B. Parrott (Cambridge University Press, Cambridge, UK and New York), 360–408.

Findlay, A. and Lawless, R. (1984). *North Africa: Contemporary Politics and Economic Development* (St. Martin's Press, New York).

Finn, P. (2004). Russian oil firm buys mysterious bid winner. *Washington Post* (December 23), A01.

Foley, M. (1997). *Labor Market Dynamics in Russia*. Center Discussion Paper No. 780, Economic Growth Center, Yale University.

Freinkman, L., Gyulumyan, G., and Kyurumyan, A. (2003). *Quasi-Fiscal Activities, Hidden Government Subsidies, and Fiscal Adjustment in Armenia* (World Bank, Washington DC).

Friedman, T. (2006). The first law of petropolitics. *For. Policy* (May/June), 28–36.

Frye, T. (2006). Original sin, good works, and property rights in Russia. *World Polit.* 58 (July), 479–504.

Frynas, J. (2004). The oil book in Equatorial Guinea. *African Aff.* 103 (413), 527–46.

Furubotn, E.G. and Pejovich, S. (1972). Property rights and economic theory: a survey of recent literature. *J. Econ. Lit.* 10 (4), 1137–62.

Gaddy, C.G. (2007). The Russian economy in the year 2006. *Post-Soviet Affairs* 23 (1), 38–49.

Gaddy, C.G. and Ickes, B.W. (1998). Russia's virtual economy. *For. Aff.* (September/October), 53–67.

Gaddy, C.G. and Gale, W.G. (2005). Demythologizing the Russian flat tax. *Tax Notes International* (March 14), 983–8.

Gaiduk, I. (2006). Year 2005 Summary. *Russian Petroleum Investor* (March), 6–12.

Gale, B. (1981). Petronas: Malaysia's national oil corporation. *Asian Survey* 21 (11), 1129–44.

Gary I. and Karl, T.L. (2003). *Bottom of the Barrel: Africa's Oil Boom and the Poor*. Catholic Relief Services.

Garrett, G. (1998). *Partisan Politics in the Global Economy* (Cambridge University Press, New York).

Gause III, F.G. (2000). Saudi Arabia: over a barrel. *For. Aff.* (May/June), 80–94.

Gavin, M. (1993). Adjusting to a terms of trade shock: Nigeria, 1972–88, in *Policymaking in the Open Economy: Concepts and Case Studies in Economic Performance*, ed. R. Dornbusch (Oxford University Press: Oxford), 172–219.

Gazprom (2008). *The Impossible is Possible.*

Gazprom. (2006). *Annual Report 2005.*

(2004). *Annual Report 2003.*

(2003). *Annual Report 2002.*

(2002). *Annual Report 2001.*

(2001). *Annual Report 2000.*

Gelb, A.H. and Associates. (1988). *Oil Windfalls: Blessing or Curse?* (Oxford University Press, New York/Oxford).

Gelb, B.A. (2002). *Caspian Oil and Gas: Production & Prospects.* CSR Report for Congress, April 9.

Gereffi, G., Garcia-Johnson, R., and Sasser, E. (2001). The NGO-industrial complex. *For. Policy* 125 (July–August), 56–65.

Gershenkron, A. (1962). *Economic Backwardness in Historical Perspective: A Book of Essays* (Harvard University Press, Cambridge, MA).

Gibb, G.S. and Knowlton, E.H. (1956). *The Resurgent Years, 1911–1927, History of Standard Oil Company (New Jersey)* (Harper & Brothers, New York).

Giddens, A. (1987). *The Nation-State and Violence* (University of California Press, Berkeley and Los Angeles).

Gleason, G. (2003). *Markets and Politics in Central Asia* (Routledge, London).

(1990). Marketization and migration: the politics of cotton in Central Asia. *Journal of Soviet Nationalities* 1 (Summer), 66–98.

Goldman Sachs. (2004). *Global Energy–Goldman Sachs Energy Environmental and Social Index* (Goldman Sachs, London).

Global Witness. (2006). *It's a Gas: Funny Business in the Turkmen Ukraine Gas Trade* (Global Witness Publishing Inc., Washington DC).

(2004). *Time for Transparency: Coming Clean on Oil, Mining and Gas Revenues.* (Global Witness, London).

Glych, M. (2001). Going it alone? Turkmenistan takes back oil fields assigned to foreign operators. *Russian Petroleum Investor* (February), 43–6.

Golden, T. (1991). Company news; Mexico pries open its oil industry. *New York Times* (September 25), D1.

Goldman, M.I. (2004). Putin and the oligarchs, *For. Aff.* 83 (6), 33–44.

(1999). Russian energy: a blessing and a curse. *J. Int. Aff.* 53 (1), 73–84.

(1980). *The Enigma of Soviet Petroleum* (George Allen & Unwin, London).

Gorenburg, D. (1999). Regional separatism in Russia: ethnic mobilization or power grab. *Europe-Asia Stud.* 51 (2), 245–74.

Gorst, I. (2008). Burning ambition to compete on global stage. *Financial Times* (January 25), 3.

Goskomstat. (1996). *Rossiia v tsifrakh* [Russia in figures]. Moscow: Goskomstat (State Committee of the Russian Federation on Statistics).

Gould, J.A. and Winters, M.S. (2007). An obsolescing bargain in Chad: shifts in leverage between the government and the World Bank. *Bus. Politic.* 9 (2), 1–34.

Government of Azerbaijan (GoA). 2005. *State Programme on Poverty Reduction and Economic Development 2003–2005.* Baku.

Grigoryev, I. (2002). New law narrows foreign investment rights: provisions may encourage foreign companies to seek alliances with local companies. *Russia/Central Europe Executive Guide* (January 31).

(2001). Suffering setbacks: negative results of exploration drilling in new projects may complicate Baku's export plans. *Russian Petroleum Investor* (August), 32–4.

Grigoryev, Y. (2007). The Russian gas industry, its legal structure, and its influence on world markets. *Energy Law Journal* 28, 125–45.

Guadagni M., Raiser M., Crole-Rees A., and Khidirov D. (2005). *Cotton Taxation in Uzbekistan: Opportunities for Reform*. ECSSD Working Paper No. 41 (World Bank, Washington, DC).

Gulbrandsen, L.H. and Moe, A. (2007). BP in Azerbaijan: a test case of the potential and limits of the CSR agenda? *Third World Quarterly* 28 (4), 813–30.

(2005). Oil company CSR collaboration in "new" petro-states. *Journal of Corporate Citizenship* 20, 53–64.

Gupta, S., Leruth, L., De Mello, L., and Chakravarti, S. (2003). Transition economies: how appropriate is the size and scope of government? *Compar. Econ. Stud.* 45, 554–76.

Gustafson, T. (1999). *Capitalism Russian Style* (Cambridge University Press, Cambridge).

(1989). *Crisis amid Plenty: The Politics of Soviet Energy under Brezhnev and Gorbachev* (Princeton University Press, Princeton NJ).

Gylfason, T. (2001). Nature, power, and growth. *Journal of Political Economy* 48 (5), 558–88.

Haber, S. and Menaldo, V. (2008). *Do Natural Resources Fuel Authoritarianism? A Reappraisal of the Resource Curse*. Draft, December 24.

Haaparanta, P., Juurikkala, T., Lazareva, O., Pirttilä, J., Solanko, L., and Zhuravskaya, E. (2003). *Firms and Public Service Provision in Russia*. BOFIT Discussion Paper No. 16. Helsinki: Finland.

Hart, J.A. (1983). *The New International Economic Order* (St. Martin's Press, New York).

Hartshorn, J.E. (1967). *Oil Companies and Governments: An Account of the International Oil Industry in Its Political Environment* (Faber and Faber, London).

Harvey, C. and Lewis Jr., S. (1980). *Policy Choice and Development Performance in Botswana* (Macmillan, London).

Haufler, V. (2006). *Corporate Transparency: International Diffusion of a Policy Idea?* Paper Prepared for the IR Field Workshop, University of Maryland.

Hausmann R. and Rigobon R. (2003). An alternative interpretation of the "resource curse": theory and policy implications, in *Fiscal Policy Formulation and Implementation in Oil-Producing Countries*, ed. J. Davis, R. Ossowski, and A. Fedelino (IMF, Washington DC), 13–44.

Heilbrunn, J. R. (2002). *Governance and Mineral Funds*. World Bank (mimeo).

Hellman, J. (1998). Winners take all: the politics of partial reform in post-communist transitions. *World Polit.* 50 (2), 203–34.

Herb, M. (2005). No representation without taxation? Rents, development, and democracy. *Comp. Polit.* 37, 297–317.

(2003). Taxation and representation. *Stud. Comp. Int. Dev.* 38 (3), 3–31.

Herrera, Y. (2006). *Transforming Bureaucracy: Conditional Norms and the International Standardization of Statistics in Russia*. Paper presented at the annual meeting of the American Political Science Association, Philadelphia, PA, August/September.

Hersh, S.M. (2001). The price of oil. *New Yorker* 77 (July 9), 48–65.

Herszenhorn, D.M. (2008). Senators sharply question oil officials. *New York Times* (May 22).

Hill, F. (2004). *Energy Empire: Oil, Gas, and Russia's Revival* (Foreign Policy Centre, London).

Hines, J. , and Sievers, E. (2001). Legal regime for hydrocarbon development in Uzbekistan. *Journal of Energy and Natural Resources Law* 19 (4), 387–402.

Hines, J.H. and Varanese, J.B. (2001). Turkmenistan's oil and gas sector: overview of the legal regime for foreign investment. *Journal of Energy and Natural Resources Law* 19(1), 44–63.

Hinz, R.P., Zviniene, A., and Vilamovska, A.M. (2005). *The New Pensions in Kazakhstan: Challenges in Making the Transition.* SP Discussion Paper No. 0537 (World Bank, Washington DC).

Hirschman, A.O. (1958). *The Strategy of Economic Development* (Yale University Press, New Haven CT).

Hoffman, D. (2002). *The Oligarchs: Wealth and Power in the New Russia* (Public Affairs, New York).

  (1998). Yeltsin demands action on economy. *Washington Post Foreign Service* (June 24), A19.

Hoffman, D.I. (2000a). Azerbaijan: the politicization of oil, in *Energy and Conflict in Central Asia and the Caucasus*, ed. R. Ebel and R. Menon (Rowman & Littlefield, Lanham MD), 55–78.

  (2000b). *Oil and State-Building in Post-Soviet Azerbaijan and Kazakhstan.* Ph.D. dissertation, University of California, Berkeley.

Holzman, F.D. (1950). Commodity and income taxation in the Soviet Union. *The Journal of Political Economy* 58 (5), 425–33.

Horiuchi, Y. and Waglé, S. (2008). *100 Years Of Oil: Did It Depress Democracy and Sustain Autocracy?* Paper presented at the annual meeting of the APSA 2008 Annual Meeting, Hynes Convention Center, Boston, Massachusetts, August 28.

Hubbert, M.K. (1956). *Nuclear Energy and the Fossil Fuels.* Paper presented before the Spring Meeting of the Southern District, American Petroleum Institute, San Antonio, Texas.

Hughes, H. ed. (1988). *Achieving Industrialization in East Asia* (Cambridge University Press, Cambridge).

Human Rights Watch. (2003). *Sudan, Oil, and Human Rights* (Human Rights Watch, New York).

Humphreys, M., Sachs, J.D, and Stiglitz, J.E. ed. (2007). *Escaping the Resource Curse.* (Columbia University Press, New York).

Huntington, S. P. (1991). *The Third Wave: Democratization in the Late Twentieth Century* (University of Oklahoma Press, Norman OK).

Ikelegbe, A. (2001). The perverse manifestation of civil society: evidence from Nigeria. *Journal of Modern African Studies* 39 (1), 1–24.

International Bank for Reconstruction and Development and the International Development Association. (2007). *Fiscal Policy for Growth and Development: Further Analysis and Lessons from Country Case Studies.* March 22.

International Budgetary Project (IBP). (2008). *Open Budget Initiative 2006.* Center on Budget and Policy Priorities, Washington DC.

International Crisis Group. (2007). *Central Asia's Energy Risks.* Asia, Report No. 133. Brussels/Bishkek.

  (2005). *The Curse of Cotton: Central Asia's Destructive Monoculture.* Report No. 93.

International Energy Agency (IEA). (2002). *Russia Energy Survey* (OECD/IEA, Paris).
　(1999). *World Energy Outlook Looking at Energy Subsidies: Getting the Prices Right* (IEA, Paris).
　(1998). *Caspian Oil and Gas: The Supply Potential of Central Asia and Transcausia* (IEA, Paris).
International Finance Corporation (IFC). (2009). *Study of Small and Medium Enterprises in Azerbaijan*. (IFC, Baku, Azerbaijan).
International Monetary Fund (IMF). (2008). *Republic of Uzbekistan: 2008 Article IV Consultation*. IMF Country Report No. 08/235 (IMF, Washington DC).
　(2007a). *Guide on Resource Revenue Transparency* (IMF, Washington DC).
　(2007b). *Country Profile for Turkmenistan* (IMF, Washington DC).
　(2007c). *Staff Report for the 2007 Article IV Consultation* (IMF, Washington DC).
　(2006a). *Republic of Kazakhstan: 2006 Article IV Consultation–Staff Report; and Public Information Notice on the Executive Board Discussion*. IMF Country Report No. 06/244 (IMF, Washington, DC).
　(2006b). *Russian Federation: Selected Issues Country Report*. December (IMF, Washington DC).
　(2005a). *Azerbaijan Republic: Selected Issues*. IMF Country Report No. 05/17 (IMF, Washington DC).
　(2005b). *Republic of Kazakhstan: Selected Issues*. IMF Country Report No. 05/240 (IMF, Washington DC).
　(2005c). *Republic of Kazakhstan: Statistical Appendix*. IMF Country Report No. 05/239 (IMF, Washington DC).
　(2005d). *Russian Federation: Selected Issues*. Country Report No.05/379 (IMF, Washington DC).
　(2004a). *Azerbaijan Republic: Poverty Reduction Strategy Paper Progress Report*. IMF Country Report No. 04/322 (IMF, Washington DC).
　(2004b). *Republic of Kazakhstan: Selected Issues*. July (IMF, Washington DC).
　(2004c). *Russian Federation: Report on the Observance of Standards and Codes–Fiscal Transparency Module*. IMF Country Report No. 04/288. (IMF, Washington DC).
　(2003a). *Azerbaijan Republic: Poverty Reduction Strategy Paper*. IMF Country Report No. 03/105 (IMF, Washington DC).
　(2003b). *Azerbaijan Republic: Selected Issues and Statistical Appendix*. IMF Country Report No. 03/130 (IMF, Washington DC).
　(2003c). *Republic of Kazakhstan: Selected Issues and Statistical Appendix*. IMF Country Report No. 03/211(IMF, Washington DC).
　(2002). *Azerbaijan Republic: Selected Issues and Statistical Appendix*. IMF Country Report No. 02/41 (IMF, Washington DC).
　(2001). *Republic of Kazakhstan: Selected Issues and Statistical Appendix*. IMF Country Report No. 01/20 (IMF, Washington DC).
　(2000a). *Azerbaijan Republic: Recent Economic Developments and Selected Issues*. IMF Staff Country Report No. 00/121 (IMF, Washington DC).
　(2000b). *Republic of Uzbekistan: Recent Economic Developments*. IMF Staff Country Report No. 00/36 (IMF, Washington DC).
　(2000c). *Russian Federation: Selected Issues*. IMF Staff Country Report No. 00/150 (IMF, Washington DC).

(1999). *Turkmenistan: Recent Economic Developments*. IMF Staff Country Report No. 99/140 (IMF, Washington DC).

(1992). *Economic Review Uzbekistan* (IMF, Washington DC).

Irwin, D.A. (2000). *How Did the United States Become a Net Exporter of Manufactured Goods?* Working Paper 7638 (National Bureau of Economic Research, Cambridge, MA).

Isham J., Woolcock M., Pritchett L., and Busby, G. (2003). *The Varieties of Resource Experience: How Natural Resource Export Structures Affect the Political Economy of Economic Growth*. Economic Discovery Paper No. 03–08, April, Middlebury College.

Ivanenko, V. (2005). The statutory tax burden and its avoidance in transitional Russia. *Europe-Asia Studies* 57 (7), 1021–45.

Ivanova, A., Keen, M., and Klemm, A. (2005). *The Russian Flat Tax Reform*. IMF Working Paper WP/05/16 (IMF, Washington DC).

Izvestiya. (2003). Stabilization fund: What should it be like? February 4.

(2002). Mikhail Zadornov: Sledushei Osen'iu Nam Pridetsya Peresmatrivat' Byudzhet (Next Fall We Will Be Forced to Take Up Budget Again). Interview with Yelena Korop. (October 17).

Jarmuzek, M. (2006). Does Fiscal Transparency Matter? The Evidence from Transition Economies, June. www.cerge.cuni.cz/pdf/gdn/RRCV_77_paper_03.pdf

Jarmuzek et.al. (2006). *Fiscal Transparency in Transition Economies* (Center for Social and Economic Research, Warsaw).

Jensen, N. and Wantchekon, L. (2004). Resource wealth and political regimes in Africa. *Compar. Polit. Stud.* 37 (7), 816–41.

Johnson, C. (1982). *MITI and the Japanese Miracle: The Growth of Industrial Policy, 1925–1975* (Stanford University Press, Stanford CA).

Johnson, J. (1997). Understanding Russia's emerging financial-industrial groups. *Post-Soviet Aff.* 13 (4), 333–65.

Johnston, D. (1994). *International Petroleum Fiscal Systems and Production Sharing Contracts* (PennWell Books, Tulsa, OK).

Jones, G.G. (1977). The British government and the oil companies 1912–2024: the search for an oil policy. *The Historical Journal* 20 (3), 647–72.

Jones Luong, P. (2003a). Economic decentralization in Kazakhstan: causes and consequences, in *The Transformation of Central Asia: States and Societies from Soviet Rule to Independence*, ed. P. Jones Luong (Cornell University Press, Ithaca NY), 182–210.

(2003b). *Political Obstacles to Economic Reform in Uzbekistan, Kyrgyzstan, and Tajikistan: Strategies to Move Ahead*. World Bank Working Paper (World Bank, Washington DC).

(2002). *Institutional Change and Political Continuity in Post-Soviet Central Asia: Power, Perceptions, and Pacts* (Cambridge University Press, New York).

(2000a). The use and abuse of Russia's energy resources: Implications for state-societal relations, in *Building the Russian State: Institutional Crisis and the Quest for Democratic Governance*, ed. V. Sperling (Westview, Boulder CO), 27–45.

(2000b). Kazakhstan: The long-term costs of short-term gains, in *Energy and Conflict in Central Asia and the Caucasus*, ed. R. Ebel and R. Menon (Rowman & Littlefield, Lanham MD), 79–106.

Jones Luong, P. and Weinthal, E. (2004). Contra coercion: Russian tax reform, exogenous shocks and negotiated institutional change. *Amer. Polit. Sci. Rev.* 98 (1), 139–52.

—— (2001). Prelude to the resource curse: explaining oil and gas development strategies in the Soviet successor states and beyond. *Comp. Polit. Stud.* 34 (4), 367–99.

Jordan, L. and Van Tuijl, P. (2000). Political responsibility in transnational NGO advocacy. *World Devel.* 28 (12), 2051–65.

Jordan, M. and Schleifer, Y. (2008). A new 'neighborhood watch': Azeri horsemen guard BP pipeline. *Christian Science Monitor* (March 12).

Kaiser, M.J. and Pulsiper, A.G. (2007). A review of the oil and gas sector in Kazakhstan. *Energy Pol.* 35, 1300–14.

Kaiser, R.G. (2002). Personality cult buoys 'father of all Turkmen' Central Asian leader nurtures nationhood. *The Washington Post* (July 8), A1.

Kaiser, R.J. (1994). *The Geography of Nationalism in Russia and the USSR* (Princeton University Press, Princeton NJ).

Kalyuzhnova, Y. (2006). Overcoming the curse of hydrocarbon: goals and governance in the oil funds of Kazakhstan and Azerbaijan. *Compar. Econ. Stud.* 48, 583–613.

—— (1998). *The Kazakhstani Economy* (Macmillan Press, London).

Kalyuzhnova, Y. and Kaser, M. (2006). Prudential management of hydrocarbon revenues in resource-rich economies. *Post-Communist Economies* 18 (2), 167–87.

Kalyuzhnova, Y. and Nygaard, C. (2009). Resource nationalism and credit growth in FSU countries. *Energy Pol.* 37, 1–11.

—— (2008). State governance evolution in resource-rich transition economies: an application to Russia and Kazakhstan. *Energy Pol.* 36, 1829–42.

Kamenev, S. (2002). Turkmenistan's economy today. *Central Asia and the Caucasus* 3 (15): 169–78.

—— (2001). Turkmenistan's fuel and energy complex: present state and development prospects. *Central Asia and the Caucasus* 6 (12), 160–79.

Kamp, M. (2003). Between women and the state: Mahalla committees and social welfare in Uzbekistan, in *The Transformation of Central Asia: States and Societies from Soviet Rule to Independence*, ed. P. Jones Luong (Cornell University Press, Ithaca NY), 29–58.

Kang, D.C. (2002). *Crony Capitalism: Corruption and Development in South Korea and the Philippines* (Cambridge University Press, New York).

Kapeliouchnikov, R. (1999). *Russia's Labor Market: Adjustment without Restructuring.* (unpublished mimeo), Moscow.

Karl, T.L. (2000). Crude calculations: OPEC lessons for the Caspian region, in *Energy and Conflict in Central Asia and the Caucasus*, ed. R. Ebel and R. Menon (Rowman & Littlefield, Lanham, MD), 29–54.

—— (1999). The perils of the petro-state: reflections on the paradox of plenty. *J. Int. Aff.* 53 (1), 31–48.

—— (1997). *The Paradox of Plenty: Oil Booms and Petro-States* (University of California Press, Berkeley).

Karl, T.L. and Gary, I. (2004). *The Global Record.* Foreign Policy in Focus-PetroPolitics Special Report (January).

Katz M., Bartsch U., Malothra H., and Cuc M. (2004). *Lifting the Oil Curse: Improving Petroleum Revenue Management in Sub-Saharan Africa* (IMF, Washington DC).

Kaufman, R.F. and Hardt, J.P., ed. (1993). *The Former Soviet Union in Transition* (M.E. Sharpe, New York).

Kaufman, R.R. and Segura-Ubiergo, A. (2001). Globalization, domestic politics, and social spending in Latin America, *World Polit.* 53 (4), 553–88.

Kazakhstan International Business Magazine. (2005). The largest oil project in Kazakhstan. No. 1. Online. http://www.investkz.com/en/journals/42/8.html

(2003). Tengizchevroil: Ten years of success. No. 1. Online. http://www.investkz.com/en/journals/34/220.html

Keen, M., Kim, Y., and Varsano, R. (2006). *The "Flat Tax(es)": Principles and Evidence.* IMF Working Paper WP/06/218 (IMF, Washington DC).

Keohane, R.O. (1988). International institutions: two approaches. *Int. Stud. Quart.* 32 (4), 379–96.

(1984). *After Hegemony* (Princeton University Press, Princeton, NJ).

Keohane, R.O. and Ooms, V.D. (1972). The multinational enterprise and world political economy. *Int. Organ.* 26 (1), 84–120.

Khadduri M. (1969). *Republican Iraq: A Study in Iraqi Politics since the Revolution of 1958* (Oxford University Press, London).

Khanlou, P. (1998). Facing the future: an interview with Natig Aliyev. *Azerbaijan International* (Winter), 75.

Khartukov, E. (2002). Russia's oil majors: engine for radical change. *Oil and Gas Journal* (May), 27.

Khodorova, J. (2006). Philanthropy in Russian society today. *International Journal of Not-for- Profit Law* 8 (3), 13–5.

Khusainov, B. and Berentaev, K. (2004). Kazakhstan: problems of developing the oil and gas sector and improving the system for taxing subsurface users. *Central Asia and the Caucasus* 5 (29), 70–81.

Khusainov, B. and Turkeeva, K. (2003). Kazakhstan's energy potential today and tomorrow. *Central Asia and the Caucasus* 4 (22). http://www.ca-c.org/online/2003/journal_eng/cac-04/13.khueng.shtml

Killick, N. (2006). BP and Azerbaijan, in *Putting Partnerships to Work*, ed. M. Warner and R. Sullivan (Greenleaf Publishing, Sheffield).

Kjaernet, H. and Overland, I. (2007). The trajectory of reform in Turkmenistan: implications for foreign oil companies. *Oil, Gas, and Energy Law Intelligence* 6 (3), 6–18.

Klapp, M.G. (1987). *The Sovereign Entrepreneur: Oil Policies in Advanced and Less Developed Capitalist Countries* (Cornell University Press, Ithaca NY).

Klebnikov, P. (1994). The quietly determined American. *Forbes* 154 (10), 48–50.

Knight, J. (1992). *Institutions and Social Conflict* (Cambridge University Press, Cambridge).

Kobrin, S. (2004). Oil and politics: Talisman Energy and Sudan. *New York University's J. Int. Law Politic.* 36, 425–56.

Kommersant. (2005). The oil and gas industry 2000–2004.

Kostikov, I. (2003). *Improving Corporate Governance in Russia*. Presentation at the 2003 Annual Conference on International Corporate Governance, Amsterdam, July 9–11.

Kotz, D.M. (2003). Sources and features of the 'Uzbek growth puzzle,' in *Growth and Poverty Reduction in Uzbekistan in the Next Decade*. A Report Commissioned by the Poverty Group, Bureau for Development Policy, UNDP, September, 32–50.

Krasner, S. (1978). *Defending the National Interest* (Princeton University Press, Princeton NJ).

Krasnov, G.V. and Brada, J.C. (1997). Implicit subsidies in Russian-Ukrainian energy trade. *Europe-Asia Studies* 49 (5), 825–43.

Krueger, A.O., Schiff, M., and Valdes, A. (1988). Agricultural incentives in developing countries: measuring the effect of sectoral and economywide policies. *The World Bank Econ. Rev.* 2 (3), 255–71.

Kuliev, H. (2000). Myths and realities: oil strategy of Azerbaijan. *Central Asia and the Caucasus* 1, 88–96.

Kuralbayeva, K., Kutan, A.M., and Wyzan, M.L. (2001). *Is Kazakhstan Vulnerable to the Dutch Disease?* ZEI Working Paper B01–29.

Kurbanova, A. (2003). Niyazov signs resolution on free supply of population with power, gas, water. *ITAR-TASS Weekly News*, 08–15.

Kurlyandskaya, G. 2007. Sharing the pie. *Federations* 6, 1 (February/March).

Kusainov, A. (2002). A struggle over energy may alter Kazakhstan's national fund, *Eurasianet*. http://www.eurasianet.org/departments/business/articles/eav111302.shtml

Kutan, A.M. and Wyzan, M.L. (2005). Explaining the real exchange rate in Kazakhstan, 1996–2003: is Kazakhstan vulnerable to the Dutch disease? *Economic Systems* 29, 242–55.

Kuz'min, B., Vorob'eva, L., and Vorob'eva, O. (2008). Corporate governance and Gazprom: problems and prospects. *Russian Social Science Review* 49 (2), 60–76.

Kuznetsov, A., Kuznetsova, O., and Warren, R. (2009). CSR and the legitimacy of business in transition economies: the case of Russia. *Scandinavian Journal of Management* 25 (1), 37–45.

Lane, D., ed. (1999). *The Political Economy of Russian Oil* (Rowman & Littlefield, Lanham, MD).

Larson, H.M., Knowlton, E.H. and Popple, C.S. (1971). *New Horizons 1927–1950, History of Standard Oil Company (New Jersey)* (Harper & Row, New York).

Larsen, B. and Shah, A. (1992). *World Fossil Fuel Subsidies and Global Carbon Emissions*. World Bank Working Papers WPS 1002, October.

Lederman, D. and Maloney, W.F. (2003). *Trade Structure and Growth*. World Bank Policy Research Working Paper 3025 (World Bank, Washington DC).

Leite, C. and Weidman, J. (1999). *Does Mother Nature Corrupt? Natural Resources, Corruption, and Economic Growth*. IMF Working Paper 99/85 (IMF, Washington DC).

Lelyveld, M. (2003). Kazakhstan energy project resumes, but questions remain. *RFE/RL Weekday Magazine–Kazakhstan* (January 28).

(2002). Heavy fine levied against Tengiz oil field developer. *RFE/RL* (March 29).

Levi, M. (1988). *Of Rule and Revenue* (University of California Press, Berkeley).

LeVine, S. (2007). *The Oil and the Glory: The Pursuit of Empire and Fortune on the Caspian Sea* (Random House, New York).

Levinsky, A. (2002). Shadows grow shorter at noon. *Izvestiya*, December 4 (published in Johnson's Russia List #6586).

Lewis, S.R. (1984). Development problems of the mineral-rich countries, in *Economic Structure and Performance*, ed. M. Syrquin, L. Taylor, and L.E. Westphal (Academic Press, New York), 157–77.

Lianguong, F. and N. Kuleshova. (1999). New changes in the tax code of the Republic of Kazakhstan and affects on export and import of crude oil and fuel products *Oil & Gas of Kazakhstan* (April), 36–41.

Lieberman, E.S. (2002). Taxation data as indicators of state–society relations: possibilities and pitfalls in cross-national research. *Stud. Int. Compar. Devel.* 36 (4), 89–115.

Lieuwen, E. (1954). *Petroleum in Venezuela: A History* (University of California Press, Berkeley).

Lindert, P.H. (2005a). *Growing Public: Social Spending and Economic Growth since the Eighteenth Century, Vol. 1* (Cambridge University Press, Cambridge).

(2005b). *Growing Public: Social Spending and Economic Growth since the Eighteenth Century, Vol. 2.* (Cambridge University Press, Cambridge).

Lipset, S.M. (1960). *Political Man: The Social Bases of Politics* (Doubleday, Garden City NY)

Lipson, C. (1985). *Standing Guard* (University of California Press, Berkeley).

Lissovolik, Y. (2008). It's not all about high oil prices. *The St. Petersburg Times* (April 15).

Litvan, D. (2003). *Empires of Profit: Commerce, Conquest, and Corporate Responsibility* (Texere Press, New York).

Locatelli, C. (2006). The Russian oil industry between public and private governance: obstacles to international oil companies' investment strategies. *Energy Pol.* 34, 1075–85.

(1995). The reorganization of the Russian hydrocarbons industry. *Energy Pol.* 23 (9), 809–19.

Lorie, H. (2003). *Priorities for Further Fiscal Reforms in the Commonwealth of Independent States.* IMF Working Paper WP/03/209 (IMF, Washington DC).

Luecke, M. and Trofimenko, N. (2008). Whither oil money? Redistribution of oil revenue in Azerbaijan, in *The Economics and Politics of oil in the Caspian Basin: the Redistribution of Oil Revenues in Azerbaijan and Central Asia,* ed. B. Najman, R. Pomfret, and G. Raballand (Routledge, New York), 132–56.

Lukoil. 2001. *Annual Report of 2000.* Online. http://www.lukoil.com/

Lydolph, P.E. and Shabad, T. (1960). The oil and gas industries in the USSR, *Annals of the Association of American Geographers* 50 (4), 461–86.

Mackenzie, G.A. and Stella, P. (1996). *Quasi-Fiscal Operations of Public Financial Institutions,* IMF Occasional Paper No. 142 (IMF, Washington DC).

Madelin, H. (1975). *Oil and Politics* (Saxon House, London and Lexington Books, Lexington).

Mahdavy H. (1970). The patterns and problems of economic development in rentier states: the case of Iran, in *Studies in the Economic History of the Middle East,* ed. M.A. Cook (Oxford University Press, London), 428–67.

Makhmutova, M. (2007). The budget process in Caspian countries. *Problems of Economic Transition* 50 (4), 24–65.

(2006). Kazakhstan expenditure on public health. *Beyond Transition* (The World Bank and CEFIR), 19–20 [in Russian].

(2005). *Implementation of Extractive Industries Transparency Initiative in Kazakhstan: Problems and Prospects.* Policy Studies 5 (10) (Public Policy Research Center, Almaty).

(2001). Local government in Kazakhstan, in *Developing New Rules in the Old Environment: Local Governments in Eastern Europe, the Caucasus, and Central Asia*, ed. I. Munteanu and V. Popa (Open Society Institute, Budapest), 403–68.

Malloy, J.M. and Borzutzky, S. (1982). Politics, social welfare policy, and the population problem in Latin America. *Int. J. Health Serv.* 12 (1), 77–98.

Maloney, W. (2002). *Innovation and Growth in Resource Rich Countries.* Central Bank of Chile Working Papers, No. 148 (February).

Manzano, O. and Rigobon, R. (2001). *Resource Curse of Debt Overhang?* National Bureau of Economic Research Working Paper (July).

Marathon. (2006). *Living Our Values: 2006 Corporate Social Responsibility Report.*

Marcel, V. (2006). *Oil Titans: National Oil Companies in the Middle East* (Chatham House, London).

Mares, D. and Altimirano, N. (2007). *Venezuela's PDVSA and World Energy Markets: Corporate Strategies and Political Factors Determining Its Behavior and Influence.* Paper prepared for the James Baker III Institute for Public Policy, Rice University (March).

Mares, I. (2001). Firms and the welfare state: when, why and how does social policy matter to employers, in *Varieties of Capitalism: The National Foundations of Comparative Institutional Advantage*, ed. P. Hall and D. Soskice (Oxford University Press, Oxford), 184–212.

Martinez-Vazquez, J. and McNab, R. (2000). *The Tax Reform Experiment in Transitional Countries.* International Studies Program Working Paper Series No. 0001. International Studies Program, Andrew Young School of Policy Studies, Georgia State University.

Martz, J.D. (1987). *Politics and Petroleum in Ecuador* (Transaction Books Press, New Brunswick NJ).

Marvin, C. (1884). *The Region of the Eternal Fire: An Account of a Journey to the Petroleum Region of the Caspian in 1883* (W.H. Allen and Co., London).

Mastrangelo, E. (2007). *An Analysis of Price Volatility in Natural Gas Markets* (Energy Information Administration, Washington DC).

Matsen, E. and Torvik, R. (2005). Optimal Dutch disease. *J. Devel. Econ.* 78(2), 494–515.

Matthews, D. (2001). Evolution of Azeri PSAs. *Caspian Investor* (April).

Matzke, R.H. (1994). Challenges of Tengiz oil field and other FSU joint ventures. *Oil and Gas Journal* (July 4), 62–5.

Mazalov, I. (2001). *Oil Taxation Changes* (Troika Dialog Research, Moscow).

McAllen, J. (2003). Milestone: BP and owners of Tyumen Oil Co. to form major Russian oil company in landmark deal, *Russian Petroleum Investor* (April), 69–75.

McKay, J.P. (1984). Baku oil and Transcaucasian pipelines, 1883–1891: a study in Tsarist economic policy. *Slavic Review* 43 (4), 604–23.

McKern, B. (1996). TNCs and the exploitation of natural resources, in *Transnational Corporations and World Development* (UNCTAD).

McLure, C.E. (1998). Tax reform in Kazakhstan. *Bulletin for International Fiscal Documentation* 52 (8/9).

(1992). Income Tax reform in Colombia and Venezuela: A comparative history. *World Devel.* 20 (3), 351–67.

McMahon, G. (1997). *The Natural Resource Curse: Myth or Reality?* World Bank Institute (mimeo).

McMann, K.M. (2009). Market reform as a stimulus to particularistic politics. *Compar. Polit. Stud.* 42 (7), 971–94.

McPherson, C. (2003). National oil companies: Evolution, issues, outlook, in *Fiscal Policy Formulation and Implementation in Oil-Producing Countries*, ed. J. Davis, R. Ossowski, and A. Fedelino (IMF, Washington DC), 184–203.

Mehlum, H., Moene, K.O., and Torvik, R. (2006). Cursed by resources or institutions? *The World Economy* 29 (8), 1117–31.

Mertens, J.B. and Tesche, J.E. (2002). VAT revenue in the Russian Federation: the role of tax administration in their decline. *Public Budgeting and Finance* 22, 87–113.

Meyer, L. and Morales, I. (1990). *Petróleo y nación (1900–1987): La política petrolera en México* (Fondo de Cultura Económica, Mexico City).

Migdal, J.S., Kohli, A., and Shue, V. (1994). *State Power and Social Forces: Domination and Transformation in the Third World* (Cambridge University Press, New York).

Migdal, J.S. (1988). *Strong Societies and Weak States: State-Society Relations and State Capabilities in the Third World* (Princeton University Press, Princeton NJ).

Mikesell, J.L. and Mullins, D.R. (2001). Reforming budget systems in countries of the former Soviet Union. *Public Admin. Rev.* 61 (5), 548–68.

Mikesell R.F. (1997). Explaining the resource curse with specific reference to mineral exporting countries. *Resources Pol.* 23 (4), 191–99.

Milov, V. (2007). *The Growing Role of the State in Russian Oil and Gas Industries.* Presentation at the Centre for Global Energy Studies, United Kingdom, May 23.

Mir-Babayev, M.Y. (2004). Baku baron days: foreign investment in Azerbaijan's oil. *Azerbaijan International* 12 (2), 82–5.

  (2003). Azerbaijan's oil history: brief oil chronology since 1920, part 2. *Azerbaijan International* 11 (3), 56–63.

Mitchell, D., Harding, A., and Gruen, F. (1994). Targeting welfare. *The Economic Record* 70 (210), 315–40.

Mitra P.K. (1994). *Adjustment in Oil-Exporting Developing Countries* (Cambridge University Press, Cambridge/New York).

Moe, A. and Kryukov, V. (1994). Observations on the reorganization of the Russian oil industry. *Post-Soviet Geogr.* 35 (2), 89–101.

Mommer, B. (2002). *Global Oil and the Nation State* (Oxford Institute for Energy Studies, Oxford).

Moore, B. (1966). *Social Origins of Dictatorship and Democracy: Lord and Peasant in the Making of the Modern World* (Beacon, Boston).

Moran, T.H. (1996). Governments and TNCs, in *Transnational Corporations and World Development* (UNCTAD).

  (1974). *Multinational Corporations and the Politics of Dependence: Copper in Chile* (Princeton University Press, Princeton NJ).

Morgan, T. (2007). *Energy Subsidies: Their Magnitude and How they Affect Energy Investment.* Final Report, June 10, (UNFCCC Secretariat, New York).

Morse, E. (1999). A New Political Economy of Oil? *J. Int. Aff.* 53 (1), 1–29.

Musgrave, R.A. (1969). *Fiscal Systems* (Yale University Press, New Haven CT).

Musgrave, R.A. and Peacock, A.T. (1958). *Classics in the Theory of Public Finance* (St. Martin's Press, New York).

Mydans, S. and Arnold, W. (2007). Lee Kuan Yew, founder of Singapore, changing with times. *New York Times* (August 29).

Najman, B., Pomfret, R., Raballand, G., and Sourdin, P. (2008). Redistribution of oil revenue in Kazakhstan, in *The Economics and Politics of Oil in the Caspian Basin: The Redistribution of Oil Revenues in Azerbaijan and Central Asia*, ed. B. Najman, R. Pomfret, and G. Raballand (Routledge, New York), 111–31.

Nazarov, I. (2005). Chinese companies expanding into Uzbekistan. *Caspian Investor* (August), 16–21.

Nefte Compass. (2004). Gentle persuasion: Kazakhstan urged to ease investment terms to unlock potential. (October 7).

(2003). Kazakhstan: Kashagan partners pay the price of preemption. (May 21).

Newcity M.A. (1986). *Taxation in the Soviet Union* (Praeger Publishers, New York).

New York Times. (1997). Central Asia Petroleum Buys Kazak Oil Stake. (May 13).

Nezhina, V. (2000). Change is the constant: Kazakhstan continues to alter the rules of the game, now hiking taxes as oil prices rise. *Russian Petroleum Investor* (April), 32–4.

Nichol, J. (2004). *Turkmenistan: Recent Developments and U.S. Interests.* CRS Report for Congress, May 13.

Nobatova, M. (2003a). Shell on the shelf: foreign investors seek best way to gain access to Kazakhstan's Caspian Sea shelf 's reserves. *Russian Petroleum Investor* (February), 57–60.

(2003b). Uzbekistan liberalizes oil legislation, instituting PSA law and revising law on subsoil. *Russian Petroleum Investor* (January), 63–5.

(2002). Rehabilitation redux: Azeri efforts to revive old offshore fields opens new opportunities for investors. *Russian Petroleum Investor* (May).

North, D. (1990). *Institutions, Institutional Change and Economic Performance* (Cambridge University Press, Cambridge).

(1981). *Structure and Change in Economic History* (W.W. Norton & Company, New York).

North, D. and Weingast, B. (1989). Constitutions and commitment: the evolution of institutions governing pubic choice in seventeenth-century England. *J Econ. Hist.* 49 (4), 803–32.

Nurshayeva, R. (2007). UPDATE 1-Kazakhstan to review energy contracts. *Reuters* (April 17). http://www.reuters.com/article/companyNewsAndPR/idUSL1757814920070 41

Ochs, M. (1997). Turkmenistan: The quest for stability and control, in *Conflict, Cleavage, and Change in Central Asia and the Caucasus*, ed. K. Dawisha and B. Parrott (Cambridge University Press, New York), 312–59.

Odell, P.R. (1968). The significance of oil. *Journal of Contemporary History* 3 (3), 93–110.

Organisation for Economic Cooperation and Development (OECD). (2006). *Economic Survey–Russian Federation* (OECD, Paris, France).

(2005). *Economic Survey–Russian Federation* (OECD, Paris, France).

(2004). *Economic Survey–Russian Federation* (OECD, Paris, France).

Ofer, G. (1999). *Trade, Trade Policy, and Foreign Exchange Regime under Transition: Russia and the Dutch Disease.* Paper presented at the Trade and Development Workshop (Economics 750b), Yale University, March.

Oil & Gas of Kazakhstan. (1996). The first tender: failure or success? (October), 20–3.

Oil of Russia. (2006). Getting Off to a Good Start. Oil of Russia magazine talks to Andrey Podbolotov, regional director of Lukoil Overseas Holding Ltd. for Uzbekistan. No. 1.

Oil Revenues–Under Public Oversight! (2007). *Two Years of Implementation of Extractive Industries Transparency Initiative (EITI) in Kazakhstan: Conclusions and Recommendations* (Soros Foundation–Kazakhstan Revenue Watch Program, Almaty, Kazakhstan).

Okruhlik, G. (1999). Rentier wealth, unruly law, and the rise of opposition: the political economy of oil states. *Comp. Polit.* 31 (3), 295–315.

O'Lear, S. (2007). Azerbaijan's resource wealth: political legitimacy and public opinion. *Geograph. J.* 173 (3), 207–23.

O'Lear, S. and Gray, A. (2006). Asking the right questions: environmental conflict in the case of Azerbaijan. *Area* 38 (4), 390–401.

Olcott, M.B. (2007). *Kazmunaigaz: Kazakhstan's National Oil and Gas Company* (The James A. Baker III Institute for Public Policy, Rice University, Houston TX), March.

  (2004). *International Gas Trade in Central Asia: Turkmenistan, Iran, Russia and Afghanistan*, Working Paper #28. Prepared for the *Geopolitics of Natural Gas Study*, a joint project of the Program on Energy and Sustainable Development at Stanford University and the James A. Baker III Institute for Public Policy of Rice University.

  (1997). Democratization and the growth of political participation in Kazakhstan, in *Conflict, Cleavage, and Change in Central Asia and the Caucasus*, ed. K. Dawisha and B. Parrott (Cambridge University Press, Cambridge/New York), 201–41.

  (1993). Kazakhstan: republic of minorities, in *Nation and Politics in the Soviet Successor States*, ed. I. Bremmer and R. Taras (Cambridge University Press, Cambridge/New York), 313–30.

Olien, D.D. and Olien, R.M. (2002). *Oil in Texas: The Gusher Age, 1895–1945* (University of Texas Press, Austin TX).

Orenstein, M. (2008). *Privatizing Pensions: The Transnational Campaign for Social Security Reform* (Princeton University Press, Princeton NJ).

Ostrom, E. (1990). *Governing the Commons: The Evolution of Institutions for Collective Action* (Cambridge University Press, Cambridge).

Ostrom, E. and Schlager, E. (1996). The formation of property rights, in *Rights to Nature: Ecological, Economic, Cultural, and Political Principles of Institutions for the Environment*, ed. S.S. Hanna, C. Folke, and K.G. Mäler (Island Press, Washington DC), 127–56.

Ostrowski, W. (2007). *Regime Maintenance in Post-Soviet Kazakhstan: The Case of the Regime and Oil Industry Relationship (1991–2005).* Ph.D. dissertation, University of St. Andrews.

Page, J. (2005). Black gold brings hope of return to the glory days of a century ago. *The Times* (May 25). http://www.timesonline.co.uk/tol/news/world/article526207.ece

Pala, C. (2002). Kazakhstan concerned on TCO's taxes: government officials surprised by project suspension. *Platt's Oilgram News* 80 (226), 2.

  (2003). Talks continue on Tengiz financing terms: Chevron Texaco has resumed work. *Platt's Oilgram News* 81 (38), 3.

  (2004). Investors recoil from oil terms in Kazakhstan. *New York Times* (October 27), W1.

Palley, T.I. (2003). Combating the natural resource curse with citizen revenue distribution funds: oil and the case of Iraq. *Foreign Policy in Focus* (December), 1–12.

Pavlova, L.P. (1999). *Problemy rascheta i oplaty federal'nykh nalogov yuridiches-kimi litsami.* (Problems Calculating and Collecting Taxes by Law Enforcement Personnel.) Moscow Financial Academy.

Pearce, R. (2003). In search of stability: stability of contract and risk of renegotiation upon transfers of subsurface rights. *Russian Petroleum Investor* (February), 61–3.

Peck, A.E. (2004). *Economic Development in Kazakhstan: The Role of Large Enterprises and Foreign Investment* (Routledge, London).

Penrose, E.T. (1968). *The Large International Firm in Developing Countries: The International Petroleum Industry* (MIT Press, Cambridge MA).

Peters, B.G. (1991). *The Politics of Taxation: A Comparative Perspective* (Blackwell, Cambridge MA).

Petersen, C.E. and Budina, N. (2002). *Governance Framework of Oil Funds: The Case of Azerbaijan and Kazakhstan* (World Bank, Washington DC).

Petri, M. and Taube, G. (2003). Quasi-fiscal activities in the energy sectors of the former Soviet Union. *Emerging Markets, Finance and Trade* 39 (1), 24–42.

Petri, M., Taube, G., and Tsyvinski, A. (2002). *Energy Sector Quasi-Fiscal Activities in the Countries of the Former Soviet Union.* IMF Working Paper WP/02/60 (IMF, Washington DC).

Petroleum. (2002). "Black gold" of Atyrau. (February), 12–5.

    (2001). Kazakhstan's oil 1991–2001. (December), 8–11.

    (2000a). A stable partner in the Kazakhstan oil and gas industry. (May), 24–6.

    (2000b). Marlo Thomas: we are committed to our shareholders, to our employees and Kazakhstan. (May), 12–9.

PFC Energy. (2006). PFC Energy 50: A Ranking of the World's Largest Listed Firms in the Oil & Gas Industry. Online. http://www.pfcenergy.com

Philip, G. (1994). *The Political Economy of International Oil* (Edinburgh University Press, Edinburgh).

Pierson, P. (2000). Increasing returns, path dependence, and the study of politics. *Amer. Polit. Sci. Rev.* 94 (2), 251–67.

Pinto, B., Drebentsov, V., and Morozov, A. (2000). *Give Growth and Macro Stability in Russia A Chance: Harden Budgets by Dismantling Nonpayments.* Economics Unit, World Bank Office, Moscow, Russia.

Pirog, R. (2007). The Role of National Oil Companies in the International Oil Market. CSR Report for Congress, August 21.

Polgreen, L. (2008). World Bank ends effort to help Chad ease poverty. *New York Times* (September 11), A12.

Pomfret, R. (2008a). *Turkmenistan after Turkmenbashi.* Paper presented at the conference Institutions, Institutional Change, and Economic Performance in Central Asia, Göttingen, September 25–26.

    (2008b). Tajikistan, Turkmenistan, and Uzbekistan, in *Distortions to Agricultural Incentives in Europe's Transition Economies*, ed. K. Anderson and J. Swinnen (World Bank, Washington DC), 297–338.

    (2006). *The Central Asian Economies since Independence* (Princeton University Press, Princeton NJ).

    (2005a). Kazakhstan's economy since independence: does the oil boom offer a second chance for sustainable development? *Europe-Asia Studies* 57 (6), 859–76.

    (2005b). *Resource Abundance and Long-Run Growth: When Is Oil a Curse? The Effects of Oil Discoveries on Kazakhstan's Economy.* Paper presented at the Canadian Network for Economic History Conference, April 15–17.

(2004). *Resource Abundance, Governance and Economic Performance in Turkmenistan and Uzbekistan.* ZEF-Discussion Papers on Development Policy, Number 79 (Zentrum für Entwicklungsforschung Center for Development Research, Bonn).

(2003). Economic performance in Central Asia since 1991: macro and micro evidence. *Compar. Econ. Stud.* 45, 442–65.

(2001). Turkmenistan: from communism to nationalism by gradual economic reform. *MOST* 11, 165–76.

(2000). The Uzbek model of economic development 1991–1999. *Econ. Transition* 8 (3), 733–48.

(1995). *The Economies of Central Asia* (Princeton University Press, Princeton NJ).

Post, A. (2008). *Liquid Assets and Fluid Contracts: Explaining the Uneven Effects of Water and Sanitation Privatization.* Ph.D. dissertation, Harvard University.

Prebisch, R. (1950). *The Economic Development of Latin America and Its Principal Problems* (United Nations, New York).

Presley, J. (1983). *Saga of Wealth: The Rise of the Texas Oilmen* (Texas Monthly Press, Austin TX).

Przeworski, A., Alvarez, M.E., Cheibub, J.A., and Limongi, F. (2000). *Democracy and Development: Political Institutions and Well-being in the World, 1950–1990* (Cambridge, University Press, New York).

Pulsipher, A. and Kaiser, M. (2006). Kazakhstan's outlook-3: business environment still seen as risky in Kazakhstan. *Oil & Gas Journal* (July 17).

Quinn, J.J. (2002). *The Road Oft Traveled: Development Policies and Majority State Ownership of Industry in Africa* (Praeger, Westport CT).

Raballand, G. and Genté, R. (2008). Oil in the Caspian Basin, in *The Economics and Politics of oil in the Caspian Basin: the Redistribution of Oil Revenues in Azerbaijan and Central Asia*, ed. B. Najman, R. Pomfret, and G. Raballand (Routledge, New York), 9–29.

Rabushka, A. (2005). Real tax reform. *Hoover Digest*, 1.

Radon, J. (2007). How to negotiate an oil agreement, in *Escaping the Resource Curse*, ed. M. Humphreys, J.D. Sachs, and J.E. Stiglitz (Columbia University Press, New York), 89–113.

(2005). The ABCs of petroleum contracts: license-concession agreements, joint ventures, and production-sharing agreements, in *Covering Oil Report: A Reporter's Guide to Energy and Development*, ed. S. Tsalik and A.Schiffrin (OSI, New York), 61–86.

Ramamurthy, S. and Tandberg, E. (2002). *Treasury Reform in Kazakhstan: Lessons for Other Countries.* IMF Working Paper No. 02/129 (IMF, Washington DC).

Rechel, B. and McKee, M. (2007). The effects of dictatorship on health: the case of Turkmenistan. *BMC Medicine* 5 (21), 1–10.

Reddaway, P. and Glinski, D. (2001). *The Tragedy of Russia's Reforms: Market Bolshevism against Democracy* (U.S. Institute of Peace Press, Washington DC).

Remington, T. (2001). *The Russian Parliament: Institutional Evolution in a Transitional Regime, 1989–1999* (Yale University Press, New Haven CT).

Repkine, A. (2004). Turkmenistan: economic autocracy and recent growth performance, in *The Economic Prospects of the CIS, Sources of Long Term Growth*, ed. G. Ofer and R. Pomfret (Edward Elgar, Cheltenham, UK/Northampton, MA), 154–76.

Reporters Without Borders. (2007). *Press Freedom in Russia*. Online. http://www.europarl.europa.eu/meetdocs/2004_2009/documents/fd/droi20071001_russia_004/droi20071001_russia_004en.pdf

Riding, A. (1979). Spill hurts credibility of Pemex. *New York Times* (August 22), D3.

Ritchie, M. (2005). Steppe dancing: Kazakhstan sends a tough message to investors. *Nefte Compass* (October 12),1.

Robert, C. and Sherlock, T. (1999). Bringing the Russian state back in: explanations of the derailed transition to market economy. *Compar. Polit.* 31 (4), 477–98.

Robinson, J.A., Torvik, R., and Verdier, T. (2006). Political foundations of the resource curse. *J. Devel. Econ.* 79, 447–68.

Rodman, K.A. (1988). *Sanctity versus Sovereignty: The United States and the Nationalization of Natural Resource Investments* (Columbia University Press, New York).

Rodriguez, F. (2008). An empty revolution: The unfulfilled promises of Hugo Chavez. *For. Aff.*, 87 (2), 49–62.

Roland, G. (2006). The Russian economy in the year 2005. *Post-Soviet Aff.* 22 (1), 90–8.

Root, H.L. (1989). Tying the king's hands: credible commitments and royal fiscal policy during the old regime. *Rationality and Society* 1 (2), 240–58.

Rose, R. (2007). *New Russia Barometer XV: Climax of the Putin Years*. Studies in Public Policy Number 426, University of Averdeen, Scotland.

Rosenberg, C.B. and De Zeeuw, M. (2001). Welfare effects of Uzbekistan's foreign exchange rate. *IMF Staff Papers* 48 (1), 160–78.

Rosenberg, C.B., Ruocco, A., and Wiegard, W. (1999). Explicit and implicit taxation in Uzbekistan. *Regensburger Diskussionsbeiträger* 325 (June).

Ross, M.L. (2008). Oil, Islam and women. *Amer. Polit. Sci. Rev.* 101 (1), 107–23.

  (2004). How does natural resource wealth influence civil wars: evidence from thirteen cases. *Int. Organ.* 58 (1), 35–67.

  (2001a). Does oil hinder democracy? *World Polit.* 53 (3), 325–61.

  (2001b). *Extractive Sectors and the Poor: An Oxfam America Report* (Oxfam America, Boston, MA).

  (2001c). *Timber Booms and Institutional Breakdown in Southeast Asia* (Cambridge University Press, Cambridge/New York).

  (1999). The political economy of the resource curse. *World Polit.* 51 (2), 297–322.

Roth G, and Wittich, C. eds. (1978). *Economy and Society, Volume II* (University of California Press, Berkeley).

Rueschemeyer, D. and Evans, P.B. (1985). The state and economic transformation: toward an analysis of the conditions underlying effective intervention, in *Bringing the State Back In*, ed. P.B. Evans, D. Rueschemeyer, and T. Skocpol (Cambridge University Press, Cambridge), 44–77.

Rumer, B. (1992). Fueling the post-Soviet economies: oil and gas. *Challenge* 35 (4), 36.

  (1989). *Soviet Central Asia* (Unwin Hyman, Boston).

Russian Economic Trends. (1998). December 8. http://www.blackwellpublishers.co.uk/ruet/

Russian Petroleum Investor (RPI). (2004). BP increasing investments in social sector (May), 62.

  (2000). Socar wins battle with foreign shareholders over project timing. (February), 29–32.

(1999). Waste not: Astana is compelling oil investors to stop burning associated gas. (October), 23–6.

(1997/1998). Foreign investors combine forces to develop Kazakhstan's offshore oil resources. (December/January), 41–3.

(1997). Minister of oil and gas Nazdhanov sheds light on Turkmenistan's foreign investment policy. (March), 35–8, 46.

(1996a). Ashgabat's 'framework' energy legislation signals even tougher times for foreign investors. (March), 63–7.

(1996b). Having lost its patience, Bridas takes Turkmenistan to international arbitration. (May), 54–7.

(1996c). Kazakhstan moves to create a more stable–but not necessarily more attractive–tax regime. (June/July), 40–4.

(1996d). Turkmenistan's oil minister on the republic's new policy for attracting foreign investment. (April), 55–61.

(1995a). Kazakhstan abruptly offers three of its oil companies for sale. (July/August).

(1995b). Kazakhstan's oil legislation is no panacea for western investors. (September).

(1995c). Offering a mixed blessing to foreign investors, Rosneft collapses before it gets off the ground. (October), 11–15.

(1994a). Turkmenistan revises JV contracts, seeking greater profits. (November), 48–9.

(1994b). Westerners stay on sidelines as Russian oil producers auction shares (March), 28–30.

Rutland, P. (1997a). Lost opportunities: energy and politics in Russia. *NBR Analysis* 8, 5.

(1997b). Battle rages over Russia's natural monopolies. *Transition Newsletter* (The World Bank, May/June).

Sabonis-Helf, T. (2004). The rise of the post-Soviet petro-states: Energy exports and domestic governance in Turkmenistan and Kazakhstan, in *In the Tracks of Tamerlane: Central Asia's Path to the 21st Century*, D.L. Burghart and T. Sabonis-Helf (National Defense University, Washington DC), 159–86.

Sachs, J.D. and Warner, A.M. (2001). Natural resources and economic development: the curse of natural resources. *Europ. Econ. Rev.* 45, 827–38.

(1995). *Natural Resource Abundance and Economic Growth*. NBER Working Paper No. 5398.

Sagers, M.J. (1995). The Russian natural gas industry in the mid-1990s. *Post-Soviet Geogr.* 36 (9), 521–64.

(1994). The oil industry in the southern-tier former Soviet republics. *Post Soviet Geogr.* 35 (5), 267–98.

Sagers, M.J., Kryukov, V.A., and Shmat, V.V. (1995). Resource rent from the oil and gas sector and the Russian economy. *Post-Soviet Geogr.* 36 (7), 389–425.

Sagheb, N. and Javadi, M. (1994). Azerbaijan's "contract of the century" finally signed with western oil consortium. *Azerbaijan International* 2 (4), 26–8.

Sakwa, R. (2009). *The Quality of Freedom: Khodorkovsky, Putin and the Yukos Affair* (Oxford University Press, Oxford).

Sala-I-Martin, X. and Subramanian, A. (2003). *Addressing the Natural Resource Curse: An Illustration from Nigeria*. International Monetary Fund Working Paper WP/03/139 (IMF, Washington DC).

Samoilov, B.V. (2003). Developing Kazakhstan's Tengiz field will be a tough task. *World Oil* (July), 161–5.

Samoylenko, V.A. (2006). Russian update. *ITIC Bulletin* (May–June), 1–2.

(2003). Reforming the Russian tax system. *Russia Business Watch*, 10th Anniversary Special Edition.

(1998). Tax reform in Russia: Yesterday, today and in the near future. *ITIC Commentary*, April.

Saparov, V. (2003). Summary of oil and gas legislation in Uzbekistan–what's the state of play? *Russian Petroleum Investor* (May), 52–5.

Sarraf M. and Jiwanji, M. (2001). *Beating the Resource Curse: The Case of Botswana*. Environmental Economics Series. Paper No. 83 (World Bank, Washington DC).

Save the Children. (2005). *Beyond Rhetoric, Measuring Revenue Transparency: Company Performance in the Oil and Gas Industries* (Save the Children, London).

(2003). *Lifting the Curse, Extractive Industry, Children and Governance* (Save the Children, London).

Sawyer, S. (2004). *Crude Chronicles: Indigenous Politics, Multinational Oil and Neoliberalism in Ecuador* (Duke University Press, Durham NC).

Saunders, P. (1994). *Welfare and Inequality. National and International Perspectives on the Australian Welfare State* (Cambridge University Press, Melbourne).

Schneider, F. (2005). Shadow economies around the world: what do we really know? *Europ. J. Polit. Economy* 21(3), 598–642.

(2002). *Size and Measurement of the Informal Economy in 110 Countries around the World* (World Bank, Washington DC).

Schubert, S.R. (2007). *Being Rich in Energy Resources–a Blessing or a Curse?* MPRA Paper No. 10108, January. Online. http://mpra.ub.uni-muenchen.de/10108/

Schultz, T. (1961). Investment in human capital, *Amer. Econ. Rev.* 51 (1), 1–17.

Shafer, M.D. (1994). *Winners and Losers: How Sectors Shape the Developmental Prospects of States* (Cornell University Press, Ithaca NY).

(1983). Capturing the mineral multinationals: advantage or disadvantage? *Int. Organ.* 37 (1), 93–119.

Shambayati, H. (1994). The rentier state, interest groups, and the paradox of autonomy: state and business in Turkey and Iran. *Comp. Polit.* 26 (3), 307–31.

Shanahan, E. (1974). Plan for oil 'windfall tax' seen stirring Senate fight. *New York Times* (January 22), 26.

Shanklemen, J. (2006). *Oil, Profits, and Peace: Does Business Have a Role in Peacemaking?* (United States Institute of Peace Press, Washington DC).

Sharipova, E. (2001). The efficiency of public expenditure in Russia. *Russian Economic Trends* 10 (2), 27–33.

Sharma, R., Brefort, L., Iskakov, M., and Thomson, P. (2003). *Uzbekistan Energy Sector: Issues, Analysis, and an Agenda for Reform* (World Bank, Washington DC).

Shatalov, S. (2006). Tax reform in Russia: history and future, *Tax Notes International*, May 29, 775–93.

Shleifer A. (1998). State versus private ownership. *J. Econ. Perspect.* 12 (4), 133–50.

Shleifer A. and Vishny, R. (1994). Politicians and firms. *Quart. J. Econ.* 109 (4), 995–1025.

Shleifer, A. and Treisman, D. (2000). *Without a Map: Political Tactics and Economic Reform in Russia* (MIT Press, Cambridge MA).

Shyngyssov, A. (2004). Changing tax scene: tax stability and assurances for petroleum operations in Kazakhstan. *Russian Petroleum Investor* (May), 58–61.

Simons, G. (1993). *Libya: The Struggle for Survival* (Macmillan, London).

Skagen, O. (1997). *Caspian Gas* (Royal Institute of International Affairs, London).

Skocpol, T. (1985). Bringing the state back in: current research, in *Bringing the State Back In*, ed. P.B. Evans, D. Rueschemeyer, and T. Skocpol (Cambridge University Press, Cambridge), 3–42.

Skocpol, T. and Amenta, E. (1986). States and social policies. *Annual Review of Sociology* 12, 131–57.

Slade, D. (2001). Contracts: myth vs. reality, comparative survey of the legal regimes for PSAs in Azerbaijan, Kazakhstan, and Russia. *Russian Petroleum Investor* (August), 42–8.

Slater, I.P. (2002). Taxing times in Kazakhstan: an analysis of the new tax code. *Tax Issues for the Energy Sector in Russia and the Caspian Region* (World Trade Executive, Inc, Concord, MA).

Slemod, J. (1990). Optimal taxation and optimal tax systems. *J. Econ. Perspect.* 4 (1), 157–78.

Slezkine, Y. (1994). The USSR as a communal apartment, or how a socialist state promoted ethnic particularism. *Slavic Review* 53 (2): 245–70.

Slone, D.K. and Lain, J.M. (1995). Open for business: the legislative framework of the Republic of Kazakhstan. *Caspian Crossroads Magazine* 1 (3).

Smith, B. (2007). *Hard Times in the Land of Plenty: Oil Politics in Iran and Indonesia* (Cornell University Press, Ithaca NY).

(2004). Oil Wealth and Regime Survival in the Developing World, 1960–1999. *Amer. J. Polit. Sci.* 48 (2), 232–46.

Smith, D.N. and Wells, L.T. Jr. (1975). *Negotiating Third-World Mineral Agreements: Promises as Prologue* (Ballinger Publishing Co, Cambridge, MA).

Smith, E.E. and Dzienkowski, J.S. (1989). *A Fifty-Year Perspective on World Petroleum Arrangements* (University of Texas at Austin School of Law Publications, Austin TX).

Solnick, S. (1998). *Stealing the State: Control and Collapse in Soviet Institutions* (Harvard University Press, Cambridge, MA).

Spanjer, A. (2007). Russian gas price reform and the EU–Russia gas relationship: incentives, consequences and European security of supply. *Energy Pol.* 35 (5), 2889–98.

Stolyarov, B. (2000). The creative works of the oil barons. *Novaya gazeta*, No. 56 (August 7).

Starobin, P. (2008). Send me to Siberia: oil transforms a Russian outpost. *National Geographic Magazine* (June), 60–80.

Stepanyan, V. 2003. *Reforming Tax Systems: Experience of the Baltics, Russia, and Other Countries of the Former Soviet Union.* IMF Working Paper WP/03/173 (IMF, Washington DC).

Stern, J. (2005). *The Future of Russian Gas and Gazprom* (Oxford University Press, Oxford).

Stevens, P. (2007). National Oil Companies: Good or Bad?–A Literature Survey. http://www.dundee.ac.uk/cepmlp/journal/html/Vol14/article14_10.html

(2003). *Resource Impact–Curse or Blessing?* A Literature Survey, IPIECA, March 25.

Stiglitz, J.E. (2007). What is the role of the state? in *Escaping the Resource Curse*, ed. M. Humphreys, J.D. Sachs, and J.E. Stiglitz (Columbia University Press, New York), 23–52.

Stijns, J.C. (2005). Natural resource abundance and economic growth revisited. *Resources Pol.* 30 (2), 107–30.

Struyk, R., O'Leary, S.O., and Dmitrieva, I. (1996). Enterprise housing divestiture in Russian Federation. *Economic Reform Today Market Solutions to Social Issues*, 4.

Suleimenov, M. (2003). Kazakh oil and gas legislation and the energy charter treaty, in *Oil and Gas Law in Kazakhstan: National and International Perspectives*, ed. I. Bantekas, J. Paterson, and M. Suleimenov (Kluwer Law International, The Hague), 51–62.

Sultanova, A. (2001). Lower-risk approach: Azerbaijan and foreign investors accent efforts to boost onshore production. *Russian Petroleum Investor* (November/ December), 31–3.

Sunley, E.M., Baunsgaard, T., and Simard, D. (2003). Revenue from the oil and gas sector: issues and country experience, in *Fiscal Policy Formulation and Implementation in Oil-Producing Countries*, ed. J. Davis, R. Ossowski, and A. Fedelino (IMF, Washington DC).

Suny, R. (1993). *The Revenge of the Past: Nationalism, Revolution, and the Collapse of the Soviet Union* (Stanford University Press, Stanford CA).

Surovtsev, D. (1996). Gazprom follows unique course to privatization. *Oil & Gas Journal* 94 (13), 62–5.

Surowiecki, J. (2001). The real price of oil. *The New Yorker* (December 3), 41.

Tanguy, E. (2002). Russian oil companies face challenges to access 'BB' rating category. Standard and Poor Ratings Direct 33 (February 14), Paris.

Tanzer, M. (1969). *The Political Economy of International Oil and the Underdeveloped Countries* (Beacon Press, Boston).

Tanzi, V. and Schuknecht, L. (2000). *Public Spending in the 20th Century: A Global Perspective* (Cambridge University Press, Cambridge).

Tasmagambetov, I. (1999). *One Hundred Years of the Oil and Gas Industry in Kazakhstan* (in Russian). (Birlik, Almaty, Kazakhstan).

Taube, G. and Zettelmeyer, J. (1998). *Output Decline and Recovery in Uzbekistan: Past Peformance and Future Prospects*. IMF Working Paper WP/98/132 (IMF, Washington DC).

Thelen, K. (1999). Historical institutionalism in comparative politics, in *Historical Institutionalism in Comparative Analysis*, ed. K. Thelen and S. Steinmo (Cambridge University Press, New York).

Thiessen, U. (2006). Fiscal federalism in Russia: theory, comparisons, evaluations. *Post-Soviet Aff.* 22 (3), 189–224.

Thompson, J.W. (1921). *Petroleum Laws of all America* (Bureau of Mines, United States).

Thomson, J.E. (1995). State sovereignty in international relations: bridging the gap between theory and empirical research. *Int. Stud. Quart.* 39, 213–33.

Thurman, M. and Lundell, M. (2001). *Agriculture in Uzbekistan: Private, Dehqan, and Shirkat Farms in the Pilot Districts of the Rural Enerprise Support Project* (World Bank, Washington DC).

Tilly, C. (1975). *The Formation of National States in Europe* (Princeton University Press, Princeton NJ).

Tkatchenko, L. (2002). *Corporate Social Responsibility of Russian Oil Companies: Driving Force Behind Corporate Social Responsibility in Russia or Why Russian Oil Companies Behave Responsibly.* Dissertation submitted to the Faculty of Economics, Moscow State University.

Tompson, W. (2008). Back to the Future? Thoughts on the Political Economy of Expanding State Ownership in Russia. The Russia Papers No. 6. Paris: Sciences Po.

Townsend, D. (2002). Azerbaijan Country Update. *ITIC Bulletin* (April 19).

Toxanova, A.N. (2007). *The Country of Kazakhstan Barriers of Entrepreneurship and Support for Entrepreneurship.* Paper for the European Economic Commission. Geneva, June 18–19. Online. http://www.unece.org/ceci/ppt_presentations/2007/eed/tox_e.pdf

Transparency International. (2008). *Promoting Revenue Transparency: 2008 Report on Revenue Transparency of Oil and Gas Companies* (Transparency International, Berlin, Germany).

Treakle, K. (1998). Ecuador: Structural adjustment and indigenous and environmental resistance, in *The Struggle for Accountability*, ed. J.A. Fox and L.D. Brown (MIT Press, Cambridge MA), 219–64.

Treisman, D. (1998). Russia's taxing problem. *For. Policy* (September), 55–66.

Tsalik, S. (2003). *Caspian Oil Windfalls: Who Will Benefit?* (Open Society Institute, New York).

Ulmishek, G. (2004). *Petroleum Geology and Resources of the Amu-Darya Basin, Turkmenistan, Uzbekistan, Afghanistan, and Iran.* U.S. Geological Survey Bulletin 2201-H. (Department of Interior, U.S. Geological Survey Reston, VA).

UNCTAD. (1999). *Foreign Direct Investment and Development* (United Nations, New York/Geneva).

UNDP. (2007). *Gender Attitudes in Azerbaijan: Trends and Challenges.* Azerbaijan Human Development Report. (UNDP, Azerbaijan).

(2006/2007). *Russia's Regions: Goals, Challenges, Achievements.* National Human Development Report. (UNDP, Russian Federation).

(2005a). *The Great Generation of Kazakhstan: Insight into the Future.* National Human Development Report. (UNDP, Almaty, Kazakhstan).

(2005b). *Reforming Tax System and Developing New Revision of Tax Code.* Online. http://www.undp.uz/projects/project.php?id=58

UNICEF. (2008). *Country Profile: Education in Uzbekistan.*

Umbeck, J. (1981). Might makes right: a theory of the formation and initial distribution of property rights. *Econ. Inquiry.* 19 (1), 38–59.

Umurzakov, K. (2003). *Investment Climate in Azerbaijan, Country Report.* United Nations Economic and Social Commission for Asia and the Pacific.

United States Agency for International Development (USAID). (2005). *Kazakhstan: Economic Performance Assessment.*

Usui, N. (2007). *How Effective Are Oil Funds? Managing Resource Windfalls in Azerbaijan and Kazakhstan.* ERD Policy Brief Series No. 50 (ADB, Manila, Philippines).

van der Linde, C. (2000). *The State and the International Oil Market: Competition and the Changing Ownership of Crude Oil Assets.* Studies in Industrial Organization, Vol. 23 (Kluwer Academic Publishers, Boston/Dordrecht).

Vandewalle, D. (1998). *Libya since Independence: Oil and State Building* (Cornell University Press, Ithaca NY).

van de Walle, D. (1998). Targeting Revisited. *World Bank Research Observer* 13 (2), 231–48.

Van der Berg, S. (1998). Consolidating South African democracy: the political arithmetic of budgetary redistribution. *African Aff.* 97, 251–64.

Vasiliev, S.A. (2000). *Overview of Structural Reforms in Russia after the 1998 Financial Crisis.* Paper prepared for the Conference and Seminar on Investment Climate and Russia's Economic Strategy (April 5–7), Moscow. Online. http://www.imf.org/external/pubs/ft/seminar/2000/invest/pdf/vasil.pdf

Vasilieva, A., Gurvich, E., and Subbotin, V. (2003). Economic analysis of tax reform. *Voprosy Economiki* 6 (3).

Verleger, P. K. (1993). *Adjusting to Volatile Energy Prices* (Institute for International Economics, Washington DC).

Vernon R. (1971). *Sovereignty at Bay* (Basic Books, New York).

Viakhirev, R. I. (1999). Samoe slozhnoe v predvybornoi kampanii–eto predvybornaia zima. (The hardest part about an election campaign is pre-election winter.) *Delovoi vtornik*, 36 (2).

Viner J. (1952). *International Trade and Economic Development* (Free Press, New York).

Von Hagen, J. and Harden, I. (1996). *Budget Processes and Commitment to Fiscal Discipline.* IMF Working Paper WP/96/78 (IMF, Washington DC).

von Hirschhausen, C. and Engerer H. (1998). Post-Soviet gas sector restructuring in the CIS: a political economy approach–consequences for European gas markets. *Energy Pol.* 26 (15), 1113–23.

(1999). Energy in the Caspian Sea region in the late 1990s: the end of the boom? *OPEC Review* (December), 273–91.

Wacziarg, R. and Horn Welch, K. (2008). Trade liberalization and growth: New evidence. *World Bank Econ. Rev.* 22 (2), 187–231.

Wade, R. (1990). *Governing the Market: Economic Theory and the Role of Government in East Asia Industrialization* (Princeton University Press, Princeton NJ).

Wakeman-Linn, J., Mathieu, P. and van Selm, B. (2003). Oil funds in transition economies: Azerbaijan and Kazakshtan, in *Fiscal Policy Formulation and Implementation in Oil-Producing Countries*, ed. J. Davis, R. Ossowski, and A Fedelino (IMF, Washington DC), 339–58.

Wakeman-Linn, J., ed. (2004). *Managing Oil Wealth: The Case of Azerbaijan* (IMF, Washington, DC).

Wall, T. (2003). IMF warns Azerbaijan assistance program "off track." January 3. Online. http://www.eurasianet.org

Wantchekon, L. (1999). *Why Do Resource Dependent Countries Have Authoritarian Governments?* Leitner Working Paper, 99–12 (Yale University, New Haven CT).

Waterbury, J. (1997a). From social contracts to extraction contracts: the political economy of authoritarianism and democracy, in *Islam, Democracy and the State in North Africa*, ed. J.P. Entelis (Indiana University Press, Bloomington IN), 141–76.

(1997b). Fortuitous byproducts. *Comp. Polit.* 29 (3), 383–402.

Watkins, M. (1963). A staple theory of economic growth. *Can. J. Econ. Polit. Sci.* 29, 141–58.

Watters, K. (2000). Environment and the development of civil society in the Caspian Region: the role of NGOs, in *The Caspian Sea: A Quest for Environmental Security*, ed. W. Ascher and N. Mirovitskaya (Kluwer, Dordrecht), 203–18.

Watts, M.J. (2005). Righteous oil? Human rights, the oil complex, and corporate social responsibility. *Annual Review of Environment and Resources* 30, 373–407.

Webber, C. and Wildavsky, A. (1986). *A History of Taxation and Expenditure in the Western World* (Simon and Schuster, New York).

Weinthal, E. (2003). Beyond the state: transnational actors, NGOs, and environmental protection in Central Asia, in *The Transformation of States and Societies in Central Asia*, ed. P. Jones Luong (Cornell University Press, Ithaca NY), 246–70.

 (2002). *State Making and Environmental Cooperation: Linking Domestic and International Politics in Central Asia* (MIT Press, Cambridge MA).

Weinthal, E. and Jones Luong, P. (2006a). The paradox of energy sector reform in Russia, in *The State after Communism: Governance in the New Russia*, ed. T. Colton and S. Holmes (Rowman and Littlefield, New York), 225–60.

 (2006b). Combating the resource curse: an alternative solution to managing mineral wealth. *Perspect. Politics* 4 (1), 37–55.

 (2001). Energy wealth and tax reform in Russia and Kazakhstan. *Resources Pol.* 27 (4), 215–23.

Wells, D.A. (1971). Aramco: the evolution of an oil concession, in *Foreign Investment in the Petroleum and Mineral Industries: Case Studies of Investor-Host Country Relations*, ed. R.F. Mikesell (The Johns Hopkins Press, Baltimore), 216–36.

Wenar, L. (2007). Property rights and the resource curse. *Philosophy and Public Affairs* 36 (1), 2–32.

Whiting, S. (2001). *Power and Wealth in Rural China: The Political Economy of Institutional Change* (Cambridge University Press, Cambridge).

Wilkins M. (1974). Multinational oil companies in South America in the 1920s: Argentina, Bolivia, Brazil, Chile, Colombia, Ecuador, and Peru. *Bus. Hist. Rev.* 48 (3), 414–46.

Williamson, H. (2007). Deutsche Bank admits to Turkmen accounts. *Financial Times* (May 10).

Williamson, O.E. (1985). *The Economic Institutions of Capitalism: Firms, Markets, Relational Contracting* (The Free Press, New York).

 (1981). The economics of organization: The transaction cost approach, *Amer. J Sociology* 87(3), 548–77.

Witt, D.A. (2006). Promoting tax reform in Russia and Kazakhstan, *Tax Notes International* (October, 23), 297–9.

Witt, D.A. and McLure, C.E. (2001). Tax Reform: Creating the Modern System. ia.ita. doc.gov/download/kazakhstan-nme-status/itic/itic-comments-kaz.pdf

Wolfrel, R.L. (2002). North to Astana: Nationalistic motives for the movement of the Kazakh(stani) Capital. *Nationalities Papers* 30 (2): 485–506.

Woodruff, D. (2007). Russian Oil: Between state and market. Online. http://www.esai.com/pdf/Woodruff%20Russia%20PE.pdf

 (1999). It's value that's virtual: Bartles, rubles, and the place of Gazprom in the Russian economy. *Post-Soviet Aff.* 15 (2), 130–48.

Woodward, D. 2002. Interview in *Azadliq*. (August 20).

World Bank. (2008). *Republic of Kazakhstan, Tax Strategy Paper–Volume I: A Strategic Plan for Increasing the Neutrality of the Tax System in Non-Extractive Sectors*. Report No. 36494-KZ (World Bank, Washington DC).

 (2007). *Russian Economic Report* (November).

(2005a). *Azerbaijan Issues and Options Associated with Energy Sector Reform.* Report No. 32371-AZ (World Bank, Washington DC).

(2005b). *Republic of Kazakhstan Country Economic Memorandum: Getting Competitive, Staying Competitive: The Challenge of Managing Kazakhstan's Oil Boom* (World Bank, Washington DC).

(2005c). *Republic of Uzbekistan Public Expenditure Review.* Report No. 31014-UZ (World Bank,Washington DC).

(2005d). *Russia: Fiscal Costs of Structural Reforms.* Report No. 30741-RU (World Bank,Washington DC).

(2005e). *Russian Economic Report* (November).

(2005f). *Russian Federation: Reducing Poverty through Growth and Social Policy Reform.* Report No. 28923-RU (World Bank, Washington DC).

(2004a). *World Development Indicators 2003* (World Bank, Washington DC).

(2004b). *Extractive Industries Review* (World Bank,Washington DC).

(2003a). *Azerbaijan: Public Expenditure Review.* Report No. 25233-AZ (World Bank, Washington DC).

(2003b). *Republic of Uzbekistan Country Economic Memorandum.* Report No. 25625-UZ (World Bank, Washington DC).

(2003c). *Russia Development Policy Review.* Report No 26000. (World Bank, Washington DC).

(2003d). *Russian Economic Report* (March).

(2002). *Transition: The First Ten Years. Analysis and Lessons for Eastern Europe and the Former Soviet Union* (World Bank, Washington DC).

(2001a). *Russian Economic Report* (October).

(2000). *Kazakhstan: Public Expenditure Review.* Volume 2: Main Report. Report No. 20489-KZ (World Bank, Washington DC).

(1998). *Kazakhstan: Living Standards* (World Bank, Washington DC).

(1994a). *Kazakhstan Agricultural Sector Review* (World Bank, Washington DC).

(1994b). *Turkmenistan* (World Bank, Washington DC).

(1993a). *The East Asian Miracle: Economic Growth and Public Policy* (Oxford University Press, New York and World Bank Group, Washington DC).

(1993b). *Kazakhstan: The Transition to a Market Economy* (World Bank, Washington DC).

(1993c). *Uzbekistan: An Agenda for Economic Reform* (World Bank, Washington DC).

(1990). *World Development Report 1990* (Oxford University Press, New York).

Wright, G. and Czelusta, J. (2004). Why economies slow: the myth of the resource curse. *Challenge* 47 (2), 6–38.

Wright, G. (2001). *Resource Based Growth Then and Now.* Paper prepared for the World Bank Project "Patterns of Integration in the Global Economy."

Wright J. (1982). *Libya: A Modern History* (Croom Helm, London).

Yakovlev, A. (2004). Evolution of corporate governance in Russia. *Post Communist Economies* 16 (4), 387–403.

Yakovleva, M. (2005a). PetroKazakhstan–from court to the auction block. *Caspian Investor* 8 (1), 10–5.

(2005b). Uzbekistan to add gas resources by exploring promising Ustyurt Oil and-Gas Province. *Caspian Investor* (November/December), 27–31.

Yates, D.A. (1996). *The Rentier State in Africa: Oil Rent Dependency and Neocolonialism in the Republic of Gabon* (Africa World Press, Trenton, NJ).

Yergin, D. (2006). Ensuring energy security. *For. Aff.* (March/April), 69–82.

(1991). *The Prize: The Epic Quest for Oil, Money, and Power* (Simon and Schuster, New York).

Yessenova, S. (2008). Tengiz crude: A view from below, in *The Economics and Politics of Oil in the Caspian Basin: The Redistribution of Oil Revenues in Azerbaijan and Central Asia*, ed. B. Najman, R. Pomfret, and G. Raballand (Routledge, New York), 176–98.

Young, O.R. (1986). International regimes: toward a new theory of institutions. *World Polit.* 39 (1), 104–22.

Yukos Oil Company. (2003). *Annual Report for 2002.*

Zaitseva, Y. and Nikolaeva, N. (2005). VAT changes at a glance. *St. Petersburg Times* (August 2). Online. http://www.sptimesrussia.com

Zettelmeyer, J. (1999). The Uzbek growth puzzle. *IMF Staff Papers* 46 (3), 274–92.

Zürn, M. (2002). From interdependence to globalization, in *Handbook of International Relations*, ed. W. von Carlsnaes, T. Risse, and B. Simmons (Sage, London), 235–254.

Index

ACG PSA, expenditures by, 233–34
Achncarry Agreement ("As Is" system),
  205n. 33
Adams, Terry, 244–45, 254–55
Africa
  petroleum reserves in, 202, 209
  taxation in mineral-rich rentier states of,
    332–33
Agip Kazakhstan North Caspian Operating
  Company, 265, 265n. 15
Agricultural Development Fund (ADF),
  (Turkmenistan), 100–05
agricultural sector
  in Azerbaijan, 237–42, 307n. 5
  in Kazakhstan, 269–74, 305–06
  in Russia, 149
  in Turkmenistan, 90, 99–100
  in Uzbekistan of, 90, 99–100, 110–14
Alekperov, Vagit, 24–25
Aleskerov, Valekh, 225, 244–45
Algeria, 207n. 37
Aliyev, Heydar, 222, 225n. 13, 227, 239–42,
  241n. 36, 246–52
Aliyev, Ilham, 219, 249–50
Alt, James, 9n. 7
American Independent Oil Company
  (AMINOL), 190
Amoco, merger with BP, 209n. 40, 252–53
Anglo-Iranian Oil Company, 205
Angola, petroleum industry in, 192, 201, 311,
  311n. 11
Arabian Oil Company, 183n. 7
Aramco, Saudi Arabia contract with, 190,
  196–97, 199n. 26
Arch of Neutrality (Turkmenistan), 104
ARCO oil company, 202–03, 203n. 31
Argentina, 326n. 2

Arkhangelskgeologia oil company, 131n. 11
Armenia, Azerbaijani war with, 236n. 29
Asanbayev, Yerik, 269
Asia Barometer Survey, 107–08, 110–14
Atyrau Bonus Fund Program, 274–81
authoritarian regimes. *See also* ownership
    structure; state-run government
    structures
  mineral rents and, 32–33, 34–38, 43–44,
    331–35
  in mineral-rich states, 2, 327–30
  resource curse thesis and, 323–27
  societal expectations and, 58–70
  in Turkmenistan and Uzbekistan, 81–87
Auty, Richard, 75
Azerbaijan
  agricultural production in, 307n. 5
  coercion in, 252–56
  distributional conflict in, 307
  expenditures in, 220–22, 233–37
  foreign investment in, 202n. 30, 218–258,
    219
  hybrid fiscal regime in, 220–22, 226,
    256–58
  integrated pipeline systems in, 26n. 26
  mineral sector taxation in, 226–29
  nationalization of petroleum by, 219n. 1
  natural resource fund in, 220–22, 227–29,
    246–52, 331–32
  non-mineral sector expenditures and
    taxation in, 229–33, 242–44
  oil reserve estimates in, 25–26
  ownership structure in, 19n. 14, 19–27
  petroleum wealth in, 20–27, 24n. 22,
    24n. 23
  production-sharing agreements in,
    138n. 33, 222n. 6, 222n. 8, 222–26

Azerbaijan (*cont.*)
  SOCAR expenditures in, 237–42
  societal expectations in, 246–52
  SOFAZ expenditures in, 237–42
  state ownership without control (S₂) in,
      119–20, 123n. 1, 219–58
  transaction costs, 244–45
Azerbaijani Charity Fund, 235
Azerbaijan International Operating Company
      (AIOC), 222n. 6, 222–26, 225n. 12,
      226n. 14, 227n. 15
  coercion and, 252–56, 254n. 49
  expenditures by, 233–37
  tax policy for, 227
Azerineft, 224–26
Azizbekov Institute of Oil and Chemistry,
      24–25
Azneftkimiya, 224–26

Bagirov, Sabit, 244–45
"Baikalfinansgroup," 131n. 12, 131–32
Baku oil fields, 221
  history of, 24n. 22, 24–25
Balgimbayev, Nurlan, 260, 265–66, 295–96
banking reforms, Russian private sector
      growth and, 148–49
bargaining. *See also* explicit bargaining;
      implicit bargaining; obsolescing bargain
      theory
  implicit *vs.* explicit, 71
  lack of transparency in, 72
  ownership structures and, 70–71
Bashneft oil company, 129–31
behavioral economics
  state ownership with control and, 51–55
  transaction costs and, 50n. 11, 50–58
Berdimuhammedov, Gurbanguly, 119
Berezovsky, Boris, 128–29
Blair, Tony, 181
Bolivia, 238, 326n. 2, 331n. 8
Bolshevik Revolution, history of petroleum
      production and, 24–25, 221
bonuses, in production-sharing agreements
      (PSAs), 191n. 16
boom and bust cycles
  domestic private owners' behavior during,
      70
  Dutch disease and, 327–30
  excess profits taxes and, 67–68
  fiscal regime stability and, 48–49
  foreign investment vulnerability to, 208
  Kazakhstan coercion of foreign oil
      companies during, 293–96
  in petroleum industry, 20–21, 21n. 16

public spending and societal expectations
      and, 60–61, 64
  in Russian gas sector, 172
Botswana, 123n. 1
  developmental exceptionalism of, 3
  economic growth in, 2–3, 330n. 7
"Boycott Shell" campaign, 200–01
Brazil, private domestic ownership in, 46n. 3,
      121
Bridas oil company, 78n. 3, 82–83
British Gas(BG)/Agip, 265–69, 274–75, 293
British Petroleum (BP)
  in Azerbaijan, 219, 221n. 4, 224, 227,
      247–48
  coercion in Azerbaijan and, 252–56
  corporate social responsibility and, 211
  Enterprise Center established by, 233n. 22,
      233–34, 235–37
  expenditures in Azerbaijan by, 234n. 23,
      234n. 24, 234, 235
  foreign investment activities of, 182,
      183n. 6, 201–02, 205
  hybrid fiscal regime in Azerbaijan and,
      256–58
  international NGO collaboration with,
      235–37
  merger with Amoco, 209n. 40, 252–53
  Russian investment by, 129–31
broad-based tax systems, revenue generation
      from, 34–38
Bromley, Daniel, 10
Browne, John, 247–48
brown fields, 261–63, 263n. 4, 263n. 5
Brunnschweiler, Christa N., 329–30
Buckee, Jim, 181
budgetary stability and transparency
  in Azerbaijan, 220–22, 226–33, 242–44,
      252–56
  expenditures, 39–43
  extrabudgetary funds and, 100n. 43,
      100–05
  foreign investment influence on, 208–15
  implicit bargaining and, 114–16
  in Kazakhstan, 266–69, 274–84
  National Fund of the Republic of
      Kazakhstan and, 278–81
  private domestic ownership and, 57–58,
      66–67
  Russian budgetary surplus policy and,
      122–24, 138–52, 161–63, 165–68,
      177–80
  SOCAR expenditures, 237–42, 240n. 35
  societal expectations of foreign investment
      and, 200, 201–04

SOFAZ expenditures, 237–42, 240n. 35
Turkmenistan/Uzbekistan comparisons,
    80–81, 88, 114–16
Bush, George H. W., 61n. 26
Business Development Alliance, 233n. 22,
    235–37, 236n. 28
Business Environment and Enterprise
    Performance Survey (BEEPs), 117,
    117n. 59–116

capital investment patterns
    in mineral-rich states, 6
    national oil companies and, 54–55, 55n. 19
CARE relief organization, 237
Caspian Basin, petroleum reserves in,
    22n. 18, 22–23, 209
Caspian Development Advisory Panel
    (CDAP), 235
Caspian International Petroleum Company,
    253–56
Central Asia Petroleum, 264
central bank financing, in Turkmenistan/
    Uzbekistan, 95
central planning
    in mineral-rich states, 6
    retention in Turkmenistan/Uzbekistan of,
    96
    Uzbekistani popular support for, 110–14
Chad-Cameroon Oil and Pipeline Project, 40,
    215, 215n. 44
Chavez, Hugo, 54, 76
    control of petroleum industry by, 54–55
Chernomyrdin, Viktor, 132n. 17, 132–34,
    133n. 19
Cheung, S., 50n. 12
Chevron, 183n. 6
    Kazakhstan investments by, 263, 266–69
    merger with Texaco, 209n. 40
Chile, 2–3, 123n. 1, 182n. 1
China
    foreign investment in petroleum by, 203
    fuel subsidies in, 52
    information asymmetry in, 71n. 34
    mineral development delay and internal
        consumption in, 47
    ownership structure in, 182n. 1
China National Offshore Oil Corporation,
    293
China National Petroleum Corporation
    (CNPC), 86–87, 203, 211, 263–64,
    264n. 11, 293–96
claimant status
    of domestic private owners (DPOs),
        55–58

foreign investment and societal
    expectations and, 195–204
ownership structures and, 10
power relations and, 70–76, 204–15
societal expectations and, 58–70
of state ownership structures, 208
transaction costs and, 51–55, 189–94
CNPS-Aktobemunaigas, 292
Coase, Ronald, 50, 50n. 10
coercion
    Azerbaijan and foreign oil companies,
        220, 252–56, 254n. 49
    Kazakhstan and foreign oil companies,
        293–96
    ownership structures and, 70–71, 204–15
collective action problem (CAP)
    in Azerbaijan, 252–56
    in Kazakhstan coercion, 291–96
    power relations in foreign investment and,
        211n. 42, 211–12
    power relations with foreign investors,
        188–89
collusion. *See* intra-elite agreements
colonialism
    domestic politics and ownership structures
        in, 300–01
    ownership structure preferences and, 309–16
    path dependency of ownership structure
        and, 315, 315n. 16
    resource curse thesis in context of, 6–7
commercial banking, Russian oil sector
    privatization and, 127–32
common property resources (CPRs), resource
    curse thesis concerning, 27–28
Commonwealth of Independent States (CIS).
    See also Russia; Soviet successor states
    countries in, 17n. 10
    foreign investment in, 202n. 30
    map of, 5
    oil and gas production and proven reserves
        in, 17, 22–23
    petroleum wealth and fiscal regime in,
        16–27
Compañia Venezolana de Petróleo, 46n. 5
concession agreements
    foreign investment in petroleum and, 190,
        190n. 10, 191n. 14
    independent petroleum contracts and,
        206–07
    private foreign ownership and, 305
Conoco oil company, 131n. 11
constitutional reforms
    in Turkmenistan, 81–84
    in Uzbekistan, 85–87

constraint mechanisms, on competition, foreign investment use of, 205, 205n. 33
consumer subsidies
  in Kazakhstan, 282–83
  Russian economic reforms and reduction of, 149
  in Turkmenistan, 101, 102n. 44
  in Uzbekistan, 102–04
"Contract of the Century," 222–26, 247–48
contractual relations
  in Azerbaijan, 224–26, 225n. 13, 244–45, 252–56
  foreign investors and host countries, 42–43, 189–94
  historical context for, 206
  institutional outcomes and, 70–76
  in Kazakhstan, 285–86, 291–96
  obsolescing bargain theory and, 207–08
  transaction costs and, 50n. 12, 50–58, 285–86
cooperative agreements
  consortia building in Azerbaijan and, 252–56
  power relations in foreign investment and, 209
corporate income taxes (CIT)
  in Azerbaijan, 228–33, 230n. 18
  in Kazakhstan, 269–74
  mineral-rich and rentier states and, 331–35
  in production-sharing agreements (PSAs), 191n. 16
  in Russia, 135n. 26, 137n. 30, 137–44, 140n. 36, 167–68
  state-owned enterprises and, 36n. 8, 36–38
corporate social responsibility (CSR)
  Azerbaijan foreign investment and and, 220–22, 235–37, 252–56
  of domestic private owners, 68–69
  by Gazprom, 169–72
  historical context for, 28
  international norms of, 14–16
  in Kazakhstan, 293–96
  model contracts and, 187–89, 193–94, 210–15
  origins of, 193n. 21
  ownership structures and, 48, 48n. 9
  proxy state creation and, 217–184
  Russian oil companies' attitudes concerning, 163n. 66, 163–65, 164n. 67, 164n. 68
  societal expectations of foreign investment and, 199n. 26, 199–204
  in Turkmenistan, 87

Uzbekistan foreign investment and lack of, 87, 119–20
Corruption Perceptions Index (CPI), 17n. 12, 17–19, 118n. 62
  in Kazakhstan, 296–98
cost oil
  private foreign ownership and, 305, 305n. 4
  in production-sharing agreements, 191n. 16
cotton exports
  extrabudgetary funds and, 100n. 43
  production quotas and price controls in, 90
  in Turkmenistan, 88n. 30, 99–100
  Uzbekistan reliance on, 80, 89–90, 99–100, 116, 303–04
crude oil, commodity trading activity of, 23n. 19
cult of personality, Niyazov's establishment of, 81–84

D'Arcy Concession, 190, 190n. 10
dataset characteristics
  ownership structure in petroleum-rich countries, 309–16, 310n. 6, 310n. 8
  ranking basis for countries, 357
  resource curse thesis and, 323–27
  wealth and path dependence and, 327–30
debt burden
  mineral sector taxation and, 34–38
  Russian expenditure reforms and, 145–46
debt service payments, extrabudgetary funds for, 100–05
decision-making by elites. *See also* governing elites; sovereign decision-making
  Azerbaijan non-mineral sector expenditures and, 242–44
  in Kazakhstan, 259–98
  ownership structures and, 75–76
  SOCAR expenditures and, 239–42
  transaction costs and, 51, 51n. 13
deficit spending, Russian fiscal regime and, 135
demand
  institutions as product of, 11–13
Democratic Republic of Congo, 52
democratization
  absence in Turkmenistan/Uzbekistan of, 118, 118n. 63
  mineral-rich rentier states and, 331–35
  resource curse thesis and, 323–27
  revenue generation, 31–32
deregulation of business, Russian economic growth and, 148–49
developing countries

domestic politics and ownership structures
in, 300
history of foreign investment in, 190
international norms concerning
involvement in, 206–07
mineral abundance in, 1–4, 75
ownership structure variation in, 345
private domestic ownership in, 70n. 33
societal expectations of foreign investment
in, 195–204
sovereign decision-making criteria in,
311–12
direct distribution schemes, 208–15
direct taxation, 33–34, 34n. 3
Azerbaijan non-mineral sector, 229–33
constraints on state from, 34–38, 35n. 6
economic growth and state-owned
enterprises and, 63
in mineral-rich countries, 37n. 9
rentier states and, 332–33
Russian tax reform and, 140–44
in Turkmenistan/Uzbekistan, 93
distributional conflict
international diffusion effect, 314n. 13
in mineral-rich states, 32–33
non-petroleum alternative revenues and,
312–13
ordinary least squares (OLS) model and,
316n. 19, 316–19
ownership structure and, 301–09, 319–21
regime type and, 316, 316n. 18
in rentier states, 334–35
Doing Business in 2005, 117–18
Doing Business in 2006, 119n. 65, 232–33
Doing Business in 2007, 119n. 65
domestic constraints, absence in mineral-rich
states of, 6
domestic private owners (DPO). *See* private
domestic ownership structure (P$_i$)
Dubov, Vladimir, 166–67
Dunning, Thad, 334–35
Durán, Esperanza, 63
Dutch disease
effects in Russia of, 122–24
export collapse and, 2
National Fund of the Republic of
Kazakhstan and, 278–81
SOFAZ expenditures and, 239–42
state ownership with control and, 63
wealth and dependence and, 327–30

Early Oil Project (Azerbaijan), 234
East Asian economic growth, mineral-rich
states compared with, 75–76

"East Asian tigers," import substitution and,
63n. 30, 316
economic development
Gazprom's role in, 177
government legitimacy tied to, 75–76
human capital development, 34
Kazakhstan expenditures and, 274–81
mineral development delay and internal
consumption and, 47
multistakeholder approach to, 208–15
natural resource funds and, 41–42
ownership structures and, 316
path dependency and, 327–30
resource curse thesis and, 3–4, 323–27
revenue generation and, 31–32
in Russia, 123n. 2, 140–44, 159, 174,
174n. 79, 178n. 83
state role in, 62–64
in Uzbekistan, 110–14
Ecuador
Amazon for Life campaign in, 195n. 24
democratization and petroleum wealth in,
326n. 2
foreign investment in petroleum in,
202–03, 203n. 31
fuel subsidies in, 238
rent-seeking behavior in, 64
education spending
Azeribaijan foreign oil company
expenditures on, 235
by Gazprom, 169–72
Kazakhstan foreign oil company
expenditures on, 274–81
by Russian oil companies, 164n. 69
in Uzbekistan, 102–04, 103n. 45, 104n. 46
Elchibey, Abulfez, 224, 224n. 9
employment
Azerbaijan expenditures outside mineral
sector, 242–44
Russian expenditure declines and, 147
Russian public opinion concerning state
role in, 159
SOCAR (Azerbaijan) labor productivity
and, 238–39, 239n. 31
in Turkmenistan/Uzbekistan, 117–18,
119–20
energy rents
in Soviet successor states, 78–79
Turkmenistan/Uzbekistan taxation on, 90
ENI/AGIP company, 183n. 7
Enron Oil and Gas Company, 57
investment in post-Soviet Turkmenistan
and Uzbekistan, 78
Entelis, John, 53

Ente Nazionale Idrocarburi (ENI), 183n. 7,
    206–07
enterprise bureaucrats
    in fiscal regime stability, 11–13
    governing elites and, 11
    in Soviet Union, 20
enterprise profit taxes (EPT)
    in Soviet Union, 19
    state-owned enterprises and, 36n. 7, 36–38
Entrepreneurship Development Foundation
    (EDF), 247, 247n. 38
Entreprise de Recherches et d'Activités
    Pétrolières (ERAP), 206–07
Environmental and Social Impact
    Assessments (ESIA), Azerbaijan's
    societal expectations and, 251
environmental protection
    corporate social responsibility and, 68–69
    foreign investment commitment to,
        191–94
    in Kazakhstan, 266–69, 289–90
Esso oil company, 205
Eurasia Partnership Foundation (EPF),
    252n. 45
European Bank for Reconstruction and
    Development (EBRD), 84, 86
    socio-economic indicators from, 17n. 11
excess profits taxes
    on domestic private owners, 67–68, 70
    on foreign oil companies, 193n. 19
    Kazakhstan tax revenue from, 273,
        273n. 21
    Russian tax reform and, 140–44
    Turkmenistan/Uzbekistan reliance on, 93
exchange rate
    in Botswana, 2–3
    export windfalls, 2
excise taxes
    in Azerbaijan, 231
    in Uzbekistan, 88n. 30, 90
expatriates, personal income tax on, 230
expenditures. *See* public sector spending
    in Azerbaijan, 233–37, 242–44
    coercion and, 293–96
    fiscal regime stability and, 11–13, 38–43
    foreign investment in petroleum and,
        183–89, 192, 194, 195–204
    fuel subsidies in Turkmenistan/Uzbekistan
        as portion of, 98–100
    Gazprom public sector spending, state
        pressure for, 177
    hybrid fiscal regimes and, 220–22
    implicit bargaining in Turkmenistan/
        Uzbekistan fiscal regimes and, 114–16

in Kazakhstan, by foreign oil companies,
    16–27, 274–81, 293–96
Kazakhstan non-mineral sector
    expenditures and, 281–84
in mineral-rich and rentier-states, 331–35
national oil companies' mismanagement of,
    52–53, 60
ownership structures and historical
    patterns of, 13–16
in Russia, 144–52, 159, 169–72, 177–80
by SOCAR, 237–42
societal expectations and, 58–70, 60n. 23,
    195–204
by SOFAZ, 237–42
in Soviet successor states, 16–27
taxation and, 31–44, 61n. 26, 61–70
transparency and, 32–33
in Turkmenistan, 95–116, 118–19
in Uzbekistan public opinion concerning,
    95–116, 118–19
explicit bargaining
    defined, 71
    fiscal regime strength and, 73
    Russian fiscal regime and, 165–68
    Turkmenistan/Uzbekistan secrecy
        concerning, 114–16
explicit taxes, 34
    in Russia, 134–36, 169–72
    in Turkmenistan, 88
    in Uzbekistan, 90
export revenues
    coercion in Kazakhstan concerning,
        293–96
    exchange rate and, 2
    extrabudgetary funds and, 100n. 42,
        100–05
    for Gazprom, 174–77, 175n. 80
    in mineral-rich and rentier states, 331–35
    ordinary least squares (OLS) model and,
        316n. 19, 316–19
    ownership structure and, 319–21
    path dependency and, 327–30, 328n. 4
    petroleum wealth based on, 309–16
    public spending and societal expectations
        and, 60–61
    in Russia, 138–44, 139n. 34, 308–09
    state ownership with control structure and,
        47, 79–80
    in Turkmenistan, 81–84, 82n. 9, 88, 90
    Uzbekistan taxes on, 89–90
extrabudgetary funds (EBTs)
    Kazakhstan expenditures outside the
        mineral sector, 281–84
    Russian fiscal regime and use of, 135

SOFAZ expenditures in Azerbaijan and, 239–42
in Turkmenistan/Uzbekistan, 100n. 42, 100–05, 114–16
Extractive Industries Review, 200n. 27, 200–01
Extractive Industries Transparency Initiative (EITI), 43n. 18
Azerbaijan membership in, 240n. 34, 252–56
British Petroleum in Azerbaijan and, 254–55
Kazakhstan reluctance concerning, 295n. 40, 295–96
National Fund of the Republic of Kazakhstan and, 278–81
Exxon Corporation, 183n. 6, 201, 202. *See also* Standard Oil of New Jersey
corporate social responsibility and, 211
merger with Mobil, 209n. 40
social spending in Azerbaijan by, 235, 237

Federal Budget Law (Russia), 144–45, 177–80
financial reserve fund *(Reservny Fond)*
creation in Russia of, 145, 146
Russian transparency concerning, 166
fiscal regimes. *See also* hybrid fiscal regimes; strong fiscal regimes; weak fiscal regimes
in Azerbaijan, 220–22
expenditures and, 11–13, 38–43
explicit bargaining and, 165–68
foreign investment in petroleum and, 193–94, 215–184
implicit bargaining in Turkmenistan/ Uzbekistan and, 114–16
institutions and, 3–4
in Kazakhstan petroleum industry, 259–98
in mineral-rich states, 31–44, 324n. 1
ownership structure and, 9–16, 74–76, 116–20
power relations and, 70–76, 206–15
private domestic ownership and, 48–49, 122
private foreign ownership and, 183–86
research methodology concerning, 28–30
resource curse thesis concerning, 1–4, 27–28
in Russia, 121–22, 134n. 25, 134–36, 135n. 26, 152–80
societal expectations and, 58–70
in Soviet successor states, petroleum wealth and, 16–27

state ownership with control and, 48–49, 116–20
state ownership without control and, 183–86
tax systems in, 33–38, 87–94
transactions costs and, 50–58
Turkmenistan/Uzbekistan comparisons of, 80–81, 87–120
flat taxes, 38n. 11
Russian oil companies' support for, 167–68
foreign exchange regimes (FER), in Turkmenistan and Uzbekistan, 90, 100–05
Foreign Investors Council (Kazakhstan), 291–96, 292n. 36
foreign oil companies (FOCs)
Azerbaijan expenditures and taxation and, 226–29, 233–37, 246–52
Azerbaijan hybrid fiscal regime and, 226
coercion of, 252–56, 291–96
corporate social responsibility and, 187–89, 331–35
fiscal regimes and ownership structure and, 181–189
historical patterns of, 13–16
host government, contractual relations with, 42–43
international diffusion effect, 314n. 13
international norms concerning, 14–16
in Kazakhstan, 86, 259–98
in mineral-rich states, 6
minimization of, in state ownership with control, 79–80
ownership structures and, 193–94, 215–184
power relations in petroleum industry and, 183–86, 204–15
private domestic ownership and, 48, 69
private foreign ownership and, 182–89
production-sharing agreements and, 191–94
regional diffusion effect, 314
in Russian gas sector, 132n. 15, 132–34, 133n. 18, 172
in Russian oil sector, 26, 129n. 9, 129–31, 155n. 55, 155–56
societal expectations and, 183–86, 195–204
state ownership with control, 48
state ownership without control and, 183–89
transaction costs and, 183–86, 188–89, 244–45

foreign oil companies (FOCs) (*cont.*)
in Turkmenistan, 25n. 25, 77–79, 78n. 3, 82–85, 84n. 15, 114–16
in Uzbekistan, 25n. 25, 77–79, 78n. 3, 85n. 23, 85–87, 114–16, 119–20
foreign trade
Soviet successor state petroleum industry access to, 26, 26n. 26
Turkmenistan/Uzbekistan taxation of, 93
former Soviet Union (FSU). *See* Soviet successor states
Freedom House Index, 118n. 63
Friedman, Thomas, 322
fuel subsidies
Azerbaijan tax revenue for, 228–29
coercion and, 293–96
for domestic private owners, 65–70, 66n. 32
governing elites' use of, 52
in Kazakhstan, 282–83, 293–96
public spending and societal expectations and, 60–61
Russian economic reforms and, 149, 169–72, 170n. 74, 170n. 76
SOCAR expenditures on, 228–29, 237–42
in Turkmenistan, 77, 98–100
in Uzbekistan, 98–100
Fund for Children's Sports Development (Uzbekistan), 120
Fund for Settlements for Agricultural Products Purchased for State Needs (Uzbekistan), 116

G-77, formation of, 206–07
Gaidar, Yegor, 168
gas quotas. *See also* natural gas
in Turkmenistan/Uzbekistan, 98–100
Gazprom, 23, 56–57
formation of, 124
governing elites' ties to, 174–77
lost assests of, 134, 134n. 24
media holdings of, 176, 176n. 81
monopoly structure of, 122, 173n. 77
pipeline network of, 134n. 22
privatization of, 132–34, 133n. 19, 133n. 20, 134n. 23, 168–77, 319–21
state takeover of Yukos oil company and, 131n. 12
undercapitalization and mismanagement of, 172
Gazprom Joint Stock Company, 124
generally accepted accounting principles (GAAP), Russian acceptance of, 166, 166n. 71

geographic isolation
democratization and petroleum wealth and, 326–27
foreign investment in petroleum and, 196–97
Gershenkron, Alexander, 1, 335
Giffen, James, 295–96
Global Witness, 200, 201–02
Goldman Sachs Energy Environmental and Social Index, 211, 254–55
goods and services
Azerbaijan foreign oil companies' expenditure, 235
foreign investment as source of, 201–04
private property rights legitimation, 69
public spending in Turkmenistan/Uzbekistan on, 100–05
Russian expenditure reforms and public spending reductions on, 150–51
Russian gas sector revenues for, 169–72
Russian privatization of, public opinion concerning, 157–65
state ownership with control and, 61–62
Goskomstat (Russian statistics collection bureau), 165–66
governing elites. *See also* intra-elite agreements; leadership structure; patronage networks
in Azerbaijan, 220–22, 226–33, 242–45, 246–56, 247n. 39
budget stability and transparency and, 66–67
coercion and, 252–56, 291–96
distributional conflict and, 301–09
enterprise bureaucrats and, 11
explicit bargaining by ROCs and, 165–68
fiscal regime stability and, 48–49
Gazprom ties with, 174–77, 179–80
geographical distribution of petroleum wealth and, 186–87
implicit bargaining by, 72–73, 114–16
import substitution embraced by, 63
interviews with, 337–43
in Kazakhstan, 259–98, 281n. 29, 305–06
in mineral-rich and rentier states, 334–35
National Fund of the Republic of Kazakhstan and, 278–81
in national oil companies' management structure, 48n. 7, 53n. 15, 53n. 16, 53
ownership structure preferences of, 21–22, 74–76, 301–09
power relations with foreign investors, 70–76, 204–15

private domestic ownership, 11–13, 47–49, 55–58

private foreign ownership and, 182n. 4, 182–89

resource curse thesis and, 319–21

Russian gas sector privatization and, 132–34, 133n. 18, 133n. 19, 133n. 20, 134n. 23, 174–77

Russian oil sector privatization and, 127–32

Russian public sector spending and, 145n. 43, 148, 160, 160n. 63

Russian tax system and, 134n. 25, 134–36, 135n. 26, 160–63

societal expectations of foreign investment and, 195–204

state ownership with control and, 46, 53–54, 301–09

state ownership without control and, 183n. 5, 183–89, 301–09

transaction costs for, 51–55, 134–36, 152–56, 189–94

in Turkmenistan, 81–84, 82n. 8, 105–14

in Uzbekistan, 105–07, 113, 305

government borrowing, taxation and, 61–70

Guatemala, private domestic ownership in, 46n. 3, 121

Gulf of Mexico Foundation, 48n. 9

Gulf Oil, 183n. 6, 205

"Gulf-plus formula" for petroleum pricing, 204–05, 205n. 32, 205n. 33

Gusinsky, Vladimir, 176

Haber, Stephen, 326–27

health care spending
Azeribaijan foreign oil company expenditures on, 235
foreign investment commitment to, 191–94
private sector growth in Russia and, 150

Herb, Michael, 326–27

Herrera Campins, Luis, 54n. 17

Horiuchi, Y., 323–27

host countries. *See also* specific countries, e.g. Azerbaijan
foreign investor contractual relations with, 14–16, 42–43, 194n. 22
IFI/INGO influence in, 208–15
obsolescing bargain theory and, 207–08
oil pricing controls of, 208
power relations of foreign investors with, 204–15
production-sharing agreements in, 191–94
societal expectations of foreign investment and, 195–204

transaction costs and, 189–94

housing subsidies, termination in Russia of, 167–68

human capital development
expenditures on, 38–43
Kazakhstan government expenditures on, 283, 283n. 31
requirements for, 34
in Uzbekistan, 102–04, 104n. 46, 117–18

Human Development Index (HDI)
Kazakhstan government expenditures and, 283n. 31
Russian expenditure reforms and, 151
in Soviet successor states, 17, 17n. 9
in Turkmenistan/Uzbekistan, 117–18

Hurricane Hydrocarbons (Canada), 264, 266–69, 274–81, 292, 293–96

hybrid fiscal regimes
foreign investment in Azerbaijan and, 220–22, 226, 256–58
in Kazakhstan, 265–66, 296–98
Kazakhstan transaction costs and, 285–86
ownership structures and, 13–16
power relations and foreign investors, 210–15

Illarionov, Andrei, 167–68

implicit bargaining
defined, 71
information concealment and, 72
in private domestic ownership, 72–73
Russian oil and gas sectors and, 168–77
in Turkmenistan/Uzbekistan, 114–16

implicit taxes, 34, 38
for domestic private owners, 65–70
fuel subsidies as, 98–100
governing elites' use of, 52
mismanagement linked to, 52–53
in Russia, 134–36, 169–72
in Turkmenistan and Uzbekistan, 88, 90

import substitution (ISI)
economic growth linked to, 62–64, 63n. 30, 315–316
human capital development and, 103–04
industrialization in Turkmenistan/Uzbekistan and, 80–81, 96–97, 99–100
private enterprise development and, 67
textile industry and, 97
in Uzbekistan, 80–81, 103–04

income inequality
Kazakhstan redistribution and, 284
Russian expenditure reforms and, 151n. 52
in state ownership with control, 74–76

income taxes. *See also* personal income taxes
    (PIT)
  Azerbaijan revenue from, 228–29
  in Kazakhstan, 269–74
  revenue generation from, 37–38
independent oil companies, power relations
    and foreign investment by, 206–07
indirect taxation, 33–34, 34n. 3
  Azerbaijan non-mineral sector, 229–33
  invisibility of, 68n.10n.5, 34–38
  petroleum-rich states and, 332–33
  Russian Tax Code and, 137–44
  in Turkmenistan/Uzbekistan, 93
Indonesia
  democratization in, 323–24
  foreign investment in, 211–12
  fuel subsidies in, 238
  petroleum development in, 311n. 9,
    311n. 10, 311
  production-sharing agreements in,
    191n. 15, 191–94, 192n. 18
industrialization
  state sponsorship of, 62–64
  in Turkmenistan/Uzbekistan, 96–97,
    99–100
informal economy
  in Azerbaijan, 231–32, 232n. 20
  in Kazakhstan, 269–274
  Russian tax reforms and, 138–44, 139n. 35
  in Uzbekistan, 117n. 62, 117–18
information asymmetry
  domestic private owners and, 72–73
  power relations and, 70–76
  Russian transparency concerning explicit
    bargaining and, 165–68
  societal expectations of foreign investment
    and, 201–04
  state *vs.* private ownership structures and,
    71n. 34
  transaction costs and, 50n. 10, 50–58
institution building
  economic growth linked to, 3–4
  government spending and, 38–43
  negative economic/political outcomes and, 2
  ownership structures and, 74–76
  power relations with foreign investors and,
    204–15
  as product of supply and demand, 11–13
  state ownership with control *vs.* private
    domestic ownership and, 48–49
  transaction costs as incentives for, 50–58
internal energy consumption
  Azerbaijan mineral sector expenditures
    and, 234

Gazprom production and, 174–77,
    175n. 80
import substitution and, 63
in mineral-rich states, 47, 79–80
societal expectations for public spending
    and taxation and, 62
wealth creation and, 327–30
internally displaced persons (IDPs),
    Azerbaijan mineral sector expenditures
    on, 235–37, 236n. 29
International Alert organization, 233n. 22,
    235–37
international diffusion effect, ownership
    structure and, 311n. 11, 314n. 13
International Federation of Red Cross and
    Red Crescent Societies, 237
international financial institutions (IFIs)
  in Azerbaijan, 220, 242–44, 246–52
  export dependency advocacy by, 327–330,
    328n. 4
  foreign investment norms and, 14–16,
    183–89, 208–15
  government spending and, 38–43
  in Kazakhstan, 285–86, 289–90, 295–96
  model contracts and, 193–94
  petroleum revenue management and,
    215–184
  rentier states and, 331–35
  resource curse thesis and, 322–23
  societal expectations and role of, 195–204
  state ownership with control and private
    domestic ownership structures and,
    48, 183–89
  transparency goals of, 33
  Uzbekistan taxation system and, 119–20
international loan programs
  Turkmenistan oil and gas sector and, 84,
    86
  in Uzbekistan, 86, 95
international market conditions, oil prices
    and, 314–15, 315n. 15
International Monetary Fund (IMF)
  on Kazakhstan tax revenue, 269–74
  National Fund of the Republic of
    Kazakhstan and, 278–81
international non-governmental
    organizations (INGOs)
  in Azerbaijan, 220, 235–37, 246–56,
    252n. 45
  coercion and, 252–56
  export dependency advocacy by, 328n. 4
  foreign investment norms and, 14–16,
    183–89, 193–94, 208–15
  in Kazakhstan, 285–86, 289–90, 295–96

model contract and, 285–86
petroleum revenue management and,
    215–184
power relations of foreign investors and,
    14–16, 208–15
rentier states and, 331–35
resource curse thesis and, 322–23
societal expectations of foreign investment
    and role of, 195n. 24, 195–204
state ownership with control and private
    domestic ownership structures and, 48
transaction costs and, 285–86
transparency goals of, 33
in Uzbekistan, 119–20
International Petroleum Company (IPC),
    190n. 11, 201n. 29, 205, 206–07
International Rescue Committee, 235–37
intra-elite agreements
foreign investment influence in, 211n. 42,
    211–12
local governments and Russian oil
    companies, 163–65
national oil companies and, 54
power relations and, 70–76
private domestic ownership and, 55–58
private foreign ownership and, 182–89
transaction costs in state ownership with
    control and, 51–55
investment decision-making
centralization in Turkmenistan/Uzbekistan
    of, 96
by governing elites, 52–53
institutional influence on, 3–4
Russian economic growth and, 148n. 48,
    148–49
Iran
independent petroleum contracts with,
    206–07
petroleum production quotas in, 205
Turkmenistan pipeline agreement with,
    81–84, 82n. 10
Iraq
independent petroleum contracts in,
    206–07
IPC oil contract with, 190n. 11
Tripoli Agreement and, 207n. 37
U.S. influence on petroleum contracts in,
    205n. 33
Iraqi constitution of 2005, Article 108, 10
Iraqi Draft Oil and Gas Law, 193
ISAR (NGO), 246–52
Ishanov, Khekim, 82–83
ITIC tax group, Kazakhstan transaction
    costs and, 285–86

Japan Export-Import Bank, 84, 86
JGC company, 86
Joint Stock Society Gazprom (RAO
    Gazprom), 132–34
joint ventures
in Azerbaijan petroleum industry, 224n. 10
foreign investment participation in, 205
state ownership with control and, 7–9
in Turkmenistan petroleum sector, 82–85
in Uzbekistan, 86–87
Jones-Luong-McMann survey, 110n. 56,
    110–14
Kazakhstan societal expectations and,
    286–91

Kamenev, Sergei, 110n. 56
Kamp, Marianne, 103
Karachaganak consortium, 295–96
Karimov, Islam, 77, 77n. 2, 85–87, 118–20
public addresses by, 113–14
Karl, Terry Lynn, 1, 31
Kazakhgazprom, 261–66
Kazakhoil, formation of, 264–65
Kazakhstan, 123n. 1
coercion of foreign oil companies in,
    291–96
distributional conflict in, 305–06
emergence as petroleum-rich state, 20–27
expenditures within mineral sector, 274–81
fiscal regime in, 16–27, 281–84
foreign investment in, 86, 202n. 30, 211–12
fuel subsidies in, 98
history of petroleum production in,
    24n. 23, 24–25
hybrid fiscal regime in, 265–66
mineral sector taxation in, 266–69
non-mineral sector expenditures and
    taxation in, 269–74, 281–84
oil reserve estimates in, 25–26
ownership structure in, 19n. 14, 19–27
petroleum quality and extraction difficulty
    in, 26
poverty reduction in, 151–52
private foreign ownership in, 259–98
private sector growth in, 148n. 47
production-sharing agreements in,
    138n. 33, 225–26
public opinion surveys in, 110n. 56
societal expectations in, 286–91, 331–35
tax system in, 112, 227, 230n. 18, 232–33
transaction costs, 285–86
Kazakhstanmunaigas, 261–66
Kazakhstan Petroleum Association (KPA),
    294, 294n. 39, 295–96

Kazhegeldin, Akezhan, 260
KazMunaiGaz (KMG), 293, 293n. 38,
  296–98
kerb rate, in Turkmenistan, 90, 90n. 36
Khalk Maslakhaty (Turkmenistan annual
  presidential address), 108–10
Khodorkovsky, Mikhail, 131–32, 158, 160,
  166, 176, 179
Kiriyenko Sergei, 121
Komitek oil company, 129–31
Kuwait, American Independent Oil contract
  with, 190
Kuwait Reserve Fund, 100
Kyrgyzstan, 110n. 56

Larmag oil company, 78n. 3, 82–83
Latin America, democratization and
  petroleum wealth in, 323–27, 326n. 2
Law of Petropolitics, current paradigms
  concerning, 1–4
Law on Concessions (Turkmenistan), 82n. 11
Law on Energy (Azerbaijan), 225–26
Law on Foreign Investment (Kazakhstan),
  263
Law on Hydrocarbon Resources
  (Turkmenistan) (Petroleum Law), 83,
  83n. 14, 84–85, 106
Law on Petroleum (Kazakhstan), 263–64
Law on Property (Uzbekistan), 85n. 20
Law on Subsoil (Uzbekistan), 85–87
Law on Subsoil Reserves (Azerbaijan),
  225–26
Law on the Protection of Foreign Investments
  (Azerbaijan), 225–26
Law on the Subsurface (Turkmenistan), 82n. 8
leadership structure
  absence of domestic constraints on, 6
  in mineral-rich states, 6–9
  revenue-cost relationships and, 301–09
legislation
  Azerbaijan production-sharing agreements
    and, 225–26
  change in ownership structure and, 8n. 6,
    8–9
  foreign investor influence on, 211–12
  Kazakhstan petroleum industry, foreign
    investment and, 263–64, 264n. 7,
    264n. 8, 264n. 9
Levi, Margaret, 31
Libya
  independent petroleum contracts with,
    206–07, 207n. 37
  public spending from oil revenues in,
    61n. 25, 65

Lieberman, E. S., 37n. 9
Life in Transition Survey (LiTS), 21–22
  Azerbaijan societal expectations and,
    246–52
  Kazakhstan societal expectations and,
    286–91
  responses by age group, 351
  Russian societal expectations and, 157–65
  Turkmenistan societal expectations and,
    107n. 51
  Uzbekistan public opinion and, 110–14
living standards
  foreign investment in petroleum and,
    187–89
  Russian public sector spending and,
    161–63
  in Turkmenistan, 101–02, 102n. 44
  Turkmenistan societal expectations and,
    108–10
  in Uzbekistan, 102–04, 104n. 46
"loans for shares program," Russian oil
  sector privatization and, 128n. 7, 128–29
local and regional government structures.
  See also regionally-based agreements
  in Azerbaijan of, 234n. 23, 234n. 24, 234,
    252–56
  in Kazakhstan, 284, 284n. 32, 293–96
  Russian oil companies' relations with,
    163–65
  societal expectations of foreign investment
    and, 196–97, 200–01, 202–04
"local content," in production-sharing
  agreements, 192, 192n. 17
López Contreras, Eleazar, 195n. 23
Lukoil Overseas Holding Ltd., 24–25, 86–87,
  119–20
  in Kazakhstan, 265–66
  as vertically integrated joint-stock oil
    company, 121, 127–32
Luong, Pauline Jones, 110n. 56

Madelin, H., 71n. 35–72
Majors ("Seven Sisters") of petroleum
  industry
  domestic politics and influence of, 300,
    319–21
  foreign investment by, 183n. 6, 190n. 12,
    319–21
  independent companies' competition with,
    206–07
  Iraqi oil contracts and, 205n. 35
  power relations in host countries and,
    204–15
Malaysia, 2–3

malhallas (community associations) in
  Uzbekistan, 102–04
Mangistaumunaigas (Kazakhstan), 264,
  264n. 11, 292
Marathon oil company, 48n. 9
market-based reforms, in Soviet successor
  states, 17–19
Marubeni company, 86
Masimov, Karim, 298
McMann, Kelly, 110n. 56
McPherson, C., 239n. 31
means testing, for targeted public spending,
  39–43, 40n. 13
Medvedev, Dmitry, 134n. 23, 177
Menaldo, Victor, 326–27
Menatep Bank (Russia), 128–29
Mexico
  corporate social responsibility of private
    companies in, 68–69
  governing elites' mismanagement in, 52–53
  mineral development delay and internal
    consumption in, 47
  national oil companies in, 55
Middle East, taxation in mineral-rich rentier
  states of, 332–33
military intervention, foreign investment in
  petroleum and, 205–06
Millennium Development Goals (MDGs),
  public sector spending in Azerbaijan
  and, 235
Miller, Alexei, 133n. 19
Mineral Resources Development Fund
  (Uzbekistan), 100–05
mineral wealth. *See also* petroleum industry
  in Azerbaijan, 226–29, 233–37, 246–52
  corporate income taxes and, 36–38,
    37n. 10
  corporate social responsibility and, 210–15
  dataset characteristics for, 309–16, 310n. 6
  delayed development of resources and, 47,
    79–80
  democratization and, 323–27
  distributional conflict and, 301–09
  domestic private owners and, 65–70
  economic development and, 1–4
  fiscal regime-ownership structure link and,
    74–76, 116–20, 181–89
  foreign investment and societal
    expectations and, 195–204
  IFI/INGO influence over, 208–15,
    210n. 41
  Kazakhstan taxation of, 266–69
  "lock-in" of regime structure and, 324n. 1
  national oil companies and, 46

ownership structure classification and, 6–9,
  45–46, 46n. 2, 46n. 3, 181–89, 309–16
path dependency and, 327–30
politics and ownership structure and,
  299–321
power relations and foreign investors and,
  208–15
private foreign ownership and, 182–89
property rights issues and, 9–10
of rentier states, 32–33, 43–44, 331–35
resource curse thesis concerning, 1–4,
  27–28, 322–36
in Russia, 138–44, 147, 161–63, 162n. 65,
  179
SOCAR expenditures and, 237–42
societal expectations and, 58–70, 195–204
SOFAZ expenditures and, 237–42
in Soviet successor states, 16–27
state leaders' decision-making and, 301–09
state ownership without control and,
  183–89
taxation *vs.* expenditure and, 31–44
tax revenue dependence on, 88
mining subsidies, Russian tax revenues for,
  144n. 41
Mobil Oil Corporation, 205
  corporate social responsibility and, 211
  Kazakhstan expenditures by, 274–75,
    291–96
  merger with Exxon, 209n. 40
  production statistics for, 239n. 31
  TengizChevroil (TCO) and, 263, 263n. 6
model contract
  foreign investors and host countries,
    189–94, 190n. 9
  historical context for foreign investment
    and, 206
  Kazakhstan transaction costs and,
    285n. 33, 285–86
  power relations and changes to, 204–15
  transaction costs and societal expectations
    with, 208
Moldova, quasi-fiscal activities in, 98
moral hazard, transaction costs and,
  50n. 11
Moran, Theodore, 205–06
multinational corporations (MNCs)
  corporate social responsibility of
    foreign investment and, 199–204,
    200n. 27
  country bonuses from, 37n. 10
  private foreign ownership and, 182
  taxes on, 36–38
Mutallibov, Ayaz, 224n. 9

"mutual hostage taking"
  domestic private owners (DPOs) and,
    72–73
  national oil companies and, 72
  obsolescing bargain theory and, 207n. 38
Mynbaev, Sauat, 277

Nadymgasprom, 171
National Oil Academy (Azerbaijan), 233
national oil companies (NOCs)
  in Azerbaijan, 224–29
  bankruptcy of, 75–76
  borrowing power of, 61–62
  economic development and, 330
  foreign investment and societal
    expectations and, 195–204
  fuel subsidies as implicit taxes on, 98–100
  Gazprom transformation into, 168–77
  governing elites and, 11
  hybrid fiscal regimes and, 226
  implicit bargaining and, 114–16
  information asymmetry and, 71n. 35–72
  in Kazakhstan, 261–66, 291–96
  management structure of, 48n. 7, 53n. 15,
    53n. 16, 53
  overreliance for economic development
    linked to, 62–64
  pilfering during boom and bust cycles of,
    61
  power relations and, 70–76, 188–89
  private domestic ownership and, 47–48,
    48n. 6, 55–58
  production-sharing agreements, 191–92,
    192n. 18
  public spending financing by, 60, 60n. 24
  rent-seeking behavior and, 63–64
  revenue inefficiencies of, 63n. 29
  Russian transaction costs for, 134–36,
    152–56
  state ownership with control and, 46,
    46n. 4, 197–99
  state ownership without control and,
    183n. 5, 183–89, 197–99
  transaction costs and, 51–55, 134–36,
    152–56
  in Turkmenistan, 105–07, 114–16
  in Uzbekistan, 79n. 6, 85–87, 105–07,
    114–16
"national prestige" projects, 14
  absence in Russia of, 148
  Gazprom spending on, 177
  Kazakhstan expenditures on, 278–81
  in mineral-rich states, 32
  national oil companies and, 52–53
  as newfound wealth benefit, 80

in Soviet successor states, 17
  in Turkmenistan, 104
  in weak fiscal regimes, 87
Nations Energy company, 274–75
  Kazakhstan taxation of, 266–69
natural gas industry
  Azerbaijan production-sharing agreements
    for, 222n. 8, 222–26
  extrabudgetary funds and, 100n. 42
  in Kazakhstan, private foreign investment
    in, 261n. 3, 261–66
  price fluctuations in, 23
  in Russia, 122, 132–34, 133n. 18, 168–77
  SOCAR expenditures and, 237–42
  SOFAZ expenditures and, 237–42
  in Turkmenistan, 79–80, 81–84, 88,
    89n. 31, 98–100, 105–07, 106n. 47
  in Uzbekistan, 98–100, 105–07
natural resource funds (NRF)
  in Azerbaijan, 220–22, 227–29, 246–52,
    331–32
  budget stability and transparency and,
    66–67
  domestic private owners and, 65–70
  excess profits taxes and, 67–68
  foreign investors and, 187–89, 215–184
  governing elites' support for, 54–55, 57–58
  Kazakhstan mineral sector expenditures
    and, 260–61, 278–81, 296–98
  model contract as equivalent of, 206
  in non-OECD countries, 123n. 1
  power relations and foreign investors,
    210–15
  in Russia, 122–24, 144–52, 161–63,
    331–35
  SOCAR expenditures in Azerbaijan and,
    239–42
  societal expectations of foreign investment
    and, 199, 202–04
  SOFAZ expenditures in Azerbaijan and,
    239–42
  tax relief and protection of, 68
  in Turkmenistan, 100–05
natural resources extraction tax (TENR)
  (Russia), 138–44, 144n. 42, 147
Navoi Opera and Ballet Theater, 120
Nazarbayev, Nursultan, 263–64, 264n. 7,
  264n. 8, 269, 277, 278–81, 287–88,
  290–91, 292, 295–96, 298
Neft Dashlari (Oily Rocks) oil complex,
  25–26, 224–26
"New Civilization" education program
  (Russia), 164n. 69
New International Economic Order,
  206–07

Nigeria
democratization in, 323–24
fuel and food subsidies in, 60
governing elites' mismanagement in, 52–53
rent-seeking behavior in, 64
"wealth" curse in, 1
Nigeria-Sao Tome and Principe Joint
Development Authority, 193n. 20
Niyazov, Sapurmurat
authoritarian regime of, 96, 118–20
cult of personality and, 81–84
death of, 119
fuel subsidies under, 77, 77n. 2, 101
lack of private sector growth and, 97
"national prestige" projects under, 104
oil and gas sector management and,
106n. 47
public addresses of, 108–10
secrecy in regime of, 114–16
tax system and, 88, 88n. 30
Nobel, Ludwig, 221
Nobel Brothers Petroleum Company, 221
Norilsk Nickel company, 128–29
North, D., 31n. 1, 51n. 13
North Apsheron Operating Company
(NAOC), 253–56
Norway, economic growth in, 3n. 4

obsolescing bargain theory, 14
coercion in Azerbaijan and, 252–56
corporate social responsibility and, 15–16
foreign investors and strategies to counter,
188–89, 209
historical context for, 28
Kazakhstan petroleum industry and,
259–98
mineral-rich rentier states, 331–35
sunk costs and foreign investors, 207–08
Occidental Petroleum Company, 183n. 7,
206–07
Offshore Kazakhstan International
Operating Company (OKIOC), 266–69,
274–75
oil. *See* petroleum
Oil and Gas Journal Database, 310, 310n. 6
oil prices
fluctuations in, 23, 23n. 19
international market conditions, 314–15
petroleum boom and bust cycles and,
20–21, 21n. 16
Oil Stabilization Fund (OSF) (Russia), 124,
134–36, 144–52, 146n. 44
governing elites' attitudes concerning,
161–63
restructuring of, 177–80, 178n. 86–179

Russian transparency concerning, 165–68
oligarchs
Russian governing elites and, 122, 179
Russian tax code reform and, 167–68
state takeover of Gazprom and, 174–77
Oliy Majlis (Uzbekistan's legislature), 113–14
Onako oil company, 129–31
Oneksimbank (Russia), 128–29
Open Budget Index, 147
Open Society Institute (OSI), 200, 210n. 41,
246–52
ordinary least squares (OLS) regression,
hypothesis testing of ownership structure
selection and, 316n. 19, 316–19,
317n. 20, 318n. 21
Organization of Petroleum Exporting
Countries (OPEC)
domestic politics and, 300
foreign investment competition from,
206–07
founding of, 14, 183–89
international diffusion effect, 314n. 13,
314n. 13
production-sharing agreements and,
191–92
reliance on mineral exports and, 16–17
rentier model and, 118–20
Turkmenistan/Uzbekistan comparisons to,
80–81
ownership structure. *See also* specific
ownership categories, e.g., private
domestic ownership
characteristics in mineral-rich states, 6–9
claimant status under, 10
coding for, 7n. 29–8
dataset characteristics of, 309–16
in developing countries, variation in, 345
distributional conflict and, 309–16
domestic determinants of, 299–321
economic development strategy and, 315–316
fiscal regimes and, 9–16, 116–20, 181–89
foreign investment influence on, 193–94,
215–184
historical context of, 13–16, 182, 182n. 2
international diffusion effect, 314,
314n. 13
international market conditions, 314–15
mineral wealth and, 6–9, 45–46, 46n. 2,
46n. 3, 181–89, 309–16
obsolescing bargain theory and, 207n. 38,
207–08
ordinary least squared model, 316–19
path dependency and, 315n. 16, 315n. 17,
315
power relations and, 70–76

ownership structure (*cont.*)
  regime type (polity) and, 316
  regional diffusion effect, 314
  in rentier states, 331–35
  research methodology concerning, 28–30
  resource curse thesis and, 1–4, 27–28,
    74–76, 319–21, 322–36
  in Russia, 121–80
  social relations and, 9–11
  in Soviet successor countries, 19–27
  state ownership with control (S_1) *vs.* private
    domestic ownership (P_1), 45–76
  state ownership without control (S_2) *vs.*
    private foreign ownership (P_2),
    181–84
  transaction costs and, 50–58
  Turkmenistan/Uzbekistan comparisons of,
    77–120
  variations in, 7–9
  wealth development and, 6–9
Oxfam, 200

path dependency
  mineral wealth and, 327–30
  ownership structure and, 315n. 16,
    315n. 17, 315
  resource curse thesis and, 323–27
patronage networks
  in Kazakhstan, 305–06
  state leaders' decision-making and,
    301–09, 302n. 2
"peak oil" premise, ownership structures
  and, 315n. 14
Pension Fund (Uzbekistan), 100–05
pension guarantees
  in Kazakhstan, 296–98
  Kazakhstan government expenditures on,
    282n. 30, 282–83
  private sector growth in Russia and, 150
  Russian public opinion concerning state
    role in, 159
  in Turkmenistan, 101–02
per capita subsoil wealth measurements,
  economic growth and, 329–30
Persian Gulf states, fuel subsidies in, 52,
  52n. 14
personal income taxes (PIT)
  administrative capacity and, 36
  in Azerbaijan, 229–33
  in Kazakhstan, 269–74
  revenue generation from, 37–38
  in Russian Tax Code, 135n. 26, 137–44
  Turkmenistan/Uzbekistan reliance on
    revenue from, 93

Pertamina oil company, 192n. 18
Peru
  foreign investment in, 201n. 29
  nationalization of petroleum in, 206–07
Petrobras, 57
PetroChina, 55n. 19, 203, 211
PetroKazakhstan, 298
Petróleos de Venezuela Sociedad Anónima
    (PdVSA), 54, 54n. 17, 54n. 18, 61, 76
Petróleos Mexicanos (Pemex), 46, 55,
    60n. 24, 63, 68–69
petroleum industry. *See also* mineral wealth;
    natural gas industry
  abundance *vs.* wealth in, 1–4, 309–16
  in Azerbaijan, 222–29
  boom and bust cycles in, 20–21, 21n. 16,
    48–49
  CIS oil and gas production and proven
    reserves, 17, 22–23
  corporate social responsibility in, 210–15
  in developing countries, 1–4
  domestic politics and, 299–321
  excess profits taxes in, 67–68
  foreign investment and development of, 26,
    26n. 26, 181–189
  foreign market access in Soviet successor
    states and, 26, 26n. 26
  history of changes in, 189–94
  Kazakhstan private foreign ownership in,
    259–98
  mergers in, 209, 209n. 40
  national oil companies and, 46
  in Persian Gulf States and, 52, 52n. 14
  private foreign ownership and, 182,
    182n. 3
  production-sharing agreements in, 191–94
  property rights issues and, 9–10
  quality and extraction difficulty in Soviet
    successor states, 26
  rents allocation and, 20–27, 58–70, 78
  reserve estimates for, 25–26
  revenue management norms in, 200,
    210–15
  in Russia, 121–80, 139n. 34
  in Soviet successor states, 16–27, 77–79
  state-owned oil companies (Russia),
    129–31
  tax revenue dependence on, 88
  terminology, 1n. 1
  in Turkmenistan, 82–85, 88, 105–07,
    106n. 47, 106n. 50, 114–16,
    116n. 58
  in Uzbekistan, 85–87, 86n. 25, 89–90,
    114–16, 116n. 58

wealth *vs.* dependence in, 310, 310n. 6, 327–30
Petronas Carigali Overseas, 86–87
pipeline development
  Azerbaijan taxation of mineral sector and, 227–29
  foreign investment in Azerbaijan on, 234, 253n. 46
  SOFAZ expenditures in Azerbaijan on, 239–42
  Turkmenistan gas exports and, 81–84, 82n. 10
point source resources
  revenue generation and, 34–38
  weak institutions and, 2
Polar Lights Company (Russia), 131n. 11
policy failure, resource curse thesis and, 327–30
political action
  distributional conflicts and, 301–09
  governing elites' mismanagement linked to, 52–53
  implicit bargaining in Turkmenistan/ Uzbekistan fiscal regimes and, 114–16
  ownership structure and, 299–321
  petroleum rents and, 23
  state leaders' decision-making and, 301–09
polity data sets, regime type and, 316, 316n. 18
postcolonial analysis, resource curse thesis in context of, 6–7
poverty reduction
  Azerbaijan government expenditures on, 235, 242–44
  contractual agreements with foreign investors and, 188–89, 210–15
  corporate social responsibility of foreign investors, 199–204
  Kazakhstan government expenditures on, 284
  ownership structures and lack of, 74–76
  Russian expenditure reforms and, 151–52
  Russian public opinion concerning state role in, 159
  targeted public spending and, 39–43, 41n. 15, 41n. 16
power relations
  coercion in Azerbaijan and, 252–56
  foreign investment in petroleum industry and, 204–15
  with foreign investors, 13–16
  foreign investors *vs.* state leaders, power shifts between, 188–89

international diffusion effect and, 314, 314n. 13
model contract paradigm and, 189–94, 190n. 9
ownership structures and, 70–76
private foreign ownership and (P_2), 183–86
regional diffusion effect, 314
research methodology concerning, 28–30
revenue-cost relationships and, 301–09
Soviet successor states' ownership structure and, 20–27
state leaders' decision-making and domestic politics and, 301–09
state ownership with control *vs.* private domestic ownership and, 48–49
state ownership without control and, 183–86
Prebisch, Raúl, 328n. 5
presidential public addresses
  Azerbaijan's societal expectations and, 246–52
  Kazakhstan societal expectations and, 290n. 35, 290–91
  Russian societal expectations and, 160–63
  societal expectations reflected in, 21–22, 96
  Turkmenistan societal expectations and, 108–10, 119
  Uzbekistan societal expectations and, 113–14
price controls
  foreign investors and world market price, 204–15, 205n. 32
  in Turkmenistan and Uzbekistan, 90
private domestic ownership (P_1)
  in boom and bust cycles, 68
  corporate social responsibility norms and, 48, 68–69
  fiscal regime stability and, 11–13, 48–49
  foreign investor minimization and, 48, 48n. 7
  governing elites and, 47–48, 319–21
  historical context for, 13–16
  implicit bargaining in, 72–73
  in low-income countries, 70n. 33
  in mineral-rich states, 331–35
  mineral rights and shareholder majority and, 8
  Natural Resource Fund and, 57–58
  negative outcomes linked to, 74–76
  petroleum-rich states adoption of, 46n. 3
  power relations and, 70–76
  property rights legitimation and, 68–69
  public relations concerns of, 48n. 8

private domestic ownership (P₁) (*cont.*)
research methodology concerning, 28–30
in Russia, 121–80
societal expectations and, 65–70
in Soviet successor states, 19n. 14, 19–27
state leaders' decision-making and, 301–09
state mineral sector regulations and,
65n. 31
state ownership with control (S₁) *vs.*, 45–76
taxation and, 57n. 20, 57n. 21, 57, 65–70,
66n. 32
transaction costs and, 55–58
triadic relationships in, 11
private foreign ownership (P₂)
domestic politics and, 299–321
fiscal regime stability and, 11–13, 183–86
foreign investors and, 193–94, 215–184
governing elites and, 182n. 4, 182–89
historical context for, 13–16
hybrid fiscal regimes and, 210–15
in Kazakhstan, 259–98, 261n. 3
leadership preferences and, 301–09
in mineral-rich states, 331–35
model contracts and, 189–94
number of petroleum-rich states with,
46n. 2
path dependency of, 315n. 16, 315n. 17,
315
research methodology concerning, 28–30
revenue-cost relationships and, 301–09
societal expectations and, 195–204
in Soviet successor states, 19n. 14, 19–27
state leaders' decision-making and, 301–09
state ownership without control (S₂) and,
181–84
transaction costs and, 183–86, 189–94
triadic relationships in, 11
private sector growth
in Azerbaijan, 232–33, 235–37
ownership structures and, 67
in Russia, 148n. 48, 148–49, 157n. 59,
157–65
social welfare spending and, 150
state control over, 9–10
in Turkmenistan/Uzbekistan, comparisons
of, 97, 116–20, 119n. 65, 157
privatization
to domestic private owners, 65–70
foreign investment and societal
expectations and, 195–204
of Kazakhstan petroleum industry,
261n. 3, 261–66
popular support in Uzbekistan for, 110–14
in Russia, 121–80, 157n. 59

of Russian gas sector, 132–34, 133n. 18,
168–77
of Russian oil sector, 127–32, 168–77
Turkmenistan ban on, 84
production quotas
Azerbaijan petroleum sector taxation and,
226–29, 227n. 15
foreign investment imposition of, 205,
205n. 34
in Turkmenistan and Uzbekistan, 90
production-sharing agreements (PSAs)
in Azerbaijan petroleum industry, 222n. 6,
222n. 8, 222–26, 226n. 14, 227–29,
239–42, 244–45, 253–56
foreign investment in petroleum industry
and, 191–94
Kazakhstan petroleum industry and,
265–69
"local content" in, 192, 192n. 17
properties of, 191n. 16
in Russian oil sector, 129n. 10, 129–31,
131n. 11, 138n. 33
SOFAZ and, 239–42
state ownership without control and, 7–9
in Turkmenistan, 84n. 15, 84n. 18, 84–85
in Uzbekistan, 86–87, 119–20
profit oil
private foreign ownership and, 305,
305n. 4
in production-sharing agreements (PSAs),
191n. 16
property rights
domestic private owners and, 65–70
resource curse thesis concerning, 27–28
Russian societal expectations and,
157–65
social relations and, 9–10
societal expectations and, 58–70
tax system and protection of, 68–69
property taxes, Azerbaijan revenue from,
229–33
proxy states, foreign investors and, 188–89,
217–184
public opinion surveys
Azerbaijan societal expectations and,
246n. 37, 246–52
Kazakhstan societal expectations and,
286–91
Russian societal expectations and,
157n. 59, 157–65, 158n. 60
on Soviet successor states' ownership
structure, 21–22
Turkmenistan societal expectations and,
107n. 51, 107–08

Uzbekistan societal expectations and,
110–14
public ownership, role of the state and, 9–10,
10n. 8
public sector spending. *See* expenditures
"Publish What You Pay," 211, 254–55
Pudakov, Amangeldy, 105–07
Putin, Vladimir, 129–32, 134n. 23, 148,
159, 160–63, 162n. 65, 166–68, 174–77,
319–21

quasi-fiscal activities (QFAs)
in Azerbaijan, 220–22, 226
energy subsidies and, 39–43
governing elites' preference for, 74–76
hybrid fiscal regimes and, 226
Russian economic reforms and reduction
of, 134–36, 149, 170
SOCAR and, 238
societal expectations of foreign investment
and, 197–99
SOFAZ and, 238
in Soviet Union, 20
transaction costs and, 54–55
Turkmenistan/Uzbekistan reliance on,
80–81, 97–101
quasi-fiscal deficit (QFD), in Uzbekistan, 99
quasi-voluntary compliance, transaction
costs and, 50–58

real exchange rate, in Kazakhstan, 278–81
Red Line Agreement of 1928, 205n. 33
refugee services, foreign oil companies'
expenditure on, 235–37, 239n. 32
Regional Development Initiative (RDI), 235,
235n. 26
regionalism, state leaders' decision-making
and domestic politics and, 301–09
regionally-based agreements
foreign investment in petroleum and,
206–07
regional diffusion effect, 314
regulatory structures
foreign investors' influence on, 211–12
state control and, 9–10
Relief International, 237
rentier states
defined, 6, 6n. 5
democratization and petroleum wealth
and, 326–27
mineral-rich states as, 32–33, 43–44,
331–35
societal expectations and, 58–70, 60n. 23,
75–76

state ownership with control and, 77–120
Turkmenistan as example of, 80–81,
118–20
Uzbekistan as example of, 118–20
rent-seeking behavior
boom and bust cycles and, 64
distributional conflict and, 306
power relations and, 70–76
private enterprise development and, 67
state ownership with control and, 63–64
resource curse thesis
country exceptions to, 2–3
current paradigms concerning, 1–4, 27–28
democratization and, 323–27
fiscal regimes of mineral-rich states and,
31–44, 116–20
historical view of, 322–36
mineral wealth and, 1–4, 27–28, 322–36
ownership structures and, 1–4, 27–28,
74–76, 319–21
petroleum wealth dataset and, 309–16
postcolonial historical context for, 6–7, 28
research methodology concerning, 28–30
Russian fiscal regime strength and, 134–36
in Soviet successor states, 16–27
state ownership with control *vs.* private
domestic ownership and, 48–49
retail turnover tax, in Soviet Union, 19
revenue generation
alternative sources for, 62, 62n. 28
Azerbaijan taxation of mineral sector and,
227–29
citizen detachment from, 65
claimant status and ownership structure,
10
corporate income taxes and, 36–38,
37n. 10
democratization and economic
development, 31–32
foreign investors as source of, societal
expectations concerning, 199,
199n. 25, 201–04
Kazakhstan non-mineral taxes as source
of, 269–74
multiple revenue sources for, 34–38
by national oil companies, 62–64,
63n. 29
non-petroleum alternative revenues,
312–13, 331–35
power relations and, 301–09
production-sharing agreements, 192,
192n. 17
public spending and societal expectations
and, 58–70

revenue generation (*cont.*)
from Russian gas sector, 169n. 73, 169–72, 170n. 75
Russian tax code reforms and, 137–44, 142n. 39, 152–56, 178n. 83
small and medium enterprises (SMEs) and, 34, 34n. 4
in state ownership with control, 46, 79–80
taxation and expenditure in mineral-rich states and, 31–44
transaction costs and state ownership with control, 51–55
Turkmenistan/Uzbekistan reliance on taxes for, 93
Revenue Watch Program (OSI), 210n. 41, 246–52
Road Fund (Uzbekistan), 100–05
road users' tax, in Russian Tax Code, 138n. 32, 138–44
robber barons, in Russia, 122
Rodman, K. A., 206n. 36
Romania
private domestic ownership in, 46n. 3, 121
Standard Oil investment in, 196
Rosneftgas Corporation/Rosneft, privatization of, 124, 127–32, 128n. 4, 128n. 5, 129n. 8, 131n. 12, 176
Royal Dutch Shell, 174–77, 182, 183n. 6
in Azerbaijan, 221
corporate social responsibility and, 211
in Indonesia, 311, 311n. 9
royalties
Azerbaijan revenue from, 228–29
Kazakhstan tax revenue from, 273, 273n. 20, 292
in production-sharing agreements (PSAs), 191n. 16
ruling elite, institutional constraints on, 3–4
rural poor, targeted spending for, 39–43, 40n. 14
Russian Federation. *See* Commonwealth of Independent States (CIS); Russia/Russian Federation
Russian Fund for Federal Property (RFFI), 129–31
Russian General Oil Society, 221
Russian oil companies (ROCs)
economic growth of, 174, 174n. 79
explicit bargaining by, 165–68
foreign investment discouraged in, 129–31
foreign investment increased in, 173–74
Gazprom and, 168–77

governing elites as representatives in, 160, 160n. 63
management restructuring of, 173n. 78, 173–74
Russian expenditure reforms and, 151
societal expectations and attitudes of, 163n. 66, 163–65, 164n. 67, 164n. 68
tax reform and, 122–24
transaction costs for, 134–36, 152–56, 153n. 54
Russian Tax Code, reformation of, 135n. 26, 137–44, 158–59, 166–68
Russia/Russian Federation
bankruptcy and insolvency regulations in, 155–56, 156n. 56
broadening of tax base in, 137–44
commodity crisis in, 136, 136n. 27
compliance rates for taxation in, 140–44, 142n. 38, 143n. 40, 158–59, 159n. 62, 331–35
democratization in, 323–27
distributional conflict in, 308–09
domestic private owners, 121–80
economic diversification in, 123n. 2, 140–44
expenditure reforms in, 144–52, 331–35
explicit bargaining in fiscal regime of, 165–68
fiscal regime strength in, 134n. 25, 134–36, 135n. 26, 152–68
foreign invesment in oil sector of, 26, 129n. 9, 129–31, 131n. 11, 155n. 55, 155–56, 202n. 30
gas sector privatization in, 56–57, 132n. 16, 132–34, 133n. 18, 168–77
history of petroleum industry in, 24
integrated pipeline systems in, 26n. 26
oil boom in, 136, 136n. 28
oil reserve estimates in, 25–26, 202
oil sector privatization in, 127–32, 168–77
ownership structure in, 19n. 14, 19–27
petroleum rents as political weapon in, 23
petroleum wealth in, 26, 323–27
private domestic ownership in, 46n. 3
private sector growth in, 148n. 48, 148–49, 159–60
privatization potential in, 122
regional oil fields in, 24n. 21
shadow economy and tax reforms in, 138–44, 139n. 35
societal expectations in, 157–65
state takeover of oil sector companies in, 131n. 12, 131n. 13, 131–32

tax reform in, 122–24, 134–36, 135n. 26, 232–33

transaction costs and fiscal regime, 134–36, 152–56

Sachs, Jeffrey, 322

safety regulations, foreign investor commitment to, 191–94

Sakhalin Energy Investment Company Ltd. (SEIC) (Russia), 174–77

Sakhalin Island oil reserves, foreign investment in, 26

Samruk, 298, 298n. 43

Saudi Arabia
  Aramco contract with, 190, 196–97, 199n. 26
  rent-seeking behavior in, 64
  tax system in, 61–62, 62n. 27
  Tripoli Agreement and, 207n. 37

SaudiAramco, 63n. 29

Save the Children, 200, 256, 322

savings funds, economic impact of, 41–42

Schlumberger, Turkmenistan oil and gas service agreements, 84

scope of tax base, in mineral-rich states, 33–34

Securities and Exchange Commission (SEC), 166n. 71

Seko, Mobutu Sese, 52

shadow economy. *See* informal economy

Sharifov, Samir, 239–42

Shatalov, Sergey Dimitrievich, 121, 154, 166–68

Sibneft oil company, 128–31, 154, 174–77

Sidanco oil company, 128–31

Sinopec, 293

Slavneft oil company, 129–31

small and medium enterprises (SMEs)
  Azerbaijan hybrid fiscal regime and, 256–58
  Azerbaijan taxes on, 230, 231–32
  Kazakhstan tax revenue from, 269–74
  Russian tax reductions for, 137–44, 159–60, 177–80
  targeting of Azerbaijan refugee population for, 237
  tax system and, 34, 34n. 4
  Turkmenistan/Uzbekistan taxation of, 93, 116–20

small foreign oil companies, historical rise of, 13–16

Sobyanin, Sergei Semyonovich, 151

SOCAR (Azerbaijani oil company), 24–25, 224n. 10, 224–26, 225n. 13

coercion of, 252–56, 256n. 51

expenditures by, 237–42

internal energy consumption requirements and, 234

revenue generation from taxation of, 228–29

societal expectations concerning, 246–52

transaction costs for, 244–45

workforce size and labor productivity in, 238–39, 239n. 31

social infrastructure maintenance tax, in Russian Tax Code, 138n. 32, 138–44

social relations, ownership structure and, 9–11

social spending. *See* expenditures

social transfers, geographical distribution of petroleum wealth and, 186–87

societal expectations
  in Azerbaijan, 220–22, 246–52
  corporate social responsibility of foreign investment and, 199n. 26, 199–204
  domestic private owners and, 65–70
  foreign investment influence on, 204–15
  governing elites' perceptions of, 74–76
  historical evolution of, 13–16
  in Kazakhstan, 286–91
  in mineral-rich and rentier-states, 331–35
  model contract and, 208
  ownership structure and, 11–13
  private foreign ownership and (P_2), 183–89, 195–204
  research methodology concerning, 28–30
  Russia's fiscal regime and, 157–65, 168–77
  in Soviet successor states, 20–27
  state ownership with control *vs.* private domestic ownership, 58–70
  state ownership without control and, 183–89, 195–204
  in Turkmenistan, 107–14
  Uzbekistan petroleum development and, 79–80, 107–14

Socony-Vacuum (Mobil), 183n. 6

Soiunov, Nazar, 82–83

Sonangol (Angola oil company), 192

Sonatrach oil company, 53, 53n. 16

South Caucasus Pipeline (SCP), 253n. 46

Southeast Asia, petroleum reserves in, 202, 209

Soviet successor states. *See also* specific states, e.g., Russia/Russian Federation
  comparisons of petroleum wealth in, 18
  democracy scores for, 323–27, 326n. 3
  energy rents in, 78
  lack of private sector growth in, 97

Soviet successor states (*cont.*)
  oil reserve estimates in, 25–26
  ownership structures in, 319–21
  petroleum quality and extraction difficulty
    in, 26
  petroleum wealth and fiscal regimes in,
    16–27
  tax systems in, 87–94
Soviet Union. *See also* Russia/Russian
    Federation
  gas sector production and revenues in,
    169–72
  history of petroleum production and,
    24n. 23, 24–25
  ownership structure in, 182n. 1
  petroleum wealth in, 323–27
"Sow the Petroleum" proclamation
    (Venezuela), 195n. 23
stabilization funds, economic impact of,
    41–42
standardization, transaction cost
    minimization and, 189n. 8
Standard Oil of California, 183n. 6, 205
Standard Oil of New Jersey, 182, 183n. 6
state formation
  revenue generation and, 31, 31n. 1
  social spending and, 58n. 22, 58–70
State Fund Finally, for the Development of
    the Oil and Gas Industry and Mineral
    Resources (SFDOG) (Turkmenistan),
    100–05, 116, 118–20
State Investment Committee (Kazakhstan),
    264–65, 265n. 12
  transaction costs and, 285–86
state leaders' decision-making.
    See also decision-making by elites
  criteria in developing countries for, 311–12,
    312n. 12
  distributional conflict and, 301–09
  transaction costs and, 51, 51n. 13
State Oil Fund of Azerbaijan Republic
    (SOFAZ), 227–29
  expenditures by, 237–42
  National Fund of the Republic of
    Kazakhstan and, 278–81
  societal expectations concerning, 246–52
  transfers to state budget from, 242–44
state-owned enterprises (SOEs)
  Azerbaijan tax revenue for support of,
    228–29
  economic growth linked to, 62–64
  enterprise profit taxes and, 36n. 7, 36–38
  foreign investors and, 193–94, 215–184
  governing elites' revenue transfer to, 52

Kazakhstan expenditures and, 274–81
  in mineral-rich states, 6
  mineral sector taxation and, 34–38
  normative bias toward, 27–28
  oil sector shareholding and, 129–31
  personal income taxes and, 36
  power relations with foreign investors and,
    206–07
  revenue-cost relationships and, 301–09
  Russian economic reforms and subsidy
    reduction to, 131–132, 149
  in Russian gas sector, 132n. 16, 132–34,
    133n. 18, 133n. 19, 133n. 20
  Russian mineral wealth privatization and,
    124, 159, 161–63
  Russian oil sector takeover by, 131n. 12,
    131n. 13, 131–32
  social relations and, 9–11
  societal expectations and, 197–99
  Soviet-era activities of, 164, 164n. 70
  state ownership without control and,
    183–89
  transaction costs and, 50–58
  Turkmenistan/Uzbekistan comparisons of,
    81–87, 116–20
  Uzbekistan popular support for, 110–14
  variations in, 7–9
state ownership with control (S_1)
  boom and bust cycles and, 60–61, 64
  defined, 8
  delayed development of resources in, 47,
    79–80
  domestic politics and, 299–321
  economic growth linked to, 62–64
  fiscal regime stability and, 11–13, 48–49,
    116–20
  foreign investment and, 48, 48n. 7
  historical context for, 13–16, 28
  internal consumption of resources in, 47,
    79–80
  Kazakhstan transition to, 296–98
  leadership preferences and, 301–09
  mineral development delay and internal
    consumption under, 47
  national oil companies under, 46
  negative outcomes linked to, 74–76
  number of petroleum-rich states with,
    46n. 2
  in Persian Gulf States, 52, 52n. 14
  petroleum-rich countries' adoption of, 219,
    219n. 2
  power relations and, 70–76
  private domestic ownership *vs.*,
    45–76

privatization of Russian petroleum and,
124
relationships under, 11
research methodology concerning, 28–30
resource curse thesis and, 322–23
of Russian oil and gas sectors, 127–32,
168–80
societal expectations under, 58–70
in Soviet successor states, 19n. 14, 19–27
state leaders' decision-making and,
301–09
taxation systems and, 61n. 26, 61–70
transaction costs and, 51–55
Turkmenistan authoritarian regime and,
77–120
Uzbekistan authoritarian regime and,
77–120
state ownership without control (S₂)
in Azerbaijan, 219–58
defined, 8
domestic politics and, 299–321
fiscal regime stability and, 11–12, 183–86
foreign investment and, 193–94, 215–184
governing elites and, 183–89
historical context for, 13–16, 28
hybrid fiscal regimes and, 210–15
Kazakhstan petroleum industry and,
259–98
leadership preferences and, 301–09
in Persian Gulf States, 52n. 14
petroleum-rich countries' adoption of, 219,
219n. 2
private foreign ownership and, 181–84
rentier-state expenditures and, 331–35
research methodology concerning, 28–30
resource curse thesis and, 322–23
societal expectations and, 195–204
sovereign decision-making and, 301–09
in Soviet successor states, 19n. 14, 19–27
transaction costs of, 183–86, 189–94
triadic relationships in, 11
in Uzbekistan, 119–20
StatoilHydro
Azerbaijan hybrid fiscal regime and,
256–58
coercion in Azerbaijan and, 252–56
corporate social responsibility and, 211
foreign oil company expenditures in
Azerbaijan by, 235, 237
management structure of, 48n. 7
South Caucasus Pipeline (SCP) and,
253n. 46
St. John, Karen, 233–34
Stolichnyi Bank, 128–29

"Strategy for the Social and Economic
Transformation of Turkmenistan," 96,
96n. 40
"Strategy for Turkmenistan Development to
2020," 96
strong fiscal regime
characteristics of, 11–13
emergence in Russia of, 134–36, 152,
177–80
oil and gas industries and presence of,
168–77
power relations and, 70–76, 204–15
private domestic ownership and, 320
societal expectations and, 58–70
state ownership without control *vs.* private
ownership and, 188–89, 212
tax systems and, 121–24
Subsurface Law (Kazakhstan), transaction
costs and, 285n. 34, 285–86
sunk costs of foreign investment, obsolescing
bargain theory and, 207–08
supply
domestic private owners and incentive of,
65–70
institutions as product of, 11–13
"supra-sovereign" constraints, 205, 205n. 33
Surgutneftegaz
"loans for shares program" and, 128n. 7,
128–29
as vertically integrated joint-stock oil
company, 121, 127–32
Surowiecki, James, 45
Swarnim, W., 323–27

targeted spending, 39–43, 40n. 13, 40n. 14
Tasmagambetov, Imangaly, 269, 278–81, 291
Tatneft oil company, 129–31
taxation
in Azerbaijan, 220–22, 226–33, 252–56
broad-based tax systems, 34–38
coercion and, 252–56
compliance rate comparisons, 140–44,
142n. 38, 143n. 40, 158–59, 159n. 62,
231–32, 232n. 19
composition of, 33–34
direct *vs.* indirect taxes, 33–34, 34n. 3
domestic private owners and, 65–70,
66n. 32
economists' view of, 33n. 2
expenditures and, 31–44, 61n. 26, 61–70
fiscal regime stability and, 11–13, 33–38,
74–76
foreign investor influence on, 183–86,
210–15

taxation (*cont.*)
  implicit bargaining and, 114–16
  implicit *vs.* explicit taxation, 34
  institutional support for, 3–4
  in Kazakhstan, 266–74, 285–86
  in mineral-rich states and rentier states,
    331–35, 334n. 9
  multiple revenue sources for, 34–38
  in private domestic ownership structure,
    57, 57n. 20
  production-sharing agreement revenues
    and, 192, 192n. 17
  profit-sharing in, 14
  in Russia, 122–24, 134n. 25, 134–36,
    135n. 26, 137–44, 152–56, 153n. 53,
    153n. 54, 157–65, 158n. 60, 169n. 73,
    169–72, 170n. 75
  scope of, 33–34
  societal expectations of foreign investment
    and, 197–99, 201–04
  in Soviet successor states, 19–27
  state control structures and, 34–38
  state formation and, 31, 31n. 1
  transaction costs and, 50–58, 152–56,
    153n. 53, 153n. 54, 285–86
  transparency and, 32–33
  Turkmenistan/Uzbekistan comparisons of,
    87n. 27, 87–94, 110–20
Technip company, 86
technology, ownership structures and,
  314–15, 315n. 15
Tehran Agreement, 206–07
TengizChevroil (TCO), 263, 266–69, 274–81,
  292–93, 295–96
Texaco oil company, 78n. 3, 183n. 6, 205
  in Kazakhstan, 265–66
  merger with Chevron, 209n. 40
Thomas, Marlo, 268
time horizons, societal expectations for
  public spending and taxation and, 62
transaction costs
  foreign investment in Azerbaijan and,
    244–45
  historical context of ownership structures
    and, 13–16
  of information disclosure, 72–73
  Kazakhstan fiscal regime and, 285–86
  model contracts and, 208
  ownership structure and, 11–13
  private domestic ownership and, 45, 55–58,
    122, 134–36
  private foreign ownership and, 183–86,
    189–94
  research methodology concerning, 28–30

  Russian fiscal regime strength and, 134–36,
    152–56
  of Russian oil and gas sectors, 168–77
  Soviet successor states' ownership structure
    and, 20–27
  state ownership with control and, 45,
    54–55
  state ownership without control and,
    183–86, 189–94
  theory of, 50–58
  in Turkmenistan/Uzbekistan fiscal regimes,
    105–07
transfer pricing, Russian oil companies' use
  of, 152–56
Transocean oil company, 48n. 9
transparency
  foreign investors and host countries
    relations and, 42–43
  Natural Resource Funds and, 17, 41–42
  tax/expenditure systems and, 32–33
triadic relationships
  fiscal regimes and ownership structure
    and, 181–189
  historical evolution of, 13–16
  national oil companies and, 46
  in private domestic ownership structure,
    47–48
  private foreign ownership and, 182–89
  in state ownership with control, 11
  state ownership without control and,
    183–89
Tripoli Agreement, 206–07, 207n. 37
Triton-Vuko oil company, 264
Tunisia, 328
Turkmen Foreign Exchange Reserve Fund
  (FERF), 88, 100–05, 116
Turkmengaz, 83–84, 105–07, 106n. 49
Turkmengeologiya, 83–84
Turkmenistan
  bribery and corruption in, 117–18
  central planning in, 96, 96n. 40
  consumer subsidies in, 101, 102n. 44
  direct *vs.* indirect taxation in, 93
  emergence as petroleum-rich state, 20–27
  extrabudgetary funds in, 100n. 42,
    100–05
  fiscal regime and petroleum wealth in,
    16–27, 87–120
  foreign exchange regime in, 90
  foreign investment in petroleum in,
    25n. 25, 77–79, 78n. 3, 82–85,
    84n. 15, 202n. 30
  fuel subsidies in, 77, 98–100, 237–42
  gas sector development in, 79–80

implicit bargaining in fiscal regime of,
114–16
implicit taxes in, 90
"national prestige" projects in, 104
oil reserve estimates in, 25–26
ownership structure in, 19n. 14, 19–27
petroleum sector growth in, 78–79, 81–87,
82n. 8, 326n. 3
private sector growth limitations in, 97,
148n. 47
production quotas and price controls in, 90
public addresses as reflection of societal
expectations in, 108–10
public opinion surveys in, 107n. 51,
107–08
public sector spending in, 95–116, 96n. 41,
118–19, 242–44
quasi-fiscal activities in, 80–81, 97–101
Russian expenditure reforms compared
with, 144–52
societal expectations in, 107–14
state ownership with control (S₁) in,
81–84
taxation in, 87n. 27, 87–94, 88n. 28,
88n. 30, 116–20
transaction costs of fiscal regime in,
105–07
value-added tax in, 88, 91n. 39, 91–93
Turkmenistan Central Bank, 100n. 42
Turkmenneft, 83–84, 84n. 16, 85n. 19,
105–07
Turkmenneftegaz, 83–84
Turkmenneftegazstroy, 83–84
turnover taxes
in Kazakhstan, 269–74
in Russian Tax Code, 137–44, 138n. 32
Tyumen Oblast, 151, 151n. 51
Tyumenskaya Neftyanaya Kompaniya
(TNK), 129–31, 154

Ukraine
natural gas delivery crisis in, 23
private sector growth in, 148n. 47
Turkmenistan gas exports to, 82, 82n. 9
UMID (NGO), 235–37, 236n. 27
UN Global Compact, 209
Unified Energy Systems (UES) (Russia), 170
unified social tax (UST), in Russian Tax
Code, 135n. 26, 137–44
United Heavy Machinery, 174–77
United States
excess profits taxes in, 67–68
internal mineral and petroleum
consumption in, 47

private domestic ownership in, 47–48
universal benefits
Kazakhstan non-mineral sector
expenditures on, 282–83
Russian economic reforms and reductions
in, 149–51, 150n. 50
societal expectations and, 58–70
state ownership without control and,
183–89
targeted spending *vs.*, 39–43
Turkmenistan societal expectations and,
108–10
Unocal oil company, 78n. 3
UN Resolution on Permanent Sovereignty
over Natural Resources, 10
Urengoigazprom, 171
utility maximization, power relations and, 71
Uzbekistan
bribery and corruption in, 117n. 60,
118–20
consumer subsidies in, 102–04
delayed development of petroleum in,
79–80
direct *vs.* indirect taxation in, 93
distributional conflict in, 303–04
emergence as petroleum-rich state, 20–27
energy rents in, 78
extrabudgetary funds in, 100–05
fiscal regime in, 16–27, 87–120
foreign exchange regime in, 90, 91n. 37
foreign investment rejected in, 25n. 25,
77–79, 78n. 3, 85n. 23, 85–87,
202n. 30
fuel subsidies in, 98–100, 237–42
history of petroleum production in,
24n. 23, 24–25
implicit bargaining in fiscal regime of,
114–16
implicit taxes in, 90
imports into, 79–80
informal economy in, 117n. 62, 117–18
internal petroleum consumption in,
21n. 15, 80–81
lack of private sector growth in, 97,
116–20, 119n. 65, 157
mineral development delay and internal
consumption in, 47
ownership structure in, 19n. 14, 19–27
petroleum reserve estimates in, 25–26, 78
petroleum sector growth in, 78–79, 79n. 6,
79n. 7, 85–87, 86n. 25, 301–09,
326n. 3
popular support for state-owned
enterprises in, 110–14

Uzbekistan (*cont.*)
  production quotas and price controls in,
    90n. 34, 90n. 35, 90
  public opinion surveys in, 107–08,
    110n. 56, 110–14, 159
  public sector spending in, 95–116, 118–19,
    242–44
  quasi-fiscal activities in, 80–81, 97–101
  Russian expenditure reforms compared
    with, 144–52
  societal expectations in, 107–14, 246
  state ownership with control in, 85,
    225–26
  state ownership without control in, 119–20
  taxation in, 87n. 27, 87–94, 88n. 29,
    116–20, 232–33
  transaction costs of fiscal regime in,
    105–07
  value-added tax in, 88, 91n. 38, 91–93
Uzbekneftegaz, 79n. 6, 85–87, 90, 105–07
Uzneftegazpererabotka, 86

value-added tax (VAT)
  Azerbaijan revenue from, 228–33, 232n. 19
  increased reliance on, 35n. 5, 37, 38n. 12
  in Kazhkstan, 266–74, 292
  in Russian Tax Code, 135n. 26, 137–44,
    140n. 36, 141n. 37
  in Turkmenistan and Uzbekistan, 88,
    91n. 38, 91n. 39, 91–93
Venezuela
  democratization and petroleum wealth in,
    326n. 2
  economic decline in, 76
  foreign investment in petroleum in,
    195n. 23
  governing elites' mismanagement in, 52–53
  national oil company management in, 54,
    54n. 17, 54n. 18, 61
  private domestic ownership in, 121
Venezuelan Investment Fund, 54–55
Vernon, R., 207–08
vertically integrated companies (VICs)
  power relations in, 205
  privatization of Russian petroleum
    industry and, 124
  Russian government support for, 131n. 14
  Russian oil sector reforms and, 127–32
Viakhirev, Rem, 172
Vostochnaya Neftyanaya Kompaniya (VNK)
    oil company, 129–31
voucher privatization
  in Russian gas sector, 132–34, 133n. 18
  in Russian oil sector, 127–32

Vyakhirev, Rem, 133n. 19, 133n. 21,
    133–34

wages as state expenditures, Uzbekistan
    reliance on, 119n. 66
Waterbury, John, 37n. 9, 332–33
weak fiscal regime
  characteristics of, 11–13
  emergence of, 87–120
  Gazprom restructuring and, 173
  governing elites' preference for, 74
  Natural Resource Fund creation and,
    54–55
  power relations and, 70–76, 204–15
  private domestic ownership and, 48–49
  rentierism and, 43–44
  resource curse and, 1–4, 27–28
  societal expectations and, 58–70
  in Soviet successor states, 19–27
  state ownership with control and, 15–16,
    48–49, 53, 188–89
  in Turkmenistan/Uzbekistan, 29, 80–81,
    179
"wealth" curse
  democratization and, 323–27
  in Nigeria, 1
  ownership structure and, 6–9
  path dependency and, 327–30
  petroleum abundance *vs.*, 309–16
Weber, Max, 31
welfare spending
  in Azerbaijan, 220–22
  Azerbaijan non-mineral sector
    expenditures on, 242–44
  governing elites' benefits from, 74–76
  Russian economic reforms and reductions
    in, 149–51, 150n. 50, 161–63,
    162n. 65, 167–68
  societal expectations and historical trends
    in, 58–70
wheat subsidies, in Turkmenistan/
    Uzbekistan, 99–100
"white elephant" public projects, societal
    expectations and, 52–53, 60
windfall profits taxes. *See* excess profits
    taxes
Woodward, David, 219, 227, 253–56
World Bank, 40, 200n. 27, 200–01
  on Kazakhstan taxation, 269–74
  National Fund of the Republic of
    Kazakhstan and, 278–81
  on SOCAR financial performance, 228–29
  wealth and path dependence
    measurements, 327–30

Yacimientos Proliferos Fiscales (YPF), 46
Yamburggazprom, 171
Yeltsin, Boris, 127, 135, 137, 148, 158,
    160–63, 308–09
Yemen ownership structure, 315n. 16
Yew, Lee Kwan, 45
Young, Oran, 58n. 22
Yugduskneftegaz, 131–32, 176, 176n. 82
Yukos oil company, 25n. 24, 158, 160,
    174n. 79

corporate social responsibility (CSR) in,
    163–65, 164n. 69
state takeover of, 131n. 12, 131–32,
    177–80
transaction costs for, 154
as vertically integrated joint-stock oil
    company, 121, 127–32
Yuzhneftegaz, 263, 274–75, 293–96

Zaire. *See* Democratic Republic of Congo

Other Books in the Series *(continued from page iii)*

Valerie Bunce, *Leaving Socialism and Leaving the State: The End of Yugoslavia, the Soviet Union, and Czechoslovakia*

Daniele Caramani, *The Nationalization of Politics: The Formation of National Electorates and Party Systems in Europe*

John M. Carey, *Legislative Voting and Accountability*

Kanchan Chandra, *Why Ethnic Parties Succeed: Patronage and Ethnic Headcounts in India*

José Antonio Cheibub, *Presidentialism, Parliamentarism, and Democracy*

Ruth Berins Collier, *Paths toward Democracy: The Working Class and Elites in Western Europe and South America*

Christian Davenport, *State Repression and the Domestic Democratic Peace*

Donatella della Porta, *Social Movements, Political Violence, and the State*

Alberto Diaz-Cayeros, *Federalism, Fiscal Authority, and Centralization in Latin America*

Thad Dunning, *Crude Democracy: Natural Resource Wealth and Political Regimes*

Gerald Easter, *Reconstructing the State: Personal Networks and Elite Identity*

Margarita Estevez-Abe, *Welfare and Capitalism in Postwar Japan: Party, Bureaucracy, and Business*

Henry Farrell, *The Political Economy of Trust: Institutions, Interests, and Inter-Firm Cooperation in Italy and Germany*

M. Steven Fish, *Democracy Derailed in Russia: The Failure of Open Politics*

Robert F. Franzese, *Macroeconomic Policies of Developed Democracies*

Roberto Franzosi, *The Puzzle of Strikes: Class and State Strategies in Postwar Italy*

Geoffrey Garrett, *Partisan Politics in the Global Economy*

Scott Gehlbach, *Representation through Taxation: Revenue, Politics, and Development in Postcommunist States*

Miriam Golden, *Heroic Defeats: The Politics of Job Loss*

Jeff Goodwin, No *Other Way Out: States and Revolutionary Movements*

Merilee Serrill Grindle, *Changing the State*

Anna Grzymala-Busse, *Rebuilding Leviathan: Party Competition and State Exploitation in Post-Communist Democracies*

Anna Grzymala-Busse, *Redeeming the Communist Past: The Regeneration of Communist Parties in East Central Europe*

Frances Hagopian, *Traditional Politics and Regime Change in Brazil*

Henry E. Hale, *The Foundations of Ethnic Politics: Separatism of States and Nations in Eurasia and the World*

Mark Hallerberg, Rolf Ranier Strauch, and Jürgen von Hagen, *Fiscal Governance in Europe*

Gretchen Helmke, *Courts Under Constraints: Judges, Generals, and Presidents in Argentina*

Yoshiko Herrera, *Imagined Economies: The Sources of Russian Regionalism*

J. Rogers Hollingsworth and Robert Boyer, eds., *Contemporary Capitalism: The Embeddedness of Institutions*

John D. Huber and Charles R. Shipan, *Deliberate Discretion? The Institutional Foundations of Bureaucratic Autonomy*

Ellen Immergut, *Health Politics: Interests and Institutions in Western Europe*

Torben Iversen, *Capitalism, Democracy, and Welfare*

Torben Iversen, *Contested Economic Institutions*

Torben Iversen, Jonas Pontussen, and David Soskice, eds., *Unions, Employers, and Central Banks: Macroeconomic Coordination and Institutional Change in Social Market Economies*

Thomas Janoski and Alexander M. Hicks, eds., *The Comparative Political Economy of the Welfare State*

Joseph Jupille, *Procedural Politics: Issues, Influence, and Institutional Choice in the European Union*

Stathis Kalyvas, *The Logic of Violence in Civil War*

David C. Kang, *Crony Capitalism: Corruption and Capitalism in South Korea and the Philippines*

Junko Kato, *Regressive Taxation and the Welfare State*

Orit Kedar, *Voting for Policy, Not Parties: How Voters Compensate for Power Sharing*

Robert O. Keohane and Helen B. Milner, eds., *Internationalization and Domestic Politics*

Herbert Kitschelt, *The Transformation of European Social Democracy*

Herbert Kitschelt, Kirk A. Hawkins, Juan Pablo Luna, Guillermo Rosas, and Elizabeth J. Zechmeister, *Latin American Party Systems*

Herbert Kitschelt, Peter Lange, Gary Marks, and John D. Stephens, eds., *Continuity and Change in Contemporary Capitalism*

Herbert Kitschelt, Zdenka Mansfeldova, Radek Markowski, and Gabor Toka, *Post-Communist Party Systems*

David Knoke, Franz Urban Pappi, Jeffrey Broadbent, and Yutaka Tsujinaka, eds., *Comparing Policy Networks*

Allan Kornberg and Harold D. Clarke, *Citizens and Community: Political Support in a Representative Democracy*

Amie Kreppel, *The European Parliament and the Supranational Party System*

David D. Laitin, *Language Repertoires and State Construction in Africa*

Fabrice E. Lehoucq and Ivan Molina, *Stuffing the Ballot Box: Fraud, Electoral Reform, and Democratization in Costa Rica*

Mark Irving Lichbach and Alan S. Zuckerman, eds., *Comparative Politics: Rationality, Culture, and Structure, second edition*

Evan Lieberman, *Race and Regionalism in the Politics of Taxation in Brazil and South Africa*

Pauline Jones Luong, *Institutional Change and Political Continuity in Post-Soviet Central Asia*

Julia Lynch, *Age in the Welfare State: The Origins of Social Spending on Pensioners, Workers, and Children*

Lauren M. MacLean, *Informal Institutions and Citizenship in Rural Africa: Risk and Reciprocity in Ghana and Côte d'Ivoire*

Beatriz Magaloni, *Voting for Autocracy: Hegemonic Party Survival and Its Demise in Mexico*

James Mahoney, *Colonialism and Postcolonial Development: Spanish America in Comparative Perspective*

James Mahoney and Dietrich Rueschemeyer, eds., *Historical Analysis and the Social Sciences*

Scott Mainwaring and Matthew Soberg Shugart, eds., *Presidentialism and Democracy in Latin America*

Isabela Mares, *The Politics of Social Risk: Business and Welfare State Development*

Isabela Mares, *Taxation, Wage Bargaining, and Unemployment*

Anthony W. Marx, *Making Race, Making Nations: A Comparison of South Africa, the United States, and Brazil*

Doug McAdam, John McCarthy, and Mayer Zald, eds., *Comparative Perspectives on Social Movements*

Bonnie Meguid, *Party Competition between Unequals: Strategies and Electoral Fortunes in Western Europe*

Joel S. Migdal, *State in Society: Studying How States and Societies Constitute One Another*

Joel S. Migdal, Atul Kohli, and Vivienne Shue, eds., *State Power and Social Forces: Domination and Transformation in the Third World*

Scott Morgenstern and Benito Nacif, eds., *Legislative Politics in Latin America*

Layna Mosley, *Global Capital and National Governments*

Wolfgang C. Müller and Kaare Strøm, *Policy, Office, or Votes?*

Maria Victoria Murillo, *Labor Unions, Partisan Coalitions, and Market Reforms in Latin America*

Maria Victoria Murillo, *Political Competition, Partisanship, and Policy Making in Latin American Public Utilities*

Monika Nalepa, *Skeletons in the Closet: Transitional Justice in Post-Communist Europe*

Ton Notermans, *Money, Markets, and the State: Social Democratic Economic Policies since 1918*

Aníbal Pérez-Liñán, *Presidential Impeachment and the New Political Instability in Latin America*

Roger Petersen, *Understanding Ethnic Violence: Fear, Hatred, and Resentment in Twentieth-Century Eastern Europe*

Simona Piattoni, ed., *Clientelism, Interests, and Democratic Representation*

Paul Pierson, *Dismantling the Welfare State? Reagan, Thatcher, and the Politics of Retrenchment*

Marino Regini, *Uncertain Boundaries: The Social and Political Construction of European Economies*

Marc Howard Ross, *Cultural Contestation in Ethnic Conflict*

Lyle Scruggs, *Sustaining Abundance: Environmental Performance in Industrial Democracies*

Jefferey M. Sellers, *Governing from Below: Urban Regions and the Global Economy*

Yossi Shain and Juan Linz, eds., *Interim Governments and Democratic Transitions*

Beverly Silver, *Forces of Labor: Workers' Movements and Globalization since 1870*

Theda Skocpol, *Social Revolutions in the Modern World*

Regina Smyth, *Candidate Strategies and Electoral Competition in the Russian Federation: Democracy Without Foundation*

Richard Snyder, *Politics after Neoliberalism: Reregulation in Mexico*

David Stark and László Bruszt, *Postsocialist Pathways: Transforming Politics and Property in East Central Europe*

Sven Steinmo, Kathleen Thelen, and Frank Longstreth, eds., *Structuring Politics: Historical Institutionalism in Comparative Analysis*

Susan C. Stokes, *Mandates and Democracy: Neoliberalism by Surprise in Latin America*

Susan C. Stokes, ed., *Public Support for Market Reforms in New Democracies*

Duane Swank, *Global Capital, Political Institutions, and Policy Change in Developed Welfare States*

Sidney Tarrow, *Power in Movement: Social Movements and Contentious Politics*

Kathleen Thelen, *How Institutions Evolve: The Political Economy of Skills in Germany, Britain, the United States, and Japan*

Charles Tilly, *Trust and Rule*

Daniel Treisman, *The Architecture of Government: Rethinking Political Decentralization*

Lily Lee Tsai, *Accountability without Democracy: How Solidary Groups Provide Public Goods in Rural China*

Joshua Tucker, *Regional Economic Voting: Russia, Poland, Hungary, Slovakia, and the Czech Republic, 1990–1999*

Ashutosh Varshney, *Democracy, Development, and the Countryside*

Jeremy M. Weinstein, *Inside Rebellion: The Politics of Insurgent Violence*

Stephen I. Wilkinson, *Votes and Violence: Electoral Competition and Ethnic Riots in India*

Jason Wittenberg, *Crucibles of Political Loyalty: Church Institutions and Electoral Continuity in Hungary*

Elisabeth J. Wood, *Forging Democracy from Below: Insurgent Transitions in South Africa and El Salvador*

Elisabeth J. Wood, *Insurgent Collective Action and Civil War in El Salvador*

Made in the USA
San Bernardino, CA
25 February 2018